SALES MANAGEMENT

The new ninth edition of *Sales Management* continues the tradition of blending the most recent sales management research with real-life "best practices" of leading sales organizations. The authors teach sales management courses and interact with sales managers and sales management professors on a regular basis. Their text focuses on the importance of employing different sales strategies for different consumer groups, as well as integrating corporate, business, marketing, and sales strategies. *Sales Management* includes current coverage of the trends and issues in sales management, along with numerous real-world examples from the contemporary business world that are used throughout the text to illuminate chapter discussions.

Key changes in this edition include:

- updates in each chapter to reflect the latest sales management research, and leading sales management trends and practices;
- an expanded discussion on trust-building and trust-based selling as foundations for effective sales management;
- all new chapter-opening vignettes about well-known companies that introduce each chapter and illustrate key topics from that chapter;
- new or updated comments from sales managers in "Sales Management in the 21st Century" boxes.

An online instructor's manual with test questions and PowerPoint presentations is available to adopters.

Thomas N. Ingram is a Partnership of Excellence Fellow and Professor of Marketing at Colorado State University, USA.

Raymond W. (Buddy) LaForge is the Brown-Forman Professor of Marketing (retired) at University of Louisville, USA.

Ramon A. Avila is the George and Frances Ball Distinguished Professor of Marketing and the founding director of the HH Gregg Center for Professional Selling at Ball State University, USA.

Charles H. Schwepker, Jr. is the Mike and Patti Davidson Distinguished Marketing Professor at University of Central Missouri, USA.

Michael R. Williams is Professor of Marketing and director of the Academy of Customer Excellence and Sales at Oklahoma City University, USA.

Sales Management
Analysis and Decision Making

NINTH EDITION

Thomas N. Ingram
Raymond W. LaForge
Ramon A. Avila
Charles H. Schwepker, Jr.
Michael R. Williams

Routledge
Taylor & Francis Group
NEW YORK AND LONDON

Ninth edition published 2015
by Routledge
711 Third Avenue, New York, NY 10017

and by Routledge
2 Park Square, Milton Park, Abingdon, Oxon, OX14 4RN

Routledge is an imprint of the Taylor & Francis Group, an informa business

Eighth edition published by M. E. Sharpe 2012

Library of Congress Cataloging in Publication Data
A catalog record for this book has been requested

ISBN: 978-1-138-85802-2 (hbk)
ISBN: 978-0-7656-4451-0 (pbk)
ISBN: 978-1-315-71798-2 (ebk)

Typeset in Galliard
by Swales and Willis Ltd, Exeter, Devon, UK

Printed and bound in the United States of America by Edwards Brothers Malloy
on sustainably sourced paper

BRIEF CONTENTS

CONTENTS

Our objective in writing the ninth edition of *Sales Management: Analysis and Decision Making* was to continue to present comprehensive and rigorous coverage of contemporary sales management in a readable, interesting, and challenging manner. Findings from recent sales management research are blended with examples of current sales management practice into an effective pedagogical format. Topics are covered from the perspective of a sales management decision maker. This decision-making perspective is accomplished through a chapter format that typically consists of discussing basic concepts, identifying critical decision areas, and presenting analytical approaches for improved sales management decision making. Company examples from the contemporary business world are used throughout the text to supplement chapter discussion.

STRENGTHS OF THIS EDITION

The ninth edition of *Sales Management: Analysis and Decision Making* continues what has been effective in previous editions, but contains changes that improve the content and pedagogy in the book. The authors teach sales management courses, are involved in sales management research, and interact with sales managers and professors on a regular basis. These activities ensure that the text covers the appropriate sales management topics and employs the most effective pedagogy. The key strengths of the ninth edition include:

- The 10 chapters and paperback format from the previous edition have been maintained. This makes it easy for professors to cover the text in a semester or quarter, and still have sufficient time to use active learning exercises throughout the course. Students can purchase the ninth edition for much less than the cost of a typical hardcover sales management book.

- New Opening Vignettes generate student interest in the chapter content by providing recent examples of leading sales organizations employing the chapter material.

- "Sales Management in the 21st Century" boxes include new sales executives or updated personal comments that reinforce important sales management concepts in each chapter.

- New "Ethical Dilemma" boxes provide students the opportunity to address important ethical issues facing sales managers with many set up as role-play exercises.

- Chapter cases with related role plays put students in the role of a sales manager in a specific sales organization situation. The cases require students to analyze the situation, decide on the appropriate action, and then implement their decisions through role-play scenarios.

- New and revised pedagogy is available in the "Developing Sales Management Knowledge" and "Building Sales Management Skills" activities at the end of each chapter.

- All chapters have been updated to incorporate the latest findings from sales management research and the best practices from leading sales organizations. Topics receiving new or expanded coverage include: using social networking in recruiting and selecting, value creation, sales productivity, mobile learning and self-directed training.

- Chapters 1 and 7 have been substantially revised to reflect current trends, improve clarity and enhance student learning.

LEVEL AND ORGANIZATION

This text was written for the undergraduate student enrolled in a one-semester or one-quarter sales management class. However, it is sufficiently rigorous to be used at the MBA level.

A sales management model is used to present coverage in a logical sequence. The text is organized into five parts to correspond with the five stages in the sales management model.

Part One, "Describing the Personal Selling Function," is designed to provide students with an understanding of personal selling prior to addressing specific sales management areas. We devote one chapter at the beginning of the text to this topic.

Part Two, "Defining the Strategic Role of the Sales Function," consists of two chapters. One discusses important relationships between personal selling and organizational strategies at the corporate, business, marketing, and sales levels. This chapter focuses on how strategic decisions at different organizational levels affect sales management decisions and personal selling practices.

The second chapter in this part investigates alternative sales organization structures and examines analytical methods for determining salesforce size, territory design, and the allocation of selling effort.

Part Three, "Developing the Salesforce," changes the focus from organizational topics to people topics. The two chapters in this part cover the critical decision areas in the recruitment and selection of salespeople and in training salespeople once they have been hired.

Part Four, "Directing the Salesforce," continues the people orientation by discussing the leadership, management, and supervisory activities necessary for successful sales management and examining important areas of salesforce motivation and reward systems.

Part Five, "Determining Salesforce Effectiveness and Performance," concludes the sales management process by addressing evaluation and control procedures. Differences in evaluating the effectiveness of the sales organization and the performance of salespeople are highlighted and covered in separate chapters.

PEDAGOGY

The following pedagogical format is used for each chapter to facilitate the learning process.

- *Learning Objectives.* Specific learning objectives for the chapter are stated in behavioral terms so that students will know what they should be able to do after the chapter has been covered.

- *Opening Vignettes.* All chapters are introduced by an opening vignette that typically consists of a recent, real-world company example addressing many of the key points to be discussed in the chapter. These opening vignettes are intended to generate student interest in the topics to be covered and to illustrate the practicality of the chapter coverage.

- *Key Words.* Key words are highlighted in bold type throughout each chapter and summarized in list form at the end of the chapter to alert students to their importance.

- *Boxed Inserts.* Each chapter contains two boxed inserts titled "Sales Management in the 21st Century." The comments in these boxes are provided by members of our Sales Executive Panel and were made specifically for our text.

- *Figure Captions.* Most figures in the text include a summarizing caption designed to make the figure understandable without reference to the chapter discussion.
- *Chapter Summaries.* A chapter summary recaps the key points covered in the chapter by restating and answering questions presented in the learning objectives at the beginning of the chapter.
- *Developing Sales Management Knowledge.* Ten discussion questions are presented at the end of each chapter to review key concepts covered in the chapter. Some of the questions require students to summarize what has been covered, while others are designed to be more thought-provoking and extend beyond chapter coverage.
- *Building Sales Management Skills.* Application exercises are supplied for each chapter, requiring students to apply what has been learned in the chapter to a specific sales management situation. Many of the application exercises require data analysis. Many chapters also have an Internet exercise to get students involved with the latest technology. Role plays are also included in most chapters.
- *Making Sales Management Decisions.* Each chapter concludes with two short cases. Most of these cases represent realistic and interesting sales management situations. Several require data analysis. Most are designed so that students can role-play their solutions.

CASES

The book contains a mixture of short and long cases. The 18 short cases at the end of the chapters can be used as a basis for class discussion, short written assignments, or role plays. The three longer cases are more appropriate for detailed analysis and class discussions or presentations by individuals or student groups. The longer cases are located at the end of the book.

SUPPLEMENTS

Instructor's Resources

The Instructor's Resources (at www.routledge.com/cw/ingram) deliver all the traditional instructor support materials in one handy place. Electronic files are provided for the complete Instructor's Manual, Test Bank, computerized Test Bank and computerized Test Bank software (ExamView), and chapter-by-chapter PowerPoint presentation files that can be used to enhance in-class lectures.

Instructor's Manual

The Instructor's Manual for the ninth edition of *Sales Management: Analysis and Decision Making* contains many helpful teaching suggestions and solutions to text exercises to help instructors successfully integrate all the materials offered with this text into their class. Each chapter includes the following materials designed to meet the instructor's needs.

- Learning objectives
- Chapter outline and summary
- Ideas for student involvement
- Possible answers to review sections in the text, *Developing Sales Management Knowledge* and *Building Sales Management Skills*
- Ideas for how to incorporate the role-play exercises found in the text into the classroom setting, as well as suggestions for conducting the role plays

(The Instructor's Manual files are located at: www.routledge.com/cw/ingram)

Test Bank

The revised and updated Test Bank includes a variety of multiple choice and true/false questions, which emphasize the important concepts presented in each chapter. The Test Bank questions vary in levels of difficulty so that each instructor can tailor his/her testing to meet his/her specific needs. The Test Bank files are located at: www.routledge.com/cw/ingram

ExamView (Computerized) Test Bank

The Test Bank is also available in computerized format (ExamView), allowing instructors to select problems at random by type, customize or add test questions, and scramble questions to create up to 99 versions of the same test.

PowerPoint Presentation Slides

Created by an expert in the field of sales, Scott Inks of Ball State University, this package brings classroom lectures and discussions to life with the Microsoft PowerPoint presentation tool. Extremely professor-friendly and organized by chapter, these chapter-by-chapter presentations outline chapter content. The eye-appealing and easy-to-read slides are, in this new edition, tailored specifically to the *Sales Management* text from the Ingram author team. The PowerPoint presentation slides are available at: www.routledge.com/cw/ingram.

ACKNOWLEDGMENTS

We are delighted to publish the ninth edition of *Sales Management: Analysis and Decision Making* with Routledge. Our hope is that this is one of many editions we work on together. A great deal of credit for this edition should go to all of the wonderful people at Routledge. Their expertise, support, and constant encouragement turned an extremely difficult task into a very enjoyable one. We are thankful for the expertise and support of the many publishing professionals who have worked with us on previous editions of this book. In particular, we appreciate the efforts of Harry Briggs, Rob Zwettler, Mike Roche and Becky Ryan. We would also like to thank our production manager Mhairi Bennett and our editor Victoria Brown for their work on the ninth edition of this book. Without their efforts this edition would not have seen the light of day. However, we also want to thank the many individuals with whom we did not have direct contact but who assisted in the development and production of this book.

We are also very appreciative of the support provided by our colleagues at Colorado State University, the University of Louisville, Ball State University, University of Central Missouri, and Oklahoma City University.

Thomas N. Ingram
Raymond W. LaForge
Ramon A. Avila
Charles H. Schwepker, Jr.
Michael R. Williams

To Jacque
—Thomas N. Ingram

To Susan, Alexandra, Kelly, and
in memory of my Mom and Dad
—Raymond W. LaForge

To Terry, Anne, Ryan, Laura, Kate,
Sarah, Nathan, Ella, Jack, Henry, and my loving parents
—Ramon A. Avila

To Laura, Charlie III, Anthony, Lauren, my Mom,
and in memory of my Dad, "Big C"
—Charles H. Schwepker, Jr.

To Marilyn, Aimee and Royce, Kerri, Bart and Gage,
and in memory of my Mom and Dad
—Michael R. Williams

Thomas N. Ingram (Ph.D., Georgia State University) is the Partnership for Excellence Professor of Business Administration in the Marketing Department at Colorado State University. Before commencing his academic career, Tom worked in sales, product management, and sales management with ExxonMobil. Professor Ingram has received numerous awards for contributions to sales research and teaching, most recently as a recipient of the Lifetime Achievement Award from the American Marketing Association Selling and Sales Management Special Interest Group. He has also been honored as the Marketing Educator of the Year by Sales and Marketing Executives International (SMEI), as a Distinguished Sales Educator by the University Sales Center Alliance, and as the first recipient of the Mu Kappa Tau National Marketing Honor Society Recognition Award for Outstanding Scholarly Contributions to the Sales Discipline. Tom has served as the Editor of *Journal of Personal Selling & Sales Management*, Chair of the SMEI Accreditation Institute, and as Editor of the *Journal of Marketing Theory and Practice*. Professor Ingram's published work has appeared in *Journal of Marketing, Journal of Marketing Research, Journal of Personal Selling & Sales Management,* and *Journal of the Academy of Marketing Science,* among others. One of his co-authored articles which appeared in the *Journal of Marketing* was recognized by the American Marketing Association Selling and Sales Management Special Interest Group as one of the "Top Ten Articles of the 20th Century" in the sales discipline.

Raymond W. (Buddy) LaForge (DBA, University of Tennessee) is the Brown-Forman Professor of Marketing at the University of Louisville (retired). He is the founder of the *Marketing Education Review*; has co-authored *Marketing: Principles and Perspectives,* 5th ed. (2007); *Professional Selling: A Trust-Based Approach,* 4th ed. (2008); *Sell,* 4th ed. (2015); *The Professional Selling Skills Workbook* (1995); *Strategic Sales Leadership: Breakthrough Thinking for Breakthrough Results* (2006); and co-edited *Emerging Trends in Sales Thought and Practice.* His research is published in many journals, including the *Journal of Marketing, Journal of Marketing Research, Decision Sciences, Journal of the Academy of Marketing Science, International Journal of Research in Marketing,* and *Journal of Personal Selling & Sales Management.* Buddy has received numerous awards, including the Outstanding Sales Scholar Award from Mu Kappa Tau, a Special Recognition Award from the American Marketing Association Sales Interest Group, a Top Thirteen Faculty Favorite Award from the University of Louisville, the Distinguished Scholar Award from the Research Symposium on Marketing and Entrepreneurship, the Distinguished Sales Educator Award from the University Sales Center Alliance, the Undergraduate Teaching Award from the College of Business, the Beta Alpha Psi Outstanding College of Business Faculty Award, and the American Marketing Association Sales Interest Group Lifetime Achievement Award. The Sales Program at the University of Louisville has been recognized as a Top University Sales Education Program by the Sales Education Foundation from 2007 to 2014.

Ramon A. Avila (Ph.D., Virginia Polytechnic Institute and State University) is the George and Frances Ball Distinguished Professor of Marketing and the founding director of the H.H. Gregg Center for Professional Selling, and earned his bachelor's degree and MBA from Ball State University. He completed his Ph.D. at Virginia Polytechnic

Institute and State University in 1984. He joined the Ball State faculty in 1984. Before coming to Ball State, he worked in sales with the Burroughs Corporation. Dr. Avila was presented with Mu Kappa Tau's Outstanding Contributor to the Sales Profession in 1999 and is the only the third person to receive this award. Dr. Avila has also received the University's Outstanding Faculty award in 2001, the Outstanding Service award in 1998, the University's Outstanding Junior Faculty award in 1989, the College of Business's Professor of the Year, and the Dean's Teaching award every year it was given from 1987 to 2002. Dr. Avila has presented numerous papers at professional conferences and has been the program chair and the director for the National Conference in Sales Management, and has published research in *Journal of Marketing Research, Journal of Euromarketing, Industrial Marketing Management, Journal of Management, Journal of Marketing Theory and Practice, Journal of Personal Selling & Sales Management, The Review of Business,* and *Mid-American Journal of Business.* A frequent consultant, he has worked with major corporations, including AT&T, Burroughs, Honeywell, Indiana Gas, Indiana Michigan Power, Indiana Bell, Midwest Metals, and Lees Inn. Dr. Avila serves on the editorial review boards of four business-related journals. He is also the former associate editor for the *Mid-American Journal of Business.* Dr. Avila's teaching focuses on industrial marketing, professional selling, and sales management.

Charles H. Schwepker, Jr. (Ph.D., University of Memphis) is the Mike and Patti Davidson Distinguished Marketing Professor at the University of Central Missouri. He has experience in wholesale and retail sales. His primary research interests are in sales management, personal selling and marketing ethics. Dr. Schwepker's articles have appeared in the *Journal of the Academy of Marketing Science, Journal of Business Research, Journal of Public Policy and Marketing, Journal of Personal Selling & Sales Management, Journal of Service Research,* and *Journal of Business Ethics,* among other journals, and various national and regional proceedings. Edited books in which his articles have appeared include *Marketing Communications Classics* (2000), *Environmental Marketing* (1995), *The Oxford Handbook of Sales Management and Sales Strategy* (2011) and the *Handbook of Unethical Work Behavior* (2013). He has received several honors for both teaching and advising, including the Hormel Teaching Excellence award and the Alumni Foundation Harmon College of Business Administration Distinguished Professor award. Dr. Schwepker received the James Comer award for best contribution to selling and sales management theory awarded by the *Journal of Personal Selling & Sales Management* and three "Outstanding Paper" awards at the National Conference in Sales Management, among others. He is on the editorial review boards of the *Journal of Personal Selling & Sales Management, Journal of Marketing Theory & Practice, Journal of Business & Industrial Marketing, Journal of Relationship Marketing,* and *Journal of Selling & Major Account Management,* and has five times won an award for outstanding reviewer. Dr. Schwepker is a co-author of *Sell,* 4th ed. (2015).

Michael R. Williams (Ph.D., Oklahoma State University) is Associate Dean for Academic Affairs and Professor of Marketing at Oklahoma City University. His previous academic associations include Professor of Marketing at Illinois State University and Director of the Professional Sales Institute. Prior to his academic career, Dr. Williams established a successful 30-plus-year career in industrial sales, market research, and sales management and continues to consult and work with a wide range of business organizations. He has co-authored *Sell,* 4th ed. (2015); *Professional Selling: A Trust-based Approach,* 4th ed. (2008); *The Professional Selling Skills Workbook* (1995); and a variety of executive monographs and white papers on sales performance topics. Dr. Williams' research has been published in national and international journals including *Journal of Personal Selling & Sales Management, International Journal of Purchasing and Materials Management, Journal of Business and Industrial Marketing, Quality Management Journal,* and *Journal of Industrial Technology.* His work has also received numerous honors, including Outstanding Article for the Year in *Journal of Business and*

Industrial Marketing, the AACSB's Leadership in Innovative Business Education award, the Marketing Science Institute's Alden G. Clayton competition, and the Mu Kappa Tau Marketing Society recognition award for Outstanding Scholarly Contribution to the Sales Discipline. He has also received numerous university, college, and corporate teaching and research awards including Old Republic Research Scholar, the presentation of a seminar at Oxford's Brasenose College, *Who's Who in American Education,* and *Who's Who in America.* Mike has and continues to serve in leadership roles as an advisor and board member for sales and sales management associations and organizations.

Sales Management
Analysis and Decision Making

CHANGING WORLD OF SALES MANAGEMENT

Personal selling is an important component of marketing strategies for many firms. Companies in the United States spend over $800 billion on their salesforces which represents an average of 10 percent of sales.[1] The 500 largest U.S. salesforces employ almost 24 million salespeople with each salesperson supporting an average of 13.7 other jobs within a company. The 200 largest manufacturing and service companies employ about 1.1 million salespeople who generate more than $6.4 trillion in sales.[2] These statistics indicate the tremendous impact of personal selling in today's business world.

Sales Management is concerned with managing a firm's personal selling function. Sales managers are involved in both the strategy (planning) and people (implementation) aspects of personal selling, as well as evaluating and improving personal selling activities. Research indicates that sales managers can increase profitable sales growth by 5 percent to 20 percent or more by moving from average to excellent salesforce effectiveness.[3] Sales managers are involved in a variety of activities and must be able to interact effectively with people in the personal selling function, with people in other functional areas in their firm, and with people outside their company, especially customers and other business partners.

Most sales organizations employ sales managers at various levels within the sales organization. These sales managers have different titles and may not have direct responsibility for specific salespeople, but all perform sales management activities that affect the salespeople in a sales organization. Illustrative titles for sales managers include chief sales officer, vice president of sales, divisional sales manager, regional sales manager, sales leader, branch manager, area director, and field sales manager.

Our objective in this chapter is to introduce the exciting world of sales management. We begin by identifying challenges in the sales organization environment and suggesting effective sales management responses to these challenges. Then, the characteristics of the best sales organizations and most effective sales managers are discussed. We conclude by presenting a general sales management model that provides a framework for the book, describing the format of each chapter, and introducing the members of our Sales Executive Panel. The goal is to "set the stage" for your journey into the dynamic and exciting world of sales management.

CHALLENGES IN THE SALES ORGANIZATION ENVIRONMENT

The internal and external environment facing sales organizations presents a variety of challenges.[4] Changes in customers, competitors, and technology are external factors that have an important impact on sales organizations. The purchasing and supply function is increasingly viewed as an effective way for organizations to lower costs and increase profits. Therefore, buyers are more demanding, better prepared, and more skilled. These customers have higher expectations in terms of customized products and services that solve their problems and offer good value. Many sales organizations face fierce global competition in both domestic and international markets. Technology affects many sales organization processes and it is changing rapidly.

The internal environment also presents challenges. The increase in mergers and acquisitions, the introduction of new products, and expanded product mixes add to the complexity of sales operations. Recent scandals in the business press have focused more attention on ethical issues within firms with a special focus on sales organizations. The costs of maintaining salespeople in the field are escalating, so firms are pressuring sales organizations to increase sales while decreasing selling costs. These internal and external environmental influences require sales organizations to make significant changes in how the sales function is managed.

SALES MANAGEMENT RESPONSES

Sales organizations are responding to these challenges in different ways. Some are making dramatic changes in their sales operations and transforming most aspects of sales management. Others are focusing on improving a few sales management areas to increase sales organization effectiveness. As indicated in Figure 1.1, these sales management responses typically emphasize ways to create customer value, increase sales productivity, and/or improve sales leadership.

Many of these responses are the result of a more strategic perspective toward sales organizations. As companies adopt a market orientation, the role of sales managers and salespeople becomes strategically more important. Market-oriented firms typically develop customer-centric cultures and establish organizational structures around customers rather than products. Market segmentation and prioritizing customers within target markets becomes increasingly important. Selling is viewed more as a core business process rather than a tactical activity. This strategic perspective considers the sales organization as critical in delivering value to customers and generating profits for the firm. Sales managers and salespeople need to change many of their activities to be successful in a more strategic role.[5]

FIGURE 1.1   Sales Management Responses

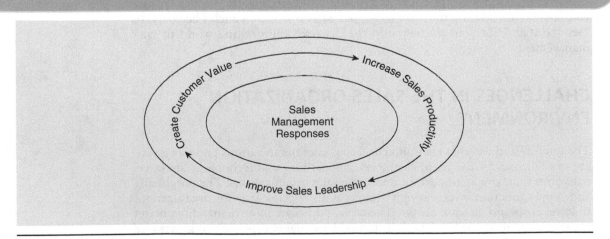

Many sales organizations are responding to the challenges facing them by making changes in their sales operations.

Create Customer Value

Many sales organizations are moving from an emphasis on merely selling products to solving customer problems and adding value to customer businesses over the long term. This change typically requires a major transformation as indicated in the following examples:

- Wausau Paper operates in a very price-conscious market which makes it difficult to maintain profit margins. The company decided to try to develop strategic relationships with key customers through a Value Delivery Framework. Salespeople focus on collaborating with customers to increase sales through marketing innovations and to reduce costs through supply chain efficiencies. These customers agree to multiyear partnerships and supply agreements which include a price dimension. Wausau would like to generate 35 percent of its sales from these strategic relationships. Achieving this objective requires a number of changes in sales management. The company focuses on hiring experienced salespeople with strong business acumen, trains them to run their sales territory as a business, and compensates them based on a variety of business-related metrics.[6]

- Ecolab operates in the industrial and institutional cleaning and sanitizing business with sales of over $6 billion and operations in more than 160 countries. Its new strategy is "Circle the Customer—Circle the Globe." This strategy is implemented through a sales-and-service model where salespeople spend most of their time with existing customers. The salespeople install systems, make sure the customer's equipment is working properly, train customer employees, audit results, and solve customer problems. They also sell existing customers additional Ecolab products. Because these salespeople do not have much time to acquire new customers, the company created a sales specialist position focused on developing new business. It also established a major accounts salesforce to serve large, multiunit customers. The success of these strategies depends upon effective sales management, so sales managers spend a great deal of time in recruiting the best salespeople, training them well, offering career development opportunities, incorporating technology to increase sales effectiveness, and providing attractive compensation. Sales managers emphasize the development and retention of their salespeople.[7]

A focus on creating customer value can lead to effective sales management strategies that do not require a complete sales organization transformation. For example, many buyers are very busy and are less willing to meet with salespeople than in the past.[8] Blue Ridge Partners (BRP) found this to be the case with its private equity firm customers. Salespeople found it increasingly difficult to set up client meetings and were also not getting as many new business referrals. Sales leaders at BRP decided to create customer value by writing a book that presented the BRP system for growing a business and then giving the book to top customers and prospects for free. This approach was extremely successful. Customers and prospects that had not been willing to meet with BRP were now contacting BRP to set up meetings. The value provided by the book opened many doors and led to more business from existing customers and new business from prospects.[9]

The key is to identify value as defined by the customer and then to create and deliver this value. Changes in the environment often result in changes in how customers define value. Salespeople must identify the new value definitions and deliver the value desired by customers. Consider the following examples:

- Strict and costly regulations in the pharmaceutical industry are driving a focus on cost reduction for many firms. Customers of Minnesota Thermal Science (MTS) used to be most interested in the technology of pharmaceutical packaging. But, now the emphasis is on reducing costs. Salespeople must now make a stronger business case for their packaging solutions, because this is what is valued most by customers.

A recent deal was closed by showing a customer how $1 million in packaging and $1 million in distribution costs could be saved by using MTS packaging.[10]

- RS Medical sells physician-prescribed home electrotherapy devices. Salespeople typically talked about the features of their products with physicians. Although product features are still important, many physicians value information that will help improve their practice as a business. RS Medical salespeople identified this shift, and began to emphasize ways to educate physicians on how to make their practices more efficient. The value provided by this approach led to an increase in device sales for RS Medical.[11]

- Spiris focuses on the aviation and healthcare markets in the highly competitive insurance industry. Salespeople sell insurance products, but spend a lot of time on helping customers reduce their insurance and other business costs. For example, one customer was not willing to pay $10 for preemployment drug testing, because of the high overall cost. However, an analysis by a salesperson showed the customer that the drug testing was a good investment and would save thousands of dollars by weeding out bad hires early. This value provided by the salesperson strengthened the relationship with the customer and led to more insurance business in the future.[12]

The importance of creating customer value is likely to increase in the future. But, how customers define value is also likely to continue to change in the future. The most successful sales organizations will be those that are able to identify how their customers define value over time and then to deliver this value to them. Changes in value creation will typically require changes in many aspects of sales management.

Increase Sales Productivity

Even as sales organizations try to create more value for customers, sales managers are under pressure to increase sales productivity. The basic role of a sales organization has typically been to sell with sales managers and salespeople normally evaluated and rewarded for growing sales volume. Generating sales is still important, but the profitability of these sales is increasingly more important. Therefore, the focus for sales managers has moved from sales volume only to sales productivity. Sales productivity includes the costs associated with generating sales and serving customers and emphasizes producing more sales for a given level of costs. Sales managers must "do more with less" by being more effective and more efficient throughout the sales organization.

Sometimes a major sales transformation is needed to increase sales productivity. Take the case of Con-way Freight. A new executive vice president of sales realized that the company needed to make major changes in sales operations to increase both sales and sales productivity. The most important changes were the creation of a new sales process; the creation and integration of new sales software into iPads; and the use of the iPads by salespeople to plan and execute the new sales process effectively. After a period of training and coaching, salespeople were able to increase sales and sales productivity significantly. In fact, the sales organization has increased customer interactions by 45 percent and yet reduced the size of its salesforce by 27 percent.[13]

Leading sales organizations look for ways to increase sales productivity in all areas of sales management. The changes in sales training at Newell Rubbermaid illustrate an example of increasing sales productivity in the sales training area. Newell Rubbermaid has 1,500 salespeople operating in 90 countries producing around $5.6 billion in annual sales. The success of these salespeople depends upon their ability to provide market insights and merchandising solutions to retail customers located in developed and developing countries. This requires continuous training of entry-level, midcareer, and senior salespeople. The company provides effective and productive training online. One approach is to use avatars as online representations of salespeople to engage trainees in the learning process. Audiocasts are also used so salespeople can be involved in training even when they are traveling. Newell Rubbermaid finds this approach to be a cost-effective way to train a global salesforce.[14]

The use of social media can be an effective way to increase sales productivity. Even though recent studies indicate that most sales organizations are in the early stages of social media use, the benefits of social media can be significant for sales organizations. For example, research suggests that salespeople continue to focus on cold calling and spend almost 25 percent of their time researching prospects. Many buyers do not respond to cold calls or email blasts, so much of this time is wasted. The use of Twitter, LinkedIn, Facebook, and blogs can be a more productive way to generate prospects and could reduce the amount of time researching prospects significantly. More productive prospecting would free up more time for salespeople to sell and increase overall sales productivity.[15]

The common element in all these situations is that changes were made to increase sales productivity, often using sales technology. Some things were done differently to get "more bang for the sales buck." This pressure to increase sales productivity is likely to intensify in the future for most sales organizations.

Improve Sales Leadership

Many sales organizations use a hierarchical, bureaucratic structure. Sales managers operate at different levels with direct supervisory responsibility for the level below and direct accountability to the management level above. Thus, field sales managers operate as the "boss" for the salespeople who report to them. They are responsible for the performance of these salespeople and exercise various types of control to get salespeople to produce desired results.

Although this approach might work well in very stable environments, many sales organizations realize that this approach makes it difficult for them to be responsive in a rapidly changing environment. These sales organizations are "flattening" the hierarchy and empowering salespeople to make more decisions in the field. This changes the role of sales managers and their relationship with salespeople. The basic trend is for a sales manager to lead more and manage less. Sales managers are playing more of a leadership role by emphasizing:

- collaboration rather than control
- coaching instead of criticism
- salesperson empowerment rather than domination
- sharing information rather than withholding it
- adapting to individual salespeople rather than treating everyone the same[16]

This emphasis on leadership means that a sales manager's job is more to help salespeople perform better and less to control and evaluate salespeople. This change in orientation is illustrated in Exhibit 1.1.[17]

The Chally World Class Sales Excellence Research Report supports the increasing importance of sales leadership for many firms. One interesting finding is that

Leadership Trends EXHIBIT 1.1	
Yesterday	**Today**
Natural resources defined power.	Knowledge is power.
Leaders commanded and controlled.	Leaders empower and coach.
Leaders were warriors.	Leaders are facilitators.
Managers directed.	Managers delegate.

Several important changes in effective leadership have occurred over the years.

salespeople who get at least one half day a week of coaching from their sales manager are twice as productive as other salespeople.[18] King Pharmaceuticals provides a specific example of effective sales leadership at one company. The complex and changing environment requires pharmaceutical salespeople to work smarter, not harder. Sales managers at King Pharmaceuticals are using a competency model to help salespeople assess their strengths and weaknesses in four important areas. Based on these assessment results, a sales manager works with each salesperson to create and execute a customized development plan for each salesperson. The objective is to improve overall sales effectiveness by having sales managers help develop the needed competencies of each salesperson.[19]

Consistent with the move from less management to more leadership, there is a trend from less emphasis on administrative activities to more of an entrepreneurial orientation throughout a sales organization. This shift requires sales managers to be more entrepreneurial in their sales management and marketplace activities.

Sales managers and salespeople need to view themselves as entrepreneurs with the sales function driving value creation and innovation within their firms. The entrepreneurial sales organization has been defined as one that focuses on creativity, innovation, empowerment, strategy, technology, and collaboration. These are not the typical characteristics used to define sales organizations. Therefore, significant change is often required to make the transformation to an entrepreneurial sales organization.[20] Some recent sales management innovations represent important entrepreneurial activities: harnessing social media, strategically aligning marketing and sales efforts, establishing a customer-centric sales process, profiting from a customer relationship management (CRM) system, embracing online collaboration, improving sales forecasting and performance metrics, coaching for sales success, leveraging mobile technology, giving salespeople access to the collective intelligence of the sales organization, and improving sales performance and compensation management.[21]

BEST SALES ORGANIZATIONS[22]

Sales consulting firms and academic researchers have studied the best sales organizations to identify the practices that make them successful now and position them for success in the future. A synthesis of this research indicates that the best sales organizations tend to:

- Create a customer-driven culture throughout the sales organization and align sales operations with business and marketing strategies.
- Recruit, hire, and retain the best talent for their specific sales situation.
- Train and coach the right skill set, and leverage the best practices of top performers to improve everyone else.
- Focus on key strategic issues by segmenting accounts and providing differentiated offerings to find, win, and retain the best customers.
- Develop an appropriate and adaptable structure and implement formal sales and relationship-building processes with an emphasis on continuous improvement.
- Use technology effectively to learn about customers, build market intelligence, and enable salesperson and sales manager success.
- Integrate sales with other business functions, especially marketing, to deliver superior customer value.

It is clear that the best sales organizations address all stages of the sales management process. There is no "silver bullet" that will lead to high performance. Many activities have to be performed and coordinated. For example, the impressive turnaround at Honeywell Business Systems was achieved by integrated efforts to develop and execute a structured sales process, a comprehensive sales training program, an attractive compensation plan, and an effective system for measurement and performance accountability.[23]

It is important to note the critical role that sales managers, especially field sales managers, play in the success of a sales organization.

EFFECTIVE SALES MANAGERS

Sales managers work with the systems and processes and interact with the people involved in making a sales organization successful. Research indicates that the most effective sales managers possess specific skills and focus on particular activities. The most important sales management skills are: communication and listening skills; human relations skills; organization and time management skills; industry, company, product, and general business knowledge; coaching, motivating, and leadership skills; and honest and ethical tendencies.[24]

In addition to these general skills, the best sales managers focus on a number of specific activities in their interactions with salespeople:[25]

- Prepare their sales team for constant change by being a role model and mentoring salespeople.
- Earn the trust of salespeople by being dependable and competent, and exhibiting integrity.
- Give salespeople continuous feedback in a positive manner.
- Build enthusiasm throughout the sales team.
- Get involved by being accessible to salespeople and visible to customers.
- Grow and develop salespeople by emphasizing continuous job improvement and career development.

As you can see, sales management is a complex and constantly evolving field. The most effective sales managers possess a variety of skills and are involved in many different activities. We now present a sales management model that captures all aspects of sales management and provides a framework for the remainder of the book.

SALES MANAGEMENT PROCESS

The sales management model presented in Figure 1.2 illustrates the major stages in the sales management process. This model is valuable to sales organizations and provides the basic framework for the study of sales management. We discuss the components of each stage in the sales management process and indicate how the remaining chapters in the book address the important areas of sales management.

Describing the Personal Selling Function

Because sales managers are responsible for managing the personal selling function, they must thoroughly understand it. This text therefore devotes a chapter to that subject before discussing sales management activities. Chapter 2 (Overview of Personal Selling) provides background information about the personal selling function with an emphasis on customer dialogue, value, and relationships. This discussion captures the key changes in personal selling being implemented by many companies. These changes have a direct impact on sales management activities as examined throughout the text.

Defining the Strategic Role of the Sales Function

Many firms in the contemporary business world consist of collections of relatively autonomous business units that market multiple products to diverse customer groups. These multiple-business, multiple-product firms must develop and integrate strategic decisions at different organizational levels. Chapter 3 (Organizational Strategies and the Sales Function) discusses the key strategic decisions at the corporate, business, marketing, and

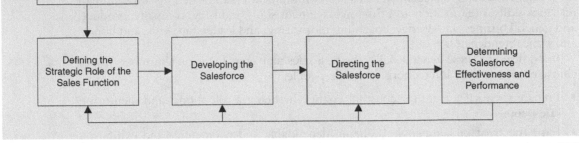

The four major stages of the sales management process and an understanding of personal selling are the focus of the book.

sales levels and the basic relationships between these decisions and the personal selling and sales management functions. Corporate- and business-level strategic decisions typically provide guidelines within which sales managers and salespeople must operate. This is especially true for firms focusing on a CRM strategy. By contrast, personal selling is an important component of marketing strategies in specific product market situations. The role of personal selling in a given marketing strategy has direct and important implications for sales managers.

Strategic decisions at the corporate, business, and marketing levels must be translated into strategies for individual accounts. We discuss the major elements of a sales strategy: account targeting strategy, relationship strategy, selling strategy, and sales channel strategy. Because personal selling is typically important in organizational marketing situations, we provide an explanation of organizational buyer behavior as a foundation for the development of sales strategies.

Sales strategies are designed for individual accounts or groups of similar accounts. Therefore, an account targeting strategy is needed to identify and classify accounts into useful categories. Then, the type of relationship, the desired selling approach, and the most productive mix of sales channels are determined for each account category. These decisions result in an integrated sales strategy for each targeted account and account group.

The development and integration of corporate, business, marketing, and sales strategies establishes the basic strategic direction for personal selling and sales management activities. However, an effective sales organization is necessary to implement these strategies successfully. Chapter 4 (Sales Organization Structure and Salesforce Deployment) presents the basic concepts in designing an effective sales organization structure: specialization, centralization, span of control versus management levels, and line versus staff positions. Different decisions in any of these areas produce different sales organization structures. The appropriate structure for a firm depends on the specific characteristics of a given selling situation. If strategic account selling programs are used, specific attention must be directed toward determining the best organizational structure for serving these major accounts.

Closely related to sales organization decisions are decisions on the amount and allocation of selling effort. We present specific methods for making salesforce deployment decisions. Because the decisions on selling effort allocation, salesforce size, and territory design are interrelated, they should be addressed in an integrative manner. A number of different analytical approaches can assist in this endeavor, but "people" issues must also be considered.

Developing the Salesforce

The sales strategy, sales organization, and salesforce deployment decisions produce the basic structure for personal selling efforts and can be considered similar to the "machine" decisions in a production operation. Sales managers must also make a number of "people" decisions to ensure that the right types of salespeople are available and have the skills to operate the "machine" structure effectively and efficiently.

Chapter 5 (Acquiring Sales Talent: Recruitment and Selection) discusses the key activities involved in planning and carrying out salesforce recruitment and selection programs. These activities include determining the type of salespeople desired, identifying prospective salesperson candidates, and evaluating candidates to ensure that the best are hired. Legal and ethical issues are important considerations in the recruitment and selection process. The ramifications of this process for salespeople's subsequent adjustment to a new job (socialization) are also examined.

Chapter 6 (Continual Development of the Salesforce: Sales Training) emphasizes the need for continuous training of salespeople and the important role that sales managers play in this activity. The sales training process consists of assessing training needs, developing objectives, evaluating alternatives, designing the training program, carrying it out, and evaluating it. Sales managers face difficult decisions at each stage of the sales training process, because it is not only extremely important but also expensive, and there are many sales training alternatives available.

Directing the Salesforce

Hiring the best salespeople and providing them with the skills required for success is one thing; directing their efforts to meet sales organization goals and objectives is another. Sales managers spend a great deal of their time in motivating, supervising, and leading members of the salesforce.

Chapter 7 (Sales Leadership, Management, and Supervision) distinguishes between the leadership, management, and supervisory activities of a sales manager. *Leadership activities* focus on influencing salespeople through communication processes to attain specific goals and objectives. *Management activities* include all aspects of the sales management process, such as recruiting, selecting, and training salespeople. *Supervisory activities* are concerned with day-to-day control of the salesforce under routine operating conditions. Key issues and problems in sales leadership, management, and supervision are discussed.

Chapter 8 (Motivation and Reward System Management) presents several content and process theories of motivation that attempt to explain how individuals decide to spend effort on specific activities over extended periods of time. Sales managers can use these theories as a foundation for determining the best ways to get salespeople to spend the appropriate amount of time on the right activities over a period of time. These theories provide the basis for specific salesforce reward systems. Both compensation and non-compensation rewards are examined. The advantages and disadvantages of different compensation programs are investigated, as well as methods for sales expense reimbursement. Specific guidelines for developing and managing a salesforce reward system are suggested.

Determining Salesforce Effectiveness and Performance

Sales managers must continually monitor the progress of the salesforce to determine current effectiveness and performance. This is a difficult task, because these evaluations should address both the effectiveness of units within the sales organization and the performance of individual salespeople.

Chapter 9 (Evaluating the Effectiveness of the Organization) focuses on evaluating the effectiveness of sales organization units, such as territories, districts, regions, and zones. The *sales organization audit* is the most comprehensive approach for evaluating the effectiveness of the sales organization as a whole. Specific methods are presented for assessing the effectiveness of different sales organization units with regard to sales, costs, profitability, and productivity. Skill in using these analyses helps a sales manager to diagnose specific problems and develop solutions to them.

Chapter 10 (Evaluating the Performance of Salespeople) changes the focus to evaluating the performance of people, both as individuals and in groups. These performance evaluations are used for a variety of purposes by sales managers. Specific criteria to be evaluated and methods for providing the evaluative information are examined, and the use of this information in a diagnostic and problem-solving manner is described. A method for measuring salesperson job satisfaction, which is closely related to salesperson performance, is presented as well.

CHAPTER FORMAT

Sales Management: Analysis and Decision Making was written for students. Therefore, its aim is to provide comprehensive coverage of sales management in a manner that students will find interesting and readable. Each chapter blends recent research results with current sales management practice in a format designed to facilitate learning.

At the beginning of each chapter, "Objectives" highlight the basic material that the student can expect to learn. These learning objectives are helpful in reviewing chapters for future study. An opening vignette then illustrates many of the important ideas to be covered in the chapter, using examples of companies in various industries to illustrate the diversity and complexity of sales management. Most of the companies described in the vignettes are well known, and most of the situations represent real actions by these firms.

Key words in the body of each chapter are printed in bold letters, and figures and exhibits are used liberally to illustrate and amplify the discussion in the text. Every figure contains an explanation so that it can be understood without reference to the text.

Each chapter contains two boxed inserts entitled Sales Management in the 21st Century. The examples in both boxes have been provided specifically for this textbook by sales executives from various companies whom we recruited to serve as a Sales Executive Panel. To ensure that the textbook includes the latest practices from leading sales organizations, each executive was asked to provide specific examples of "best practices" in their company. Backgrounds of each executive are provided at the end of this chapter.

Sales managers are confronted with various ethical issues when performing their job activities. Many of these ethical issues are addressed in the Ethical Dilemma boxes that appear in the remaining chapters. You will be presented with realistic ethical situations faced by sales managers and asked to recommend appropriate courses of action.

A chapter summary is geared to the learning objectives presented at the beginning of the chapter. Understanding Sales Management Terms lists the key words that appear in bold throughout the chapter. Developing Sales Management Knowledge presents 10 questions to help you develop an understanding of important sales management issues and relationships. Building Sales Management Skills consists of exercises in which you can apply the sales management knowledge learned in the chapter. Making Sales Management Decisions includes two interesting case situations that allow you to make important sales management decisions. If you understand sales management terms, develop sales management knowledge, and build sales management skills, you will be prepared to make successful sales management decisions.

CONCLUDING STATEMENT

This brief overview of contemporary sales management and summary of the contents and format of *Sales Management: Analysis and Decision Making* set the stage for your journey into the dynamic and exciting world of sales management. This should be a valuable learning experience as well as an interesting journey. All the information contained in this textbook should prove very relevant to those of you who begin your career in personal selling and progress through the ranks of sales management.

SALES EXECUTIVE PANEL

Chris Aiken started with Pfizer Pharmaceuticals as a sales representative in San Angelo, Texas in 1991 and is currently a Senior Professional Healthcare Representative in Oklahoma City. His primary customer base includes primary care and specialty physicians as well as group and account management. In addition, he serves on a variety of advisory boards both on a regional and national basis with Pfizer. Chris has a B.B.A. in marketing from Texas Tech University and an MBA from Oklahoma City University.

Tom Cassidy, Director of Polymer Platforms for Northbrook, IL-based Stepan Company, integrates sales, operations planning, and manufacturing in his management of everyday operations and preparation for future global strategic growth. With over 20 years' experience managing polymer sales in the Americas, he is a strong advocate of listening to customers to understand their needs and gain suggestions for improvement. Tom has a B.A. from Lake Forest College in Lake Forest, IL, where he dual-majored in Economics and Psychology, both of which have been advantageous in his sales career.

Rich Clasby is a Vice President General Manager for Maxon, a Honeywell Company. He manages global operations for the Maxon line of business including a worldwide network of sales offices. Rich has a B.S. in Mechanical Engineering from the University of Cincinnati.

Kim Davenport is a District Sales Manager with Merck Pharmaceuticals. He leads a team of nine sales representatives who sell in the greater Phoenix area. Kim has a B.S. in Marketing from Ball State University.

Chris Fergen is vice president of sales, service, and customer contact for Hach Company, a global leader in the water quality, analysis, and testing industry. His experience includes industrial engineering, product management, marketing and sales, and general management. Based in Loveland, Colorado, Chris directs more than 200 employees worldwide. He holds degrees from Arizona State University, an undergraduate degree in engineering and a MBA.

Jerry Heffel started with the Southwestern Company as a college student salesperson in 1965. He served as president of the company for many years and is now president emeritus. Jerry has a B.A. in History from Oklahoma State University and an MBA from the University of Oklahoma.

Jennifer Johnson-Kenny is a Sales Account Manager for Verailla. She manages a portfolio of business customers in the food, beverage, and spirits industry. Jennifer has a B.S. in Chemical Engineering from Purdue University and an MBA from the Krannert School of Management.

Joe Kemp is a District Marketing Manager with Federated Mutual Insurance. He leads a team of eight salespeople. Joe has a B.S. in Marketing from the University of Kentucky.

Michael Maretich is Global Sales Manager-Development and Effectiveness for the Northbrook, IL-based Stepan Company. Mike works with all sales, operations, and product groups on a global basis to enhance the organization's overall industry leadership and sales effectiveness in the fast paced and competitive industrial chemicals industry. Mike has a B.S. in Biology from Aquinas College, Grand Rapids, MI, along with an MBA from Lake Forest Graduate School of Management, Lake Forest, IL.

John Schwepker is the former Vice President of Sales and Marketing for Reality Systems, a St. Louis, MO-based document imaging company that was acquired by Cintas. He is responsible for sales and marketing throughout the United States. John has a B.S. in Marketing from Southeast Missouri State University and an MBA from the University of Phoenix.

Troy Secchio has been in industrial sales for over 28 years. Currently, Troy is the Director of Corporate Strategy and Account Acquisition for Ironwear, a manufacturer of value-added personal protective gear. Throughout Troy's career he has provided leadership in key areas of sales and marketing, including management of national strategic sales, directing both inside and outside sales, and setting corporate sales strategy. His successful experience within account, people, and product management has honed his leadership skills, enabling him to develop relevant value propositions that truly impact customer relationships through value-added results.

Tom Simpson is Vice President and COO for Elite PS. He leads the sales and operation efforts for the company which includes more than 20 direct sales and support staff members. Tom has a B.S. in Telecommunications from Ball State University.

Marty Zucker is Regional Office Coffee Services Manager for W.B. Mason Office Products, the largest independent office supply company in the world. He is responsible for increasing revenues and margins for 14 locations located in New Jersey, New York, Pennsylvania, Delaware, and Maryland. Marty has been in the office products industry for 44 years. He has held such positions as Regional Vice President National Accounts, Midwest Region; Vice President/General Manager Chicago; Vice President Sales New York/New Jersey; and Director of Operations for the Long Island division. Marty studied Marketing and Business Administration at the State University of New York, Delhi.

Describing the Personal Selling Function

The chapter in Part 1 describes the personal selling function. A clear understanding of personal selling is essential to gain a proper perspective of the issues facing sales managers. Chapter 2 discusses the role of personal selling in marketing, including the significance of personal selling, types of sales jobs, and the key job roles fullfilled by salespeople. The trust-based relationship selling process, with a focus on understanding, creating and communicating, and continually increasing customer value, is illustrated. This includes a discussion of knowledge, skills, and trust-building as foundations of the selling process. Selling strategy and several personal selling approaches such as consultative selling are also discussed as part of trust-based relationship selling. The chapter discusses sales professionalism with key themes of complexity, collaboration, and accountability and concludes with career insights for future salespeople and sales managers.

OVERVIEW OF PERSONAL SELLING

OBJECTIVES

After completing this chapter, you should be able to

1. Describe the role of personal selling in marketing.

2. Discuss the key roles of salespeople as financial contributors, change agents, communications agents, and customer value agents.

3. Explain the trust-based relationship selling process and how it differs from transactional selling.

4. Understand the concept of selling strategy with its key elements of customer value and alternative personal selling approaches.

5. Explain adaptive selling and five alternative approaches to selling: stimulus response, mental states, problem solving, needs satisfaction, and consultative.

6. Discuss current trends in sales professionalism: complexity, collaboration, and accountability.

PERSONAL SELLING: IT'S ALL ABOUT THE CUSTOMER

Historically, salespeople have been known for taking their story on the road and trying to convince buyers to "buy now." While persuasion remains an important element in personal selling, it is increasingly important to develop sales messages that resonate with specific customers. This means that salespeople must do a more thorough job determining the customer's needs, purchasing motives and processes, and how specific customers define customer value. Salespeople have a lot more customer information at their fingertips, so pre-call research is recommended, followed by conversations with the customer to be sure that the prescribed products and/or services are a good fit for the customer.

SunGard, one of the world's leading software and technology companies, expects its salespeople to become long-term partners and trusted advisors for both current and prospective customers. To fulfill this role, SunGard's salespeople must go beyond sales presentations that focus on product features and pricing options. They must be able to understand the buyer's decision process, tailor sales conversations to specific customer needs, and react to changing customer requirements. In a nutshell, SunGard sales representatives must develop keen insights into their customer's world and differentiate themselves from competitors based on experience and expertise. With SunGard, selling from a strong knowledge base is supported by a market research department that furnishes an "insight vault." The vault is easily accessed by salespeople where they can stay up to date on industry events and relevant marketplace trends.

Creating value by focusing on the customer's most important needs is not always an easy task. Inexperienced salespeople typically understand their own products before they learn the in and outs of their customers' businesses. Experienced salespeople may rely too much on their own view of what is best for their customers. To maximize value creation with customers, salespeople must achieve clarity in their sales dialogues. Customers are extremely busy and don't have the patience to intuit the seller's value. According to popular sales blogger Geoffrey James, customers are in a constant state of information overload and will quickly tune out of the conversation if the salesperson strays from topics of interest to the customer. Further, Mr. James adds that salespeople who unnecessarily complicate the dialogue or lapse into seller jargon will be ineffective.

Sources: Henry Canady, "Selling the New SunGard Way," *Selling Power* (October/November/ December 2013): 27–30; and Geoffrey James, "3 Slam-Dunk Ways to Give Customers Exactly What They Want," *Inc.*, January 31, 2014, www.inc.com/geoffrey-james/the-future-is-in-being-easy.html (accessed March 26, 2014).

THE ROLE OF PERSONAL SELLING IN MARKETING

Marketing is the activity, set of institutions, and processes for creating, communicating, delivering, and exchanging offerings that have value for customers, clients, partners, and society at large.[1] Personal selling, a crucial part of marketing, involves interpersonal communications between buyers and sellers to initiate, develop, and enhance customer relationships. In the best sales organizations, salespeople earn the trust of their customers and utilize selling strategies that satisfy customer needs. In such organizations, salespeople help create customer value and, over time, increase the value delivered to customers.

The Significance of Personal Selling

Personal selling has always been an important part of marketing, particularly for companies that operate in business-to-business markets where purchasing situations often involve complex technical products, large dollar amounts, professional buyers, and multiple parties who influence purchase decisions. The importance of personal selling is reflected in the numbers of salespeople employed by major companies as shown in Exhibit 2.1.[2] Consumer goods companies such as Coca-Cola, Procter & Gamble, and PepsiCo rely heavily on advertising and sales promotion to boost sales at the retail level. But these companies also have huge salesforces that sell to retailers, wholesalers, and other channel intermediaries. As shown in Exhibit 2.1, for example, PepsiCo has 36,000 salespeople.

In terms of money spent, personal selling is the most important part of marketing communications, especially in business-to-business markets. The general public is accustomed to seeing salespeople in some sectors, including retailing, automotive, real estate, insurance and financial services, and service organizations that serve the ultimate consumer. In the business-to-business arena, however, salespeople's significant contributions to marketing go largely unnoticed by the general public. Business purchases far exceed those in consumer markets, with wholesalers, retailers, government agencies, manufacturers, homebuilders, professional services firms, transportation providers, and schools and hospitals being among key customers in the business market.

Types of Sales Jobs

There is considerable variety among sales jobs, with distinctions sometimes made according to what is sold (products vs. services, industrial vs. consumer) or to whom the product is sold (e.g., ultimate consumers, manufacturers, resellers, institutions, the government). Sales jobs can also be classified according to the relative emphasis placed on gaining new customers versus servicing existing customers. Salespeople who focus on gaining new customers are sometimes referred to as hunters, pioneers, and order-getters. These salespeople increase market share for their companies by adding new customers. These new customers may subsequently be turned over to account-servicing salespeople referred to as farmers and *order-takers*. This latter category of salespeople try to increase sales as they build customer share, that is, they seek to improve the seller's position within each account.

Selected Companies with Large Salesforces EXHIBIT 2.1		
Company	**Industry Sector**	**Approximate Number of Salespeople**
PepsiCo	Consumer Goods	36,000
American Express	Financial Services	23,400
AT&T	Communications	25,000
Microsoft	Computer & Office Equipment	16,000
Xerox	Computer & Office Equipment	15,000
IBM	Computer & Office Equipment	14,000
Citigroup	Financial Services	12,700
Johnson & Johnson	Medical Products	8,500
Pfizer	Pharmaceuticals	7,600

Some salespeople are not responsible for making the actual sale, but support the sales effort by providing information and performing other supplemental services. For example, missionary salespeople support the overall sales effort by "spreading the gospel" at the grassroots level. An example of this in the pharmaceutical industry is the detailer, a salesperson who provides physicians, nurses, and other medical professionals with pertinent information about drugs to support the overall sales effort. In the retail sector, merchandisers support the sales effort by setting up point-of-purchase displays, rotating stock, and keeping store personnel informed about new products and sales promotions.

In many companies, salespeople combine these roles in a single job. For example, the national accounts salespeople for Tyco Integrated Security, a multinational company, are expected to contact and secure major new business and maintain existing business at a rate consistent with Tyco's strategic business plan. National accounts salespeople at Tyco also do sales support work such as providing current market information to their employer and attending trade shows and other customer events. In this case, the Tyco salesperson is a hunter for new business, a farmer, or cultivator, of existing business, and also fulfills a sales support role.[3] As a reference point for this book, when we use the term *salesperson*, we are typically referring to a business-to-business combination salesperson that has new business, existing business, and sales support responsibilities. It should also be noted that some salespeople work as part of a sales team. Team selling is discussed in Chapter 3.

Key Roles of Salespeople

To make their investment in personal selling pay off, companies expect a lot from their sales organizations. The expectations of salespeople can be viewed as achieving four key roles: financial contributor, change agent, communications agent, and customer value agent. Salespeople are important financial contributors to their organizations as they assume a key role in revenue production. An emphasis on achieving profit goals, i.e., a healthy bottom line, is well known in business. To support the bottom line, salespeople are expected to achieve revenue goals or a healthy "top line" on the profit and loss statement. Most salespeople are charged with specific dollar goals or quotas, and their job performance and compensation are typically tied closely to whether or not they achieve these revenue goals. While sales organizations are expected to achieve overall revenue targets, they are also increasingly being held accountable for improving overall profitability by enhancing sales organization productivity.

Salespeople are also expected to act as change agents as they stimulate sales cycles and help customers reach buying decisions as soon as reasonably possible. In this sense, salespeople are catalytic agents, that is, when they are added to the economic process, their role is to make something happen. More specifically, they are expected to educate potential customers and advance toward an ultimate sale. In their change agent role, salespeople are heavily involved in the diffusion of innovation, which frequently leads to improved quality of life for consumers and improved business practices. The change agent role can also positively impact economic cycles, assisting in recovery from slow economic periods and extending periods of relative prosperity.

Another key role fulfilled by salespeople is that of communications agent. Basic economics holds that information has utility, and the value of information is widely recognized in the business world. Salespeople are heavily involved as two-way communications agents between their customers and their employers. Customers depend on salespeople for their knowledge of products and services, as well as developments in the marketplace. Sales organizations typically rely on their salespeople to be the eyes and ears of the company, reporting back to the company on competitive activity, buyer preferences, and ideas for new products. Despite the possibility that such communications activities could take away from selling time, most companies find it extremely beneficial to rely on the salesforce to provide valuable information back to the company. Sales organizations consolidate market information from individual salespeople to get a larger picture about competitive activity across the entire market area. Thus it is important that salespeople are careful to report information accurately and in a timely fashion. See "An Ethical Dilemma" for a scenario in which the salesperson must think about the proper way to report competitive activity.

AN ETHICAL DILEMMA

Kelsey Alexander is a sales representative for a large industrial distributor of electrical components in a highly competitive sales territory in upstate New York. She has learned that Connection Central, one of her major competitors, is opening a new distribution center in her territory. Kelsey wanted to be better informed about her competitor's products and distribution capabilities, so she checked out Connection Central's Web site, where she found an invitation to a grand opening for the distribution center. The invitation was directed to Connection Central customers, local government officials, and the business press. The invitation also stated that the general public would be welcome on a space available basis. Kelsey filled out an RSVP form on Connection Central's Web site, pretending to be in the "general public" category. She used a fictitious name for herself and her company. She figured that, as a competitor, she would not be welcome at the open house and she thought her actions were justifiable. As she completed the registration form for the open house, Kelsey reminded herself that "all is fair in love and war," and that she was at war with Connection Central. What do you think of Kelsey's actions?

The fourth key role fulfilled by salespeople is that of customer value agent, with salespeople helping to create, communicate, deliver, and continually increase customer value. Customer value previously discussed in Chapter 1, depends on the buyer's situations, needs, and priorities, but essentially it can be defined as the customer's perception of what they receive (e.g., products, services, information) in exchange for what they give up (e.g., time, effort, and money). Customer value is determined in part by product/service capabilities and the support given by the sales organization to the customer. In addition, salespeople's expertise and behaviors can also be an important dimension of customer value. Salespeople can add to or detract from customer value depending on criteria such as:

- Customer and market knowledge: is the salesperson knowledgeable about the customer's business, competition, and market conditions?

- Coordination: does the salesperson coordinate with others in their company to solve customer problems or provide opportunities to the customer?

- Efficiency: is time spent with this salesperson worthwhile, and can he or she get things done?
- Strategic alignment: does the salesperson understand and contribute to achieving the customer's strategic priorities?
- Trustworthiness: can the salesperson be trusted, i.e., is this person competent, customer-oriented, honest, dependable and compatible with customers?

TRUST-BASED RELATIONSHIP SELLING PROCESS

The sales process shown in Figure 2.1 is representative of sales processes that are customer-oriented. It is not representative of sales approaches that advocate putting pressure on the customer to "say yes" rather than truly satisfy the customer's needs. The latter approaches to selling are referred to as transactional selling. With transactional selling, salespeople focus on maximizing the outcomes of individual transactions rather than on longer-term relationships with customers. Put another away, transactional salespeople try to make a sale on every call, have little regard for the customer's unique needs or priorities, and typically are not very engaged in the service aspects that follow the sale. Transactional selling focuses more on one-way sales presentations, often called sales pitches, in which the salesperson strives to persuade the buyer to make an immediate purchase. These sales pitches vary little from customer to customer, and salespeople are not particularly interested in seeking feedback from buyers during their sales calls.

Trust-Based Relationship Selling Process   **FIGURE 2.1**

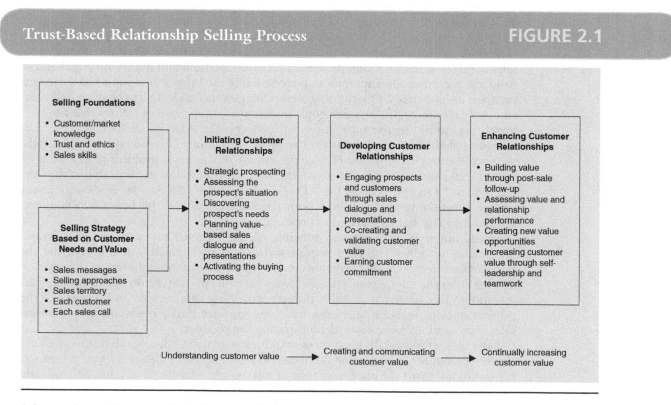

Salespeople must have certain attributes and behave appropriately to inspire trust in their customers and they must be able to adapt their selling strategies to the situation. One or more personal selling approaches are used in the sales process. The major phases in the sales process are initiating, developing, and enhancing customer relationships. Salespeople must understand, help create and communicate, and continually increase customer value during the sales process.

In contrast to transactional selling, trust-based relationship selling, as shown in Figure 2.1, seeks to initiate, develop, and enhance long-term customer relationships by earning customer trust, focusing on customer needs, and having the salesperson play a key role in building the value received by the customer. With trust-based relationship selling, salespeople rely on questioning and listening to establish dialogue with customers. With this approach, communications between buyers and sellers are much more two-way and collaborative than with the transactional approach.

Selling Foundations: Knowledge, Skills, and Trust-Building

As shown in Figure 2.1, the trust-based sales process requires salespeople with the right knowledge and skills who employ an ethical, trust-building approach to selling. This process also requires salespeople whose actions are based on strategies that focus on customer needs and customer value.

Sales Knowledge and Skills

The particular knowledge and skill components required for successful selling will be somewhat dependent on the sales situation. For example, technical products typically require a different knowledge and skill base than would be necessary for selling simple products and selling to government buyers is different from selling to retailers. Despite situational differences, there are some skill and knowledge areas that are commonly required for success in a broad range of sales jobs. Salespeople must understand their customers, including what motivates their customers to make purchases and customer purchasing processes and protocols. They should be experts on their products and services, and be able to link the features (facts and specifications) and benefits (what those features do for their customers) of their offerings to buyer motives. Salespeople also need to be knowledgeable about their competitors and developments in the marketplace.

Specific skills that are important in the sales process include listening, questioning, sales dialogue skills, and sales presentation skills. Listening and questioning go hand in hand and are extremely important in understanding the buyer's viewpoint and determining their unique needs. Questioning methodologies such as SPIN (to be discussed later) and *ADAPT* are helpful to salespeople in determining relevant questions that can ultimately lead to productive interactions with buyers. The ADAPT method suggests that questions should be used to *A*ssess the buyer's situation, *D*iscover the buyer's needs, *A*ctivate the buying process, *P*roject the impact of solving a problem or realizing an opportunity, and make a *T*ransition to the sales presentation or the next step in the buying process.[4] One purpose of the ADAPT method is to develop an efficient, relevant line of questioning that will help both the salesperson and the buyer find common ground for sales dialogue and sales presentations.

In addition to questioning and listening, salespeople must have sales presentation and sales dialogue skills. The term *sales presentation* is traditionally used to describe the face-to-face interactions between buyers and sellers. The term implies more information flowing from the salesperson, though buyers certainly participate during most sales presentations. Key presentation skills include explaining the features and benefits of the product, producing additional information to reinforce claims made, using audiovisual sales aides, and, in some cases, demonstrating the product.

Sales presentation skills remain essential for salespeople, but sales dialogue skills are also important for an increasing number of salespeople. Sales dialogue involves business conversations that take place over time as salespeople attempt to initiate, develop, and enhance relationships with customers. Common sales dialogues include:

- determining if a prospective customer has the financial resources and an adequate interest in making a future purchase to warrant additional follow-up
- assessing the prospective customer's situation and buying processes

- discovering the prospective customer's specific needs and requirements
- confirming the prospective customer's strategic priorities
- illustrating how the sales organization can create and deliver customer value
- negotiating an agreement to do business
- building customer value by providing additional opportunities
- assessing the extent to which the customer is satisfied with the value received

These and other business conversations comprising sales dialogue should be driven by a clear purpose and should be customer-focused. Otherwise, time can be wasted, something both buyer and sellers would like to avoid. Sales dialogue features a back-and-forth, two-way conversation between buyers and sellers, with both parties benefiting from their participation.

Trust-Building as a Sales Foundation

To be successful at trust-building with their customers, research indicates that salespeople should demonstrate five key attributes: customer orientation, competence or expertise, dependability, candor or honesty, and compatibility.[5] Carew International, a leading sales training and consulting company, understands the importance of trust-building. Noting that business relationships seek mutual benefit, profits, efficiency, and growth for both buyers and sellers, Carew emphatically states that the foundation for these beneficial relationships is trust. Carew urges salespeople to demonstrate on a daily basis a firm commitment to doing the right thing. According to Carew, the right thing is a multidimensional concept, with telling the truth, being reliable, and dedication to the customer's well-being as key sales behaviors.[6] It is important to note that salespeople's trustworthiness and overall reputation is easily shared within buyers' networks of professional acquaintances. With communications technology making salespeople's actions more transparent, being trustworthy is more important than ever for sales success.

A customer orientation can be demonstrated through certain behaviors such as determining the buyer's unique needs before recommending a purchase, preventing and correcting problems, and sincere listening during sales calls. HR Chally, a large, widely respected sales consulting and training organization, has studied customer expectations of salespeople. The Chally findings reflect a strong customer orientation, as customers report that they appreciate salespeople who:

- are personally accountable for the customer's desired results
- understand the customer's business
- will be an advocate for the customer so the customer receives maximum value from the selling company
- will be a business consultant who thinks beyond the current transaction
- will solve customer problems
- will be creative in responding to customer needs[7]
- will be easily accessible

Having a strong customer orientation is necessary to build trust, but it is not enough. Salesperson competence, or expertise, is another important dimension required to build customer trust. While most customers will give new salespeople a little time to come up to speed, they rightfully expect salespeople to know what they are doing and to get answers if they don't already know the answer. In any interpersonal relationship, whether it is in the business world or not, candor, or honesty, is essential. Should a customer find that his or her salesperson has been dishonest, the relationship is likely ruined, perhaps never to be resurrected. Dependability, another important trust-builder, should be the easiest to achieve for all salespeople. It is as simple as doing what you say you will do. Yet many salespeople fail on this dimension by over-promising and under-delivering or simply forgetting to fulfill an obligation such as getting back to a customer with requested information by a specified time. Finally, customer compatibility can help build trust. Compatibility is less about the personal dynamics between buyers and sellers than it is about the salesperson being viewed as a good person to do business with. While some personal characteristics, e.g., pleasant personality and a positive attitude, can enhance compatibility, professionalism and making it easy for the customer to do business with the selling firm also determine compatibility. While we say that it is not necessary for a customer to like a salesperson in order to trust the salesperson, it is harder to trust someone whom one dislikes.

In addition to consistently exhibiting trust-building behaviors, it is important that salespeople be aware of pertinent laws and potentially troublesome ethical pitfalls. Some suggestions for playing it safe from an ethical and legal perspective are shown in Exhibit 2.2.

Selling Strategy

Selling strategy involves the planning of sales messages and interactions with customers. Selling strategy can be defined at three levels: for a group of customers, i.e., a sales territory; for individual customers; and for specific customer encounters, referred to as sales calls. Variations in selling strategy across these three levels are tied largely to how much alteration there is in sales messages at the territory, customer, and sales call levels and the extent to which unique customer needs and customer value are factored into these sales messages.

Personal Selling Approaches

Salespeople can use one or more personal selling approaches to interact with their customers. As shown in Figure 2.2, these approaches vary according to how much salespeople adapt their messages from customer to customer, and the extent to which the sales message is based on unique buyer needs, customer value, and the customer's strategic priorities. The five personal selling approaches shown in Figure 2.2 are: stimulus response; mental states; problem solving; need satisfaction, and consultative selling.[8]

EXHIBIT 2.2   Ethical and Legal Guidelines

1. Adhere to sales organization and company codes of ethics and codes of conduct.
2. Be truthful. Use facts and be able to substantiate performance claims made for products and services.
3. Accurately depict competitors. Do not disparage competitors.
4. Obtain competitive information only through ethical and legal means.
5. Be aware of and obey relevant laws and regulations, including local laws.
6. Do not create false expectations by over-promising. Remember that promises and verbal agreements can be as binding as a written contract.
7. Ensure that customers are aware of stipulations for proper usage of products and any safety issues and limitations.
8. Observe the need for confidentiality with sensitive information provided by customers and employers.
9. Avoid conflicts of interests, or even the appearance of conflicts of interests.
10. Avoid discussions with competitors that deal with pricing, profit margins, bids or intent to bid, terms of sale, discounts, promotional allowances, sales territories or markets to be served, and the rejection or termination of customers.
11. Do not make the purchase of one product a condition of making another product available to customers.
12. If selling to competing retailers or competing wholesalers who are buying similar quantities of like products, ensure a level playing field in terms of prices, terms of sale, and promotional support offered.
13. Be aware of and comply with customer codes of ethics, purchasing protocol and guidelines.
14. Report unethical and illegal activities to supervisors, and, if appropriate, to law enforcement and regulatory personnel.

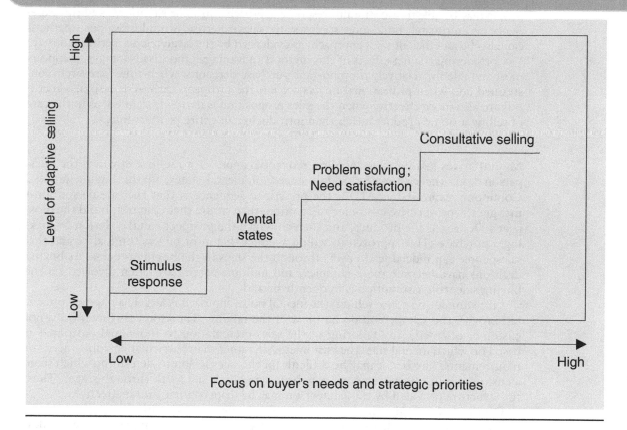

Personal Selling Approaches   FIGURE 2.2

The five personal selling approaches are stimulus response, mental states, problem solving, need satisfaction, and consultative. These approaches vary according to how much the sales message focuses on unique customer needs and strategic priorities, and the level of adaptive selling from one customer to the next.

Since personal selling involves interpersonal communication, salespeople can practice adaptive selling, which means they can modify their sales messages and behaviors during a sales presentation or as they encounter unique sales situations and customers. Because salespeople often encounter buyers with different personalities, communications styles, and needs and goals, adaptive selling is an important concept. With adaptive selling, the salesperson could use one or more of the selling approaches shown in Figure 2.2 or could develop hybrid selling approaches that draw from the illustrated approaches.

Stimulus Response Selling

Of the five selling approaches shown in Figure 2.2, stimulus response selling is the least flexible and least focused on the buyer's unique needs and strategic priorities. With only minor variations, all customers get the same sales presentation. The logic behind stimulus response selling comes from lab experiments with animal behavior in which various stimuli would elicit desired behavior. Extended into the sales context, salespeople using this approach furnish the stimuli (words and actions) to produce the desired response (a customer purchase). Stimulus response selling is the dominant approach used by telemarketing salespeople, who work from a script or use a memorized canned sales presentation.

Buyers, especially professional buyers, do not like stimulus response sales approaches. Most buyers like to take an active role in the sales interaction, and stimulus response selling calls for the salesperson to do most of the talking. Further, buyers may have difficulty getting the information they want unless their questions and concerns fit the preplanned script. Should questions go unanswered, a positive purchase decision is unlikely.

Stimulus response sales strategies offer some advantages to sellers. Through pre-planning, key selling points can be sequenced in a logical order and likely questions and objections can be addressed before they are voiced by the buyer. Inexperienced salespeople may be able to use stimulus response approaches in some situations, and this experience may ultimately build more sophisticated sales expertise. Stimulus response methods can also be an efficient sales approach, as evidenced by the large telemarketing industry.

Considering the net effects of this method's advantages and disadvantages, it appears most suitable for relatively unimportant purchase decisions, when time is severely constrained and when professional buyers are not the prospects. Stimulus response methods are also more effective when the sales proposition is narrowly defined, as in the case of selling a single product rather than introducing an entire product line.

Mental States Selling

Mental states selling is essentially a sequential approach to selling in which the salesperson leads the customer through stages, or mental states, in the buying process. Commonly expressed as AIDA, the prescribed sequence is that the salesperson must first get the prospective customer's *A*ttention, then secure their *I*nterest, build the prospect's *D*esire for the product, and then convince the prospect to take *A*ction by making a purchase. This approach to selling assumes that most buyers think alike and that salespeople can indeed lead buyers through the steps in the buying process. As buying decisions have become more complex, and multiple parties are often involved on the buying side, this assumption is frequently invalid.

Like stimulus response selling, the mental states approach is largely a one-way presentation with the salesperson doing most of the talking. Therefore, this method is not customer-oriented. Any tailoring of the sales presentation to individual customers is based on which mental state the customer is in, rather than particular customer needs or requirements. Further, it may be difficult for the salesperson to determine which stage a customer is in, or the customer may be moving back and forth through stages. Thus, the structure provided by the salesperson may be inappropriate and ineffective.

On the positive side, this method does force some pre-planning by the salesperson, who comes to realize that timing is an important aspect of the purchase process. Salespeople using this method are listening to the customer to determine what stage they are in. As the salesperson listens, it is highly likely that he or she will realize that a more customer-oriented approach is in order if customer needs are to be met. See "An Ethical Dilemma" for a situation in which the salesperson is contemplating the movement of the prospect into the "action" stage.

AN ETHICAL DILEMMA

Kyle Burklin, a sales representative for PAY-SOURCE, a payroll-processing software company, has been working for two months to secure a contract with Catskill Mountains Surgical Center. His primary contact at the surgical center is Rebecca Keith, the office manager. Rebecca currently processes the employee payroll with an antiquated time-consuming manual system, and has agreed with Kyle that it is time for a change. Even so, Rebecca continually says she is too busy to make the change. She repeatedly has told Kyle that she will make the change when the time is right. When Kyle follows up and suggests implementation of the new system, Rebecca puts him off until "things settle down and I have time to deal with the new system." Kyle is under pressure from his sales manager, Ray Gould, to close the deal by the end of the week. Ray told Kyle, "Enough is enough. Tell Rebecca that the $200 installation fee we quoted will expire this Friday. After that, the installation fee will be $400." Kyle knew that new customers were never charged more than $200 for installation, but he was frustrated with waiting so long for Rebecca to make a decision. Further, if he closed the sale by Friday, Kyle would qualify as the month's top salesperson in his office. What should Kyle do?

Need Satisfaction Selling

The logic of need satisfaction selling is that customers will be motivated to buy to satisfy particular needs. Salespeople using this method help customers identify their needs if customers are not already aware of their needs, and then sell customers products and services to meet the needs. In contrast to the stimulus response and mental states methods, need satisfaction selling focuses on the customer. Salespeople use questions to uncover buyer needs, and the customer typically dominates the sales interaction until needs have been established. At that point, the salesperson moves to a more active selling role, describing how his or her offering can satisfy the buyer's needs.

Customers appreciate this approach to selling, as they feel that their point of view and unique circumstances are being addressed. Although it may take a fair amount of time to fully define customer needs, both customers and salespeople think this is often time well spent, especially if a major purchase is pending. Also, this sales approach can minimize the resistance from the prospect that sometimes surfaces when a salesperson rushes to the persuasive part of the sales message without adequate attention to the buyer's needs. Just as it is when we visit our doctor, we appreciate diagnosis before prescription.

Problem-Solving Selling

Problem-solving selling extends need satisfaction selling beyond identifying needs to developing alternative solutions for satisfying these needs. This approach has been popularized by the commercial success of SPIN selling, conceived by Neil Rackham.[9] With SPIN selling, the salesperson investigates the customer's *Situation*, determines a *Problem*, discusses the *Implications* of the problem if it is left unattended, and shows how the salesperson's offering can solve the problem (*Need payoff*). An important reality for salespeople using problem-solving selling in a business world with competing priorities and limited resources is that not all customer problems are worth solving—at least in the short term. To be effective, the SPIN method and other problem-solving approaches typically require that salespeople clearly illustrate the significance of the existing problem and how the customer can receive significant customer value from the problem solution.

Consultative Selling

Consultative selling is the process of helping customers reach their strategic goals by using the products, services, and expertise of the sales organization.[10] Consultant Mack Hanan is credited with introducing the concept of consultative selling to the business world in 1970. In his most recent book on the topic, Hanan distinguishes between consultative sellers and suppliers or vendors by stating that "no matter what vendor suppliers make, they sell it; no matter what consultative sellers make, they sell the value that it adds."[11] Consultative selling requires that the salesperson be an expert on the customer's business, competitors, and market developments. This expertise ultimately puts the salesperson in a consultant, or advisor role, in which educating the customer is an important activity.

Consultative selling has become a popular approach across many industries, as indicated by job postings on employment Web sites. A recent review of a recent review of the popular job posting site www.indeed.com revealed more than 7,000 jobs in which consultative selling was specified as a key job activity. Hiring companies included FedEx, Facebook, Xerox, Fender Musical Instruments, AT&T, and Wells Fargo.[12]

Consultative selling is differentiated from other sales approaches because it focuses on achieving strategic goals of customers. A consultative process may also solve customer problems, meet customer needs, and provide additional customer opportunities. But unless the process is focused on strategic priorities of the customer, it is not truly a consultative process.

To illustrate consultative selling, consider how Wal-Mart screens out potential suppliers. Before a company has an opportunity to attempt to sell to Wal-Mart, it must answer key questions that would require some knowledge of Wal-Mart's strategic priorities. For example, one question is: "How can Wal-Mart gain market share with your product and, at the same time, control the cost of doing business to maximize sales?" Gaining market share and controlling costs have been and continue to be strategic priorities for Wal-Mart, facts that are readily available from annual reports, press releases, and other sources.

Consultative selling often requires that the salesperson be a coordinator, arranging for others in the selling company to play a role in the sales process. For example, logistics and manufacturing personnel might lend their expertise at the request of a software salesperson to help redesign the customer's supply chain. In this example, the customer might purchase the software for use in its supply chain, while the redesign of the supply chain helps the customer achieve a strategic priority of cutting overall operating expenses. The importance of consultative salespeople working with others within their own companies to create customer value is evident to Randall Murphy of Acclivus R3, a consulting firm whose clients include IBM, Shell, and Verizon. Mr. Murphy notes that it takes a high level of business expertise to practice consultative selling, and that salespeople and the sales organization typically need additional expertise and proactive support from coworkers and top management to succeed with a consultative approach. Mr. Murphy counsels sales managers to get buy-in from all-important parties within their own companies before implementing consultative selling.[13]

Consultative sellers must also commit to being partners with their customer over a long-time horizon rather than being focused on making short-term sales. Such a commitment means that the sales organization must also be committed to the consultative selling approach and design its salesperson performance evaluation and reward systems accordingly. Consultative selling is not appropriate for all sales situations. Some customers are not interested in such a collaborative approach and may not wish to share their strategic priorities with sellers. Some products, including many commodities, are purchased more on price basis. In such cases, unless value can be defined beyond price considerations, consultative selling is likely to be an inefficient sales approach. For more on consultative selling, see "Sales Management in the 21st Century: Consultative Selling."

SALES MANAGEMENT IN THE 21ST CENTURY

Consultative Selling

Chris Fergen, senior vice president of sales for X-Rite, a global leader in color science and technology, comments on the importance of consultative selling in technical markets.

The salesperson's role as a strategic orchestrator is critical in consultative selling. The salesperson is at the hub of the interaction between sales, product management, and marketing. At the point of impact with the customer, salespeople represent our combined expertise as a company and are expected to add to the customer value equation. The value of our salespeople is identified more by the information they gather from customers than the information they dispense. We strive to be more than vendors to our customers. We want to be their trusted advisors. To accomplish trusted advisor status, we constantly focus on improving our efficiency and effectiveness so we can maximize customer value.

CURRENT TRENDS IN SALES PROFESSIONALISM

The current emphasis on sales professionalism has been widely embraced by progressive sales organizations, professional groups, sales consultants, educators, and sales trainers. The term has various meanings, but common elements of sales professionalism include the use of customer-oriented, truthful, non-manipulative sales strategies and tactics to satisfy the long-term needs of customers and the selling firm. Sales professionalism also requires that salespeople work from a dynamic, ever-changing knowledge base. New products, technologies, and market developments require a dedication to career-long learning to avoid obsolescence. There is an old saying that applies in this case: "If you think you have figured out the permanent formula for success, you are probably one step away from becoming obsolete."

As we look to the future of the sales profession, three key themes are evident. Sales organizations, including salespeople, sales managers, and sales executives must be:

- Capable of working in an increasingly complex business environment;
- Strong collaborators, both within their own organizations and with their customers;
- Accountable for their actions and results from an ethical and fiscal responsibility point of view.[14]

DHL Global Forwarding (DGF), an international airfreight company with headquarters in Bonn, Germany, typifies a successful sales organization dealing with complexity, collaboration, and accountability. DGF's 8,000 salespeople in the company's 850 branches deal with complex logistical projects in industrial settings across the globe. To remain competitive in a highly competitive marketplace, DGF invests heavily in sales training for different sales roles in 13 languages. A virtual team of 105 sales trainers work with the global salesforce to certify salespeople as specialists in international logistical operations. DFG's training utilizes a wide variety of delivery mechanisms, including online self-paced learning, classroom sessions, and sales management review sessions. Sales training is reinforced through newsletters, online magazines, video and email messages, and internal competitions inspire continual learning. Cigdem Wondergem, global head of sales training, received an international award from industry executives for her innovative sales training programs. To win the award, Ms. Wondergem exemplified the ability to deal with complexity, accountability, and collaboration. The CEO of DHL specifically praised Ms. Wondergem's strengths in communication and collaboration as keys to the successful sales training program.[15] For some of the key changes and salesforce responses related to the themes of complexity, collaboration, and accountability, see Exhibit 2.3.

Complexity

The business environment is becoming more complex, and, for sales organizations, increasing complexity is particularly acute. This is because sales organizations operate across organizational boundaries, working with customers and typically facing numerous competitors. Further, technology advances, growing dominance of large buyers such as Wal-Mart, slow-growth economies in much of the world, and increasing globalization and diversity in the customer base all contribute to a more complex sales environment. To succeed in such a complex setting, sales organizations must focus on the customer and strive for more trust-based, long-term relationships. Sales must become a "smarter" business function, meaning that sales strategy becomes more important. As will be discussed in Chapter 3, this often means developing new sales channels, or ways of reaching customers. To keep abreast of an ever-changing environment, sales organizations must become continual learning organizations and recruit salespeople who can adapt to diverse cultures, languages, and business practices.

Collaboration

The sales function is finding it increasingly important to collaborate with other functional areas within their companies and with customers. Within their own companies, the need for sales to integrate and cooperate more with production, finance, and marketing is getting a lot of attention in the business world. In particular, the importance of better alignment between sales and marketing is widely acknowledged as indicated by the American Marketing Association's training seminars on the topic. To improve collaboration between sales and marketing, the two parties should agree on critical customer issues such as identification of customer segments and the related needs, buying motives, purchasing processes, and relevant value dimensions within those segments.[16] Clearly, this need for more collaboration should be addressed by cross-functional training and communications programs.

EXHIBIT 2.3   Current Trends in Sales Professionalism: Complexity, Collaboration, and Accountability

Complexity Issues	Salesforce Responses
Increasing customer expectations driven by buyer dominance, slow-growth economies, and increasing competition	Focus on the customer; use salespeople to monitor market developments; emphasize trust-based, long-term customer relationships
Significant change occurring more frequently, e.g., sales technology advancing rapidly, markets often in a state of flux	Sales must become more strategic; sales organizations must become learning organizations; complement initial training with ongoing sales training; use sales specialists for specific customer types; develop multiple sales channels such as major accounts programs and electronic networks
Increasing customer diversity and globalization	Recruiting and developing salespeople who understand diverse cultures, languages, and business practices

Collaboration Issues	Salesforce Responses
More internal collaboration needed between sales, marketing, and other functional units	Implement cross-functional programs to foster communication and cooperation
Sales managers and salespeople need to collaborate more, rather than sales managers relying on authority to direct the salesforce	Sales managers should build trust with salespeople; ensure that salespeople know how to manage themselves and play a leadership role when required
Need for more customer-oriented selling	Focus on trust-based relationship selling; train salespeople in problem solving, conflict resolution, and how to recover from service failures

Accountability Issues	Salesforce Responses
Increasing the efficiency and effectiveness of sales operations	Appropriate use of sales technology; lower-cost contact methods, e.g., telemarketing for some customers; implementing more effective sales organization structures
Customer demands for ethical, trustworthy salespeople	Ensure that salespeople know the ethical and legal framework for their markets, including cultural and global market variations

Sources: Thomas N. Ingram, "Future Themes in Sales and Sales Management: Complexity, Collaboration, and Accountability," *Journal of Marketing Theory and Practice* (Fall 2004): 1–11; Thomas N. Ingram, Raymond W. LaForge, William B. Locander, Scott B. MacKenzie, and Philip M. Podsakoff, "New Directions in Sales Leadership Research," *Journal of Personal Selling & Sales Management* 25 (Spring 2005): 137–154.

Greater collaboration is also needed between sales managers and salespeople, and sales managers should strive to earn the trust of their salespeople rather than over-relying on the authority provided by their supervisory position. With customers, collaboration should extend the concept of customer-oriented selling to include problem solving and involving the salesforce in recovering from service problems that may arise. For more about the importance of collaboration, see "Sales Management in the 21st Century: The Importance of Teamwork."

The Importance of Teamwork

Jerry Heffel, president emeritus of the Southwestern Company, offers his perspective on teamwork:

Sometimes the salesperson is referred to as the lead car in the business train. But just having a lead car doesn't make a train. For this reason, a salesperson who is effective long term is also an effective team player—he or she realizes they need coordinated involvement from many different parts of the orga-nization in order to serve the customer. At some time, whenever they see themselves as part of the customer's team, and that they are both striving for the same outcome, they become an indispensable part of the value chain for that customer. Southwestern's sales training philosophy stresses this team aspect: we tell our salespeople that they are the gas and oil of the free enterprise system, but they also need tires, the car body, the drive train, and what's in the trunk to get anywhere significant.

Accountability

More than ever, sales organizations are being scrutinized under a sharp lens. The scrutiny focuses on two areas: ethics and fiscal responsibility. We have spoken at length in this chapter about the need for ethical, trustworthy salespeople. Companies and salespeople who do not practice ethical selling are increasingly subject to extreme criticism, customer dissatisfaction, and in some cases, legal sanctions.

Some of the current focus on sales ethics comes from unethical sales behavior. As an example, the Do Not Call restrictions imposed on telemarketers by the Federal Trade Commission were implemented primarily because unscrupulous sales organizations were acting contrary to the tenets of sales professionalism. Putting it bluntly, the incorporation of sales professionalism into an organization's sales practices is good business. To do otherwise puts the sales organization into a vulnerable position that may lead to its demise.

As we pointed out early in this chapter, the sales function represents a substantial investment for many firms. In the past, the sales function was more concerned about generating sales revenue than the costs of generating that revenue. Things have changed, and most sales managers and executives, along with an increasing number of salespeople, are being held accountable not only for achieving revenue targets, but doing so at a reasonable cost. The proper utilization of technology, careful travel planning, and control of other direct selling costs is definitely part of most sales managers' and salespeople's job.

SALES CAREER INSIGHTS

Since this is a college textbook, a few comments about sales careers are in order. Professional selling offers excellent career opportunities, and the U.S. Department of Labor projects growth over the next decade in the total number of salespeople in all industry categories. For many newly minted college graduates, professional selling is one of the most popular entry-level jobs. In larger companies, some new hires will make a career in sales and sales management and others will branch out into other areas, including marketing management and general management.

For new college graduates, starting in sales can be an attractive opportunity. The pay is good and can rapidly become great for those who excel, because pay is closely tied to performance in selling. In the early years of their careers, salespeople become experts on their company's products, competitive offerings, and customer behavior. They learn to work independently and as a team member while sharpening their communications skills and problem-solving skills. All of this helps prepare young salespeople for management positions should they want to move in that direction.

One of the most important elements of leadership is persuading others to your point of view, and salespeople are involved in persuasive communications on a daily basis.

Further, running a sales territory has some parallels with running your own company in terms of achieving measurable outcomes, meeting obligations to others, and being accountable from a perspective that blends ethics and profitable business practices. For the many young people who aspire to be entrepreneurs, selling experience can be indispensable. Entrepreneurs spend a lifetime selling their ideas to others, including investors, resellers, and customers.

On a daily basis, salespeople encounter a great deal of variety in their jobs, calling on different customers, perhaps selling different products depending on the situation, and facing ever-changing competitive activities. Salespeople rarely complain about job boredom, as the variety and fast pace in most sales jobs make the job challenging rather than boring. Salespeople constantly know how they are doing in terms of job performance, as they are getting immediate feedback on every sales call. They play a critical role for their customers and their employers, so there is some pressure to perform at an acceptable level.

Like most professions, a key to success in sales and sales management is how well an individual is suited to a particular job. For those interested in learning more about sales careers, there are a variety of ways to proceed. Visit with professional salespeople and sales managers. Check out professional organizations such as the Sales Management Association (www.salesmanagement.org) and publications such as *Sales and Marketing Management* (www.salesandmarketing.com) and *Selling Power* (www.sellingpower. com). Read the free materials of leading sales training and consulting firms such as HR Chally (www.chally.com), Forum (www.forum.com), and Miller Heiman (www.miller-heiman.com). Become familiar with a variety of sales positions and requirements of sales job applicants from university career centers and employment listing services such as Indeed (www.indeed.com). In addition, there are excellent books on professional selling available through university libraries and commercial bookstores for those who want to explore various dimensions of selling and sales management.

SUMMARY

1. **Describe the role of personal selling in marketing.** Personal selling involves interpersonal communications between buyers and sellers to initiate, develop, and enhance customer relationships. It is widely used in consumer goods companies, and plays an especially critical role in business-to-business markets. More money is spent on personal selling than any other form of marketing communications, including advertising and sales promotion. Some salespeople, referred to as hunters, pioneers, and order-getters, focus more on building market share with new customers, while others (e.g., missionary salespeople, detailers, and merchandisers) focus more on selling to existing customers. In many companies, salespeople have a combination of responsibilities to attract new customers, enhance relationships with existing customers, and perform some service activities to support the overall sales effort.

2. **Discuss the key roles of salespeople as financial contributors, change agents, communications agents, and customer value agents.** Salespeople perform a key role by making sales and thus generating revenue for their employers. Increasingly, salespeople are also expected to contribute to the bottom line by being more productive with their sales activities. Salespeople are change agents, meaning, when added to the process, they are expected to make positive things happen. In this role, salespeople facilitate diffusion of innovation and improved business practices. As communications agents, salespeople are involved in the two-way flow of information between their customers and their employer. Salespeople do more than communicate customer value. They can be part of customer value by impacting the value received by the customer. Salespeople can also be an important element in delivering increasing levels of customer value by providing additional opportunities to customers and by solving problems and providing ongoing service to their customers.

3. **Explain the trust-based relationship selling process and how it differs from transactional selling.** Transactional selling is focused more on the seller's desire to make an immediate sale than it is on the customer's needs and strategic priorities. Trust-based relationship selling, as shown in Figure 2.1, seeks to initiate, develop, and enhance customer relationships by earning customer trust, focusing on customer needs, and having the salesperson play a key role in building the value received by the customer. Communications with this approach are much more two-way and collaborative than with the transactional approach.

4. **Understand the concept of selling strategy with its key elements of customer value and alternative personal selling approaches.** Selling strategy involves the planning of sales messages and interaction with customers. Customer value is defined differently by different customers, but essentially it is what the customer gets (products, services, solutions) for what the customer gives up (typically time and money). Selling strategies can be set for a group of customers or for a specific customer. In addition, selling strategies can vary from one sales call to the next as salespeople engage in sales dialogue with their customers. In developing selling strategies, salespeople may use various approaches as illustrated in Figure 2.2.

5. **Explain adaptive selling and five alternative approaches to selling: stimulus response, mental states, problem solving, need satisfaction, and consultative.** Adaptive selling takes place when salespeople modify their sales messages and behaviors during sales presentations and sales dialogues, or when they encounter unique sales situations and customers. Adaptive selling might draw from one or more of the basic approaches to personal selling, or the adaptive salesperson might develop a unique selling approach in a given sales situation. The approaches to personal selling shown in Figure 2.2 range from stimulus response (not focused on unique customer needs or strategic priorities, not adaptive) to consultative selling (high on both customer focus and level of adaptive selling). Between these two extremes, other approaches to selling are mental states, problem solving, and need satisfaction selling.

6. **Discuss current trends in sales professionalism: complexity, collaboration, and accountability.** The business world is becoming more complex, as indicated by increasing buyer expectations, slow-growth economies, and increasing levels of competitive activity. Significant change is occurring more frequently, and customers are increasingly diverse and global in their operation and perspectives. As a result, salesforces must focus on the customer and seek to build trust-based, long-term relationships. The sales function is becoming more strategic, and recruiting and training salespeople with the capacity to learn is important for success. More collaboration is needed within the selling company and with customers to ensure future success. More customer-oriented selling is required and salespeople should be trained in problem solving, conflict resolution, and how to recover from service failure. Salesforces are being held more accountable now than in the past. Accountability is important from efficiency/effectiveness and ethics/trust-building perspectives. Sales organizations are using new technologies, process improvements, and alternative sales organization structures to become more efficient and effective. Sales training on ethical and legal frameworks is recommended.

UNDERSTANDING SALES MANAGEMENT TERMS

personal selling	sales dialogue
hunters	trust-building
pioneers	customer orientation
order-getters	salesperson competence
farmers	candor
order-takers	dependability

missionary salespeople	customer compatibility
detailer	selling strategy
merchandiser	adaptive selling
financial contributor	stimulus response selling
change agent	mental states selling
communications agent	need satisfaction selling
customer value agent	problem-solving selling
customer value	SPIN selling
transactional selling	consultative selling
trust-based relationship selling	sales professionalism
ADAPT	

DEVELOPING SALES MANAGEMENT KNOWLEDGE

1. Personal selling is especially critical for companies that sell to other businesses. Does this mean that personal selling is unimportant to retailers and others who sell directly to ultimate consumers?

2. Fielding a large salesforce is an expensive proposition. In terms of the key roles fulfilled by salespeople, how do companies make this investment pay off?

3. What is customer value? How can salespeople add to the value received by customers?

4. Review the five approaches to personal selling in Figure 2.2. Which of the five approaches require strong listening and questioning skills? Which of the five approaches would require sales dialogue?

5. How can salespeople earn the trust of their customers?

6. Explain how the ADAPT and SPIN questioning methods can be used in the sales process. How are the two methods similar? How are they different?

7. What is adaptive selling? Can a salesperson practice consultative selling without practicing adaptive selling?

8. How does consultative selling differ from problem-solving selling?

9. When do you think stimulus response selling would be most effective?

10. In consultative selling, how important is collaboration with the customer and within the sales organization?

BUILDING SALES MANAGEMENT SKILLS

1. Successful salespeople and sales managers must continue to learn about their profession, especially trends and best practices. One way to learn about new developments is to monitor leading sales training and consulting firms. Visit the following Web sites and develop a listing of the 10 ideas or trends that you think are particularly useful for improving the performance of a sales organization. The Web sites are:

   - HR Chally, www.chally.com
   - Forum Corporation, www.forum.com
   - Miller Heiman, www.millerheiman.com

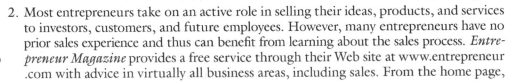

2. Most entrepreneurs take on an active role in selling their ideas, products, and services to investors, customers, and future employees. However, many entrepreneurs have no prior sales experience and thus can benefit from learning about the sales process. *Entrepreneur Magazine* provides a free service through their Web site at www.entrepreneur.com with advice in virtually all business areas, including sales. From the home page,

click on the "Marketing" link, then the "Sales" link. From there, click on the "How-To Guides." Select one of the guides that you think is a good example of customer-oriented selling, prepare a short written summary of the guide, and be prepared to share your findings in a class discussion.

3. Many major corporations provide useful information on their Web sites for potential vendors (suppliers). For example, go to Best Buy's portal for vendors at www.extending thereach.com. Click on the link "Become a Partner," then click on "New Merchandising Vendor Inquiry Form." Based on the key questions for potential vendor which of the following personal selling approaches do you think would be most appropriate for selling to Best Buy: problem solving, need satisfaction, or consultative? Explain your reasoning.

ROLE PLAY

4. **Role-Play**

    Situation: Review the ADAPT questioning method on p. 22.

    Characters: One student is the seller, and one student is the potential buyer.

    Scene: As the seller, you are trying to determine if one of your classmates has any unmet needs or problems with their cell phone or smart phone. Use ADAPT questions prepared in advance to see if your classmate would consider switching to another phone, coverage plan, or data plan. Afterwards, the buyer and seller should critique the seller's performance and discuss how thoughtful questions can be useful in the sales process. Repeat the exercise with the roles reversed.

ROLE PLAY

5. **Role-Play**

    Situation: Review the ethical and legal guidelines in Exhibit 2.2.

    Characters: One sales manager and one salesperson for ABC, an athletic shoe manufacturer that sells to sporting goods retailers.

    Scene: The salesperson is a good performer in terms of meeting sales quotas, but the sales manager is concerned about some the salesperson's behaviors. Specifically, the salesperson sometimes makes promises that cannot be kept. Second, the salesperson tends to exaggerate the market growth and potential profitability of ABC's products when trying to secure new accounts. Role play a meeting in which the sales manager coaches the salesperson to take a trust-based approach to selling. The salesperson sees no harm in his/her current approach and sincerely believes that stretching the truth helps increase sales. Afterwards, discuss the pros and cons of trust-based selling in a competitive environment.

MAKING SALES MANAGEMENT DECISIONS

CASE 2.1: PROFOOD SUPPLY COMPANY

Background

ProFood Supply Company was founded in New York in 1960 to supply professional catering companies with a wide variety of institutional food products, including canned vegetables and meats. The company had grown steadily over the decades, and is now one of the largest full-service institutional food suppliers in the nation, selling perishable and nonperishable foods and foodservice supplies such as tablecloths, napkins, and tableware. In the past year, ProFood had begun an aggressive push into a new market segment, the hotel/motel restaurant market.

Current Situation

Jon Menzes is the ProFood sales representative in Nashville, Tennessee. Jon has been with the company for almost two years. He is a recent college graduate and looks forward to proving himself in his sales position, then moving into management with the company. Jon's sales manager, Emily Lewis, has told Jon that if he finishes the year over 100 percent on his sales versus quota target that he would enter the pool of candidates for promotion sometime in the following 12 months. Jon is doing quite well with his existing accounts, and has added a couple of new accounts. He believes that he will finish the year a little over 100 percent of quota, but he needs to add some of the new hotel/motel business to be sure he achieves his sales goals.

Jon has been attempting to secure the restaurant business of Sleep Tight Inns, a regional chain of 16 moderately priced motels in Tennessee. Sleep Tight's corporate headquarters are in Nashville and the chain currently buys all of its food and restaurant supplies from Swanson's Food Supply, a well-established wholesale restaurant supplier. Swanson's has its own salesforce, most of whom are veteran salespeople who have established good relationships with the restaurant operators in their sales territories.

ProFood has not been a supplier for Swanson's for more than 10 years. Jon has been told that ProFood and Swanson's had some friction over service problems, with Swanson's head buyer claiming that ProFood was not a reliable supplier. The buyer reportedly withheld partial payment on several invoices, and ultimately ProFood refused to sell to Swanson's. Jon and the ProFood sales representative who preceded him had tried to get reestablished with Swanson's, but Swanson's buyers had steadfastly refused to buy from ProFood.

Jon was determined to get the Sleep Tight Inn's business, so he made sales calls on the 16 motels to gauge their interest in switching to Baker Brothers, another foodservice wholesaler with whom Jon had a strong working relationship. The Sleep Tight operators were unanimous—they had no intention of leaving Swanson's for Baker Brothers. In making the rounds to the 16 motels, Jon learned that the individual hotel managers had no authority to buy from suppliers that had not been previously approved by their corporate headquarters in Nashville. Jon then called on Sleep Tight's corporate headquarters, where he learned that becoming an approved supplier would take a minimum of 60 days—if approval was granted. Sleep Tight's director of purchasing was frank with Jon, telling him: "We have been extremely satisfied with Swanson's, and don't see much need to add Baker Brothers to the list of approved suppliers. If I were in your shoes, I would try to sell through Swanson's."

Jon went back to Swanson's, trying once again to become one of their suppliers. He decided to use a foot-in-the-door strategy, meaning that he would only try to sell one small part of his product line, with hopes that if this proved to be successful, he would be able to expand his sales through Swanson's. Jon presented the newest version of ProFood, a very attractive tablecloth/napkin package that could be customized with Sleep Tight's logo. Bill Wilson, the Swanson's buyer, turned Jon down, saying, "Jon, don't take this personally, but we simply are not ready to do business with ProFood again. You guys are doing some impressive things in the marketplace, and next year we may get together with you. But that's not in the plan for this year."

Disappointed, Jon felt he had but one choice if he wanted to make his year-end numbers. He arranged sales calls with the three Baker Brothers sales representatives who called on Sleep Tight Inns. Jon planned to work with the Baker Brothers salespeople to present the ProFood packages, cut the price to stimulate interest, and try to convince all 16 of the Sleep Tight operators to buy the packages from Baker Brothers. If the motel operators liked the packages, Jon figured he could use their interest to speed up the supplier approval process back at Sleep Tight's headquarters and book the additional sales volume before year-end.

It was now Friday night, and Jon was heading home. It had been a tough week, and he was looking forward to the weekend. The Swanson's situation with Sleep Tight had not gone the way he hoped it would, but now that he had decided what to do, he was feeling better. Jon did not like to lose, and as he drove home, more than once he thought, "I'll show Swanson's. If you don't play ball with me, I'll take the business through Baker Brothers." Jon planned to call Emily Lewis over the weekend and run the plan by her. Next week, he planned on hitting all of the Sleep Tight Inns with the Baker Brothers salespeople.

Questions

1. How likely is it that Jon Menzes will be successful in the short term with this strategy?
2. What are the longer-run implications of this strategy for Jon Menzes and ProFood?
3. If you were Emily Lewis, what advice would you give Jon?

Role Play

Situation: Read Case 2.1.

Characters: Jon Menzes, ProFood sales representative; Emily Lewis, ProFood sales manager.

Scene: *Location*—Jon and Emily talk on the phone on Saturday morning. *Action*—Emily expresses some concerns about Jon's plans for gaining the Sleep Tight business. She thinks that it is important that ProFood rekindle its relationship with Swanson's and feels that Jon's plan could have a major negative impact on any chance of doing business with Swanson's in the future. Jon is focused on making his numbers and thinks that Emily is unfairly holding him back.

ROLE PLAY

Upon completion of the role play, address these questions:

1. With an existing customer (Baker Brothers) and two potential customers (wholesaler Swanson's and end user Sleep Tight Inns), how would you assess Jon's focus? Is it customer-oriented? Is it based on delivering customer value?
2. Assume that Jon proceeds with his plan to call on Sleep Tight Inns with the Baker Brothers salespeople. Would this preclude any chance that he would be able to sell to Swanson's in the future?

CASE 2.2: SPECIALIZED BUSINESS COMPUTERS

Background

Specialized Business Computers (SBC) is a 10-year-old company operating throughout the United States, providing large retail customers with handheld computers and proprietary software to support the retail sales effort. The basic idea is that SBC works with electronics and home improvement retailers to store information that help retail salespeople as they attempt to make or facilitate sales in the store. Typical information includes product availability, specifications and technical information, pricing, product reviews and comparisons, and installation guidance when appropriate.

Current Situation

Elizabeth Manning is a major accounts representative for SBC, serving five states in the Midwest. She is responsible for sales to multi-store electronics retail chains that are headquartered in Illinois, Indiana, Ohio, Wisconsin, and Michigan. Elizabeth is responsible for securing new retail customers, upgrading and reselling to existing customers, and working with technical support personnel to ensure smooth installation and ongoing operations in the retail stores.

A month ago, Elizabeth heard about an interesting new sales opportunity. Smart Office, a Web-based office supply retailer, had announced plans to build five stores in Illinois and Michigan over the next 18 months. In addition to office supplies, computers, and furniture, Smart Office announced that its stores would move aggressively into several consumer electronics categories, including televisions and related audio-video items. SBC had not previously sold to office supply retailers, but Elizabeth had been given the go-ahead to pursue the Smart Office account.

Elizabeth moved quickly to set up introductory meetings with several Smart Office executives to explore the possible use of SBC handheld computers by Smart Office salespeople. Over the course of two weeks, she met with Ron Bachus, director of purchasing, Shannon Fields, director of management information systems, Kelsy Kramer, director of retail sales operations, and Bill Jameson, chief financial officer. After meeting with these four people individually, she met with them together in an hour-long session to be sure that she fully understood what Smart Office hoped to achieve with the electronics category and what they expected if a decision was made to utilize handheld computers as a retails sales tool.

Following the meeting, Elizabeth made some notes about her impressions of the key players from Smart Office:

- Ron Bachus, director of purchasing—Ron is the key contact person and was helpful in setting up the group meeting. He will not have much to say about the go or no-go decision on handhelds, but he will expect prompt delivery and installation, mistake-free billing, and reassurances before the sale that SBC will be a reliable source of supply.
- Shannon Fields, director of management information systems—she will be very influential in

making the go or no-go decision and selecting a supplier if it is a go. She is an information technology expert and seemed rather impatient when other Smart Office personnel expressed opinions about how the handhelds should be utilized. In particular, Shannon wants all the information stored on the corporate server and have it accessible on a password-protected portion of the Smart Office home page. The handheld computers would be used only to access the Smart Office home page. She thinks that handheld may be an unnecessary expense, and thinks that the retail sales associates can access the Smart Office home page from a small number of stationary computers located in scattered positions in the stores.

- Kelsy Kramer, director of retail sales operations—Kelsy couldn't care less about the details of the handheld technology, and he was quick to point out that he needed to know how these "gadgets" would increase sales and customer satisfaction. He seemed worried that retail operations would be charged for the expense of the handhelds and he is very interested in the payback. In a nutshell, will the handhelds be a worthwhile investment? He is somewhat concerned that, if Smart Office does not go with the handhelds, the company may be perceived as lagging in technology.

- Bill Jameson, chief financial officer—hard to read him. He said very little during the meetings and would not reveal whether Smart Office had a budget allocated for handhelds, or even a general category for retail sales support. He gave no indication if a lease arrangement might be a possibility if an outright purchase was not feasible.

Questions

1. What additional information does Elizabeth Manning need before she can attempt to make the sale to Smart Office?

2. Using the ADAPT questioning method discussed in this chapter, develop 5–7 questions for the first two stages—A (assess the buyer's situation) and D (discover the buyer's needs)—that could be directed to Shannon Fields and Kelsy Kramer. Note that there may be some questions that would be appropriate for both Fields and Kramer, but some unique questions for both Fields and Kramer would definitely be appropriate.

Role Play

Situation: Read Case 2.2.   **ROLE PLAY**

Characters: Elizabeth Manning, SBC sales representative; Shannon Fields, Smart Office director of management information systems.

Scene 1:   *Location*—Shannon Fields' office. *Action*—Using the questions previously developed for question 2, Elizabeth Manning tries to learn more about Shannon Fields' situation and her particular needs.

Scene 2:   *Location*—Kelsy Kramer's office. *Action*—Using the questions previously developed for question 2, Elizabeth Manning tries to learn more about Kelsy Kramer's situation and his particular needs.

Upon completion of the role play, answer these questions:

1. Did the Elizabeth Manning character adequately assess the situation and determine the buyer's needs for both Shannon Fields and Kelsy Kramer?

2. What should Elizabeth Manning try to accomplish in her next sales calls on Smart Office?

Defining the Strategic Role of the Sales Function

The two chapters in Part 2 discuss the sales function from a strategic perspective. Chapter 3 investigates strategic decisions at different levels in multibusiness, multiproduct firms. The key elements of corporate strategy, business strategy, marketing strategy, and sales strategy are described, and important relationships between each strategy level and the sales function are identified. Special attention is directed toward the role of personal selling in a marketing strategy and sales strategy development. Account targeting strategy, relationship strategy, selling strategy, and sales channel strategy are the key elements of a sales strategy.

Chapter 4 emphasizes the importance of sales organization design and salesforce deployment in successfully executing organizational strategies. The concepts of specialization, centralization, span of control, management levels, and line/staff positions are critical considerations in sales organization design. Special attention is directed toward the use of different sales organization structures in different selling environments. Salesforce deployment decisions include allocating selling effort to accounts, determining the appropriate salesforce size, and designing sales territories. The key considerations and analytical approaches for each of these decisions are discussed.

ORGANIZATIONAL STRATEGIES AND THE SALES FUNCTION

OBJECTIVES

After completing this chapter, you should be able to

1. Define the strategy levels for multibusiness, multiproduct firms.

2. Discuss how corporate and business strategy decisions affect the sales function.

3. List the advantages and disadvantages of personal selling as a marketing communications tool.

4. Specify the situations in which personal selling is typically emphasized in a marketing strategy.

5. Describe ways that personal selling, advertising, and other tools can be blended into effective integrated marketing communications programs.

6. Discuss the important concepts behind organizational buyer behavior.

7. Define an account targeting strategy.

8. Explain the different types of relationship strategies.

9. Discuss the importance of different selling strategies.

10. Describe the advantages and disadvantages of different sales channel strategies.

SELLING THE NEW SUNGARD WAY

How much is at stake in sales transformation? According to extensive research by global sales and marketing consulting firm ZS Associates, companies that move their salesforce effectiveness metrics from average to excellent as part of a sales transformation can increase profitable growth by 5 to 15 percent—and sometimes by 20 percent or more.

Those numbers would make almost any sales leader sit up and take notice. On the other hand, a sales transformation is a staggering endeavor. Not only does an overhaul of this scale take several months to plan and execute, it requires strategic and coordinated effort among a team of senior leaders whose priorities are tightly aligned. And, of course, successful change requires consistent, crystal-clear communication companywide. Everyone on the lowest to the highest rung on the ladder must be a stakeholder and understand how change will result in a better, brighter future.

In December 2011, Jim Neve was appointed senior vice president of global sales and marketing operations at SunGard. In February 2012, Neve brought Ken Powell on board as vice president of global sales enablement. The two had worked together on other successful, large-scale sales transformations, and their aim at SunGard was to create similar success. Neve and Powell understood that SunGard needed to address problems familiar to most enterprise sales organizations: globalization, the explosion of the Internet and its effects on buyers' access to information, increased compliance requirements imposed by governments, and tighter budgets imposed on IT departments.

SunGard also faced some unique challenges, however. On the way to building its existing reputation as one of the world's leading software and technology services companies, SunGard grew largely by acquisition. Since its founding in 1982, more than 160 acquisitions have taken place. When Neve and Powell came on board, SunGard's go-to-market approach was highly fragmented, left to the individual businesses to define. Frequently, multiple sales reps pursued the same clients. The company had thousands of consultants engaged in professional services work, yet its main selling focus was licensed software.

"We were moving from a holding company to an operating company," Powell says. "We needed to maximize our channels, sell the broadest set of solutions possible, and go to market in a coordinated manner. We needed to build a sustainable growth engine."

It was vital that reps be capable of becoming long-term partners and trusted advisors for both current and prospective customers. The transformation would lead to selling solutions that combine leading technology and services from across all SunGard units, not just the product divisions. Moreover, sales presentations would deliver not just product information, but also insight into improving each customer's business. The SunGard rep's ability to make the sales experience a beneficial one for the customer would rise above product functionality and price.

One of the key starting points was to administer a global sales-productivity survey to 500 sales associates to gain insight on the current and desired state of sales readiness across the firm. Among many findings, the survey revealed that 80 percent of reps were concerned with getting better training, as well as good, competitive analyses and more effective sales campaigns. They also wanted better data, fewer administrative tasks, and a simplified salesforce interface. This survey helped SunGard develop and shape a detailed transformation plan.

To support this plan for change, SunGard needed to overhaul a number of different practices. For example, in addition to improving and refining its value proposition with the assistance of Corporate Visions, SunGard also needed to alter how sales reps are selected, trained, managed, and compensated. Senior leaders determined that the plan would require an investment totaling in the millions—a steep price tag; however, the more senior executives realized the value of the proposed changes, the more eager they were to find ways to finance them. In some cases, they shifted budgets from ineffective programs and reallocated funds to projects related to the sales transformation. "The whole organization gravitated toward change," Powell says. "[Everyone] knew it had to happen."

In fact, a major goal in the transformation was to establish a consistent set of procedures, metrics, and tools, as well as a cohesive training infrastructure that could be used throughout the sales organization. One of the most obvious resources to tap was SunGard's CRM and sales-management tool, Salesforce, which was reconfigured to guide salespeople through all the necessary steps they need to take to more effectively close a sale. Accordingly, SunGard has made a number of resources easily available from within this system. For example, Launch International has built a set of assets, sales tools and a framework, to help guide SunGard sales associates to key content and sales tools (case studies, white papers, market data, etc.) to help them with situational selling challenges. To serve up this content in a seamless manner, SunGard partnered with SAVO to create a one-stop shop to access it all directly from inside Salesforce.

To keep the salesforce informed about the latest market happenings, SunGard has built and integrated its market research and analyst-relations strategy into a sales enablement support infrastructure. This includes publishing an "insights vault," where reps can search for facts, figures, and trends, and a schedule of quarterly briefings, so subject matter experts can inform the sales associates about noteworthy events taking place in the industry and emphasize how they relate to SunGard solutions.

Partnering with such firms as data provider OneSource, for example, or global sales-training and performance-improvement firm Richardson has helped SunGard's salespeople become savvier about customer buying habits, possible opportunities for sales, and the selling approaches that work best. Such improvements have made SunGard a more appealing stomping ground for new sales reps. With rep turnover peaking in 2012, SunGard has since shifted away from hiring based purely on industry experience and a well-stocked list of contacts. Instead, the company now uses a talent-assessment tool provided by Chally

Group Worldwide to define ideal job profiles and evaluate the skills and performance patterns of existing and prospective salespeople. The Chally tool also gives managers insight into areas in which sales associates need the most guidance, and is used to create individual development plans and a common set of role expectations.

SunGard holds a live kickoff sales meeting once a year and invests in enhancing first-year sales rep training so that new reps can bring value quicker. Salespeople are now on boarded through SunGard's Sales Academy, a structured program that includes curriculum and related support materials in the areas of product knowledge, market understanding, and selling skills. A combination of informational videos, self-paced e-learning, and field-based activities ensures that the learning is relevant and real-world for each salesperson.

During the sales transformation, SunGard established a common method to measure sales associates' productivity, including how often they won or lost business and individual sales forecasts. These metrics are visible to all relevant stakeholders throughout the company; this increases accountability and inspires a competitive spirit. By adopting Xactly as an automated tool to manage incentives and commissions (previously tracked manually), reps can quickly see what they have sold and how they will get paid. They can also run through what-if scenarios, determining potential earnings based on various sales situations.

Thus far, SunGard is on target for significant growth on a $1 billion sales plan. To Neve, the contents of the sales pipeline, combined with an attractive win rate, signal a favorable future. Many financial firms are exploring the possibility of outsourcing many back-office tasks. This is demonstrated through an increase in professional-service and managed-service opportunities in the pipeline. With an arsenal of assets, SunGard is well positioned to address this market demand of each of the markets. Some unprecedented and significant deals have already begun to close.

Source: Selling Power (Fall 2013).

One of the primary goals for the initiative was to shift to what was branded internally as "Selling the SunGard Way." SunGard leaders wanted reps that could understand the buyer's journey, anticipate customer needs, and tailor interactions to meet shifting concerns. In sum, they wanted reps to be equipped to sell based on insight. In doing so, they hoped to create a salesforce that could differentiate SunGard from competitors by leveraging knowledge, experience, and expertise.

Many firms consist of multiple business units that market multiple products to different customer groups. Strategy development in these multibusiness, multiproduct firms is extremely complex. Strategy decisions must be made at many levels of the organization. In just over 30 years, SunGard made more than 160 acquisitions resulting in a go-to-market approach that was highly fragmented. SunGard needed to go to market in a coordinated manner. However, the strategies must be consistent with each other and integrated for the firm to perform successfully. We now examine the key strategic decisions at each organizational level and highlight the impact of these strategic decisions on the sales organization.

ORGANIZATIONAL STRATEGY LEVELS

The key strategy levels for multibusiness, multiproduct firms are presented in Exhibit 3.1. Corporate strategy consists of decisions that determine the mission, business portfoio, and future growth directions for the entire corporate entity. A separate business strategy must be developed for each strategic business unit (SBU) (discussed later in this chapter) in the corporate family, defining how that SBU plans to compete effectively within its industry. Because an SBU typically consists of multiple products serving different markets, each product/market combination requires a specific marketing strategy. Each marketing strategy includes the selection of target market segments and the development of a marketing mix to serve each target market. A key consideration is the role that personal selling will play in the marketing communications mix for a particular marketing strategy.

EXHIBIT 3.1   Organizational Strategy Levels

Strategy Level	Key Decision Areas	Key Decision Makers
Corporate strategy	Corporate mission Strategic business unit definition Strategic business unit objectives	Corporate management
Business strategy	Strategy types Strategy execution	Business unit management
Marketing strategy	Target market selection Marketing mix development Integrated marketing communications	Marketing management
Sales strategy	Account targeting strategy Relationship strategy Selling strategy Sales channel strategy	Sales management

The corporate, business, and marketing strategies represent strategy development from the perspective of different levels within an organization. Although sales management may have some influence on the decisions made at each level, the key decision makers are typically from higher management levels outside the sales function. Sales management does, however, play the key role in sales strategy development. An example of one approach for strategy development at different organizational levels is presented in "Sales Management in the 21st Century: Integrating Organizational Strategy throughout Each Business Unit."

CORPORATE STRATEGY AND THE SALES FUNCTION

Strategic decisions at the topmost level of multibusiness, multiproduct firms determine the corporate strategy for a given firm, which is what provides direction and guidance for activities at all organizational levels. Developing a corporate strategy requires the following steps:

1. Analyzing the corporate situation to identify potential opportunities and threats

2. Determining corporate mission and objectives

3. Defining strategic business units

4. Setting objectives and resource allocations for each strategic business unit

Once the corporate strategy has been developed, management is concerned with implementation, evaluation, and control of the corporate strategic plan. Although the corporate strategy has the most direct impact on business-level operations, each element does affect the sales function.

Corporate Mission

The development of a corporate mission statement is an important first step in the strategy formulation process. This mission statement provides direction for strategy development and execution throughout the organization. Sales managers and salespeople must operate within the guidelines presented in the corporate mission statement. Furthermore, they can use these corporate guidelines as a basis for establishing specific policies for the entire sales organization. Thus, in this way, the corporate mission statement has a direct effect on sales management activities.

Despite its importance, it has been estimated that only about 20 percent of companies have a clear mission statement that is articulated to salespeople by sales managers.

The most successful corporate mission statements are simple, complete, and communicated directly to salespeople. Siebel Systems changed its mission statement to "Make one hundred percent customer satisfaction Siebel's overriding priority." This simplified version expressed the company's values succinctly and was easy for the salespeople to understand and adopt.[1]

Definition of Strategic Business Units

Defining strategic business units, often called SBUs, is an important and difficult aspect of corporate strategy development. The basic purpose is to divide the corporation into parts to facilitate strategic analysis and planning. An SBU is a designated unit within a corporation that operates like an individual business. SBUs typically consist of a single product or line of related products marketed to defined market segments. Most SBUs include all of the basic business functions with managers responsible for the performance of each function and the SBU. Some functions, however, might be provided at the corporate level and shared across SBUs. For example, centralizing parts of the purchasing function at the corporate level is a trend in many companies. Thus, an SBU usually has its own sales organization with sales managers and salespeople.

The definition of SBUs is an important element of corporate strategy. An example of defining strategy broadly to apply to all the operations of a corporation is presented in "Sales Management in the 21st Century: Integrating Organizational Strategy throughout Each Business Unit." Changes in SBU definition may increase or decrease the number of SBUs, and these changes typically affect the sales function in many ways. Salesforces may have to be merged, new salesforces may have to be established, or existing salesforces may have to be reorganized to perform different activities. These changes may affect all sales management activities from the type of salespeople to be hired to how they should be trained, motivated, compensated, and supervised.

Restructuring at General Electric (GE) provides a typical example. GE had considered lighting and appliances to be separate SBUs. The company, however, decided it could cut costs and better focus sales resources by combining lighting and appliances into a new business unit called GE Consumer Products. Except for some financial services at GE

SALES MANAGEMENT IN THE 21ST CENTURY

Integrating Organizational Strategy throughout Each Business Unit

Rich Clasby, VP general manager of Maxon, A Honeywell Company, discusses the importance of integrating organizational strategy throughout each business unit:

Typically in large corporations with a number of different strategic groups or strategic business units, corporate management will define strategy broadly to apply to all the operations of the corporation. Some examples of these broadly defined strategies are "great positions in good industries" or "industry leader with energy saving solutions." Effective corporate strategy should define the path to corporate growth and shareholder return. Corporate management would then review and approve more specific strategy as developed by the management of each business unit and allocate resources based on opportunities and longer-term vision. Specific strategic objectives of each business unit should definitely support the broad corporate strategy. If a business unit has not been able to improve a poor position, for example, they may move to divest out of a particular business or product offering. Marketing management would also set a specific strategy to support the business unit and corporate strategy. Marketing management could look to add sales operations, direct and/or indirect channels, in specific regions in order to improve their position to better serve a good industry. Or marketing management could develop strategic objectives to promote more product lines that offer customers energy efficiency, while sales management sets objectives to call on more customers within the segment that is looking for energy savings. Each level of management in the organization, and management across functions should be working together to develop and execute on strategic objectives that are consistent with corporate strategy.

Capital Corp., all of the products GE sold to consumers were now included in GE Consumer Products. This change gave the GE sales organization more leverage in the consumer marketplace and increased the productivity of selling resources.[2] For example, Home Depot carried GE appliances, but not GE light bulbs. Wal-Mart sold many GE light bulbs, but few GE appliances. Because the same salesperson now sold both appliances and light bulbs, selling costs were reduced and the opportunity to get Home Depot to carry GE light bulbs and Wal-Mart to sell more GE appliances was increased.[3]

Objectives for Strategic Business Units

Once SBUs have been defined, corporate management must determine appropriate strategic objectives for each. Many firms view their SBUs collectively as a portfolio of business units. Each business unit faces a different competitive situation and plays a different role in the business unit portfolio. Therefore, specific strategic objectives should be determined for each SBU. Corporate management has ultimate responsibility for establishing strategic objectives for each SBU. As illustrated in Exhibit 3.2, the strategic objective assigned to a business unit has a direct effect on resource allocations, as well as personal selling and sales management activities.

EXHIBIT 3.2   SBU Objectives and the Sales Organization

SBU Objectives	Sales Organization Objectives	Primary Sales Tasks	Recommended Compensation
Build market share	Increase sales volume Expand distribution	Get new accounts Increase sales to existing accounts	Salary plus sales-based incentives
Hold market share	Maintain sales volume	Maintain sales to current accounts Replace lost sales with new accounts	Salary plus commission and/or bonus
Harvest market share	Reduce selling costs Target profitable accounts	Service most profitable accounts Eliminate unprofitable accounts Reduce service levels Reduce inventory	Salary plus profit-based incentives
Divest/liquidate market share	Minimize selling costs and clear out inventory	Dump inventory Eliminate service	Salary

AN ETHICAL DILEMMA

Darotec Pharmaceuticals has several products coming off patent at the end of second quarter. It is fairly obvious sales will fall off once the generics hit the market. Jenny Baker, your district sales manager, has decided to start a sales contest to possibly offset some of the sales decline. Industry analysts believe sales will fall 30 to 35 percent during the third quarter on these products. Baker has told you district sales can only fall 20 percent if everyone wants to get their yearly bonus. Over the past five years the bonus has averaged 30 percent of each rep's salary. Baker's contest has not only stated that it is critical not to lose doctors who are writing your products, but it is equally important to grow your business with new doctors. Baker has put up some attractive prizes (trips, big-screen TVs, etc.) but the salesforce already looks at all of this as a lose-lose. That is, it is going to be tough to win the contest, and everyone is looking at losing their bonus. You have a sales meeting on Friday at 8 a.m. What would you do? Why?

Determining strategic objectives for each SBU is an important aspect of corporate strategy. These strategic objectives affect the development of the sales organization's objectives, the selling tasks performed by salespeople, and the activities of sales managers. All sales organization policies are designed to help salespeople achieve the business unit strategic objective. However, too much emphasis on business unit objectives can place salespeople in uncomfortable situations, as illustrated in "An Ethical Dilemma."

Corporate Strategy Summary

Strategic decisions at the topmost levels of multibusiness corporations provide guidance for strategy development at all lower organizational levels. Even though the sales function is often far removed from the corporate level, corporate strategy has direct and indirect impacts on personal selling and sales management. The corporate mission, definition of SBUs, and determination of SBU objectives all affect sales organization operations. However, corporate strategy decisions have their most immediate impact on business unit strategies.

BUSINESS STRATEGY AND THE SALES FUNCTION

Whereas corporate strategy addresses decisions across business units, a separate strategy must be designed for each SBU. The essence of business strategy is competitive advantage: How can each SBU compete successfully against competitive products and services? What differential advantage will each SBU try to exploit in the marketplace? What can each SBU do better than their competitors? Answers to these questions provide the basis for business strategies.

Business Strategy Types

Although creating a business unit strategy is a complex task, several classification schemes have been developed to aid in this endeavor. One of the most popular is Porter's generic business strategies,[4] presented in Exhibit 3.3. Each of these generic strategies—**low**

Generic Business Strategies and Salesforce Activities   EXHIBIT 3.3

Strategy Type	Role of the Salesforce
Low-cost supplier Aggressive construction of efficient-scale facilities, vigorous pursuit of cost reductions from experience, tight cost, and overhead control, usually associated with high relative market share.	Servicing large current customers, pursuing large prospects, minimizing costs, selling on the basis of price, and usually assuming significant order-taking responsibilities.
Differentiation Creation of something perceived industrywide as being unique. Provides insulation against competitive rivalry because of brand loyalty and resulting lower sensitivity to price.	Selling nonprice benefits, generating orders, providing high quality of customer service and responsiveness, possibly significant amount of prospecting if high-growth industry, selecting customers based on low price sensitivity, usually requires a high-quality salesforce.
Niche Service of a particular target market, with each functional policy developed with this target market in mind. Although market share in the industry might be low, the firm dominates a segment within the industry.	Becoming experts in the operations and opportunities associated with the target market, focusing customer attention on nonprice benefits and allocating selling time to the target market.

cost, **differentiation**, or **niche**—emphasizes a different type of competitive advantage and has different implications for a sales organization. The sales function plays an important role in executing a generic business strategy.[5] As indicated in Exhibit 3.3, the activities of sales managers and salespeople differ depending on whether the business unit is using a low-cost, differentiation, or niche business strategy. The sales function can often provide the basis for differentiation.

Many companies are adopting customer relationship management (CRM) as a business strategy:

> CRM is a strategy resulting in developing the most appropriate relationship with a customer, a process that is supported by technology and that may not necessarily yield deep or strategic partnerships with all customers. Technology is used to analyze customer and market information, automate specific business processes, and facilitate the development of customer relationship strategies. The salesforce is imbedded in the context of an organization-wide focus on the customer as the center of the firm.[6]

A critical aspect of this definition is that CRM is a business strategy. However, the effective implementation of a CRM strategy requires integrated, cross-functional business processes, specific organizational capabilities, an appropriate business philosophy, and the right technology to make everything work.[7] AB Phone Works founder, Anneke Seley, states: "CRM is evolving to much more personalized and tailored capabilities." She believes "companies need to start from scratch with their CRM because social media fundamentally change the model that companies use for effective customer relationships."[8] Successful firms address the strategy, philosophy, process, and capability issues first, and then find the best technology for implementation. Unsuccessful firms tend to focus on the technology first and then try to adapt their strategy, philosophy, process, and capability to fit the technology.[9]

Deere & Company represents an example of a successful approach to CRM. Faced with the consolidation of customers within the agriculture industry, Deere responded by crafting a CRM strategy. The essence of the strategy was for its dealers to develop stronger relationships with the largest accounts using a consultative selling process. Different types of relationships and selling processes were used to serve smaller accounts. The strategic focus was to establish stronger relationships with fewer, but larger accounts. The appropriate technology to support the CRM strategy was then implemented by dealers. This approach produced strong sales and profit gains for Deere.[10]

Business Strategy Summary

Business strategies determine how each SBU plans to compete in the marketplace. Several strategic approaches are available, each placing its own demands on the sales function. The role of the sales function depends on how an SBU plans to compete in the marketplace, with the activities of sales managers and salespeople being important in executing a business strategy successfully.

MARKETING STRATEGY AND THE SALES FUNCTION

Because SBUs typically market multiple products to multiple customer groups, separate marketing strategies are often developed for each of an SBU's target markets. These marketing strategies must be consistent with the business strategy. For example, marketers operating in an SBU with a differentiation business strategy would probably not develop marketing strategies that emphasize low price. The marketing strategies for each target market should reinforce the differentiation competitive advantage sought by the SBU.

Figure 3.1 illustrates the major components of a marketing strategy and highlights the position of personal selling within the marketing communications portion of a marketing strategy. The key components of any marketing strategy are the selection of a target market and the development of a marketing mix. Target market selection

Marketing Strategy and Personal Selling   FIGURE 3.1

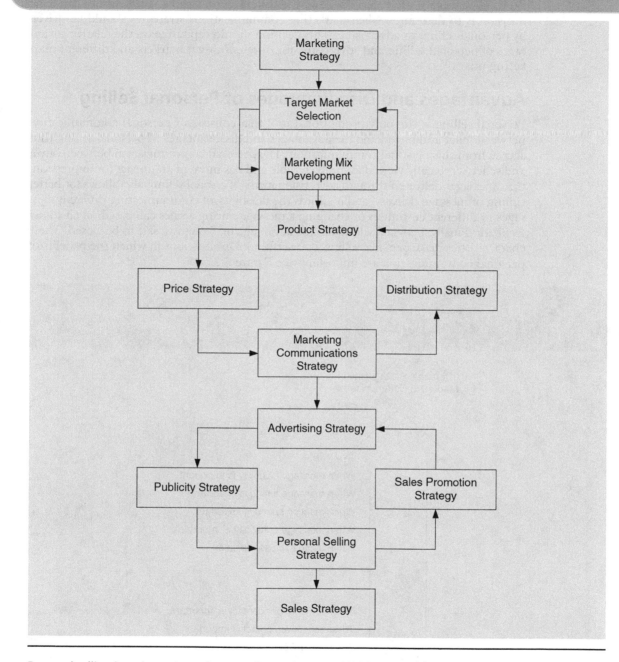

Personal selling is an important element of a marketing communications strategy. The marketing communications strategy is one element of a marketing mix designed to appeal to a defined target market. A marketing strategy can be defined in terms of target market and marketing mix components.

requires a definition of the specific market segment to be served. The marketing mix then consists of a marketing offer designed to appeal to the defined target market. This marketing offer contains a mixture of product, price, distribution, and marketing communications strategies. The critical task for the marketing strategist is to develop a marketing mix that satisfies the needs of the target market better than competitive offerings.

Personal selling may be an important element in the marketing communications portion of the marketing mix. The marketing communications strategy consists of a mixture of personal selling, advertising, sales promotion, and publicity, with most strategies emphasizing either personal selling or advertising as the main tool. Sales promotion and publicity are typically viewed as supplemental tools. Thus, a key strategic decision is to determine when marketing communications strategies should be driven by personal selling or advertising. This decision should capitalize on the relative advantages of personal selling and advertising for different target markets and different marketing mixes.[11]

Advantages and Disadvantages of Personal Selling

Personal selling is the only promotional tool that consists of personal communication between seller and buyer, and the advantages and disadvantages of personal selling thus accrue from this personal communication. The personal communication between buyer and seller is typically viewed as more credible and has more of an impact (or impression) than messages delivered through advertising media. Personal selling also allows for better timing of message delivery, and it affords the flexibility of communicating different messages to different customers or changing a message during a sales call based on customer feedback. Finally, personal selling has the advantage of allowing a sale to be closed. These characteristics make personal selling a powerful tool in situations in which the benefits of personal communication are important (see Figure 3.2).

FIGURE 3.2	Personal Selling–Driven versus Advertising-Driven Marketing Communications Strategies

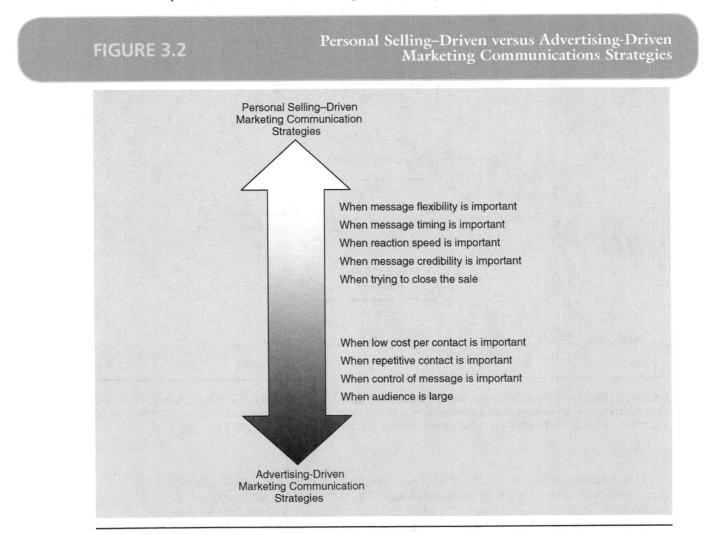

Personal selling–driven marketing communications strategies are most appropriate in situations in which the benefits of personal communication are important.

The major disadvantage of personal selling is the high cost to reach each member of the audience. Contrast this with the pennies that it costs to reach an audience member through mass advertising. The benefits of personal selling do not come cheap. They may, however, outweigh the costs for certain types of target market situations and for specific marketing mixes.

Target Market Situations and Personal Selling

The characteristics of personal selling are most advantageous in specific target market situations. Personal selling–driven strategies are appropriate when (1) the market consists of only a few buyers that tend to be concentrated in location, (2) the buyer needs a great deal of information, (3) the purchase is important, (4) the product is complex, and (5) service after the sale is important. The target market characteristics that favor personal selling are similar to those found in most business purchasing situations. Thus, personal selling is typically the preferred tool in business marketing, whereas advertising is normally emphasized in consumer marketing situations (see Figure 3.3).

An effective marketing communications mix capitalizes on the advantages of each promotional tool. Moreover, characteristics of the target market must be considered, and the promotional mix must also be consistent with the other elements of the marketing mix to ensure a coordinated marketing offer.

Marketing Mix Elements and Personal Selling

One of the most difficult challenges facing the marketing strategist is making sure that decisions concerning the product, distribution, price, and marketing communications areas result in an effective marketing mix. There are any number of ways that these elements can be combined to form a marketing mix. However, some combinations tend to represent logical fits. Exhibit 3.4 shows when a personal selling emphasis might fit well with the other marketing elements. Again, these suggestions should be considered only as guidelines, because the development of unique marketing mixes may produce competitive advantages in the marketplace.

An interesting example is Best Buy. Best Buy is the largest consumer electronics retailer in the nation. It is, however, beginning to face increased competition from new

Targeting Market Characteristics and Marketing Communications Strategy   FIGURE 3.3

Business Target Markets	→	Personal Selling–Driven Marketing Communications Strategies

Characteristics
• Few buyers
• Buyers concentrated geographically
• Purchase information needs high
• Purchases made in large amounts
• High-importance purchases
• Complex products purchased
• Postpurchase service important

Consumer Target Markets	→	Advertising–Driven Marketing Communications Strategies

Characteristics
• Many buyers
• Buyers dispersed geographically
• Purchase information needs low
• Purchases made in small amounts
• Low-importance purchases
• Low-complexity products purchased
• Postpurchase service not important

Personal selling–driven marketing communications strategies are most appropriate for target markets that have characteristics typical of business markets.

EXHIBIT 3.4	Marketing Mix Elements and Personal Selling

Marketing Mix Area	Characteristics
Product or service	• Complex products requiring customer application assistance (computers, pollution control systems, stream turbines) • Major purchase decisions, such as food items purchased by supermarket chains • Features and performance of the product requiring personal demonstration and trial by the customer (private aircraft)
Channels	• Channel system relatively short and direct to end users • Personal selling needed in "pushing" product through channel • Channel intermediaries available to perform personal selling function for supplier with limited resources and experience (brokers or manufacturers' agents) • Product and service training and assistance needed by channel in intermediaries
Price	• Final price negotiated between buyer and seller (appliances, automobiles, real estate) • Selling price or quantity purchased enable an adequate margin to support selling expenses (traditional department store compared with discount house)

sources. Wal-Mart, the world's largest retailer, is moving aggressively into high-end consumer electronics. In addition, Dell is also expanding its product mix to include MP3 players and flat-panel TVs. Best Buy's marketing strategy to compete with these giants is to focus more on the personal selling component of its marketing mix. Its salespeople, called "blueshirts," are implementing a CARE Plus sales process to increase sales by connecting more deeply with customers and providing attention, know-how, service, and complete solutions to meet customer needs. This personal selling–driven strategy is intended to differentiate Best Buy from Wal-Mart, with its low price strategy, and Dell, which has a direct selling Internet model.[12]

Integrated Marketing Communication

Although marketing communication strategies are typically driven by advertising or personal selling, most firms use a variety of tools in their marketing communication mix. The key task facing both business and consumer marketers is deciding how and when to use these tools. Integrated marketing communication (IMC) is the increasingly popular term used by many firms to describe their approach. IMC is the strategic integration of multiple marketing communication tools in the most effective and efficient manner. The objective is to use the most cost-effective tool to achieve a desired communication objective and to ensure a consistent message is being communicated to the market.

A typical approach is to use some form of advertising to generate company and product awareness and to identify potential customers. These sales leads might then be contacted and qualified by telemarketers. The best prospects are then turned over to the salesforce to receive personal selling attention. This approach uses relatively inexpensive tools (advertising and telemarketing) to communicate with potential customers early in the buying process and saves the more expensive tools (personal selling) for the best prospects later in the buying process.

One of the keys to integrating marketing communications successfully is greater coordination between the marketing and sales functions. Figure 3.4 presents the basic activities undertaken by the marketing function with input from sales on the left, and important sales tasks with input from marketing on the right.[13] The activities in the middle require the marketing and sales functions to work closely together. Although this may seem easy to achieve, it is often very difficult. Marketers tend to focus on products, analysis, projects, processes, the office, and take a long-term perspective. The sales function, in contrast, emphasizes customers, personal relationships, daily activity, results, the field, and a short-term perspective. Integrating these different orientations requires the creation of business structures, processes and systems, cultures, and employees designed to facilitate communication and coordination between the marketing and sales functions.

Marketing Strategy Summary

Selecting target markets and designing marketing mixes are the key components in marketing strategy development. Marketing strategies must be developed for the target markets served by an SBU and must be consistent with the business unit strategy. One important element of the marketing mix is marketing communications. The critical task is designing a mix that capitalizes on the advantages of each tool. Personal selling has the basic advantage of personal communication and is emphasized in target market situations and marketing mixes in which personal communication is important.

SALES STRATEGY FRAMEWORK

Corporate, business, and marketing strategies view customers as aggregate markets or market segments. These organizational strategies provide direction and guidance for the sales function, but then sales managers and salespeople must translate these general organizational strategies into specific strategies for individual customers.

A sales strategy is designed to execute an organization's marketing strategy for individual accounts. For example, a marketing strategy consists of selecting a target market and developing a marketing mix. Target markets are typically defined in broad terms,

---

Marketing and Sales Activities   **FIGURE 3.4**

Marketing   Sales

Sales to Marketing Inputs

- Competitive analysis
- Market research
- Market segmentation
- Product development
- Product positioning
- Pricing
- Packaging
- Advertising

- Target marketing
- Sales forecasting
- Customer account selection
- Value proposition development/ Customer messaging
- Promotions

- Competitive market intelligence
- Personal selling
- Distributor management
- Account management
- Merchandising
- Installation
- After-sales service

Marketing to Sales Inputs

The coordination of sales and marketing activities is important to integrated marketing communication strategies.

such as the small business market or the university market. Marketing mixes are also described broadly in terms of general product, distribution, price, and marketing communications approaches. All accounts within a target market (e.g., all small businesses or all universities), however, are not the same in terms of size, purchasing procedures, needs, problems, and other factors. The major purpose of a sales strategy is to develop a specific approach for selling to individual accounts within a target market. A sales strategy capitalizes on the important differences among individual accounts or groups of similar accounts.

A firm's sales strategy is important for two basic reasons. First, it has a major impact on a firm's sales and profit performance. Second, it influences many other sales management decisions. Salesforce recruiting, selecting, training, compensation, and performance evaluation are affected by the sales strategies used by a firm.

Because personal selling–driven promotion strategies are typical in business marketing, our discussion of sales strategy focuses on organizational (also called industrial or business) customers. Specific customers are referred to as accounts. Thus, a sales strategy must be based on the important and unique aspects of organizational buyer behavior. A framework that integrates organizational buyer behavior and sales strategy is presented in Figure 3.5.

ORGANIZATIONAL BUYER BEHAVIOR

Organizational buyer behavior refers to the purchasing behavior of organizations. Although there are unique aspects in the buying behavior of any organization, specific types of organizations tend to share similarities in their purchasing procedures (see Exhibit 3.5). Most of our attention is focused on business organizations classified as users or original equipment manufacturers (OEM). However, we provide examples of resellers, government organizations, and institutions throughout the book.

As indicated in Figure 3.5, the development of sales strategy requires an understanding of organizational buyer behavior. The unique aspects of organizational buyer behavior revolve around the buying situation, buying center, buying process, and buying needs.

Buying Situation

One key determinant of organizational buyer behavior is the buying situation faced by an account. Three major types are possible, each representing its own problems for the buying firm and each having different strategic implications for the selling firm.

A new task buying situation, in which the organization is purchasing a product for the first time, poses the most problems for the buyer. Because the account has little knowledge or experience as a basis for making the purchase decision, it will typically use a lengthy process to collect and evaluate purchase information. The decision-making process in this type of situation is often called extensive problem solving.

A modified rebuy buying situation exists when the account has previously purchased and used the product. Although the account has information and experience with the product, it will usually want to collect additional information and may make a change when purchasing a replacement product. The decision-making process in this type of situation is often referred to as limited problem solving.

The least complex buying situation is the straight rebuy buying situation, wherein the account has considerable experience in using the product and is satisfied with the current purchase arrangements. In this case, the buyer is merely reordering from the current supplier and engaging in routinized response behavior.

Sales Strategy Framework   FIGURE 3.5

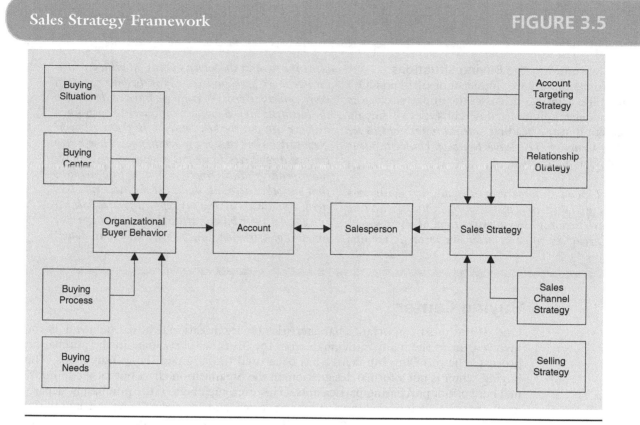

Salesperson interaction with accounts is directed by a sales strategy. The sales strategy, which defines how specific accounts are to be managed and covered, must be based on an understanding of the buying situation, buying center, buying process, and buying needs of the account.

Types of Organizations   EXHIBIT 3.5

Major Category	Types	Example
Business or industrial organizations	Users—purchase products and services to produce other products and services	HP purchasing facsimile machines from Sharp for their corporate offices
	Original equipment manufacturers (OEM)—purchase products to incorporate into products	HP purchasing microcomputer chips from Intel to incorporate into their personal computers
	Resellers—purchase products to sell	Best Buy purchasing HP personal computers to sell to organizations
Government organizations	Federal, state, and local government agencies	Virginia State Lottery purchasing HP personal computers for managers
Institutions	Public and private institutions	United Way purchasing HP personal computers for their offices

SALES MANAGEMENT IN THE 21ST CENTURY

Understanding the Buying Situations

Tom Simpson, vice president of sales and COO for Elite Printing, discusses the important factors in understanding the different types of buying situation in the heading *Sales Management in the 21st Century: The Importance of Understanding the Buying Situation.*

"I spend time with each of my reps going over their accounts and assessing their understanding of each account's buying situation. Straight rebuys are great; we must be attentive to the buyer and

continue to meet the buyer's needs. Modified rebuys become more problematic; why is the buyer seeking more information? What do we have to do to keep the business? How do we get the buyer to open up to us so we can put the best solution in front of them? New task buyers can be big challenges. How much time and resources do we put toward their bid? We may spend so much time on a new task account that our other accounts don't get the attention they need. I'm always asking my reps if they are balancing each of their buying situations with the proper amount of attention, much easier said than done."

Buying Center

One of the most important characteristics of organizational buyer behavior is the involvement of the many individuals from the firm that participate in the purchasing process. The term buying center has been used to designate these individuals. The buying center is not a formal designation on the organization chart but rather an informal network of purchasing participants. (However, members of the purchasing department are typically included in most buying centers and are normally represented in the formal organizational structure.) The difficult task facing the selling firm is to identify all the buying center members and to determine the specific role of each.

The possible roles that buying center members might play in a particular purchasing decision are

- *initiators,* who start the organizational purchasing process
- *users,* who use the product to be purchased
- *gatekeepers,* who control the flow of information between buying center members
- *influencers,* who provide input for the purchasing decision
- *deciders,* who make the final purchase decision
- *purchasers,* who implement the purchasing decision

Each buying center role may be performed by more than one individual, and each individual may perform more than one buying center role.

The members of a buying center are often from different functional areas and desire different benefits from a purchasing decision. Exhibit 3.6 presents an example. Notice that each function requires unique benefits, but some benefits are important to several functional areas. For example, a competitive price is important to both the chief financial officer and the purchasing manager, and the logistics manager and manufacturing manager are both interested in dependable delivery. The challenge is to understand both the role and benefits desired by each member of the buying center. Knowing the functional area of buying center members can help determine the relevant benefits.

Buying Process

Organizational buyer behavior can be viewed as a buying process consisting of several phases. Although this process has been presented in different ways, the following phases represent a consensus.

Phase 1. Recognition of a problem or need

Phase 2. Determination of the characteristics of the item and the quantity needed

	Buying Center Members and Benefits Desired EXHIBIT 3.6
Buying Center Member	**Benefits Desired**
Purchasing manager	Electronic ordering Competitive price Warranty
Logistics manager	Dependable delivery Order tracking
Chief financial officer	Competitive price Payment terms
Manufacturing manager	Dependable delivery Product quality Customized products

Phase 3. Description of the characteristics of the item and quantity needed

Phase 4. Search for and qualification of potential sources

Phase 5. Acquisition and analysis of proposals

Phase 6. Evaluation of proposals and selection of suppliers

Phase 7. Selection of an order routine

Phase 8. Performance feedback and evaluation

These buying phases may be formalized for some organizations and/or for certain purchases. In other situations, this process may only be a rough approximation of what actually occurs. For example, government organizations and institutions tend to have more formal purchasing processes than most business or industrial organizations. Viewing organizational buying as a multiple-phase process is helpful in developing sales strategy. A major objective of any sales strategy is to facilitate an account's movement through this process in a manner that will lead to a purchase of the seller's product.

Buying Needs

Organizational buying is typically viewed as goal-directed behavior intended to satisfy specific buying needs. Although the organizational purchasing process is made to satisfy organizational needs, the buying center consists of individuals who are also trying to satisfy individual needs throughout the decision process. Individual needs tend to be career related, whereas organizational needs reflect factors related to the use of the product.

Even though organizational purchasing is often thought to be almost entirely objective, subjective personal needs are often extremely important in the final purchase decision. For example, an organization may want to purchase a computer to satisfy data-processing needs. Although a number of suppliers might be able to provide similar products, some suppliers at lower cost than others, buying center members might select the most well-known brand to reduce purchase risk and protect job security.

We discussed how the influence of buying center members varies at different buying phases in the preceding section. Couple this with the different needs of different buying center members, and the complexity of organization buying behavior is evident. Nevertheless, sales managers must understand this behavior to develop sales strategies that will satisfy the personal and organizational needs of buying center members.

SALES STRATEGY

Sales managers and salespeople are typically responsible for strategic decisions at the account level. Although the firm's marketing strategy provides basic guidelines—an overall game plan—the battles are won on an account-by-account basis. Without the design and execution of effective sales strategies directed at specific accounts, the marketing strategy cannot be successfully implemented.

The success of Hill-Rom illustrates the importance of developing effective sales strategies. Hill-Rom markets beds and other medical equipment to medical care facilities. The salesforce typically treated all customers about the same, although larger facilities received more attention than smaller facilities. The company performed an extensive customer segmentation analysis and identified two types of customers: key customers and prime customers. These customer groups differed in their buying needs and processes, and not just in size. Hill-Rom found that their current approach provided too much attention to prime customers and not enough to key customers. Based on this analysis, the company developed a specific sales strategy for each customer group. Key customers were assigned multifunctional sales teams under the direction of an account manager. Prime customers were served by territory managers. The results from the new sales strategies are higher sales, more satisfied customers, and lower selling costs.[14]

Our framework suggests four basic sales strategy elements: account targeting strategy, relationship strategy, selling strategy, and sales channel strategy. We consider each of these as a separate, but related, strategic decision area. Sales strategies are ultimately developed for each individual account; however, the strategic decisions are often made by classifying individual accounts into similar categories.

Account Targeting Strategy

The first element of a sales strategy is defining an account targeting strategy. As mentioned earlier, all accounts within a target market are not the same. Some accounts might not be good prospects because of existing relationships with competitors. Even those that are good prospects or even current customers differ in terms of how much they buy now or might buy in the future, how they want to do business with sales organizations, and other factors. This means that all accounts cannot be effectively or efficiently served in the same way.

An account targeting strategy is the classification of accounts within a target market into categories for the purpose of developing strategic approaches for selling to each account or account group. The account targeting strategy provides the foundation for all other elements of a sales strategy. Just as different marketing mixes are developed to serve different target markets, sales organizations need to use different relationship, selling, and sales channel strategies for different account groups.

The experience of an electronic products distributor provides a good example of the value of account targeting. The 10 inside and 12 outside salespeople emphasized excellent service to all 5,000 customers. An analysis of the customer base indicated that the top 400 customers accounted for 80 percent of sales with a gross profit of $150/order. The bottom 3,800 customers accounted for 5 percent of sales with a gross profit of $8/order, with the remaining customers in between these extremes. A consultant helped the company develop an account targeting strategy with four segments:

1. Key accounts—top 400 accounts

2. Target accounts—next best 400 accounts

3. Maintenance accounts—next best 400 accounts

4. Why bother accounts—remaining 3,800 accounts

The new account targeting strategy provided the basis for developing sales strategies for each account segment.[15]

Relationship Strategy

As discussed in previous chapters, there is a clear trend toward a relationship orientation between buyers and sellers, especially in business markets. However, some accounts want to continue in a transaction mode, whereas others want various types of relationships between buyer and seller. A relationship strategy is a determination of the type of relationship to be developed with different account groups. A specific relationship strategy is developed for each account group identified by a sales organization's account targeting strategy.

Any number of relationship strategies might be developed, but typically an account targeting strategy defines three to five target groups, each requiring a specific relationship strategy. We illustrate with the general approach established by a large industrial manufacturer. The firm's account targeting strategy identified four different account groups and determined a specific relationship strategy for each group. Exhibit 3.7 presents the characteristics of each relationship strategy.

The relationship strategies range from a transaction relationship based on selling standardized products to a collaborative relationship in which the buyers and sellers work closely together for the benefit of both businesses. In between these extremes are intermediate types of relationships. A solutions relationship emphasizes solving customer problems, and a partnership relationship represents a preferred supplier position over the long term. As a sales organization moves from transaction to collaborative relationships, the time frame becomes longer, the focus changes from buying/selling to creating value, and the products and services offered move from simple and standardized to more complex and customized.

The different characteristics of the different relationship strategies are further illustrated in Figure 3.6. The move from transaction to collaborative relationships requires a greater commitment between buyer and seller, because they will be working together much more closely. Some buyers and sellers are not willing to make the required commitments. In addition, the selling costs are increased to serve accounts with higher-level relationships. Therefore, sales organizations must consider the sales and costs associated with using different relationship strategies for different account groups. The critical task is balancing the customer's needs with the cost to serve the account.

Selling Strategy

Successfully executing a specific relationship strategy requires a different selling approach. A selling strategy is the planned selling approach for each relationship strategy. Chapter 2 presented five basic selling approaches: stimulus response, mental states, need satisfaction, problem solving, and consultative. These selling approaches represent different selling strategies that might be used to execute a specific relationship strategy. We illustrate this by continuing the example of the large industrial manufacturer and the relationship strategies presented in Exhibit 3.7 and Figure 3.6.

Exhibit 3.8 matches the appropriate selling strategy with the appropriate relationship strategy. As indicated, the stimulus response and mental states approaches typically fit with a transaction relationship strategy. The need satisfaction and problem-solving selling strategies are normally used with a solutions relationship strategy. The consultative approach is most effective with the partnership and collaborative relationship strategies.

Characteristics of Relationship Strategies   EXHIBIT 3.7

	Transaction Relationship	Solutions Relationship	Partnership Relationship	Collaborative Relationship
Goal	Sell products	⟶		Add value
Time frame	Short	⟶		Long
Offering	Standardized	⟶		Customized
Number of customers	Many	⟶		Few

FIGURE 3.6 Relationship Strategy Selling Costs

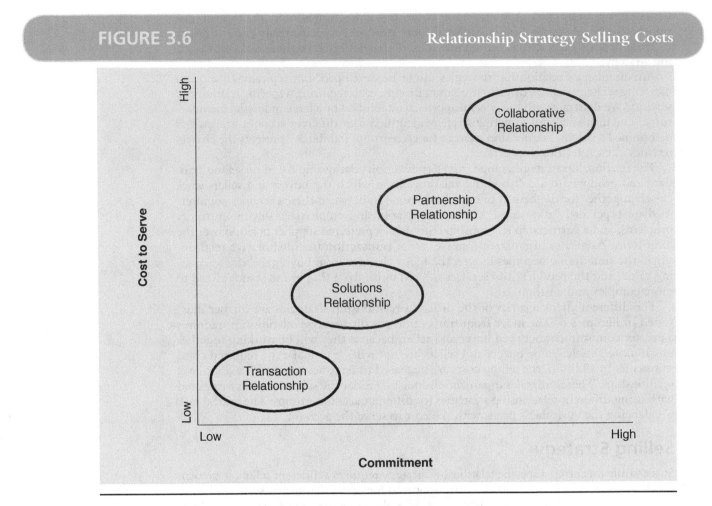

Each relationship strategy represents an increasing commitment between the buyer and seller and a higher cost to serve the customer.

Sometimes, a collaborative relationship strategy requires a selling strategy that is completely customized to the specific buyer-seller situation. The important point is that achieving the desired type of relationship in a productive manner requires using different selling strategies. Matching selling strategies and relationship strategies is an important sales management task.

EXHIBIT 3.8 Matching Selling and Relationship Strategies

Relationship Strategy			
Transaction	**Solutions**	**Partnership**	**Collaborative**
Stimulus response Mental states			
	Need satisfaction Problem solving		
		Consultative	Consultative Customized

Sales Channel Strategy

Sales channel strategy—ensuring that accounts receive selling effort coverage in an effective and efficient manner—is a necessary component of sales strategy. Various methods are available to provide selling coverage to accounts, including a company salesforce, the Internet, distributors, independent representatives, team selling, telemarketing, and trade shows. Many firms use multiple distribution channels and multiple sales channels for their products. The critical challenge is to balance customer needs and the costs of serving customers. A firm's account targeting strategy, relationship strategy, and selling strategy provide a basis for the sales channel strategy. In general, the most important account segments requiring the closest relationships and requiring the most complex sales process are served by the most expensive sales channels. In contrast, the least important, most transaction-oriented account segments receive the least expensive sales channels. The sales channel strategy for customers between these extremes should employ the most effective and efficient sales channel at each stage of the sales process. Because most of this book is concerned with management of a company field salesforce, our discussion of sales channel strategy focuses on alternatives to the typical company field salesforce.

The Internet

The Internet is rapidly becoming an important sales channel in selling to organizations. The focus is using this electronic channel in a way that meets customer needs and reduces selling costs. As technology continues to develop, opportunities to use the Internet effectively increase. Although the smallest accounts with the least profit potential might be served completely by electronic channels, most sales organizations integrate the Internet with other sales channels in various ways. The following examples illustrate different approaches:

- Cisco Systems uses field salespeople to generate new customers and then employs the Internet to serve customer needs for product information and reordering.[16]

- National Semiconductor uses a company salesforce for its largest accounts, but a distributor network for smaller accounts. However, private extranets are developed for each large account and distributor to access purchase information. Smaller accounts have access to an open Web site that links them to distributors.[17]

- Hewlett-Packard's Image and Printing Unit serving small and medium businesses uses customer support representatives to interact with customers trying to solve problems from its Web site. These potential customers can click a pop-up and will be connected with an HP representative online. This representative will try to help solve the problem or refer callers to another sales channel, such as an HP reseller, if appropriate.[18]

- Pragmatech asks Web site visitors five questions. Based on the responses to these questions and other information, the company determines whether the visitor represents a good potential opportunity or not. The best prospects are passed on to field salespeople. The others are interacted with electronically.[19]

These examples illustrate how the Internet is being used as an electronic sales channel by different companies. These and most other companies are focusing on ways to integrate the Internet into a multiple sales channel strategy that provides value to customers in a cost-effective manner. Thus, the Internet is being blended with field selling effort but also with other sales channels such as industrial distributors, independent representatives, and telemarketing.

Distributors

One alternative sales channel is distributors—channel middlemen that take title to the goods that they market to end users. These distributors typically employ their own salesforce and may carry (1) the products of only one manufacturer, (2) related but non-competing products from different manufacturers, or (3) competing products from different manufacturers. Firms that use distributors normally have a relatively small company salesforce to serve and support the efforts of the distributor.

The use of distributors adds another member to the distribution channel. Although these distributors should not be considered as final customers, they should be treated like customers. Developing positive long-term relationships with distributors is necessary for success. Indeed, the development of a partnership with distributors can be the key to success.

Herman Miller, the furniture manufacturer, has 300 direct salespeople and 240 distributors. Herman Miller salespeople call on customers directly but also work with distributors to make sure customers are satisfied. In large markets, the salespeople are usually the lead on accounts, with the distributors responsible for smaller accounts. Herman Miller also provides the distributors with market information to help them succeed, and the salespeople maintain continuous contact to motivate the distributors to emphasize Herman Miller products.[20]

Dell represents an interesting example in the use of distributors in various ways. The cornerstone of its sales channel strategy has been to sell computers directly to customers through the Internet or by phone. However, personal computer sales from these channels have been decreasing and these channels are not well suited for developing countries. Dell is responding to this situation by adding kiosks in malls, creating its own stores, and selling its products through other resellers. This is a big change in sales channel strategy for the global leader in personal computer market share. Although this new strategy is intended to have a positive impact in the U.S., it should also help Dell increase sales in international markets, such as Russia, China, and Hungary, where customers are just learning to buy online and home delivery services do not support the direct sales model well.[21]

Independent Representatives

Firms using personal selling can choose to cover accounts with independent representatives (also called *manufacturers' representatives* or just *reps*). Reps are independent sales organizations that sell complementary, but noncompeting, products from different manufacturers. In contrast to distributors, independent representatives do not normally carry inventory or take title to the products they sell. Manufacturers typically develop contractual agreements with several rep organizations. Each rep organization consists of one or more salespeople and is assigned a geographic territory. It is typically compensated on a commission basis for products sold.

Most independent rep agencies are small with an average of six employees, although a few have up to 100 salespeople and support staff. Independent reps are typically compensated on a commission basis for products sold. There is, however, a trend toward paying larger commissions and even stipends for opening new territories and shifting some compensation toward paying for rep activities rather than just for sales results. Some rep agencies are performing direct mail, telemarketing, newsletter publishing, and Web-site design services for clients.[22]

Why would so many manufacturers use reps instead of company salesforces? As indicated in Exhibit 3.9,[23] reps have certain advantages over company salesforces, especially for small firms or for smaller markets served by larger firms. Because reps are paid on a commission basis, selling costs are almost totally variable, whereas a large percentage of the selling costs of a company salesforce are fixed. Thus, at lower sales levels a rep organization is more cost-efficient to use than a company salesforce. However, at some level of sales, the company salesforce will become more cost-efficient, because reps typically receive higher commission rates than company salespeople (see Figure 3.7).

Marley Cooling Tower capitalizes on the different cost structure between company salesforces and independent reps. Tim Wigger, vice president of sales, manages a company salesforce of 40, plus 70 manufacturers' reps. The company started with only a field

---

Advantages of Independent Representatives   EXHIBIT 3.9

Independent sales representatives offer several advantages over company salesforces:

- Reps provide a professional selling capability that is difficult to match with company salespeople.
- Reps offer in-depth knowledge of general markets and individual customers.
- Reps offer established relationships with individual customers.
- The use of reps provides improved cash flow because payments to reps are typically not made until customers have paid for their purchases.
- The use of reps provides predictable sales expenses because most of the selling costs are variable and directly related to sales volume.
- The use of reps can provide greater territory coverage because companies can employ more reps than company salespeople for the same cost.
- Companies can usually penetrate new markets faster by using reps because of the reps' established customer relationships.

Independent Representatives versus Company Salesforce Costs   FIGURE 3.7

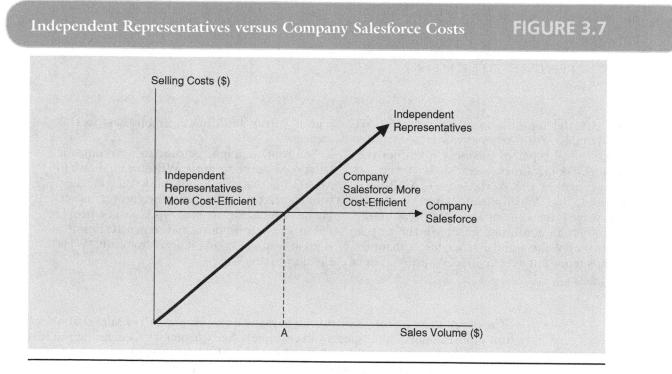

Independent representatives are typically more cost-efficient at lower sales levels, because most of the costs associated with reps are variable. However, at higher sales levels (beyond point A) a company salesforce becomes more efficient.

---

salesforce but began adding reps to capitalize on growth outside the original salesperson territories. This approach has been a cost-effective way for Marley to grow in new geographic areas.[24]

Although reps may cost less in many situations, management also has less control over their activities. The basic trade-off is cost versus control. There are two aspects to control. First, because reps are paid a commission on sales, it is difficult to get them to engage in activities not directly related to sales generation. Thus, if servicing of accounts is important, reps may not perform these activities as well as a company salesforce. Second, the typical rep represents an average of 10 manufacturers or principals. Each manufacturer's products will therefore receive 10 percent of the rep's time if it is divided equally. Usually, however, some products receive more attention than others. The biggest complaints that manufacturers seem to have with reps is that they do not spend enough time with their products and thus do not generate sufficient sales. The use of reps limits the amount of control that management has over the time spent selling their products. The relationship with manufacturers' representative organizations can also produce some complex situations as indicated in "An Ethical Dilemma."

Team Selling

Our earlier discussion of organizational buyer behavior presented the concepts of buying centers and buying situations. If we move to the selling side of the exchange relationship, we find analogous concepts. As discussed in Chapter 1, firms often employ multiple-person sales teams to deal with the multiple-person buying centers of their accounts. Figure 3.8[25] illustrates the basic relationships between sales teams and buying centers. A company salesperson typically coordinates the activities of the sales team, whereas the purchasing agent typically coordinates the activities of the buying center. Both the sales team and buying center can consist of multiple individuals from different functional areas. Each of these individuals can play one or more roles in the exchange process.

AN ETHICAL DILEMMA

You are the national sales manager for WC Electronics. Your company serves manufacturers of all types of business machines (i.e., copiers, fax machines, etc.). Most of your customers are on the West Coast in California, Oregon, and Washington. These customers are served by a company salesforce. Other customers in adjoining states are the responsibility of Walton and Associates, a manufacturer's representative agency. Walton has done a good job in building your business in this area.

You think it might be time to hire company salespeople for these areas. When you indicate to Mr. Walton that you do not think you will renew your contract with his agents, he gets very upset. He talks about all the hard work his salespeople did to sell your products and, now that business is good, you are taking it away from him. What should you do? Why?

The use of **team selling** is increasing in many firms, especially as a sales channel for a firm's most important prospects and customers (see Chapter 1). Generating the best new customers and expanding relationships with the best existing customers often requires the participation of many individuals from the selling firm. The software company DataCert provides an interesting example of team selling. The company employs sales teams consisting of employees from different departments to meet with prospects at crucial stages of the sales process. Regional sales managers determine which employees attend which meetings with each prospect. This is a very expensive sales channel approach, but prospects seem to appreciate the attention they receive. The team selling strategy has helped DataCert obtain top clients, such as UPS, Microsoft, and AT&T.[26]

Telemarketing

An increasingly important sales channel is **telemarketing** (also called *telesales)*, which consists of using the telephone as a means for customer contact, to perform some of, or all, the activities required to develop and maintain account relationships. This includes both outbound telemarketing (the seller calls the account) and inbound telemarketing (the account calls the seller).[27]

Team Selling and Buying Centers   FIGURE 3.8

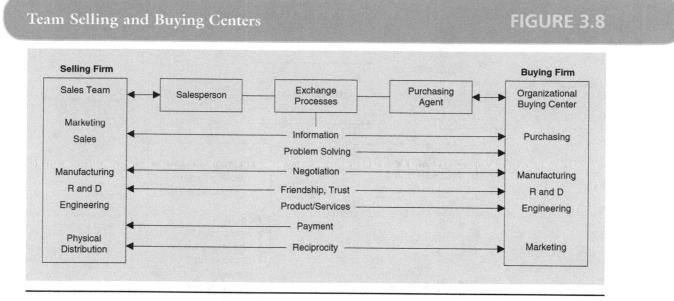

The salesperson coordinates the activities of a sales team to interact with the members of an account's buying center. The size, composition, and activities of the sales team depend on the buying situation faced by the seller.

Firms typically use telemarketing to replace field selling for specific accounts or integrate telemarketing with field selling to the same accounts (see Figure 3.9). The major reason for replacing field selling with telemarketing at specific accounts is the low cost of telemarketing selling. Telemarketing salespeople are able to serve a large number of smaller accounts. This lowers the selling costs to the smaller accounts and frees the field salesforce to concentrate on the larger accounts. Sometimes telemarketing can be used effectively to serve all accounts. For example, SecureWorks once used a field salesforce to bring its Internet security services to distributors and resellers. The company changed to salespeople selling directly to end users over the phone. Results of the change have been spectacular, with the number of clients going from 50 to 850 and annual sales from $700,000 to over $8.5 million.[28]

More typical approaches are to use telemarketing to serve smaller accounts or to integrate telemarketing with other sales channels for most accounts. For example, infoUSA sells its lead development services to small businesses over the phone. Large companies receive the attention of field salespeople. Both the telemarketing and field salespeople focus on meeting customer needs, but the lower cost of phone sales produces more profit from smaller accounts.[29] A typical example of integrating telemarketing with other sales channels is for leads to be developed and appointments made by phone with field salespeople, distributor salespeople, or independent sales representatives making the personal sales call. Once a customer relationship is established, the telemarketing and field salespeople often share the responsibility for and perform different activities to build relationships with customers.

The development of telemarketing salesforces to serve some accounts or to support field selling operations can be difficult. One of the keys to success appears to be consistent communication with the field salesforce throughout all stages of telemarketing development. Field salespeople must be assured that the telemarketing operations will help them improve their performance. Specific attention must also be directed toward developing appropriate compensation programs for both salesforces and devising training programs that provide the necessary knowledge and skills for the telemarketing and field salesforces to be able to work effectively together.

FIGURE 3.9   Uses of Telemarketing

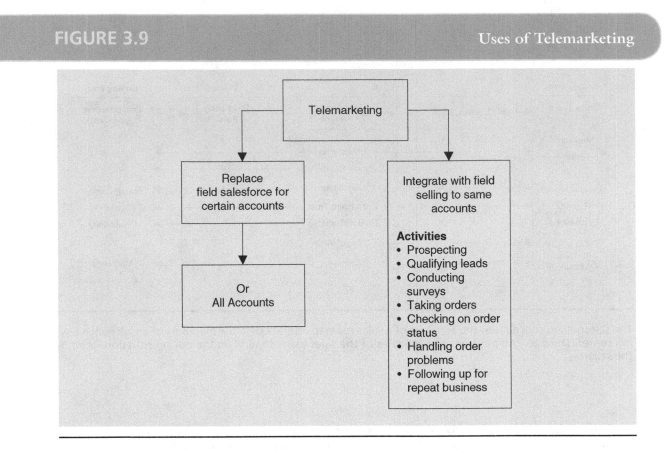

Telemarketing is typically used either to replace field selling or be integrated with field selling by performing specific activities.

Trade Shows

The final sales channel to be discussed here, trade shows, is typically an industry-sponsored event in which companies use a booth to display products and services to potential and existing customers. Because a particular trade show is held only once a year and lasts only a few days, trade shows should be viewed as supplemental methods for account coverage, not to be used by themselves, but integrated with and supported by other sales channels.

Statistics show that trade shows are popular. Company budgets for trade shows have nearly doubled in recent years. The number of trade shows in the United States has increased from around 4,500 in 1999 to more than 10,000 in 2015. Attendance at some shows has decreased in recent years as companies move to online ads and other events. Companies are, however, spending more time and effort on ways to improve their returns from trade show investments.[30] For example, Biovail Pharmaceuticals used an interactive game with physicians at the American College of Cardiology show to increase the number of leads generated to 900 from the 250 leads the year before.[31]

Trade shows are used to achieve both selling and nonselling objectives. Relevant selling objectives are to test new products, to close sales, and to introduce new products. Nonselling objectives include servicing current customers, gathering competitive information, identifying new prospects, and enhancing corporate image. Successful trade shows tend to be those where firms exhibit a large number of products to a large number of attendees, where specific written objectives for the trade show are established, and where attendees match the firm's target market.

The potential value of trade shows can be illustrated through several examples. Express Personnel Services spent $50,000 to exhibit at the Society of Human Resource

Managers Conference and generated about 400 sales leads and an increase in sales of $1.2 million. Azanda Network Devices garnered three new customers and $3 million to $5 million in extra sales from a $70,000 investment at the NetWorld-Interprop Conference. Orion International gained 125 new clients and $245,000 in new sales from its exhibit at the National Manufacturers Association Conference.[32]

Channel Conflict

Developing an effective sales channel strategy is a challenging task. Sales managers must determine the right mix of sales channel alternatives to meet the needs of all their customers in a cost-effective manner. Once a sales channel strategy is created, sales managers are faced with managing multiple channels and the channel conflict that emerges. Channel conflict occurs when the interests of different channels are not consistent. Typical examples of channel conflict include introducing an Internet sales channel that takes sales away from distributors or independent reps, determining which accounts are served by the field salesforce and which accounts are served by a distributor, or taking accounts from field salespeople and turning them over to telemarketers. The development and integration of corporate, business, marketing, and sales strategies sets the strategic direction for a company and its sales organization. Sales strategies are of most direct concern to sales managers and salespeople. The effective implementation of sales strategies requires an appropriate sales organization structure and the productive deployment of selling resources. Chapter 4 examines these important areas.

SUMMARY

1. **Define the strategy levels for multibusiness, multiproduct firms.** Multibusiness, multiproduct firms must make strategic decisions at the corporate, business, marketing, and sales levels. Corporate strategy decisions determine the basic scope and direction for the corporate entity through formulating the corporate mission statement, defining strategic business units, setting strategic business unit objectives, and determining corporate growth orientation. Business strategy decisions determine how each business unit plans to compete effectively within its industry. Marketing strategies consist of the selection of target markets and the development of marketing mixes for each product market. Personal selling is an important component of the marketing communications mix portion and business of marketing strategies and a key element in sales strategies.

2. **Discuss how corporate and business strategy decisions affect the sales function.** Corporate strategy decisions provide direction for strategy development at all organizational levels. The corporate mission statement, definition of strategic business units, determination of strategic business unit objectives, and establishment of the corporate growth orientation provide guidelines within which sales managers and salespeople must operate. Changes in corporate strategy typically lead to changes in sales management and personal selling activities. Business strategy decisions determine how each strategic business unit intends to compete. Different business strategies place different demands on the sales organization.

3. **List the advantages and disadvantages of personal selling as a marketing communications tool.** Personal selling is the only tool that involves personal communication between buyer and seller. As such, personal selling has the advantage of being able to tailor the message to the specific needs of each customer and to deliver complicated messages. The major disadvantage of personal selling is the high cost to reach individual buyers.

4. **Specify the situations in which personal selling is typically emphasized in a marketing strategy.** Marketing strategies tend to be either personal selling driven

or advertising driven. Personal selling is normally emphasized in business markets where there are relatively few buyers, usually in concentrated locations, who make important purchases of complex products and require a great deal of information and service. Personal selling is also typically emphasized in marketing mixes for complex expensive products that are distributed through direct channels, or through indirect channels by using a "push" strategy, and when the price affords sufficient margin to support the high costs associated with personal selling.

5. **Describe ways that personal selling, advertising, and other tools can be blended into effective integrated marketing communications strategies.** Effective strategies typically consist of a mixture of personal selling, advertising, and other tools. Firms often use advertising to generate company and brand awareness and to identify potential customers. Personal selling is then used to turn these prospects into customers of the firm's products or services. Other tools are normally used to supplement the advertising and personal selling efforts.

6. **Discuss the important concepts behind organizational buyer behavior.** The key concepts behind organizational buyer behavior are buying situation, buying center, buying process, and buying needs. Buying situations can be characterized as new task, modified rebuy, or straight rebuy. The type of buying situation affects all other aspects of organizational buyer behavior. The buying center consists of all the individuals from a firm involved in a particular buying decision. These individuals may come from different functional areas and may play the role of initiators, users, gatekeepers, influencers, deciders, and/or buyers. Organizational purchasing should be viewed as a buying process with multiple phases. Members of the buying center may be involved at different phases of the buying process. Organizational purchases are made to satisfy specific buying needs, which may be both organizational and personal. These concepts are highly interrelated and interact to produce complex organizational purchasing phenomena.

7. **Define an account targeting strategy.** An account targeting strategy is the classification of accounts within a target market into categories for the purpose of developing strategic approaches for selling to each account or account group.

8. **Explain the different types of relationship strategies.** A sales organization might use any number of different relationship strategies to serve targeted accounts. Transaction, solutions, partnership, and collaborative relationship strategies are examples used by some sales organizations.

9. **Discuss the importance of different selling strategies.** A selling strategy is the planned selling approach for each relationship strategy. Selling strategies might include stimulus response, mental states, need satisfaction, problem solving, consultative, or a completely customized strategy. Different selling strategies are needed to successfully execute different relationship strategies.

10. **Describe the advantages and disadvantages of different sales channel strategies.** A sales channel strategy consists of decisions as to how to provide selling effort coverage to accounts. The sales channel strategy depends on the firm's marketing strategy. If indirect distribution is used, then distributors become the main focus of selling effort coverage. Firms might decide to employ independent representatives instead of having a company salesforce. The concept of team selling is analogous to the buying center concept. Depending on whether the seller faces a new task selling situation, a modified resell situation, or a routine resell situation, different individuals will be included in the sales team. Telemarketing is a sales channel that can be used to replace or support field selling operations. Finally, trade shows can be used to achieve specific objectives and supplement the other sales channels.

UNDERSTANDING SALES MANAGEMENT TERMS

corporate strategy
business strategy
strategic business unit (SBU)
marketing strategy
corporate mission statement
business unit portfolio
generic business strategies
low-cost strategy
differentiation strategy
niche strategy
customer relationship
 management (CRM)
target market
marketing mix
business marketing
integrated marketing
 communication (IMC)
user
original equipment
 manufacturer (OEM)
reseller

government organization
institution
new task buying situation
extensive problem solving
modified rebuy buying situation
limited problem solving
straight rebuy buying situation
routinized response behavior
buying center
buying process
buying needs
account targeting strategy
relationship strategy
selling strategy
sales channel strategy
distributors
independent representatives
team selling
telemarketing
trade shows
channel conflict

DEVELOPING SALES MANAGEMENT KNOWLEDGE

1. How does the corporate mission statement affect personal selling and sales management activities?

2. How can sales promotion and publicity be used to supplement a personal selling–driven strategy?

3. Why is personal selling typically emphasized in business markets and advertising emphasized in consumer markets?

4. Why do most firms use both personal selling and advertising in their strategies?

5. How would sales management activities differ for an SBU following a differentiation strategy versus an SBU using a low-cost strategy?

6. Discuss how the buying situation affects the buying center, the buying process, and buying needs.

7. How is the management of relationships with distributors different from the management of relationships with end-user customers?

8. How can trade shows be used to supplement other sales channels?

9. How might telemarketing be used when accounts are covered by distributors?

10. What are the most important organizational buyer behavior trends, and how might these trends affect sales strategies in the future?

BUILDING SALES MANAGEMENT SKILLS

1. Visit the library or use the Internet to find the annual report or similar information about a company of your choice. Try to choose a firm with whom you might like to work after graduation. Use the information in the annual report to describe the firm's corporate strategy, marketing strategy, and sales function.

2. You are the sales manager for WorldPub, a textbook publishing company. You believe it would be a good idea to get involved on the Internet to help move your company's line of college business textbooks. Discuss your strategy for using the Internet and other sales channels to sell textbooks.

3. Protech Athletics Manufacturing currently markets a line of sporting goods equipment through independent sales representatives. The company has grown considerably since its inception seven years ago. Recently, Protech has become frustrated with its independent reps. It believes its products are not getting the attention they deserve. Protech is wondering if there is something it can do to help motivate the reps. However, given its recent disappointment with the reps, Protech is entertaining the idea of developing its own salesforce. What do you suggest Protech do and why? What are the advantages and disadvantages associated with your solution?

4. A salesperson leaving a sales meeting was heard to remark, "If we didn't have to spend so much of our time with all this planning, we could spend our time on something productive like selling." What advice would you give this salesperson about the purposes of planning?

ROLE PLAY

5. **Role Play**

   Situation: Read the Ethical Dilemma on p. 64.

   Characters: National Sales Manager for WC Electronics and the President of Walton and Associates.

   Scene: *Location*—conference room at WC Electronics
   Action—Role-play the meeting between the two company representatives about ending the relationship with Walton and Associates.

MAKING SALES MANAGEMENT DECISIONS

CASE 3.1: FAMILY VIDEO AND PARTY STORES

Background

Family Video and Party Stores (FVPS) is a well-established company with over 150 outlets scattered along the West Coast. A little over 100 of their outlets are in California. Each outlet is a combination video store with a larger than usual party store. The party store side of the business has expanded over the past 10 years to carry almost anything a convenience store might carry. The party store items can be anything from balloons and streamers for a birthday to seasonal holiday items. This combination has worked quite well for FVPS. Of the 150 stores, 47 are company-owned stores with the remaining stores leased to independent owners in a quasi-franchising agreement. The independent owners agree to buy their DVDs and party supplies from Family Video's parent company, Entertainment Inc. through their designated distributors. They also agree to uphold uniformity and facilitate appearance standards as set by Family Video. Every store's layout is exactly the same throughout the entire West Coast. The independent owners are encouraged to buy their convenience store merchandise from Family Video's designated distributor, but they are not required to do so. Lease payments are collected from independent owners when DVD deliveries are made each month when new releases come out.

Current Situation

In the past 12 months, Family Video and Party Store's growth rate has slowed considerably. This has been a major concern to FVPS's upper management, including Marcie Gaines, vice president for sales. Gaines has analyzed the declining growth rate and found that sales volume at company-owned stores is growing at a very acceptable 12 percent on an annualized basis. In contrast, stores run by independent dealers are lagging behind with an annual growth rate of only 2 percent. Gaines believes the independent category is underperforming for three basic reasons. First, the independent stores are generally not kept as clean and professional looking as the company-owned stores. Second, many of the larger independent operators have begun buying a larger share of their party store merchandise from low-cost distributors other than FMPS's designated distributors. This hurts sales volume results, since FVPS's retail operation gets rebates from their designated distributors, which counts as sales volume in the Family Video financial system. Third, FVPS has suffered volume losses from closed outlets. Competition has intensified, and turnover among dealers has

become more commonplace. It was taking FVPS an average of 60 days to find new dealers when existing dealers decided to leave the business. When a dealer operation closed, FVPS rarely converted it to a company-owned store, as their aggressive growth strategy at the corporate level left little capital for acquisition of existing outlets.

Marcie Gaines called her five regional managers into her California headquarters office to discuss the problem with declining sales volume and possible remedies to the problem. Given that the corporate strategy would continue to be to build market share and sales volume, Gaines outlined the following five-point plan:

1. Each salesperson would continue to supervise company-owned stores and independent dealers.

2. Salespeople would be given specific objectives for facilities appearance and a percentage of sales of convenience store merchandise purchases from FVPS's designated distributors.

3. Salespeople would be given mandates that no retail outlet would remain closed for more than 30 days.

4. Sales volume objectives for salespeople would remain in place. Current year volume objectives would not change.

5. Regional sales managers' annual objectives would be revised to be consistent with salespeople's new objectives.

The regional managers saw the need for the revised strategy but raised several concerns. They felt that the corporate strategy focused on building market share, but that the sales organization was expected to both build and hold market share. They complained that the new-dealer team, a corporate group, should be adding new dealers at a faster rate, and that part of the volume shortfall was due to poor performance of the new dealer team, not the salesforce. They also pointed out that FVPS salespeople were paid on a straight salary basis, primarily because they had previously functioned more as managers of multiple retail outlets than as pure salespeople. The discussion became heated, and finally Tucker Hanley spoke for the regional managers: "Look, Marcie, we know that corporate strategy can shift, and we know we have to adapt when that happens. But this drop in sales volume is partly the fault of the corporate new-dealer team. We don't see them having to change their ways. And we are really concerned that without some incentive pay, it will be hard to redirect our salespeople." Gaines, having heard enough at this point, replied,

"Tell your salespeople that their incentive is that if they succeed, they get to keep their jobs!" With that, the meeting quickly came to a conclusion.

Questions

1. Is it reasonable to charge FVPS's salesforce with simultaneously building and holding market share?

2. What are the pros and cons of Marcie Gaines' five-point plan?

3. Since the meeting with the regional managers ended on a sour note, what should Gaines do now? What should the regional managers do?

ROLE PLAY

Role Play

Situation: Read Case 3.1.

Characters: Marcie Gaines, Vice President of Sales; five regional managers.

Scene: *Location*—Conference room at Family Video Headquarters. *Action*—Role-play meeting among Marcie Gaines and the five regional managers to discuss the five-point plan and to decide on a strategy to increase sales at independent stores.

CASE 3.2: GLOBAL POSITIONING PRODUCTS

Background

Global Positioning Products (GPP) is a Kansas City-based manufacturer of GPS systems. In recent years, these devices have exploded in popularity as prices dropped to affordable levels. This is due to advancing technology and low-cost production outside the United States. Although GPP continues to manufacture a few of its own products, most production is outsourced to manufacturers in South Korea.

A key element in the GPP success story is the growth of dominant retail chains and club wholesalers such as Wal-Mart, Target, Best Buy, Sam's Club, and Costco. GPP uses major account teams to serve these and other large discounters, which accounts for 75 percent of GPP's annual sales. The remaining 25 percent comes from smaller retail accounts that buy either from GPP's manufacture representative or directly from GPP's Web site.

Current Situation

Andy Chulrane, GPP's national sales manager, is working on two major issues. First, he is fighting to keep GPP's direct cost of sales at 5 percent of total sales. The 5 percent target has been part of GPP's sales culture for more than 30 years, reflecting the belief that a low-cost operation translates into a more competitive position in the marketplace. Over the past few years, Andy's sales organization has reduced cost in various ways.

E-mail and texting, instead of long-distance phone calls, staying in budget motels, cutting overnight travel to a minimum were just a few of the measures taken to stay within the 5 percent guideline. In spite of Andy's diligent efforts, cost of sales was running at 7 percent for the major account team. Commissions remained fixed for several years at 4.5 percent.

The second issue currently demanding Andy's attention ironically stemmed from a GPP cost-cutting measure that was implemented one year ago. In an attempt to reduce manufacturer's representative costs, GPP has established a Web site as an alternative channel for smaller retailer customers. The reps have protested vehemently, but GPP insisted that selling on the Internet was an essential part of their selling strategy. Not all of GPP's products were available on the Web, a fact that did little to make happy the disgruntled representatives. Cost of sales of the Web site was a modest 2 percent of sales. Sales volume on the Web amounted to 3 percent of GPP's total sales during the past year, but current projections were for volume to increase to 5 percent of total sales this year and perhaps as much as 10 percent the following year. Some of the stronger reps were threatening to leave GPP in favor of the major competitor, which offered its reps a partial commission on all Web sales.

As Andy thought about the situation, he began to wonder if he could hit the 5 percent cost of sales target this year. Ninety percent of the cost of his major account teams was compensation-related salaries and incentive pay. Good salespeople were hard to find, and Andy had found that GPP had to pay the going rate or else GPP's top performers would look for new opportunities. Andy still regretted the recent loss of Barb Sherman, a major account manager, to a competitor who offered a better pay percentage. Sales volume at Sherman's former account had dropped 15 percent after her departure.

Andy didn't like to think about changing his major account strategy, but he wondered if he could move some of his large retail chain accounts to the manufacturers' rep organization. After all, representative commissions ran only 4.5 percent, and essentially there were no other direct sales costs associated with the reps. As he headed home after a long day at the office, Andy thought that the next morning he would try to build a case with the CEO of GPP to revise the 5 percent cost-of-sales target to reflect reality. If the answer is no, Andy thought he just might explore the idea of consolidating his major account teams and handing one selected large retail account to some of the more capable representative firms. He hated the idea of laying people off, but he told himself it may be necessary in this case.

Questions

1. Should Andy request a revision of the 5 percent cost-of-sales target? If so, what sort of information would he need to convince his CEO?

2. What factors should Andy consider as he contemplates a change in major account sales strategy, especially a change that assigns independent reps to some major accounts?

3. How would you assess GPP's alternative sales channel on the Web? Can you recommend any changes to minimize conflict with the independent reps?

Role Play

ROLE PLAY

Situation: Read Case 3.2.

Characters: Andy Chulrane, GPP's National Sales Manager; CEO of GPP; President of Manufacturers' rep agency.

Scene 1:   *Location*—Office of GPP CEO. *Action*—Role-play meeting between Andy Chulrane and GPP CEO to discuss 5 percent cost-of-sales target and to arrive at a decision.

Scene 2:   *Location*—Andy Chulrane's office. *Action*—Role-play meeting between Andy Chulrane and president of manufacturers' rep agency concerning the practice of selling over the Internet by GPP to arrive at a decision.

SALES ORGANIZATION STRUCTURE AND SALESFORCE DEPLOYMENT

OBJECTIVES

After completing this chapter, you should be able to

1. Define the concepts of specialization, centralization, span of control versus management levels, and line versus staff positions.

2. Describe the ways salesforces might be specialized.

3. Evaluate the advantages and disadvantages of sales organization structures.

4. Name the important considerations in organizing strategic account management programs.

5. Explain how to determine the appropriate sales organization structure for a given selling situation.

6. Discuss salesforce deployment.

7. Explain three analytical approaches for determining allocation of selling effort.

8. Describe three methods for calculating salesforce size.

9. Explain the importance of sales territories and list the steps in the territory design process.

10. Discuss the important "people" considerations in salesforce deployment.

KEY ACCOUNT MANAGEMENT

There's a big push in sales organizations today for reps to become "trusted advisors" and "collaborative partners" with their customers. But nudging your reps in this direction is a lot like asking them to write a book: It seems like a fairly straightforward process until you actually sit down to do it. Then you come face-to-face with a paralyzing onslaught of questions. How do you shift from selling to advising? Does it take a different approach for each account? Does—gulp!—your entire sales process need to change, or are you simply looking at a change in the kinds of conversations your reps are having?

While there's no one-size-fits-all road map for moving from vendor to trusted advisor, here's a look at how one company, a global manufacturing organization, tackled those questions. It is now so intertwined in its major customers' long-term business planning that in many cases the manufacturer is able to sidestep the Request For Proposal (RFP) process entirely.

The company's strategy shift began in 2004 when leaders recognized a major vulnerability: More than 50 percent of their revenues were coming from fewer than 10 percent of their clients, yet many of the company's interactions with these customers were reactionary. Customers would issue RFPs and the manufacturer would respond. With each RFP, the company risked losing a key account.

Though the manufacturer often won these bids, they knew this wasn't the way to lock in their key accounts and become trusted advisors to them. They knew they should be sitting down and planning collaboratively with them, but they had no formal process in place for doing so and no precedent for creating one. That's when they brought in Performance Methods, Inc. (PMI) and asked them to build a process that would enable them to shift into a collaborative planning role with each of their key global accounts.

A Four-Step Process

PMI conducted a series of in-depth customer assessment interviews to understand how the company's global accounts defined value in a strategic supplier. The feedback revealed two interesting dynamics. First, it appeared the manufacturing organization and its clients wanted to get to the same point. Customers expressed a desire to look into the future and share go-to-market strategies with a strategic partner, but just as the manufacturer had no process in place for doing this kind of planning with its customers, neither were customers sure how to go about it with their strategic vendors.

Second, while each customer had some unique needs, overall there was a huge amount of overlap in their value definitions. PMI's research uncovered 16 common requirements in a strategic supplier, including the need for those suppliers to have knowledge of the customer's business and industry, an ability to solve the customer's business problems, resources dedicated to the customer's account, proactive planning sessions with the customer, and an executive-level relationship between customer and supplier.

Armed with this information, PMI created the following four-step process that the manufacturer undertook with its strategic customers. As a result of this process, the company is becoming entrenched as a trusted advisor and strategic partner for many of those key accounts.

1. Internal Account-Planning Meeting

Starting in 2005, the company held a series of meetings, each one focused on a single key account. Everyone from around the world who was dedicated to a certain customer—sales reps, sales leadership, customer service reps, and customer support staff—flew in to meet with others working on that same account. Depending on the customer, groups ranged in size from six on the low end to as many as 16 participants on the high end.

The initial meeting lasted two to three days. Participants arrived having completed a brief pre-work package about their experiences with the customer. Drawing from that information, the team held detailed discussions about the customer, the customer's unique value profile according to PMI's research, and the manufacturer's strategy for working collaboratively with that customer.

2. Customer Validation

Armed with an initial plan for a collaborative partnership, the manufacturer next requested the opportunity to present its new strategy to the customer. Three or four people from the manufacturing organization, including an executive sponsor, the key salesperson, and PMI, participated in the presentation; in most cases, roughly the same number from the customer side attended.

During the presentation, the manufacturing team presented a summary of the work it had done during that initial account-planning meeting, explained its desire to work in a collaborative planning role with the customer, and detailed the benefits of such a relationship for the customer.

"It was very interesting to see how few customers understood what it means to be a strategic account," says PMI President Steve Andersen. He added that once customers understood how the manufacturing organization wanted to work with them and the value that a vendor who was an integral part of go-to-market planning could provide, they were overwhelmingly on board.

3. Collaborative Planning

Once customers agreed to work collaboratively with the company, the two sides scheduled an initial collaborative planning session. There, they discussed the customer's potential value targets and business objectives and broke out into round-table groups to brainstorm how the manufacturer could help the customer attain its value targets. Here's the six-step collaborative planning approach PMI implemented to provide the framework for each collaborative planning meeting:

- Identify potential areas of value creation.
- Qualify mutual value targets for appropriate levels of fit.
- Strategize and brainstorm together to determine best approaches.
- Prioritize value targets together.
- Execute action plans to proactively pursue value targets.
- Assess progress together and adjust value creation plans as needed.

The key to these meetings, says Andersen, is to hold them on a regular basis, regardless of whether there is a problem or specific opportunity on the table. Most teams meet quarterly.

4. Recap

After each collaborative planning session, key players on the manufacturer's team meet to confirm action items and evaluate how they're doing relative to their objectives.

Andersen points out that this strategy, properly executed, can completely circumvent the RFP process. By way of example, he cites one of the manufacturing firm's early collaborative planning sessions with a strategic customer. During the session, the customer brought up its plans to expand into a new region representing many millions of dollars in potential revenue. Before it could expand, however, it needed to acquire the type of business services and solutions the manufacturer provided.

In the past, the customer would have issued an RFP for those services and handled the rest of the expansion independently. Working collaboratively with the manufacturer, however, the two sides were able to short-circuit what could have been a lengthy search and RFP process, and got right to solving the expansion problems. In so doing, they both saved months of work as well as the hundreds of thousands of dollars it would have cost to prepare, issue, respond to, and review the RFP.

Obviously, this kind of strategic collaboration isn't possible with every account, says Andersen. But for those key accounts that make up the biggest percentage of your business, a collaborative planning strategy is not only possible, it's a necessity in today's business environment.

Source: "Manage Your Sales Team," Interview with Steve Andersen by Heather Baldwin. *Selling Power* (September 2007, republished 2014).

One important area of sales force structure is strategic account management. The opening vignette demonstrates a four-step process that can be used with strategic customers. The end result of this process is for the selling organization to become a trusted advisor and strategic partner for their key accounts.

Chapter 3 discussed the close relationships among corporate, business, marketing, and sales strategies. The strategic levels must be consistent and integrated to be effective. Strategic changes at one organizational level typically require strategic changes at other organizational levels.

The development of effective strategies is one thing, successfully implementing them another. In one sense, the remainder of this book is concerned with the development and management of a sales organization to implement organizational strategies successfully. This chapter begins the journey into successful implementation by investigating the key decisions required in sales organization structure and salesforce deployment.

SALES ORGANIZATION CONCEPTS

The basic problem in sales organization structure can be presented in simple terms. The corporate, business, marketing, and sales strategies developed by a firm prescribe specific activities that must be performed by salespeople for these strategies to be successful. Sales managers are also needed to recruit, select, train, motivate, supervise, evaluate, and control salespeople. In essence, the firm has salespeople and sales managers who must engage in a variety of activities for the firm to perform successfully. A sales organization structure must be developed to help salespeople and sales managers perform the required activities effectively and efficiently. This structure provides a framework for sales organization operations by indicating what specific activities are performed by whom in the sales organization. The sales organization structure is the vehicle through which strategic plans are translated into selling operations in the marketplace.[1]

The important role of a sales organization structure for a firm has been described as follows:

> The role of organization in sales has been compared to that of the skeleton in the human body; it provides a framework within which normal functions must take place. There is, however, a degree of uniformity in the human skeleton that does not characterize the sales organization. Each firm has its own objectives and problems, and the structure of the sales organization reflects this diversity.[2]

Developing a sales organization structure is difficult. Many different types of structures might be used, and many variations are possible within each basic type. Often the resultant structure is complex, with many boxes and arrows. The basic concepts involved are specialization, centralization, span of control versus management levels, and line versus staff positions.[3]

Specialization

Our earlier discussion suggested that a sales organization structure must ensure that all required selling and management activities are performed. In the simplest case, each salesperson could perform all selling tasks, and each sales manager could perform all management activities. Most sales organizations, however, are too complex for this structure and require instead some degree of specialization, in which certain individuals concentrate on performing some of the required activities to the exclusion of other tasks. Thus, certain salespeople might sell only certain products or call on certain customers. Some sales managers might concentrate on training, others on planning. The basic idea behind specialization is that, by concentrating on a limited number of activities, individuals can become experts on those tasks, leading to better performance for the entire organization. This approach can produce difficult situations as indicated in "An Ethical Dilemma."

A useful way to view salesforce specialization is from the perspective of the continuum presented in Figure 4.1. At one extreme, salespeople act as generalists, performing all selling activities for all the company's products to all types of customers. Moving toward

FIGURE 4.1   Salesforce Specialization Continuum

Generalists
All selling activities and all products to all customers

Some specialization of selling activities, products, and/or customers

Specialists
Certain selling activities for certain products to certain customers

A broad range of alternatives exists for specializing salesforce activities.

AN ETHICAL DILEMMA

Premier Copier Company, PCC, has spent a lot of money reorganizing their salesforce. From the beginning, PCC's salespeople were responsible for all their products and all customer types. The company had recently seen rapid growth and the sales management team had decided their customers needed specific attention given to them depending on the type of market the customer served. PCC divided their salesforce into four groups: government, educational, medical (GEM) and general accounts (GA). On paper this looked good, until the general account salespeople started to outperform the other market sales reps (GEM). The GA reps were bringing home monthly commission checks two to three times larger than their GEM counterparts at PCC. The GEM reps thought their territories were too restrictive and, when budgets were low, not much was spent on copier equipment. On the other hand, the GA reps could call on financial institutions, manufactures, wholesalers, etc., and this left them with a lot more opportunity according to the GEM reps. The GA reps were on record that the other GEM reps were not working hard enough! To further complicate things, when GA territories came open, the GEM reps applied for the open territory and were upset when they didn't get the GA opportunity. The sales managers from the four divisions are about to meet. What should they do? Why?

the right of the continuum, salespeople begin to specialize by performing only certain selling tasks, selling only certain types of products, or calling on only specific types of accounts.

Centralization

An important characteristic of the management structure within a sales organization is its degree of centralization—that is, the degree to which important decisions and tasks are performed at higher levels in the management hierarchy. A centralized structure is one in which authority and responsibility are placed at higher management levels. An organization becomes more decentralized as tasks become the responsibility of lower-level managers. Centralization is a relative concept in that no organization is totally centralized or totally decentralized. Organizations typically centralize some activities and decentralize others. However, most organizations tend to have a centralized or decentralized orientation. There is no single greater influence over the success of the sales organization than how the sales leadership creates the sales culture and environment for the people who will work for them. In this regard, the best organizations have strong leaders who exercise authoritarian control, dictate team direction, and establish the codes of behavior that all team members must abide by. Although these tenets are similarly used within military units to enforce chain of command, sales leaders prefer to use motivation and the force of their personal character before employing the power associated to their title.

The senior leadership team typically does not micromanage its sales teams below. Instead, there is independent and autonomous local decision making that operates within the guidelines and protocols established by the leaders above. But rest assured, the actions of the lower levels of the organization always take into account the goals and desires of the senior leaders.[4]

The trends from transactions to relationships, from individuals to teams, and from management to leadership, are producing a more decentralized orientation in many sales organizations. Salespeople and other sales team members who have contact with customers must be able to respond to customer needs in a timely manner. They must be empowered to make decisions quickly. A decentralized structure facilitates decision making in the field and encourages the development of relationships with customers.

Span of Control versus Management Levels

Span of control refers to the number of individuals who report to each sales manager. The larger the span of control, the more subordinates a sales manager must supervise. Management levels define the number of different hierarchical levels of sales management within the organization. Typically, span of control is inversely related to the number of sales management levels. This relationship is illustrated in Figure 4.2.

In the flat sales organization structure, there are relatively few sales management levels, with each sales manager having a relatively large span of control. Conversely, in the tall structure, there are more sales management levels and smaller spans of control. Flat organization structures tend to be used to achieve decentralization, whereas tall structures are more appropriate for centralized organizations. The span of control also tends to increase at lower sales management levels. Thus, as one moves down the organization chart from national sales manager to regional sales manager to district sales manager, the number of individuals to be supervised directly increases.

FIGURE 4.2   Span of Control versus Management Levels

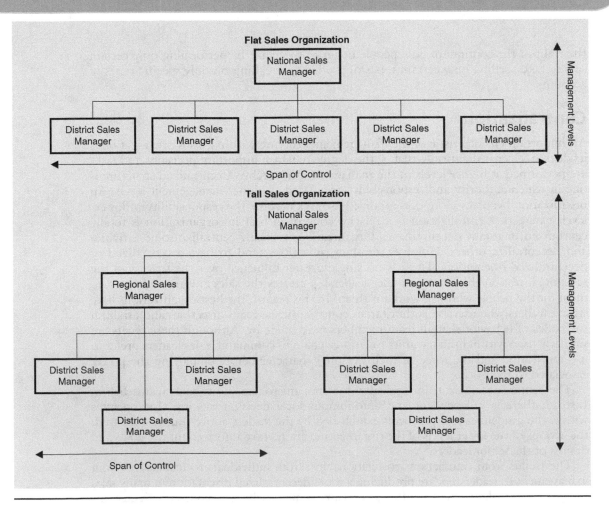

The flat sales organization has only two sales management levels, giving the national sales manager a span of control of 5. The tall sales organization has three sales management levels, giving the national sales manager a span of control of only 2.

Line versus Staff Positions

Sales management positions can be differentiated as to line or staff positions. Line sales management positions are part of the direct management hierarchy within the sales organization. Line sales managers have direct responsibility for a certain number of subordinates and report directly to management at the next highest level in the sales organization. These managers are directly involved in the sales-generating activities of the firm and may perform any number of sales management activities. Staff sales management positions, however, are not in the direct chain of command in the sales organization structure. Instead, those in staff positions do not directly manage people, but they are responsible for certain functions (e.g., recruiting and selecting, training) and are not directly involved in sales generating activities. Staff sales management positions are more specialized than line sales management positions.

A comparison of line and staff sales management positions is presented in Figure 4.3. The regional and district sales managers all operate in line positions. The district sales managers directly manage the field salesforce and report to a specific regional sales manager. The regional sales managers manage the district sales managers and report to the national sales manager. Two staff positions are represented in the figure. These training managers are located at both the national and regional levels and are responsible for sales training programs at each level. The use of staff positions results in more specialization of sales management activities. Staff managers specialize in certain sales management activities.

In sum, designing the sales organization is an extremely important and complex task. Decisions concerning the appropriate specialization, centralization, span of control versus management levels, and line versus staff positions, are difficult. Although these decisions should be based on the specifics of each selling situation, several trends appear to be emerging. Many sales organizations are moving to some type of specialization, usually a

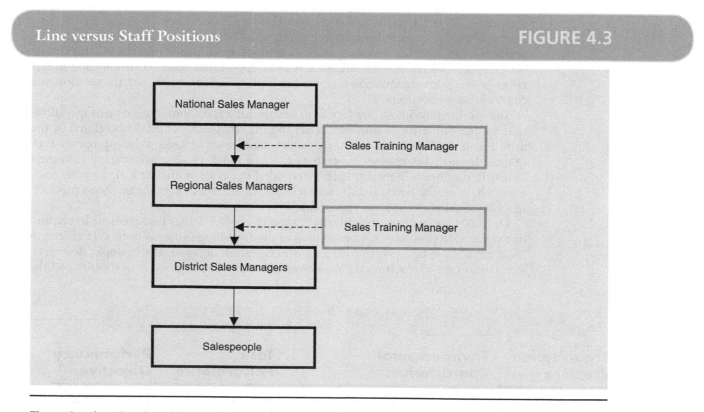

Line versus Staff Positions   FIGURE 4.3

The national, regional, and district sales managers occupy line positions, whereas the sales training managers represent staff positions.

structure that allows salespeople to concentrate on specific types of customers. The downsizing and restructuring of entire companies have affected the sales function. Sales management levels have been eliminated and replaced by sales organization structures that are flatter and that increase the span of control exercised by the remaining sales managers. This restructuring has influenced the trend toward more decentralized orientations and has resulted in the elimination of some staff positions. For example, some sales organizations have outsourced the sales training function to sales training firms, thereby either eliminating or greatly reducing the number of sales training staff positions.

SELLING SITUATION CONTINGENCIES

Determining the appropriate type of sales organization structure is as difficult as it is important. There is no one best way to organize a salesforce. The appropriate organization structure depends, or is contingent, on the characteristics of the selling situation. As a selling situation changes, the type of sales organization structure may also need to change. One key decision in sales organization design relates to specialization. Two basic questions must be addressed:

1. Should the salesforce be specialized?

2. If the salesforce should be specialized, what type of specialization is most appropriate?

The decision on specialization hinges on the relative importance to the firm of selling skill versus selling effort. Thus, if sales management wants to emphasize the amount of selling contact, a generalized salesforce should be used. If sales management wants to focus on specific skills within each selling contact, then a specialized salesforce should be used. Obviously, there must be some balance between selling effort and selling skill in all situations. But sales management can skew this balance toward selling effort or selling skill by employing a generalized or specialized salesforce.

Some guidelines for sales organization structure and selling situation factors are presented in Exhibit 4.1.[5] This exhibit suggests that a specialized structure is best when there is a high level of environmental uncertainty, when salespeople and sales managers must perform creative and nonroutine activities, and when adaptability is critical to achieving performance objectives. Centralization is most appropriate when environmental uncertainty is low, sales organization activities are routine and repetitive, and the performance emphasis is on effectiveness.

Two of the most important factors in determining the appropriate type of specialization are the similarity of customer needs and the complexity of products offered by the firm. Figure 4.4[6] illustrates how these factors can be used to suggest the appropriate type of specialization. For example, when the firm has a simple product offering but customers have different needs, a market-specialized salesforce is recommended. If, however, customers have similar needs and the firm sells a complex range of products, then a product-specialized salesforce is more appropriate.

Decisions concerning centralization, span of control versus management levels, and line versus staff positions, require analysis of similar selling situation factors. Decisions in these areas must be consistent with the specialization decision. For example, decentralized organization structures with few management levels, large spans of control, and the

EXHIBIT 4.1	Selling Situation Factors and Organizational Structure		
Organization Structure	**Environmental Characteristics**	**Task Performance**	**Performance Objective**
Specialization	High environmental uncertainty	Nonroutine	Adaptiveness
Centralization	Low environmental uncertainty	Repetitive	Effectiveness

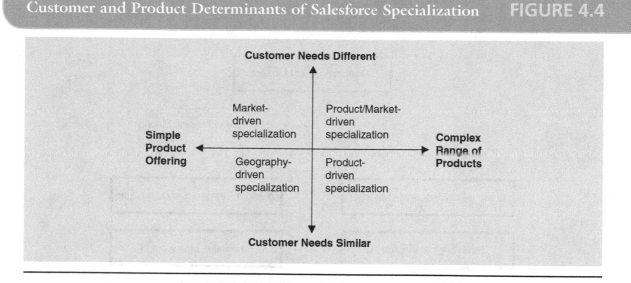

Customer and Product Determinants of Salesforce Specialization   FIGURE 4.4

Analysis of the similarity of customer needs and the complexity of a firm's product offering can provide general guidelines for determining the appropriate type of salesforce specialization.

use of staff positions may be consistent with a specialized salesforce in some selling situations but not in others.

Although the appropriate sales organization structure depends on the specific characteristics of a firm's selling situation, research evidence suggests that the structures need to change as a business goes through its life cycle. As firms move from start-up to growth to maturity to decline, the size and structure of the sales organization needs to adapt to the different situations at each life cycle stage. For example, specialization is most important in the growth and maturity stages and much less important at the start-up and decline stages. Sales managers should be alert to the need to examine their sales organization structure as their firm grows and matures.[7]

SALES ORGANIZATION STRUCTURES

Designing the sales organization structure requires integration of the desired degree of specialization, centralization, span of control, management levels, line positions, and staff positions. Obviously, there are a tremendous number of ways a sales organization might be structured. Our objective is to review several of the basic and most often used ways and to illustrate some variations in these basic structures.

To provide continuity to this discussion, each type of sales organization is discussed from the perspective of the ABC Company. The ABC Company markets office equipment (e.g., printers, furniture) and office supplies (e.g., paper, pencils) to commercial and government accounts. The firm employs 200 salespeople, who operate throughout the United States. The salespeople perform various activities that can be characterized as being related either to sales generation or account servicing. Examples of sales organization structures that the ABC Company might use are presented and discussed.

Geographic Sales Organization

Many salesforces emphasize geographic specialization. This is the least specialized and most generalized type of salesforce. Salespeople are typically assigned a geographic area and are responsible for all selling activities to all accounts within the assigned area.[8] There is no attempt to specialize by product, market, or function. An example of a geographic sales organization for the ABC Company is presented in Figure 4.5. Again, note

FIGURE 4.5   Geographic Sales Organization

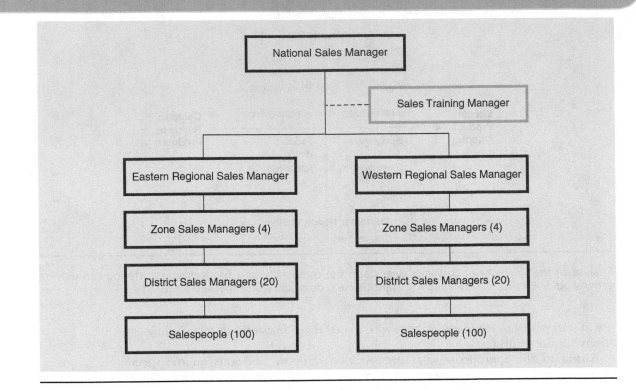

This geographic sales organization structure has four sales management levels, small spans of control, and a staff position at the national level.

that this type of organization provides no salesforce specialization except by geographic area. Because of the lack of specialization, there is no duplication of effort. All geographic areas and accounts are served by only one salesperson.

The structure in this example is a rather tall one and thus somewhat centralized. There are four levels of line sales management with relatively small spans of control, indicated in parentheses: national sales manager (2), regional sales managers (4), zone sales managers (5), and district sales managers (5). Note the sales management specialization in the sales training staff position. Because this staff position is located at the national sales manager level, training activities tend to be centralized.

Product Sales Organization

Product specialization has been popular in recent years, but it seems to be declining in importance, at least in certain industries. Salesforces specializing by product assign salespeople selling responsibility for specific products or product lines. The objective is for salespeople to become experts in the assigned product categories.

An example of a product sales organization for the ABC Company is presented in Figure 4.6. This organization structure indicates two levels of product specialization. There are two separate salesforces: One salesforce specializes in selling office equipment, and the other specializes in selling office supplies. Each of the specialized salesforces performs all selling activities for all types of accounts. The separate salesforces are each organized geographically. Thus, there will be duplication in the coverage of geographic areas, with both office equipment and office supplies salespeople operating in the same areas. In some cases, the salespeople may call on the same accounts.

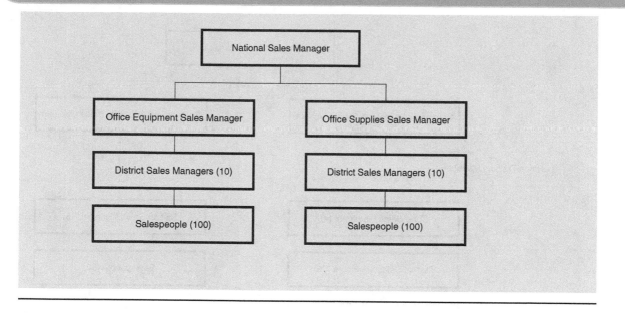

Product Sales Organization   **FIGURE 4.6**

This product sales organization structure has three sales management levels, large spans of control, and no staff positions.

The example structure in Figure 4.6 is flat and decentralized, especially when compared with the example presented in Figure 4.5. There are only three line management levels, with wide spans of control: national sales manager (2), product sales managers (10), and district sales managers (10). This structure has no staff positions and thus no management specialization beyond product specialization. The office equipment and office supplies salesforces are organized in exactly the same manner.

Market Sales Organization

An increasingly important type of specialization is market specialization. Salespeople are assigned specific types of customers and are required to satisfy all needs of these customers. The basic objective of market specialization is to ensure that salespeople understand how customers use and purchase their products. Salespeople should then be able to direct their efforts to satisfy customer needs better. There is a clear trend toward market specializations by many sales organizations.[9] For example, Yahoo! recently merged its search and display advertising salespeople into one salesforce. Instead of just selling search or display advertising, the salespeople now can focus on meeting all of the advertising needs of its customers from brand awareness to direct response.[10]

The market sales organization shown for the ABC Company in Figure 4.7 focuses on account types. Separate salesforces have been organized for commercial and government accounts. Salespeople perform all selling activities for all products but only for certain accounts. This arrangement avoids duplication of sales effort, because only one salesperson will ever call on a given account. Several salespeople may, however, operate in the same geographic area.

The example in Figure 4.7 presents some interesting variations in sales management organization. The commercial accounts salesforce is much more centralized than the government accounts salesforce. This centralization is due to more line management levels, shorter spans of control, and a specialized sales training staff position. This example structure illustrates the important point that the specialized salesforces within a sales organization do not have to be structured in the same manner.

FIGURE 4.7   Market Sales Organization

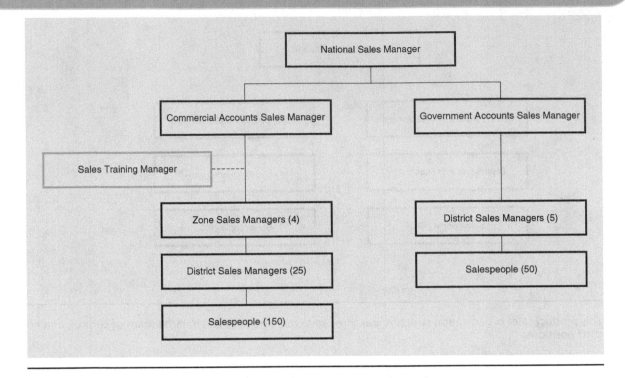

This market sales organization structure organizes its commercial accounts salesforce differently from its government accounts salesforce. The commercial accounts salesforce has three sales management levels, small spans of control, and a staff position. The government accounts salesforce has two sales management levels, large spans of control, and no staff positions.

Functional Sales Organization

The final type of specialization is functional specialization. Most selling situations require a number of selling activities, so there may be efficiencies in having salespeople specialize in performing certain of these required activities. As already discussed in Chapter 3, many firms are using a telemarketing salesforce to generate leads, qualify prospects, monitor shipments, and so forth, while the outside salesforce concentrates on sales-generating activities. These firms are specializing by function.

An example of a functional sales organization for ABC Company is presented in Figure 4.8. In this structure, a field salesforce performs sales-generating activities and a telemarketing salesforce performs account-servicing activities. Although the salesforces will cover the same geographic areas and the same accounts, the use of telemarketing helps to reduce the cost of this duplication of effort. The more routine and repetitive activities will be performed by the inside telemarketing salesforce. The more creative and nonroutine sales-generating activities will be performed by the outside field salesforce.

The field salesforce is more centralized than the telemarketing salesforce, but both salesforces tend to be decentralized. The cost-effectiveness of telemarketing is illustrated by the need for only two management levels and three managers to supervise 40 salespeople. This example does not include any staff positions for sales management specialization.

Strategic Account Organization

Many firms receive a large percentage of their total sales from relatively few accounts. These large-volume accounts are obviously extremely important and must be considered

Functional Sales Organization   FIGURE 4.8

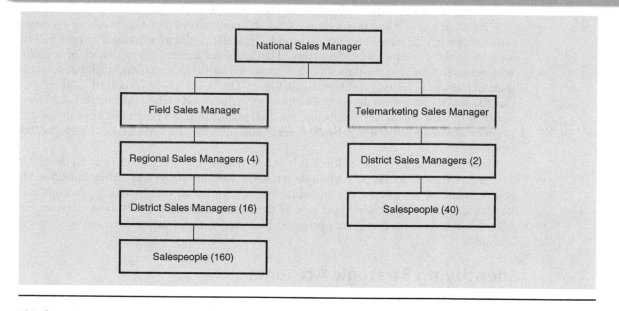

This functional sales organization structure organizes its field salesforce differently from its telemarketing salesforce. The field salesforce has three sales management levels, with small spans of control, and the telemarketing salesforce has two sales management levels, with large spans of control. Neither salesforce uses staff positions.

when designing a sales organization. The term strategic account is used to refer to large, important accounts that should receive special attention from the sales organization. Some firms use the terms *key account* or *major account* instead. Although the terms *strategic account*, *key account*, and *major account* are often used interchangeably, we emphasize strategic account, because the relevant professional association is named the Strategic Account Management Association (www.strategicaccounts.org). One approach for serving strategic accounts is presented in "Sales Management in the 21st Century: Organizing Strategic Accounts."

A strategic account organization represents a type of market specialization based on account size and complexity. Two types of strategic account organizations are of particular importance. National account management (NAM) focuses on meeting the

SALES MANAGEMENT IN THE 21ST CENTURY

Organizing Strategic Accounts

Jennifer Johnson-Kenny, manager of account sales for Verallia, a division of Saint-Gobain, discusses her company's perspective for serving strategic accounts:

Verallia is a manufacturer of glass packaging for the food, beverage, spirits, beer, and wine markets. Large consumer product companies are considered strategic accounts because they have a high potential for product exposure and sales. Depending on
the scope of the consumer product company, Verallia has either a national or international sales account manager assigned to each customer. The manager is responsible for working with a team of Verallia colleagues to meet the high standards that strategic accounts require. Strategic account sales managers must be astute front-line managers, and have the ability to interface effectively with marketing, production planning, packaging, quality, and manufacturing departments.

needs of specific accounts with multiple locations throughout a large region or entire country. For example, Cintas has both national and regional accounts. National accounts have locations throughout the U.S. Regional accounts, in contrast, might have 10–15 locations within a specified geographical area, such as a state.

Global account management (GAM), by contrast, serves the needs of strategic customers with locations around the world. Typically, a global account manager will be located at the customer's headquarters. This manager directs the activities of account representatives in that customer's other locations worldwide. Often, a global account management team is assigned to each customer. This team might consist of product specialists, applications specialists, sales support specialists, and others. Although GAM programs take time and effort to develop, research results indicate that a GAM program can improve customer satisfaction by 20 percent and increase sales and profits by 15 percent or more.[11]

Strategic account organization has become increasingly important in both domestic and international markets. Although strategic account programs differ considerably across firms, all firms must determine how to identify their own strategic accounts and how to organize for effective coverage of them. Steve Andersen of PMI in the opening vignette describes his company's program to organize for effective coverage of strategic accounts.

Identifying Strategic Accounts

All large accounts do not qualify as strategic accounts. As illustrated in Figure 4.9, a strategic account should be of sufficient size and complexity to warrant special attention from the sales organization. An account can be considered complex under the following circumstances:[12]

- There are multiple buying locations.
- Top management heavily influences its purchasing decisions.
- Multiple functions are involved in buying decisions.
- Its purchasing process is complex and diffuse.
- Some purchasing activities are centralized.
- It requires special services.

FIGURE 4.9   Identifying Strategic Accounts

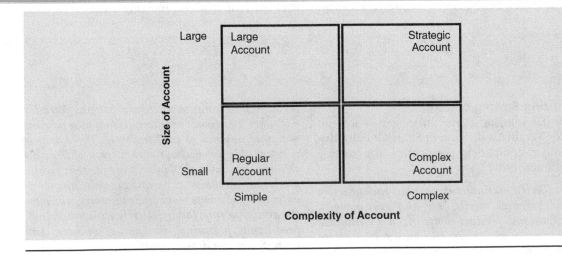

Strategic accounts are both large and complex. They are extremely important to the firm and require specialized attention.

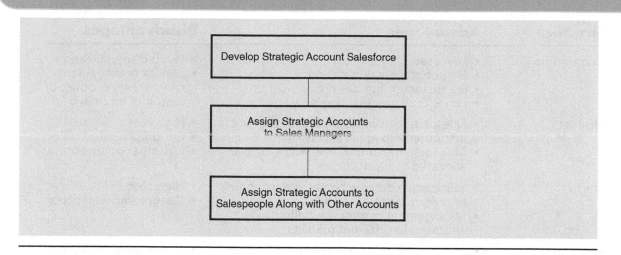

Strategic Account Options   FIGURE 4.10

Once identified, strategic accounts can be served in three basic ways. The development of a strategic account salesforce is the most comprehensive approach and is being used increasingly often for customers in domestic and international markets.

Organizing for Strategic Account Coverage

Accounts that are not both large and complex are typically served adequately through the basic sales organization structure, but those identified as strategic accounts pose problems for organization design that might be handled in a variety of ways. The basic options are shown in Figure 4.10. In one option, strategic accounts, although identified, are assigned to salespeople, as are other accounts. This approach may provide some special attention to these accounts but is not a formal major account management program.

Many firms have found that formal strategic account management programs can strengthen account relationships and improve communications between buyers and sellers. These formal programs are designed in several ways. One approach is to assign strategic accounts to sales executives, who are responsible for coordinating all activities with each assigned account. This strategic account responsibility is typically in addition to the executives' normal management activities.

An increasingly popular approach is to establish a separate strategic account salesforce. This approach is a type of market specialization in which salespeople specialize by type of account based on size and complexity. Each salesperson is typically assigned one or more strategic accounts and is responsible for coordinating all seller activities to serve the assigned accounts. In other cases, formal sales teams are created to serve specific strategic accounts. Research indicates that the effectiveness of the strategic account salesforce depends on the esprit de corps of those serving the major account, access to sales and marketing resources, the number of activities performed with the strategic account, and top management involvement. Interestingly, the formalization of the strategic account salesforce approach was not related to effectiveness.[13]

COMPARING SALES ORGANIZATION STRUCTURES

The sales organization structures described in the preceding section represent the basic types of salesforce specialization and some examples of the variations possible. A premise of this chapter is that no one best way exists to structure a sales organization. The appropriate structure for a given sales organization depends on the characteristics of the selling situation. Some structures are better in some selling situations than in others. Exhibit 4.2 summarizes much of what has been discussed previously

EXHIBIT 4.2   Comparison of Sales Organization Structures

Organization Structure	Advantages	Disadvantages
Geographic	• Low cost • No geographic duplication • No customer duplication • Fewer management levels	• Limited specialization • Lack of management control over product or customer emphasis
Product	• Salespeople become experts in product attributes and applications • Management control overselling effort allocated to products	• High cost • Geographic duplication • Customer duplication
Market	• Salespeople develop better understanding of unique customer needs • Management control overselling effort allocated to different markets	• High cost • Geographic duplication
Functional	• Efficiency in performing selling activities	• Geographic duplication • Customer duplication • Need for coordination

by directly comparing the advantages and disadvantages of each basic sales organization structure.

As is evident from this exhibit, the strengths of one structure are weaknesses in other structures. For example, the lack of geographic and customer duplication is an advantage of a geographic structure but a disadvantage of the product and market structures. Because of this situation, many firms use hybrid sales organization structures that incorporate several of the basic structural types. The objective of these hybrid structures is to capitalize on the advantages of each type while minimizing the disadvantages.

An example of a hybrid sales organizational structure is presented in Figure 4.11. This structure is extremely complex in that it includes elements of geographic, product, market, function, and major account organizations. Although Figure 4.11 represents only one possible hybrid structure, it does illustrate how the different structure types might be combined into one overall sales organization structure. The example also illustrates the complex nature of the task of determining sales organization structure. As noted before, the task is an extremely important one; sales management must develop the appropriate sales organization structure for its particular selling situation to ensure the successful implementation of organizational and account strategies. This task becomes increasingly more difficult as firms operate globally.

SALESFORCE DEPLOYMENT

The important sales management decisions involved in allocating selling effort, determining salesforce size, and designing territories are often referred to as salesforce deployment. These decisions are closely related to the sales organization structure decisions. Changes in structure often require adjustments in all three areas of salesforce deployment—selling effort allocation, salesforce size determination, and territory design.

Salesforce deployment decisions can be viewed as providing answers to three interrelated questions.

1. How much selling effort is needed to cover accounts and prospects adequately so that sales and profit objectives will be achieved?

2. How many salespeople are required to provide the desired amount of selling effort?

Hybrid Sales Organization Structure   FIGURE 4.11

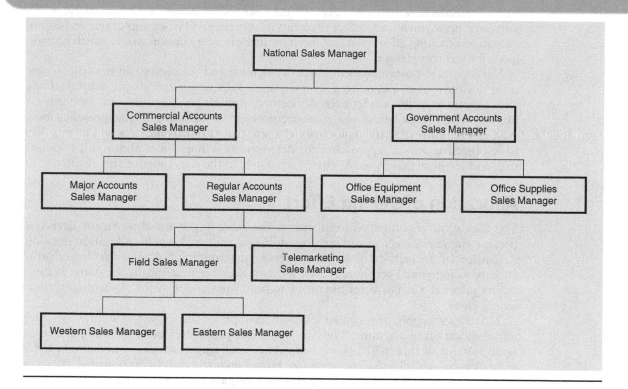

This complex sales organization structure incorporates market, product, functional, and geographic specialization.

Interrelatedness of Salesforce Deployment Decisions   FIGURE 4.12

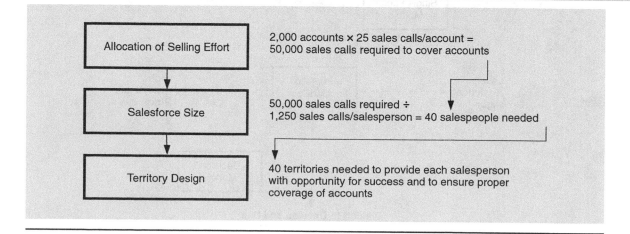

Determining how much selling effort should be allocated to various accounts provides a basis for calculating the number of salespeople required to produce the desired amount of selling effort. The salesforce size decision then determines the number of territories that must be designed. Thus, decisions in one deployment area affect decisions in other deployment areas.

3. How should territories be designed to ensure proper coverage of accounts and to provide each salesperson with a reasonable opportunity for success?

The interrelatedness of these decisions is illustrated in Figure 4.12. Decisions in one salesforce deployment area affect decisions in other areas. For example, the decision on allocation of selling effort provides input for determining salesforce size, which provides input for territory design.

Despite the importance of salesforce deployment and the need to address the deployment decisions in an interrelated manner, many sales organizations use simplified analytical methods and consider each deployment decision in isolation—an approach not likely to result in the best deployment decisions. Even such simplified approaches, however, can typically identify deployment changes that will increase sales and profits. The basic objectives of and approaches for determining selling effort allocation, salesforce size, and territory design are discussed separately in the remainder of this chapter.

Allocation of Selling Effort

The allocation of selling effort is one of the most important deployment decisions, because the salesforce size and territory decisions are based on this allocation decision. Regardless of the method of account coverage, determining how much selling effort to allocate to individual accounts is an important decision strategically speaking, because selling effort is a major determinant of account sales and a major element of account selling costs.

U.S. Paper Supply provides an excellent example of the impact of improved selling effort allocation to accounts. The company's salespeople had been spending about the same amount of time with all accounts. After analyzing customer data from its CRM technology system, clients were categorized based on revenue and sales potential. Based on these categories, salespeople plan the type and frequency of contacts with each customer

---

FIGURE 4.13   Analytical Approaches to Allocation of Selling Effort

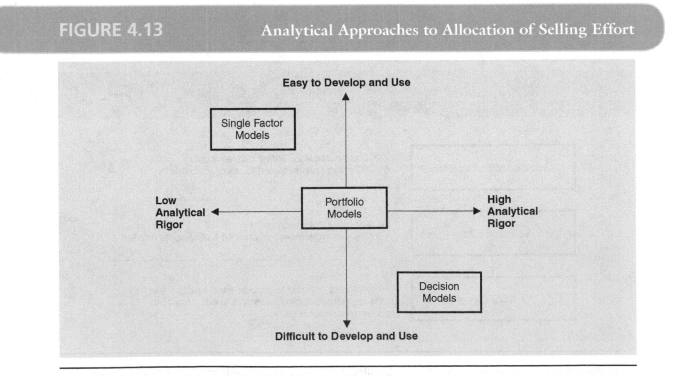

The single factor, portfolio, and decision model approaches for performing a deployment analysis differ in terms of analytical rigor and in ease of development and use. Typically, the more rigorous the approach, the more difficult it is to develop and use.

	Examples of Single Factor Model EXHIBIT 4.3

The single factor model was applied to evaluate the market potential of each account and then classify all accounts into A, B, C, and D market potential categories. The average number of sales calls to an account in each market potential category was calculated and evaluated. Based on this analysis, changes in the account effort allocation strategy were made. A summary of the results follows:

Market Potential Categories	Average Sales Calls to an Account Last Year	Average Sales Calls to an Account Next Year
A	25	32
B	23	24
C	20	16
D	16	8

for a 12-month period. The best accounts get the most face-to-face selling effort. Other accounts receive a blend of personal sales calls, telephone sales calls, e-newsletters, and product updates. This change in selling effort allocation produced a 25 percent increase in sales.[14]

Although decisions on the allocation of selling effort are difficult, several analytical tools are available to help. The three basic analytical approaches are single factor models, portfolio models, and decision models. These three are compared in Figure 4.13[15] and discussed in detail throughout the remainder of this section.

Single Factor Models

Easy to develop and use, single factor models do not, however, provide a very comprehensive analysis of accounts. The typical procedure is to classify all accounts on one factor, such as market potential, and then to assign all accounts in the same category the same number of sales calls. An example of using a single factor model for sales call allocation is presented in Exhibit 4.3.

Although single factor models have limitations, they do provide sales managers with a systematic approach for determining selling effort allocation. Sales managers are likely to make better allocation decisions by using single factor models than when relying totally on judgment and intuition. Because of their ease of development and usage, single factor models are probably the most widely used analytical approach for making these allocation decisions.

Portfolio Models

A more comprehensive analysis of accounts is provided by portfolio models, but they are somewhat more difficult to develop and use than single factor models. In a portfolio model, each account served by a firm is considered as part of an overall portfolio of accounts. Thus, accounts within the portfolio represent different situations and receive different levels of selling effort attention. The typical approach is to classify all accounts in the portfolio into categories of similar attractiveness for receiving sales call investment. Then, selling effort is allocated so that the more attractive accounts receive more selling effort. The typical attractiveness segments and basic effort allocation strategies are presented in Figure 4.14.[16]

Account attractiveness is a function of account opportunity and competitive position for each account. *Account opportunity* is defined as an account's need for and ability to purchase the firm's products (e.g., grocery products, computer products, financial services). *Competitive position* is defined as the strength of the relationship between the firm and an account. As indicated in Figure 4.14, the higher the account opportunity and the stronger the competitive positions, the more attractive accounts become.

FIGURE 4.14   Portfolio Model Segments and Strategies

Competitive Position

	Strong	**Weak**
High (Account Opportunity)	**SEGMENT 1** **Attractiveness:** Accounts are very attractive because they offer high opportunity, and sales organization has strong competitive position. **Selling Effort Strategy:** Accounts should receive a heavy investment of selling effort to take advantage of opportunity and maintain/improve competitive position.	**SEGMENT 2** **Attractiveness:** Accounts are potentially attractive due to high opportunity, but sales organization currently has weak competitive position. **Selling Effort Strategy:** Additional analysis should be performed to identify accounts where sales organization's competitive position can be strengthened. These accounts should receive heavy investment of selling effort, while other accounts receive minimal investment.
Low (Account Opportunity)	**SEGMENT 3** **Attractiveness:** Accounts are moderately attractive due to sales organization's strong competitive position. However, future opportunity is limited. **Selling Effort Strategy:** Accounts should receive a selling effort investment sufficient to maintain current competitive position.	**SEGMENT 4** **Attractiveness:** Accounts are very unattractive; they offer low opportunity, and sales organization has weak competitive position. **Selling Effort Strategy:** Accounts should receive minimal investment of selling effort. Less costly forms of marketing (for example, telephone sales calls, direct mail) should replace personal selling efforts on a selective basis, or the account coverage should be eliminated entirely.

Accounts are classified into attractiveness categories based on evaluations of account opportunity and competitive position. The selling effort strategies are based on the concept that the more attractive an account, the more selling effort it should receive.

Using portfolio models to develop an account effort allocation strategy requires that account opportunity and competitive position be measured for each account. Based on these measurements, accounts can be classified into the attractiveness segments. The portfolio model differs from the single factor model in that many factors are normally measured to assess account opportunity and competitive position. The exact number and types of factors depend on a firm's specific selling situation. Thus, the portfolio approach provides a comprehensive account analysis that can be adapted to the specific selling situation faced by any firm.

Sales organizations can apply the portfolio model approach in different ways. For example, one approach used successfully by firms in a variety of industries divides accounts into categories based on types of sales opportunities. The four account opportunity categories are: repurchase, replacement, expansion, and innovation. Each category requires different amounts and types of selling effort. Salespeople focus their selling effort on managing sales opportunities across accounts and not just on selling products. Companies employing this portfolio approach report significant sales increases.[17]

Portfolio models can be valuable tools for helping sales managers improve their account effort allocation strategy. They are relatively easy to develop and use (although more difficult than single factor models) and provide a more comprehensive analysis than single factor models.

Decision Models

The most rigorous and comprehensive method for determining an account effort allocation strategy is by means of a decision model. Because of their complexity, decision models are somewhat difficult to develop and use. However, today's computer hardware and software make decision models much easier to use than before. Research results have consistently supported the value of decision models in improving effort allocation and salesforce productivity.[18]

Although the mathematical formulations of decision models can be complex, the basic concept is simple—to allocate sales calls to accounts that promise the highest sales return from the sales calls. The objective is to achieve the highest level of sales for any given number of sales calls and to continue increasing sales calls until their marginal costs equal their marginal returns. Thus, decision models calculate the optimal allocation of sales calls in terms of sales or profit maximization.

Salesforce Size

Research results have consistently shown that many firms could improve their performance by changing the size of their salesforce. In some situations, the salesforce should be increased. In other situations, firms are employing too many salespeople and could improve performance by reducing the size of their salesforce. Determining the appropriate salesforce size requires an understanding of several key considerations as well as a familiarity with the analytical approaches that might be used.

Key Considerations

The size of a firm's salesforce determines the total amount of selling effort that is available to call on accounts and prospects. The decision on salesforce size is analogous to the decision on advertising budget. Whereas the advertising budget establishes the total amount that the firm has to spend on advertising communications, the salesforce size determines the total amount of personal selling effort that is available. Because each salesperson can make only a certain number of sales calls during any period, the number of salespeople times the number of sales calls per salesperson defines the total available selling effort. For example, a firm with 100 salespeople who each make 500 sales calls per year has a total selling effort of 50,000 sales calls. If the salesforce is increased to 110 salespeople, then total selling effort is increased to 55,000 sales calls. Key considerations in determining salesforce size are productivity, turnover, and organizational strategy.

Productivity

In general terms, *productivity* is defined as a ratio between outputs and inputs. One way the sales productivity of a salesforce is calculated is the ratio of sales generated to selling effort used. Thus, productivity is an important consideration for all deployment decisions. However, selling effort is often expressed in terms of number of salespeople. This suggests that the critical consideration is the *relationship* between selling effort and sales, not just the total amount of selling effort or the total level of sales. For example, sales per salesperson is an important sales productivity measure.

Sales will generally increase with the addition of salespeople, but not in a linear manner. With some exceptions, costs tend to increase directly with salesforce size. This produces the basic relationship presented in Figure 4.15. In early stages, the addition of

FIGURE 4.15   **Sales and Cost Relationships**

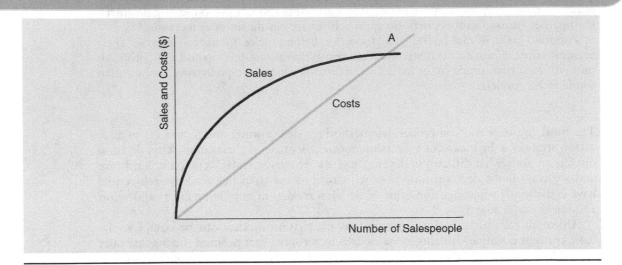

Although costs tend to increase in a linear manner with the addition of salespeople, the associated sales increases are typically nonlinear. In general, the increases in sales tend to decrease as more salespeople are added. A point (A) is reached when the sales from adding a salesperson are not sufficient to cover the additional costs.

salespeople increases sales considerably more than the selling costs. However, as salespeople continue to be added, sales increases tend to decline until a point is reached when the costs to add a salesperson are more than the revenues that salesperson can generate. In fact, the profit maximization point is when the marginal costs of adding a salesperson are equal to the marginal profits generated by that salesperson. It typically becomes more difficult to maintain high sales productivity levels at larger salesforce sizes. This makes it imperative that management consider the relationship between sales and costs when making decisions on salesforce size.

Turnover

Salesforce turnover is extremely costly. Because some turnover is going to occur for all firms, it should always be considered when determining salesforce size. Once the appropriate salesforce size is determined—that is, one sufficient for salespeople to call on all the firm's accounts and prospects in a productive manner—this figure should be adjusted to reflect expected turnover. If an increase or maintenance of current salesforce size is desired, excess salespeople should be in the recruiting-selecting-training pipeline. If a decrease is desired, turnover might be all that is necessary to accomplish it. For example, a grocery products marketer that found that its salesforce should be reduced from 34 to 32 salespeople achieved the two-salesperson reduction through scheduled retirements in the near future instead of firing two salespeople.

Organizational Strategy

Salesforce size decisions must also be consistent with the firm's organizational strategy. Companies that focus on serving current customers and achieving limited growth during slow economic times might reduce salesforce size as a way to lower costs. In contrast, companies trying to gain market share, capture new customers, and take advantage of market opportunities are likely to increase salesforce size. In fact, increasing salesforce size at the right time can provide a firm with a competitive advantage. For example, when Rilston Electrical Components sensed that economic conditions were improving, it added three salespeople to its salesforce of eight. Because it responded to opportunities before its competitors did, the company was able to increase market share and grow sales by 25 percent.[19]

The pharmaceutical industry provides an interesting example. Most pharmaceutical companies find sales calls to doctors a more effective way to increase prescriptions than consumer advertising. Thus, the number of pharmaceutical salespeople tripled to over 90,000 in the past decade. Merck is typical. It added 1,500 salespeople, bringing its salesforce to about 7,000. The increased number of salespeople increased drug sales, but there are problems. Sales organization costs are up significantly. Many doctors feel bombarded by pharmaceutical salespeople and have refused to see them or have severely limited their access. This has lowered sales productivity as the number of meetings with a doctor for an average pharmaceutical salesperson has dropped from 808 per year to around 529 per year.[20]

Pharmaceutical companies are responding to pressure from doctors, consumer groups, and government regulators by reducing the size of their salesforces. The 100,000 pharmaceutical salespeople in the United States is expected to decrease by about 20 percent in the next few years. Pfizer cut 2,200 salespeople in the United States and is decreasing its European salesforce by 20 percent. Other pharmaceutical companies are doing the same.[21]

Analytical Tools

The need to consider sales, costs, productivity, and turnover makes salesforce size a difficult decision. Fortunately, some analytical tools are available to help management process relevant information and evaluate salesforce size alternatives more fully. Before describing these analytical tools, we want to make it clear that there are several types of salesforce size decisions (see Figure 4.16). The most straightforward situation is when a firm has one generalized salesforce. However, as discussed earlier, many firms employ multiple specialized salesforces, in which case both the total number of salespeople employed by the firm and the size of each individual salesforce are important. Both generalized and specialized salesforces are normally organized into geographic districts, zones, regions, and so on. The number of salespeople to assign to each district, zone, region, and so on is a type of salesforce size decision.

These decisions are similar conceptually and can be addressed by the same analytical tools, provided that the type of salesforce size decision being addressed is specified. Unless stated otherwise, you can assume the situation of one generalized salesforce in the following discussion.

Salesforce Size Decisions	FIGURE 4.16

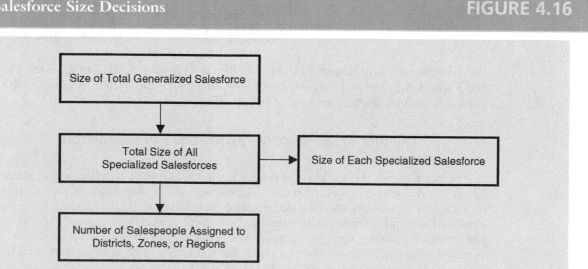

Depending on the sales organization structure of a firm, sales managers may be faced with several different types of salesforce size decisions. Each requires the same basic concepts and analytical methods.

Breakdown Approach

A relatively simple approach for calculating salesforce size, the breakdown approach, assumes that an accurate sales forecast is available. This forecast is then "broken down" to determine the number of salespeople needed to generate the forecasted level of sales. The basic formula is

$$\text{Salesforce size} = \text{Forecasted sales/Average sales per salesperson}$$

Assume that a firm forecasts sales of $50 million for next year. If salespeople generate an average of $2 million in annual sales, then the firm needs 25 salespeople to achieve the $50 million sales forecast:

$$\text{Salesforce size} = \$50{,}000{,}000/\$2{,}000{,}000 = 25 \text{ salespeople}$$

The basic advantage of the breakdown method is its ease of development. The approach is straightforward, and the mathematical calculations are simple. However, the approach is conceptually weak. The concept underlying the calculations is that sales determine the number of salespeople needed. This puts the cart before the horse, because the number of salespeople employed by a firm is an important determinant of firm sales. A sales forecast should be based on a given salesforce size. The addition of salespeople should increase the forecast, and the elimination of salespeople should decrease it.

Despite this weakness, the breakdown method is probably the one most often used for determining salesforce size. It is best suited for relatively stable selling environments in which sales change in slow and predictable ways, and no major strategic changes are planned, and for organizations that use commission compensation plans and keep their fixed costs low. However, in many selling situations the costs of having too many or too few salespeople are high. More rigorous analytical tools are recommended for calculating salesforce size in these situations.

Workload Approach

The first step in the workload approach is to determine how much selling effort is needed to cover the firm's market adequately. Then the number of salespeople required to provide this amount of selling effort is calculated. The basic formula is

$$\text{Number of salespeople} = \frac{\text{Total selling effort needed}}{\text{Average selling effort per salesperson}}$$

For example, if a firm determines that 37,500 sales calls are needed in its market area and a salesperson can make an average of 500 annual sales calls, then 75 salespeople are needed to provide the desired level of selling effort:

$$\text{Number of salespeople} = 37{,}500/500 = 75 \text{ salespeople}$$

The key factor in the workload approach is the total amount of selling effort needed. Several workload methods can be used, depending on whether single factor, portfolio, or decision models were used for determining the allocation of effort to accounts. Each workload method offers a way to calculate how many sales calls to make to all accounts and prospects during any time period. When the sales call allocation strategies are summed across all accounts and prospects, the total amount of selling effort for a time period is determined. Thus, the workload approach integrates the salesforce size decision with account effort allocation strategies.

The workload approach is also relatively simple, although its simplicity depends on the specific method used to determine total selling effort needs. The approach is conceptually sound, because salesforce size is based on selling effort needs established by account effort allocation decisions. Note, however, that we have presented the workload approach in a simplified manner here by considering only selling effort. A more realistic presentation would incorporate nonselling time considerations (e.g., travel time, planning time) in the analysis. Although incorporating these considerations does not change the basic workload concept, it does make the calculations more complex and cumbersome.

The workload approach is suited for all types of selling situations. Sales organizations can adapt the basic approach to their specific situation through the method used to calculate total selling effort. The most sophisticated firms can use decision models for this purpose, whereas other firms might use portfolio models or single factor approaches.

Incremental Approach

The most rigorous approach for calculating salesforce size is the incremental approach. Its basic concept is to compare the marginal profit contribution with the marginal selling costs for each incremental salesperson. An example of these calculations is provided in Exhibit 4.4. At 100 salespeople, marginal profits exceed marginal costs by $10,000. This relationship continues until salesforce size reaches 102. At 102 salespeople, the marginal profit equals marginal cost, and total profits are maximized. If the firm added one more salesperson, total profits would be reduced, because marginal costs would exceed marginal profits by $5,000. Thus, the optimal salesforce size for this example is 102. The major advantage of the incremental approach is that it quantifies the important relationships between salesforce size, sales, and costs, making it possible to assess the potential sales and profit impacts of different salesforce sizes. It forces management to view the salesforce size decision as one that affects both the level of sales that can be generated and the costs associated with producing each sales level.

The incremental method is, however, somewhat difficult to develop. Relatively complex response functions must be formulated to predict sales at different salesforce sizes (sales=f[salesforce size]). Developing these response functions requires either historical data or management judgment. Thus, the incremental approach cannot be used for new salesforces where historical data and accurate judgments are not possible.

Turnover

All the analytical tools incorporate various elements of sales and costs in their calculations. Therefore, they directly address productivity issues but do not directly consider turnover in the salesforce size calculations. When turnover considerations are important, management should adjust the recommended salesforce size produced by any of the analytical methods to reflect expected turnover rates. For example, if an analytical tool recommended a salesforce size of 100 for a firm that experiences 20 percent annual turnover, the effective salesforce size should be adjusted to 120. Recruiting, selecting, and training plans should be based on the 120 salesforce size.

Continually in Hiring Mode

Kim Davenport, District Sales Manager for over 30 years in the pharmaceutical industry, states:

Turnover is a real problem for any sales manager. I have managed between 10 and 20 salespeople in my district and I know I must always be recruiting. If I wait for a salesperson to resign I have put myself behind the eight ball. Every day I have an open territory my competitors are in the doctors' offices detailing their products and I know these same doctors are not hearing

a thing about our products. I must continually work with our human resources department to identify top candidates that are ready to move into one of our open territories. It can take three to six months to bring one our new hires up to speed on our products. Our goal is to get the new hire productive in their territory as quickly as possible. I work with district managers from other areas of the country to place a new hire if I don't have an open territory at the time of a hire. It is not unusual for our industry to have 10 to 15 percent turnover. I must be ready to respond to our anticipated turnover. That is why I am continually in hiring mode.

EXHIBIT 4.4   Incremental Approach

Number of Salespeople	Marginal Salesperson Profit Contribution	Marginal Salesperson Cost
100	$85,000	$75,000
101	$80,000	$75,000
102	$75,000	$75,000
103	$70,000	$75,000

Failure to incorporate anticipated salesforce turnover into salesforce size calculations can be costly. Evidence suggests that many firms may lose as much as 10 percent in sales productivity due to the loss in sales from vacant territories or low initial sales when a new salesperson is assigned to a territory. Thus, the sooner that sales managers can replace salespeople and get them productive in their territories, the less loss in sales within the territory. An example of staying ahead of turnover is presented in "Sales Management in the 21st Century: Continually in Hiring Mode."

Outsourcing the Salesforce

The salesforce size decisions we have been discussing apply directly to an ongoing company salesforce. However, there may be situations where a company needs salespeople quickly, for short periods of time, for smaller customers, or for other reasons, but does not want to hire additional salespeople. An attractive option is to outsource the salesforce. A growing number of companies can provide salespeople to a firm on a contract basis. These salespeople only represent the firm and customers are typically not aware that these are contracted salespeople. Contracts can vary as to length, customer assignment, and other relevant factors. This gives the client firm a great deal of flexibility.

The situation at GE Medical Systems is illustrative. Salespeople at GE Medical Systems called on hospitals with 100 or more beds in major metropolitan areas. This left the market for smaller hospitals in rural areas to competitors. GE decided it needed to pursue these smaller markets, but did not want to hire additional salespeople or to have existing salespeople take time away from their large customers. So, GE contracted with a firm to provide seven salespeople experienced in capital equipment sales to serve the smaller markets. The salespeople were hired, trained on GE products, and in the field within three months. These contracted reps grew annual GE sales in the smaller markets to $260 million within five years. The results were so spectacular that GE has renewed the outsourcing contract and continues to use the contracted salespeople.[22]

Designing Territories

As discussed earlier, the size of a salesforce determines the total amount of selling effort that a firm has available to generate sales from accounts and prospects. The effective use of this selling effort often requires that sales territories be developed and each salesperson be assigned to a specific territory. A territory consists of whatever specific accounts are assigned to a specific salesperson. The overall objective is to ensure that all accounts are assigned salesperson responsibility and that each salesperson can adequately cover the assigned accounts. Although territories are often defined by geographic area (e.g., the Oklahoma territory, the Tennessee territory), the key components of a territory are the accounts within the specified geographic area.

The territory can be viewed as the work unit for a salesperson. The salesperson is largely responsible for the selling activities performed and the performance achieved in a territory. Salesperson compensation and success are normally a direct function of territory performance; thus, the design of territories is extremely important to the individual salespeople of a firm as well as to management.

Territory Considerations

The critical territory considerations are illustrated in Exhibit 4.5.[23] In this example, Andy and Sally are salespeople for a consumer durable goods manufacturer. They have each been assigned a geographic territory consisting of several trading areas. The exhibit compares the percentage of their time currently spent in each trading area with the percentages recommended from a decision model analysis. A review of the information provided in the exhibit highlights territory design problems from the perspective of the firm and of each salesperson.

The current territory design does not provide proper selling coverage of the trading areas. The decision model analysis suggests that the trading areas in Andy's territory should require only 36 percent of his time, yet he is spending all his time there. Clearly, the firm is wasting expensive selling effort in Andy's territory. The situation in Sally's territory is just the opposite. Proper coverage of Sally's trading areas should require more than two salespeople, yet Sally has sole responsibility for these trading areas. In this situation the firm is losing sales opportunities because of a lack of selling attention.

From the firm's perspective, the design of Andy's and Sally's territories limits sales and profit performance. Sales performance in Sally's territory is much lower than it might be if more selling attention were given to her trading areas. Profit performance is low in Andy's territory because too much selling effort is being expended in his trading areas. The firm is not achieving the level of sales and profits that might be achieved if the territories were designed to provide more productive market coverage. Thus, one key consideration in territory design is the productive deployment of selling effort within each territory.

From the perspective of Andy and Sally, the poor territory design affects their level of motivation. Andy is frustrated. He spends much of his time making sales calls in trading areas where little potential exists for generating additional sales. Andy's motivational level is low, and he may consider resigning from the company. By contrast, Sally's territory has so much sales potential that she can limit her sales calls to the largest accounts or the easiest sales. She is not motivated to develop the potential of her territory but can merely "skim the cream" from the best accounts. The situations facing Andy and Sally illustrate how territory design might affect salesperson motivation,

	Trading Area[a]	**Present Effort (%)**[b]	**Recommended Effort (%)**[b]
Andy	1	10	4
	2	60	20
	3	15	7
	4	5	2
	5	10	3
Total		100	36
Sally	6	18	81
	7	7	21
	8	5	11
	9	35	35
	10	5	11
	11	30	77
Total		100	236

Territory Design Example   **EXHIBIT 4.5**

[a]Each territory is made of up several trading areas.
[b]The percentage of salesperson time spent in the trading area (100% = 1 salesperson). Thus, the deployment analysis suggests that Andy's territory requires only 0.36 salespeople, whereas Sally's territory needs 2.36 salespeople for proper coverage.

morale, and even turnover. These potential effects are important considerations when designing territories.

Recent research results support the example. Studies of sales managers in several countries found positive relationships between satisfaction with territory design and salesperson performance. These results are confirmed in a study of salespeople. The study concluded that salespeople who are satisfied with the design of their sales territory worked harder, performed better, and were more satisfied with their job. This research provides strong evidence for the impact of sales territory design on the attitudes, behavior, and performance of salespeople.[24]

Procedure for Designing Territories

A general procedure for designing territories is presented in Figure 4.17. Each step in the procedure can be performed manually or by using computer models. The procedure is illustrated manually by using Andy's and Sally's territories as an example application. The basic problem is to organize the 11 trading areas into three territories that provide proper market coverage of accounts in each territory and fair performance opportunities for each salesperson. Three territories are developed because the decision model results presented in Exhibit 4.5 indicate that two salespeople cannot adequately cover these trading areas. The data needed to design the sales territories are presented in Exhibit 4.6.

Select Planning and Control Unit

The first step in territory design is to select the planning and control unit that will be used in the analysis—that is, some entity that is smaller than a territory. The total market area served by a firm is divided into these planning and control units, then they are analyzed and grouped together to form territories.

Examples of potential planning and control units are illustrated in Figure 4.18. In general, management should use the smallest unit feasible. However, data are often not available for small planning and control units, and the computational task becomes more complex as more units are included in the analysis. The selection of the appropriate planning and control unit therefore represents a trade-off between what is desired and what is possible under the given data or computational conditions. In our example, trading areas have been selected as the planning and control unit.

Analyze Opportunity of Planning and Control Unit

First, determine the amount of opportunity available from each planning and control unit. Specific methods for performing these calculations will be covered in the appendix to Chapter 4. However, the most often used measure of opportunity is *market potential*. The market potentials for the 11 trading areas in our example are provided in Exhibit 4.6. Everything else being equal, the higher the market potential, the more opportunity is available.

FIGURE 4.17   Territory Design Procedure

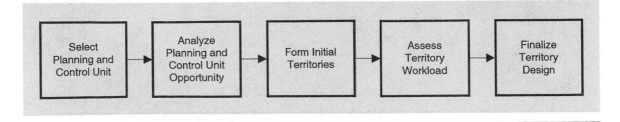

Designing territories requires a multiple-stage approach. Although most territory design approaches follow the stages presented in this figure, the methods used at each stage differ considerably, depending on the analytical tools used.

Trading Area	Market Potential	Number of Sales Calls
	Territory Design Data	EXHIBIT 4.6
1	$250,000	25
2	$700,000	100
3	$350,000	35
4	$150,000	15
5	$200,000	20
6	$2,000,000	175
7	$750,000	65
8	$500,000	50
9	$1,000,000	100
10	$500,000	50
11	$1,750,000	175

Potential Planning and Control Units   FIGURE 4.18

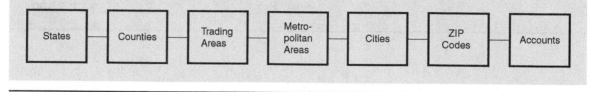

Planning and control units represent the unit of analysis for territory design. Accounts are the preferred planning and control unit. However, often it is not possible to use them as such, in which case a more aggregate type of planning and control unit is used.

Form Initial Territories

Once planning and control units have been selected and opportunity evaluated, initial territories can be designed. The objective is to group the planning and control units into territories that are as equitable as possible in opportunity. This step may take several iterations, as there are probably a number of feasible territory designs. It is also unlikely that any design will achieve complete equality of opportunity. The best approach is to design several territory arrangements and evaluate each alternative. Each alternative must be feasible in that planning and control units grouped together are contiguous. This can be a cumbersome task when done manually, but is much more efficient when computer modeling approaches are used.

Two alternative territory designs for our example are presented and evaluated in Exhibit 4.7. Although the first design is feasible, the territories are markedly unfair in opportunity. However, a few adjustments produce reasonably equal territories.

Assess Territory Workloads

The preceding step produces territories of nearly equal opportunity. It may, however, take more work to realize this opportunity in some territories than in others. Therefore, the workload of each territory should be evaluated by (1) the number of sales calls required to cover the accounts in the territory, (2) the amount of travel time in the territory, (3) the total number of accounts, and (4) any other factors that measure the amount of work required by a salesperson assigned to the territory. In our example, workload for each trading area and territory is evaluated by the number of sales calls required. This information is presented in Exhibit 4.8.

EXHIBIT 4.7   Initial Territory Design

	Alternative 1		Alternative 2	
	Trading Area	Market Potential	Trading Area	Market Potential
Territory 1	1	$250,000	1	$250,000
	2	700,000	2	700,000
	3	350,000	5	200,000
	4	150,000	8	500,000
	5	200,000	9	1,000,000
		$1,650,000		$2,650,000
Territory 2	6	$2,000,000	6	$2,000,000
	7	750,000	7	750,000
	8	500,000		$2,750,000
		$3,250,000		
Territory 3	9	$1,000,000	3	$350,000
	10	500,000	4	150,000
	11	1,750,000	10	500,000
		$3,250,000	11	1,750,000
				$2,750,000

Finalize Territory Design

The final step is to adjust the initial territories to achieve equal workloads for each sales-person. The objective is to achieve the best possible balance between opportunity and workload for each territory. Typically, both of these objectives cannot be completely achieved, so management must decide on the best trade-offs for its situation. Any inequalities in the final territories can be addressed when quotas are established, as discussed in Chapter 10.

Achieving workload and opportunity balance for our example is illustrated in Exhibit 4.9. The equal opportunity territories resulted in somewhat unequal workloads (see

EXHIBIT 4.8   Workload Evaluations

	Trading Area	Sales Calls
Territory 1	1	25
	2	100
	5	20
	8	50
	9	100
		295
Territory 2	6	175
	7	65
		240
Territory 3	3	35
	4	15
	10	50
	11	175
		275

	Trading Area	Market Potential	Sales Calls
Final Territory Design			EXHIBIT 4.9
Territory 1	1	$250,000	25
	5	200,000	20
	7	750,000	65
	8	500,000	50
	9	1,000,000	100
		$2,700,000	260
Territory 2	2	$700,000	100
	6	2,000,000	175
		$2,700,000	275
Territory 3	3	$350,000	35
	4	150,000	15
	10	500,000	50
	11	1,750,000	175
		$2,750,000	275

Exhibit 4.8). The final territory design moved trading area 7 to territory 1 and trading area 2 to territory 2. This produces territories that are reasonably equal in both opportunity and workload.

Performing territory design analyses manually is difficult and time-consuming. Fortunately, advances in computer hardware and software make it possible to consider multiple factors and rapidly evaluate many alternatives when designing territories.

Assigning Salespeople to Territories

Once territories have been designed, salespeople must be assigned to them. Salespeople are not equal in abilities and will perform differently with different types of accounts or prospects. Some sales managers consider their salespeople to be either farmers or hunters. *Farmers* are effective with existing accounts but do not perform well in establishing business with new accounts. *Hunters* excel in establishing new accounts but do not fully develop existing accounts. Based on these categories, farmers should be assigned to territories that contain many ongoing account relationships, and hunters should be assigned to territories in new or less-developed market areas.

Using Technology

We have taken you through the territory design process manually so that you understand what is involved in each step. Many sales organizations still perform this process manually using maps, grease pencils, and calculators. There are, however, several software programs that automate the process. Most of these programs make it easy to design potential territories, print maps, and compare opportunity and workload. Then, changes can be made easily and new maps and comparisons produced quickly. This allows sales managers to evaluate many possible territory designs and to assess the impact of territory design changes easily. Examples of available software include Sales Territory Configurator (www.rochestergroup.com), Tactician® (www.tactician.com), and TerrAlign (www.terralign.com).

"PEOPLE" CONSIDERATIONS

Our discussion of salesforce deployment decisions has, to this point, focused entirely on analytical approaches. This analytical orientation emphasizes objective sales and cost considerations in evaluating different allocations of sales calls to accounts, different salesforce sizes, different territory designs, and different assignments of salespeople to territories. Although such analytical approaches are valuable and should be used by sales managers, final deployment decisions should also be based on "people" considerations. These "people" considerations can produce some problems as presented in "An Ethical Dilemma." Statistics are numbers, whereas sales managers, salespeople, and customers are people. Analysis of statistical data provides useful but incomplete information for deployment decisions. Models are only representations of reality, and no matter how complex, no model can incorporate all the people factors that are important in any salesforce deployment decision. Accordingly, while using the appropriate analytical approaches, sales managers should temper the analytical results with people considerations before making final deployment decisions.

What are the important people considerations in salesforce deployment? The most important ones concern relationships between salespeople and customers and between salespeople and the sales organization. Consider the allocation of selling effort to accounts. The analytical approaches for making this decision produce a recommended number of sales calls to each account based on some assessment of expected sales and costs for different sales call levels. Although these approaches may incorporate a number of factors in developing the recommended sales call levels, there is no way that any analytical approach can use the detailed knowledge that a salesperson has about the unique needs of individual accounts. Therefore, an analytical approach may suggest that sales calls should be increased or decreased to a specific account, whereas the salesperson serving this account may know that the account will react adversely to any changes in sales call coverage. In this situation, a sales manager would be wise to ignore the analytical recommendation and not change sales call coverage to the account because of the existing relationship between the salesperson and customer.

Salesforce size decisions also require consideration of people issues. A decision to reduce the size of a salesforce means that some salespeople will have to be removed from the salesforce. How this reduction is accomplished can affect the relationship between salespeople and the sales organization. Achieving this reduction through attrition or offering salespeople other positions is typically a better approach than merely firing salespeople.

Increasing salesforce size means that the new salespeople must be assigned to territories. Consequently, some accounts will find themselves being served by new salespeople. These changes in assignment can have a devastating effect on the existing customer-salesperson relationship. Not only should that relationship be considered, but also the issue of fairness in taking accounts from one salesperson and assigning them to another. The situation can be a delicate one, requiring careful judgment as to how these people considerations should be balanced against analytical results.

AN ETHICAL DILEMMA

Business has been great for the past five years for Hi-Tech Media out of Atlanta, Georgia. Hi-Tech has developed media products such as large screens, LCD projectors, and home theaters, etc. Their domestic reps have been doing well but their international reps have been earning large paychecks with their recent orders. Sales have really been rising up overseas. Dubai, UAE has recently been awarded the World Expo for 2020. The rep in Dubai has earned as much in one month as the domestic reps usually make in one year! Jane Todd, Hi-Tech's National Sales Manager, has proposed a 10 percent commission on each year's first $3 million in sales and 2 percent thereafter. This commission structure will even up the paychecks for both international and domestic sales reps. A national sales meeting has been planned for next month to go over the plan. Even though reps will still be making between $300,000 and $400,000 per year, Jane is hearing the international reps are upset. Is Jane on the right track? Why?

In sum, sales managers should integrate the results from salesforce deployment analysis with people considerations before implementing changes in sales call allocation, salesforce size, or territory design. A good rule of thumb is to make salesforce deployment changes that are likely to have the least disruptive effect on existing relationships.

SUMMARY

1. **Define the concepts of specialization, centralization, span of control versus management levels, and line versus staff positions.** *Specialization* refers to the division of labor such that salespeople or sales managers concentrate on performing certain activities to the exclusion of others. *Centralization* refers to where in the organization decision-making responsibility exists. Centralized organizations locate decision-making responsibility at higher organizational levels than decentralized organizations. Any sales organization structure can be evaluated in terms of the types and degrees of specialization and centralization afforded by the structure. Sales management organization design also requires decisions concerning the number of management levels, spans of control, and line versus staff positions. In general, more *management levels* result in smaller *spans of control*, and more *staff positions* result in more sales management specialization.

2. **Describe the ways salesforces might be specialized.** A critical decision in designing the sales organization is determining whether the salesforce should be specialized and, if so, the appropriate type of specialization. The basic types of salesforce specialization are geographic, product, market (including major account organization), and functional. The appropriate type of specialization depends on the characteristics of the selling situation. Important selling situation characteristics include the similarity of customer needs, the complexity of the firm's product offering, the market environment, and the professionalism of the salesforce. Specific criteria of importance are affordability and payout, credibility and coverage, and flexibility. The use of different types and levels of specialization typically requires the establishment of separate salesforces.

3. **Evaluate the advantages and disadvantages of sales organization structures.** Because each type of sales organization structure has certain advantages and disadvantages, many firms use hybrid structures that combine the features of several types. Usually, the strengths of one structure are weaknesses in other structures.

4. **Name the important considerations in organizing strategic account management programs.** Identifying strategic accounts (which should be both large and complex) and organizing for coverage of them are the important considerations in strategic account management.

5. **Explain how to determine the appropriate sales organization structure for a given selling situation.** There is no one best way to structure a sales organization. The appropriate way to organize a salesforce and sales management depends on certain characteristics of a particular selling situation. Also, because the sales organization structure decision is dynamic, it must be adapted to changes in a firm's selling situation that occur over time.

6. **Discuss salesforce deployment.** Salesforce deployment decisions entail allocating selling effort, determining salesforce size, and designing territories. These decisions are highly interrelated and should be addressed in an integrated, sequential manner. Improvements in salesforce deployment can produce substantial increases in sales and profits.

7. **Explain three analytical approaches for determining allocation of selling effort.** Single factor, portfolio, and decision models can be used as analytical tools to determine appropriate selling effort allocations. The approaches differ in terms of analytical rigor and ease of development and use. Sales organizations should use the approach that best fits their particular selling situation.

8. **Describe three methods for calculating salesforce size.** The breakdown method for calculating salesforce size is the easiest to use but the weakest conceptually. It uses the expected level of sales to determine the number of salespeople. The workload approach is sounder conceptually, because it bases the salesforce size decision on the amount of selling effort needed to cover the market appropriately. The incremental method is the best approach, although it is often difficult to develop. It examines the marginal sales and costs associated with different salesforce sizes.

9. **Explain the importance of sales territories from the perspective of the sales organization and from the perspective of the salespeople, and list the steps in the territory design process.** Territories are assignments of accounts to salespeople. Each becomes the work unit for a salesperson, who is largely responsible for the performance of the assigned territory. Poorly designed territories can have adverse effects on the motivation of salespeople. From the perspective of the firm, territory design decisions should ensure that the firm's market area is adequately covered in a productive manner. The first step in the territory design process is to identify planning and control units. Next, the opportunity available from each planning and control unit is determined, initial territories are formed, and the workloads of each potential territory are assessed. The final territory design represents management's judgment concerning the best balance between opportunity and workload.

10. **Discuss the important "people" considerations in salesforce deployment.** Although analytical approaches provide useful input for salesforce deployment decisions, they do not address people considerations adequately. Sales managers should always consider existing relationships between salespeople and customers, and between salespeople and the sales organization, before making salesforce deployment changes. Many of these people considerations have ethical consequences.

UNDERSTANDING SALES MANAGEMENT TERMS

specialization
centralization
span of control
management levels
line sales management
staff sales management
geographic specialization
product specialization
market specialization
functional specialization
strategic account
strategic account organization
national account management (NAM)

global account management (GAM)
hybrid sales organization
salesforce deployment
single factor models
portfolio models
decision models
sales productivity
breakdown approach
workload approach
incremental approach
territory
planning and control unit

DEVELOPING SALES MANAGEMENT KNOWLEDGE

1. Discuss the situational factors that suggest the need for specialization and centralization. Provide a specific example of each factor discussed.

2. Why do you think there is a trend toward more salesforce specialization?

3. What are the advantages and disadvantages of structuring a sales organization for strategic account management?

4. What are some problems that a firm might face when undertaking a major restructuring of its sales organization?

5. What are the important relationships between span of control, management levels, line positions, staff positions, specialization, and centralization?

6. How are salesforce deployment decisions related to decisions on sales organization structure?

7. How can the incremental method be used to determine the number of salespeople to assign to a sales district?

8. How are salesforce size decisions different for firms with one generalized salesforce versus firms with several specialized salesforces?

9. How can computer modeling assist sales managers in designing territories?

10. Should firms always try to design equal territories? Why or why not?

BUILDING SALES MANAGEMENT SKILLS

1. Assume that you are the national sales manager for Replica Inc., a manufacturer and marketer of photocopy equipment and supplies. The firm's products are sold both nationally and internationally by a salesforce of 5,000. Replica sells to accounts of various sizes across several industries. Prepare a proposal that illustrates your recommended sales organization structure. Be sure to justify your recommended structure.

2. As an organization, your university has a specified structure. Identify this structure (draw it or obtain a copy of it). How specialized is this structure? What is its degree of centralization? What does the span of control look like and how appropriate is it? How many levels of management exist? Is this enough or too much? What are the relationships between line and staff positions? Are they appropriate? Assuming you would like the university to run as efficiently and effectively as possible, what changes would you recommend making to this structure and why? If no changes are recommended, why not?

3. Give an example of why a firm might want to organize around a geographic, product, market, or a functional specialization.

4. Using the following information, calculate the total salesforce size necessary by using each of the following approaches: breakdown, workload, and incremental. (Your answers may vary because each piece of information does not apply to the same company.) Be sure to show your work. Also, explain the advantages and disadvantages of each approach. Which approach would you recommend using to determine salesforce size? Why?

   • Sales of $80 million are forecast for next year.

   • Fifteen thousand calls are needed in the market area to be covered.

- Salespeople generate an average of $2 million in annual sales.
- A salesperson can make an average of 500 annual sales calls.
- Marginal salesperson cost is $65,000. With 88 salespeople, the marginal salesperson profit contribution is $75,000. This profit contribution decreases by $5,000 with each additional salesperson added to the base of 88 salespeople. Marginal salesperson cost remains constant.
- Turnover is 10 percent annually.

ROLE PLAY

5. **Role Play**

Situation: Read the Ethical Dilemma on p. 79.

Characters: Four sales managers: government, education, medical, and general account managers.

Scene: *Location*—Headquarters' conference room.
Action—Role-play a meeting between the sales managers concerning the sales teams competing against each other.

MAKING SALES MANAGEMENT DECISIONS

CASE 4.1 IMPACT PACKAGING, INC.

Background

Impact Packaging, Inc. (IPI) is a national manufacturer of a wide variety of polyethylene and polystyrene packaging products, including food and ice bags; Styrofoam egg cartons, meat trays, and food service products; laundry and dry-cleaning packaging; trash bags, and construction film and plastic shipping pallets. IPI is a strong competitor in all of its product lines. Not an innovative company, IPI leverages its large manufacturing capacity to drive its costs down, which allows the company to sell its products at highly attractive price levels.

IPI operates five regional offices: Charlotte, Boston, Minneapolis, Denver, and San Francisco. These offices are located at manufacturing plants that serve each region. IPI is organized by product line, with each product line run by a regional product manager and a regional sales manager. Eight to 10 sales representatives report to each of the five regional sales managers. The product managers and sales managers in each region report to a regional marketing manager. The key products and customers for each product line are shown in Exhibit 4.10.

Current Situation

Jack Saddler, Western Region marketing manager, has called his four sales managers and four product managers to San Francisco to discuss alternative approaches to organizing the IPI salesforce. Thirty days earlier, Saddler and his managers had hosted a key customer roundtable at the annual meeting of the Plastics Packaging Manufacturers' Association. Saddler was troubled by several themes that emerged from the roundtable. Some of the most influential paper and plastic distributors are disturbed by the fact that IPI sells to grocery chains, garment manufacturers, egg packers/processors, and uniform rental companies on a direct basis. This is puzzling to Saddler, since IPI has always sold through distributors when feasible. Further, distributors are informed before stocking IPI products that if end users meet certain sales volume requirements and request that they be sold on a direct basis, IPI will sell direct rather than risk losing the business.

Saddler is also concerned that many of the grocery chain buyers and paper and plastic distributors complained about the amount of time it takes for them to see several IPI salespeople. These

	PPI Product Lines and Key Customer Types	EXHIBIT 4.10
Product Line	**Key Products**	**Key Customer Types**
Food Packaging	Produce bags	Grocery chains Food coops Paper and plastic distributors
	Foam meat trays	Grocery chains Meat and poultry processors Food coops Paper and plastic distributors
Institutional	Trash bags	Paper and plastic distributors Restaurant wholesalers Janitorial wholesalers
	Food service (plastic plates, bowls)	Restaurant wholesalers Grocery store delis Institutional food wholesalers Paper and plastic distributors
Agricultural	Egg cartons	Grocery chains Egg packers/processors
Garment	Poly bags	Laundries and dry cleaners Uniform rental companies Garment manufacturers Paper and plastic distributors

customers wanted to deal with a single IPI representative, not one from each product line. An additional concern was that IPI did not allow aggregation of products across product lines to make it easier for these buyers to achieve the maximum quantity discounts.

To prepare for the meeting, Jack Saddler asked each product manager/sales manager team to come ready to discuss these issues:

1. Is it time for IPI to reconsider its salesforce organization by product line?

2. What are the advantages and disadvantages of organizing the IPI salesforce by product line?

3. What are the advantages and disadvantages of developing a new sales organization for the Western Region that would organize according to these customer types: (a) grocery chains and food coops; (b) distributors, including paper and plastic distributors, restaurant wholesalers, institutional food wholesalers, and janitorial wholesalers; and (c) end users, including meat and poultry processors, grocery store delis, egg packers/processors, laundries and dry cleaners, uniform rental companies, and garment manufacturers?

Assume you are the sales manager for the food packaging product line. Address the preceding questions as if you will attend the upcoming meeting. In addition, outline your thoughts on other alternatives for organizing the salesforce.

Role Play

ROLE PLAY

Situation: Read Case 4.1.

Characters: Jack Saddler, Western Region marketing manager; sales manager for food packing product line; one or more other product/sales managers.

Scene 1: *Location*—Saddler's office. *Action*—Role-play between Saddler and sales manager for food packing product line, discussing the advantages and disadvantages of a salesforce organized by product line.

Scene 2: *Location*—Meeting room. *Action*—Role-play meeting with Saddler and all product/sales managers, discussing the advantages and disadvantages of different alternatives for organizing IPI's salesforce and arriving at a decision.

CASE 4.2: ADDISON INSURANCE CONSULTING
Background

Addison Insurance Consulting (AIC) is a 30-year-old company that specializes in providing small businesses with supplemental insurance benefits that aren't covered with normal insurance plans. AIC focuses on small businesses with 20 or fewer employees such as machine shops, law firms, account firms, and small restaurants. AIC has three sales representatives serving the Cincinnati, Ohio metropolitan market.

Joe Morgan, AIC's founder and current president, was the company's first salesperson. When the company grew to the point that Morgan had a hard time serving all of his accounts, he added Tom Foster as a sales representative. Morgan gave Foster 15 of his existing accounts and instructed him to go after potential customers not yet in contact with AIC. A few years later, Karen Seaver was hired as a sales representative and added in much the same fashion. Seaver was not quite as experienced as Foster, so Morgan and Foster turned over 20 accounts to Seaver, 10 each. She also was instructed to add new customers not already doing business with AIC. Both Karen Seaver and Tom Foster report directly to Joe Morgan. Of AIC's total sales volume, Joe Morgan accounted for approximately 60 percent. The remaining 40 percent was split evenly between Seaver and Foster. Seaver and Foster are paid a percentage of AIC's billings to their clients.

Current Situation

Morgan is planning to retire in another year as a sales producer. In this so-called semi-retirement Morgan plans to continue as sales manager and president. Morgan has decided to bring in his son Tony as his replacement. Tony has no prior sales experience, so he will learn the business over the next three months, then step full-time into a sales role. Joe Morgan is gathering information that will help him decide how to design AIC's territories after he gives up his sales responsibilities. He is not comfortable turning over all of his accounts to his son, Tony. Although he is hard working, Tony is inexperienced in the insurance consulting industry. A recent graduate of Xavier University in Cincinnati and a double major in Finance and Accounting, Tony has a goal of becoming president of AIC, then expanding company operations into other markets.

Morgan has been contemplating the sales performance of Seaver and Foster. Both had been solid, dependable performers over the years, but Foster had recently slowed down a bit. While his sales volume compared favorably to Seaver's, Foster was selling in a higher potential sales territory. Further, he had a five-year head start on Seaver in developing new accounts, yet Seaver had brought in almost as much new business as Foster during the past year. Morgan had talked to Foster about the lack of sales growth in his territory but only heard excuses about why his sales had leveled off (i.e., slow economy). Foster promised to try harder to bring in new business. Morgan suspected that Foster was comfortable with his earnings and simply did not want to work much harder, even if he could make more money.

After several weeks of analysis, Joe Morgan finally had a rough draft of a new territory design policy that would go into effect at the start of the next new quarter. The key points of the new policy are:

1. Half of Joe Morgan's accounts will be split between Tom Foster and Karen Seaver. Joe Morgan's remaining accounts will be assigned to Tony Morgan.

2. After one year, sales territories will be redesigned so that the three territories will be comparable in terms of workload and sales potential.

3. For the current year, AIC salespeople will continue to earn a commission based on AIC billings to their clients.

4. After the sales territories are redesigned in a year, the commission rate for existing clients will be reduced, and a higher commission rate will be implemented for new accounts added within the past year.

Joe Morgan distributed the draft plan to Karen, Tom, and Tony. Both Karen and Tom questioned the idea of assigning half of Joe's accounts to Tony. Tom came right to the point, saying, "Look, Joe, he's your son and he will do just fine with some seasoning. But I think he ought to start with a smaller group of accounts. He'll learn the

business a lot faster if he has to build it by adding his own accounts."

Karen and Tom were also concerned that they would have some of Joe's former accounts for a year, and then lose them to Tony. Tony remained neutral on these issues, and voiced neither support nor opposition to the draft plan.

Questions

1. What are the implications for Karen Seaver and Tom Foster if the draft plan is implemented?

2. What are the implications for AIC's customers if the draft plan is implemented?

3. What are the pros and cons of Morgan's draft plan?

4. What changes and additions would you make to the draft plan?

ROLE PLAY

Role Play

Situation: Read Case 4.2.

Characters: Joe Morgan, president; Tony Morgan, son and salesperson; Tom Foster, company's first salesperson; Karen Seaver, company's second salesperson.

Scene 1:   *Location*—Meeting room. *Action*—Role-play discussion among Joe Morgan, Tony Morgan, Tom Foster, and Karen Seaver about the draft territory design plan.

Scene 2:   *Location*—Meeting room. *Action*—Role-play discussion among Joe Morgan, Tony Morgan, Tom Foster, and Karen Seaver about alternatives to the draft territory design plan and a final territory design decision.

A meteorologist used all the latest technology to predict a bright and sunny day in the mid-80s. It rained most of the day and never got warmer than 70 degrees. The weather forecast missed the mark on this particular occasion, but the meteorologist will continue to make weather forecasts and to work on improving weather forecasting procedures.

Sales managers face a situation similar to that of the meteorologist. The business environment is complex and dynamic, there are a number of forecasting methods available, and often forecasts are incorrect. Nevertheless, sales managers must continue to forecast and to work on improving their forecasting procedures.

Why is forecasting so important to sales managers? In one sense, all sales management decisions are based on some type of forecast. The sales manager decides on a certain action because he or she thinks that it will produce a certain result. This expected result is a forecast, even though the sales manager may not have quantified it or may not have used a mathematical forecasting procedure. More specifically, forecasts provide the basis for the following sales management decisions:

1. Determining salesforce size

2. Designing territories

3. Establishing sales quotas and selling budgets

4. Determining sales compensation levels

5. Evaluating salesperson performance

6. Evaluating prospective accounts

FORECASTING BY SALES MANAGERS

Although top management levels are most concerned with total firm forecasts, sales managers are typically interested in developing and using forecasts for specific areas, such as accounts, territories, districts, regions, and/or zones. For example, a district sales manager would be concerned with the district forecast as well as forecasts for individual territories and accounts within the district. There are, however, different types of forecasts that sales managers might use in different ways, and different approaches and methods might be used to develop these forecasts.

Types of Forecasts

The term *forecast* is ordinarily used to refer to a prediction for a future period. Although this usage is technically correct, it is too general for managerial value. As illustrated in Figure 4A.1, at least three factors must be defined when referring to a forecast: the product level, the geographic area, and the time period. The figure presents 90 different forecasts that might be made, depending on these factors. Thus, when using the term *forecast*, sales managers should be specific in defining exactly what is being forecast, what geographic area is being targeted, and what period is being forecast.

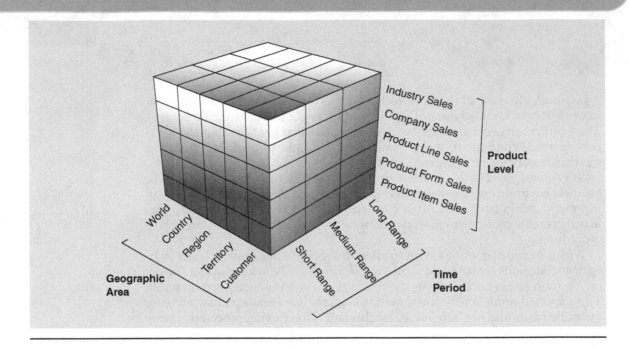

Many different types of forecasts are possible. Every forecast should be defined in terms of geographic area, product level, and time period.

A useful way for viewing what is being forecast is presented in Exhibit 4A.1. This exhibit suggests that it is important to differentiate between industry and firm levels and to determine whether the prediction is for the best possible results or for the expected results given a specific strategy. Four different types of forecasts emerge from this classification scheme:

1. *Market potential*—the best possible level of industry sales in a given geographic area for a specific period.

2. *Market forecast*—the expected level of industry sales given a specific industry strategy in a given geographic area for a specific period.

3. *Sales potential*—the best possible level of firm sales in a given geographic area for a specific period.

4. *Sales forecast*—the expected level of firm sales given a specific strategy in a given geographic area for a specific period.

Notice that the geographic area and period are defined for each of these terms and that a true *sales forecast* must include the consideration of a specific strategy. If a firm changes this strategy, the sales forecast should change also.

As an example, assume that you are the district sales manager for a firm that markets personal computers (PCs) to organizational buyers. Your district includes Missouri, Kansas, Iowa, and Nebraska. You are preparing forecasts for 2016. You might first try to assess market potential. This market potential forecast would be an estimate of the highest level of PC sales by all brands in your district for 2016. Then, you might try to develop a market forecast, which would be the expected level of industry PC sales in your district for 2016. This forecast would be based on an assumption of the strategies that would be used by all PC firms operating in your district. If you think that new firms are going to enter the industry or that existing firms are going to leave it or change their

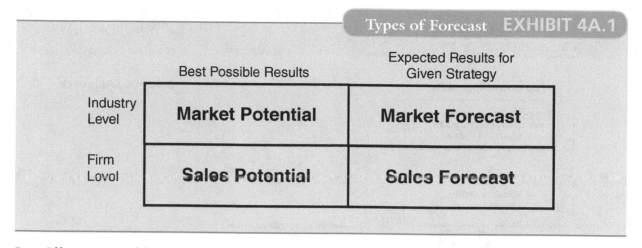

Four different types of forecasts are typically important to sales managers depending upon whether a forecast is needed for the industry or firm, and whether the best possible or expected results are forecast.

strategies, your industry forecast will change. Another type of forecast might be a determination of the best possible level of 2016 sales for your firm's PCs in the district. This would be a sales potential forecast. Finally, you would probably want to predict a specific level of district sales of your firm's PCs given your firm's expected strategy. This would result in a sales forecast that would have to be revised whenever strategic changes were made.

Uses of Forecasts

Because different types of forecasts convey different information, sales managers use certain types for specific sales management decisions. Forecasts of market potential and sales potential are most often used to identify opportunities and to guide the allocation of selling efforts. Market potential provides an assessment of overall demand opportunity available to all firms in an industry. Sales potential adjusts market potential to reflect industry competition and thus represents a better assessment of demand opportunity for an individual firm. Both of these forecasts of potential can be used by sales managers to determine where selling effort is needed and how selling effort should be distributed. For example, as discussed earlier, designing territories requires an assessment of market potential for all planning and control units. Specific territories are then designed by grouping planning and control units together and evaluating the equality of market potential across the territories.

Market forecasts and sales forecasts are used to predict the expected results from various sales management decisions. For example, once territories are designed, sales managers typically want to forecast expected industry and company sales for each specific sales territory. These forecasts are then used to set sales quotas and selling budgets for specific planning periods. Thus, it is important to develop accurate forecasts. Furthermore, inaccurate forecasts may result in detrimental effects such as increased inventory costs due to over-forecasting or lost sales and profits resulting from under-forecasting.[1]

Top-Down and Bottom-Up Forecasting Approaches

Forecasting methods can be classified in a variety of ways.[2] Specific examples of two basic approaches are presented in Figure 4A.2. Top-down approaches typically consist of different methods for developing company forecasts at the business unit level. Sales managers then break down these company forecasts into zone, region, district, territory, and account forecasts. Bottom-up approaches, by contrast, consist of different methods for developing sales forecasts for individual accounts. Sales managers then combine the

Forecasting Approaches   FIGURE 4A.2

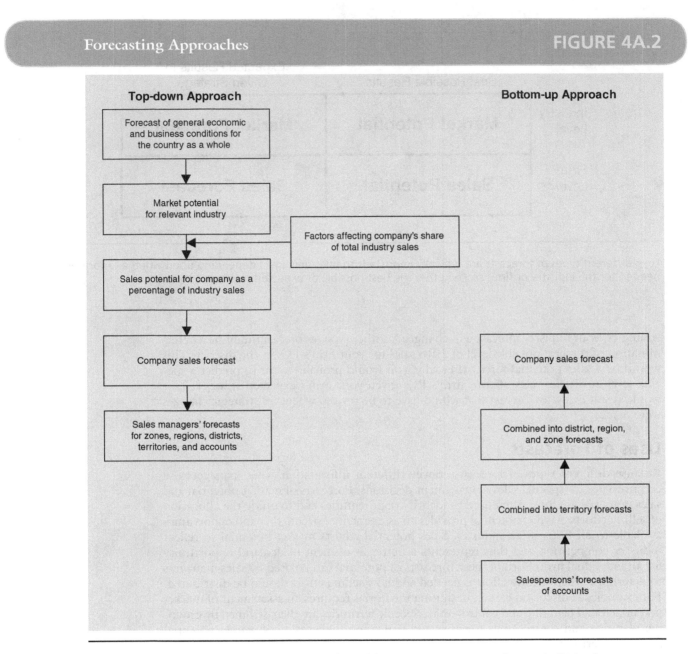

In top-down approaches, company personnel provide aggregate company forecasts that sales managers must break down into zone, region, district, territory, and account forecasts. In bottom-up approaches, account forecasts are combined into territory, district, region, zone, and company forecasts.

account forecasts into territory, district, region, zone, and company forecasts. The top-down and bottom-up approaches represent entirely different perspectives for developing forecasts, although some forecasting methods can be used in either approach. However, the focus is on the most popular forecasting methods for each approach.

Top-Down Approach

Implementing the top-down approach requires the development of company forecasts and their breakdown into zone, region, district, territory, and account levels. Different methods are used to develop company forecasts and break them down to the desired levels.

Company Forecasting Methods

Although a variety of methods is available for developing company forecasts, this discussion is limited to three popular time series methods: moving averages, exponential smoothing, and decomposition methods.

Moving averages is a relatively simple method that develops a company forecast by calculating the average company sales for previous years. Thus, the company sales forecast for next year is the average of actual company sales for the past three years, past six years, or some other number of years. An example of calculating a moving averages company sales forecast for two and four-year time frames is presented in Exhibit 4A.2. This exhibit shows that the forecast predicted for 2010 was derived by adding actual sales in 2008 of $8,400,000 to actual sales in 2009 of $8,820,000 and then dividing by two ([$8,400,000 + $8,820,000]/2 = $8,610,000). This was repeated to get the projected forecast for each successive year. To get the forecast for 2016, actual sales for 2014 and 2015 were added together and divided by two ([$9,674,000 + $10,060,000]/2 = $9,868,000). The same procedure is used to calculate the four-year moving average, but rather than using two years of actual sales and dividing by two, four years are summated and then divided by four (e.g., sales forecast for 2016 is [$8,622,000 + $9,484,000 + $9,674,000 + $10,060,000]/4 = $9,460,000).

As illustrated in this example, the moving averages method is straightforward and requires simple calculations. Management must, however, determine the appropriate number of years to include in the calculations. In addition, this method weights actual company sales for previous years equally in generating the forecast for the next year. This equal weighting may not be appropriate if company sales vary substantially from year to year or if there are major differences in the business environment between the most recent and past years.

Exponential smoothing is a type of moving averages method, except that company sales in the most recent year are weighted differently from company sales in past years.[3] An example of the exponential smoothing method is provided in Exhibit 4A.3. This exhibit shows that the sales forecast predicted for 2016 using an alpha of 0.2 was derived by multiplying actual sales in 2015 by 0.2 and adding it to 0.8 times the forecasted sales in 2015 ([.2 × $10,060,000 + .8 × $8,884,000] = $9,119,000). Each of the previous years' forecasts was derived in the same manner.

A critical aspect of this method involves determining the appropriate weight (α) for this year's company sales. This is typically accomplished by examining different weights for historical sales data to determine which weight would have generated the most accurate

---

EXHIBIT 4A.2   Moving Averages Example

Moving Averages Forecast

Year	Actual Sales	Two-Year	Four-Year
2008	$8,400,000		
2009	8,820,000		
2010	8,644,000	$8,610,000	
2011	8,212,000	8,732,000	
2012	8,622,000	8,428,000	$8,520,000
2013	9,484,000	8,418,000	8,574,000
2014	9,674,000	9,054,000	8,740,000
2015	10,060,000	9,579,000	8,998,000
2016	?	9,868,000	9,460,000

where

$$\text{Sales forecast for next year} = \frac{\text{Actual sales for past two or four years}}{\text{Number of years (two or four years)}}$$

EXHIBIT 4A.3   Exponential Smoothing Example

		Sales Forecast for Next Year		
Year	Actual Sales	$\alpha = 0.2$	$\alpha = 0.5$	$\alpha = 0.8$
2008	$8,400,000			
2009	8,820,000	$8,400,000	$8,400,000	$8,400,000
2010	8,644,000	8,484,000	8,610,000	8,736,000
2011	8,212,000	8,516,000	8,627,000	8,662,000
2012	8,622,000	8,455,000	8,420,000	8,302,000
2013	9,484,000	8,488,000	8,521,000	8,558,000
2014	9,674,000	8,687,000	9,003,000	9,299,000
2015	10,060,000	8,884,000	9,339,000	9,599,000
2016	?	9,119,000	9,700,000	9,968,000

where

Sales forecast for next year = (α)(actual sales this year) + (1 − α)(this year's sales forecast)

sales forecasts in the past. Based on the analysis in Exhibit 4A.3, management should probably use a weight of 0.8 for this year's company sales.

Decomposition methods involve different procedures that break down previous company sales data into four major components: trend, cycle, seasonal, and erratic events. These components are then reincorporated to produce the sales forecast. An example of a decomposition method is presented in Exhibit 4A.4. Notice that the trend, cycle, and erratic events components are incorporated into the annual forecast but that the seasonal component is used only when forecasting sales for periods of less than a year, such as months or quarters. Decomposition methods are sound conceptually but often require complex statistical approaches for breaking down the company sales data into the trend components. Once this decomposition has been completed, it is relatively easy to reincorporate the components into the development of a company forecast.

EXHIBIT 4A.4   Decomposition Method Example

Assume that various analyses have decomposed previous sales data into the following components:

A 5% growth in sales is predicted due to basic developments in population, capital formation, and technology (trend component). A 10% decrease in sales is expected due to a business recession (cycle component). Increased tensions in the Middle East are expected to reduce sales by an additional 5% (erratic events component). Sales results are reasonably consistent throughout the year except for the fourth quarter, where sales are expected to be 25% higher than the other quarters (seasonal component).

A marketer of consumer products might recombine the different components in the following manner to forecast sales for 2016:

Sales in 2015 were $10,060,000. The trend component suggests that 2016 sales will be $10,563,000 ($10,060,000 × 1.05). However, incorporating the expected business recession represented in the cycle component changes the sales forecast to $9,506,700 ($10,563,000 × 0.90). The annual sales forecast is reduced to $9,031,365 when the erratic events component is introduced ($9,056,700 × 0.95). Quarterly sales forecasts would initially be calculated as $2,257,841 ($9,031,365 ÷ 4). However, incorporating the seasonal component suggests fourth-quarter sales of $2,822,302 ($2,257,841 × 1.25) and sales for the other three quarters of $2,069,688 ($9,031,365−$2,822,302 ÷ 3).

Breakdown Methods

Once sales managers receive a company forecast, they can use different market factor methods to break it down to the desired levels. Market factor methods typically involve identifying one or more factors that are related to sales at the zone, region, district, territory, or account levels and using these factors to break down the overall company forecast into forecasts at these levels.

One approach is for a firm to develop a buying power index for its specific situation. For example, a general aviation aircraft marketer developed a buying power index for its products in each county in the United States. The basic formula was

$$\text{Index} = (5I + 3AR + 2P) \div 10$$

where

I = Percentage of U.S. disposable income in county

AR = Percentage of U.S. aircraft registrations in county

P = Percentage of U.S. registered pilots in county

These calculations produced an index for each county. The index calculated for each county can then be multiplied by the total company sales forecast to break it into a forecast for each county. The firm could take U.S. forecasts provided by the industry trade association and convert them to market and sales forecasts for each county by using their calculated indices and market shares.

The use of market factor methods is widespread in the sales management area. Indices developed by specific firms and other market factor methods can be extremely valuable forecasting tools for sales managers. These indices and market factors should be continually evaluated and improved. They can be assessed by comparing actual sales in an area to the market factor value for the area. For example, the general aviation aircraft marketer found high correlations between actual aircraft sales in a county and the county indices. This finding provided support for the use of the calculated index as an indirect forecasting tool.

Bottom-Up Approach

Implementing the bottom-up approach requires various methods to forecast sales to individual accounts and the combination of these account forecasts into territory, district, region, zone, and company forecasts. This section focuses on the survey of buyer intentions, jury of executive opinion, Delphi, and salesforce composite methods as used in a bottom-up approach.

The survey of buyer intentions method is any procedure that asks individual accounts about their purchasing plans for a future period and translates these responses into account forecasts. The intended purchases by accounts might be obtained through mail surveys, telephone surveys, personal interviews, or other approaches. For example, companies such as Dow Chemical and Hewlett-Packard have asked their business customers for feedback regarding intended future needs. At times, forecasts based on customer intentions may be distorted due to buyers' unwillingness to put much effort into predicting future needs. Moreover, buyers are often unwilling to reveal plans for selling a vendor's product out of fear competitors may retaliate if they find out.[4]

The jury of executive opinion method involves any approach in which executives of the firm use their expert knowledge to forecast sales to individual accounts. Separate forecasts might be obtained from managers in different functional areas. These forecasts are then averaged or discussed by the managers until a consensus forecast for each account is reached. Team-based approaches such as this are believed to result in more accurate long-range industry-level forecasts than individually based approaches.[5]

The Delphi method is a structured type of jury of executive opinion method. The basic procedure involves selection of a panel of managers from within the firm. Each member of the panel submits anonymous forecasts for each account. These forecasts are

Quarterly Forecasting Form for Salespeople   FIGURE 4A.3

Account	Projected Sales by Product Group for Quarter Beginning 7/5/2015								Totals
	364-60	364-80	28B	460	28				
Ace	1,250	960	1,400	2,100	160				5,870
Sentry	950	1,250	1,930	470	968				5,568
Cutter	—	2,110	—	960	1,750				4,820
Grossman	—	—	—	—	364				364
Paycass	400	1,800	—	—	720				2,920
American	—	—	—	—	1,230				1,230
Pro	—	—	—	—	—				700
Totals	2,600	6,820	3,330	3,530	5,192				21,472

This is an example of a form used by a firm to get salespeople to forecast sales for each account and product group.

summarized into a report that is sent to each panel member. The report presents descriptive statistics concerning the submitted forecasts with reasons for the lowest and highest forecasts. Panel members review this information and then again submit anonymous individual forecasts. The same procedure is repeated until the forecasts for individual accounts converge into a consensus. Because this procedure involves written rather than verbal communication, such negatives as domination, undue conservatism, and argument are eliminated, while team members benefit from one another's input.[6]

The salesforce composite method involves various procedures by which salespeople provide forecasts for their assigned accounts, typically on specially designed forms (see Figure 4A.3), electronically via computer, or through the company's CRM system. At Cisco Systems, reps submit data electronically to a company database that provides information about their pipelines, including opportunity size, customer technology requirements, and competitors. Managers then use this data to develop weekly, monthly, and quarterly forecasts.[7] Research results suggest that salesperson forecasts can be improved by developing detailed instructions about the forecasting procedures and providing salespeople with detailed information about their accounts and feedback concerning the accuracy of previous forecasts.[8]

Forecasting with Regression Analysis

Regression analysis is a statistical technique that can be used to develop sales forecasts at all organizational levels, as well as company wide.[9]

A market response framework to guide this type of approach is presented in Figure 4A.4.[10] Depending on the planning and control unit of interest (territory, district, region, or zone), different determinants of market response (e.g., sales, market share) might be important. However, these determinants can be classified as either environmental, organizational, or salesperson factors. Once the determinant and market response factors are identified, their values for each planning and control unit in the previous period must be measured.

Statistical packages such as SPSS can then be used to estimate the parameters of the regression equation. For example, if you are a district sales manager interested in forecasting territory sales, you would identify and measure specific environmental, organizational, and salesperson factors, as well as sales for each territory in the previous year. You could then develop a regression model of the following form:

$$\text{Territory sales} = a + (b1)(\text{environmental factor}) + (b2)(\text{organizational factor}) + (b3)(\text{salesperson factor})$$

The a, $b1$, $b2$, and $b3$ values are the model parameters supplied by the regression procedure to define the relationship between the determinant factors and territory sales.

Although this type of model might be useful, it suffers from two basic weaknesses. First, it incorporates only the independent effects of the determinant variables, yet these variables are highly interrelated. Second, this type of equation is linear, yet the determinant variable relationships are probably nonlinear. These weaknesses can be addressed by performing the linear regression on the logarithms of the actual data, producing a multiplicative power function of the following form:

$$\text{Territory sales} = (a)(\text{environmental factor}^{b1})(\text{organizational factor}^{b2})(\text{salesperson factor}^{b3})$$

Market Response Framework   **FIGURE 4A.4**

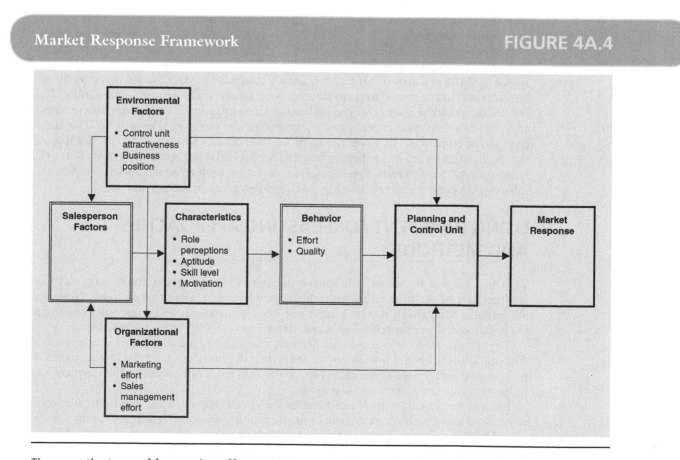

These are the types of factors that affect market response for any planning and control unit, whether it be accounts, territories, districts, regions, or zones. Market response might be profits, market share, or some other response, but sales is usually the market response variable of interest to sales managers.

EXHIBIT 4A.5   Regression Model Examples

Territory sales = (800.82)(potential$^{.53}$)(concentration$^{.03}$)(experience$^{.08}$)
(span of control$^{-.55}$)

	Territory 1	Territory 2	Territory 3
Potential (number of persons employed by firms in customer industry located in territory)	114,000	125,000	87,000
Concentration (number of persons employed by the large plants in customer industry located in territory)	94,000	52,000	12,000
Experience (months salesperson has been with company)	30	10	20
Span of control (number of salespeople supervised by sales manager)	5	8	10
Territory sales forecast	$586,000	$238,400	$173,200

This function is nonlinear and incorporates interactions through the multiplication of determinant variables.

A specific example illustrating this type of function is presented in Exhibit 4A.5.[11] The environmental factors are *potential* and *concentration*, the salesperson factor is *experience*, and the organizational factor is *span of control*. The data are for three territories and are used in the model to generate sales forecasts for each territory individually. This regression model indicates that the higher the territory potential, account concentration, and level of salesperson experience are, the higher the territory sales will be. The larger the span of control is, the lower the territory sales. The exponents in the model suggest that territory sales are most affected by territory potential and span of control. Thus, the regression model generates a specific sales forecast for each territory, and it also provides information concerning relationships between determinant factors and sales.

USING DIFFERENT FORECASTING APPROACHES AND METHODS

This discussion of top-down and bottom-up approaches and several forecasting methods is illustrative of the forecasting procedures used by many sales organizations. However, all available forecasting methods have not been introduced, and some sales organizations may use the approaches and methods in different ways than discussed here.

The actual usage of forecasting methods discussed is presented in Exhibit 4A.6.[12] Although this study did not ask respondents their degree of usage of the Delphi method, it remains a very viable approach.[13] Notice the differences that exist in the frequency of usage depending on the forecast period.

Because forecasting is such a difficult task and each approach and method has certain advantages and disadvantages, most firms use multiple forecasting approaches and methods. Then, various approaches are used to combine the results from each method into a final forecast.[14] If different approaches and methods produce similar sales forecasts, sales managers can be more confident in the validity of the forecast. If extremely divergent forecasts are generated from the different approaches and methods, additional analysis is

Forecasting Method	Usage of Forecasting Methods EXHIBIT 4A.6		
	Percentage of Firms Using Method by Forecast Period		
	Less than 3 months	**3 months to 2 years**	**More than 2 years**
Top-Down			
Moving average	9	45	11
Exponential smoothing	8	92	16
Decomposition	2	40	10
Bottom-Up			
Survey of buyer intentions	5	38	15
Jury of executive opinion	4	77	55
Salesforce composite	5	38	15
Regression Analysis	4	69	30

required to determine the reasons for the large differences and to make the adjustments necessary to produce an accurate sales forecast. Some firms even take advantage of available sales forecasting software, such as ForecastPro (www.forecastpro.com), to help them in the forecasting process. Microsoft provides a premade sales forecasting template (http://office.microsoft.com/en-us/templates/TC011347871033.aspx?pid=Ct101441951033) that can help streamline the forecasting process.

Even though firms use multiple forecasting methods, research evidence indicates that several criteria are used to select specific forecasting methods.[15] The most important criterion identified in this study was the accuracy of the forecasting method. Other criteria that were considered in decreasing importance were ease of use, data requirements, cost, and familiarity with methods. These results suggest that the selection of forecasting methods often represents a trade-off between the accuracy of the method and the ease with which it can be implemented. Some of the more accurate forecasting methods are difficult to use and have substantial data requirements. Thus, firms may have to sacrifice some accuracy by selecting methods that they are able to readily implement. This situation is illustrated in Exhibit 4A.6, where some of the more accurate methods (e.g., decomposition) are not used by many firms. Strengths and weaknesses of each forecasting method are found in Exhibit 4A.7.

EXHIBIT 4A.7   Strengths and Weaknesses of Forecasting Methods

Technique	Strengths	Weaknesses
Moving averages	Well suited to situations in which sales forecasts are needed for a large number of products Good for products with fairly stable sales Smoothes out small random fluctuations Can compensate to some degree for trend if double moving average model is used	Requires a large amount of historical data Adjusts slowly to changes in sales Assigns equal weight to each period, ignoring the fact that more recent periods usually have more impact on future sales Results cannot be tested statistically
Exponential smoothing	Fairly simple to understand and use Provides more weight to recent data points Requires little data storage Generally accessible software packages are available Fairly good accuracy for short-term forecasts	Much searching may be needed to find appropriate weight Poor for medium- and long-term forecasts Erroneous forecasts can result due to large random fluctuations in recent data Requires a large amount of past data
Decomposition method	Simple to understand Included in most computer packages Acknowledges three key factors affecting sales—trend, seasonal, cycles Breaks past sales into component parts, making it easier to understand the sales pattern	Does not lend itself to longer-range forecasts Does not lend itself to statistical analysis of forecast values (no confidence limits or tests of significance)
Survey of buyer intentions	Forecasts are based on customers' buying plans Contacts with customers can also provide feedback about possible problems with the firm's products Relatively inexpensive if only a few key customers need to be contacted	Intentions frequently do not culminate in actual purchases Some firms may not be willing to disclose buying intentions, especially if they are not regular customers
Jury of executive opinion	Provides input from the firm's key functional areas Executives usually have a solid understanding of broad-based factors and how they affect sales Can provide fairly quick forecasts	May require excessive amounts of executives' time Executives removed from the marketplace may not understand the firm's sales situation Not well suited to firms with a large number of products One or two influential people may dominate the process

Strengths and Weaknesses of Forecasting Methods—*continued*   EXHIBIT 4A.7

Technique	Strengths	Weaknesses
Delphi method	Eliminates the need for committee or group meetings Eliminates group decision-making pitfalls, such as specious persuasion or a bandwagon effect Participants receive input from other "experts" in an isolated environment Allows for voicing of unusual opinions and anonymous mind changing Proper facilities (email) enable rapid exchange of ideas	Participants are often selected more on their willingness to participate and their accessibility than on their real knowledge or representativeness Can take a great deal of time to arrive at a consensus Process may suffer because of high dropout rate of participants
Salesforce composite	Uses input from persons closest to actual markets Provides reasonably detailed forecasts (by product, customer, or territory) May enhance salesforce morale by letting their input guide decisions	Salespeople may underestimate sales when their forecasts are being used to set sales quotas Can take excessive amounts of salespeople's time if done too often Salespeople often lack the knowledge to evaluate the economic situation and how it might affect future sales
Regression analysis	Identifies unknown factors affecting market response Provides an objective forecasting method Develops sales forecasts that explicitly consider the characteristics of a control unit, making them easy to translate into sales quotas	Requires a large amount of data to produce a reliable model Requires some technical skill and expertise to use Factors affecting market response must be accurately identified Does not consider effects of seasonal variations

3

Developing the Salesforce

The two chapters in Part 3 concentrate on the development of a productive salesforce. In Chapter 5, we review the process of acquiring sales talent through recruitment and selection. Standard recruitment and selection tools such as advertising, job interviews, and tests are discussed. Legal and ethical issues are also raised, and the topic of salesforce socialization is introduced.

Chapter 6 focuses on the continual development of salespeople through sales training. A model of the sales training process provides a framework for discussing needs assessment; training objectives; alternatives for training; and the design, performance, and evaluation of sales training.

ACQUIRING SALES TALENT: RECRUITMENT AND SELECTION

OBJECTIVES

After completing this chapter, you should be able to

1. Explain the critical role of recruitment and selection in building and maintaining a productive salesforce.

2. Describe how recruitment and selection affect salesforce socialization and performance.

3. Identify the key activities in planning and executing a program for salesforce recruitment and selection.

4. Discuss the legal and ethical considerations in salesforce recruitment and selection.

ACQUIRING SALES TALENT: DIVERGENT APPROACHES AMONG COMPANIES

While most companies hope to find the best available talent, doing so is not necessarily an easy task. The path to finding the perfect hire varies among companies, and is both time-consuming and expensive. However, failing to do an adequate job can be even more costly.

Companies take different approaches to recruiting the best available sales talent. For instance, the owners of Clarkston-based Chase Plastics Services, Kevin and Carole Chase, like to hire engineers as salespeople because they can speak the customers' language. They have found that building and maintaining relationships with universities and high schools has allowed them to develop relationships with engineering students early in their education, which has led to the successful recruiting and hiring of several salespeople for their firm. Jim Schubert, president of Southern States Insurance, an independent agency with offices in Georgia and Florida, is searching for talented young insurance agents. To recruit a younger audience, he relies on social media recruiting sites such as LinkedIn and Craigslist, which he has found invaluable in starting conversations with job candidates. He has also found that involving young agents in the interview process has been extremely helpful in attracting young recruits, who have found it comforting knowing "there are others like me here," he says.

Companies likewise take different approaches to selection. Take for instance Delta Rigging & Tools, a provider of rigging and lifting products located in Houston, Texas. When it determined that it was using different hiring practices at each of its 12 offices, it decided to standardize its hiring practices. To do so, it solicited the help of Rise Performance, an organization specializing in employment assessment. Rise provided them with a sales assessment tool that measures how well a person fits specific sales jobs in a company. Working with Rise, Delta Rigging & Tools analyzed the attributes of their best sales performers and used this information to develop a model for new hires. Sales candidates for hire are assessed based on these attributes. According to Tom Hudgins, vice president of sales and marketing at Delta Rigging & Tools, "We see this adding good insight and giving us one more useful tool to use. It is already helping us in making the final decision among the best two or three candidates." Mike Nagel, VP of sales & marketing, from Neomed, Inc., a medical device company, has taken a similar approach to selecting his salespeople. He utilizes a sales assessment tool developed by Caliper, an employment selection and development company, to help him determine salespeople who are the best fit for Neomed. According to Nagel, this has resulted in a happier and more productive salesforce. Brent Hadaway, vice president of sales & marketing at Service Today, Inc., adds that it is important to conduct a background check when hiring. He uses this, along with drug testing, when screening sales candidates to hire.

Sources: Gary Anglebrandt, "Fastest Growing Companies: Chase Plastic Services, Inc.," *Crain's Detroit Business*, July 15, 2013, 16; David Port, "Desperately Seeking Young Agents," *LifeHealthPro*, November 4, 2013; Kevin Tanzillo, "Delta Rigging & Tools Implements Rise Performance Group Assessment Tool to Improve Sales Staff Hiring," press release, May 24, 2013, www.pr.com/press-release/493134 (accessed January 9, 2014); Mike Nagel, client testimonial, *Caliper*, www.calipercorp.com/home-3/client-testimonials/ (accessed on January 9, 2014); Kimberly Schwartz, "Do You Know When to Grow?" *Air Conditioning, Heating & Refrigeration News* (October 2013): 1, 15–17.

As illustrated in the opening vignette, the recruitment and selection process can involve various approaches. However, investing the necessary resources to hire the right sales talent is essential. Recruiting and selecting those best qualified for a position can make the difference between a firm's long-run ultimate success and failure. Although many factors influence sales performance, sales managers cannot survive without doing a competent job in recruiting and selecting salespeople. The vital and complex nature of the job is summarized by Munson and Spivey:

> The process is complicated by various conflicting factors—the need to select applicants with characteristics related to job success, the difficulty of determining these characteristics, inadequacies inherent in the various selection techniques themselves, and the need to simultaneously insure that the selection process satisfies existing governmental regulations pertaining to discrimination in hiring practices.[1]

Today, the recruitment and selection process must be adjusted to the demographics of an older salesforce with a higher proportion of women and minorities than in the past.[2] Sales managers also face challenges associated with acquiring talent for an international salesforce, as well as with recruiting and selecting for team selling. Proper staffing of the salesforce is critical given the strong impact of the recruiting process on a firm's performance and profits.[3] Today's sales manager's role in recruitment and selection is explored in this chapter. Before examining a basic model of the process, let's discuss further the importance of recruitment and selection.

IMPORTANCE OF RECRUITMENT AND SELECTION

In most sales organizations, sales managers with direct supervisory responsibilities for salespeople have the primary responsibility for recruitment and selection. They may have the support of top management or coordinate their efforts with human resource personnel or other managers within the firm, but it is the sales manager who generally retains primary recruitment and selection responsibilities. To emphasize the importance of recruitment and selection, consider a few of the problems associated with inadequate implementation:

1. Inadequate sales coverage and lack of customer follow-up

2. Increased training costs to overcome deficiencies

3. More supervisory problems

4. Higher turnover rates

5. Difficulty in establishing enduring relationships with customers

6. Suboptimal total salesforce performance

Clearly, salesforce performance will suffer if recruitment and selection are poorly executed. Other sales management functions become more burdensome when the sales manager is handicapped by a multitude of "bad hires." The full costs of unsuccessful recruitment and selection are probably impossible to estimate. In addition to sales trainee salaries, advertising fees; screening, interviewing, and assessment costs; and employment agency fees, among others, there are hidden costs associated with salesforce turnover, such as the loss of the relationships that salespeople build with their customers over time and increased managerial problems that defy calculation. (For a more detailed look at the costs of a bad hire, go to Salestestonline.com, "The Cost of Failure Calculator," http://salestestonline.com/calculator.asp). Estimates suggest that it costs a firm anywhere from one third to five times a worker's annual salary to replace a bad hire.[4] Federated Insurance estimates it invests nearly $225,000 in each new marketing development trainee before the trainee is assigned to his/her own marketing representative territory.[5] For a bad hire, such an investment represents sunk costs that may be nonrecoverable. And in view of studies that tell us that a significant number of salespeople should not be in sales for one reason or another,[6] it is apparent that recruitment and selection are among the most challenging and important responsibilities of sales management.

INTRODUCTION TO SALESFORCE SOCIALIZATION

Salesforce socialization (sometimes referred to as *onboarding*) refers to the process by which salespeople acquire the knowledge, skills, and values essential to perform their jobs. The process begins when the sales recruit is first exposed to the organization and may extend for several years. A model of salesforce socialization is shown in Figure 5.1.

Proposed Model of Salesforce Socialization   **FIGURE 5.1**

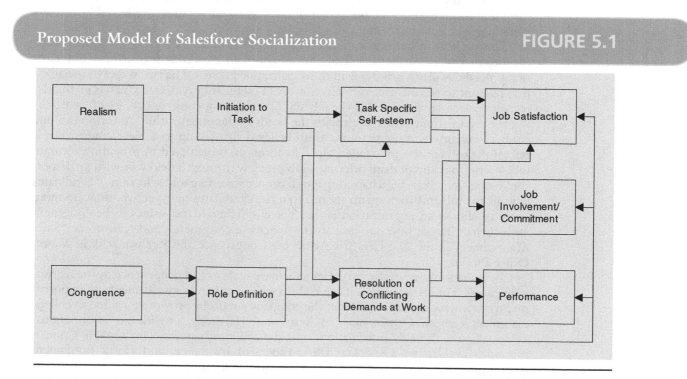

Sales organizations must present accurate portrayals of the sales job (achieving realism) to sales recruits, who must possess skills and needs compatible with the needs and offerings of the organization (achieving congruence). If these objectives of recruiting and selection are met, salesforce socialization is enhanced, and ultimately, salesforce performance, job satisfaction, and job involvement and commitment are improved.

Achieving Congruence and Realism at W.B. Mason Office Products

Marty Zucker, Regional Office Coffee Services Manager for W.B. Mason Office Products, comments on achieving congruence and realism:

W.B. Mason Office Products is the world's largest independent office supply company. Operating out of 11 New England States and an additional 20 Breakpoints throughout the U.S.A., competing against the nation's largest publicly held office supply companies, requires a highly talented salesforce to be successful. This requires hiring salespeople who are a good fit with our organization. As a 116-year-old company, we have a track record that attracts candidates with a desire to sell for a company with a long history and great reputation in the industry. New college recruits must have a four-year degree *with extracurricular activities. We are looking for those young men and women that show the desire to excel. We prefer that the candidate is involved with sports, music or business clubs. These people are accustomed to being inspired and motivated in order to excel. They are willing to put forth the extra effort and work well in a team environment. However, we will not exclude anybody from the interview or hiring process just because they do not have these specific extracurricular activities, but they must have a desire to excel. Prior to a formal offer, however, the candidate must do a one-day drive along with one of our sales trainers. This is the reality check! This is the first time our candidates will see first-hand what is expected of them. If this preview does not match the candidate's job expectations, we are not likely to have a good fit.*

This model suggests that important job outcomes such as job satisfaction, job involvement and commitment, and performance are directly and indirectly affected by recruitment and selection procedures.

The socialization process is discussed again in subsequent chapters. For now, accept the idea that socialization affects salesforce performance and that recruitment and selection procedures play a major role in the socialization process. The two stages of socialization relevant to recruitment and selection are (1) achieving realism, which is giving the recruit an accurate portrayal of the job and (2) achieving congruence, which is matching the capabilities of the recruit with the needs of the organization. According to one study of executives, more than one third believed that failing to achieve congruence is one of the top reasons for a failed hire.[7] Realism can be achieved by providing accurate job descriptions and perhaps offering a job preview through a field visit with a salesperson. Congruence can be achieved through proper screening and selection of candidates who fit the job and the organization. From the candidates' perspective, they are more likely to choose an organization if they perceive its goals and values to be congruent with theirs.[8] To see how one firm works to achieve congruence and realism see "Sales Management in the 21st Century: Achieving Congruence and Realism at W.B. Mason Office Products."

Companies take several approaches to achieve realism and congruence in the recruiting process. For instance, to achieve realism some companies give students an opportunity to view what a career in sales at the company entails by providing a video to college placement centers. Others, such as Xerox and Hershey's, provide an informational video, along with other information, on a job applicant gateway on the Web. Companies such as Hershey Chocolate USA, Federated Insurance, and Hertz Equipment Rental provide candidates with a comprehensive brochure describing the company, its philosophy, and its products. Some companies provide informational sessions on college campuses for recruits, while others offer a ride-along on a sales call. Congruence is achieved through various selection tools, such as interviewing and testing, which will be discussed later in this chapter.

RECRUITMENT AND SELECTION PROCESS

Figure 5.2 illustrates the steps in the recruitment and selection process. The first step involves **planning activities**: conducting a job analysis, establishing job qualifications, completing a written job description, setting recruitment and selection objectives, and developing a recruitment and selection strategy. These planning activities are conducted within the overall planning framework of the organization to ensure consistency with the objectives, strategies, resources, and constraints of the organization.

The second step is **recruitment**, which, simply put, is the procedure of locating a sufficient number of prospective job applicants. A number of internal (within the company) and external (outside the company) sources may be used to develop this pool of candidates.

The next step in the model is **selection**, the process of choosing which candidates will be offered the job. Many screening and evaluation methods, including evaluation of resumes and job application forms, interviews, tests, assessment centers, background investigations, and physical exams, are used in this step. A more detailed discussion of each step in the recruitment and selection process follows.

Planning for Recruitment and Selection

Given the critical nature of recruitment and selection, it would be difficult to overstate the case for careful planning as part of the process. Sales managers are concerned with the current staffing needs of their organizations; but perhaps more important, they are also concerned with future staffing needs, which is what makes planning so essential.

Proper planning provides more time for locating the best recruits. Upper management can be alerted in advance to probable future needs, rather than having to be convinced quickly when the need becomes imminent. Also, training can be planned more effectively when the flow of new trainees into the organization is known. Overall, the main benefit of adequate planning for the recruitment and selection process is that it helps prevent the kind of poor decisions that often prove so expensive both emotionally and financially. According to a study of 1,600 hiring managers by a global human resources consulting firm, 20 percent of new hires turn out to be a poor choice.[9] Proper planning could help reduce this number. The key tasks in planning for recruitment and selection are the following:

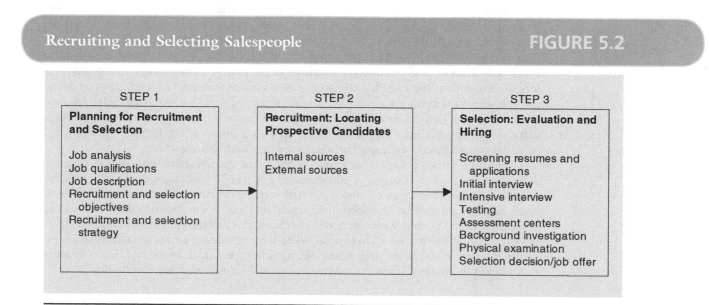

Recruiting and Selecting Salespeople   **FIGURE 5.2**

STEP 1	STEP 2	STEP 3
Planning for Recruitment and Selection	**Recruitment: Locating Prospective Candidates**	**Selection: Evaluation and Hiring**
Job analysis Job qualifications Job description Recruitment and selection objectives Recruitment and selection strategy	Internal sources External sources	Screening resumes and applications Initial interview Intensive interview Testing Assessment centers Background investigation Physical examination Selection decision/job offer

Three main steps are involved in recruiting and selecting salespeople: planning, recruiting, and selection.

Job Analysis

To effectively recruit and select salespeople, sales managers must have a complete understanding of the job for which candidates are sought. Because most sales managers have served as salespeople in their companies before entering management, it is reasonable to think that they would have a good understanding of the sales jobs for which they are recruiting. However, some have lost touch with changing conditions in the field and thus have an obsolete view of the current sales task to be accomplished.

To ensure an understanding of the sales job, the sales manager may need to conduct, confirm, or update a job analysis, which entails an investigation of the tasks, duties, and responsibilities of the job. For example, will the selling tasks include responsibilities for opening new accounts as well as maintaining existing accounts? Will the salesperson be responsible for collecting account receivables or completing administrative reports? The job analysis defines the expected behavior of salespeople, indicating which areas of performance will be crucial for success. In most larger companies, the job analysis is completed by human resource managers or other corporate managers, but even then, the sales manager may have input into the job analysis.

Job Qualifications

The job analysis indicates what the salespeople are supposed to do on the job, whereas job qualifications refer to the aptitude, skills, knowledge, personal traits, and willingness to accept occupational conditions necessary to perform the job. For example, when hiring a new business sales representative, ADP looks for candidates who have a BSBA or equivalent education, three to seven years of business-to-business sales experience, excellent prospecting, presentation and selling skills, keen business savvy, maturity, competitiveness and an excellent work ethic.[10]

Common sales job qualifications address sales experience, educational level, willingness to travel, willingness to relocate, interpersonal skills, communication skills, problem-solving skills, relationship management skills, organizational skills, ability to overcome objections, tenacity, persistence, time management skills, follow-up skills, adaptability, attitude, enthusiasm, work ethic, empathy, ego drive, ego strength, integrity, self-motivation, and ability to work independently. Consistent with our earlier discussion of the diversity of personal selling jobs, there is a corresponding variance in job qualifications for different sales jobs. Therefore, each sales manager should record the pertinent job qualifications for each job in the salesforce. A generic list of job qualifications for all the salespeople in the organization may not be feasible. Some research, however, has consistently found that more successful salespeople tend to be more empathetic and motivated, have a strong ego drive, are able to build trust quickly, are willing to ask for commitments, and in some sales roles possess more acute problem-solving and organizational skills.[11] Forward-looking organizations would be wise to go beyond their current list of qualifications and outline characteristics of the ideal sales candidate. This profile may look different than the one describing current salesforce members as it attempts to define the salesperson necessary to move the organization into the future. Sage Software analyzed data compiled on its top 25 salespeople to create a profile of the most successful software salespeople and then used this profile as a guide when hiring.[12] Exhibit 5.1 provides guidelines for creating the ideal sales candidate profile.[13]

For a given sales job within the same company, the qualifications may vary in different selling situations. For example, a multinational company whose salespeople sell the same products to the same types of customers may require different qualifications in different countries. Qualifications considered unimportant, and even discriminatory, in hiring salespeople in the United States, such as social class and religious and ethnic background, are important in hiring overseas.[14] In general, when sending salespeople on international assignments, it is helpful if they are patient, flexible, confident, persistent, motivated, and tolerant of new ways of doing things; have a desire to work abroad; and have a sense of humor.[15]

Job Description

Based on the job analysis and job qualifications, a written summary of the job, the job description, is completed by the sales manager or, in many cases, the human resource

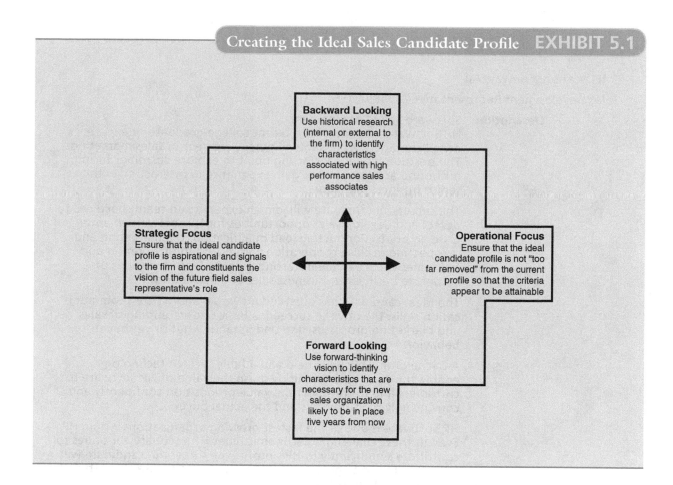

Creating the Ideal Sales Candidate Profile   EXHIBIT 5.1

Backward Looking
Use historical research (internal or external to the firm) to identify characteristics associated with high performance sales associates

Strategic Focus
Ensure that the ideal candidate profile is aspirational and signals to the firm and constituents the vision of the future field sales representative's role

Operational Focus
Ensure that the ideal candidate profile is not "too far removed" from the current profile so that the criteria appear to be attainable

Forward Looking
Use forward-thinking vision to identify characteristics that are necessary for the new sales organization likely to be in place five years from now

manager. Job descriptions for salespeople could contain any or all of the following elements:

1. Job title (e.g., sales trainee, senior sales representative)

2. Duties, tasks, and responsibilities of the salesperson

3. Administrative relationships indicating to whom the salesperson reports

4. Types of products to be sold

5. Customer types

6. Significant job-related demands, such as mental stress, physical strength or stamina requirements, travel requirements, or environmental pressures to be encountered

Job descriptions are an essential document in sales management. Their use in recruitment and selection is only one of their multiple functions. They are used to clarify duties and thereby reduce role ambiguity in the salesforce, to familiarize potential employees with the sales job, to set objectives for salespeople, and eventually, to aid in evaluating performance by setting performance standards. A typical job description for a sales representative is shown in Exhibit 5.2.[16]

Recruitment and Selection Objectives

To be fully operational, recruitment and selection objectives should be specifically stated for a given period. The following general objectives of recruitment and selection could be converted to specific operational objectives in a given firm:

• Determine present and future needs in terms of numbers and types of salespeople (as discussed in Chapter 4).

EXHIBIT 5.2

Job Location: Conway, AR

Sales Development Representative-1170892

Description

Software Sales Development

HP Software is looking for a recent college graduate or experienced candidate who wants to pursue a career in sales/marketing. The position is an ideal starting point to explore customer facing, outbound activities and to gain experience in interacting with senior business managers.

The successful candidate will join an experienced team chartered to detect and develop sales opportunities for HP Software in enterprise accounts. Conducting lead qualification, telemarketing and prospecting in close cooperation with outbound marketing and field sales will be an ideal starting point to learn the ropes of corporate business-to-business sales and marketing.

The ideal candidate has outstanding verbal and written communication skills, the drive to succeed, a basic understanding of sales and marketing processes, and understands what drives buyer behavior.

A Bachelor in a business field and a fable [sic] for technology enable the candidate to quickly grasp the value of HP Software to customers and to transport the value proposition confidently and convincingly to influencers and the actual buyer.

HP Software is one of the fastest-growing organizations within HP. Even in these challenging economic times HP Software continues to contribute significantly to HP's profit. The successful candidate will have the chance to grow with HP Software and to use HP Software as a launch pad into a career at HP.

Responsibilities
- Conduct marketing campaign/event follow-up.
- Manage a prospecting pipeline within the Software sales database and maintain accurate information about suspects, prospects, and their companies.
- Promote the HP Software value proposition and create demand for all of software products within designated markets.
- Work closely with inside and outside sales, and marketing.
- Act as a liaison between marketing and sales orgs.
- Disposition/qualify all incoming opportunities and assign qualified opportunities to appropriate sales representative to maximize their time (SAL—Sales Accepted Leads).
- Event telemarketing (attendance driving).
- Create pipeline activity by qualifying raw leads driven from marketing generated events and campaigns.
- Develop outbound call campaigns with product, event and campaign marketing managers to bolster registration and attendance to various events.

Qualifications
- B.A./B.S. or equivalent.
- One to two years' lead development experience in a competitive high tech environment (preferably the software marketplace).
- Proven track record and methodology of achieving/exceeding measurable goals.
- Ability to communicate articulately, confidently, and professionally with senior level managers and executives, both in writing and verbally.
- Understanding of the sales process and what drives a buyer's behavior.

continued EXHIBIT 5.2

- Knowledge of marketing principles and campaigns.
- Ability to conduct research via the Internet.
- Prior Siebel database usage a plus.

Job—Sales Operations
Primary Location—United States-Arkansas-Conway
Schedule—Full-time
Job Type—Early Career
Shift—Day Job
Travel—No
Job Posting—Sep 26, 2013

Job ID: 1170892

- Meet the company's legal and social responsibilities regarding composition of the salesforce.
- Reduce the number of underqualified or overqualified applicants.
- Increase the number of qualified applicants at a specified cost.
- Evaluate the effectiveness of recruiting sources and evaluation techniques.

By setting specific objectives for recruitment and selection, sales managers can channel resources into priority areas and improve organizational and salesforce effectiveness.

Recruitment and Selection Strategy

After objectives have been set, a recruitment and selection strategy can be developed. Formulating this strategy requires the sales manager to consider the scope and timing of recruitment and selection activities as follows:

- When will the recruitment and selection be done?
- How will the job be portrayed?
- How will efforts with intermediaries, such as employment agencies and college placement centers, be optimized?
- What are the most likely sources for qualified applicants?
- What type of salespeople will be hired when developing an international salesforce?
- How much time will be allowed for a candidate to accept or reject an offer?

Recruitment and selection are perpetual activities in some sales organizations but in others are conducted only when a vacancy occurs. Some recruit seasonally. For example, large companies often concentrate their efforts to coincide with spring graduation dates on college campuses. However, most sales organizations could benefit by ongoing recruitment to facilitate selection when the need arises.

A strategic decision must be made in terms of how the job will be portrayed, particularly in advertisements. Initial descriptions of the job in the media are necessarily limited. Should earnings potential be featured, or perhaps the opportunity for advancement? Or is this job correctly portrayed as ideal for the career salesperson? Consider how the advertisement in Exhibit 5.3[17] portrays the salesperson's job at Heartland Payment Systems.

Strategy also involves coordinating recruiting needs and activities with employment agencies and college placement centers. For instance, dates and times for interviewing on campus must be arranged. If an employment agency is to be used, it will need a job description and job qualifications for the position to be filled.

When developing an international salesforce, the sales manager must consider the type of salesperson best suited for selling outside the home country. Options include hiring expatriates, who are salespeople from the firm's home country, hiring host-country nationals, or hiring third-country nationals. Advantages and disadvantages of hiring each type of salesperson are shown in Exhibit 5.4.[18]

EXHIBIT 5.3 Example of an Individual Company's Advertisement to Recruit Salespeople

This ad is from *Selling Power* (August/September 2013).

Advantages and Disadvantages of Salesperson Types for International Salesforce Development		EXHIBIT 5.4
Salesperson Type	**Advantages**	**Disadvantages**
Expatriates	High product knowledge Good follow-up service Good training for promotion Greater home-country control	Highest maintenance costs High turnover rates High training costs

Host-Country Nationals	Easy and inexpensive to hire
	Significant market
	  knowledge
	Speak the native language
	Cultural understanding
	Quickly penetrate market
		Need extensive product training
		Sales often considered
		  low-esteem position
		Difficult to instill organization's
		  culture
		Hard to ensure organizational
		  loyalty

Third-Country Nationals	Possible cultural understanding
	  and language skills if from
	  similar region
	Economical labor force
	Allows regional sales coverage
	May allow sales to country in
	  conflict with home country
		Nationality unrelated to
		  organization or place of
		  work
		Low promotion potential
		Need extensive product and
		  company training
		Sales often considered
		  low-esteem position
		Potential difficulty of adapting
		  to new environments
		Difficult to instill organization's
		  culture
		Hard to ensure organizational
		  loyalty

Another strategic decision is the length of time a candidate will be given to accept an offer. This time element is important, because other recruitment and selection activities may be temporarily suspended until the decision is made. Strategy also involves identifying the sources that look most promising for recruitment. This subject is discussed in detail in the following section.

Recruitment: Locating Prospective Candidates

As Figure 5.2 showed, the next step in recruitment and selection is to locate a pool of prospective job candidates. This step, the actual recruiting, may use a variety of internal and external sources.

Internal Sources

One of the most popular methods of locating sales recruits is through employee referral programs. These programs are relatively quick and inexpensive compared with other recruiting methods, such as advertising, using employment agencies, and visiting college campuses. Referral programs also may be very effective. In a survey of company recruiters, 75 percent report that employee referral programs are effective or very effective tools.[19] Another study found that applicants who are referred by current employees are more likely to receive job offers and become employees than those recruited by other sources.[20] In addition, those hired as a result of an employee referral tend to stay in their position longer than those hired from other sources.[21] An employee who furnishes a referral may be paid a "finder's fee." For example, Federated Insurance provides its current Marketing Representatives with a $2,400 referral bonus when a referred candidate is hired and an additional $1,600 bonus when the referred candidate completes his or her first 12 months in the field.[22] Existing salespeople are obviously good sources for referral programs because they have a good understanding of the type of person sought for a sales position. Purchasing agents within the company may also be helpful in identifying prospective sales candidates. Employee referral programs can be enhanced by publicly recognizing successful referrals, by regularly providing incentives and promptly rewarding successful referrals, by offering a proactive program that encourages employee participation, and by providing feedback concerning the status of referrals to those making them.[23] Be sure, however, not to rely solely on an employee referral program when recruiting, as doing so could be discriminatory according to the Civil Rights Act of 1964.[24]

Other internal methods include announcing sales job openings through newsletters, on the company's intranet, in meetings, or on the bulletin board. Internal transfers or promotions may result from announcing an opening on the salesforce. One study found that employees of the firm who transfer to sales positions can be expected to yield more long-run profits than salespeople from any other source.[25]

External Sources

Although it is a good idea to include internal sources as part of a recruitment and selection program, there may not be enough qualified persons inside the organization to meet the human resource needs of the salesforce. The search then must be expanded to external sources. Marty Zucker, Regional Office Coffee Services Manager for W.B. Mason Office Products, comments on its sources for sales candidates in "Sales Management in the 21st Century: Locating Sales Candidates at W.B. Mason Office Products."

SALES MANAGEMENT IN THE 21ST CENTURY

Locating Sales Candidates at W.B. Mason Office Products

Marty Zucker, Regional Office Coffee Services Manager for W.B. Mason Office Products, comments on its sources for sales candidates.

Staying in business for 116 years as an independent office supply company requires an effective recruitment and selection strategy. The W.B. Mason model calls for constant sales recruitment at every one of its locations. The recruiting process teams our human resource managers and our sales managers in a neverending quest to hire the best people available. We heavily recruit college students, but look for industry veterans as well. W.B. Mason's recruiting teams attend numerous college job fairs every month. In addition, we host several open houses. It is not unusual to make offers to college seniors in their first semester and hold the position open until graduation. When considering hiring industry veterans, we look for those who have a following of loyal customers. This provides them with a lot of potential customers when joining W.B. Mason.

Online

The Internet provides an effective and relatively inexpensive way to recruit. Companies can list job openings on bulletin boards or in job banks such as monster.com, beyond.com or careerbuilder.com, as well as several sales-specific job sites such as salesjobs.com and replocate.com, where candidates seeking a position can reply to an ad online. Employers also might consider advertising on a site such as Glassdoor.com, an employee-generated site that job seekers use to investigate the work culture of prospective employers. Most newspapers have added Web versions of their classified sections. Furthermore, many companies are using their Web site to advertise job openings and allow candidates to apply online. A company Web site should provide ample information about the position and the company, make it easy to apply, and give the candidate a favorable impression overall.[26] Companies can even create a Web page specifically for their job listings under the ".jobs" domain. It may be useful to follow guidelines such as those found in Exhibit 5.5[27] when writing for online recruitment. Since Web recruiting can produce a tremendous number of resumes, it may be helpful to use an automated applicant tracking system, such as that provided by Peoplefluent (www.peoplefluent.com), to identify the applicants who are most appropriate for the position.

Independent recruiting services are also widely available. For example, Wonderlic Inc. offers sales managers an automated application service that allows them to screen applicants before taking a phone call or handling a resume or application. Applicants call a special toll-free phone number included in the firm's recruiting ad, or are sent to a designated Web site and respond to questions related to the job. Wonderlic forwards the completed applications to the client company the next day for their review. Jobs in Pods (www.jobsinpods.com) will develop an audio podcast interview of a company's employees answering typically asked questions by job candidates (e.g., What's it like to work here?), publish it on its site, and broadcast it to sites such as iTunes and YouTube. Resume-search services such as CIRS (www.cirssearch.com) are likewise useful for finding qualified candidates. These services sort through thousands of resumes they have on file looking for candidates who match the specific qualifications a firm desires. They generally guarantee qualified candidates and charge only when a match is made.

Recruiting software, such as that provided by Oracle (www.oracle.com) and PCRecruiter (www.PCRecruiter.net), are available to help manage the recruitment process. This application allows for automating much of the recruiting process from posting the position online, to screening and contacting candidates, to scheduling interviews and assigning in-house interviewing responsibilities such as prescreening.

Increasingly, social networking sites such as LinkedIn, Facebook and Twitter are being used to recruit job candidates. One survey of recruiters found that 94 percent of respondents use social media as a tool to recruit potential job candidates, with one-third reporting it has helped to improve the quantity and quality of candidates. Moreover, 42 percent report using such sites to vet job candidates.[28] LinkedIn, for instance, allows

---

Writing for Online Recruitment   EXHIBIT 5.5

Writing for the online medium is a different art than writing for print.

Job summary. Online job boards show a position summary before the potential applicant sees the full ad. Be sure to present the job opportunity in terms of the outcomes the position will produce for the prospective applicant.

Keep it brief. It is much harder to read on screen than paper, and experts say you should cut the number of words by 50 percent compared to print.

Key words. Include key words and phrases you believe candidates would use to search for your position.

Job titles. Job titles commonly used in the industry tend to be picked up more readily by search engines than company-specific job titles.

Job skills. The relevance of your ad in search results can be increased by including all important job skills.

Job description. Provide brief but clear company and job descriptions.

Access points. Draw one's attention to different parts of the ad by using crossheadings and bullet points.

Mind your language. Minimize ambiguity by avoiding long sentences, using plain English, and being consistent in tone and style throughout.

Link up—but sparingly. Word count may be minimized by providing a link to a corporate career site for additional information.

How to apply. Provide contact details and be specific about how applicants should apply.

millions of professionals to post career profiles and find prospective employees globally online via company placed recruiting ads. Furthermore, companies can participate in industry-specific group discussion forums provided by LinkedIn in order to attract talent. When Bob Greenberg, regional sales manager for Agilent Technologies vacuum products division, put the word out on LinkedIn that he was hiring, he received responses from higher-quality candidates than those he typically received from his human resources department and ended up hiring a candidate he had previously met from a competing firm.[29] Jobcast.com offers a recruiting app that allows companies to build a fully branded career page in Facebook that can be used to post jobs and embed YouTube videos in order to attract passive job candidates. Some companies, such as Sodexo, a food services company, are acquiring talent by "tweeting" (text broadcasting) position openings via Twitter.[30] Related, online career communities, such as Sales Gravy (www.salesgravy.com), allow recruiters to reach professionals who use such sites to learn more about their career or industry, read white papers, blog, connect, and look for jobs.

Recruiting online offers several benefits. For one, it has the potential for fast turnaround. While a week may pass by the time an ad appears in the Sunday paper and the first applications are received, an opening can be posted online and applications received as early as the same day. There is also a cost saving, as ads posted on national job Web sites tend to run significantly less than similar offline classified ads. Finally, given the large number of job seekers who use the Internet, having a presence there appears critical. Nevertheless, this method should not be used exclusively since portions of the population may be excluded. Not all demographics use the Internet on an equally proportional basis. As such, strictly relying on online sources to recruit may result in violating antidiscrimination laws.[31]

Print Advertisements

Although less extensively used, print advertisements may be used to attract qualified applicants in the form of classified or display ads. Classified ads are often found in print and online, and require a relatively short lead time for ad placement. Advertisements in trade publications can attract those already in a specified field. In the case of trade magazines, lead time to place an advertisement in the next issue is longer than with newspapers—typically six to eight weeks. Other specialty publications provide nationally distributed employment listings, such as those published by the *Wall Street Journal.*

Research suggests that printed advertising material should provide important information regarding the job, otherwise applicants view the organization as being less concerned about their needs. Furthermore, the ads must be distinctive and stand out from others through physical representation or the presentation of unusual information (e.g., promise uncommon benefits such as pet insurance). By focusing on job candidates' needs and interests and emphasizing unique aspects of the job, print ads are likely to garner greater attention.[32]

Private Employment Agencies

A commonly used source when recruiting is the private employment agency. The fee charged by the agency may be paid by the employer or the job seeker, as established by contract before the agency begins work for either party. Fees vary, but typically amount to 15 to 35 percent (generally around 25 percent) of the first-year earnings of the person hired through the agency. The higher the caliber of salesperson being sought, the greater the probability the employer will pay the fee.

Many agencies, such as the Porter Group, Inc. (www.portergroup.com), and Salestalentinc (www.salestalentinc.com), specialize in the placement of salespeople. Such agencies can be extremely useful in national searches, particularly if the sales manager is seeking high-quality, experienced salespeople. This is true because high-performing salespeople are usually employed but may contact an agency just to see if a better opportunity has arisen.

Employment agencies usually work from a job description furnished by the sales manager and can be instructed to screen candidates based on specific job qualifications. The professionalism of private employment agencies varies widely, but there are enough good agencies that a sales manager should not tolerate an agency that cannot refer qualified candidates.

Employment agencies that specialize in part-timers are sometimes used when a need arises to hire part-time salespeople to support or supplant the full-time salesforce. In most cases, part-time salespeople are not eligible for fringe benefits, so the cost of sales coverage can be reduced by using them.

Colleges and Universities

A popular source for sales recruits, especially for large companies with extensive training programs, are colleges and universities. College students usually can be hired at lower salaries than experienced salespeople, yet they have already demonstrated their learning abilities. Some universities even provide professional selling programs designed to specifically train students for a career in sales. Companies seeking future managers often look here for sales recruits.

Campus placement centers can be helpful in providing resumes of applicants, arranging interviews, and providing facilities for screening interviews. Some campus placement centers offer videoconferencing systems that allow corporate recruiters to interview students from the home office. Some universities allow employers to post job vacancies directly to their career services Web site, which is accessible by all students. College campuses are also common sites for career conferences in which multiple companies participate in trade show fashion to familiarize students with sales job opportunities. Most placement centers also provide access to alumni in addition to the current student body. In some instances, contacts with faculty members may provide sales recruits. Federated Insurance, Inc., for instance, works closely with university faculty to identify strong sales candidates.

Another campus recruiting method is to offer sales internships, which allow both the company and the student an opportunity to see whether a match exists. The internship as a recruiting vehicle is gaining popularity. Northwestern Mutual Financial Network's internship program is designed to develop college students personally and professionally. Likewise, Vector Marketing, Xerox, and AFLAC all offer sales internships in hopes of developing future reps for the company. To facilitate their university recruiting efforts, State Farm, Inc. has even gone as far as sponsoring a university sales competition and offering sales scholarships as a mechanism for getting closer to students.

On the international scene, college campuses are gaining in popularity as a source of sales recruits. College students in foreign countries are beginning to see United States–based firms as viable alternatives to home-country firms.

Career Fairs

Several employers are brought together in one location for recruiting purposes by career fairs. Candidates visit the booths of employers they are interested in, or companies request a meeting with a candidate based on a favorable reaction to the candidate's resume. Career fairs are best conducted in the evening hours so that currently employed salespeople can attend. However, virtual career fairs on the Internet circumvent this problem. Companies can participate in online career fairs hosted by companies such as VirturalEvents365 by CGS (www.cgsinc.com). The company provides a virtual medium for keynote speakers and presentations where applicants can gather information about career choices and possible employers. Hosted career fairs offer employers the opportunity to interact with job seekers in real time or on demand, provide collateral, presentations and videos, and list job openings and position descriptions.

Professional Organizations

Another worthwhile source of sales recruits is professional organizations. A primary reason sales executives join professional organizations is to establish a network of colleagues who have common interests. Organizations such as Sales and Marketing Executives International meet regularly and provide the opportunity to establish contacts with professional sales executives, who may provide the names of prospective salespeople. Some professional organizations publish newsletters or operate a placement service, which could also be used in recruiting.

Selection: Evaluation and Hiring

The third step in the recruitment and selection model shown in Figure 5.2 is selection. As part of the selection process, various tools are used to evaluate the job candidate in terms of job qualifications and to provide a relative ranking compared with other candidates. Exhibit 5.6 provides an example of how characteristics of an ideal sales candidate might be assessed using different selection tools.[33] Keep in mind that the characteristics of the ideal sales candidate may vary by position and by company. In this section, commonly used evaluation tools are presented and some of the key issues in salesforce selection are discussed.

Screening Resumes and Applications

The pool of prospective salespeople generated in the recruiting phase often must be drastically reduced before engaging in time-consuming, expensive evaluation procedures such as personal interviews. Initially, sales recruits may be screened based on a review of a resume or an application form.

EXHIBIT 5.6   Linking Ideal Sales Candidate Profile Characteristics to the Selection Process

Ideal Sales Candidate Profile Characteristic	Selection Tools Used to Assess Profile Characteristic
Listening skills	Individual interviews with: Sales representatives Human resources personnel Others in the sales organization (trainer, sales support, etc.)
Follow-up skills	Assessment center exercises or simulations Application form (previous sales- or service-related work)
Adaptable communication/social style	Panel interviews (including several "layers" of personnel) Selection test on social style
Organizational skills	Application form Reference checks
Verbal communication skills	Individual interviews with internal parties Job sampling activities
Written communication skills	Assessment center exercises or simulations Application form
Proficiency in social connections across "levels"	Panel interview in a social setting (e.g., over a meal) Selection tests
Able to overcome objections	Individual interviews with trainer (including role-play exercise) Assessment center simulation Job sampling activities
Closing skills	Individual interviews Assessment center exercise
Tenacity and persistency	Reference checks Job sampling activities
Time management/planning	Reference checks Job sampling activities

In analyzing resumes, sales managers check job qualifications (e.g., education or sales experience requirements), the degree of career progress by the applicant, and the frequency of job change. Depending on the format and extensiveness of the resume, it may be possible to examine salary history and requirements, travel or relocation restrictions, and reasons for past job changes. Also, valuable clues about the recruit may be gathered from the appearance and completeness of the resume. Recruiters, however, should be cautious to inadvertently infer the candidate's personality based on his or her resume. Research indicates that such inferences tend to be unreliable and invalid, leading to poor assessments of applicants' employability.[34]

Technology makes it possible to screen resumes electronically. Screening software helps select the best applicants by screening for certain words or phrases, thus eliminating the need to examine every single resume received.[35] In addition, companies such as Oracle and PeopleFluent offer advanced search and artificial intelligence to locate top candidates. Caution, however, should be exercised when using screening software. If the screening criteria are not carefully chosen, groups of people from various protected categories may be eliminated.[36] Companies are increasingly exploring personal Web sites, blogs, message boards, and social networking sites to determine if a candidate is a good fit.

A job application form can be designed to gather all pertinent information and exclude unnecessary information. There are three additional advantages of application forms as a selection tool. First, the application form can be designed to meet antidiscriminatory legal requirements, whereas resumes often contain such information. For example, if some applicants note age, sex, race, color, religion, or national origin on their resumes and others do not, a legal question as to whether this information was used in the selection process might arise. A second advantage of application forms is that the comparison of multiple candidates is facilitated because the information on each candidate is presented in the same sequence. This is not the case with personalized resumes. Finally, job applications are usually filled out in handwriting, so the sales manager can observe the attention to detail and neatness of the candidate. In some sales jobs, these factors may be important for success.

Interviews

Interviews of assorted types are an integral part of the selection process. Because interpersonal communications and relationships are a fundamental part of sales jobs, it is only natural for sales managers to weigh interview results heavily in the selection process.

Although sales managers agree that interviews are important in selecting salespeople, there is less agreement on how structured the interviews should be and how they should be conducted. For example, some sales managers favor unstructured interviews, which encourage the candidates to speak freely about themselves. Others favor a more structured approach in which particular answers are sought, in a particular sequence, from each candidate. Research suggests, however, that interviews are improved as a selection tool when using a structured approach.[37]

Initial Interviews

Interviews are usually designed to get an in-depth look at the candidate. In some cases, however, they merely serve as a screening mechanism to support or replace a review of resumes or application forms. These initial interviews are typified by the on-campus interviews conducted by most sales recruiters. They are brief, lasting less than an hour. The recruiter clarifies questions about job qualifications and makes a preliminary judgment about whether a match exists between the applicant and the company. Such interviews may also be conducted one-on-one over the telephone or through teleconferencing or video-conferencing if there is a need to involve multiple parties.

A promising time-saving technique for initially interviewing candidates involves them responding to a series of questions on the Internet or over the telephone. Companies such as Interview Connect (www.interviewconnect.com) provide a means for companies who are recruiting to record interview questions, each as a separate digital clip. These questions are then presented via the Web to candidates anywhere throughout the world who respond to the digital clips and have their answers automatically recorded using a digital camera. The results are then forwarded to the hiring company. These interviews alleviate some of the costs involved in conducting a personal interview, as unqualified applicants are omitted prior to the personal interview.

During this phase of selection, sales managers should be careful to give the candidate an accurate picture of the job and not oversell it. Candidates who are totally "sold" on the job during the first interview only to be rejected later suffer unnecessary trauma.

Intensive Interviews

One or more intensive interviews may be conducted to get an in-depth look at the candidate. Often, this involves multiple sequential interviews by several executives or several managers at the company's facilities. The interview process at Federated Insurance for Marketing Representative candidates, for example, includes six to eight interviews, two days of field observations with current Federated Marketing Representatives, and a one-day field observation with a District Marketing Manager.[38] Another variation on the theme, used less often, is to interview several job candidates simultaneously in a group setting.

When a candidate is to be interviewed in succession by several managers, planning and coordination are required to achieve more depth and to avoid redundancy. Otherwise, each interviewer might concentrate on the more interesting dimensions of a candidate and some important areas may be neglected. An interviewing guide such as the one in Exhibit 5.7[39] could be used with multiple interviewers, each of whom would delve into one or more of the seven categories of information about the candidate. Or questions such as those in Exhibit 5.8,[40] which are useful for identifying sales-related competencies based on the premise that past performance/behavior is the best predictor of future performance/behavior, might also be used.

Given the emphasis placed today on developing enduring customer relationships, it is important to hire salespeople who value honesty and integrity, characteristics necessary for developing such relationships. Exhibit 5.9[41] outlines some sample questions (along with potential responses) geared toward gathering information on past behaviors that illustrate whether a candidate's ethical values are compatible with those of the organization. Most interview situations would require using only two or three such questions. The "rightness" or "wrongness" of the answers is up to the interviewer's judgment. As such it's important to train interviewers to follow up with more questions to pin down behavior and the thinking behind the behavior as well as to ask for additional examples. Interviewers then meet so that multiple interpretations of the answers can be obtained and discussed. The interviewers would then agree on a rating for the candidate's level of integrity.

Interviews, like any other single selection tool, may fail to predict adequately applicants' future success on the job. Interviewer bias, or allowing personal opinions, attitudes, and beliefs to influence judgments about a candidate, can be a particularly acute problem with some interviewers. Sales managers, like other human beings, tend to have preferences in candidates' appearances and personalities—and any number of other subjective feelings that may be irrelevant for a given interview situation.

AN ETHICAL DILEMMA

Bob Jones, sales manager for Steelhouse Industries, a manufacturer and marketer of heavy-duty industrial construction equipment, has just finished evaluating several different sales candidates for a vacant position. He has narrowed the list to two candidates that stand out. Both Russ and Susan meet the job qualifications. In fact, on paper Susan appears to be a stronger candidate, having nearly twice as much industry-related sales experience as Russ. Bob, however, believes that the construction industry is a man's world. He fears that many of Steelhouse's customers (and even its own employees) may not respect a woman salesperson. Thus, even though Susan appears to be the most qualified for the position, Bob is leaning toward hiring Russ. What should Bob do? Why?

Meeting the Candidate

At the outset, act friendly but avoid prolonged small talk—interviewing time costs money.
- Introduce yourself by using your name and title.
- Mention casually that you will make notes. ("You don't mind if I make notes, do you?")
- Assure the candidate that all information will be treated in confidence.

Questions
- Ask questions in a conversational tone. Make them both concise and clear.
- Avoid loaded and negative questions. Ask open-ended questions that will force complete answers. "Why do you say that?" (Who, what, where, when, how?)
- Don't ask direct questions that can be answered "yes" or "no."

Analyzing
- Attempt to determine the candidate's goals. Try to draw the candidate out, but let him or her do most of the talking. Don't sell—interview.
- Try to avoid snap judgments.

Interviewer Instructions
You will find two columns of questions on the following pages. The left-hand column contains questions to ask yourself about the candidate. The right-hand column suggests questions to ask the candidate. During the interview it is suggested that you continually ask yourself, "What is this person telling me about himself or herself?" What kind of person is he or she? In other parts of the interview, you can cover education, previous experience, and other matters relating to specific qualifications.

Ask Yourself	Ask the Candidate
I. Attitude	
• Can compete without irritation?	1. Ever lose in competition? Feelings?
• Can bounce back easily?	2. Ever uncertain about providing for your
• Can balance interest of both company and self?	family?
• What is important to him or her?	3. How can the American way of business be improved?
• Is he or she loyal?	4. Do you think that you've made a success of life to date?
• Takes pride in doing a good job?	5. Who was your best boss? Describe the person.
• Is he or she a cooperative team player?	6. How do you handle customer complaints?
II. Motivation	
• Is settled in choice of work?	1. How does your spouse (or other) feel about a selling career?
• Works from necessity, or choice?	2. When and how did you first develop an interest in selling?
• Makes day-to-day and long-range plans?	3. What mortgages, debts, etc., press you now?
• Uses some leisure for self-improvement?	4. How will this job help you get what you want?
• Is willing to work for what he or she wants in face of opposition?	5. What obstacles are most likely to trip you up?
III. Initiative	
• Is he or she a self-starter?	1. How (or why) did you get (or want to get) into sales?
• Completes own tasks?	2. Do you prefer to work alone or with others?
• Follows through on assigned tasks?	3. What do you like most and like least about selling?
• Works in assigned manner without leaving own trademark?	

(continued)

EXHIBIT 5.7   **Interview Guide** *continued*

Ask Yourself	Ask the Candidate
• Can work independently?	4. Which supervisors let you work alone? How did you feel about this? 5. When have you felt like giving up on a task? Tell me about it.

IV. Stability

Ask Yourself	Ask the Candidate
• Is he or she excitable or even-tempered? • Impatient or understanding? • Uses words that show strong feelings? • Is candidate poised or impulsive; controlled or erratic? • Will he or she broaden or flatten under pressure? • Is candidate enthusiastic about job?	1. What things disturb you most? 2. How do you get along with customers (people) you dislike? 3. What buyers' actions irritate you? 4. What were your most unpleasant sales (work) experiences? 5. Most pleasant sales (work) experiences? 6. What do you most admire about your friends? 7. What things do some customers do that are irritating to other people?

V. Planning

Ask Yourself	Ask the Candidate
• Ability to plan and follow through? Or will depend on supervisor for planning? • Ability to coordinate work of others? • Ability to think of ways of improving methods? • Ability to fit into company methods? • Will he or she see the whole job or get caught up in details?	1. What part of your work (selling) do you like best? Like least? 2. What part is the most difficult for you? 3. Give me an idea of how you spend a typical day. 4. Where do you want to be five years from today? 5. If you were manager, how would you run your present job? 6. What are the differences between planned and unplanned work?

VI. Insight

Ask Yourself	Ask the Candidate
• Realistic in appraising self? • Desire for self-improvement? • Interested in problems of others? • Interested in reaction of others to self? • Will he or she take constructive action on weaknesses? • How does he or she take criticism?	1. Tell me about your strengths and weaknesses. 2. Are your weaknesses important enough to do something about them? Why or why not? 3. How do you feel about those weaknesses? 4. How would you size up your last employer? 5. Most useful criticism received? From whom? Tell me about it. Most useless? 6. How do you handle fault-finders?

VII. Social Skills

Ask Yourself	Ask the Candidate
• Is he or she a leader or follower? • Interested in new ways of dealing with people? • Can get along best with what types of people? • Will wear well over the long term? • Can make friends easily?	1. What do you like to do in your spare time? 2. Have you ever organized a group? Tell me about it. 3. What methods are effective in dealing with people? What methods are ineffective? 4. What kind of customers (people) do you get along with best? 5. Do you prefer making new friends or keeping old ones? Why? 6. How would you go about making a friend? Developing a customer? 7. What must a person do to be liked by others?

Sales-Related Competencies Interview   EXHIBIT 5.8

Goal Setting/Accomplishment/Focus

1. Give me an example of a time when you set a goal and were able to meet or achieve it.
2. Describe how you set your goals for last year and how you measured your work. Did you achieve your goals? If not, why not?
3. Give me an example of a time when you used a systematic process to define your objectives even though you were not prompted or directed to do so. What type of system did you use? What payoff did you get from using the process?
4. Tell me about a time you were assigned a goal that you believed would be impossible to attain.

Oral Communication

1. Tell me about the most difficult or complex idea, situation or process you have ever had to explain to someone. How did you explain it? Were you successful?
2. Describe a time when you had difficulty communicating your thoughts clearly to another person or group. What message were you trying to convey? Where did the difficulty in communicating lie? How did you end up getting your point across?
3. Give me an example of a time when you were able to successfully communicate with a customer you personally did not like.

Presentation Skills

1. Describe a situation where, after a presentation, you were faced with a hostile questioner. What did you do? What were the results?
2. Give me an example of a time when a presentation you were making wasn't working and you were able to switch tactics to make it work. How did you know the presentation wasn't working?
3. Tell me about an oral presentation you made to a group within the last year. What was the most difficult aspect of the presentation?
4. Describe the most significant presentation you have had to complete.

Research confirms the subjective nature of interviewing, concluding that different interviewers will rate the same applicant differently unless there is a commonly accepted stereotype of the ideal applicant.[42] For instance, research suggests that race bias is a potential concern.[43] Bias related to attractiveness and gender also is a common problem.[44] Sales managers must not let bias interfere with the hiring decision. To see how bias may influence one's decision, see "An Ethical Dilemma" on p. 148.

Testing

To overcome the pitfalls of subjectivity and a potential lack of critical analysis of job candidates, many firms use tests as part of the selection process. Selection tests may be designed to measure intelligence, aptitudes, personality, and other interpersonal factors.

Historically, the use of such tests has been controversial. In the late 1960s, it appeared that testing would slowly disappear from the employment scene under legal and social pressure related to the lack of validity and possible discriminatory nature of some testing procedures. Instead, selection tests have changed, and perhaps managers have learned more about how to use them as a legitimate part of the selection process. Therefore, they are frequently used today.

Those who have had success with tests suggest they are useful for identifying candidates' strengths and weaknesses, as well as for revealing candidates who possess key personality traits associated with successful salespeople.[45] For example, the traits "conscientiousness," "learned optimism," and "playfulness" appear to be valid predictors of sales performance,[46] as does the need for cognition (i.e., the desire to engage in effortful thinking) and self-monitoring (i.e., the degree to which one engages in impression management).[47] The Caliper Profile Employee Assessment Tool, for instance, measures 25 personality traits that influence salesperson performance. It can be taken online or

EXHIBIT 5.9   Interviewing for Integrity

1. "We are often confronted with the dilemma of having to choose between what is right and what is best for the company. Give at least two examples of situations in which you faced this dilemma and how you handled them."

Good answer: Once, we discovered a technical defect in a product after it had been shipped and used by a client. The client did not notice the defect. We debated whether to tell the client and admit we had made a stupid error, or just let things go because the client seemed to be using the product with no problem. We decided to tell the client and replace the product at no cost.

Questionable answer: We discovered that our sales clerks were making errors in charging for certain combinations of products and that the errors were almost always in favor of the company. In no way were the clerks encouraged or trained to make these errors. We also learned that, with training, the errors could be eliminated, but the training would be fairly expensive. I decided not to institute the training.

2. "Have you ever observed someone stretching the rules at work? What did you do about it?"

Good answer: One of my fellow executives took a company car to use for a weekend vacation. I spoke to him, and he agreed that it was not right and that he would not do it again.

Questionable answer: Everybody stretches the rules sometimes.

3. "Have you ever had to bend the rules or exaggerate a little bit when trying to make a sale?"

Good answer: My experience is that when salespeople misrepresent products and services, customers buy less from them. Having credibility with customers brings in better long-term sales. For example, when I was selling servers, we had a proprietary server and operating system. The client asked me why my machine was really worth the higher cost. I listed the advantages and disadvantages, which indicated for him that the cheaper solution would work. I lost that sale but came back to win a much larger sale six months later.

Questionable answer: Sometimes when selling to a doctor, the doctor will state that he's heard that one of my products is effective against a certain disease. I listen and nod my head and say, "Interesting." I don't correct him, even though I know that the drug is not recommended for that purpose. I'm not saying that it does work the way he thinks it does; I'm just not disagreeing with the doctor. You can't give advice to physicians.

4. "We've all done things that we regretted. Can you give me an example that falls into this category for you? How would you handle it differently today?"

Good answer: When I first took over my job, I let seven people go without a whole lot of knowledge about their skills and contributions. Later I found that three of them were actually outstanding employees who should not have been let go. My jumping to conclusions hurt them and the company's operations. It took us several years to replace their knowledge of our equipment.

Questionable answer: I've never regretted anything about business. It's a game. I play the game to win.

5. "There are two philosophies about regulations and policies. One is that they are to be followed to the letter; the other is that they are just guidelines. What is your opinion?"

Good answer: Regulations and policies are made for important reasons. A regulation seems to me to be stronger than a policy, and I feel that I follow all regulations, such as getting reports in at a certain time and accounting for expenses in a certain way. Policies are a little bit more indefinite. They express more of a guideline and a philosophy. There are circumstances when you fall into the "gray area" when applying a policy. When I have had questions, I've checked with my boss.

Questionable answer: In order to get things done, you can't be held back by old-fashioned policies of your organization. You have to know what's right and do the right thing. You have to have good ethics and make decisions based on those ethics. You may have to bend the rules sometimes.

on paper and its results offer objective information on a sales candidate's limitations, strengths, motivation and potential performance in a specific sales role.[48] Sales Success Profile (www.salessuccessprofile.com), a 50-question, multiple-choice test, measures salespeople's strengths and weaknesses in 13 critical areas, including the ability to approach, involve, and build rapport; the ability to identify a buyer's needs and motivations; skill at overcoming objections; and time management. An Internet-based test offered by ANOVA Communications Group called Profile Sales Indicator measures sales performance and attempts to predict behavior by benchmarking a company's successful salespeople and then identifying candidates whose answers to the test approximate those of successful performers. Intelligence tests are likewise useful, as they tend to predict cognitive ability, which has been found to predict future salesperson performance.[49] Valid tests measuring certain personality traits, sales skills, strengths, or cognitive ability may be used to supplement other salesforce selection tools. They can often be completed online at relatively little expense.

Those who remain reluctant to use tests ask three questions: (1) Can selection tests really predict future job performance? (2) Can tests give an accurate, job-related profile of the candidate? (3) What are the legal liabilities arising from testing? In addressing the first question, one must admit it is sometimes difficult to correlate performance on a test at a given point in time with job performance at a later date. For example, how can sales managers account for performance variations caused primarily by changes in the uncontrollable environment, as might be the case in an unpredictable economic setting?

Question 2 really is concerned with whether the tests measure the appropriate factors in an accurate fashion. The precise measurement of complex behavioral variables such as motivation is difficult at best, so it is likely that some tests do not really measure what they purport to measure.

Answers to question 3 depend largely on the complete answers to questions 1 and 2. The capsule response to the third question is that, unless test results can be validated as a meaningful indicator of performance, there is a strong possibility that the sales manager is in a legally precarious position.

Suggestions to sales managers to improve the usefulness of tests as selection tools include:[50]

1. Do not attempt to construct tests for the purpose of selecting salespeople. Leave this job to the testing experts and human resource specialists.

2. If psychological tests are used, be sure the standards of the American Psychological Association have been met.

3. Use tests that have been based on a job analysis for the particular job in question.

4. Select a test that minimizes the applicant's ability to anticipate desired responses.

5. Use tests as part of the selection process, but do not base the hiring decision solely on test results.

Tests can be useful selection tools if these suggestions are followed. In particular, tests can identify areas worthy of further scrutiny if they are administered and interpreted before a final round of intensive interviewing. For example, Federated Insurance requires applicants to take a written personality test as part of the application process.

Sales managers may use commercial testing services in selecting salespeople. For example, Wonderlic, Inc. (www.wonderlic.com) offers a computer-scored test called the 7-Factor Personality Profile that assesses personality from a job compatibility perspective. This extensively validated test can be used to analyze candidates' strengths and weaknesses related to a position in sales. Companies such as Cardinal Health, for instance, test job candidates' sales skills utilizing online assessment and testing services provided by the HR Chally Group (www.chally.com).[51] Chally works with companies to determine specific job requirements and then tailors an assessment to determine candidates who meet these requirements.

Tests may prove useful for selecting among local candidates when operating in a foreign country. Tests such as the Occupational Personality Questionnaire (OPQ), which measures 32 factors, including sociability and the ability to persuade others, can be created on a country-by-country basis.[52] One must be careful when testing globally, however, as tests do not always translate well into other languages and cultures.

Assessment Centers

An assessment center offers a set of well-defined procedures for using techniques such as group discussion, business game simulations, presentations, and role-playing exercises for the purpose of employee selection or development. The participant's performance is evaluated by a group of assessors, usually members of management within the firm. Although somewhat expensive because of the high cost of managerial time to conduct the assessments, such centers are being used more often in the selection of salespeople. Research finds that assessment center ratings correlate with general intelligence, achievement motivation, social competence, and self-competence, all desirable salesperson characteristics.[53]

An interesting report on the use of an assessment center to select salespeople comes from the life insurance industry, well known for its continual need for new salespeople. Traditional selection methods used in this industry apparently leave something to be desired because turnover rates are among the highest for salespeople. An assessment-center approach was used by one life insurance firm to select salespeople based on exercises simulating various sales skills, such as prospecting, time management, and sales presentation skills. Results of the study indicated that this program was superior to traditional methods of selecting salespeople in the insurance industry in terms of predicting which salespeople would survive and which would drop out within six months of being hired.[54] Some companies are even using sales simulation software to assess candidates' selling skills. Sales reps from a large U.S. transportation firm who scored highly on AlignMark's sales simulator, AccuVision, reached 130 percent of their sales quota, as opposed to 90 percent for low scorers one year after being hired.[55]

Background Investigation

Job candidates who have favorably emerged from resume and application screening, interviewing, testing, and perhaps an assessment center may next become the subject of a background investigation. This may be as perfunctory as a reference check or comprehensive if the situation warrants it. For instance, Federated Insurance reviews each Marketing Representative applicant's motor vehicle and credit reports, conducts a criminal background check, and conducts at least 10 reference checks.[56] In conducting background investigations, it is advisable to request job-related information only and to obtain a written release from the candidate before proceeding with the investigation.

If a reference check is conducted, two points should be kept in mind. First, persons listed as references are biased in favor of the job applicant. As one sales manager puts it, "Even the losers have three good references—so I don't bother checking them." Second, persons serving as references may not be candid or may not provide the desired information. This reluctance may stem from a personal concern (i.e., Will I lose a friend or be sued if I tell the truth?) or from a company policy limiting the discussion of past employees. One suggestion for conducting a reference check is to ask your finalists to provide 10 references. Call the references when they will not be available and leave a voice mail indicating that your company is hiring for an important position and that they should only call back if the candidate is really outstanding.[57] Another option involves using an automated system such as ChequedReference, offered by Chequed.com. This automated system sends emails to references from candidates asking them to complete a short online survey about their experience together. This approach has improved reference response rate from 30 to more than 80 percent.[58]

Despite these and other limitations, a reference check can help verify the true identity of a person and possibly confirm his or her education and employment history. Learning that an applicant or employee lied on the application form can also be used as a defense in a hiring or firing discrimination suit.[59] With personal misrepresentation and resume fraud being very real possibilities, (experts estimate that 20 percent to 50 percent of job applicants lie to enhance their credentials) a reference check is recommended.[60] Furthermore, a valid reference check may be useful in helping a company prevent a lawsuit resulting from a negligent hire.[61] Exhibit 5.10[62] provides techniques for getting valid information in a background check. When questioning references, be sure to avoid any questions that could be discriminatory, such as those referencing age, race, color, religion, marital status, sexual orientation and other protected classifications. Also, avoid questions concerning arrests, financial disclosure matters, family and medical history, as well as those questions as to whether the applicant filed any lawsuits or claims against the employer.[63]

Physical Examination

Requiring the job candidate to pass a physical examination is often a formal condition of employment. In many instances, the insurance carrier of the employing firm requires a physical examination of all incoming employees. The objective is to discover any physical problem that may inhibit job performance.

Drug testing also may be required as a condition for employment. When instituting a drug testing program as part of the hiring process, the company should first develop a written policy stating when and how the testing will be performed, the types of drugs for which testing will be performed, and what will happen to an applicant who tests positive for drug use (e.g., reject or require employer-sponsored drug counseling as a condition for employment).[64] The need for the drug testing should be reasonably related to potential job functions and all applicants should be required to be tested. Furthermore, applicants should be informed of the test before taking it and the results should be kept confidential.[65]

Selection Decision and Job Offer

When making the selection decision, the sales manager must evaluate candidates' qualifications relative to characteristics considered most important for the job. It may be helpful to design a form similar to the one shown in Exhibit 5.11 to track each sales candidate through the selection process.[66] A decision must be made about whether a candidate's strength in one characteristic can compensate for a weakness in another characteristic, whether a characteristic is so important that a weakness in it cannot be tolerated, or whether the candidate must meet certain minimum levels to be successful.[67] At times, the sales manager may face a dilemma similar to that found in "An Ethical Dilemma" on p. 157.

After evaluating the available candidates, the sales manager may be ready to offer a job to one or more candidates. Some candidates may be "put on hold" until the top candidates have made their decisions. Another possibility is that the sales manager may decide to extend the search and begin the recruitment and selection process all over again.

In communicating with those offered jobs, it is now appropriate for the sales manager to "sell" the prospective salesperson on joining the firm. In reality, top salespeople are hard to find, and the competition for them is intense. Therefore, a sales manager should enthusiastically pursue the candidate once the offer is extended. As always, an accurate portrayal of the job is a must. In addition to standard enticements, such as salary, performance bonuses, company car, and fringe benefits, certain extra incentives are sometimes offered to prospective salespeople. Candidates may be offered relocation assistance and reimbursement for other expenses. Another incentive is the market bonus paid on hiring to salespeople having highly sought-after skills and qualifications. This one-time payment recognizes an existing imbalance in supply and demand in a given labor market. Using a market bonus could be a reasonable alternative if the supply-demand imbalance is thought to be temporary, because the bonus is a one-time payment and not a permanent addition to base compensation.

The offer of employment should be written, but can be initially extended in verbal form. Any final contingencies, such as passing a physical examination, should be detailed in the offer letter. Candidates not receiving a job offer should be notified in a prompt, courteous manner. A specific reason for not hiring a candidate need not be given. A simple statement that an individual who better suits the needs of the company has been hired is sufficient.

EXHIBIT 5.10   How to Get Valid Information in a Background Check

The HR Chally Group's experience shows that many employers never really check references, or else they do it hastily and it becomes little more than a rubber stamp. Here are 10 techniques to make the background check a useful and productive tool in aiding the selection process. While it is often difficult to get references to cooperate because of cautious internal policies or other legal concerns, many will comment orally or off the record, but not in writing.

1. **Be wary of first-party references.**
   Good sales candidates are not going to name references who will describe them negatively. Such first-party references are not as valuable as the candidate's past customers, who will probably be more candid. These references can indicate how loyal and satisfied the customers were with the candidate, which is a good indication of a prospective employee's past performance.

2. **Radial search referrals might be used.**
   The radial search for referrals is a method of reference checking that requires getting additional references from the first-party references. Such "second generation" references will not be carefully selected to present only a positive impression. **Remember:** Ask references to help you out; don't ask them just to criticize. Ask them to highlight strengths and let them build up the salesperson, and see how high they are willing to go.

3. **Use an interview background check.**
   This will show whether or not the salesperson is likely to change in terms of work performance. In other words, what degree of reliability do the references suggest? What "odds" do they give for the person's future success?

4. **Use the critical incident technique.**
   Determine the one trait or incident for which the candidate is best remembered. Could this be described as primarily good, bad, or neutral? Does it indicate an individual who is results-oriented or service-oriented?

5. **Pick out problem areas.**
   Determine the candidate's customers who were the most difficult to handle, and those problems that were the toughest to solve. Even first-party references may reveal difficulties that can be indicative of future sales performance. Find out if the candidate eventually overcame the difficulties.

6. **Obtain a numerical scale reference rating.**
   Keep in mind that 70 points on a 100-point scale is "passing" to most people; 50 points would be "failing." Reference rating scales are often easier for people to deal with. For example, references generally do not like to say negative things, but they may be willing to call a person an "85" instead of flatly saying "average."

7. **Identify an individual's best job.**
   Notice whether or not the reference needs to think excessively about identifying an individual's best job. This may suggest that the individual's behavior was consistent, but not necessarily exceptional.

8. **Check for idiosyncrasies.**
   Did the candidate have any outstanding idiosyncrasies? If so, did they help or hinder job performance?

9. **Check financial and personal habits.**
   Credit difficulties and any indication of alcoholism or gambling are clearly negative indicators for future success. A strong interest in betting, even associated with a measure of success, is frequently associated with long-term problems in sales.

10. **Get customer opinion.**
    Has the candidate kept regular customers? How loyal are customers to the candidate personally, as opposed to the product or the company? Why? Was the candidate seen as efficient, dependable, and genuinely interested in the customers?

Selection Tool	Profile Characteristic (Behavioral Indicator)	Rating 0–10
Application Form	Organizational skills (previous position)	____
	Written communication skills (application essay)	____
	Follow-up skills (previous sales/service position)	____
Interviews with Sales Associates	Fit to organizational culture (personality, citizenship assessment)	____
	Fit to sales position (describe details of position and note reactions)	____
	Listening skills (assess linking questions to comments)	____
	Verbal communication skills (persuasiveness and clarity)	____
Testing	Social style/adaptability (validated test of social styles: test score 0–100)	____
	Aptitude (cognitive intelligence test: test score 0–100)	____
Reference Checks	Organizational skills (direct question of reference)	____
	Tenacity and persistency (direct question of reference)	____
Job Sampling Activities	Verbal communication skills (feedback from ride-along with current sales representative)	____
	Overcoming objections (feedback from ride-along with current sales representative)	____
	Time management/planning (timely completion of job sampling activities)	____
Overall Score		____

AN ETHICAL DILEMMA

You are the district sales manager for an electronics manufacturing company and are responsible for all the recruitment and selection decisions in your district. The company's national sales manager has asked you to interview his daughter for a sales position that has just opened up in your district. Coincidentally, he mentions that a regional sales manager position (which you desire very much) is about to open up. On interviewing the national sales manager's daughter, along with several other candidates, you find that she is not the best qualified for the position. What would you do? Explain.

LEGAL AND ETHICAL CONSIDERATIONS IN RECRUITMENT AND SELECTION

Key Legislation

The possibility of illegal discrimination permeates the recruitment and selection process, and a basic understanding of pertinent legislation can be beneficial to the sales manager. Some of the most important legislation is summarized in Exhibit 5.12.[68] The legislative acts featured in Exhibit 5.12 are federal laws applicable to all firms engaged in interstate commerce. Companies not engaging in interstate commerce are often subject to state and local laws that are similar to these federal laws.

EXHIBIT 5.12   Legislation Affecting Recruitment and Selection

Legislative Act	Purpose
Fifth and Fourteenth Amendments to the U.S. Constitution	Provide equal protection standards to prevent irrational or unreasonable selection methods.
Equal Pay Act (1963)	Requires that men and women be paid the same amount for performing similar job duties.
Civil Rights Act (1964)	Prohibits discrimination based on age, race, color, religion, sex, or national origin.
Age Discrimination in Employment Act (1967; amended 1987)	Prohibits discrimination against people of ages 40 and older.
Fair Employment Opportunity Act (1972)	Founded the Equal Employment Opportunity Commission to ensure compliance with the Civil Rights Act.
Rehabilitation Act (1973)	Requires affirmative action to hire and promote handicapped persons if the firm employs 50 or more employees and is seeking a federal contract in excess of $50,000.
Vietnam Veterans Readjustment Act (1974)	Requires affirmative action to hire Vietnam veterans and disabled veterans of any war. Applicable to firms holding federal contracts in excess of $10,000.
Pregnancy Discrimination Act (1978)	Prohibits discrimination based on pregnancy or pregnancy-related conditions.
Americans with Disabilities Act (1990)	Prohibits discrimination against qualified disabled people in all areas of employment. Prohibits the use of employment tests, qualification standards, and selection criteria that tend to screen out individuals with disabilities unless the standard is job related or consistent with business necessity.
Civil Rights Act (1991)	Prohibits employers from adjusting scores of, using different cutoff scores for, or otherwise altering the results of employment-related tests on the basis of race, color, religion, sex, or national origin.
Amendment to Fair Credit Reporting Act (1997)	When seeking background information from a reporting service company, employers must inform job applicants or employees in writing that a report on them will be procured and must obtain their signature authorizing the move.
Genetic Information Nondiscrimination Act of 2008	Makes it illegal to discriminate against employees or applicants because of genetic information.

Guidelines for Sales Managers

The legislation reviewed in Exhibit 5.12 is supported by various executive orders and guidelines that make it clear that sales managers, along with other hiring officials in a firm, have legal responsibilities of grave importance in the recruitment and selection process. In step 1 of the process, planning for recruitment and selection, sales managers must take care to analyze the job to be filled in an open-minded way, attempting to overcome any personal mental biases.

Job descriptions and job qualifications should be accurate and based on a thoughtful job analysis. The planning stage may also require that the sales manager consider fair employment legislation and affirmative action requirements before setting recruitment and selection objectives.

In step 2 of the process, recruitment, the sources that serve as intermediaries in the search for prospective candidates should be informed of the firm's legal position. The firm must be careful to avoid sources that limit its hiring from protected classes.[69] It is also crucial that advertising and other communications be devoid of potentially discriminatory content. For example, companies that advertise for "young, self-motivated salesmen" may be inviting an inquiry from the Equal Employment Opportunity Commission on the basis of age and gender discrimination.

Finally, all applicants should be treated equally. A variety of selection tools related to job performance should be used and generally must be applied to all applicants.[70] When interviewing, one must be careful not to violate the law. Exhibit 5.13[71] provides some basic rules for legally interviewing job applicants. Munson and Spivey summarize legal advice for selection by stating, "At each step in the selection process, it would be advisable to be as objective, quantitative, and consistent as possible, especially because present federal guidelines are concerned with all procedures suggesting employment discrimination."[72]

To more fully appreciate the sensitivity necessary in these matters, consider the following list of potentially troublesome information often found on employment applications.[73]

- Age or date of birth
- Length of time at present address
- Height and/or weight
- Marital status
- Ages of children
- Occupation of spouse
- Relatives already employed by the firm
- Person to notify in case of an emergency
- Type of military discharge

These topics leave the employer open to charges of discrimination, as would a request for a photograph of the applicant, a birth certificate, or a copy of military discharge papers. Further questions to avoid are those concerning the original name of the applicant, race or color, religion (including holidays observed), nationality or birthplace of the applicant, arrests, home ownership, bankruptcy or garnishments, disabilities, handicaps and health problems, and memberships in organizations that may suggest race, religion, color, or ancestral origin of the applicant.

Ethical Issues

Two ethical issues of particular importance are (1) how the job to be filled is represented and (2) how interviews are conducted. Misrepresentation of the job does not always extend into the legal domain. For example, earnings potential may be stated in terms of

---

Basic Rules of the Job Interview   EXHIBIT 5.13

Rule 1—Questions should focus on job-related topics, such as job requirements and applicant qualifications and credentials.

Rule 2—Properly phrase questions. Good questions are based on the job description and advertised position requirements; relate to genuine job qualifications; go beyond a yes/no response; and are understandable and succinct.

Rule 3—You do not have to ask every applicant the same questions.

Rule 4—With regards to religion and disability, reasonable accommodations must be made to the interviewee, even at the pre-employment stage. For example, if a candidate could not interview on a certain day, due to religious observance, the interview must be rescheduled, unless doing so would cause an "undue hardship."

what the top producer earns, not expected first-year earnings of the average salesperson. Or perhaps the opportunities for promotion are somewhat overstated but no completely false statements are used. As simple as it may sound, the best policy is a truthful policy if the sales manager wants to match the applicant to the job and avoid later problems from those recruited under false pretenses.

Some ethical issues also arise in interviewing, especially regarding the stress interview. This technique is designed to put job candidates under extreme, unexpected, psychological duress for the purpose of seeing how they react. A common tactic for stress interviewing in the sales field is to demand an impromptu sales presentation for a convenient item such as a ballpoint pen. Such requests may seem unreasonable to a professional salesperson who is accustomed to planning a presentation before delivering it. Another stress interviewing tactic is to ridicule the responses of the job candidates or to repeatedly interrupt the candidates' responses to questions before they have an adequate opportunity to provide a complete response.

Sales managers who use stress interviewing justify its use by pointing out that salespeople must be able to think on their feet and react quickly to unanticipated questions from customers. Although this is true, there would seem to be better ways of assessing a candidate's skills. The stress interview may create an unfavorable image of the company, and it may alienate some of the better candidates.[74] It appears to be a risky, and ethically questionable, approach.

SUMMARY

1. **Explain the critical role of recruitment and selection in building and maintaining a productive salesforce.** Recruitment and selection of salespeople can be an expensive process, characterized by uncertainty and complicated by legal considerations. If the procedures are not properly conducted, a multitude of managerial problems can arise, the worst of which being that salesforce performance is suboptimal. The sales manager is the key person in the recruitment and selection process, although other managers in the hiring firm may share responsibilities for staffing the salesforce.

2. **Describe how recruitment and selection affect salesforce socialization and performance.** Socialization, the process by which salespeople adjust to their jobs, begins when the recruit is first contacted by the hiring firm. Two stages of socialization should be accomplished during recruitment and selection: achieving realism and achieving congruence. Realism means giving the recruit an accurate portrayal of the job. Congruence refers to the matching process that should occur between the needs of the organization and the capabilities of the recruit. If realism and congruence can be accomplished, future job satisfaction, involvement, commitment, and performance should be improved. These relationships are shown in a model of the socialization process in Figure 5.1.

3. **Identify the key activities in planning and executing a program for salesforce recruitment and selection.** Figure 5.2 depicts a model of the recruitment and selection process. There are three steps in the process: planning, recruitment, and selection. *Planning* consists of conducting a job analysis, determining job qualifications, writing a job description, setting objectives, and formulating a strategy. *Recruitment* involves locating prospective job candidates from one or more sources within or outside the hiring firm. The third step, *selection*, entails an evaluation of the candidates culminating in a hiring decision. Major methods of evaluating candidates include resume and job-application analysis, interviews, tests, assessment centers, background investigations, and physical examinations.

4. **Discuss the legal and ethical considerations in salesforce recruitment and selection.** Every step of the recruitment and selection process has the potential to discriminate illegally against some job candidates. Federal laws and guidelines provide the basic antidiscriminatory framework, and state and local statutes may also be

applicable. The most important legislation that applies are the Civil Rights Act and the Fair Employment Opportunity Act. Two primary ethical concerns are (1) misrepresentation of the job to be filled and (2) using stress interviews in the selection stage.

UNDERSTANDING SALES MANAGEMENT TERMS

salesforce socialization	private employment agency
achieving realism	career fairs
achieving congruence	professional organizations
job preview	job application form
planning activities	initial interviews
recruitment	intensive interviews
selection	interviewer bias
job analysis	assessment center
job qualifications	background investigation
job description	market bonus
recruitment and selection strategy	misrepresentation
employee referral programs	stress interview

DEVELOPING SALES MANAGEMENT KNOWLEDGE

1. What are some of the problems associated with improperly executed recruitment and selection activities?

2. To enhance salesforce socialization, recruitment and selection should ensure realism and congruence. How can this be accomplished?

3. Refer to p. 134 to "Sales Management in the 21st Century: Achieving Congruence and Realism at W.B. Mason Office Products." What does W.B. Mason Office Products do to help it achieve congruence and realism in its salesforce?

4. Describe the relationship between conducting a job analysis, determining job qualifications, and completing a written job description.

5. What are the advantages of using employee referral programs to recruit salespeople? Can you identify some disadvantages?

6. Refer to p. 142 to "Sales Management in the 21st Century: Locating Sales Candidates at W.B. Mason Office Products." Where does W.B. Mason Office Products find its sales candidates?

7. How can private employment agencies assist in the recruitment and selection of salespeople? Who pays the fee charged by such agencies: the hiring company or the job candidate?

8. What can be learned about a job candidate from analyzing a job application that cannot be learned from the candidate's resume?

9. Summarize the primary legislation designed to prohibit illegal discrimination in the recruitment and selection process.

10. What is stress interviewing? How do some sales managers justify using stress interviews?

BUILDING SALES MANAGEMENT SKILLS

1. Access HR-Guide.com at http://www.hr-guide.com. Click on "2000 interview questions" and then go to the section (bottom of the page) that has these organized by

topics. Put together a list of 25 questions (five for each category) that could be used to assess a sales candidate's creativity, analytical thinking, organization, achievement, and flexibility in a job interview. Be sure to consider questions that would be most appropriate to ask a sales candidate. Please label the category for each set of five questions.

2. Find job qualifications and a position description for a sales position at a company of your choice. Design a series of questions that you could use as a guide to interview a candidate for this position. Now, find a classmate who also has found job qualifications and a position description for a sales position, and swap information. Using your interview guide, take turns interviewing each other. (The information you swapped with your classmate serves as a guide for the interviewee.) Make an audio or video recording of your interview. Finally, listen to or view your recording and write a critique of your interview, explaining what went well and what did not.

3. The Web is filled with many sites that could be beneficial in the recruitment and selection process. Using an Internet search engine, type in a key word from this chapter such as "recruitment." This should provide you with several sites that could be useful in the recruitment and selection process. Explore some of these sites, and then choose three that you believe would be helpful to a sales manager involved in recruitment and selection. First, provide each site address. Second, provide a description of each site. Finally, explain how each site or the information it contains could be useful in the recruitment and selection process.

4. Access the following video that provides direction for interviewing sales candidates: Selling Power, "How to Interview Sales Candidates," YouTube, May 20, 2008, www.youtube.com/watch?v=4rs0NaybFFk. Watch the video and answer the following questions:

   a. When interviewing a salesperson, why should a sales manager focus on past experiences rather than hypotheticals?

   b. Why is it important to probe into a person's responses when interviewing him or her?

   c. Why should testing be used at the beginning of the interview process?

   d. What are the three elements of sales drive?

5. The Strong Corporation's main competitor, Leadrod Company, just filed for bankruptcy, presenting a potential opportunity for an increase in customers and revenue at Strong. As a result, several of Leadrod's salespeople have contacted Sam Smith, Strong's vice president of sales, inquiring about employment with Strong. Currently Smith has no openings on his 10-person salesforce. However, he does not want to dismiss the Leadrod reps, some of whom are top performers that might be able to enhance Leadrod's revenue stream that has been falling for the past year.

   After speaking to his CEO about adding a position to his salesforce, Smith was given permission to do so as long as the new salesperson made more of his salary in commissions than base salary. Smith, however, would like to add three of Leadrod's salespeople. Currently there are four salespeople on Smith's staff that outperform the other six, who are approximately equal in talent. Yet, Smith is hard-pressed to identify a clear laggard whom he would dismiss in favor of the competition's salespeople. Smith is also concerned that he could disrupt the team chemistry he has worked hard to build the past two years by firing some of his current salespeople and hiring those from Leadrod. However, he does not know if he can pass up this opportunity to upgrade his salesforce.

   How should Smith approach this dilemma? Should he hire the new reps and deal with the ramifications of letting two of his people go, or can he afford to pass on the new reps altogether?[75]

ROLE PLAY

6. This exercise consists of a series of different role plays involving two characters: a sales manager and a candidate seeking a sales position. Find another classmate to assume one of the roles. Role-play the following situations:

1. The sales manager misrepresents the job in an interview.

2. The sales manager employs a stress interview.

3. The sales manager opens him/herself up to charges of discrimination during an interview.

On completion of the role plays, address the following questions:

1. What are the dangers of misrepresenting the position during an interview?

2. What are the pros and cons of using a stress interview?

3. How can you avoid possible discrimination charges as a result of interviewing?

ROLE PLAY

7. **Role Play**

Situation: Read the Ethical Dilemma on p. 157.

Characters: District sales manager; national sales manager.

Scene: *Location*—National sales manager's office. *Action*—Having completed the interview process, the district sales manager explains to the national sales manager who will be hired and why.

8. Search the Web for an online testing service. Print the home page of this site. Analyze the pros and cons of using this testing service as a selection tool in the hunt for sales talent. Would you recommend using this service? Why or why not? Attach a copy of the home page you printed to your analysis.

9. Find three advertisements for sales positions (one from a newspaper, one from a trade magazine, and one from the Internet). After examining each ad, list the job qualifications for the position being advertised. Then, develop a job description based on the ad's contents. Finally, provide your suggestions for improving each ad. Please attach your ads to your write-up.

10. Due to the high costs associated with turnover, it is critical that companies do a good job in the recruitment and selection process. The HR Chally Group has devised a method to help estimate the costs of turnover. Access the Chally Group's turnover cost calculator at http://chally.com/solution-suite/tools/. Given the following information, calculate the annual turnover cost for the salesforce:

- The company employs 100 salespeople.
- Annual turnover is 10 percent.
- Average annual compensation is $50,000.
- Average tax and benefit cost as a percent of salary is 20.
- Average number of candidates interviewed per opening is 15.
- Average number of candidates assessed per opening is five.

MAKING SALES MANAGEMENT DECISIONS

CASE 5.1: HELP WANTED!

Background

Fred Sutton, sales manager for Batops, a small regional manufacturer and marketer of various grades of batteries based out of Kansas City, has been experiencing a difficult time filling an open sales rep position that was vacated by a rep who quickly left the company due to his spouse's job transfer. As the weeks and months passed, Fred began to feel significant pressure and was becoming anxious about filling this position. Reps in his district were complaining that helping to service customers in the open territory was taking a toll on relationships with their existing customers. Consequently, Fred was concerned with the level of service current customers in the vacated territory were receiving. Moreover, no prospecting had been conducted in the territory since it was vacated, making it difficult to increase sales volume. To compound matters, Fred has been helping to cover the vacated territory and it was starting to detrimentally affect his ability to properly manage his salesforce. Fred realized that the longer the position was left vacant, the greater the chances for damaged customer relationships and the larger the lost sales opportunity. Fred's boss, Sean Lexington, was a tolerant individual, but his patience was wearing thin. Fred knew that if he did not fill the position soon, not only would his personal income be hurt, but he risked receiving a poor performance appraisal. Given that his last appraisal was less than stellar he wanted to avoid this at all costs.

Fred has been undertaking an extensive search to fill the vacant position. He placed a classified ad in the local newspaper, the *Kansas City Star*. Additionally, he contacted the career placement offices of local colleges and universities to see whether they had any leads on potential candidates. This attracted a limited pool of candidates, several of which were interviewed for the position. However, Fred was having a difficult time finding a proper fit. Some candidates were simply unqualified for the position. The qualified candidates seemed to lose interest upon learning more about what the position entailed.

The vacant position is demanding. It requires extensive overnight travel and some weekend travel. The job is also physically demanding, requiring lifting heavy product, assembling displays and spending grueling hours on the road driving from account to account. The salary is primarily commission-based, with the average salesperson earning about $45,000 his or her first year. Within five years, the average salesperson with the company makes about $75,000 a year. However, the earnings potential is great for star performers, with some earning $150,000 annually. Although there was money to be made as a salesperson, the company's size limited the opportunities for promotion. The company offers little formal training. Salespeople are provided a training manual and most of the training occurs on the job.

Salespeople at Batops are required to be very customer-oriented. In addition, they need good prospecting skills since the company is constantly trying to acquire new customers given its relatively high customer turnover rate. Furthermore, the person who fills this position must have outstanding planning and organizing skills, leadership skills, be persuasive, show initiative, and possess strong communication skills, including the ability to write, speak and listen.

Current Situation

Fred believes that his inability to fill the vacant position stems from not making the position look attractive enough to potential candidates. Thus, to increase the attractiveness of the position, he decided to rewrite his newspaper ad, neglecting to mention some of the responsibilities of the job. In particular, he downplayed the travel associated with the position and emphasized the high earnings potential. In doing so, he noticed an increase in job applications. Fred reasoned that if he could make the job sound attractive enough he could persuade someone to take it, who surely later would find it a rewarding opportunity.

What follows are some excerpts from a recent interview with Victor Shell, a candidate attracted by the new round of advertising. Victor recently graduated with a degree in marketing from a well-respected university in the area. Although he has limited sales experience, he otherwise appears to be qualified for the position.

Fred: Victor, you'll be responsible for selling various lines of batteries to retailers throughout the Midwest. You'll service existing accounts in your territory as well as prospect for new accounts. We participate in two trade shows a year, which should provide you with good opportunities to prospect.

Victor: Does the position entail overnight stay?

Fred: Yes, there's some overnight travel involved, depending upon where your customers are located. However, we pay for all your travel expenses, including your lodging and meals. I haven't heard many complaints from our salesforce regarding travel requirements.

Victor: Do you have a training program?

Fred: We have a fine training program. Our current salespeople have been through our training program and each one is performing quite well right now. Our training manual is particularly helpful for learning new product knowledge. Once you get into the field, you will find the product practically sells itself.

Victor: Are there ample opportunities for promotion?

Fred: We try to promote from within as much as possible. There is no reason why a hardworking ambitious person should not be able to get promoted in this company. In fact, I began my career as a delivery person for Batops, was promoted to sales, and from there moved into sales management.

Victor: I understand the job pays a salary plus commission.

Fred: That's correct. Our starting base salary is $25,000. However, with commission, you could earn as much as $150,000! With little effort you should have no problem making about $50,000–$60,000 your first year.

After interviewing two candidates for the position resulting from his new approach, Fred decided he would forgo any more interviews and make a job offer to Victor, given his apparent interest, and Fred's strong desire to quickly fill the position. Victor was very excited about the offer Fred extended to him. Two days ago he interviewed for a sales position at another company that also extended him an offer. Although this company was reputable, and the offer sounded like a solid opportunity, it did not sound as appealing as the opportunity at Batops. He is leaning toward accepting the offer from Batops, but he wants to talk it over with his wife. He likes the fact that there is not much overnight travel. He and his wife recently had a baby son and Victor does not want to be away from his new family too much. The fact that the company provides training also appeals to him. Although he took a sales class in college, he believes he can be more successful with additional company training. The other company Victor interviewed with offered a one-week training program, which he thought might not be enough. The compensation is particularly appealing. The offer from the other company included a higher base salary, but first-year earnings were expected to be only about $45,000 and there was no mention of earning $150,000. With student loans to pay off, Victor is interested in earning as much as he can as quickly as possible. Although Victor is eager to sell, he wants to land a job with a company that provides ample opportunity for promotion. Based on his conversation with Fred, Victor sensed such opportunity existed at Batops.

Questions

1. Assess Fred's interview with Victor.

2. How are the key concepts of socialization related to this situation? Explain.

3. What do you think might happen to Victor should he accept the position?

4. What responsibility does Victor have when interviewing for a position such as this?

5. How do you think that Fred could improve his recruitment and selection process?

Role Play

Situation: Read Case 5.1.

Characters: Fred Sutton, sales manager; Sean Lexington, Fred's boss; Victor Shell, sales candidate.

Scene 1:   *Location*—Sean's office. *Action*—Fred meets with Sean to discuss the actions that have been taken to date to fill the vacant sales position. Sean provides Fred with advice on how to improve his recruitment and selection strategy.

Scene 2:   *Location*—Fred's office. *Action*—Fred interviews Victor for the position. This time he is careful to avoid misrepresentation and takes actions to achieve realism and congruence.

CASE 5.2: STUCK IN THE PAST
Background

Steelrock Industries manufactures and markets industrial equipment throughout the United States. Last year, Steelrock did more than $2 billion in sales and appeared to be in an upward growth trend. The company has grown considerably since its inception in 1974. Founder and CEO Carman Pulte is proud of the progress the company has achieved over the years, despite considerable aggressive competition. He attributes much of Steelrock's success to his management team, most of whom have been with him since the company's founding.

David Winston had been vice president of sales and marketing at Steelrock since 1977. Two months ago, he retired and was replaced by Duane Rowland. Duane had been in product design and engineering at Steelrock since 1989. Well-educated, articulate, and likable, Rowland was believed to be the best candidate for the position.

Rowland, a very methodical individual, set as his first task an assessment of the marketing program.

One of the main things concerning him was the composition of the salesforce. In particular, he was concerned about two items. First, the salesforce was aging, with the average age being 51. Several salespeople were nearing retirement. Only a small percentage were in their twenties or thirties. Second, he noticed that the salesforce did not include any minorities or women. Rowland scheduled a meeting to discuss these issues with Titan's national sales manager, Tommy Ashton.

Ashton loves his job. He has been with Steelrock for nearly 25 years. He began as a salesperson and worked his way up to national sales manager. Surprisingly, many of his salespeople have been with the company for 20 years or more. Ashton takes pride in the accomplishments of his salesforce. He believes they have been instrumental in Steelrock's growth over the years.

Current Situation

At their scheduled meeting, Rowland explained to Ashton his ideas concerning the composition of the salesforce. The following are excerpts from their meeting:

Ashton: I realize we will have several salespeople soon retiring, but could you explain why it is necessary to hire women and minorities to replace these individuals?

Rowland: Many of the companies we sell equipment to are now being closely monitored and regulated by federal and state governments. Several companies in our industry have recently come under attack from the Equal Employment Opportunity Commission. The Commission is putting pressure on these companies to hire women and minorities. It is only a matter of time before they take aim at us. We need to get women and minorities into the salesforce so that they can eventually work their way up into management positions.

Ashton: I can't imagine a woman going into the field trying to sell a large piece of industrial equipment. How seriously do you think a woman will be taken in this business? Not very, I can assure you. Our customers want to speak to someone who really understands how this equipment operates.

Rowland: Women can learn to sell our equipment. Just because they may not operate it doesn't mean they can't understand how it works. As a matter of fact, a few months ago a woman was involved in selling us a piece of manufacturing equipment for our operations. She did an outstanding job.

Ashton: Maybe so. However, when we hire a replacement, we try to find the best person for the job. As a result, I believe we currently have some of the best salespeople in the business.

Rowland: Unfortunately, that person always seems to be a white male. There are plenty of intelligent and motivated women and minorities graduating from business schools today who are capable of performing the job. Regardless of governmental threats, it is still the right thing to do, and the profitable one. I would like to see us take a leadership role in this area in our industry and begin to make an effort to hire women and minorities.

Ashton was not convinced. He was very concerned that minorities, and women in particular, would not be positively accepted by buyers. The industrial equipment business is largely male-dominated. This, in turn, could have a negative impact on sales. Moreover, given that much of his salesforce was composed of "old-timers," he was concerned about how hiring these groups might affect salesforce morale.

Turnover in the salesforce was relatively low. Thus, specific hiring procedures were not well developed. Ashton decided he would recruit women and minorities to appease Rowland but would develop an entrance test that would be difficult for women and minorities to pass. This way he could actively recruit women and minorities but tell Rowland they did not qualify because they did not pass the entrance test. Ashton was only a few years from retirement and was unwilling to change his current practices at this juncture, particularly in light of the success his salesforce had experienced over the years.

Questions

1. Should Rowland be concerned about the present composition of the salesforce? Explain.

2. How do you evaluate Ashton's method for dealing with the salesforce composition issue?

3. What steps could be taken to effectively bring about a salesforce comprised of more women and minorities?

ROLE PLAY

Role Play

Situation: Read Case 5.2.

Characters: Duane Rowland, vice president of sales and marketing; Tommy Ashton, national sales manager.

Scene 1: *Location*—Rowland's office. *Action*—Role-play the meeting between Ashton and Rowland.

Scene 2: *Location*—Ashton's office. *Action*—Rowland gets a copy of the selection test, figures out what Ashton is up to, and decides to confront him.

OBJECTIVES

After completing this chapter, you should be able to

1. Understand the role of sales training in salesforce socialization.

2. Explain the importance of sales training and the sales manager's role in sales training.

3. Describe the sales training process as a series of six interrelated steps.

4. Discuss six methods for assessing sales training needs and identify typical sales training needs.

5. Name some typical objectives of sales training programs, and explain how setting objectives for sales training is beneficial to sales managers.

6. Identify the key issues in evaluating sales training alternatives.

7. Identify key ethical and legal issues in sales training.

SALES TRAINING AT MOHAWK INDUSTRIES: AN ONGOING PROCESS

Facing ever increasing competition, flooring manufacturer Mohawk Industries, Inc., decided to take its sales training to a new level. To improve the performance of its salespeople, Mohawk developed consistent and ongoing sales training around the areas of new hire orientation, customer relationship management, team collaboration/accountability and personal and professional development.

A six-month, three-phase salesperson new hire orientation was developed by Mohawk Sales Academy, which serves Mohawk's Commercial Carpet division. As part of the process, sales trainees take part in Mohawk's online university, where they learn product knowledge and selling skills by utilizing video, audio and published training tools. Since its inception in 2012, sales amongst newly hired salespeople have increased on average 10 percent per new hire in the first 18 months of entering their new position. Moreover, Mohawk developed new hire orientation for internal sales associates and external customer partners in its ceramic division. This training involves providing nine unique multicourse, position-specific training tracks with online courses ranging from company information, benefits, product knowledge, sales training and safety training, to legacy online information systems.

In terms of customer relationship management, Mohawk divisions use either an internally developed app called Navigator or the commercially available salesforce.com to help salespeople execute daily tasks. Providing sales reps with training in how to utilize these systems has resulted in a 72 percent increase in weekly transactions.

To develop team collaboration and accountability, Mohawk implemented Franklin Covey's "The Four Disciplines of Execution" to accompany its in-house training programs. Over 250 sales reps commit to acting upon behaviors that produce small outcomes that contribute to the team's sales goals.

Using measurement tools in an online scorecard to assess the results of this training, Mohawk found a 20 percent year-over-year increase in strategic account sales for its Commercial Carpet division.

Mohawk also aims to personally and professionally develop its salespeople. In this regard, it utilizes part of the Franklin Covey curriculum called "The 5 Choices of Extraordinary Productivity" for its Commercial Carpet division. Attendees of the program receive a productivity coach (certified graduates of the program) who assists them in goal setting, arranging their work activities and improving personal habits. The program has been considered effective as measured by feedback from attendees who report reductions in email, enhanced manager-subordinate relations, improved marriages and greater satisfaction with work/life balance. To support the development of its internal sales associates and retail customer sales associates, Mohawk offers courses in sales fundamentals, time and territory management, strategic account management, sales negotiation skills, business operations, product knowledge, technical product installation, product claim resolution training, and retail selling skills. The company delivers these courses both in the classroom and online using its learning management system.

Mohawk's management is committed to a culture of continual learning. By addressing the four key areas outlined through a structured, consistent, ongoing training process, Mohawk is able to execute its strategies to meet its business goals.

Source: Robert Bagley, "Sales Training," *Training* (November/December 2013): 70–71.

As the opening vignette illustrates, companies often believe that sales training is necessary to successfully implement their strategy. Mohawk Industries realizes the important role its salespeople play in the success of the company and is willing to invest considerable time and money in developing them. Training can be used to achieve a number of objectives and fulfill various needs. At Mohawk, sales training is designed to orient new sales hires, teach customer relationship management skills, improve team collaboration/accountability, and enhance personal and professional development.

Today's salespeople must be prepared to meet the demands of value-conscious customers. Salespeople must do their part by providing solutions to problems, acting as strategic advisors, adding value, and meeting service requirements expected to satisfy customer needs. Proper training can prepare salespeople to meet these challenges.

In this chapter several training issues and methods are discussed. First, the role of sales training in salesforce socialization is examined. Then the importance of sales training is considered and management of the sales training process is discussed.

ROLE OF SALES TRAINING IN SALESFORCE SOCIALIZATION

Recall from Chapter 5 that salesforce *socialization* refers to the process by which salespeople acquire the knowledge, skills, and values essential to perform their jobs. Training plays a key role in this process. Newly hired salespeople usually receive a company orientation designed to familiarize them with company history, policies, facilities, procedures, and key people with whom salespeople interact. Some firms go well beyond a perfunctory company orientation in an effort to enhance salesforce socialization. By referring to Figure 5.1 in Chapter 5, you can see how sales training can affect salesforce socialization. During initial sales training, it is hoped that each salesforce member will experience a positive initiation to task—the degree to which a sales trainee feels competent and accepted as a working partner—and satisfactory role definition—an understanding of what tasks are to be performed, what the priorities of the tasks are, and how time should be allocated among the tasks.[1]

The need for socialization as part of the training process is supported by expected indirect linkages between socialization and beneficial job outcomes. As suggested in Figure 5.1, trainees who have been properly recruited and trained tend to be more confident on the job and have fewer problems with job conflicts, leading to higher job satisfaction, involvement, commitment, and performance.

The positive relationships between salespeople's job-related attitudes and perceptions and their commitment to their companies have been supported in empirical studies. For example, a study of salespeople in the food industry found that "among approaches within a company's control, programs aimed at minimizing new salespeople's role ambiguity and improving their satisfaction are most likely to be most effective in building commitment to the company."[2] Another study of manufacturers' salespeople found a positive relationship between job satisfaction and salespeople's commitment to the organization.[3] In addition, a study of industrial salespeople found that when salespeople believe the company is taking certain actions to support the salesforce and reduce the difficulties associated with a sales position, they are more committed to and satisfied with the job.[4] These studies reinforce the importance of sales managers taking an active role in socializing their salespeople to maximize overall salesforce productivity.

Newly hired salespeople should be extremely interested in learning about their jobs, peers, and supervisors. A basic orientation may be insufficient to provide all the information they desire, so more extensive socialization may be indicated. At Federated Insurance, newly hired Marketing Representatives participate in a two-week seminar that introduces them to the company's products, the corporate mission, the Federated business plan, functions and departments within the company, and many of the support people with whom they will work, as the first step in their 6–12-month training program.[5]

The need for salesforce socialization is especially likely to extend past the initial training period. This is particularly true if salesforce members have limited personal contact with peers, managers, and other company personnel.

SALES TRAINING AS A CRUCIAL INVESTMENT

A comprehensive review of sales management research concludes that whom one recruits is important, but it is probably not as important in determining salesforce performance as what sales managers do with the recruits—and to the recruits—after they have been hired.[6] Perhaps that is why 82 percent of top performing sales organizations mandate formal sales training.[7]

Sales training is a crucial investment necessary for maintaining and/or improving the performance of the salesforce. Training can help to improve the effectiveness of salespeople, which is critical. A survey of 70,000 business decision makers found that 39 percent of purchasing decisions depend on the effectiveness of the sales rep, a larger portion than any other aspect, including price, product or service.[8] Not only is training important in developing effective salespeople, but also in keeping them. One comprehensive study of salesforce effectiveness found inadequate sales training to be a driving force in turnover.[9] Online retailer Furniture@Work, for instance, credits sales training with reducing its attrition rate by nearly 90 percent in just 12 months after it implemented sales training.[10]

Most organizations need sales training of some type, perhaps because of inadequacies of current training programs and/or because new salespeople have joined the organization. Thus, an ongoing need exists to conduct sales training to improve salesforce performance. It should be stressed that the need for sales training is continual, if for no other reason than that the sales environment is constantly changing.

Companies view training as an important means for protecting their investments in their salesforces. U.S. companies spend approximately $15 billion per year on sales training, averaging about $2,000 per year for each salesperson.[11] The time and money spent on sales training varies, however, by company and industry. A survey of sales practices at 1,500 organizations found the amount spent on training, per sales rep, varied from none, at slightly over 2 percent of the respondents, to more than $7,500 at 7.5 percent respondents, with most (24.7 percent) reporting expenditures of between $1,501 to $2,500.[12]

As research shows, this training generally pays off in terms of improvement in salesforce productivity.[13] A survey of sales executives from over 1,500 companies found that sales training, when properly applied, produces a positive return on investment.[14] One survey of over 2,500 firms found that companies that invest more in training have a 45 percent higher median total stockholder return the following year than companies that spend the market average and an 86 percent higher return than those spending less than average. The survey also found that companies offering ongoing sales training are 10 times more likely to create peak-performing salespeople than companies that do not.[15] Furthermore, some research indicates a positive relationship between training expenditures and a firm's share price.[16] It is no wonder that the top 100 training companies consider training a competitive advantage to their business.[17]

One aspect of the investment in sales training is the amount of time required of the sales manager. Usually, sales managers are involved not only in the "big picture" of planning, but also in the time-consuming details of implementing training, such as the following:

- Arranging for salespeople to work with key personnel in various departments in the firm to familiarize them with the functions of those departments
- Selecting literature, sales aids, software, and materials for study
- Enrolling salespeople in professional workshops or training programs
- Accompanying salespeople in the field to critique their sales behavior and reinforce other training
- Conducting periodic training meetings and professional training conferences

Sales training is indeed expensive, and sales managers should take special care to see that time and money are wisely spent. With these thoughts in mind, let's examine a model for the judicious analysis, planning, and implementation of a sales training program.

MANAGING THE SALES TRAINING PROCESS

The sales training process is depicted as six interrelated steps in Figure 6.1: assess training needs, set training objectives, evaluate training alternatives, design the sales training program, perform sales training, and conduct follow-up and evaluation.

Assess Training Needs

The purpose of sales training needs assessment is to compare the specific performance-related skills, attitudes, perceptions, and behaviors required for salesforce success with the state of readiness of the salesforce. Such an assessment usually reveals a need for changing or reinforcing one or more determinants of salesforce performance. When assessing training needs, it is important to consider the knowledge, skills and abilities salespeople must have to fulfill both organizational level and salesforce level goals and objectives.[18]

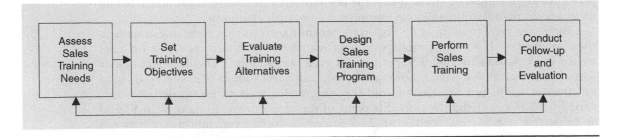

FIGURE 6.1   Sales Training Process

| Assess Sales Training Needs | → | Set Training Objectives | → | Evaluate Training Alternatives | → | Design Sales Training Program | → | Perform Sales Training | → | Conduct Follow-up and Evaluation |

The sales training process is performed in six steps, beginning with an assessment of training needs. The follow-up and evaluation step provides feedback that may alter future sales training.

All too often, the need for sales training becomes apparent only after a decline in salesforce performance is revealed by decreasing sales volume, rising expenses, or perhaps low morale. Sales training for correcting such problems is sometimes necessary, but the preferred role of sales training is to prevent problems and improve salesforce productivity on a proactive, not reactive, basis.

Needs assessment requires that sales managers consider the training appropriate for both *sales trainees* and experienced salespeople. A sales trainee is an entry-level salesperson who is learning the company's products, services, and policies in preparation for a regular sales assignment. Entry-level salespeople may need basic training in sales techniques, whereas experienced salespeople could benefit from training in advanced sales techniques. For example, Avanade, a global IT consulting company, divided its company's salesforce into different skill families and accompanying job roles. The company provides a unique learning roadmap for each skill family that identifies the training activities for each level of career progression.[19] Given that top salespeople are often much more productive than many in the salesforce, it is important to continue to invest training dollars in them. In addition, the training needs of selling teams must be considered.

Methods of Needs Assessment

Proactive approaches to determining sales training needs include a salesforce audit, performance testing, observation, a salesforce survey, a customer survey, and a job analysis. Needs assessment can be conducted in-house or by companies such as Wilson Learning Corporation (http://wilsonlearning.com).

Salesforce Audit

A salesforce audit is "a systematic, diagnostic, prescriptive tool which can be employed on a periodic basis to identify and address sales department problems and to prevent or reduce the impact of future problems."[20] The salesforce audit (discussed fully in Chapter 9) includes an appraisal of all salesforce activities and the environment in which the salesforce operates. In the sales training area, the audit examines such questions as these:

- Is the training program adequate in light of objectives and resources?
- Does the training program need revision?
- Is an ongoing training program available for senior salespeople?
- Does the training program positively contribute to the socialization of sales trainees?

To be effective, a salesforce audit should be conducted annually. More frequent audits may be warranted in some situations, but the comprehensive nature of an audit requires a considerable time and money investment. As a result, other periodic assessments of sales training are suggested.

Performance Testing

Some firms use performance testing to help determine training needs. This method specifies the evaluation of particular tasks or skills of the salesforce. For example, salespeople may be given periodic examinations on product knowledge to check retention rates and uncover areas for retraining. Salespeople may be asked to exhibit particular sales techniques, such as demonstrating the product or using the telephone to set up sales appointments while the sales trainer evaluates their performance. Sales managers may even want to administer a scientifically developed measure of selling skills; this measure assesses salespeople's interpersonal, salesmanship, and technical skills.[21]

Observation

First-level sales managers spend a considerable amount of time in the field working with salespeople. They also may have direct responsibility for some accounts, acting as a salesperson or as a member of a sales team. Through observation of these field selling activities, sales managers often identify the need for particular sales training. In some instances, the training need is addressed instantaneously by critiquing the salesperson's performance after the sales call has been completed. In other situations, frequent observation of particularly deficient or outstanding sales behavior may suggest future training topics.

Salesforce Survey

The salesforce may be surveyed in an attempt to isolate sales training needs. The sales-force survey may be completed as an independent activity or combined with other sales management activities, such as field visits or even included as part of the routine salesforce reporting procedures. The weekly reports submitted by many salespeople to their sales managers often have sections dealing with problems to be solved and areas in which managerial assistance is requested. For example, a faltering new product introduction may signal the need for more product training, additional sales technique sharpening, or perhaps training needs specific to an individual salesperson.

By surveying the salesforce, the task of assessing training needs may become more complex than if sales management alone determines training needs. To ignore the salesforce in this step of the training process, however, could be a serious sin of omission. For example, when implementing a CRM strategy, a company might find resistance from its salesforce. By surveying the salesforce, the company could determine its salespeople's computer capabilities and deficiencies, and design a training program that fits its salespeople's needs. If sales managers and their salespeople should disagree on training needs, it is far better to discover this disagreement and resolve it before designing and delivering specific sales training programs.

Customer Survey

Intended to define customer expectations, a customer survey helps determine how competitive the salesforce is compared with other salesforces in the industry. If personal selling is prominent in the firm's marketing strategy, some sort of customer survey to help determine sales training needs is highly recommended. For example, upon surveying its customers, Paxar, a supplier of labels to retailers and apparel manufacturers, learned that its salespeople were miscommunicating with customers and were failing to understand their market needs.[22] Online services such as QuestionPro.com (http://questionpro.com) make it easy to design, deliver, and analyze Web-based customer surveys.

Job Analysis

The job analysis, defined in Chapter 5, is an investigation of the task, duties, and responsibilities of the sales job. In a well-run sales organization, a job analysis will be part of the recruitment and selection process and then will continue to be used in sales training and other managerial functions. Because the job analysis defines expected behavior for salespeople, it is a logical tool to be used in assessing training needs. Since sales jobs may vary within the same salesforce, job analyses may also help in determining individualized sales training needs or the needs of different groups of salespeople.

Typical Sales Training Needs

As the preceding discussion implies, the need for sales training varies over time and across organizations. However, the need for salesforce training on certain topics is widespread. A discussion of some of the more popular sales training topics follows.

Sales Techniques

There is a universal, ongoing need for training on "how to sell." Research finds that one of the highest priorities in sales training is teaching salespeople sales techniques.[23] Common mistakes salespeople make in this area include the following:

- Ineffective listening and questioning
- Failure to build rapport and trust
- Poor job of prospecting for new accounts
- Lack of preplanning of sales calls
- Reluctance to make cold calls (without an appointment)
- Lack of sales strategies for different accounts
- Failure to match call frequency with account potential
- Spending too much time with long-standing customers

- Overcontrolling the sales call
- Failure to respond to customers' needs with related benefits
- Giving benefits before clarifying customers' needs
- Ineffective handling of negative attitudes
- Failure to effectively confirm the sale

This rather lengthy list of common shortcomings is remarkable in that proper training could erase these problems entirely. In fact, most formal sales training programs spend considerable time on sales techniques. Some research indicates that nearly one-third of annual sales training hours are devoted to teaching selling skills.[24]

As mentioned previously, the basic nature of sales techniques training is changing, and more emphasis is being placed on developing trusting, enduring relationships with customers. Salespeople are receiving more training on listening and questioning skills so that they may be more effective in learning the customer's needs. Limited research supports the idea that effective listening skills are positively associated with sales performance and work satisfaction.[25] Furthermore, high-pressure sales techniques are declining in popularity and are being replaced with sales techniques based on need satisfaction, problem solving, and partnership-forming with the customer's best interests as the focus. Companies such as Motorola and Owens Corning teach their salespeople how to provide solutions to customer problems to facilitate the development of lasting relationships with customers.[26] IBM's consultative training program teaches salespeople to work with customers as consultants to jointly solve problems and build close relationships.[27] Research by the HR Chally Group highlights relationship-building characteristics at which salespeople must excel to best serve business-to-business customers and achieve sales excellence. They spent 14 years interviewing 80,000 business customers and collecting data on 300,000 sales professionals representing 7,200 salesforces from over 15 major industries. They found that customers want salespeople who (1) personally manage their desired results; (2) understand their business; (3) act as a customer advocate; (4) are knowledgeable of product applications; (5) are easily accessible; (6) solve their problems; and (7) provide innovative responses to their needs.[28] Achieving the competencies outlined in Exhibit 6.1[29] should enable salespeople to meet customer desires, while simultaneously building and strengthening customer relationships.

Product Knowledge

Salespeople must have thorough product knowledge, including its benefits, applications, competitive strengths, and limitations. Product knowledge may need updating in the event of new product development, product modification, product deletions, or the development of new applications for the product. For example, in an effort to constantly provide its distributors with the most current product knowledge available, Blue Hawk, a purchasing cooperative whose members distribute a range of HVACR-related products, such as heating, air conditioning and refrigeration units, and tools for construction markets, provides numerous online product training courses, with new ones added weekly. Blue Hawk credits increased training in product knowledge with improving overall sales results.[30]

Generally speaking, product knowledge is one of the most commonly covered topics in sales training programs. As expected, the more complex the product or service, the higher the likelihood that detailed knowledge about the offering will be stressed in the training program.

Although it is an essential requirement, adequate product knowledge will not necessarily lead to sales success. Studies have shown that product knowledge levels of high-performing salespeople are not significantly different from those of moderate performers.[31] Having product knowledge is not enough—the salesperson must know the customer and have the necessary sales skills to apply the knowledge of the product to the customer's situation. To learn the importance of training in both product and customer knowledge at Ironwear, see "Sales Management in the 21st Century: Tactical Sales Training at Ironwear."

EXHIBIT 6.1 Competencies of Successful Salespeople

Below each competency are questions that can be used to assess it. Ask salespeople to respond to each question using the following scale to indicate how often they use each behavior: 1—never, or not at all; 2—seldom or to a small extent; 3—sometimes or to a moderate extent; 4—usually or to a great extent; 5—almost always. When finished, calculate the total score for each competency by adding the responses to each question for a particular competency and then adding each competency score together to get a total score. The average score is 63. A score above average indicates the salesperson is using the competencies better than the typical business-to-business salesperson, whereas a score below average may signal a need for improvement.

Competency 1
Aligning customer/supplier strategic objectives by identifying new opportunities and applications that add value to the customer organization and enhance the value of the relationship with my organization.

1. I gather information to understand customers' business strategies and views of market opportunities.
2. I stay up-to-date with new developments and innovations in customers' markets.
3. I keep current with emerging trends and initiatives of customers' competitors.

Competency 2
Listening beyond product needs by identifying business process improvement potential and opportunities to add value to my organization and for our customers.

4. I keep the customer regularly updated with information and changes that might be important.
5. I suggest ways I can bring added value to our customers.
6. I help customers think differently about their future needs.

Competency 3
Understanding the financial impact of decisions on the customer's organization and on my organization by quantifying and communicating the value of the relationship.

7. I look actively for ways to contribute to the customer's profitability.
8. I search actively for more cost-effective ways to serve customers.
9. I focus on the financial consequences of approaches to meeting customer needs.

Competency 4
Orchestrating organizational resources by identifying key contributors; communicating relevant information; and building collaborative, customer-focused relationships.

10. I communicate customer needs, suggestions, and concerns to appropriate resources in my organization.
11. I work cooperatively with people in other parts of the customer organization who can be useful sources of ongoing information, resources, and support.
12. I ensure that my product, sales, and service units work together to deliver value.

Competency 5
Consultative problem solving to create new solutions, customized products and services, and paradigm changes while being willing and able to work outside the norm when necessary.

13. I anticipate possible problems and invite discussion about how they can be overcome.
14. I determine the cause of a problem and identify constraints before recommending a solution.
15. I propose innovative solutions that go beyond the immediate application of the product or service.

(continued)

Competencies of Successful Salespeople—*continued*   EXHIBIT 6.1

Competency 6
Establishing a vision of a committed customer/supplier relationship by identifying value-adding products, processes, and services.

16. I create a relationship that supports the goals and values of both organizations.
17. I develop relationships that recognize the needs of all contributing functions in both organizations.
18. I communicate objectives for the relationship that are achievable and challenge the creativity of both organizations.

Competency 7
Engaging in self-appraisal and continuous learning by securing feedback from customers, colleagues, and managers.

19. I demonstrate an understanding of what is working, what is not working, and how I can do things differently.
20. I stay up-to-date in my field of expertise.
21. I ask for and welcome feedback to assess my performance and the degree to which I am meeting expectations.

Customer Knowledge

Sales training may include information relating to customers' needs, buying motives, buying procedures, and personalities (i.e., customer knowledge). Faced with situational and individual differences among customers, some firms use classification methods to categorize buyers according to personality and the buying situation. An example of different types of buyers and suggested sales training topics is presented in Exhibit 6.2.[32]

As minority populations increase and companies expand their global selling efforts, training programs must address multicultural differences and business protocol in subcultures and foreign countries. For instance, female Hispanic business owners generally take longer to make decisions.[33] Such information can be useful in determining the selling cycle. Gift-giving, for example, is a sensitive area internationally because well-intentioned expressions of goodwill can backfire and instead become personal insults to a prospective customer. It is important that salespeople are trained in intercultural communication to improve their chances of developing international buyer-seller relationships.[34] Some insights for understanding foreign customers are provided in Exhibit 6.3.[35]

Competitive Knowledge

Salespeople must know competitive offerings in terms of strengths and weaknesses to plan sales strategy and sales presentations effectively and to be able to respond effectively to customer questions and objections. This area is extremely important for salespeople who are new to the industry because the competitor's salespeople may have years of experience and be quite knowledgeable. Furthermore, customers may exploit a salesperson's lack of competitive knowledge to negotiate terms of sale that may be costly to the selling firm. For example, salespeople who are not familiar with a competitor's price structure may unnecessarily reduce their own price to make a sale, thereby sacrificing more revenue and profits than they should have. Besides researching the competition, salespeople should be trained to ask customers probing questions about the competition. Exhibit 6.4[36] provides 12 areas of inquiry for determining a competitive situation. Salespeople can be trained to use these as a basis for developing questions to ask customers in order to ascertain information about competitors.

SALES MANAGEMENT IN THE 21ST CENTURY

Tactical Sales Training at Ironwear

Troy Secchio, Director of Corporate Strategy and Account Acquisition with Ironwear, comments on product and customer tactical sales training:

At Ironwear, we take our brand image seriously, thus we go through an extensive sales tactical training process in order to uphold a clear and concise message as to our worth to the marketplace. Ironwear is a manufacturer of personal protective gear that sells through distribution, which in turn sells to the end user. The end user is defined as industrial manufacturers who produce products in such verticals as food, oil and gas, construction, and automotive, just to name a few.

The key focus of our tactical sales training is based on the impact our products bring to the end users' application. An example of impacting an end user's application would be manufacturing a cut-and-slip-resistant glove specific to workers handling sharp-edged cans in a food processing plant. This focus goes along with our value statement: "we do not simply manufacture product; we produce products that impact specific plant application." In order to truly impact an end user's application, we first must structure sales into what we term verticals, meaning Ironwear has a representative or group of representatives who focus on a specific industry (i.e., food, oil and gas, construction, automotive. . .).

This investment of learning becomes critical, where representatives are being trained on all aspects of our product within their focused vertical. The representative is trained on all value points of product and engages in a product excellence process. Representatives first learn why a product was developed and how it is positioned relative to competitive brands. After a series of training modules within this process, the representative begins to study their focused vertical, which includes studying industry publications, riding with seasoned representatives to see the product working at plant locations, and afterward, sitting down with product management to discuss and reengage product to end user application. Once completed, the representative shifts to a product excellence process in which he or she keys in on specific product attributes and addresses detailed improvements needed to enhance value within their focused vertical. Not only does this help enhance the sales representative's learning curve and command for end user application, but it also provides valuable product improvements toward impacting Ironwear's marketplace image.

Tactical sales training is an intense-time-consuming investment. Depending upon the skill set of the employee, the initial baseline learning process can take up to six to nine months. Ironwear's learning and discovery investment is a continual training process due to the dynamic changes that occur within the industrial markets. Simply put, it is critical to train and manage our salesforce, along with any action put forth by the company, in order to protect and enhance Ironwear's brand image in the marketplace.

Time and Territory Management

The quest for an optimal balance between salesforce output and salesforce expenditures is a perennial objective for most sales managers. Therefore, training in time and territory management (TTM) is often included in formal sales training programs. Essentially, the purpose of TTM training is to teach salespeople how to use time and efforts for maximum work efficiency.

TTM training is important for all sales organizations but especially for those in declining, stagnant, or highly competitive industries. In such situations, salespeople are often overworked, and there comes a point when working harder to improve results is not realistic. Such circumstances call for "working smarter, not harder."[37]

Efforts to make more efficient use of time and increase salesperson productivity have been bolstered by salesforce automation. Salesforce automation (e.g., cellular phones, tablets, faxes, laptops, databases, the Internet, personal digital assistants, and electronic data interchange) can boost productivity. To do so, salespeople often need training in computer and software applications. As part of this training, attention should be given to improving salespeople's use of social media technologies (e.g., Facebook, Twitter,

Sales Training for Different Types of Buyers EXHIBIT 6.2	
Kind of Buyer	**Sales Training Topic**
1. Hard Bargainer (a difficult person to deal with)	1. Teach psychologically oriented sales strategies (e.g., transactional analysis). 2. Teach sales *negotiation* strategies (e.g., the use of different bases of power). 3. Teach listening skills and the benefits of listening to the prospect. 4. Emphasize how to handle objections. 5. Emphasize *competitive* product knowledge.
2. Sales Job Facilitator (attempts to make the sales transaction go smoothly)	1. Teach importance of a *quid pro quo.* 2. Communicate advantages of having a satisfied customer base. 3. Show how customers can assist salespeople (e.g., by pooling orders, providing leads).
3. Straight Shooter (behaves with integrity and propriety)	1. Teach importance of selling the "substance" of the product offering and not just the "sizzle." 2. Teach straightforward techniques for handling objections (e.g., a direct denial approach).
4. Socializer (enjoys personal interaction with salespeople)	1. Communicate company policy information about giving gifts and entertaining and socializing with customers. 2. Discuss ethical and legal implications of transacting business. 3. Emphasize importance of salespeople maintaining an appropriate balance between socializing with customers and performing job responsibilities.
5. Persuader (attempts to "market" his or her company)	1. Communicate importance of qualifying prospects. 2. Teach techniques for qualifying customers.
6. Considerate (shows compassion for salesperson)	1. Communicate importance of obtaining market information from customers. 2. Teach importance of a *quid pro quo.*

LinkedIn), as these methods of communicating are changing the means by which salespeople interact with prospects and customers. Furthermore, as electronic data interchange (a method for transferring information electronically between selling firms and buying firms) and CRM technology become more prominent, the need for computer literacy in the salesforce will increase. Studies indicate that proper training in salesforce automation is necessary for it to be effective.[38]

Perhaps time and territory management could be improved by training salespeople in self-management. Self-management refers to an individual's effort to control certain aspects of his or her decision making and behavior, and as such employs strategies that assist individuals in structuring the environment and facilitating behaviors necessary to achieve performance standards. This might include improving salespeople's (1) self-assessment, whereby the salesperson identifies areas that need improvement; (2) self-direction, whereby strategies for achieving desired change are identified by the salesperson; (3) self-monitoring, whereby the salesperson assesses advancement toward completing desired changes; and (4) self-reinforcement, whereby the salesperson develops strategies for reinforcement or punishment to sustain the desired changes.[39] Research suggests that salespeople trained in self-management increase both short- and long-term performance.[40]

EXHIBIT 6.3 Understanding Foreign Customers

Many selling skills that are successful in the United States will also work in other countries. However, one must be aware of cultural variations that can make the difference between closing a deal and losing a customer. Here is some advice for conducting business in certain countries around the world.

Arab Countries:

- Don't use your left hand to hold, offer, or receive materials because Arabs use their left hands to touch toilet paper. If you must use your left hand to write, apologize for doing so.
- When first meeting someone, avoid giving a gift as it might be interpreted as a bribe.

Belgium:

- Decision makers vary. In Dutch-speaking regions, group decisions are common, while in French-speaking regions executives at the highest level make the final decision.

China:

- Don't refuse tea during a business discussion. Always drink it, even if you're offered a dozen cups a day.
- Printed materials presented to Chinese business leaders should be in black and white because colors have great significance for the Chinese.
- Never begin to eat or drink before your host does in China.
- Deliver presentations in a visually neutral way.
- Present gifts privately and do not make a big issue of it.
- Expect to continue negotiations after the deal to iron out any problems that arise.

Colombia:

- Build a personal relationship and friendship with business counterparts.
- Changing salespeople in midstream can put an end to negotiations.

France:

- Don't schedule a breakfast meeting—the French tend not to meet until after 10 a.m.

Germany:

- Don't address a business associate by his or her first name, even if you have known each other for years. Always wait for an invitation to do so.
- Breakfast meetings are unheard of here also.
- Provide detail and lots of supporting documentation during presentations.
- Avoid providing prospects with flashy brochures. Keep them detailed, but avoid exaggeration.

India:

- Keep a flexible schedule given that Indians are less time sensitive and thus less concerned with punctuality.
- As a hierarchical society, decisions are only made by the highest-level boss.

Latin America:

- People here don't take the clock too seriously—scheduling more than two appointments in the same day can prove disastrous.
- People like to stand close to one another and touch during conversation.
- Give gifts after establishing a relationship and during social encounters, rather than in the course of business.

Japan:

- Don't bring up business on the golf course—always wait for your host to take the initiative.
- Don't cross your legs in Japan—showing the bottom of the foot is insulting.

(continued)

Understanding Foreign Customers—*continued*   EXHIBIT 6.3

- Deliver presentations in a visually neutral way.
- Avoid giving gifts wrapped with bows (considered unattractive) and ribbons (colors have different meanings). Do not open a gift in front of a Japanese counterpart or expect them to do so.

Mexico:

- Don't send a bouquet of red or yellow flowers as a gift—Mexicans associate those colors with evil spirits and death. Instead, send a box of premium chocolates.
- It is best to meet during breakfast or lunch.
- It is important to develop relationships with business counterparts, as these are more valuable than business experience.

Peru:

- Peruvians relate to people rather than corporations. Establish personal rapport.
- Avoid changing salespeople in the middle of negotiations.

Russia:

- Be warm and approachable during the first meeting, which is considered to be a formality.

Scotland:

- People tend to be private and soft-spoken.
- It takes time to build relationships.

South Korea:

- Since status is valued, salespeople should not meet with higher-level executives.
- One's title should be clearly indicated on his or her business card.

Thailand:

- Avoid confrontation, since the Thai culture emphasizes harmony.

Miscellaneous:

- The thumbs-up gesture is considered offensive in the Middle East, rude in Australia, and a sign of "OK" in France.
- It is rude to cross your arms while facing someone in Turkey.
- In the Middle East don't ask, "How's the family?"—it is considered too personal. Also, don't show the bottom of your foot.

Twelve Areas of Inquiry for Determining a Competitive Situation   EXHIBIT 6.4

1. With whom has the customer met?
2. What has the competitor sold to this customer to date?
3. What value did the competitor provide?
4. What does the customer perceive as the competitor's strengths and weaknesses?
5. What level of satisfaction does the competitor provide?
6. What is the customer's perception of the quality of the competitor's deliverables?
7. What customer decision makers or influences sponsored the competitor?
8. Who are the competitor's allies?
9. Who opposes the competitor?
10. How does the customer feel about the relationship?
11. How does the customer feel about the competitor's sales rep?
12. How do we compare? (Note: This is the most important question.)

Set Training Objectives

Having assessed the needs for sales training, the sales manager moves to the next step in the sales training process shown in Figure 6.1: setting specific, measurable, and obtainable sales training objectives. Because training needs vary from one sales organization to the next, so do the objectives. In general, however, one or more of the following are included.

1. Increase sales or profits.

2. Create positive attitudes and improve salesforce morale.

3. Assist in salesforce socialization.

4. Reduce role conflict and ambiguity.

5. Introduce new products, markets, and promotional programs.

6. Develop salespeople for future management positions.

7. Ensure awareness of ethical and legal responsibilities.

8. Teach administrative procedures (e.g., expense accounts, call reports).

9. Ensure competence in the use of sales and sales support tools, such as CRM technology.

10. Minimize salesforce turnover rate.

11. Prepare new salespeople for assignment to a sales territory.

12. Improve teamwork and cooperative efforts.

These objectives are interrelated. For example, if salespeople gain competence in the use of a new sales tool, sales and profit may improve, salesforce morale may be positively affected, and other beneficial outcomes may occur. By setting objectives for sales training, the manager avoids the wasteful practice of training simply for training's sake. Furthermore, objectives force the sales manager to define the reasonable expectations of sales training rather than to view training as a quick-fix panacea for all the problems faced by the salesforce. By defining expectations up-front, it is possible to later determine if objectives have been met and more reasonably calculate a return on training investment.[41] As seen in "Sales Management in the 21st Century: Fulfilling Company Objectives Through Strategic Training at Ironwear," companies use different types of training to fulfill company objectives. Additional benefits of setting objectives for sales training are as follows:

• Written objectives become a good communications vehicle to inform the salesforce and other interested parties about upcoming training.

• Top management is responsive to well-written, specific objectives and may be more willing to provide budget support for the training.

• Specific training objectives provide a standard for measuring the effectiveness of training.

• By setting objectives, the sales manager finds it easier to prioritize various training needs, and the proper sequence of training becomes more apparent.

Evaluate Training Alternatives

In the third step of the sales training process, the sales manager considers various approaches for accomplishing the objectives of training. Certainly, many more alternatives exist today than in the past, thanks to such technologies as computer-assisted instruction, video conferencing, and the Internet. The number of sales training professionals for hire also seems to be increasing, or perhaps such trainers are just doing a better job of promoting their services. Even a casual examination of a typical shopping

SALES MANAGEMENT IN THE 21ST CENTURY

Fulfilling Company Objectives Through Strategic Training at Ironwear

Troy Secchio, Director of Corporate Strategy and Account Acquisition with Ironwear, comments on strategic training at Ironwear designed to meet an important ongoing company objective:

In today's complex business environment and with the chatter of all the various types of "real time" electronic communication, staying on point with what a company represents to the marketplace is more critical than ever before. An important objective at Ironwear is to ensure that every one of the company's marketplace touch points are strategically aligned to support and reinforce the company's value proposition. Marketplace touch points include any action taken by a company that reaches, and more importantly impacts, outside the organization. These touch points include, but are not limited to, the outside sales force, inside sales, marketing, customer service, social media, warehouse, shipping, and all administration functions.

Marketplace touch points have many influencers that can misguide the company's message such as individuals from different backgrounds, personalities, age groups, and departmental functions with locations positioned throughout the country and abroad. As you can see, strategic training is a serious task to passionately embrace. In order to rein in all the chaos, companies must put forth strategic training, keeping in mind every marketplace touch point, to ensure the company's message is on point each and every time.

For Ironwear, in order to stay consistent with its brand image, strategic training is an important process. Strategic training is a cross-functional overview of how each department and action contributes to its brand image and value proposition. Tactical training is specific to the role within each department and reinforces the department's functions; this is done in order to align with Ironwear's brand image. Although strategic training is above and beyond tactical training, it is important that both training objectives blend together. Strategic training gives relevance to departmental tactical training.

mall bookstore will reveal a number of titles related to building sales skills, along with audio- and video recordings on the subject. Some associations are even offering training courses to help improve the skills of salespeople in their industry.

Critiquing all these alternatives is a monumental job, so it is recommended that fairly stringent criteria, including cost, location of the training, flexibility of prepackaged materials, opportunity for reinforcement training, and time required to implement an alternative be established for preliminary screening.

The evaluation of alternatives for training inevitably leads to three key questions. First, who will conduct the training? An answer to this question will require the consideration of internal (within the company) and external (outside the company) trainers. The second question deals with location for the training. Sales training may be conducted in the field, in the office, at a central training location, virtually, at hotels and conference centers, or at other locations. The third question is which method (or methods) and media are best suited for conducting the training?

Selecting Sales Trainers

In general, companies rely most heavily on their own personnel to conduct sales training. In this endeavor, the sales manager is the most important sales trainer. In larger companies, a full-time sales trainer is often available. Senior salespeople may also be involved as trainers. For example, Hitachi Data Systems has salespeople from each of its global locations deliver local training. Hitachi claims their salespeople love to learn through examples and war stories and tend to trust fellow salespeople more than a trainer who is not a salesperson.[42]

Why are internal sources used so often in sales training? First, and perhaps most important, company personnel are intimately aware of job requirements and can communicate in very specific terms to the sales trainee. However, outside consultants may be only superficially informed about a specific sales job and often offer generic sales training packages. Second, sales managers are the logical source for training to be conducted in the field, where valuable learning can occur with each sales call. It is extremely difficult to turn field training over to external trainers. Finally, using internal trainers simplifies control and coordination tasks. It is easier to control the content of the program, coordinate training for maximum impact, and provide continuity for the program when it is the sales manager who does the training or who designates other company personnel to do the training.

At some point, a sales manager's effectiveness may be improved by using external trainers. Internal resources, including time, expertise, facilities, and personnel, may be insufficient to accomplish the objectives of the sales training program. Also, outside trainers might be looked to for new ideas and methods. Large training firms such as, Sales Performance International (www.SPISales.com), Carew International (www. carew.com) and The Brooks Group (www.brooksgroup.com) often customize their generic programs for use within specific companies. Others, such as Wilson Learning Corporation, deliver training programs via the Web that include interactive stories, tutorials, interactive questions, online exercises, role plays, games, summaries, and post-tests. Exhibit 6.5[43] outlines attributes to consider when shopping for an outside training program.

Selecting Sales Training Locations

Most sales training is conducted in home, regional, or field offices of the sales organization. Manufacturing plants are also popular training sites, and some firms use non-company sites such as hotels or conference centers to conduct training. Central training facilities are another possibility, used by companies such as Federated Insurance, Edward Jones, and General Electric, among others.

As video broadcasting, teleconferencing and webcasting become more prevalent, many firms are enjoying some of the benefits of a centralized training facility without incurring the travel costs and lost time to transport the salesforce to and from training. Field offices arrange for video hook-up, either in-house or at video-equipped conference hotels, and trainees across the country share simultaneously in training emanating from a central location.

EXHIBIT 6.5   Choosing an Outside Training Program

Several training organizations, such as the Covey Leadership Center, the Center for Creative Leadership, Decker Communications, and the American Society of Training and Development, provide their input on what makes a useful training program.

1. The program should make it easy to master content by lessening the participant's struggle to learn new skills and knowledge and change old work habits. Content and delivery must consider the skill level, education level, and learning style of participants.
2. The program should anticipate and deal with obstacles to long-term behavior modification. It should motivate participants to drop old habits, adopt new skills, and desire continued training.
3. The program's content should be limited to what has been shown to help participants most on the job.
4. The program's development and delivery should stay within the constraints of time, money, logistics, and repeatability. Only technology that enhances training should be used.
5. Participants should be actively involved in the program to preserve the excitement that comes from self-development.
6. The trainer must clearly understand the program's objectives, as well as the concepts, behaviors, and attitudes to be acquired by participants.
7. When appropriate, the program should accommodate group dynamics and promote a sense of group membership and shared purpose.

Selecting Sales Training Methods

A variety of methods can be selected to fit the training situation. Indeed, the use of multiple methods and media for blended learning is encouraged over the course of a training program to help maintain trainee attention and enhance learning. There are four categories of training methods: classroom/conference, on-the-job, behavioral simulations, and absorption.

Classroom/Conference Training

The classroom or conference setting features lectures, demonstrations, and group discussion with expert trainers serving as instructors. This method is often used for training on basic product knowledge, new product introductions, administrative procedures, and legal and ethical issues in personal selling. At Federated Insurance, for instance, trainees spend 6–12 months in the classroom learning hands-on product knowledge and sales methodologies.[44] The format often resembles a college classroom, with regularly scheduled examinations and overnight homework assignments. When appropriate, classroom sessions may be recorded and used at a later date for refresher training. In addition to using internal facilities and personnel, some companies send their salespeople to seminars sponsored by organizations such as the American Management Association, American Marketing Association, Sales and Marketing Executives International, and local colleges and universities. These organizations offer training on practically any phase of selling and sales management.

On-the-Job Training

In the final analysis, salespeople can be taught only so much about selling without actually experiencing it. Consequently, on-the-job training (OJT) is extremely important and is a very prevalent method of training salespeople. OJT puts the trainee into actual work circumstances under the observant (it is hoped) eye of a supportive mentor or sales manager. Other OJT methods approximate a "sink or swim" philosophy and often produce disastrous results when the trainee is overwhelmed with unfamiliar job requirements.

Mentors have different objectives from company to company, but they usually strive to make the new hires feel at home in their jobs, relay information about the corporate culture, and be available for discussion and advice on topics of concern to the trainee. Coworker mentoring is popular among salesforces, and in some companies, the sales manager serves as the mentor. For instance, Lotta Laitinen, a manager at If, a Scandinavian insurance broker, decided to take more time to mentor her salespeople by listening in on client calls, observing her top salespeople and coaching them one-on-one. This resulted in a 5 percent increase in sales over a three-week period, with the largest gains coming from below average performers.[45] At California-based plumbing and HVAC wholesaler PACE Supply, reps are trained in many ways, including one-on-one defined mentor relationships.[46] Research indicates that salespeople with mentors have higher performance and less intent to leave than those with no mentors, and that manager mentors inside the organization are superior to peer mentors or those outside of the organization.[47] Mentoring tends to work best when the protégé makes clear to the mentor what he or she expects from the relationship and the mentor "shows" rather than "tells" the protégé how to do something.[48] The mentoring concept is yet another way that companies are striving to improve salesforce socialization, especially the role definition and initiation-to-task steps explained earlier in this chapter. However, mentoring programs are not without challenges, as seen in "An Ethical Dilemma."

Other than working with a senior salesperson or a mentor, common OJT assignments include the trainee's filling in for a vacationing salesperson, working with a sales manager who acts as a "coach," and job rotation. The sales manager's role as coach is discussed in Chapter 7, on supervision and leadership of the salesforce. When senior salespeople act as mentors, they too are undergoing continual training as their ideas and methods are reassessed, and sometimes refined, with each trainee. Job rotation, the exposure of the sales trainee to different jobs, may involve stints as a customer service representative, a distribution clerk, or perhaps in other sales positions. Job rotation is often used to groom salespeople for management positions.

AN ETHICAL DILEMMA

As a senior sales rep at the ABC Company, Dan is always more than willing to help out. Dan is a hard-working, high-performing salesperson who is both well liked and well respected by his colleagues. So, when sales manager Brad asked Dan to mentor a new trainee, Cindy, as part of the company's new sales mentorship program, he gladly stepped up to the challenge. Dan was asked to take Cindy, a recent college grad embarking on her first sales position, under his wings and show her the ropes. In doing so, Dan became very attracted to Cindy and wanted more than simply a "working" relationship. Cindy felt Dan was a nice guy, but she was not interested in a relationship. She began to feel uncomfortable with Dan's advances but was afraid to complain, feeling that it might jeopardize her job. Moreover, Cindy felt that her sales manager Brad, being a male, would likely brush it off as Dan just being friendly. Cindy finally got up enough nerve to approach Brad with her concern. Upon hearing this, Brad was dismayed. Having knowing Dan for five years he believed this conduct to be completely out of character for Dan. In fact, he had his doubts about the truthfulness of Cindy's accusation. What do you think about Dan's conduct? If you were Brad, what would you do?

Behavioral Simulations

Methods that focus on behavioral learning by means of business games and simulations, case studies, and role playing—where trainees portray a specified role in a staged situation—are called behavioral simulations. They focus on defining desirable behavior or in correcting behavioral mistakes, in part by allowing salespeople to experience the consequences of their actions. This is a popular method of training, as one study found that 84 percent of top-performing sales organizations use simulations.[49]

Games may come in a variety of forms. For instance, companies such as Oracle have utilized a board game called Apples and Oranges to help its sales reps better understand how executive-level decision makers think by having them run a mock manufacturing company over a simulated three-year period. During a five- to six-hour training session, reps are divided into teams of three or four. As players progress along the board, they must make decisions regarding productivity changes, resource allocation, and cash flow management. The game helps salespeople learn what customers to pursue to help build a profitable customer base.[50] International Paper credits a board game called Zodiak with helping its salesforce bring value to its customers and add profits to its bottom line. This game teaches sellers how to think like their customers by having them simulate ownership and operation of a company.[51] There is even a book available called the *The Big Book of Sales Games* that provides 50 games that reinforce selling techniques.

An interesting example of a behavioral simulation to teach product knowledge comes from B. Braun Medical Inc., a manufacturer of infusion therapy and pain management products. When they found that their salespeople did not feel that they had the clinical expertise necessary to establish credibility with their customers or correctly set expectations for use of its IV catheter, they developed a simulation to improve their reps' product understanding. To enable salespeople to understand what clinicians experienced when they used the product, salespeople were trained how to place the IV catheter through scenario-based simulation training in which they practiced inserting the catheter into a "demo arm" with blood pressure and fake blood. The company credits the simulation with improving participants' knowledge and skills by 25 percent.[52]

An example of a computer-based simulation is DialogCoach, a computer-based personal role-play system that listens to salespeople as they interact with a virtual customer. Ventiv Commercial Services, a pharmaceutical sales outsourcer, has used DialogCoach to help train its salespeople. In the simulation, reps interact with an on-screen simulated talking and moving physician. Reps receive immediate feedback and must provide appropriate responses to move forward in the simulation.[53] Such simulations provide the advantage of reaching large populations at once via the Internet, company intranet, or CD-ROM.

Along with OJT, role playing is extremely popular for teaching sales techniques. Typically, one trainee plays the role of the salesperson and another trainee acts as the buyer. The role playing is video-recorded or performed live for a group of observers who then critique the performance. This can be an extremely effective means of teaching personal selling, without the risk of a poor performance in the presence of a real customer. It is most effective when promptly critiqued with emphasis on the positive points of the performance as well as suggestions for improvement. A good way to maximize the benefits of the critique is to have the person who has played the role of the salesperson offer opinions first and then solicit opinions from observers. After role playing, the "salesperson" is usually modest about his or her performance, and the comments from observers may bolster this individual's self-confidence. In turn, future performance may be improved.[54] While role playing offers the opportunity for a positive learning experience, this may not always be the case, as seen in "An Ethical Dilemma" below.

Absorption Training

As the name implies, absorption training involves furnishing trainees or salespeople with materials that they peruse (or "absorb") without opportunity for immediate feedback and questioning. Product manuals, direction-laden memoranda, audio and video recordings and sales bulletins are used in absorption training. Federated Insurance, for example, maintains a substantial library of audio and video recordings, books, workbooks, and self-study material for employees to use.[55] One time-effective method of absorption training involves furnishing the salesforce with CDs so that driving time can be used as training time. At Newell Rubbermaid, salespeople are provided audiocasts so that they can listen to training material on the move.[56]

Companies such as Astellas, a pharmaceutical company, are using podcasts, audio recordings that can be downloaded from the Internet to an MP3 player or mobile phone, to disseminate training material.[57] Some sales training firms are now offering 15-minute podcasts on a variety of topics from "competitive smarts" to "winning sales proposals" that can be downloaded to a computer or a portable media player.[58] Companies are increasingly using technology to offer learning portals, where salespeople can log into a portal and access sales training materials, company and industry news, white papers, case studies, press releases, and current communication from top executives.[59] It should be noted that absorption training is most useful as a supplement to update salesforce knowledge, reinforce previous training, or introduce basic materials to be covered in more detail at a later date.

AN ETHICAL DILEMMA

During a recent training session, national sales manager Richard Brown was not happy with trainee Betty White's performance in a role-playing exercise. Upon conclusion of the exercise, Richard began to mock Betty's role-playing behavior in front of the other trainees to illustrate how inadequate her performance was. Richard believed that his gesture would leave a lasting impression on the trainees and help make his point stick. Furthermore, he informed Betty and the others that if they performed like that on a sales call, they would be looking for a new job very soon. What do you think about Richard's actions? How would you have handled this situation?

Selecting Sales Training Media

Communications and computer technology have expanded the range of sales training media dramatically in the past decade. Sales trainers warn against the tendency to be overly impressed with the glamorous aspects of such training media, but they agree that it is advisable to evaluate new media continually to see whether they should be incorporated into the sales training program. Among other things, electronic media typically allow trainees to learn at their own pace in a risk-free environment. The most promising new media are found at the communications/computer technology interface and are often referred to as e-learning or virtual media. This type of learning can be delivered synchronously, whereby trainees congregate simultaneously in an online classroom and training is delivered live, or asynchronously, in which participants partake in self-paced training modules comprised of instructional content, videos, and presentations that have been prepared to consume at the trainee's convenience.

The Internet offers opportunities to cost-effectively train the salesforce across different times and locations without taking salespeople out of the field. Cisco Systems, for example, has moved heavily into virtual media and conducts training sessions through the Web on a variety of topics, including understanding profit-and-loss statements, how to understand customers' business, and how to conduct an executive dialogue, among others.[60] The Web also offers an opportunity to provide video-on-demand content, whereby salespeople can review training videos at their convenience. AT&T, for instance, provides videos to trainees of top-performing sales coaches explaining how top salespeople implement key techniques. One study reports that 83 percent of top-performing sales organizations use video-based content for training.[61] At Baxter Healthcare, e-learning is used for teaching basic knowledge, but it still conducts instructor-led training by webinar, video conferencing, or in the classroom for competitive information and selling skills practice.[62] Companies such as WebEx (www.webex.com) and Inter- Call (www.InterCall .com) provide Web, video, and telephone conferencing services. Using the Web, trainers can display slides, whiteboard visual concepts, introduce real-time interaction, share desktop applications, and lead a Web tour.

Several media are particularly useful for delivering content that can be viewed or heard by salespeople on the move. Learning material can be sent by email to personal digital assistants and mobile phones. Some companies, such as Eli Lilly and Daimler-Chrysler AG, have even used video email for sales training.[63] When Sprint added GPS software to its phones, it made five-minute training videos available so that its reps could dial in and view the videos while sitting in a lobby or their car.[64] Exhibit 6.6 provides tips for designing mobile learning content.[65]

Another technology, desktop personal computer videoconferencing, allows sales managers and salespeople to see each other and trade information via their personal computers. For example, Cadence Design Systems, an electronic design tool organization, developed a program to train its global salesforce on new products and features, selling strategies, and handling competition, among other things, that was delivered through video, in-person, and online.[66] Similarly, audiographics connects the instructor simultaneously with several sites via computer displays and audio link. Or sales managers may want to set up an online chatroom to train salespeople interactively at remote locations. Baltimore Aircoil, a cooling and refrigeration equipment manufacturer for the industrial market, has had success training salespeople by setting up a chat room for its 250 independent salespeople to trade success stories.[67] These technologies can be used to simultaneously train salespeople dispersed in several remote locations.

Satellite television offers another viable training alternative. For instance, RE/MAX uses its satellite network to conduct sales training for its RE/MAX affiliates throughout the United States.[68]

EXHIBIT 6.6   Tips for Designing Mobile Learning Content

1. Limit content to two minutes.
2. Use animation, even for serious content.
3. Offer customized content in a conversational style.
4. Offer information to make the user better, smarter or faster.
5. Focus on areas of work that are done incorrectly or lack compliance.
6. Invite users to help design content to encourage participation.
7. Encourage users to look for the content, rather than push it on them.
8. Encourage users to diagnose their own training needs.
9. Make the content readily available so that users can access it when and where they need it.

E-learning or virtual media provide several benefits. First, costs of delivery and travel can be reduced (see Exhibit 6.7[69] for an example of the cost savings that can be achieved by using virtual training more heavily than the classroom). Cisco Systems claims to save more than 85 percent on each training session's delivery cost and 100 percent on travel costs through virtual media. Second, by allowing trainees to take in smaller chunks of information at once, trainees avoid fatigue, more quickly absorb the material, and retention and comprehension are improved. Third, gains in productivity can be realized, as less time is spent out of the field or office. Finally, adoption is often enhanced as electronically communicated information can be quickly put to use.[70] For tips on successfully using virtual media to train see Exhibit 6.8.[71] Although companies utilize various methods and media for sales training, 97 percent of best-in-class companies use instructor led training, while 93 percent use informal on-the-job training, 84 percent mentoring/coaching and 78 percent self-paced e-learning.[72]

Training Costs: Classroom vs. Virtual   EXHIBIT 6.7

Below are expected costs associated with training a salesforce of 500. Column 1 involves costs of hosting a training event for all 500, while Column 2 shows costs for hosting the event for 100 salespeople and having the remaining participate virtually. In this case, cost savings are nearly $600,000 by implementing virtual training. (Costs associated with travel time are included, as this time is often unproductive.) Furthermore, since the virtual event can be archived, salespeople and trainees can review the material in the future.

	Classroom only	Classroom and Virtual
Number of physical attendees	500	100
Number of virtual attendees	0	400
Travel (average 10 hrs per person)	5,000	1,000
Manpower cost (@ $50 per hour)	$250,000	$50,000
Travel (average $800 per person)	$400,000	$80,000
Venue rental	$100,000	$25,000
Totals	$750,000	$155,000

Tips for Successfully Using Virtual Media to Train   EXHIBIT 6.8

- Provide the training in short, manageable segments over a shorter time period.
- Plan material so that it fits into the time you allotted for any synchronous virtual session, and then keep training participants on schedule.
- At the beginning of each virtual training session, teach participants how to use the technology (e.g., how to use the icon to raise one's hand, use the chat window, participate in breakout sessions, or contribute to whiteboard sessions).
- After reviewing the technology, discuss the training's purpose and the skills participants are expected to learn.
- Allow time for participants to virtually socialize and get to know one another in order to build stronger teamwork.
- Use virtual breakout rooms to group participants together to work on assignments.
- Be creative and keep participants engaged. Use graphics and color and keep something moving on the screen (even if it is just a pointer) to keep participants involved. Test attentiveness by using periodic polls or asking questions where each participant must respond.
- Have senior management reinforce the importance and value of virtual training to solicit participant buy-in.

Design the Sales Training Program

The fourth step in the sales training process is a culmination of, and condensation of, the first three steps shown in Figure 6.1. Working toward selected objectives based on needs assessment and having evaluated training alternatives, the sales manager now commits resources to the training to be accomplished. At this point in the process, sales managers may have to seek budget approval from upper management.

In this step of designing the training program, the necessary responses to *what, when, where,* and *how* questions are finalized. Training is scheduled, travel arrangements are made, media is selected, speakers are hired, and countless other details are arranged. Certainly this can be the most tedious part of the sales training process, but attention to detail is necessary to ensure successful implementation of the process.

When selling globally, an additional challenge involves determining the extent to which the training program will be standardized globally. Hitachi Data Systems, a global storage solutions company, plans globally, yet acts locally, with regards to its approach to worldwide sales training. The company's global headquarters team generally develops all training with an enterprise reach, such as global sales methodology training and global product launch training. Each geographical location, however, is given the opportunity to adapt the training to the culture and selling style of a particular geographical location. For global instructor-led training, the company first trains local trainers, who in turn localize the program for their geographical location.[73]

Perform Sales Training

The fifth step in the process, actually performing the training, may take only a fraction of the time required by the previous steps. This is particularly true in better sales training programs. As the training is being conducted, the sales manager's primary responsibility is to monitor the progress of the trainees and to ensure adequate presentation of the training topics. In particular, sales managers should assess the clarity of training materials. It is also recommended that some assessment of the trainees' continuing motivation to learn be made. Motivation to learn can be increased by making sure that salespeople understand how they will benefit from the training prior to conducting it. Feedback from the trainees might be solicited on everything from the effectiveness of external trainers to the adequacy of the physical training site.

An alternative to using trainers and a specified training program is to incorporate a self-directed training program. With this program, salespeople are responsible for diagnosing their individual training needs, formulating learning goals, identifying, choosing, and implementing learning strategies, and assessing learning outcomes, all within guidelines set by supervisors.[74] Self-directed training programs may be induced, whereby management determines the training content, and evaluation of learning outcomes is measured by others; synergistic, which is essentially the same, but participation is considered optional; voluntary, in which salespeople choose their personal learning goal, as well as learning material; and scanning, in which the salesperson monitors current trends to keep up to date and remain relevant in the field.[75]

Conduct Follow-Up and Evaluation

It is always difficult to measure the effectiveness of sales training. This is a long-standing problem, due in some cases to a lack of clearly stated sales training objectives. Even with clearly stated objectives, however, it is hard to determine which future performance variations are a result of sales training. Other factors, such as motivation, role perceptions, and environmental factors, may affect performance more or less than training in different situations. Nevertheless, given that poor training not only wastes time and money, but negatively impacts sales team morale and discourages salespeople from participating in future training, follow-up and evaluation should be conducted.[76]

Although scientific precision cannot be hoped for, a reasonable attempt must nevertheless be made to assess whether current training expenditures are worthwhile and whether future modification is warranted. Evaluations can be made before, during, and after the training occurs.[77] For example, the pretraining evaluation might include an examination for sales trainees to assess their level of knowledge, corroborate or deny the need for training, and further define the objectives of the training. As suggested earlier, training can be evaluated while it is being conducted, and adjustments may be made at any point in the delivery of training. Post-training evaluations might include reactions or critiques of the trainees, "final examinations," retention examinations at later dates, observations by sales managers as they work in the field with salespeople, customer feedback, new business growth, and an examination of actual performance indicators such as sales volume. At Cisco, trainees are monitored throughout its training program by a series of assessments including role-playing activities and virtual and written tests focused on behavior, technical skills, and product knowledge. In addition, by examining results of tests, instructors identify and reinforce content that was not clearly understood.[78]

Additionally, it may be useful to determine the impact of training on both organizational level and salesforce level goals and objectives.[79] At Motorola, Inc., the effectiveness of sales training has been determined by measuring customer satisfaction, along with measuring salespeople's ability to affect customer value.[80] Dell has measured the strength of its customer relationships as a means of assessing its sales training, as has Dr Pepper/7 Up, which also gauged volume, distribution, and display.[81] Trainee reactions, however, can serve as an important measure of training effectiveness given research indicating that trainees who are satisfied with their training are more likely to retain and use what they learned, resulting in greater selling effectiveness, improved customer relations, and a stronger commitment to the organization.[82]

Despite the inherent difficulty in relating subsequent sales performance to previously conducted sales training, the effectiveness of sales training is increasingly being measured in dollars and cents. This return-on-investment approach seeks to define training effectiveness in terms of incremental sales volume from existing accounts or volume generated by new accounts.[83] Paetec, a communications technology solutions provider, performs a full ROI analysis, which includes factors such as cost of the trainer's time, time of the employees being out of the field, travel costs and opportunity costs, on 15 to 20 percent of all its training.[84]

It is also important to reinforce the training in subsequent weeks. Within 30 days of sales training, salespeople lose as much as 60 to 90 percent of the skills they were taught if the learning is not immediately and consistently reinforced.[85] Post-training implementation and reinforcement are critical to enhanced behavior change. Reinforcement should be integrated with the sales organization's daily work.[86] Some companies, for instance, reinforce their training through frequent informal coaching sessions with their salespeople. The Fort Hill Company of Wilmington Delaware connects training to priority work upon trainees' return to work. This includes three months of post-course, structured, Web-based follow-through.[87] Exhibit 6.9[88] shows results of a study identifying the most effective methods to reinforce new sales skills.

A reasonable approach to sales training is to ensure that it is not prohibitively expensive by carefully assessing training needs, setting objectives, and evaluating training alternatives before designing the training program and performing the training. Furthermore, the sales training process is incomplete without evaluation and follow-up.

ETHICAL AND LEGAL ISSUES

Ethical and legal issues are being included in sales training programs more often than in the past. One catalyst for this change has been product liability litigation that has awarded multimillion-dollar judgments to plaintiffs who have suffered as a result of unsafe products. Another is to lessen liability due to criminal violations of the Federal Sentencing Guidelines. Firms who train employees on compliance and ethics can lessen fines due to violations by up to 95 percent.[89] Research has found that salespeople face a number of ethical and legal dilemmas on the job and that salespeople want more direction from their managers on how to handle such dilemmas.[90] Companies may benefit by training salespeople how to handle the situations or practices identified in a study by buyers as being unethical, as listed in Exhibit 6.10.[91]

EXHIBIT 6.9   Methods for Reinforcing New Sales Skills Ranked by Importance

Method	Percent Indicating as Effective
Sharing sales methods and language with the sales team	49
Coaching by the sales manager	46
Follow-up training classes	43
Clear statement of management expectations	39
Incentive compensation for new sales behaviors	36
Technology reinforcement and support	33
Coaching by outside specialists	30
Participation in a community Web site based on the training	11

EXHIBIT 6.10   Sales Practices Viewed as Unethical by Buyers

1. The salesperson exaggerates how quickly orders will be delivered to get a sale.

2. The salesperson hints if order is placed, the price might be lower on the next order, when it is not so.

3. The salesperson grants price concessions to purchasing agents of company they own stock in.

4. The salesperson gives a potential customer a gift worth $50 or more at Christmas or other occasion.

5. The salesperson seeks confidential information about competitors by questioning suppliers.

6. The salesperson attempts to get the buyer to divulge competitors' bid in low-bid buying situation.

7. The salesperson gives the purchaser who was one of the best customers a gift worth $50 or more at Christmas or other occasion.

8. The salesperson seeks information from the purchaser on competitors' quotations for the purpose of submitting another quotation.

9. The salesperson in a shortage situation allocates product shipments to purchasing agents the seller personally likes.

10. In reciprocal buying situation, salesperson hints unless order is forthcoming, prospect's sales to firm might suffer.

11. The salesperson stresses only positive aspects of the product, omitting possible problems the purchasing firm might have with it.

12. The salesperson attempts to sell product to a purchasing agent that has little or no value to the buyer's company.

13. The salesperson has less competitive prices or other terms for buyers who depend on the firm as the sole source of supply.

14. The salesperson lets it be known that they have information about a competitor if purchasing agent is interested.

15. The salesperson intends to use economic power of their firm to obtain concessions from the buyer.

Note: Ranked from most to least unethical in a survey of buyers.

Legal Reminders for Salespeople	EXHIBIT 6.11

1. Use factual data rather than general statements of praise during the sales presentation. Avoid misrepresentation.

2. Thoroughly educate customers before the sale on the product's specifications, capabilities, and limitations. Remind customers to read all warnings.

3. Do not overstep authority because the salesperson's actions can be binding to the selling firm.

4. Avoid discussing these topics with competitors: prices, profit margins, discounts, terms of sale, bids or intent to bid, sales territories or markets to be served, and rejection or termination of customers.

5. Do not use one product as bait for selling another product.

6. Do not try to force the customer to buy only from your organization.

7. Offer the same price and support to all buyers who purchase under the same set of circumstances.

8. Do not tamper with a competitor's product.

9. Do not disparage a competitor's product, business conduct, or financial condition without specific evidence of your contentions.

10. Avoid promises that will be difficult or impossible to honor.

Training in the legal area is extremely difficult because laws are sometimes confusing and subject to multiple interpretations. Training salespeople in ethics is even more difficult because ethical issues are often gray, not black or white. Companies that address ethics and legal issues in their sales training programs usually rely on straightforward guidelines that avoid complexity. Salespeople should be provided with the company's code of ethics and informed of the organization's policies concerning ethical behavior. Furthermore, by providing salespeople with potentially troubling ethical scenarios, having them respond, and then explaining how a similar situation could be handled, it may be possible to lessen salespeople's concerns about such situations.[92] Salespeople are given basic training on applicable legal dimensions and advised simply to tell the truth and seek management assistance should problems arise. Owens Corning, for instance, has used a lawyer to speak to its salespeople about legal and ethical issues.[93] Another possibility includes role playing, in which trainees learn to develop consistently legal interactive scripts.[94] These guidelines may sound simplistic, but such training can greatly reduce a salesperson's ethical conflict on the job, teach salesperson behaviors that help facilitate development of profitable long-term relationships with customers, and reduce the liability of the salesperson and the organization. There is even evidence that suggests that training in sales ethics leads salespeople to experience higher levels of satisfaction with supervisors and coworkers.[95]

The legal framework for personal selling is extensive. Some of the key components of this framework are antitrust legislation, contract law, local ordinances governing sales practices, and guidelines issued by the Federal Trade Commission dealing with unfair trade practices. A partial listing of important legal reminders that should be included in a sales training program is shown in Exhibit 6.11. Salespeople must be made aware of changes in the legal environment as soon as they occur.

SUMMARY

1. **Understand the role of sales training in salesforce socialization.** Newly hired salespeople usually receive a company orientation designed to familiarize them with company history, policies, facilities, procedures, and key individuals with whom they will

interact. During initial sales training, it is hoped that each salesforce member will experience a positive initiation to task and satisfactory role definition.

2. **Explain the importance of sales training and the sales manager's role in sales training.** Most organizations have a continual need for sales training as a result of changing business conditions, the influx of new salespeople into the organization, and the need to reinforce previous training. Sizable investments in training are likely in larger companies. The sales manager has the overall responsibility for training the salesforce, although other people may also conduct sales training.

3. **Describe the sales training process as a series of six interrelated steps.** Figure 6.1 presents the sales training process in six steps: assess sales training needs, set training objectives, evaluate training alternatives, design the sales training program, perform sales training, and conduct follow-up and evaluation. The time spent to perform sales training may be only a fraction of the time spent to complete the other steps in the process, especially in well-run sales organizations.

4. **Discuss six methods for assessing sales training needs and identify typical sales training needs.** Sales managers may assess needs through a salesforce audit, performance testing, observation, a salesforce survey, a customer survey, or a job analysis. It is recommended that salesforce training needs be assessed in a proactive fashion; that is, needs should be assessed before performance problems occur rather than after problems occur. Typical sales training needs include product, customer, and competitive knowledge; sales techniques; and time and territory management.

5. **Name some typical objectives of sales training programs, and explain how setting objectives for sales training is beneficial to sales managers.** The objectives of sales training vary over time and across organizations, but they often include preparing sales trainees for assignment to a sales territory, improving a particular dimension of performance, aiding in the socialization process, or improving salesforce morale and motivation. By setting objectives, the sales manager can prioritize training, allocate resources consistent with priorities, communicate the purpose of the training to interested parties, and perhaps gain top management support for sales training.

6. **Identify the key issues in evaluating sales training alternatives.** Evaluation of alternatives is a search for an optimal balance between cost and effectiveness. One key issue is the selection of trainers, whether from outside the company (external) or inside the company (internal). Another is the potential location or locations for training. Still another important factor is the method or methods to use for various topics. Sales training methods include classroom/conference training, on-the-job training, behavioral simulations, and absorption training. The sales manager must also consider whether to use various sales training media, such as printed material, audio- and video-recordings, and computer-assisted instruction.

7. **Identify key ethical and legal issues in sales training.** Because of increasing product liability litigation, legal and ethical issues are being incorporated into salesforce training. Exhibits 6.10 and 6.11 point out several issues that should be covered in sales training. Lectures and role playing provide useful means for training in this area.

UNDERSTANDING SALES MANAGEMENT TERMS

initiation to task
role definition
needs assessment
salesforce audit
performance testing

time and territory management (TTM)
self-management
sales training objectives
sales trainer
classroom/conference training

observation
salesforce survey
customer survey
job analysis
sales techniques
product knowledge
customer knowledge
competitive knowledge

on-the-job training (OJT)
mentor
job rotation
behavioral simulations
role playing
absorption training
sales training media

DEVELOPING SALES MANAGEMENT KNOWLEDGE

1. How is sales training related to recruiting and selecting salespeople? How can sales training contribute to salesforce socialization?

2. Why is it important to invest in sales training?

3. What are six methods of assessing sales training needs? Can each of these methods be used in either a proactive or reactive approach to determining training needs?

4. Refer to "Sales Management in the 21st Century: Tactical Sales Training at Iron-wear" on p. 176. What is involved in sales tactical training at Ironwear and why is it done?

5. How is the process of setting objectives for sales training beneficial to sales managers?

6. Refer to "Sales Management in the 21st Century: Fulfilling Company Objectives Through Strategic Training at Ironwear" on p. 181. What important objective does strategic training help Ironware fulfill? What does strategic training at Ironware involve?

7. When the sales manager is evaluating sales training alternatives, what four areas should he or she consider?

8. Discuss four methods for delivering sales training.

9. What is the purpose of the follow-up and evaluation step in the sales training process? When should evaluation take place?

10. What are some of the important ethical and legal considerations that might be included in a sales training program?

BUILDING SALES MANAGEMENT SKILLS

1. Go to http://www.webex.com. What is WebEx? What are the advantages and disadvantages of using a company such as WebEx to assist a company with its sales training? What types of sales training do you believe would work best with this media and why? What types of sales training might not be as appropriate with this media and why?

2. As a sales manager, you have decided it would be a good idea to survey your customers to determine how well their needs are being met by your 50-person salesforce. Develop a series of questions that could be used to determine this and explain how your customer survey will be implemented.

3. There is a universal ongoing need for training on "how to sell." For instance, knowing how to listen effectively is an extremely important skill that contributes to the success of salespeople. Find several articles on listening. Use this information to design a training program to improve salespeople's listening skills. Assume that you will conduct the training session. Determine what you will teach, along with the methods and media you will use. Also, decide how you will assess whether the training was successful. If possible, conduct your training program on a small group such

as your fraternity, sorority, student American Marketing Association chapter, or any other student group.

ROLE PLAY

4. As the sales manager for ABC company, you have decided that as part of your training program you would like to use role playing to achieve three objectives: (1) teach salespeople how to set appointments with prospects properly via the phone, (2) teach salespeople how to approach prospects and build rapport, and (3) teach salespeople how to question prospects effectively. Design three role plays (one for each objective) to achieve these goals. Then, have a classmate play the salesperson and you play the buyer and act out each role play. On completing each role play, critique the salesperson's performance, being sure to emphasize the positive points and to make suggestions for improvements. Consider soliciting self-assessment feedback from the salesperson before making your own critique.

5. Access Rapid Learning Institute (http://rapidlearninginstitute.com) and click on the "training solutions" tab at the top and then the "sales skill training" tab. Address the following questions:

   a. What types of sales skill training needs does this company address with its online training?

   b. What are some potentially important training needs that are not addressed?

   c. What are the advantages and disadvantages of using this type of online training?

6. The Web contains various sales training Web sites. Search the Web to find a company that offers sales training. Briefly explain the types of training the company offers, the methods and media they use to deliver the training, and the pros and cons of using the company to train the salesforce.

7. As a sales manager, you would like to teach your salespeople how to handle different buyer types. Using Exhibit 6.2 on p. 177 as a guide, explain the methods and media you would use to prepare your salespeople to deal with each buyer type.

ROLE PLAY

8. **Role Play**

   Situation: Read the Ethical Dilemma on p. 185.

   Characters: Richard Brown, national sales manager; Betty White, sales trainee.

   Scene: *Location*—Company training room. *Action*—Richard acts out an alternative method for handling Betty's poor role-play performance.

9. You would like to develop a game to help train your salesforce. Choose a specific sales training learning objective and develop a game to be administered to salespeople to achieve the objective. Explain the format of the game, including its object, how it is played, who is involved, its rules, and any props necessary to implement the game.

MAKING SALES MANAGEMENT DECISIONS

CASE 6.1 DEVELOPING A TRAINING PROGRAM AT DOCUCSAN

Background

Docuscan is a small independently owned regional document imaging company located in the Southern United States. The company converts paper files, X-rays, microfilm, microfiche, and other media to electronic documents to help companies more effectively and efficiently run their business. The company has held its own in the fragmented imaging market having steadily increased sales each year of its existence. Although the company has only been in existence for about eight years, it has likewise steadily grown its salesforce to 15 members. Each salesperson brings his or her own unique set of skills and talents to the company, as Docuscan has never before offered any formal sales training, that is, until now.

Current Situation

It was a Friday afternoon when Chip Dipston, VP of sales at Docuscan, met with company owner Sharon Cooper to discuss plans for taking the salesforce to the next level. Sharon had been pressuring Chip to improve sales significantly this year. Chip felt confident that his salespeople were doing all they could. In his opinion, members of his sales team appeared highly motivated and hard working. Perhaps, he thought, they could hire a couple more salespeople. However, when he had mentioned this to Sharon a few weeks earlier she seemed lukewarm to the idea. Thus, Chip decided he would propose to Sharon the idea of conducting formal salesforce training. He believed this could help make his sales team stronger and ultimately increase company sales. Sharon was excited about the idea. Prior to starting Docuscan she had worked in sales at Xerox and had undergone extensive sales training. She felt it was instrumental in helping her develop as a salesperson. Moreover, after leaving Xerox she had developed some sales training programs herself when she served as VP of sales at a small office supply company. Therefore, Sharon accepted Chip's proposal to develop sales training and sent him on his way.

Chip was excited. Training the salesforce would surely help his team take the next step. The question was, what exactly should he teach his salespeople? Given Sharon's push to increase sales, Chip decided that if he could improve the prospecting skills of his salesforce, they could obtain more customers, and thus increase sales. Since the market is very competitive, Chip felt that it may be useful to increase the competitive knowledge of his salesforce. In addition, Chip felt that if his salespeople better understood their customers they surely would do a better job of selling. Chip also thought that his salespeople should be very customer-oriented and treat customers fairly. In doing so, it was important that salespeople closely adhered to the company's code of ethics. Therefore Chip decided that he also would conduct training in sales ethics. Finally, Chip was a big believer in being organized, as he felt this helped one to work more efficiently and effectively. Thus, he surmised that his salespeople could use training in time and territory management.

Having determined the areas in which he wanted to train the salesforce, Chip set some goals he hoped to achieve by implementing his training: (1) find more customers; (2) increase sales and profits; (3) improve teamwork and cooperative efforts; (4) improve salespeople's customer orientation; and (5) develop a smarter salesforce. If my training can accomplish these goals, Chip thought, then sales will increase and Sharon will get off my back.

Next, some details concerning the training needed to be worked out. Who would do the training? Chip considered hiring an external trainer but decided to do it himself. He felt that his intimate knowledge of the industry, his company and his sales team put him in the best position to serve as trainer. Another question involved how to conduct the training. Chip had been doing a lot of reading lately on the benefits of virtual training. He felt this would be a good way to train his busy salesforce, as it could save both time and money. He could host an interactive synchronous webinar that his salesforce could attend via a computer and an Internet connection. He was familiar with a company called WebEx that provides services for conducting virtual meetings. Having participated as an attendee in a webinar a few years ago that used WebEx he decided to go with them. Since Chip had several topics to cover, he determined that he would host a series of webinars, one on each topic for the next five Tuesdays from 10:00 to 11:30 a.m. Having hammered out these details, Chip went about designing the material that would be covered in each session.

Once the training finally got underway, Chip began to experience some problems. He found some salespeople joining the sessions late or others not at all. Many of his salespeople were not familiar with the technology, having never participated in a webinar. Several of them had no idea how to "raise their hand" to ask a question, participate in polls, or use the online whiteboard. As a result, they became confused, found it difficult to keep up, and failed to learn. Some of the sessions involved no interaction on the part of salespeople. In these sessions, some salespeople had a difficult time focusing and became disengaged. Many felt as though they simply could have read the material on their own time.

Upon concluding the training sessions, Chip wondered whether the training would pay off. Having heard some comments from his salespeople, he realized that there were some difficulties. But that's not uncommon in training, he thought. As he reflected on the training, he was just sure that his salespeople received some value. But only time would tell, he concluded. Chip then began to prepare his report that detailed the training program and its impact on the salesforce for his meeting with Sharon later in the week.

Questions

1. If you were in charge of the training for this salesforce, explain how you would have gone about designing a training program.

2. Do you believe that the training program outlined in this case will achieve its objectives? Explain.

3. What kind of reactions might Chip expect from his salespeople after implementing this training program?

ROLE PLAY

Role Play

Situation:	Read Case 6.1.
Characters:	Chip Dipston, VP of sales; Sharon Cooper, owner of Docuscan.
Scene:	*Location*—Sharon's office. *Action*—Chip meets with Sharon to discuss the sales training program. Chip overviews what he did and why, and then gives his assessment of how well the training went. Sharon interacts with Chip and provides feedback on how to improve sales training in the future.

CASE 6.2: ALICE'S SALES CALL: A NEED FOR TRAINING?

Background

Alice Befuddled joined Computing, Inc., 18 months ago. She was interested in working for a progressive company with growth potential. Computing, Inc., appeared to be such a company. The company sold a variety of business computing systems. Alice was assigned to sell computerized cash register systems.

The salesforce was taught to practice adaptive selling in which salespeople learned how to probe for customer needs and respond to customer wants. This method of selling has proven to be very successful for the company. In fact, the company credits its move in market position from number five to number three in the last three years to its implementation of adaptive selling and its salesforce's ability to build strong customer relationships.

Current Situation

Alice was running behind as usual. She had a major presentation scheduled with a well-qualified prospect that could bring a substantial payoff to both her and her company. As a result, she had to cancel her first scheduled appointment of the day so that she could finish preparing her presentation for this prospect. This was not the first time she had to cancel an appointment. Just last week she canceled an appointment because she realized she would be unable to make it to the client's firm before it closed. She had failed to budget enough time into her schedule to allow her to travel from one appointment to the next.

Alice arrived at Hometown Hardware five minutes late. Luckily for Alice the owner of Hometown, Tim Tools, had been on an important conference call that ran a little longer than anticipated. Tools was hoping to purchase a new cash register system that could track his inventory. He was concerned about inventory loss, particularly in terms of pilferage and the possibility of employees inaccurately (both on purpose and otherwise) ringing up sales. Moreover, he hoped to implement a system that would allow him to track sales better, while at the same time expedite the checkout process. Currently, he is using antiquated equipment that does not provide him with the ability to scan merchandise or systematically track inventory and sales.

After introducing herself and her company, Alice got right down to business. She went into a 30-minute presentation explaining the CR2000, a cash register system she believed would be appropriate for Tools' store. What follows are excerpts from her meeting with Tools:

Alice: Although we sell several systems, Mr. Tools, I believe the CR2000 cash registers would be good for you. They are relatively inexpensive, provide a more rapid system for checking out customers, and are superior to what you now have.

Tools: As I mentioned earlier, I want a system that provides me with the ability to track inventory and total sales. Does this system do that?

Alice: No, it doesn't. We sell systems that can monitor inventory, but they are more expensive. You presently have some type of system for tracking inventory, don't you?

Tools: Yes, but it is time-consuming and I have always been concerned about its accuracy.

Alice: We could provide you with an inventory tracking system. But, in your case, it may not be worth the extra cost.

Tools: I'd really be interested in a system that is quicker than my present system and can track sales and inventory. I would also like to begin using bar codes, rather than individually pricing each item.

Alice: We carry the CR2500. This system would provide you with the ability to do these things. However, this system runs quite a bit more.

Tools: Will this system allow me to monitor sales hourly?

Alice: I believe it will. This is a fairly new system. It's an update of an earlier model. Some changes were made, and I'm not sure exactly what has been changed.

Tools: Can the system break out sales by department?

Alice: The older version of this system could. I am sure the new version can also. If you would like, Mr. Tools, I can write you a proposal for installing the CR2500. When I finish the proposal we can meet again to further discuss the CR2500.

Questions

1. With regard to Alice, what sales training needs can you identify?

2. If you were Alice's sales manager and you discovered that several of your salespeople had training needs similar to those of Alice, what methods would you suggest for training the salesforce to improve in deficient areas?

3. What are the effects of sales training on salesforce motivation and morale?

ROLE PLAY

Role Play

Situation: Read Case 6.2.

Characters: Alice Befuddled, sales rep; Tim Tools, store owner; Donna Carin, Alice's sales manager.

Scene 1:   (optional) *Location*—Hometown Hardware. *Action*—Alice is making her presentation to Tim Tools as her sales manager Donna Carin observes.

Scene 2:   *Location*—Outside Hometown Hardware following Alice's meeting with Tim Tools. *Action*—Donna coaches Alice regarding her sales presentation (for more detail on coaching, see Chapter 7).

Directing the Salesforce

This part contains two chapters dealing with the direction of the activities of the salesforce. Chapter 7 presents a model of sales leadership. Contemporary views of sales leadership are discussed, along with important leadership functions such as coaching. The critical role of ethics in leadership is emphasized.

Chapter 8 deals with motivating the salesforce to work hard on the right activities over a sustained period of time. Reward systems, with an emphasis on financial and nonfinancial compensation, are discussed. Special issues related to team compensation and compensating a global salesforce are presented. Guidelines for motivating and rewarding salespeople are offered.

OBJECTIVES

After completing this chapter, you should be able to

1. Distinguish between salesforce leadership, management, and supervision.

2. Discuss the importance of situational factors in determining the most effective sales leadership approaches.

3. Explain how leadership style approaches contribute to contemporary sales leadership.

4. Discuss five bases of power that affect sales leadership.

5. Explain five influence strategies used in sales leadership.

6. Discuss issues related to coaching salespeople, conducting sales meetings, and promoting ethical behavior.

SALES LEADERSHIP: TRANSFORMING A SALES ORGANIZATION

SunGard is a leading software and technology services firm. The company was created in 1982 and has grown largely through 160 acquisitions since its inception. This strategy has generated sales growth over the years, but the company has not achieved the desired level of market share in many of its markets. Changes in the sales environment indicate the need for SunGard to transform its sales organization to meet its goals in the future.

The rapidly changing sales environment facing SunGard is similar to that confronting many business-to-business (B2B) sales organizations. Global competition is fierce. B2B buyers are using the Internet to become more knowledgeable about available products and services, and are working under tight purchasing budgets, especially for information technology. And, expanding regulations have increased compliance requirements.

The sales strategy being employed by SunGard was not likely to be successful in this type of environment. Each business in the SunGard portfolio defined its own sales strategy, which often led to several SunGard salespeople calling on the same customer with each salesperson selling a different product. Customers did not like dealing with several SunGard salespeople and salespeople focused on selling their assigned products and not solving customer problems. One result of this approach was that sales of technology services were growing, but sales of its flagship software products were not achieving the desired results.

Two senior sales leaders were hired to improve the SunGard sales organization. Their analyses indicated the need for a more coordinated sales strategy and an extensive sales organization transformation. This transformation would take a lot of time and would be expensive, but the senior sales leaders were convinced it was needed to position SunGard effectively for the future.

The vision was to create a sales organization that would differentiate SunGard from competitors by having salespeople become long-term partners and advisors to customers by providing insight to help improve a customer's business. Termed "Selling the SunGard Way," salespeople would offer tailored solutions to customer problems by selling the appropriate mix of SunGard products across all business units.

The first step was to communicate the importance of the sales organization transformation to the top corporate executives at SunGard and to get their support. Once this support was achieved, the senior sales leaders conducted a global sales productivity survey to get input from salespeople about the current and desired sales organization situation. The results of this survey helped to get support from salespeople and indicated the need to change many aspects of sales management at SunGard. This generated new processes, metrics, and tools that would be used throughout the sales organization. Of particular importance was the use of a talent assessment tool to identify the right sales talent and then to create individual development plans for each salesperson.

Field sales managers are working directly with salespeople to implement the desired changes within their sales team. Because the performance of first-year salespeople is critical to the success of the sales transformation, sales development managers were hired and are assisting the field sales managers in developing first-year salespeople. Salespeople are also playing a key leadership role in many areas.

Although the sales organization transformation at SunGard is continuing to evolve, initial results are promising. The company is on track to achieve its $1-billion-sales plan, and sales from first-year salespeople are projected to double from previous results. The sales transformation improvements are ongoing and position SunGard well for increased sales growth in the future.

Sources: Henry Canaday, "Selling the New SunGard Way," *Selling Power* (October/November/December 2013): 27–31; "50 Best Companies to Sell For," *Selling Power* (October/November/December 2013): 35.

The opening vignette highlights the leadership activities of senior sales leaders, field sales managers, sales development managers, and salespeople in the sales organization transformation at SunGard. Sales managers in different positions and

EXHIBIT 7.1 Sales Organization Positions and Activities

	Leadership	**Management**	**Supervision**
Senior Sales Leaders	Influencing the entire sales organization or a large subunit by creating a vision, values, culture, direction, alignment, and change, and by energizing action	Planning, implementation, and control of sales management process for entire sales organization or large subunit	Working with sales administrative personnel on day-to-day basis
Field Sales Managers	Influencing assigned salespeople by creating a climate that inspires salespeople	Planning, implementation, and control of sales management process within assigned sales unit	Working with salespeople on day-to-day basis
Salespeople	Influencing customers, sales team members, others in the company, and channel partners	Planning, implementation, and control of sales activities within assigned territory	Working with sales assistants on day-to-day basis

salespeople at many firms are involved in a variety of leadership, management, and supervisory activities. Exhibit 7.1 presents a description of typical leadership, management, and supervisory responsibilities for senior sales leaders, field sales managers, and salespeople.[1]

Senior sales leaders include all positions within a sales organization that have direct responsibility for other sales executives or field sales managers. Typical senior sales leader titles are chief sales executive, national sales manager, or regional sales manager. Field sales managers have direct responsibility for an assigned group of salespeople and normally include titles like district sales manager or sales manager. The major distinguishing characteristic between senior sales leader and field sales managers is that salespeople report directly to field sales managers but not to senior sales leaders. Notice that Exhibit 7.1 also includes salespeople. Salespeople are often involved in leadership, management, and sometimes supervisory activities.

Although the terms *leadership, management,* and *supervision* are often used interchangeably, we think it is important to differentiate among them. Sales leadership includes activities that influence others to achieve common goals for the collective good of the sales organization and the company. The leadership activities of senior sales leaders are directed at the entire sales organization or large subunits, and focus on creating the appropriate direction, environment, and alignment within the sales organization. Field sales manager leadership activities emphasize creating the right climate to inspire their assigned salespeople to achieve high levels of performance. Salespeople, in contrast, are engaged in self-leadership and sometimes play a leadership role with customers, others in the sales organization and company, and with channel partners.

Sales management activities are those related to the planning, implementation, and control of the sales management process, as presented in Exhibit 7.1. Senior sales leaders address the broader aspects of the sales management process, while field sales managers are more involved in implementing the process with their assigned salespeople. For example, senior sales leaders typically establish the recruiting and selection process for the sales organization, while field sales managers implement the process by actually recruiting, interviewing, evaluating, and often hiring salespeople. The management activities of salespeople are more focused on the planning, implementation, and control of sales activities within their assigned territory.

Sales supervision refers to working with subordinates on a day-to-day basis. Senior sales leadership and salespeople are normally not as involved with supervision as field sales managers. Sales supervision is an extremely important component of the field sales manager position, because field sales managers spend a great deal of time working with assigned salespeople on a day-to-day basis.

This chapter focuses primarily on sales leadership by sales managers, because sales leadership activities are becoming increasingly important for sales management positions at all levels in a sales organization. However, sales management and supervision are also addressed. Sales leadership, management, and supervision are interrelated and sales managers are involved in all three areas.

SITUATIONAL SALES LEADERSHIP PERSPECTIVES

Sales researchers have examined leadership from a variety of perspectives. Each perspective offers insight from a different vantage point and can help improve the leadership activities of sales managers throughout a sales organization.[2]

Many studies have tried to uncover what makes an effective leader. One popular category of this research is called the trait approach, which attempts to determine the personality traits of an effective leader. To date, trait research, however, has not been enlightening. The behavior approach, which seeks to catalog behaviors associated with effective leadership, has likewise failed to identify what makes an effective leader. As the behavior and trait studies continue to be inconclusive, it has become increasingly apparent that the situation could have a strong impact on leadership. A contingency approach to leadership recognizes the importance of the interaction between situational factors and other factors. Examples of situational contingency factors include the firm's market orientation; sales organization culture; company policies and procedures; the importance of the issue requiring attention; the time available to react; and the power, resources, and interdependencies of the parties involved. When time is at a premium, crisis management is called for, which requires totally different leadership behaviors than usual.

The difficult economic conditions beginning around 2008 and lingering today changed the situations facing many sales managers and required different sales leadership activities. One of the biggest challenges for sales managers in this type of situation is making sure salespeople continue with their sales activities, even though they are not likely to achieve the same results they have in the past. These sales activities are likely to produce results down the road when economic conditions improve. A regional sales manager for Agilent Technology addressed this situation by bringing his sales team together on a regular basis to share success stories, talk about various issues, and to improve overall morale. These sessions created a camaraderie that helped each salesperson continue to work hard during tough economic times.[3]

Sales Leadership Styles

A leadership style is the general orientation toward leadership activities. Two basic leadership styles have been examined by sales researchers: transactional and transformational. A transactional leadership style is characterized as a contingent reward or contingent punishment orientation. Sales leaders exhibiting a transactional leadership style focus on getting subordinates to perform desired behaviors and achieve high performance levels by providing rewards and punishments. A transformational leadership style, in contrast, is represented by an orientation toward inspiring subordinates to engage in desired behaviors and perform at high levels. Specific aspects of a transformational leadership style include articulating a vision, providing an appropriate model, fostering the acceptance of group goals, having high performance expectations, giving individual support, and providing intellectual stimulation.[4]

Although transactional and transformational are the two basic leadership styles, there are individual styles within each category. For example, visionary, coaching, affiliative, democratic and servant are viewed as transformational styles, and pace setting and commanding as transactional approaches. Effective leaders employ multiple leadership styles, depending on the situation. Thus, sales managers might have a general transactional or transformational leadership style, but adapt to each salesperson and situation by using the most appropriate leadership style.[5]

SALES MANAGEMENT IN THE 21ST CENTURY

Leading Salespeople at Federated Insurance

Joe Kemp, District Marketing Manager for Federated Insurance, discusses how he adapts his leadership style and relationship-building approach to different salespeople and situations:

I believe that you have to employ a leadership style that is unique to each sales rep. Some reps respond well to strict direction with specific goals and ideas, while others work better when given more of a free rein. Similarly, there are those who need to be managed with a "firm hand" and those who need a more nurturing and gentle leadership approach. I try to adapt my leadership style and provide support to meet the specific needs of each sales rep. This helps me to develop a strong personal relationship with all of my reps. I want them to know that I care about their success and any direction I give them is for their benefit. If your reps believe in you and trust you, then they will follow your advice and improve their performance.

Sales Leadership Relationships

In addition to general leadership styles, sales researchers have examined the development of relationships between sales managers and salespeople. The Leader-Member Exchange (LMX) model focuses on the relationships in each salesperson–sales manager dyad. LMX proposes that sales managers interact uniquely with individual salespeople rather than employing a specific leadership style for each situation. Studies have shown that reciprocal trust between sales managers and salespeople has a positive effect on the salesperson–sales manager relationship. This research indicates a positive relationship between trust and job satisfaction, satisfaction with the manager, a positive psychological climate, a willingness to change, goal commitment, performance, and a negative relationship with role conflict.[6]

One appealing aspect of the LMX model is that many sales organizations are reorienting their sales processes toward more long-term, trust-based relationships with customers. Salespeople and sales managers in these companies are learning the benefits of building trust in customer relationships and are likely to be motivated to engage in trust-building in the salesperson–sales manager dyad. By developing quality working relationships with salespeople, sales managers may be able to foster more adaptive selling behaviors by salespeople as a way to develop customer relationships.

The need for salespeople to play more of a sales leadership role than in the past has led sales researchers to view the development of relationships between sales managers and salespeople from vertical exchange theory perspective. This means that the relationship is based upon the exchange of information between a sales manager and salesperson. Sometimes the sales manager provides the information, but other times the salesperson is the focal point. For example, a sales manager might provide a salesperson with information about goals, strategies, and new ideas. Information from the salesperson to the sales manager could include what strategies are working or not, customer developments, and action plans. These social interactions between the sales manager and salesperson are the basis for their dyadic relationship. Thus, both the sales manager and salesperson are responsible for the sales leadership activities required to develop an effective relationship.[7]

Effective sales leadership requires many skills. Sales leaders must employ the appropriate leadership style for each salesperson and situation, as well as developing unique relationships with each salesperson. Joe Kemp, District Marketing Manager, discusses his approach in "Sales Management in the 21st Century: Leading Salespeople at Federated Insurance."

Power and Sales Leadership

In most job-related interpersonal situations, sales managers and the parties with whom they interact hold power in some form or another. The possession and use of this power will have a major impact on the quality of leadership achieved by a sales manager. To simplify discussion, the sales manager–salesperson relationship is emphasized, but keep in mind that sales managers must use their leadership skills in dealing with other personnel in the firm, as well as outside parties such as employment agencies, external trainers, customers, and suppliers.

The power held by an individual in an interpersonal relationship can be of one or more of the following five types.[8] For each type, a sample comment from a salesperson recognizing the sales manager's power is shown in parentheses.

1. Expert power—based on the belief that a person has valuable knowledge or skills in a given area. ("I respect her knowledge and good judgment because she is well-trained and experienced.")

2. Referent power—based on the attractiveness of one party to another. It may arise from friendship, role modeling, or perceived similarity of personal background or viewpoints. ("I like him personally and regard him as a friend.")

3. Legitimate power—associated with the right to be a leader, usually as a result of designated organizational roles. ("She has a legitimate right, considering her position as sales manager, to expect that her suggestions will be followed.")

4. Reward power—stems from the ability of one party to reward the other party for a designated action. ("He is in a good position to recommend promotions or permit special privileges for me.")

5. Coercive power—based on a belief that one party can remove rewards and provide punishment to affect behavior. ("She can apply pressure to enforce her suggestions if they are not carried out fully and properly.")

It should be stressed that it is the various individuals' perceptions of power, rather than a necessarily objective assessment of where the power lies, that will determine the effects of power in interpersonal relationships. For example, a newly appointed district sales manager may perceive the expert power to be extremely high, whereas more experienced salespeople may not share this perception. Such differences in perceptions regarding the nature and balance of power are often at the root of the problems that challenge sales managers.

Many sales managers have been accused of relying too much on reward and coercive power. This is disturbing for three reasons. First, coercive actions are likely to create strife in the salesforce and may encourage turnover among high-performing salespeople who have other employment opportunities. Second, as salespeople move through the career cycle, they tend to self-regulate the reward system. Senior salespeople are often seeking rewards that cannot be dispensed and controlled by sales managers, such as a sense of accomplishment on the job. As a result, rewards lose some of their impact. Third, salespeople are typically more satisfied with their sales manager, if the relationship is based on expert and referent power. Thus, it is recommended that sales managers who wish to become effective leaders develop referent and expert power bases.

At times, salespeople have more power in a situation than the sales manager. For example, senior salespeople may be extremely knowledgeable and therefore have dominant expert power over a relatively inexperienced sales manager. Or a sales manager with strong self-esteem needs may be intent on winning a popularity contest with the salesforce, which could give salespeople a strong referent power base. When a sales manager senses that the salesperson is more powerful in one of these dimensions, there is a strong tendency to rely on legitimate, coercive, or reward power to gain control of the situation. Again, it is suggested that these three power bases be used sparingly, however, and that the sales manager work instead toward developing more expert and referent power.

This recommendation is getting results in progressive sales organizations. For example, Marty Reist, National Sales Manager for MPRS Sales, has used expert and referent power to bring about double-digit sales increases. One of his salespeople at MPRS explains, "He doesn't direct his team from a throne, he gets down in the trenches with you."[9]

The concepts of teamwork and employee participation in management decision making are often used and are largely incompatible with the heavy-handed use of coercive and legitimate power. Sales managers interested in developing an effective power base might consider the advice given in Exhibit 7.2.[10]

One additional point on sales managers' use of power is that a combination of power bases may be used in a given situation. For example, it might be a sales manager's referent and expert power that allows him or her to conduct a highly effective leadership function, such as an annual sales meeting. The use of combinations of power bases more accurately reflects reality than does the exclusive use of one power base for all situations.

Sales Leadership Influence Strategies

Because sales managers have power from different sources to use in dealing with salespeople, peers, and superiors, they have the opportunity to devise different influence

How Sales Managers Can Develop Power   EXHIBIT 7.2

Suggestions for sales managers in developing their power bases:

- Decide on overall objectives.
- Listen to your sales team's wants, needs, and dreams.
- Align the sales team with the firm's corporate culture.
- Meet key customers and industry leaders.
- Make appearances at image-enhancing events.
- Secure support of upper management for sales management programs and activities.
- Use one-on-one meetings to motivate salespeople.
- Develop an information management system to minimize the flow of irrelevant information.

strategies according to situational demands. Influence strategies can be based on threats, promises, persuasion, relationships, and manipulation.[11] All are appropriate at some time with some salespeople but not necessarily with superiors or peers.

1. Threats. In a strategy based on threats, a manager might specify a desired behavior and the punishment that will follow if the behavior is not achieved. "If you do not call on your accounts at least once a week, you will lose your job," is an example. Threats should be viewed as a last resort, but they should not be eliminated as a viable influence strategy.

2. Promises. Sales managers can use reward power as a basis for developing influence strategies based on promises. Promises typically produce better compliance than threats. This would seem to be especially true for well-educated mobile employees, which many professional salespeople are. Furthermore, influence strategies based on promises as opposed to threats help foster positive feelings among salespeople and boost salesforce morale.

3. Persuasion. An influence strategy based on persuasion can work without the use of reward or coercive power. Because persuasive messages must be rational and reasonable, however, expert and referent power bases are necessary to make them effective. Persuasion implies that the target of influence must first change his or her attitudes and intentions to produce a subsequent change in behavior. For example, a sales manager might persuade the salesforce to submit weekly activity reports by first convincing them of the importance of the reports in the company's marketing information system. Generally speaking, persuasion is preferred to threats and promises, but it does require more time and skill.

4. Relationships. Two types of relationships can affect influence processes. The first type is based on referent power. It builds on personal friendships, or feelings of trust, admiration, or respect. In short, one party is willing to do what the other party desires, simply because the former likes the latter. In a salesforce setting, these kinds of relationships are consistent with the notion of the salesforce as a cooperative team.

In the second type of relationship, one party has legitimate power over the other party by virtue of position in the organizational hierarchy. Sales managers have legitimate power in dealing with salespeople. As a result, they can influence salespeople in many situations without the use of threats, promises, or persuasion.

5. Manipulation. Unlike the other influence strategies, manipulation does not involve direct communications with the target of influence. Rather, circumstances are controlled to influence behavior. For example, a salesperson lacking self-confidence might be assigned to work on a temporary assignment with a confident senior salesperson. In team selling, the sales manager might control the group dynamics within teams by carefully selecting compatible personality types to compose the teams. Manipulation might also involve "office politics" and the use of third parties to influence others. For example, a sales manager might use the backing of his or her superior in dealing with peers on the job. Sometimes manipulation influence strategies can pose moral questions as presented in "An Ethical Dilemma."

You are a field sales manager with 10 sales-people on your team. All of your salespeople are performing well, except for one. You have tried different leadership styles, relationship approaches, and influence strategies, but this problem sales-person has not responded to any of your leader-ship approaches. Feeling desperate, you are thinking about telling this problem salesperson that you are going to have to terminate one sales-person from your team, because your firm wants to reduce the size of its salesforce. The top candi-dates for termination are the problem salesperson and another salesperson who is currently per-forming better than the problem salesperson. Although none of this is true, you think it might motivate the problem salesperson to work harder and perform better. What would you do and why?

Sales Leadership Communications

Clear, consistent, and effective communication is an important sales leadership skill. Senior sales leaders must continuously communicate to the entire sales organization, especially during times of change. For example, one reason for the success of the SunGard sales transformation, presented in the opening vignette, was due to effective communication from the beginning and throughout the entire process. This included communicating the need for the transformation to top corporate executives and then to the entire sales organization, getting input from salespeople about changes that would help them improve, presenting a new vision and plan, and updating progress on a regular basis. Research suggests that at least 15 percent of a senior sales leader's time should be spent communicating a clear course for establishing and accomplishing the current sales plan.[12]

Field sales managers need to focus on communicating effectively to members of their sales team on a regular basis. In addition to coaching and sales meetings, discussed later in this chapter, field sales managers should create a communication plan that meets the needs of the sales team and the sales organization situation. Two examples illustrate different approaches:

- Mike Nelson leads a team of salespeople from ON24. The salespeople are located across the country. He communicates with them on a daily basis using a mixture of phone calls, instant messages, and emails. Sales meetings are held when needed.[13]

- Carole Levin, sales manager for Taconic, has found that a monthly conference call is an effective way for her and her 11 salespeople, scattered throughout the United States, to communicate on a regular basis. She solicits ideas from reps and publishes an agenda to keep the calls on track. The first 30 minutes of the call focus on the agenda and the remaining 30 minutes are used for discussion and feedback. Levin e-mails a call summary to everyone.[14]

A critical part of using communication in leadership processes is knowing how to use appropriate communication tools effectively. In today's productivity-driven environment, sales managers are using every conceivable device to improve the efficiency of their communication with the salesforce. Cell phones, Web conferencing, voice mail, email, Internet, company intranet, satellite, and companywide video networks are some of the more popular tools being used to speed communication to salesforces in far-flung locations. The key is to use the communication mechanisms most appropriate to the sales organization.

All communication with the salesforce must be carefully planned to ensure accuracy and clarity. The latest technological developments offer some valuable communication advantages. For example, NBC Universal uses Salesforce.com's Chatter to share information throughout the sales organization. Everyone gets automatic updates when something changes. So, if something happens with a customer, all sales managers and salespeople get the latest information. Even though this type of technology can communicate information throughout the sales organization efficiently, the personal communication between a sales manager and a salesperson is still of prime importance in sales leadership.[15] In fact, research suggests that more frequent and informal communication between a sales manager and salespeople is likely to result in better job performance and greater job satisfaction.[16]

IMPORTANT SALES LEADERSHIP FUNCTIONS

This section examines three leadership functions that are particularly relevant to sales managers: coaching salespeople, conducting sales meetings, and promoting ethical behavior.

Coaching Salespeople

One of the most critical tasks for sales managers, especially field sales managers, is coaching. Coaching includes working directly with salespeople to help them develop professionally, plan and execute sales strategies for specific customers, and improve all aspects of the sales process. The importance of coaching has been recognized for many years:

- Comcast engaged in a sales transformation to improve the ability of its inside salespeople to create more value for customers and to increase the productivity of the entire sales organization. Salespeople received training to improve the quality of its conversations with customers. Sales managers reinforced the sales training by focusing on coaching. A study of sales managers found a direct correlation between coaching time and salesperson performance. The sales managers that spent the most time coaching had the highest-performing sales teams.[17]

- A sales manager was assigned to a sales team that was consistently ranked in the bottom quartile of the 100 sales teams at the company. This team had never received coaching from a sales manager. The new manager began an intensive coaching approach and used every interaction with a salesperson as a coaching opportunity. Within 18 months, this sales team had improved to the top 10 percent of the company's sales teams.[18]

Sales managers have many opportunities to coach salespeople. Sales managers can take advantage of every interaction with a salesperson as an opportunity to develop salespeople through coaching. Sometimes, coaching can occur during short meetings of the entire sales team. For example, sales managers at Comcast have a daily "huddle" with their sales team to discuss challenges, present best practices, and recognize salesperson accomplishments.[19] Finally, the most typical coaching approach is to have one-to-one scheduled meetings with salespeople to discuss various issues and review progress concerning commitments from previous meetings.

Many sales organizations have sales managers spend time with salespeople in the field and conduct sales calls together. At the end of a field visit and after the completion of a sales call, the sales manager typically conducts a coaching session designed to help improve the salesperson's performance in the future. A typical approach is to have sales managers accompany salespeople in the field once a month. After every field ride, sales managers provide salespeople with a coaching guide that analyzes their performance in categories such as work ethic, technical knowledge, and sales skills. Managers provide suggestions for improvement along with positive feedback. By ensuring a close link between the coaching session and the appropriate event (e.g., a field visit or sales call), the sales manager is using the principle of *recency* to assist the developmental, or learning, process. Essentially this principle holds that learning is facilitated when it is immediately applied. By making a practice of holding coaching sessions after each sales call, sales managers are also using *repetition*, another powerful learning tool.

In addition to using repetition and recency to facilitate learning, sales managers should consider the type of feedback they offer to salespeople during coaching sessions. Feedback can be described as either outcome feedback or as cognitive feedback. Outcome feedback is information about whether a desired outcome is achieved. By contrast, cognitive feedback is information about how and why the desired outcome is achieved. The importance of outcome and cognitive feedback is evident in the coaching suggestions presented in Exhibit 7.3.[20]

EXHIBIT 7.3   Coaching Suggestions

1. Take a "we" approach instead of a "you" approach. Instead of telling the salesperson, "You should do it this way next time," say, "On the next call, we can do it this way."
2. Address only one or two problems at a time. Prioritize problems to be attacked, and deal with the most important ones first.
3. Instead of criticizing salespeople during coaching, help them improve by giving how-to advice. Repeatedly tell them what you like about their performance.
4. Ask questions to maximize the salesperson's active involvement in the coaching process.
5. Recognize differences in salespeople and coach accordingly. Although salespeople should work together as a team, direct some efforts toward meeting individual needs.
6. Coordinate coaching with more formal sales training. Coaching is valuable, but it cannot replace formal sales training. Train regularly to enhance skills, then reinforce with coaching.
7. Encourage continual growth and improvement of salespeople. Use team or one-on-one sessions to evaluate progress and celebrate accomplishments.
8. Insist that salespeople evaluate themselves. Self-evaluation helps develop salespeople into critical thinkers regarding their work habits and performance.
9. Reach concrete agreements about what corrective action is to be taken after each coaching session. Failure to agree on corrective action may lead to the salesperson's withdrawal from the developmental aspects of coaching.
10. Keep records of coaching sessions specifying corrective action to be taken, objectives of the coaching session, and a timetable for accomplishing the objective. Follow up to ensure objectives are accomplished.

SALES MANAGEMENT IN THE 21ST CENTURY

Coaching Salespeople at Federated Insurance

Joe Kemp, District Marketing Manager for Federated Insurance, discusses how he gets salespeople to implement his coaching suggestions.

The coaching suggestions I give to salespeople are to help improve their performance. But, they must actually do what I suggest. I have to prove to salespeople that what I suggest actually works and it is something that I do myself. What I do is travel with salespeople in the field, tell them about a sales behavior they need to implement, and then show it to them in an actual sales situation. This approach
has been very successful for me. For example, one of my newer reps was trying to close a large account. All of the competitors for this business had made their proposals. My rep was trying to call the prospect, but could not get his calls returned. I suggested that the rep just go to the business and stay until the prospect would see him. The rep was reluctant to do this, so I went with him. We waited in the office until the prospect would see us, talked about our proposal, and closed the business during this meeting. My rep got the business, but also learned that my suggestions work and that I will to do what I ask sales reps to do.

Successful coaching occurs in an environment of trust and respect between the sales manager and salesperson. By demonstrating honesty, reliability, and competency and by listening to salespeople's needs, sales managers can earn the trust and respect of salespeople and enhance their own chances of being a successful coach. As coaches, sales managers must be role models that set positive examples through their behavior. This is crucial because salespeople will emulate the work habits, positive attitudes, and goals of their managers. Joe Kemp, District Marketing Manager, discusses his approach in "Sales Management in the 21st Century: Coaching Salespeople at Federated Insurance."

Drew Cameron, President of HVAC, contends coaching is a position that carries tremendous power and responsibilities. Sales coaching should be an individualized development process designed to change a salesperson's behavior to better meet an organization's goal for customer happiness and financial performance. Through coaching, salespeople should benefit from ongoing observation, analysis, feedback, and encouragement. Cameron's basic principles for coaching are summarized in Exhibit 7.4.[21]

Conducting Sales Meetings

One of the best ways for sales managers to demonstrate leadership is to conduct a sales meeting. Sales meetings are usually held on a regular basis and intended for salespeople and sales managers, but sometimes other business functions are included. The meetings typically have multiple purposes and include a variety of activities, such as sales training, strategic planning, motivational programs, recognition events, as well as recreation and entertainment. For example, Tea Collection holds two sales meetings a year. At a summer meeting, designers were included to present new clothing lines and to brainstorm ideas for presenting as many clothing items in a sales call that typically lasts for about 90 minutes. New prospecting software was also introduced. The meeting also included a winery tour and a cookout to improve the morale of the sales organization. Most importantly, it led to increased sales. One salesperson used the new software to identify 20 new accounts and sold them significant portions of the product line.[22]

The success of sales meetings requires careful planning and execution. Salespeople and sales managers do not like to be taken out of the field for a meeting, unless the meeting is enjoyable and valuable to them. Therefore, the needs of salespeople should be taken into consideration when planning a sales meeting. Some general suggestions from salespeople for conducting a successful meeting are presented in Exhibit 7.5.[23]

Planning and conducting a sales meeting involves creative, sometimes glamorous, activities, such as selecting a theme for the meeting, arranging for the appearance of professional entertainers, or even assisting in the production of special films and other

Basic Principles for Coaching   EXHIBIT 7.4

1. A coach must be ready to make others look good. "It takes a particular level of emotional maturity, and you would be surprised at the difficulty many people have with getting over their own ego."
2. People learn from experience, not from being told. "You can tell your salespeople about selling all day long, but that doesn't mean they are going to get any better at it. They need to experience failure, rejection, and success. It is your job as the coach to introduce them to these experiences. This means going on sales calls with them, listening in on conference calls, etc."
3. A coach has to be up when others are down. It is vital that the coach sets the tone for the sales environment. It is especially important that you stay positive when things get tough, because if you're in the dumps, your salespeople will be, too.
4. Use systems, processes, and principles. "People perform better when they have a system." It's no different with sales. Establish a usable sales system and coach your salespeople on the principles of the system.
5. Finally, "You must be inspiring." As he said, "If you are a cold fish, it's just not going to work."

EXHIBIT 7.5   Suggestions from Salespeople on Conducting Meetings

1. Keep technical presentations succinct, and use visual aids and breakout discussion groups to maintain salespeople's interest.
2. Keep salespeople informed of corporate strategy and their role in it.
3. Minimize operations reviews unless they are directly related to sales. Use a combination of face-to-face exchanges and written handouts to introduce key people in advertising and customer service.
4. Set a humane schedule. Overscheduling can deter learning. Allow time for salespeople to share experiences so they learn from each other.
5. Let salespeople know what's planned. Be sure they are briefed on the purpose and content of the meeting. Distribute a written agenda.
6. Ask salespeople for their ideas on topics, speakers, and preferred recreational activities, if applicable.
7. Generate excitement with contests. Reward effort and results so that all participants can enjoy the chance to win.

---

audiovisual materials. For example, Latitude Communications, an online conferencing provider, developed the theme "Fire Up" for its national sales meeting. The meeting began with a volcano erupting with smoke and sound effects and a performance from a fire dancer, and included, among other things, the vice president of marketing performing a rap song about company sales. To foster teamwork and keep with the meeting's theme, salespeople were taken offsite to participate in exercises used to train firefighters, such as a simulated rescue from a five-story tower, a fire-victim carrying race, the passing of water buckets, and extinguishing a fire with authentic firefighting equipment.[24] However, the ultimate success of all meetings depends on the planning and execution of rather detailed activities, such as communicating with all parties before the meeting, checking site arrangements, preparing materials for the meeting, arranging for audiovisual support, and ensuring that all supplies are on hand when the meeting begins. To increase the effectiveness of a major meeting, sales managers would be well served to heed the advice given in Exhibit 7.6.[25]

Increasingly, communication technology allows off-site meeting participants to join in meetings. This is often an attractive option for salesforces that are geographically dispersed. Computer networks, groupwork software, Web meetings, and videoconferencing can replace some face-to-face meetings without any loss in meeting effectiveness. The cost is often lower, as well. For instance, Web conferencing allows participants to talk while sharing information on the Web, provides online facilities that enable participants to ask questions, and includes tools that can be used to poll attendees.[26] Nonetheless, face-to-face meetings remain a crucial sales leadership activity.

Promoting Ethical Behavior

The development of trust-based, long-term relationships between buyers and sellers requires ethical behavior by salespeople and others in the sales organization and throughout the company. Research results suggest positive relationships between salesperson ethical behavior and buyer trust and relationship commitment.[27] The importance of ethical behavior is stressed in every chapter in this book by highlighting specific ethical dilemmas faced by sales managers and salespeople. A general framework for different approaches to management ethics is presented in Exhibit 7.7.[28]

The immoral management and amoral management approaches either disregard or do not consider the morality or ethical implications of management decisions and behavior. These approaches are likely to lead to some of the troubling unethical situations presented in the business or popular press in recent years. Several studies during the past few years indicate that unethical behavior in firms and sales organizations is more prevalent today than it has been in the past.[29]

| | Sales Manager's Meeting Review List   EXHIBIT 7.6 |

Before your meeting
1. Distribute meeting notice/agenda.
2. Plan and prepare the meeting content, both text and visuals, in terms of the needs of your audience.
3. Rehearse.
4. Check out room and equipment.

At the start of the meeting
1. Review the agenda.
2. Review meeting objectives.
3. Explain what role the participants will have in the meeting.

During the meeting (encouraging participation)
1. Ask open-ended questions...that is, questions that can't be answered with "yes" or "no".
2. Ask one or two participants to bring specific relevant information to share at the meeting.
3. Reinforce statements that are on target with meeting objectives.
4. When questions are asked of you, redirect them to the group or to the questioner.
5. Use examples from your own personal experience to encourage the group to think along similar lines.

During the meeting (maintaining control)
1. Ignore off-target remarks. Do not reinforce.
2. Ask questions specifically related to the task at hand.
3. Restate relevant points of the agenda when the discussion veers from objectives.
4. When one person is dominating the discussion, tactfully, but firmly, ask him or her to allow others to speak.
5. Ask the group's opinion about whether a certain subject is on target or not with the agenda.

At the end of the meeting
1. Summarize.
2. State conclusions and relate to original meeting objectives.
3. Outline actions to be taken as a result of the meeting (who is expected to do what and by when).

Cautions
1. Encourage, don't resent, questions.
2. Be a facilitator and not a monopolizer of discussion.
3. A little humor is welcome at most any meeting, but don't attempt to be a constant comic.
4. Don't put anybody down in public. If you have a problem participant, take him or her aside at a break and ask for cooperation.
5. Coming unprepared is worse than not coming.

Moral management, in contrast, actively incorporates moral considerations into all aspects of management and takes proactive measures to promote ethical behavior throughout the firm and sales organization. Many sales organizations have created a code of ethics to communicate the values and expected behaviors of salespeople and sales managers. Professional associations often have codes of ethics and require members to adhere to these standards of ethical behavior. An example of a code of ethics for professional salespeople is presented in Exhibit 7.8.[30]

Although ethical codes can have a positive impact, sales managers have an important role to play in promoting ethical behavior. Sales managers face a number of situations with ethical implications as they interact with salespeople, customers, and others in their firm. Some of the most difficult situations are those related to a conflict of interest. One example of this type of situation is presented in "An Ethical Dilemma."

Sales leadership activities are also very important in promoting ethical behavior in a sales organization. The ethical situations faced by salespeople and sales managers are often complex. As a result, the ethical decision-making process is based on a number of

AN ETHICAL DILEMMA

You are a district sales manager for a rapidly growing technology firm. There are eight salespeople in your district. Your company has set an aggressive district quota for this year. But, if your district exceeds this quota, you will receive a nice bonus, which is what you need to make the down payment on a house that you and your wife want to purchase. As you review the performance of your district, it looks like you have a good chance of exceeding your district quota. Most of your sales reps are on track, but your star salesperson is 10 percent over quota already. It looks like this salesperson will ensure that your district quota is achieved, so you want to make sure you support this salesperson as much as you can throughout the remainder of the year. However, as you are reviewing recent expense reports, it becomes obvious to you that this star salesperson has been "padding" his expense report by claiming reimbursement for personal expenses. If true, this is a violation of your sales organization's code of ethics and could warrant termination of the salesperson. What would you do and why?

EXHIBIT 7.7   Approaches to Management Ethics

Organizational Characteristics	Immoral Management	Amoral Management	Moral Management
Ethical Norms	Management decisions, actions, and behavior imply a positive and active opposition to what is moral (ethical). Decisions are discordant with accepted ethical principles. An active negation of what is moral is implied.	Management is neither moral nor immoral, but decisions lie outside the sphere to which moral judgments apply. Management activity is outside or beyond the moral order of a particular code. May imply a lack of ethical perception and moral awareness.	Management activity conforms to a standard of ethical, or right, behavior. Management activity conforms to accepted professional standards of conduct. Ethical leadership is common on the part of management.
Motives	Selfish. Management cares only about its or the company's gains.	Well-intentioned but selfish in the sense that impact on others is not considered.	Good. Management wants to succeed but only within the confines of sound ethical precepts (fairness, justice, due process).
Goals	Profitability and organizational success at any price.	Profitability. Other goals are not considered.	Profitability within the confines of legal obedience and ethical standards.
Orientation toward Law	Legal standards are barriers that management must overcome to accomplish what it wants.	Law is the ethical guide, preferably the letter of the law. The central question is what we can do legally.	Obedience toward letter and spirit of the law. Law is a minimal ethical behavior. Prefer to operate well above what law mandates.
Strategy	Exploit opportunities for corporate gain. Cut corners when it appears useful.	Give managers free rein. Personal ethics may apply but only if managers choose. Respond to legal mandates if caught and required to do so.	Live by sound ethical standards. Assume leadership position when ethical dilemmas arise. Enlightened self-interest.

Code of Ethics for Professional Salespeople   EXHIBIT 7.8

As a certified professional salesperson, I pledge to the following people and organizations:

The Customer. In all customer relationships, I pledge to

- Maintain honesty and integrity in my relationships with customers and prospective customers.
- Accurately represent my product or service to place the customer or prospective customer in a position to make a decision consistent with the principle of mutuality of benefit and profit to the buyer and seller.
- Keep abreast of all pertinent information that would assist my customers in achieving their goals as they relate to my product(s) or service(s).

The Company. In relationships with my employer, coworkers, and other parties whom I represent, I will

- Use their resources that are at my disposal for legitimate business purposes only.
- Respect and protect proprietary and confidential information entrusted to me by my company.

The Competition. Regarding those with whom I compete in the marketplace, I promise to

- Obtain competitive information only through legal and ethical methods.
- Portray my competitors and their products and services only in a manner that is honest and truthful and that reflects accurate information that can or has been substantiated.

individual and organizational factors.[31] Sales managers need to reinforce the importance of ethical behavior in all of their leadership activities. Employing transformational leadership style, building trust-based relationships with salespeople, creating an ethical climate, addressing ethics during the socialization process, and incorporating an ethical perspective into the overall approach for managing salespeople are leadership activities related to ethical behavior in a sales organization.[32] Sales managers must orient and coordinate all aspects of their sales leadership and management activities toward promoting ethical behavior.

SUMMARY

1. **Distinguish between salesforce leadership, management, and supervision.** As noted in Exhibit 7.1, senior sales leaders, field sales managers, and salespeople can all be involved in leadership, management, and supervision activities. Sales leadership includes all activities performed by those in a sales organization to influence others to achieve common goals for the collective good of the sales organization and company. The leadership activities of senior sales leaders are directed at the entire sales organization or large subunits, while field sales manager leadership activities emphasize creating the right climate to inspire their assigned salespeople. Salespeople, in contrast, are engaged in self-leadership and sometimes play a leadership role with customers, others in the sales organization and company, and with channel partners. Sales management activities are those related to the planning, implementation, and control of the sales management process. Senior sales leaders address the broader aspects of the sales management process, while field sales managers are more involved in implementing the process with their assigned salespeople. The management activities of salespeople are more focused on the planning, implementation, and control of sales activities within their assigned territory. Sales supervision refers to working with subordinates on a day-to-day basis. Senior sales leadership and salespeople are normally not as involved with supervision activities as are field sales managers.

2. **Discuss the importance of situational factors in determining the most effective sales leadership approaches.** Research indicates that the best sales leadership

approaches depend upon the situation facing a sales manager. Different situations require the use of different sales leadership styles, relationship strategies, power bases, influence strategies, and communication approaches.

3. **Explain how leadership style approaches contribute to contemporary sales leadership.** Transformational leadership recognizes the necessity and importance of change in most sales organizations by inspiring salespeople to engage in the desired behaviors and perform at high levels. A transactional leadership style, in contrast, emphasizes rewards and punishments to get salespeople to improve performance.

4. **Discuss five bases of power that affect sales leadership.** The five power bases are coercive, reward, legitimate, referent, and expert. Coercive power is associated with punishment and is the opposite of reward power. Legitimate power stems from the individual's position in the organizational hierarchy. Referent power is held by one person when another person wants to maintain a relationship with that person. Expert power is attributed to the possession of information. A sales manager and those with whom he or she interacts may use one or more power bases in a given situation.

5. **Explain five influence strategies used in sales leadership.** Influence strategies used by sales managers could be based on threats, promises, persuasion, relationships, or manipulation. Unlike the other four strategies, manipulation does not involve face-to-face interactions with the target of influence. Threats use coercive power, whereas promises stem from the reward power base. Persuasion uses expert and referent power. Legitimate and referent power are used when influence strategy is based on interpersonal relationships.

6. **Discuss issues related to coaching salespeople, conducting sales meetings, and promoting ethical behavior.** Coaching involves the continual development of the salesforce. A most critical part of coaching is one-on-one sessions with a salesperson. Coaching relies on the learning principles of recency and repetition and is often conducted in the field before and after sales calls. Integrative meetings accomplish multiple sales management functions. Sales managers are involved in creative aspects of planning integrative meetings, but paying attention to detail is the key to successful meetings. Meeting ethical responsibilities is not necessarily easy but is essential to long-term success in a sales career.

UNDERSTANDING SALES MANAGEMENT TERMS

sales leadership
sales management
sales supervision
trait approach
behavior approach
contingency approach
leadership style
transactional leadership style
transformational leadership
Leader–Member Exchange (LMX)
  model
expert power
referent power
legitimate power
reward power

coercive power
influence strategies
threats
promises
persuasion
relationships
manipulation
coaching
outcome feedback
cognitive feedback
sales meeting
immoral management
amoral management
moral management
code of ethics

DEVELOPING SALES MANAGEMENT KNOWLEDGE

1. Explain why the following views of leadership are relevant for sales organizations: transactional leadership and transformational leadership.

2. What do you think are the most important situational factors a field sales manager should consider when determining the most effective sales leadership approaches?

3. Describe five types of power that affect leadership. What are the problems associated with overreliance on reward and coercive power?

4. How does the contingency approach to leadership differ from the trait approach and the behavior approach?

5. How can new technologies be used most effectively in sales leadership communication?

6. Describe five influence strategies, including the power bases related to each strategy.

7. What is the difference between outcome feedback and cognitive feedback? Which is most important in coaching?

8. Sales managers may learn a lot about their organizations and salespeople simply by spending time observing activities in the office or in the field and talking with the people involved. To maximize their own learning while simultaneously providing leadership, which power bases would be especially important?

9. Refer to "Sales Management in the 21st Century: Leading Salespeople at Federated Insurance" on p. 204. Explain Joe Kemp's approach to leadership in your own words.

10. Refer to "Sales Management in the 21st Century: Coaching Salespeople at Federated Insurance" on p. 210. Discuss the key aspects of Joe Kemp's strategy for coaching salespeople.

BUILDING SALES MANAGEMENT SKILLS

1. Sid Cox has been a steady contributor as an automotive parts representative with Premier Auto Parts for the past five years. Conscientious and hard-working, he has always been willing to pull his weight and then some. Customers and coworkers find that his cheerful and pleasant demeanor make him a joy to be around. Over the past month, his sales manager, Randy Ross, has noticed a significant change in Sid's behavior. Sid appears to be worn down, less than enthusiastic, and reluctant to make as many sales calls as he has in the past. His positive, upbeat demeanor seems to have been replaced with a more pessimistic attitude about things. His generally steady sales results have been on the decline. If you were Randy Ross, what would you do? Explain.

2. Choose an individual who is considered to be (or to have been) a great leader (e.g., Lee Iacocca, J.F.K.). Use library resources, the Internet, and so on, to examine this individual to determine what makes (or made) this person such a good leader. In your analysis, explain this leader's traits or characteristics and the leadership skills that contributed to his or her success. Also, attempt to identify and explain the sources of power generally used by this leader. Finally, explain what you learned about this leader that you could use to help you become a more successful leader.

3. Google "sales leadership." Select three articles from the results of this search. Read each article and discuss how it applies to one or more topics covered in this chapter.

ROLE PLAY

4. **Role Play**

Situation: Sales manager Lisa Lefton is accompanying sales rep Sherry Shorten on a sales call to a local grocery store, Price Chopper. Sherry is attempting to gain shelf space for a new flavor of Lipton bottled tea.

Characters: Lisa Lefton, sales manager; Sherry Shorten, sales representative; Jim Hopson, store manager.

Scene 1: *Location*—Price Chopper grocery store. *Action*—Sherry attempts to convince Jim Hopson to give her shelf space for a new flavor of Lipton bottled tea. She is very unenthusiastic. Furthermore, she is having trouble overcoming objections, particularly Jim's concern about the need for a new flavor and the space desired. Lisa observes the sales call.

Scene 2: *Location*—In Sherry's car on the way to their next sales call. *Action*—Lisa coaches Sherry regarding her visit with Jim Hopson.

ROLE PLAY

5. **Role Play**

Situation: Read "An Ethical Dilemma" on p. 208.

Characters: Yourself as field sales manager; the problem salesperson.

Scene: *Location*—Field sales manager's office.
Action—You are meeting with the problem salesperson again to motivate him/her to work harder and perform better. The exact discussion in this meeting will depend on whether or not you decide to use the manipulation influence strategy.

ROLE PLAY

6. **Role Play**

Situation: Read "An Ethical Dilemma" on p. 214.

Characters: Yourself as district sales manager; the star salesperson.

Scene: *Location*—District sales manager's office.

Action—You are meeting with the star salesperson to address issues related to performance and the possibility of "expense padding." The exact discussion in this meeting will depend on your decision about how to handle the possible "expense padding" situation.

7. Access the Center for Creative Leadership at http://www.ccl.org. Examine the contents of the Web site. What types of resources are available to sales managers to help them become better leaders (explain at least two of these). Be sure to explain how the resources could be utilized by sales managers.

MAKING SALES MANAGEMENT DECISIONS

CASE 7.1: TASTI-FRESH BAKERY PRODUCTS

Background

Tasti-Fresh Bakery Products has been very successful at selling breads, rolls, and other bakery products to small- and medium-sized retailers throughout the Midwest. It has built its reputation on quality products, strong service, honesty, and integrity. The company credits much of its success to its sales people, who provide the main link between it and its customers. The ability of Tasti-Fresh's salespeople to build strong customer relationships has helped keep the company profitable despite increasing competition.

Current Situation

Tasti-Fresh district sales manager Laurel Brown recently received the following letter from one of the company's biggest customers.

February 22, 2014
3242 Grand Avenue
St. Louis, MO 63441

Ms. Laurel Brown
District Sales Manager
Tasti-Fresh Bakery Products
1675 Main
St. Charles, MO 63301

Dear Laurel:

We have always been pleased with your company's products and service. The sales rep who calls on us, Curt Stanford, has gone out of his way to ensure our satisfaction. Lately, however, I have noticed some changes in Curt's behavior. Normally I would not complain, but the treatment we have been getting recently is dramatically different from that to which we are accustomed, and I am concerned about Curt.

Over the past couple of months, I have noticed a dramatic shift in Curt's behavior. Usually steady and dependable, his behavior has become erratic. He has been late, or not shown up at all, for some of his scheduled appointments. Curt also has failed to follow through on several occasions. Sometimes he visits us and he is so enthusiastic it is almost unbearable, whereas on other visits he appears very tired and worn down. I think he might be having some personal problems.

As I said earlier, over the years we have been happy with your products and service. However, if this type of behavior persists, we will be forced to look for another supplier. We simply cannot afford to jeopardize our business.

Sincerely,

Janice Miller

Janice Miller
Purchasing Agent, Flanders Groceries, Inc.

Laurel was perplexed. Curt is one of her top performers. He has worked for the company for four years and has been salesperson of the year the past two years. She had not noticed a change in Curt. Then again, she has not had much direct contact with Curt lately because she has been concentrating her efforts on three newly hired sales reps. She wonders if she should confront Curt or simply ignore it. He is making the company a lot of money, and she has not heard any other complaints. If she confronts him, he might quit. Perhaps Janice is simply exaggerating and is really upset about something else. Maybe Janice needs to be confronted. Ignoring her may result in the loss of a big customer.

Questions

1. Should Laurel confront Curt? If not, why? If so, how should she handle the situation?

2. Should Laurel speak to Janice? Why or why not? If so, what should she say to her?

3. If Curt has personal problems, what do you recommend that Laurel do? How can she prevent problems like this in the future?

Role Play

ROLE PLAY

Situation: Read Case 7.1.

Characters: Laurel Brown, district sales manager; Janice Miller, purchasing agent; Curt Stanford, sales representative

Scene 1:   *Location*—Laurel's office. *Action*—Laurel has called a meeting with Curt Stanford to confront him regarding the issue brought to her attention by Laurel Brown.

Scene 2:   *Location*—Tasti-Fresh Bakery Products. *Action*—After speaking to Curt, Laurel decides to visit Janice Miller at Tasti-Fresh to discuss the situation with her.

CASE 7.2: GLOBAL ENTERPRISE
Background

Rock Madd was a drill sergeant in the U.S. Marine Corps for five years before joining Global Enterprise seven years ago as a sales representative. In the Corps, he had been through some tough times and was always willing to face a challenge. A disciplined man, he rapidly became one of the company's best salespeople. However, his goal was to move into sales management. Because of his strong determination and hard work, he was eventually promoted to district sales manager, replacing Lucille Fagan, who recently retired.

Lucille had done an outstanding job with the district. Her district's sales figures were consistently among the top in the company. She was well liked and respected by her salespeople. Lucille practiced good management skills and was adept at planning, organizing, controlling, and leading. Although she always took the ultimate responsibility for planning, she often consulted salespeople when she thought their ideas might be helpful. When it came to organizing, her goal was to motivate her salespeople to work as a team. As a result, she was able to get salespeople to help each other when the needs arose. She had control over her salespeople, but it was primarily through self-control. By setting realistic and individual-specific goals, she was able to motivate her salespeople not only to commit to those goals but also to supervise their own efforts effectively. Finally, Lucille had a real knack for leadership. She had the ability to get salespeople to realize their true potential and then help them achieve it. It was her contention that a leader should develop people, and she did. In fact, over the years, her salespeople were consistently promoted into management positions.

Rock took a different approach to managing, primarily as a result of his military background. He was a hard-working individual who demanded respect from those around him. He wanted to make sure those he supervised knew he was the boss. His attitude toward planning was that he made the plans and others carried them out. He did not need or seek input from others. He ran a tight organization, calling all the shots. When it came to control, he liked to scrutinize his salespeople closely, making sure they were doing what they were supposed to do.

Current Situation

On Monday afternoon, Rock completed a sales call with Electra Aveshon, a three-year veteran at Global Enterprise. Although not the most outstanding salesperson in the district, Electra was a good performer. She credited much of her success to Lucille, who had helped bring her along. It was Electra's opinion that Lucille could have easily let her go after her rocky start but instead invested the time in coaching her to become a better salesperson. After the call, Rock indicated that he would like to meet with Electra on Friday to discuss the sales call. He had some other business he had to attend to right away, so they could not meet that afternoon. She agreed and an appointment was scheduled for Friday afternoon.

After finishing her appointments Friday morning, Electra met with Rock as scheduled. Following are excerpts from their meeting:

Rock: I was disappointed with your sales call on Monday. It surprised me to see a veteran such as yourself perform so sloppily. You should be ashamed.

Electra: I realize I didn't make the sale. But for the first visit, I felt I made progress in beginning to establish trust and build a relationship.

Rock: You spent too much time attempting to build rapport. You wasted valuable time that could be spent calling on other prospects or servicing current customers.

Electra: I always spend a little more time building rapport. I think it pays off in the long run.

Rock: Your handling of objections was poor. Your response to the question on pricing was totally inadequate. Your response to the question on delivery time was likewise inept. You need to work on handling objections.

Electra: My responses may not have been perfect, but I did not sense the prospect was unsure about what I was saying or had a problem with my responses.

Rock: And where did you learn to close? You need to drive the sale home. You played it a little too soft. I expect to see some real improvement on our next outing. If you can't do any better than this, maybe I'll have to find someone who can.

That evening after work Electra met with a few of her colleagues for some drinks and dinner. The following conversation ensued:

Electra: I'm sick of Madd bossing us around like we are a bunch of his soldiers. This isn't the army. We deserve to be treated with a little more respect.

Andrew: I hear you. The other day Madd went with me on a sales call. All I heard was what a horrible job I was doing. It was as if nothing I did on my call was right.

Colette: Madd always has something to say, and it's usually negative. He doesn't have any problem telling me what's wrong, but he never offers any advice on how to improve.

Matt: Come on, you guys. Give the guy a break. He's just doing what he thinks is right. He's trying to impress upper management by showing them he has everything under control down here.

Once he sees this hard-guy stuff doesn't work, he'll loosen up.

Andrew: Yeah, if half the salesforce doesn't quit first. I don't like working for a guy like him. Why should I bust my tail to make him look good? I won't put up with it for long. I've heard some of the others [salespeople] talking and they aren't happy, either. Morale really seems to be down.

Colette: Maybe Matt's right. Perhaps, soon, Madd will loosen up a bit.

Electra: I don't know, Colette. It's been eight months now. Once a sergeant, always a sergeant.

Questions

1. How would you characterize Rock's leadership style? How would you assess his sales management performance thus far?

2. What suggestions can you provide to Rock regarding coaching?

3. What would you recommend Rock do differently?

ROLE PLAY

Role Play

Situation: Read Case 7.2.

Characters: Rock Madd, district sales manager; Electra Aveshon, sales rep; Andrew, sales rep; Colette, sales rep; Matt, sales rep.

Scene 1: *Location*—Madd's office. *Action*—Role-play the meeting between Rock and Electra.

Scene 2: *Location*—A local bar and grill. *Action*—Role play the conversation between Electra, Andrew, Colette, and Matt.

Scene 3: *Location*—Madd's office on Monday morning. *Action*—Electra, Andrew, Collette, and Matt decide to confront Rock about his leadership style, letting him know their concerns about his leadership approach.

OBJECTIVES

After completing this chapter, you should be able to

1. Explain the key components of motivation: intensity, persistence, and direction.

2. Explain the difference between compensation rewards and noncompensation rewards.

3. Describe the primary financial and nonfinancial compensation rewards available to salespeople.

4. Describe salary, commission, and combination pay plans in terms of their advantages and disadvantages.

5. Explain how to determine an appropriate financial compensation level.

6. Explain the fundamental concepts in sales-expense reimbursement.

7. Discuss issues associated with sales contests, equal pay for equal work, team compensation, global compensation, and changing a reward system.

8. List the guidelines for motivating and rewarding salespeople.

ADAPTING SALES COMPENSATION TO A DYNAMIC BUSINESS ENVIRONMENT

Economic conditions have been challenging over the past several years. Most analysts believe that the widespread recession which began in 2007 has been replaced by an upswing in business activity. As a general trend, sales organizations have moved away from cost control as a primary focus and are once again placing an emphasis on sales growth and profitability. As economic conditions change, firms typically modify their sales compensation plans to better align with their strategic initiatives and goals. According to Deloitte Consulting, more than 60 percent of sales leaders surveyed in 2013 had changed their sales compensation plans during the prior two years. Sales compensation plans are often changed to increase salesforce productivity, expand services and market offerings, reformulate job roles, and to pursue new target markets.

Changing sales compensation plans to better align with the desired relationship between salespeople and their customers is an admirable step, but also can be a risky proposition. For example, banking giant HSBC changed the compensation for its financial advisors from a product-based commission plan to straight salary plus quarterly bonus based on client experience, sales quality, and values measures. According to HSBC vice president of communications, "The plan aligned with our aim of building sustainable relationships with clients based on trust and expertise, and with HSBC's strategy and values." Some industry observers applaud HSBC's customer-oriented shift in compensation, while others predict that high-producing financial advisors will leave in favor of commission-based jobs with other financial institutions. If client-based compensation plans become standard in financial planning salesforces, HSBC's reputation as a pioneer will likely pay off with increased business in the future.

As companies modify their sales compensation plans, new technologies are helping to build a sense of urgency, communicate sales results, and bring recognition to high performers. Increasingly, medium and larger-size companies are moving beyond spreadsheets to manage sales compensation in favor of automated sales performance systems that integrate customer relationship management (CRM) with compensation management and other dimensions of sales management. Integrated sales performance systems available from vendors such as Callidus, Synygy, Varicent/IBM, and Xactly can assist in optimizing compensation plans, administering sales incentive plans, encouraging desired sales behaviors, and tying sales performance to pay levels.

Sources: Kelly Liyakasa, "Sales Reps Are Falling Short of their Goals," *Customer Relationship Magazine* (April 2013): 12; Margarida Correia, "HSBC's Now Comp Structure—Insane or Prescient?" *Bank Investment Consultant* (September 2013): 7–9; and Jim Dickie, "Taking SPM Out of the Dark Ages," *Customer Relationship Management* (June 2013): 15.

The opening vignette introduces several important points regarding salesforce motivation and reward system management including tying sales compensation to a changing economic environment and changing the compensation plan to achieve emerging priorities. Firms such as HSBC are paying more attention to the desired long-term relationships between their salespeople and customers. Finally, sales organizations should take steps to administer compensation plans in an efficient manner, to include the use of appropriate technologies to communicate and analyze sales compensation.

A salesforce reward system, because of its impact on motivation and job satisfaction, is one of the most important determinants of short- and long-term sales performance. This chapter examines the sales manager's role in motivating the salesforce through the use of reward systems. We first define motivation and explain some key concepts in reward system management. In the next section of this chapter, the characteristics of an effective reward system, along with the reward preferences of salespeople in general, are discussed. The following section concentrates on financial rewards, such as salaries, commissions, and bonuses. As seen in Exhibit 8.1,[1] expenditures for financial rewards are quite substantial, often being the largest component of the sales organization's budget.

Nonfinancial rewards, such as opportunities for growth, recognition, and promotion, are reviewed. Expense reimbursement is also covered. Current issues in reward system management, such as the use of sales contests, equal pay for equal work, team compensation, global compensation, and changing reward systems, are presented. This chapter concludes with summary guidelines for managing salesforce reward systems.

EXHIBIT 8.1	Financial Compensation for Sales Managers, Sales Supervisors, and Salespeople	

Job Title	Average Annual Financial Compensation
Sales managers (nonretail)	$123,150
First-line sales supervisors (nonretail)	$82,890
Financial services salespeople	$102,510
Sales engineers	$101,790
Wholesale and manufacturing representatives (technical products)	$85,610
Wholesale and manufacturing representatives (nontechnical products)	$65,000
Insurance sales agents	$63,610
Advertising sales agents	$57,000

MOTIVATION AND REWARD SYSTEMS

An important part of sales management is motivating salespeople to accomplish organizational goals. Many factors, including job design, interactions with others on the job, personal goals and preferences of employees, and work-related rewards can impact salespeople's motivation.[2] In this chapter, we will focus on the role of reward systems as a key sales management motivational tool. Definitions of motivation often include three dimensions: intensity, direction, and persistence.[3] Intensity refers to the amount of mental and physical effort put forth by the salesperson. Direction implies that salespeople choose where their efforts will be spent among various job activities. Persistence describes the salesperson's choice to expend effort over time, especially when faced with adverse conditions.

Because salespeople are often faced with a diverse set of selling and nonselling job responsibilities, their choice of which activities warrant action is just as important as how hard they work or how well they persist in their efforts. The motivation task is incomplete unless salespeople's efforts are channeled in directions consistent with the overall strategic role of the salesforce within the firm.[4]

Motivation is an unobservable phenomenon, and the terms *intensity, persistence,* and *direction* are concepts that help managers explain what they expect from their salespeople. It is important to note that, although sales managers can observe salespeople's behavior, they can only infer their motivation. Indeed, it is the personal, unobservable nature of motivation that makes it such a difficult area to study.

Motivation can also be viewed as intrinsic or extrinsic. If salespeople find their job to be inherently rewarding, they are intrinsically motivated. If they are motivated by the rewards provided by others, such as pay and formal recognition, they are extrinsically motivated. Although a salesperson's overall motivation could be a function of both intrinsic and extrinsic motivation, some will have strong preferences for extrinsic rewards, such as pay and formal recognition awards, whereas others will seek intrinsic rewards, such as interesting, challenging work.

Reward system management involves the selection and use of organizational rewards to direct salespeople's behavior toward the attainment of organizational objectives. An organizational reward could be anything from a $5,000 pay raise to a compliment for a job well done.

Organizational rewards can be classified as compensation and noncompensation rewards. Compensation rewards are those that are given in return for acceptable performance or effort. Compensation rewards can include nonfinancial compensation, such as recognition and opportunities for growth and promotion.

Noncompensation rewards include factors related to the work situation and well-being of each salesperson. Sales jobs that are interesting and challenging can increase salespeople's motivation, as can allowing salespeople some control over their own activities. Sales managers can also improve salesforce motivation by providing performance-enhancing feedback to salespeople. Other examples of noncompensation rewards are (1) providing adequate resources so that salespeople can accomplish their jobs and (2) practicing a supportive sales management leadership style. In this chapter, the focus is on compensation rewards, including financial and nonfinancial compensation.

OPTIMAL SALESFORCE REWARD SYSTEM

The optimal reward system balances the needs of the organization, its salespeople, and its customers against one another. From the organization's perspective, the reward system should help accomplish the following results:

1. Provide an acceptable ratio of costs and salesforce output in volume, profit, or other objectives. The salesforce must deliver value equal to or greater than the costs of doing so.

2. Encourage specific activities consistent with the firm's overall, marketing, and salesforce objectives and strategies. For example, the firm may use the reward system to encourage the selling of particular products or to promote teamwork in the salesforce.

3. Attract and retain competent salespeople, thereby enhancing long-term customer relationships.

4. Reward salesperson performance based on measurable criteria that are easy to comprehend.

5. Allow the kind of adjustments that facilitate administration of the reward system. A clearly stated, reasonably flexible plan assists in the administration of the plan.

From the perspective of the salesperson, reward systems are expected to meet a somewhat different set of criteria than from the sales manager's perspective. As indicated in the previous chapter, salespeople expect to be treated equitably, with rewards comparable to those of others in the organization doing a similar job—and to the rewards of competitors' salespeople. Most salespeople prefer some stability in the reward system, but they simultaneously want incentive rewards for superior performance. Because the most productive salespeople have the best opportunities to leave the firm for more attractive work situations, the preferences of the salesforce regarding compensation must be given due consideration. The most popular sales incentive is cash.[5] Gift cards, recognition banquets, leisure trips, and merchandise are also frequently used to stimulate sales outcomes such as renewal of contracts, achieving sales quotas, selling targeted products, and adding new customers.

In recent years, the needs of the customer have become more important than the needs of the salesforce in determining the structure of reward systems in sales organizations. Companies such as IBM, General Motors, and Xerox tie compensation to customer satisfaction. A majority of technology companies tie compensation to customer satisfaction and loyalty. Some automobile dealers have tried to reduce customer dissatisfaction stemming from high-pressure sales techniques by paying their salespeople a salary instead of a commission based on sales volume. Others adjust the salesperson's commission based on customer satisfaction with the salesperson's handling of the sale.

Meeting the needs of customers, salespeople, and the sales organization simultaneously is indeed a challenging task. As you might suspect, compromise between sometimes divergent interests becomes essential for managing most salesforce reward systems. As noted by Greenberg and Greenberg, "A salesforce is comprised of individual human beings with broadly varying needs, points of view, and psychological characteristics who cannot be infallibly categorized, measured, and punched out to formula."[6]

TYPES OF SALESFORCE REWARDS

For discussion purposes, the countless number of specific rewards available to salespeople are classified into five categories: pay, promotion, sense of accomplishment, personal growth opportunities, and recognition. Each of these reward categories is discussed in the next two sections of this chapter. As we discuss salesforce rewards in the following sections, keep in mind that the motivational power of various rewards is dependent on a multitude of factors, including individual salesperson preferences, cultural variations around the world, and workplace differences between sales organizations. Even so, it is possible to generalize by saying that, for most salespeople, pay is the most sought-after reward and that all of the other rewards discussed in this chapter are important to a significant number of salespeople across a wide variety of workplaces.

FINANCIAL COMPENSATION

In many sales organizations, financial compensation is composed of current spendable income, deferred income or retirement pay, and various insurance plans that may provide income when needed. The discussion here is limited to the current spendable income because it is the most controllable, and arguably most important, dimension of a salesforce reward system. The other components of financial compensation tend to be dictated more by overall company policy rather than by sales managers.

Current spendable income includes money provided in the short term (weekly, monthly, and annually) that allows salespeople to pay for desired goods and services. It includes salaries, commissions, and bonuses. Bonus compensation may include noncash income equivalents, such as merchandise and free-travel awards. The three basic types of salesforce financial compensation plans are straight salary, straight commission, and a salary plus incentive, with the incentive being a commission and/or a bonus. A discussion of each type follows (summarized in Exhibit 8.2).

Straight Salary

Paying salespeople a straight salary (exclusively by a salary) is uncommon. Such plans are well suited for paying sales support personnel and sales trainees.

Sales support personnel, including missionaries and detailers, are involved in situations in which it is difficult to determine who really makes the sale. Because missionaries and detailers are concerned primarily with dissemination of information rather than direct solicitation of orders, a salary can equitably compensate for effort. Compensation based on sales results might not be fair.

Salaries are also appropriate for sales trainees, who are involved in learning about the job rather than producing on the job. In most cases, a firm cannot recruit sales trainees on a college campus without the lure of a salary to be paid at least until training is completed.

Advantages of Salary Plans

One advantage of using salary plans is that they are the simplest ones to administer, with adjustments usually occurring only once a year. Because salaries are fixed costs,

Summary of Financial Compensation Plans **EXHIBIT 8.2**

Type of Plan	Advantages	Disadvantages	Common Uses
Salary	Simple to administer; planned earnings facilitates budgeting and recruiting; customer loyalty enhanced; more control of nonselling activities	No financial incentive to improve performance; pay often based on seniority, not merit; salaries may be a burden to new firms or to those in declining industries	Sales trainees; sales support
Commission	Income linked to results; strong financial incentive to improve results; costs reduced during slow sales periods; less operating capital required	Difficult to build loyalty of salesforce to company; less control of nonselling activities	Real estate; insurance; wholesaling; securities; automobiles
Combination	Flexibility allows frequent reward of desired behavior; may attract high-potential but unproven recruits	Complex to administer; may encourage crisis-oriented objectives	Widely used—most popular type of financial pay plan

planned earnings for the salesforce are easy to project, which facilitates the salesforce budgeting process. The fixed nature of planned earnings with salary plans may also facilitate recruitment and selection. For example, some recruits may be more likely to join the sales organization when their first-year earnings can be articulated clearly in salary terms rather than less certain commission terms.

Salaries can provide control over salespeople's activities, and reassigning salespeople and changing sales territories is less of a problem with salary plans than with other financial compensation plans. There is general agreement that salesforce loyalty to the company may be greater with salary plans and that there is less chance that high-pressure, non-customer-oriented sales techniques will be used. Salary plans also make it easier to encourage teamwork and customer service.

Salaries are also used when substantial developmental work is required to open a new sales territory or introduce new products to the marketplace. Presumably, the income stability guaranteed by a salary allows the salesperson to concentrate on job activities rather than worry about how much the next paycheck will be. In general, salary plans allow more control over salesforce activities, especially nonselling activities.

Disadvantages of Salary Plans

The most serious shortcoming of straight-salary plans is that they offer little financial incentive to perform past a merely acceptable level. As a result, the least productive members of the salesforce are, in effect, the most rewarded salespeople. Conversely, the most productive salespeople are likely to think salary plans are inequitable. As such, it may be difficult to attract high-performing salespeople.

Differences in salary levels among salespeople are often a function of seniority on the job instead of true merit. Even so, the constraints under which many salary plans operate may cause salary compression, or a narrow range of salaries in the salesforce. Thus sales trainees may be earning close to what experienced salespeople earn, which could cause perceptions of inequity among experienced salespeople, leading to diminished motivation.

Salaries represent fixed overhead in a sales operation. If the market is declining or stagnating, the financial burden of the firm is greater with salary plans than with a variable expense such as commissions based on sales.

Straight Commission

Unlike straight-salary plans, commission-only plans (or straight commission) offer strong financial incentives to maximize performance. However, they also limit control of the salesforce. Some industries—real estate, insurance, automobiles, and securities—traditionally have paid salespeople by straight commission. In these industries, the primary responsibility of salespeople is simply to close sales; nonselling activities are less important to the employer than in some other industries.

Manufacturers' representatives, who represent multiple manufacturers, are also paid by commission. Wholesalers, many of whom founded their businesses with limited working capital, also traditionally pay their salesforce by commission.

The huge direct-sales industry, including such companies as Mary Kay Cosmetics, Tupperware, and Avon, also pays by straight commission. The large number of salespeople working for these organizations makes salary payments impractical from an overhead and administrative standpoint.

Commission Plan Variations

There are several factors to be considered in developing a commission-only plan:

1. Commission base—volume or profitability

2. Commission rate—constant, progressive, regressive, or a combination

3. Commission splits—between two or more salespeople or between salespeople and the employer

4. Commission payout event—when the order is confirmed, shipped, billed, paid for, or some combination of these events

Commissions may be paid according to sales volume or some measure of profitability, such as gross margin, contribution margin, or, in rare cases, net income. Recently, there has been more experimentation with profitability-oriented commission plans in an effort to improve salesforce productivity. Despite the gradual adoption of profitability-based commission plans by various companies, the most popular commission base appears to be sales volume.[7]

Commission rates vary widely, and determining the appropriate rate is a weighty managerial task. The commission rate, or percentage paid to the salesperson, may be a constant rate over the pay period, which is an easy plan for the salespeople to understand and provides incentive for them to produce more sales or profits (because pay is linked directly to performance). A progressive rate increases as salespeople reach pre-specified targets. This provides an even stronger incentive to the salesperson, but it may result in overselling and higher selling costs. A regressive rate declines at some predetermined point. Regressive rates might be appropriate when the first order is hard to secure but reorders are virtually automatic. Such is the case for many manufacturer salespeople who sell to distributors and retailers.

Some circumstances might warrant a combination of a constant rate with either a progressive or regressive rate. For example, assume that a manufacturer has limited production capacity. The manufacturer wants to use capacity fully (i.e., sell out) but not oversell, because service problems would hamper future marketing plans. In such a case, the commission rate might be fixed, or perhaps progressive up to the point at which capacity is almost fully used, then regressive to the point of full use.

When salespeople are paid on straight commission, the question of splitting commissions is of primary concern. To illustrate this point, consider a company with centralized purchasing, such as Delta Airlines. Delta may buy from a sales representative in Atlanta, where its headquarters are located, and have the product shipped to various hubs across the country. The salespeople in the hub cities are expected to provide local follow-up and be sure the product is performing satisfactorily. Which salespeople will receive how much commission? Procedures for splitting commissions are best established before such a question is asked.

No general rules exist for splitting commissions; rather, company-specific rules must be spelled out to avoid serious disputes. A company selling to Delta Airlines in the situation just described might decide to pay the salesperson who calls on the Atlanta headquarters 50 percent of the total commission and split the remaining 50 percent among the salespeople who serve the hub cities. The details of how commissions are split depend entirely on each company's situation.

Another issue in structuring straight-commission plans is when to pay the commission. The actual payment may be at any time interval, although monthly and quarterly payments are most common. The question of when the commission is earned is probably just as important as when it is paid. Many companies operating on the basis of sales-volume commissions declare the commission earned at the time the customer is billed for the order, rather than when the order is confirmed, shipped, or paid for.

Salesforce automation has made it easier to keep track of complicated commission systems. For instance, AccountPro (www.AccountPro.com) offers a software application called Sales Commission Platinum that enables companies to rapidly design, process, and communicate sophisticated commission programs. By communicating sales credit, performance, and earnings information, the software allows sales managers and salespeople to keep abreast of their goal progress and compensation status.[8] Furthermore, such software enables sales managers to spot trends and identify strengths and weaknesses within the salesforce.

Advantages of Commission Plans

One advantage of straight-commission plans is that salespeople's income is linked directly to desired results and therefore may be perceived as more equitable than salary plans. In the right circumstances, a strong financial incentive can provide superior results, and commission plans provide such an incentive. Thus, such plans are likely to attract competent results-oriented salespeople and eliminate incompetent reps.

From a cost-control perspective, commissions offer further advantages. Because commissions are a variable cost, operating costs are minimized during slack selling periods. Also, working capital requirements are lessened with commission-only pay plans. Before choosing a straight-commission plan, however, the disadvantages of such plans should be considered.

Disadvantages of Commission Plans

Perhaps the most serious shortcoming of straight-commission plans is that they contribute little to company loyalty, which may mean other problems in controlling the activities of the salesforce, particularly nonselling and administrative activities. A lack of commitment may lead commission salespeople to leave the company if business conditions worsen or sales drop. Or, salespeople may neglect cultivating potentially profitable long-run customers in favor of easy sales. Also, if commissions are based on sales volume, salespeople may be encouraged to discount unnecessarily, resulting in lower profitability. Another potential problem can arise if commissions are not limited by an earnings cap, in that salespeople may earn more than their managers. Not only do managers resent this outcome, but the salespeople may not respond to direction from those they exceed in earnings.

Performance Bonuses

The third dimension of current spendable income is the performance bonus, either group or individual. Both types are prevalent, and some bonus plans combine them. Bonuses are typically used to direct effort toward relatively short-term objectives, such as introducing new products, adding new accounts, or reducing accounts receivable. They may be offered in the form of cash or income equivalents, such as merchandise or free travel. At CooperVision Inc., one of the world's largest contact lens manufacturers, the top 20 percent of salespeople based on performance on annual sales quotas receive a first-class vacation for themselves and a guest, with the destination changing each year.[9] Although commissions or salary may be the financial-compensation base, bonuses are used strictly in a supplementary fashion.

Advantages of Performance Bonuses

One advantage of the performance bonus is that the organization can direct emphasis to what it considers important in the sales area. In addition, sales emphasis can be changed from period to period. Bonuses are particularly useful for tying rewards to accomplishment of objectives.

Disadvantages of Performance Bonuses

One problem with the performance bonus is that it may be difficult to determine a formula for calculating bonus achievement if the objective is expressed in subjective terms (e.g., account servicing). Furthermore, if salespeople do not fully support the established objective, they may not exert additional effort to accomplish the goal.

Combination Plans (Salary plus Incentive)

The limitations of straight-salary and straight-commission plans have led to increasing use of plans that feature some combination of salary, commission, and bonus—in other words, salary plus incentive. Combination pay plans usually feature salary as the major source of salesperson income. Salary-plus-bonus and salary-plus-commission-plus-bonus plans are popular.

When properly conceived, combination plans offer a balance of incentive, control, and enough flexibility to reward important salesforce activities. For example, a company that expects its salespeople to perform a variety of activities such as gain new customers, retain key customers, establish new products in the marketplace, and maintain a balance between sales volume and profitability might use a combination plan to direct appropriate efforts toward these various objectives. The salary component could direct the salesforce toward longer-term objectives such as retaining key customers and establishing new products in the marketplace. Commissions could be paid on all sales. An annual bonus could be paid for achieving sales volume objectives. An additional bonus could be tied to profit margins achieved in each individual salesperson's territory. In such a scenario, the compensation plan is fairly simple, and the company can direct effort toward company goals. Salespeople have some earnings stability from the salary component, while also having the opportunity for upside earnings from the commission and bonuses.

One challenging aspect of the structuring combination pay plans is determining the financial combination mix, or the relative amounts to be paid in salary, commission, and bonus.

The compensation mix should be tilted more heavily toward the salary component when individual salespeople have limited control over their own performance. When well-established companies rely heavily on advertising to sell their products in highly competitive markets, the salesforce has less direct control over job outcomes. Then a salary emphasis is logical. Furthermore, if the provision of customer service is crucial as contrasted with maximizing short-term sales volume or if team selling is used, a compensation mix favoring the salary dimension is appropriate. Finally, when the time from initial customer contact to the initial sale (sales cycle) is long, a higher proportion of salary is common.

Advantages of Combination Plans

The primary advantage of combination pay plans is their flexibility. Sales behavior can be rewarded frequently, and specific behaviors can be reinforced or stimulated quickly. For example, bonuses or additional commissions could be easily added to a salary base to encourage such activities as selling excess inventory, maximizing the sales of highly seasonal products, introducing new products, or obtaining new customers. For example, rug and home accessory manufacturer Surya paid out a total of $100,000 in bonuses to four of its 60 salespeople who led the company in opening new accounts, increasing sales in existing accounts, and increasing overall sales in an annual sales contest.[10]

Combination plans can also be used to advantage when the skill and/or experience levels of the salesforce vary, assuming that the sales manager can accurately place salespeople into various categories and then formulate the proper combination for each category. This is most commonly done with sales trainees, regular salespeople, and senior salespeople, with each category of salespeople having a different combination of salary and incentive compensation.

Combination pay plans are attractive to high-potential but unproven candidates for sales jobs. College students nearing graduation, for example, might be attracted by the security of a salary and the opportunity for additional earnings from incentive-pay components.

Disadvantages of Combination Plans

As compared with straight-salary and straight-commission plans, combination plans are more complex and difficult to administer. Their flexibility sometimes leads to frequent changes in compensation practices to achieve short-term objectives. Although flexibility is desirable, each change requires careful communication with the salesforce and precise coordination with long-term sales, marketing, and corporate objectives. A common criticism of combination plans is that they tend to produce too many salesforce objectives, many of which are of the crisis resolution "firefighting" variety. Should this occur, more important long-term progress can be impeded. Furthermore, mediocre salespeople are eliminated less rapidly than they would be under a straight-commission plan.

Determining Appropriate Financial Compensation Levels

Determining the appropriate financial compensation level depends upon an understanding of the duties expected for a particular sales position. In addition, information about competitive salaries and the requirements for attracting and keeping qualified salespeople is necessary. This information can be obtained by benchmarking earnings levels of salespeople through a variety of methods including: reviewing trade publications; using salary surveys; examining Internet sites such as Indeed.com and Salary.com; and utilizing employment agents and placement firms.

In general, sales positions that are more complicated and require more skills are compensated at a higher level. While generalizations about what defines appropriate compensation levels are difficult to make, Exhibit 8.3[11] outlines conditions typically associated with higher levels of pay.

NONFINANCIAL COMPENSATION

As indicated early in this chapter, compensation for effort and performance may include nonfinancial rewards. Examples of nonfinancial compensation include career advancement through promotion, a sense of accomplishment on the job, opportunities for personal growth, and recognition of achievement. Sometimes, nonfinancial rewards are coupled with financial rewards—for example, a promotion into sales management usually results in a pay increase—so one salesperson might view these rewards as primarily financial, whereas another might view them from a nonfinancial perspective. The value of nonfinancial compensation is illustrated by the considerable number of salespeople who knowingly take cuts in financial compensation to become sales managers. The prevalence of other nonfinancial rewards in salesforce reward systems also attests to their important role.

Opportunity for Promotion

Opportunity for promotion is a highly valued reward among salespeople. Among younger salespeople, it often eclipses pay as the most valued reward.

Receiving a promotion typically involves a pay raise, but even in cases when the net dollars associated with the promotion are insignificant, some salespeople still would prefer a promotion over a simple pay raise. This is understandable, as a promotion can

---

EXHIBIT 8.3   Conditions Associated with Higher Pay Levels

Higher pay levels are typically associated with:

1. Job experience, as most senior salespeople have built a record of success. Without a record of success, salespeople are likely to find another way to earn a living.
2. The importance of personal selling in the overall marketing effort.
3. The extent to which there is an expectation that salespeople sell new products into new markets. They deserve to be paid more than those who primarily service existing customers, fulfilling more of an order-taker status.
4. Higher skill levels, especially those that call for creativity and problem solving.
5. Responsibility for major accounts, where there is a high expectation that salespeople add considerable value for the customer.
6. Highly competitive markets where an intense personal selling effort is important for customer retention and growth.

lead to subsequent advancement where potential earnings are much higher. For example, consider a salesperson who is promoted into product management. The pay raise may be 10 percent, but our hypothetical salesperson may give up a company car and move to a new location where the cost of living is higher. The net financial change in such circumstances could be minimal or perhaps even negative. Nonetheless, many salespeople welcome such opportunities because it puts them on track for future advancement with greater financial rewards. Given the increasing number of young to middle-aged people in the workforce, the opportunities for promotion may be limited severely in nongrowth industries. (Growth industries, such as financial services and direct sales, offer reasonably good opportunities for advancement through promotion.) Because opportunities for promotion are not easily varied in the short run, the importance of matching recruits to the job and its rewards is again emphasized. It should be noted that a promotion need not involve a move from sales into management. Some career paths may extend from sales into management, whereas others progress along a career salesperson path.

Sense of Accomplishment

Unlike some rewards, a sense of accomplishment cannot be delivered to the salesperson from the organization. Because a sense of accomplishment emanates from the salesperson's psyche, all the organization can do is facilitate the process by which it develops. Although organizations cannot administer sense-of-accomplishment rewards as they would pay increases, promotions, or formal recognition rewards, the converse is not true—they do have the ability to withhold this reward, to deprive individuals of feeling a sense of accomplishment. Of course, no organization chooses this result; it stems from poor management practice.

Several steps can be taken to facilitate a sense of accomplishment in the salesforce. First, ensure that the salesforce members understand the critical role they fulfill in revenue production and other key activities within the company. Second, personalize the causes and effects of salesperson performance. This means that each salesperson should understand the link between effort and performance and between performance and rewards. Third, strongly consider the practice of management by objectives or goal setting as a standard management practice. Finally, reinforce feelings of worthwhile accomplishment in communication with the salesforce.

Opportunity for Personal Growth

Opportunities for personal growth are routinely offered to salespeople. For example, college tuition reimbursement programs are common, as are seminars and workshops on such topics as physical fitness, stress reduction, and personal financial planning. Companies that offer tuition reimbursement for salespeople and other employees include Exxon mobil, General Electric, Apple, UPS, Oracle, and Chevron.[12] Interestingly, many sales job candidates think the major reward available from well-known companies is the opportunity for personal growth. This is particularly true of entrepreneurially oriented college students who hope to "learn then earn" in their own business. In a parallel development, many companies showcase their training program during recruitment and selection as an opportunity for personal growth through the acquisition of universally valuable selling skills.

Recognition

Recognition, both informal and formal, is an integral part of most salesforce reward systems. Informal recognition refers to "nice job" accolades and similar kudos usually delivered in private conversation or correspondence between a sales manager and a salesperson. Or, it might involve a thank you letter to a salesperson's family detailing the rep's accomplishments and expressing appreciation for all his or her work, or a call from the organization's president, personally thanking the rep for a big accomplishment. Informal recognition is easy to administer, costs nothing or practically nothing, and can reinforce desirable behavior immediately after it occurs. Paul Shearstone, an internationally known author and sales trainer, emphasizes the importance of recognition as a reward for sales performance:

> At the risk of making salespeople appear shallow or monolithic (they are not), recognition amongst their peers is still the quintessential motivator, whether there is an incentive program or not. The rule again, is, there is no such thing as too much recognition! Salespeople by nature gravitate to the limelight much like other performers, and so there should be no shortage of achievement and overachievement recognitions that find their way—in a timely manner—to the public's eye.[13]

Formal recognition programs have long been popular in sales organizations. The insurance industry has the Million Dollar Roundtable, and "100%" clubs for those who exceed 100 percent of their sales quota are common. The ultimate recognition for Xerox's sales elite is to be named a member of the President's Club, while salespeople at Federated Insurance strive to be a member of the Chairman's Council.

Formal recognition programs are typically based on group competition or individual accomplishments representing improved performance. Formal recognition may also be associated with monetary, merchandise, or travel awards but is distinguished from other rewards by two characteristics. First, formal recognition implies public recognition for accomplishment in the presence of peers and superiors in the organization. Second, it includes a symbolic award of lasting psychological value, such as jewelry or a plaque. Sound advice for conducting formal recognition programs is offered in Exhibit 8.4.

As formal recognition, programs often feature lavish awards banquets and ceremonies to culminate the program and set the stage for future recognition programs. Because lavish expenditures for any salesforce activity ultimately must be well justified in this era of emphasis on productivity improvement, it is evident that many companies believe that money spent on recognition is a good investment. For more on recognition programs, see "Sales Management in the 21st Century: Recognition and Incentive Programs at W.B. Mason Office Products."

SALES EXPENSES

Most sales organizations provide full reimbursement to their salespeople for legitimate sales expenses incurred while on the job. Typical reimbursable expenses are shown in Exhibit 8.5. Selling expenses are a substantial amount in most companies, with

---

EXHIBIT 8.4   Guidelines for Formal Programs

Formal recognition programs have a better chance of success if sales managers

1. Remember that recognition programs should produce results well beyond the expected and that the program should make sense from a return-on-investment perspective.
2. Publicize the program before it is implemented. Build momentum for the program while it is underway with additional communiqués, and reinforce the accomplishments of the winners with postprogram communications both inside and outside the company.
3. Ensure that the celebration for winners is well conceived and executed. Consider the possibility of having customers and teammates join in with brief congratulatory testimonials or thanks.
4. Arrange for individual salespeople or sales teams to acknowledge the support of others who helped them win the award—as is the case with the Grammy Awards, for example. This builds the teamwork orientation.
5. Strive for fairness in structuring recognition programs so that winners are clearly superior performers, not those with less difficult performance goals.

Recognition and Incentive Programs at W.B. Mason Office Products

Marty Zucker, sales manager Northern New Jersey and NYC for W.B. Mason Office Products, discusses how the company uses recognition and incentive programs.

W.B. Mason Office Products is the largest independent office products company in the United States, selling office supplies, furniture, promotional marketing, printing and beverage services. At W.B. Mason, it is extremely important that we have a well-educated, highly talented and extremely motivated salesforce.

W.B. Mason Office Supplies believes in both recognition and incentive programs to drive sales amongst its salespeople. At the beginning of each year, sales goals are set along with standards for our highly coveted recognition awards. W.B. Mason sales professionals are amongst the most highly compensated in the industry. It is our belief

that "you get what you pay for." In other words, a highly compensated sales team will be motivated sufficiently to continually meet and beat both sales and margin budgets on a consistent basis. The sky is the limit at W.B. Mason. There are no earning caps and quite frankly sales professionals at our company can give themselves pay increases just about anytime they see fit to work a bit smarter!

The incentive plan is also designed to provide a consistent vehicle for recognition. At the beginning of our fiscal year, the entire salesforce of approximately 500 meet at the Mohegan Sun Casino and Resort for meetings and our coveted recognition program. Only the top 20 sales professionals are recognized for their outstanding performance from the prior fiscal year. They are awarded fabulous prizes, but more importantly salespeople are recognized by the owners of our company and their peers. Providing top-notch recognition and incentive programs is extremely important in the competitive times in which we live.

Typical Reimbursable Expense Items   EXHIBIT 8.5

Automobile (company-leased)	Entertainment
Automobile (company-owned)	Product samples
Mileage allowance	Local promotions
Other travel reimbursement	Office and/or clerical expenses
Lodging	Computer and related equipment
Telephone (including mobile phone)	

---

companies spending tens of billions of dollars every year on travel and entertainment. Given the magnitude of sales expenses, it is easy to understand why most companies impose tight controls to ensure judicious spending by the salesforce.

Controls used in the sales expense reimbursement process include (1) a definition of which expenses are reimbursable, (2) the establishment of expense budgets, (3) the use of allowances for certain expenditures, and (4) documentation of expenses to be reimbursed.

Covered expenses vary from company to company, so it is important for each company to designate which expenses are reimbursable and which are not. For example, some firms reimburse their salespeople for personal entertainment, such as the cost of movies and reading material while traveling, and others do not.

Expense budgets may be used to maintain expenses as a specified percentage of overall sales volume or profit. Expenditures are compared regularly to the budgeted amount, and expenditure patterns may change in response to budgetary pressures.

Allowances for automobile expenses, lodging, and meal costs are sometimes used to control expenditures. For example, one common practice is to reimburse personal automobile use on the job at a cents-per-mile allowance. Many firms use a per-diem (daily) allowance for meals and lodging.

Because of more stringent tax laws, extensive documentation in the form of receipts and other information concerning the what, when, who, and why of the expenditure has become standard procedure. Salespeople whose companies do not reimburse expenses must also provide such documentation to deduct sales expenses in calculating their income taxes. A typical form for documenting sales expenses is shown in Exhibit 8.6.[14]

The job of reporting and tracking sales expenses has become less burdensome and more cost-efficient for companies that use expense report software and Web-based programs. For example, Concur Technologies' Concur Expense Service makes it easier for salespeople to file expense reports and for sales managers to process the reports and analyze expenditures. This cloud-based application allows salespeople to easily generate reports anytime from anywhere using a computer, tablet, or smart phone. The system, which integrates with a company's back office systems, allows data to be automatically imported from a company's corporate credit card or from a photographed paper receipt. Concur's application increases accuracy and productivity while decreasing exposure to

EXHIBIT 8.6 Sales Expense Report Form

Name__________ Week Ending__________ 11______

DAY	City and State	Lodging	Transportation		Automobile Expenses	Meals Itemize Business Meals Below			Local Taxi, Carfare, Tolls, Etc.	Entertainment	Miscellaneous Expenses	Daily Total
			Air, Rail, Etc.	Limousine Car, Rental, Etc.	Itemize Below	Breakfast	Lunch	Dinner		Itemize Below	Itemize Below	
SUN												
MON												
TUE												
WED												
THU												
FRI												
SAT												
	Totals											

Totals Expenses Paid by Employee ______

Entertainment and Business Meals

Date	Name of Person(s) Entertained Company, Title	Time and Place	Nature and Purpose of Entertainment	Amount	% of $ Allocated to Business

Itemize Below Those Expenses Charged Directly to the Company

- Deduct from My Advance
- Mail to Home Address
- Mail to Branch Office

REMARKS:

Automobile and Miscellaneous Expenses

Date	Items	Amount

Expenses Charged Directly to the Company (Air, Fare, Auto Rental, Etc.)

Date	Items	Amount

Signature

Approved

AN ETHICAL DILEMMA

You have been Sherry Smith's sales manager for more than six years. Her dedication to the company, her sales team, and her customers is beyond reproach. For the past two years, she has been named salesperson of the year at your company. Besides being an outstanding performer, she is a genuinely nice person with a great personality. Looking over Sherry's latest expense report, you noticed that she had meal expenses for her and a customer last Thursday. However, you recall making a call to this customer on that very day to follow up with some information he had requested and being informed that he was out of town. Your company has very strict policies regarding business expenses. What should you do? Explain.

mistakes and fraud.[15] With this program, sales managers can easily audit salespeople's expenditures, focus on expenses in a particular area, and compare selling costs with selling budgets. It is also possible to track expenditures with particular hotels or rental car companies, which may enable the sales organization to negotiate more favorable rates.

The area of expense reimbursement is the cause of some ethical and legal concern in sales organizations. Certainly expense account padding, in which a salesperson seeks reimbursement for ineligible or fictional expenses, is not unknown. There are countless ways for an unscrupulous salesperson to misappropriate company funds. Tactics include overstating expenses, seeking reimbursement for personal expenses, inventing purchases, and filing the same expenses on separate expense reports.[16] A common ploy of expense account "padders" is to entertain friends rather than customers, then seek reimbursement for customer entertainment. Another tactic is to eat a $10 meal and report that it costs $20, since most companies do not require receipts for expenses less than $25. Others simply add a certain percentage to every expense report they file. "An Ethical Dilemma" portrays a possible problem with expense account padding.

Tight financial controls, well-publicized and enforced requirements for documentation of expenditures, an anonymous tip program, and periodic visits by highly trained financial auditors help deter expense account abuse. Although it may sound extreme, many companies have a simple policy regarding misappropriation of company funds— the minimum sanction is termination of employment, and criminal charges are a distinct possibility.

ADDITIONAL ISSUES IN MANAGING SALESFORCE REWARD SYSTEMS

In addition to the managerial issues raised thus far, four other areas of salesforce reward systems have received considerable attention: sales contests, team compensation, global considerations, and changing an existing reward system.

Sales Contests

Sales contests are temporary programs (usually lasting one sales cycle) that offer financial and/or nonfinancial rewards for accomplishing specified, usually short-term, objectives. Popular incentives include merchandise, gift certificates, cash, trendy electronics, experiential and humorous rewards, and travel. There is a long-running debate in sales management circles about whether cash or noncash incentives work best. There is no clear-cut answer, as some individuals will be more motivated by cash and others by noncash incentives. In some cases, winners who receive cash will spend the money on routine living expenses, perhaps minimizing any significant memory of their accomplishment. Those who are rewarded with trips or merchandise will likely enjoy those rewards on a guilt-free basis, since there is no alternative but to consume the award. The cash versus noncash argument for sales contests is not settled, but there is some evidence that managers prefer cash awards for increasing sales and noncash awards for a wide variety of other objectives such as motivating specific behaviors and improving teamwork, customer satisfaction, and customer loyalty.[17]

Contests may involve group competition among salespeople, individual competition whereby each salesperson competes against past performance standards or new goals, or a combination of group and individual competition. Sales contests can be instituted without altering the basic financial compensation plan.

Despite the widespread use of sales contests and the sizable expenditures for them, very little is known about their true effects. In fact, many contests are held to correct bad planning and poor sales performance, and others are held with the belief that contests must have positive effects, despite the difficulty in pinpointing these effects. There is always a concern about whether sales contests have any lasting value or simply boost short-term sales. If contests merely pull sales from a future period into the contest period, little is gained—and the expenses of running contests can be substantial.

To optimize the use of sales contests, the following guidelines are recommended.[18]

1. Minimize potential motivation and morale problems by allowing multiple winners, but do not set low expectations just so everyone can win. Salespeople should compete against individual goals and be declared winners if those goals are met.

2. Recognize that top performers will likely be motivated no matter what the incentives are. Try to structure sales contests to encourage strong efforts from the remainder of the salesforce while still appealing to the high performers.

3. Recognize that contests will concentrate efforts in specific areas, often at the temporary neglect of other areas. Plan accordingly.

4. Consider the positive effects of including nonselling personnel in sales contests to help build teamwork. Consider using team contests to enhance customer relationships.

5. Use variety as a basic element of sales contests. Vary timing, duration, themes, and rewards.

6. Ensure that sales contest objectives are clear, realistically attainable, and quantifiable to allow performance assessment and measurement of return on investment. Consider sending periodic email reminders to reps to keep them informed of their goal progress.

7. Prior to the contest, publicize it to build interest and excitement.

8. Provide both public (e.g., at a special event or banquet) and private (e.g., personal letter from management) recognition to the winners.

9. Encourage the winners to share their winning strategies with the salesforce.

Contests can be implemented to achieve a variety of objectives. For instance, Guardian Protection Services, the world's largest privately held security company, coordinates its sales contests for its dealer salespeople across the United States to ensure that company-wide and local priorities are addressed. At Guardian, annual contests are supplemented by monthly contests to spur extra effort toward generating new sales, improving the average selling price, and emphasizing the sale of specific products and services.[19]

The design, implementation, and administration of sales contests is made easier by companies such as Rymax Marketing Services, the largest U.S. manufacturer's representative in the incentive industry. Rymax operates worldwide, providing support and fulfillment that facilitates sales contest design, a Web-based interface that can be customized for each corporate client, and reports that allow managers and contestants to track their progress. The Rymax online catalog offers prizes from more than 200 brand-name companies, including Apple, Coach, Samsung and Nikon.[20]

Use of Sales Contests at Reality Systems

John Schwepker, vice president of sales and marketing for Reality Systems, St. Louis, Missouri, the leading outsourcer of document scanning solutions in the Midwest, discusses how sales contests help motivate the salesforce as well as increase revenue to the company's bottom line.

There are several ways to utilize sales contests to help motivate and compensate your salesforce. Many companies base their contests on yearly sales goals and award very expensive and luxurious prizes such as cars and trips. Although quarterly and yearly sales contests are viewed as good motivators to increase sales, sometimes these contests actually act as demotivators. Once a sales rep realizes that he or she will not win the contest or achieve the desired sales goal necessary to achieve the contest prize, his or her performance may actually go down. In many cases, the rep's performance ends up being worse than if there was no contest at all. This is why we like to have daily and weekly contests at Reality Systems. The prizes are smaller but anyone can win and more people have a chance to win. In our business, since the sales cycle is so long, it is not really fair to base a sales contest on revenue or profit generated. The amount of work that goes into a $1,500 deal is typically the same as what goes into a $500,000 deal. So we have contests that are based on such things as how many new calls or appointments our reps can make in a day, week or month. Winners receive prizes such as dinner for two to a nice restaurant, tickets to the St. Louis Cardinals baseball game, or, on a little larger scale, a weekend at the Lake of the Ozarks. Since we do not have yearly sales contests, we are able to afford more frequent smaller contests and give all of our sales reps a chance to win more often. This tends to keep the salesforce better motivated throughout the year and keeps them on track toward reaching their ultimate yearly sales goals.

It is hard to design a sales contest that will maximally motivate every member of the salesforce. Research suggests that salespeople's enthusiasm for participating in contests and their design preferences for goal type, number of winners, contest duration, and award value may vary by individual, supervisory, and sales setting characteristics.[21] Martiz Incentives offers an assessment tool for surveying the salesforce to determine how to achieve the biggest motivational effects in the most economical way.[22] Such assessment tools, in addition to input from salespeople, can be useful in designing sales contests. Postcontest feedback from salespeople and customers can also be useful in designing subsequent contests.

The precise measurement of sales contest results can also be a managerial challenge. Factors beyond the control of the salespeople can impact contest results, particularly if contests are held over a long period of time or if national or international contests are run without factoring in local market conditions. Even so, sales contests will doubtlessly continue to be a commonly used tool. By following the nine guidelines previously mentioned, sales managers can improve the odds of making justifiable investments in sales contests. For more on sales contests, see "Sales Management in the 21st Century: Use of Sales Contests at Reality Systems."

Team Compensation

Most salespeople are still paid based on their individual performance. As mentioned throughout this textbook, however, teamwork in selling and team selling are growing in importance. As a result, many sales organizations are adjusting their compensation plans to recognize team performance. This represents a real challenge to sales managers for several reasons. Existing reward systems for individual salespeople typically are not easy to adapt to team selling situations. Salespeople who are accustomed to earning commissions based on their individual efforts may not respond enthusiastically to team-based compensation. They may be concerned that rewards for high performers might be diminished by lower-performing team members. Furthermore, it is difficult to determine an individual salesperson's contribution to overall team performance.

Given these challenges, it is easy to see that experimentation is often required to find the right compensation plan for sales teams. For instance, when salespeople with different levels of experience work as a team, commissions might be split based on experience. For example, the experienced salesperson might receive 57 percent of the commission, versus 43 percent for the less-experienced salesperson. Plans could be reviewed periodically and revised based on an individual's performance on the team. In many cases, discussion among team members determines how incentive pay is distributed. When different members have different roles it is appropriate to assign different performance metrics to each and compensate accordingly. Some companies are ranking individual team members and dividing up an incentive pool based on these rankings.

There are no easy answers for structuring team pay. In general, it is a good idea to reward both individual and team performance. Some research shows that compensation packages that reward individual and team performance are more effective than pay equality (each team member receives the same pay) and pay equity (each member is compensated according to individual performance) approaches to team compensation. Other research suggests using output-sharing incentives for teams when (1) individual efforts are affected by peer monitoring and pressures; (2) salespeople's efforts are not perfect substitutes, but rather complementary; and (3) "helping effort" is reciprocal and efficient.[23]

Sales organizations that utilize team selling are leveraging information technology to encourage and reward collaboration between sales team members and other personnel within their organizations. Sales teams can learn and share knowledge with products such as Salesforce.com's Chatter and Microsoft's Yammer. With such technology, top performers not only achieve their sales objectives, but they also routinely engage with other salespeople to orchestrate sales activities and provide expertise and resources to their colleagues.[24] For example, Microchip, a global leader in the semiconductor industry, changed its commission-based pay plan for individual salespeople to a salary-based team plan with a small commission/bonus element for team performance. After the compensation plan change, Microchip reported record growth and profitability, more collaboration between salespeople, and practically zero turnover in the salesforce.[25]

Not only do social media and business communications tools foster teamwork, they also enable sales managers to monitor individual and team contributions as an input into compensation and reward programs. For example, Terryberry, an employee recognition company, offers a social media platform called Mongo Wall that allows team members to post on the wall of other team members, make suggestions, and share resources. The platform can be filtered and searched by managers who wish to reward certain collaboration behaviors.[26]

Global Considerations

Global compensation issues are receiving more attention. In many cases, sales representation in other countries is secured through a distributor or sales agent. These situations are not so complex from a compensation management point of view because commissions or discounts from list price provide the income basis for the sellers. The compensation of native salespeople is more difficult. In many countries, political or cultural factors may have a strong influence on salesforce pay practices and preferred incentives. For example, salespeople in the United States are less often paid by straight salary than their counterparts in any other part of the world.

Furthermore, what motivates salespeople can vary from country to country. A survey of nearly 41,000 salespeople in nine countries found that only salespeople in the United States, United Kingdom, and Singapore choose money as their number-one motivator. Salespeople in Australia, Canada, Chile, New Zealand, Norway, and Sweden are more motivated by the opportunity to use their talent.[27] Given such circumstances, it may be best to localize the compensation program when dealing with native salespeople. According to Mercer's Global Compensation Strategy and Administration Survey, approximately 75 percent of multinational sales organizations use local or regional compensation plans, with 25 percent using a global approach to compensation.[28]

The compensation of expatriate salespeople presents a different set of problems.[29] Often, the company is in the position of offering additional incentives to encourage salespeople to take assignments abroad. This pattern is changing somewhat as awareness increases that overseas assignments can enhance career opportunities. Furthermore, as companies cultivate "global" employees who welcome the opportunity to experience new cultures and take advantage of learning opportunities, companies are scaling back the once-lucrative incentives for foreign-based employment. Nonetheless, arriving at equitable pay for salespeople deployed around the world requires knowledge of living costs, taxes, and other factors that are not typically dealt with by sales managers. In fact, sales managers often rely on human resource professionals to assist in global compensation planning. These professionals point out that expatriates should not lose or gain in spending power as a result of an international assignment. They also point out the importance of tying a deployment plan to the sales growth strategy and specifying the particulars of the job before addressing compensation issues. Exhibit 8.7[30] provides a list of "dos and don'ts" for developing global compensation that comes from experience gained by IBM when it revamped its global compensation scheme.

Changing the Reward System

The need to change the salesforce reward system for a given company may arise periodically as companies strive for improved performance and productivity. Changes in sales compensation are often made to bring the salesforce more in line with a shift in strategy or to maximize corporate resources. If the current plan is confusing, offers little choice, fails to drive organizational cultural initiatives, or results in unhappy salespeople, it likewise may be time for a change. Sales compensation plans may also be changed to exploit a new market opportunity. Such was the case with Installation and Service Technologies, Inc. (IST), a Kansas-based company that sells point-of-sale and wireless technologies to restaurants and retail customers across the United States.[31] When IST decided to add hardware and other tangible products to its services offerings, the company created a new sales division focused on selling products. This led sales director Matt Haselhoff to search for industry best practices in blending salary and commissions to motivate his salesforce in a fair, motivational manner. By using online resources available from Makana Motivator Express, Haselhoff was able to quickly develop and implement the new sales compensation plan. Reward systems should be closely monitored and should be changed when conditions warrant. A situation similar to the one in "An Ethical Dilemma" may warrant consideration.

Minor adjustments in reward systems can be made relatively painlessly, and sometimes even pleasurably, for all concerned parties. For example, the sales manager might plan three sales contests this year instead of the customary two, or could announce a cash bonus instead of a trip to Acapulco for those who make quota.

However, making major changes in reward systems can be traumatic for salespeople and management alike if not properly handled. Any major change in financial compensation practices is likely to produce a widespread fear among the salesforce that their earnings will decline. Because many changes are precipitated by poor financial

---

DOs AND DON'Ts of Global Compensation   EXHIBIT 8.7

- Do involve reps from key countries
- Do allow local managers to decide the mix between base and incentive pay
- Do use consistent performance measures (results paid for) and emphasis on each measure
- Do allow local countries flexibility in implementation
- Do use consistent communication and training themes worldwide
- Don't design the plan centrally and dictate to local countries
- Don't create a similar framework for jobs with different responsibilities
- Don't require consistency on every performance measure within the incentive plan
- Don't assume cultural differences can be managed through the incentive plan
- Don't proceed without the support of senior sales executives worldwide

performance by the company or inequitable earnings among salesforce members, this fear is often justified for at least part of the salesforce. It might be wise to consider how any change in compensation will affect the company's top performers and attempt to avoid a change that would hurt them.

To implement a new or modified reward system, sales managers must, in effect, sell the plan to the salesforce. To do this, the details of the plan must be clearly communicated

---

AN ETHICAL DILEMMA

You have been hired by a copier supply company to replace their sales manager. Although it is a small company, its salesforce has always performed well, allowing it to hold its own against much larger competitors. The former sales manager had a unique way of motivating his salesforce. Each year all salespeople were rank-ordered, and the bottom three performers were fired, despite having performed very profitably for the company. Will you change this system? Why or why not?

---

well in advance of its implementation. Feedback from the salesforce should be encouraged and questions promptly addressed. For instance, the 260 member salesforce at Administaff formed an internal advisory board that includes top sellers as internal consultants on issues such as compensation plan changes.[32] Reasons for the change should be discussed openly, and any expected changes in job activities should be detailed.

It is recommended that, if possible, major changes be implemented to coincide with the beginning of a new fiscal year or planning period. It is also preferable to institute changes during favorable business conditions, rather than during recessionary periods.

The dynamic nature of marketing and sales environments dictates that sales managers constantly monitor their reward systems. It is not unreasonable to think that major changes could occur every few years or even more frequently.

GUIDELINES FOR MOTIVATING AND REWARDING SALESPEOPLE

Sales managers should realize that practically everything they do will influence salesforce motivation one way or another. The people they recruit, the plans and policies they institute, the training they provide, and the way they communicate with and supervise salespeople are among the more important factors. In addition, sales managers should realize that environmental factors beyond their control may also influence salesforce motivation. Like other managerial functions, motivating salespeople requires a prioritized, calculated approach rather than a futile attempt to address all motivational needs simultaneously. If for no other reason, the complexity of human nature and changing needs of salesforce members will prohibit the construction of motivational programs that run smoothly without periodic adjustment. Guidelines for motivating salespeople are as follows:

1. Recruit and select salespeople whose personal motives match the requirements and rewards of the job.

2. Attempt to incorporate the individual needs of salespeople into motivational programs.

3. Provide adequate job information and ensure proper skill development for the salesforce.

4. Use job design and redesign as motivational tools.

5. Concentrate on building the self-esteem of salespeople.

6. Take a proactive approach to seeking out motivational problems and sources of frustration in the salesforce.

Recruitment and Selection

The importance of matching the abilities and needs of sales recruits to the requirements and rewards of the job cannot be overstated. This is especially critical for sales managers who have little opportunity to alter job dimensions and reward structures. Investing more time in recruitment and selection to ensure a good match is likely to pay off later in terms of fewer motivational and other managerial problems.

Incorporation of Individual Needs

At the outset of this chapter, motivation was described as a complex personal process. At the heart of the complexity of motivation is the concept of individual needs. The demographics of the workforce is diverse, with individuals at different stages in their personal and work lives, each with varying interests and influences. Although there is considerable pressure and, in many cases, sound economic rationale for supporting mass approaches to salesforce motivation, there may also be opportunities to incorporate individual needs into motivational programs. When possible, individual consideration should be taken into account when motivating and rewarding salespeople. For instance, some companies, such as broadband equipment manufacturer Netopia, have turned to online incentive programs, such as InnergE (http://www.hinda.com/technology/InnergE.html), to meet the diverse needs of its resellers when attempting to motivate them. Resellers participating in the program log on to InnergE, where they can redeem points earned by selling Netopia products for rewards from a catalog of more than 2,000 items ranging from digital cameras and DVD players to travel certificates.[33]

Information and Skills

Salespeople must have high skill levels and be well equipped with the right information to do their jobs well. If sales managers train their people properly and give them the right information, salespeople can see how their efforts lead to the desired results. If salespeople's understanding of how their efforts produce results is consistent with that of the sales manager, reasonable goals can be set that allow performance worthy of rewards. Providing adequate information to the salesforce also enhances salesforce socialization (discussed in earlier chapters), thereby reducing role conflict and role ambiguity.

Job Design

Given the nature of sales jobs, one would expect good opportunities to stimulate intrinsic motivation without major changes in the job. Sales jobs allow the use of a wide range of skills and abilities; boredom is thus not a typical problem. And given the unique contributions of personal selling to the organization, as discussed in Chapter 2, salespeople can readily see that their jobs are critical to the organization's success. Most salespeople have considerable latitude in determining work priorities and thus experience more freedom on the job than do many other employees. Finally, feedback from sales managers or through self-monitoring is readily available. In many ways, the motivational task is easier for sales managers than for other managers. The sales job itself can be a powerful motivator.

Building Self-Esteem

Sales managers increase salesforce motivation by building salespeople's self-esteem. Positive reinforcement for good performance should be standard procedure. This may be done with formal or informal communications or recognition programs designed to spotlight good performance. When performance is less than satisfactory, it should not be overlooked but addressed in a constructive manner.

Proactive Approach

Sales managers should be committed to uncovering potential problems in motivation and eliminating them before they develop. For example, if some members of the salesforce perceive a lack of opportunity for promotion into management and are demotivated as a result, the sales manager might take additional steps to clearly define the guidelines for promotion into management and review the performance of management hopefuls in light of these guidelines. If promotion opportunities are indeed limited, the matching function of recruitment and selection again shows its importance.

SUMMARY

1. **Explain the key components of motivation: intensity, persistence, and direction.** A variety of ways exist to define motivation. Our definition includes the qualities of intensity, persistence, and direction. Intensity is the amount of mental and physical effort the salesperson is willing to expend on a specific activity. Persistence is a choice to expend effort over time, especially in the face of adversity. Direction implies that, to some extent, salespeople choose the activities on which effort is expended.

2. **Explain the difference between compensation rewards and noncompensation rewards.** Compensation rewards are those given by the organization in return for the salesperson's efforts and performance. They may include both financial and nonfinancial rewards. Noncompensation rewards are related to job design and work environment. The opportunity to be involved in meaningful, interesting work is an example of a noncompensation reward. The provision of adequate resources to do the job and a supportive management system are other examples. The focus in this chapter has been on the management of compensation rewards.

3. **Describe the primary financial and nonfinancial compensation rewards available to salespeople.** Financial compensation could include a salary component and variable pay components such as commissions and bonuses. For most salespeople, financial rewards are most important, but nonfinancial rewards also play an important role in motivating salespeople. Nonfinancial rewards include opportunities for career advancement through job promotion, a sense of accomplishment, opportunities for personal growth, and recognition. In some cases, nonfinancial rewards may be accompanied by financial rewards such as when a salesperson I promoted into management. In these instances, one salesperson might get more satisfaction out of the financial reward, while another might value the nonfinancial aspect of the reward more than the financial aspect.

4. **Describe salary, commission, and combination pay plans in terms of their advantages and disadvantages.** Straight-salary plans and straight-commission plans represent the two extremes in financial compensation for salespeople. Straight salary offers maximum control over salesforce activities but does not provide added incentive for exceptional performance. The opposite is true for straight-commission plans. The limitations of both plans have made combination plans the most popular with sales organizations. Although such plans can become too complex for easy administration, when properly conceived they offer a balance of control and incentive.

5. **Explain how to determine an appropriate financial compensation level.** In general, sales positions that are more complicated and require more skills are compensated at a higher level. Determining the appropriate financial compensation can be accomplished by benchmarking earnings levels of salespeople through a variety of methods including: reviewing trade publications; using salary surveys; examining

Internet sites such as Monster.com and Salary.com; and utilizing employment agents and placement firms.

6. **Explain the fundamental concepts in sales-expense reimbursement.** Sales expenses are usually substantial. Job-related expenses incurred by salespeople are reimbursed by a large majority of sales organizations. Companies use budgets, allowances, and documentation requirements to control sales expenses.

7. **Discuss issues associated with sales contests, team compensation, global compensation, and changing a reward system.** Sales contests are used widely to achieve short-term results, but little is known about their true effects. Companies that are new to team selling may find it difficult to move from individual-based compensation to team-based compensation. It is a challenge to determine how much of each team member's pay should be based on individual performance and how much on team performance. In most team selling situations, salary is the major compensation component, although bonuses, commissions, and other team rewards can have a positive influence on motivation. Global compensation may be dependent on different cultures and other business environment factors in varying locations around the world. Sales managers often rely heavily on human resource professionals to structure global compensation plans. Changing a reward system is a delicate procedure, requiring careful communication to the salesforce, who must "buy" the new system much like a customer would buy a product.

8. **List the guidelines for motivating and rewarding salespeople.** Six managerial guidelines for motivating salespeople are as follows: First, match the recruit to the requirements and rewards of the job. Second, incorporate individual needs into motivational programs when feasible. Third, provide salespeople with adequate information and ensure proper skill development to facilitate job performance. Fourth, use job design and redesign as motivational tools. Fifth, cultivate salespeople's self-esteem. Sixth, take a proactive approach to uncovering motivational problems by trying to eliminate problems before they become serious.

UNDERSTANDING SALES MANAGEMENT TERMS

motivation	commission splits
intensity	commission payout event
persistence	constant rate
direction	progressive rate
intrinsic motivation	regressive rate
extrinsic motivation	performance bonus
reward system management	salary plus incentive
compensation rewards	financial compensation mix
noncompensation rewards	nonfinancial compensation
current spendable income	opportunity for promotion
straight salary	sense of accomplishment
planned earnings	opportunities for personal growth
salary compression	recognition
straight commission	sales expenses
commission base	expense account padding
commission rate	sales contests

DEVELOPING SALES MANAGEMENT KNOWLEDGE

1. Identify and explain the three key dimensions of motivation.

2. Distinguish between compensation rewards and noncompensation rewards.

3. Describe an optimal salesforce reward system.

4. What are the nonfinancial compensation rewards discussed in this chapter? What suggestions can you make for administering recognition rewards?

5. Evaluate straight-salary, straight-commission, and combination pay plans in terms of their advantages and disadvantages. When should each be used?

6. Refer to "Sales Management in the 21st Century: Recognition and Incentive Programs at W.B. Mason Office Products" on p. 235. How does W.B. Mason use recognition and incentive programs to motivate its salespeople?

7. What concerns should a sales manager have regarding the use of sales contests?

8. Refer to "Sales Management in the 21st Century: Use of Sales Contests at Reality Systems" on p. 239. How often does Reality Systems have sales contests? What types of incentives do they offer? Explain the rationale for the manner in which contests are conducted at Reality Systems.

9. What challenges do sales managers face when using team-based compensation? What guidelines can sales managers follow when using team-based compensation?

10. Discuss several guidelines to improve the effectiveness of salesforce motivation and reward system management.

BUILDING SALES MANAGEMENT SKILLS

1. Assume you have been hired as the national sales manager for a newly formed electronics distributor. Your salesforce will sell directly to electronics retailers. Although the company is not widely known, it will use little other than the salesforce to promote its products in a highly competitive market. Thus, salespeople's skills are very important. Salespeople will be responsible for providing complete customer service, including handling damage claims, helping with merchandising, providing advice, and following up after the sale to ensure the customer is completely satisfied. Devise a reward system for your salesforce, being sure to address the type of financial compensation plan you will use and why, as well as the types of nonfinancial compensation you will provide. What role will recruitment and selection play in this process? Explain.

2. Most student organizations are looking for ways to raise funds. Choose a student (or any other) organization and determine a fundraising activity that involves some form of personal selling (e.g., a raffle). Then, devise a sales contest that would be appropriate for achieving predetermined fundraising objectives. Explain your fundraiser, its objectives, the contest, and the rationale behind the contest's incentives.

ROLE PLAY

3. **Role Play**

   Situation: Read and prepare your plan for a sales contest as explained in no. 2 directly above.

   Characters: One student is the salesperson, and one is the sales manager.

   Scene: The salesperson presents the sales contest plan to the sales manager and tries to convince the sales manager to support the plan by dedicating the organization's time and/or money to the sales contest. Reverse roles and repeat the role play. After each role play, the salesperson and sales manager should discuss the salesperson's presentation and record ideas for improvement in the plan and presentation of the plan.

4. This exercise is designed to expose you to differences in compensation and motivation across salespeople and companies. Interview three salespeople (in person or via telephone or the Internet) from three companies. Provide a brief report for each salesperson indicating gender, age, experience, company, industry, compensation method, financial and nonfinancial compensation rewards, and what each believes

motivates him or her to perform. Then write a summary paragraph that points to similarities and differences among the three and why these might exist. Finally, of the three, whose compensation plan would interest you the most and why?

5. Ashley Dillon, sales manager for PayWell, an automated payroll processing company, is attempting to foster teamwork in her salesforce. In particular, new salespeople often struggle to establish a customer base, and many leave their jobs during their first year of employment. PayWell compensates its sales trainees on a salary basis for three months, after which they are switched to a straight commission basis. Ashley knows that her successful senior salespeople could provide guidance to the younger salespeople, but the senior salespeople are reluctant to spend time on anything but selling. As one of the senior representatives told Ashley, "I would like to help the rookies out, but if I am not in front of customers, my commissions will drop." How can Ashley accommodate both rookie and senior salespeople to improve overall sales-force effectiveness?

6. Conduct a search using the Internet (or search for articles by some other means) to locate various incentives that might be offered to a salesforce. Explain at least three different specific incentives (e.g., an African safari trip) that could be offered to a salesforce, when and why each might be offered, and how good a motivator each might be. Attach the information that you found on the incentives to your write-up.

7. **Role Play**

    Situation: Read the Ethical Dilemma on p. 237.

    Characters: Sherry Smith, salesperson; Sherry's sales manager.

    Scene: *Location*—Sales manager's office. *Action*—Sherry's sales manager confronts her regarding meal expenses that he believes Sherry falsified on her expense report.

ROLE PLAY

MAKING SALES MANAGEMENT DECISIONS

CASE 8.1: ELITE ELECTRICAL PRODUCTS

Background

Elite Electrical Products is a market leader in the residential and commercial construction market, providing computer-controlled interfaces that allow homeowners and property managers to manage their electrical systems in an economical fashion. The company's salesforce is highly experienced, and is noted for its ability to develop sophisticated technical solutions for its customers.

Current Situation

Calvin Burns, Elite's sales manager, is contemplating the upcoming fourth quarter of the fiscal year and realizes he has two critical issues to deal with if Elite is to meet its annual growth objectives. First, Calvin has been comparing the performance of Elite's top 20 key accounts this year as compared to last year. He discovered that as a group, the top 20 accounts were ahead of last year's sales figures by an impressive 15 percent. However, when he analyzed the data more closely, he found that two of the top 20 accounts were at 80 percent of last year's year-to-date sales levels. Both of the lagging accounts were in Don Covington's territory. Don was a perennial leader among Elite's senior salespeople, and his key account performance was definitely a cause for concern. Calvin Burns had been aware of Don's lackluster performance this year, and they had discussed the issue a couple of months ago, when Don assured Calvin that he would finish the year strong. Earlier today, Calvin and Don reviewed the key account situation again, and Calvin came away with an uneasy feeling. He values Don as an opinion leader among fellow salespeople and especially needed his support in introducing Elite's new mobile application for its control system that would allow customers to manage electrical consumption anywhere and anytime. As Calvin replayed the meeting with Don in his head, he recalled this dialogue:

Calvin: So, Don, I really need you to bear down the fourth quarter and bring those two key accounts in over last year's sales levels.

Don: I understand, Calvin, and I will do what I can. This has been a tough year for me personally, and I think I may just need to catch my breath and get ready for next year. That knee replacement operation slowed me down a bit, and frankly, it sapped my energy for a while. My commissions are holding up OK, so I should be alright.

Calvin: Don, you became a sales leader for Elite through working hard and working smart. I just hope you don't lose the edge. Are you still as hungry as you used to be?

Don: Calvin, we go back too far for you to ask a question like that. Of course I am just as hungry as ever! But I am a human being too, and right now I just need a little slack.

Calvin: I just want you to reach your full potential. And I need you to help champion the roll-out of the new mobile application. You have got to help the rest of the salesforce take the mobile app over the top.

Don: Maybe you need to find another champion. I think I'd better concentrate on getting my own act together. If we are done here, I need to get out and make some key account calls.

Questions

1. How do you suggest Burns handle Covington?

2. Assess the possibility of Covington becoming a champion for the roll-out of the mobile application. Is this a good idea?

ROLE PLAY

Role Play

Situation: Read Case 8.1.

Characters: Calvin Burns, Elite Electrical sales manager, Don Covington, senior sales representative.

Scene 1:   *Location*—Calvin Burns's office. *Action*—Burns is unhappy with the way his last meeting with Covington ended. He wants to keep pushing Covington to improve his performance, but wants to do so in a positive way. Burns is meeting with Covington to talk things over and hopefully move in a positive direction. Covington is somewhat defensive, but has an open mind about how to proceed.

Scene 2:   *Location*—Calvin Burns's office. *Action*—It is year-end and Covington has returned to form as a top sales representative. Unfortunately, Covington seems to resent the extra pressure applied by Burns and now seems totally focused on maximizing total sales volume and thus his commissions. Before the meeting, Covington tells

Burns: "I am a selling machine. Spare me the rah-rah and don't ask me to be a cheerleader for any new product roll-outs." Burns doesn't like Covington's current attitude, and he is determined to retain Covington as a positive member of the salesforce. Burns is thinking about how non-commission rewards might be used in this case. Burns has called this meeting to lay out a plan of action and get Covington's buy-in. Burns is also feeling that it will be important for him to assert his control over the situation.

CASE 8.2: FLOOR-SHINE CLEANING PRODUCTS

Background

Floor-Shine Cleaning Products has been manufacturing and selling household floor cleaning products for more than 60 years. The company offers several brands that can be used to clean a variety of floor surfaces. It stands behind all its products with a "customer satisfaction guarantee." Any consumer who is not fully satisfied with the floor cleaner on applying it properly may return it to the place of purchase and receive a refund or have the product replaced with another of equal value.

Floor-Shine's products are distributed in a variety of outlets, ranging from small grocery and convenience stores to huge discounters such as Wal-Mart and Home Depot. Each customer is highly valued regardless of size. According to the company's founder, Arthur Worthington, "Every customer should be treated as if they are our only customer." For this reason, the company takes pride in establishing long-term customer relationships. In fact, several of the company's current customers have been distributing its products since the company was founded. The company's salesforce was built around this idea and to this day is well noted for its commitment to building strong and satisfying customer relationships.

Current Situation

Vince Coleman, Floor-Shine's national sales manager, recently asked regional sales manager Bob Herman to coordinate a special fourth-quarter sales push to achieve projected year-end sales goals. Herman, a committed sales manager, was confident he could develop a program that would succeed. He thought a sales contest would be an excellent way to boost fourth-quarter sales in his region. By developing a contest, he could avoid altering the current compensation package, which he believed to be satisfactory to his salespeople.

Herman has 100 salespeople in his region, about 20 percent of whom are women. The region is divided into five districts, each comprised of 20 salespeople. Rather than have all 100 salespeople compete against each other, Herman decided to have five winners, one for each district. Salespeople within each district would compete against each other, and the salesperson with the highest number of sales during the contest period would be declared the winner.

Herman recently heard about a new approach being taken by some companies to motivate their salespeople. Contest winners were awarded a trip to a fantasy baseball camp. Award winners spent a week with baseball legends who taught and coached them. The award proved to be a highly successful motivator. Herman liked this idea and decided to offer this trip to each district winner as the prize for winning the sales contest. Herman contacted the company's marketing communications group to ask them to design a set of promotional materials to be distributed to each salesperson. He then visited each district, explaining the contest rules to its salespeople. At the same time, he delivered pep talks. "Each of you has an equal chance at victory. Now is the time to seize the moment and go for the gold!"

After all the preplanning was completed, the contest finally went into effect. Most salespeople realized that they could increase their sales either by selling more to current customers or by finding new accounts. One method for increasing sales to current customers was to help them in merchandising so that they could sell more product. This seemed to work well for many salespeople. However, several concentrated on their large customers at the expense of their smaller accounts. The larger customers had much more potential and the input-to-output ratio with these customers had a much higher payoff. Several salespeople's obsession with their larger accounts got in the way of providing their smaller customers with the service they had come to expect. Some customers even threatened to take their business elsewhere. In fact, Ray's Groceries, a small but long-standing customer, was so upset with the decline in service that it dropped Floor-Shine as a supplier.

Numerous salespeople got wise to the idea that they could increase their sales by loading their customers with product toward the end of the contest period. Some salespeople asked customers to purchase and take delivery of their next scheduled order early. Others offered customers special incentives if they agreed to order more product than usual. One salesperson went so far as to offer a small kickback.

In an attempt to gain new customers, some salespeople took on customers that were poor credit risks.

For instance, salesman Larry Lynn knew a medium-sized hardware store in his territory was in financial trouble, so much so that the store had lost its paint supplier because of its inability to pay. Larry figured he could enhance his sales during the contest period by taking the customer's order. If the customer was unable to pay, it would not show up until after the contest was over, and Larry would already have these sales added to his total for the period.

About one-third of the way into the contest, Dan Tate, a sales rep in district 3, was able to land a new major account, which meant a tremendous increase in sales for him. At that point, the other salespeople in his district seemed to lose enthusiasm for the contest. As Saul Weber put it, "I don't stand a prayer of winning the contest now. The only way I would have a chance is to land a similar account. Given my present territory, that is impossible. Doug has this contest wrapped up. He might as well grab his mitt and pack his bags—he's heading for fantasy baseball camp." As the contest was drawing to a close, Herman noticed that sales had not increased nearly as much as he had anticipated. Moreover, most of the women in the salesforce did not significantly increase their sales figures. In fact, they were about the same as usual. Herman knew Coleman would want a full assessment of the contest on its completion. As he sat at his desk, he began to think about what went wrong.

Questions

1. How would you evaluate this contest? What are its pros and cons?

2. How could this contest be designed to have a better chance of success?

ROLE PLAY

Role Play

Situation: Read Case 8.2.

Characters: Vince Coleman, national sales manager; Bob Herman, regional sales manager; Larry Lynn, salesperson.

Scene 1:   *Location*—Bob Herman's office. *Action*—Herman got word of Larry Lynn's tactic of taking on customers with questionable credit risk during the contest period. He is meeting with Larry to discuss these tactics.

Scene 2:   *Location*—Vince Coleman's office. *Action*—Vince Coleman is meeting with Bob Herman to get a recap of his sales contest. Herman explains the pros and cons of the contest. Coleman then provides some advice for developing a sales contest in the future.

Determining Salesforce Effectiveness and Performance

The two chapters in Part 5 focus on determining salesforce effectiveness and performance. Chapter 9 addresses the evaluation of sales organization effectiveness. Methods for analyzing sales, costs, profitability, and productivity at different sales organization levels are reviewed. Chapter 10 addresses the evaluation of salespeople's individual performance and job satisfaction. Ways of determining the appropriate performance criteria and methods of evaluation, and of using the evaluations to improve salesperson performance and job satisfaction, are discussed.

EVALUATING THE EFFECTIVENESS OF THE ORGANIZATION

OBJECTIVES

After completing this chapter, you should be able to

1. Differentiate between sales organization effectiveness and salesperson performance.

2. Define a sales organization audit and discuss how it should be conducted.

3. Describe how to perform different methods of sales analysis for different organizational levels and different types of sales.

4. Describe how to perform a cost analysis for a sales organization.

5. Describe how to perform an income statement analysis, activity-based costing, and return on assets managed to assess sales organization profitability.

6. Describe how to perform a productivity analysis for a sales organization.

7. Define benchmarking and Six Sigma and discuss how each should be conducted.

IDENTIFY AND EVALUATE ORGANIZATIONAL COMPETENCIES: USING A SALES ORGANIZATION AUDIT

Organizational capabilities are key strategic assets—the collective skills, abilities, and expertise of an organization. They are the outcome of investments in structure, staffing, technology, processes, training, communication, and other resources. Together, an organization's capabilities define and determine what it is good at doing and, in the end, what it is. As such, it is essential for a sales manager to identify, evaluate, and understand the capabilities of the sales organization, how they impact the success of his or her organization, and what additional capabilities must be developed in order for the organization to be successful. Because the nature of capabilities makes them difficult to measure, managers have found success utilizing a structured research methodology, the organization audit, to identify capabilities and evaluate their effectiveness in terms of organizational performance.

Just as a financial audit tracks cash flow and effectiveness of financial management, a sales organization audit enables the sales manager to identify and monitor capabilities, highlight which ones are most important given the organization's effectiveness and performance, and lead to an action plan for improvement. This analysis can work for an entire sales organization, a region, business unit, or product category. Indeed, any unit of the sales organization can do an audit.

Massachusetts-based Boston Scientific has enjoyed strong growth over the past 25 years with the international division delivering 45 percent of company revenues and 55 percent of company profits. Company executives wanted to find ways to further improve the division's success and decided to engage in an organizational audit. Data was gathered from multiple groups and analyzed to identify the most critical capabilities requiring managerial action. The results of the audit resulted in an action plan to further enhance the competitiveness of the international division as well as baseline measures to use in assessing the effectiveness of managerial actions.

The sales organization audit is an objective identification and review of the structure, systems and processes, staff, technology, training, skills, and strategies of your sales organization. The focus of the audit is to advise sales management on how to hire, evaluate, coach, and develop people; how to develop effective sales strategies; how to design appropriate departmental structures and systems, and how to develop effective sales management styles.

Sources: Dave Ulrich and Norm Smallwood, "Capitalizing on Capabilities," *Harvard Business Review* (June 2004), http://hbr.org/2004/06/capitalizing-on-capabilities/ar/1 (accessed January 27, 2014).

Assessing the success of a sales organization is difficult because so many factors must be considered. For example, the success of the sales organization must be differentiated from the success of individual salespeople (see Figure 9.1).[1] Whereas sales organization effectiveness is a function of how well the sales organization achieved its goals and objectives overall, salesperson performance is a function of how well each salesperson performed in his or her particular situation. Thus, salesperson performance contributes to, but does not completely determine, sales organization effectiveness.

As illustrated by the Boston Scientific example in the opening vignette, the organizational sales audit provides sales managers with an effective tool for identifying and

FIGURE 9.1	Sales Organization Effectiveness

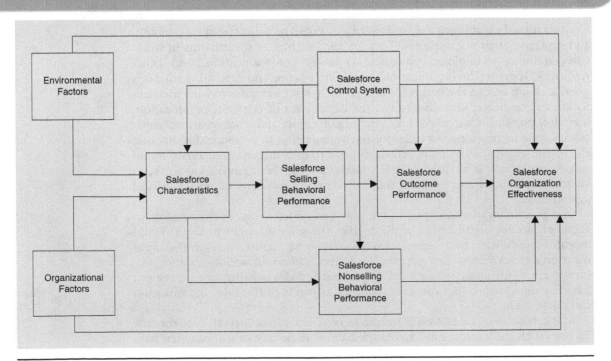

evaluating the capabilities of the sales unit and guides the development of sales strategies and action plans toward achieving sales goals and objectives. The focus of the organization's evaluation is on the overall sales organization as well as the managerial levels that comprise the organization: districts, regions, zones, territories, and individual salespeople. The results of sales organization evaluations are normally general strategic or policy changes. However, analyzing and improving salesperson performance is typically paramount to improving sales organization effectiveness.

Evaluations of salesperson performance are confined to the individuals, not the sales organization or sales organization levels. The results of these evaluations are typically tactical. In other words, they lead a sales manager to take specific actions to improve the performance of an individual salesperson. Generally, different actions are warranted for different salespeople, depending on the areas that need improvement.

Evidence for the difference between sales organization effectiveness and salesperson performance is provided in a study of 144 sales organizations in the United States. A comparison of the more-effective and less-effective sales organizations indicated that those that were more effective had achieved much better results in many areas, compared with their less effective counterparts. For example, the more effective sales organizations generated much higher sales per salesperson ($3,988,000 versus $1,755,000) and much lower selling expenses as a percentage of sales (13 percent versus 18 percent) than the less effective sales organizations. The salespeople in the more effective organizations also outperformed salespeople in the less effective ones in several areas. However, the differences in salesperson performance were not sufficient to completely explain the differences in sales organization effectiveness. Thus, sales organization effectiveness is the result of salesperson performance as well as many other factors (e.g., sales organization structure and deployment and sales management performance).[2]

This chapter addresses the evaluation of sales organization effectiveness, and Chapter 10 addresses the evaluation of salesperson performance. Chapter 9 begins with a discussion of a sales organization audit and then describes more specific analyses of sales, costs, profits, and productivity to determine sales organization effectiveness. This is followed by a discussion of how benchmarking and Six Sigma can be used to improve sales organization effectiveness.

SALES ORGANIZATION AUDIT

Although the term *audit* is most often used in reference to financial audits performed by accounting firms, the audit concept has been extended to business functions in recent years. In Chapter 6, a sales organization audit was described as a comprehensive, systematic, diagnostic, and prescriptive tool. The purpose of a sales organization audit is to assess the adequacy of a firm's sales management process and to provide direction for improved performance and prescription for needed changes. It is a tool that should be used by all firms whether or not they are achieving their goals. This type of audit is the most comprehensive approach for evaluating sales organization effectiveness.

A framework for performing a sales organization audit is presented in Figure 9.2.[3] As indicated in the figure, the audit addresses four major areas: sales organization environment, sales management evaluation, sales organization planning system, and sales management functions. The purpose of the audit is to investigate, systematically and comprehensively, each of these areas to identify existing or potential problems, determine their causes, and take the necessary corrective actions. For example, after having an agency conduct an audit, Guinness was able to redesign its salesforce to improve its structure and clarity. This resulted in a more motivated, focused, efficient, and subsequently higher-performing sales organization.[4]

The sales organization audit should be performed regularly, not just when problems are evident. One of the major values of an audit is its generation of diagnostic information that can help management correct problems in early stages or eliminate potential problems before they become serious. Because auditing should be objective, it should

FIGURE 9.2 — Sales Organization Audit Framework

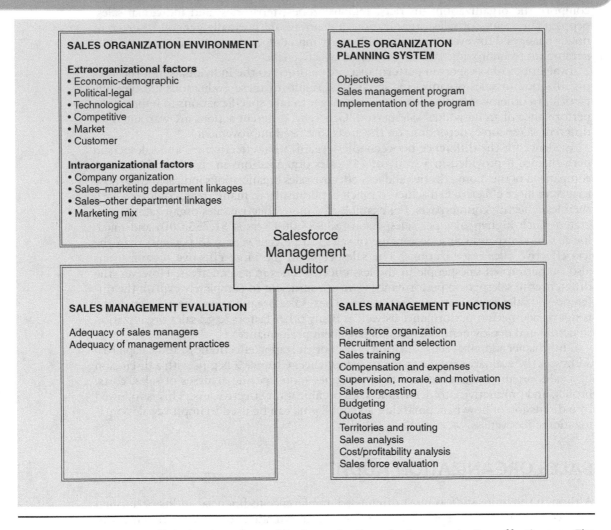

SALES ORGANIZATION ENVIRONMENT

Extraorganizational factors
• Economic-demographic
• Political-legal
• Technological
• Competitive
• Market
• Customer

Intraorganizational factors
• Company organization
• Sales–marketing department linkages
• Sales–other department linkages
• Marketing mix

SALES ORGANIZATION PLANNING SYSTEM

Objectives
Sales management program
Implementation of the program

Salesforce Management Auditor

SALES MANAGEMENT EVALUATION

Adequacy of sales managers
Adequacy of management practices

SALES MANAGEMENT FUNCTIONS

Sales force organization
Recruitment and selection
Sales training
Compensation and expenses
Supervision, morale, and motivation
Sales forecasting
Budgeting
Quotas
Territories and routing
Sales analysis
Cost/profitability analysis
Sales force evaluation

The sales organization audit is the most comprehensive evaluation of sales organization effectiveness. The audit typically provides assessments of the sales organization environment, sales management evaluation, sales organization planning system, and sales management functions.

be conducted by someone from outside the sales organization. This could be someone from another functional area within the firm or an outside consulting firm.

Although outsiders should conduct the audit, members of the sales organization should be active participants. Sales managers and salespeople provide much of the information collected. Exhibit 9.1[5] presents sample questions that should be addressed in a sales organization audit. Answers typically come from members of the sales organization and from company records.

Although obviously an expensive and time-consuming process, the sales organization audit usually generates benefits that outweigh the monetary and time costs. Potential benefits resulting from an audit include, among others, increases in productivity, and sales and profits due to improvements and efficiencies in sales operations and management. This is especially true when audits are conducted regularly because the chances of identifying and correcting potential problems before they become troublesome increase with the regularity of the auditing process.

Sample Questions from a Sales Organization Audit   EXHIBIT 9.1

IV. SALES MANAGEMENT FUNCTIONS

A. Salesforce Organization

1. How is our salesforce organized (by product, by customer, by territory)?
2. Is this type of organization appropriate, given the current intraorganizational and extraorganizational conditions?
3. Does this type of organization adequately service the needs of our customers?

B. Recruitment and Selection

1. How many salespeople do we have?
2. Is this number adequate in light of our objectives and resources?
3. Are we serving our customers adequately with this number of salespeople?
4. How is our salesforce size determined?
5. What is our turnover rate? What have we done to try to change it?
6. Do we have adequate sources from which to obtain recruits? Have we overlooked some possible sources?
7. Do we have a job description for each of our sales jobs? Is each job description current?
8. Have we enumerated the necessary sales job qualifications? Have they been recently updated? Are they predictive of sales success?
9. Are our selection screening procedures financially feasible and appropriate?
10. Do we use a battery of psychological tests in our selection process? Are the tests valid and reliable?
11. Do our recruitment and selection procedures satisfy employment opportunity guidelines?

C. Sales Training

1. How is our sales training program developed? Does it meet the needs of management and sales personnel?
2. Do we establish training objectives before developing and implementing the training program?
3. Is the training program adequate in light of our objectives and resources?
4. What kinds of training do we currently provide our salespeople?
5. Does the training program need revising? What areas of the training program should be improved or deemphasized?
6. What methods do we use to evaluate the effectiveness of our training program?
7. Can we afford to train internally or should we use external sources for training?
8. Do we have an ongoing training program for senior salespeople? Is it adequate?

D. Compensation and Expenses

1. Does our sales compensation plan meet our objectives in light of our financial resources?
2. Is the compensation plan fair, flexible, economical, and easy to understand and administer?
3. What is the level of compensation, the type of plan, and the frequency of payment?
4. Are the salespeople and management satisfied with the compensation plan?
5. Does the compensation plan ensure that the salespeople perform the necessary sales job activities?
6. Does the compensation plan attract and retain enough quality sales performers?
7. Does the sales expense plan meet our objectives in light of our financial resources?
8. Is the expense plan fair, flexible, and easy to administer? Does it allow for geographical, customer, and/or product differences?
9. Does the expense plan ensure that the necessary sales job activities are performed?
10. Can we easily audit the expenses incurred by our sales personnel?

SALES ORGANIZATION EFFECTIVENESS EVALUATIONS

There is no one summary measure of sales organization effectiveness. Sales organizations have multiple goals and objectives, and thus, multiple factors must be assessed. As illustrated in Figure 9.3, four types of analyses are typically necessary to develop a comprehensive evaluation of any sales organization. Conducting analyses in each of these areas is a complex task for two reasons. First, many types of analyses can be performed to evaluate sales, cost, profitability, and productivity results. For example, a sales analysis might focus on total sales, sales of specific products, sales to specific customers, or other types of sales and might include sales comparisons to sales quotas, to previous periods, to sales of competitors, or other types of analyses. Second, separate sales analyses need to be performed for the different levels in the sales organization. Thus, a typical evaluation would include separate sales analyses for sales zones, regions, districts, and territories.

The results from one study on methods used to measure salesforce effectiveness are presented in Exhibit 9.2.[6] While many sales organizations focus on sales analysis, customer satisfaction is also heavily relied upon to determine sales organization effectiveness. This involves surveying customers to determine their level of satisfaction with the company's products, service, and salespeople, among other things. For a look at how the Stepan Company incorporates assessments of customer satisfaction into their assessment of sales organization effectiveness, see "Sales Management in the 21st Century: Stepan Company's Sales Organization Assessment Focuses on Customer Satisfaction." Determining the level of customer satisfaction has become easier due to the Internet. Companies such as Apogee Analytics, LLC (http://www.apogeeanalytics.com) and NetReflector (http://www.netreflector.com) will create and administer Web-based customer satisfaction surveys for firms. Now we discuss how sales, cost, profitability, and productivity analyses can be conducted to evaluate sales organization effectiveness.

Sales Analysis

Because the basic purpose of a sales organization is to generate sales, sales analysis is an obvious and important element of evaluating sales organization effectiveness. The difficulty, however, is in determining exactly what should be analyzed. One key consideration is in defining what is meant by a *sale*. Definitions include a placed order, a shipped order, and a paid order. Defining a sale by when an order is shipped is probably most common.

| FIGURE 9.3 | Sales Organization Effectiveness Framework |

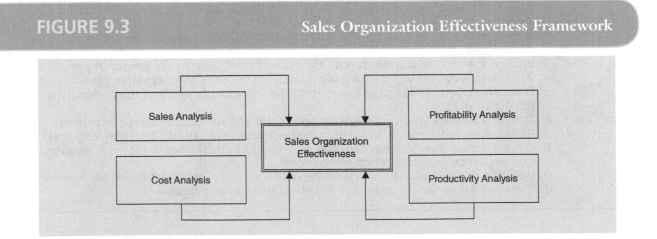

Evaluating sales organization effectiveness requires analyses of sales, cost, profitability, and productivity. Each type of analysis can be performed in several ways, should be performed at different sales organization levels, and will produce unique evaluative and diagnostic information for sales managers.

Methods Used to Measure Salesforce Effectiveness   EXHIBIT 9.2

	Percent Using
Sales results versus goal	79
Customer satisfaction	59
Profit versus goal	49
Sales manager feedback	45
Market share	39
Cost of sales	37
Sales employee feedback	28
Return on investment of sales resources	21
Other	9

SALES MANAGEMENT IN THE 21ST CENTURY

Stepan Company's Sales Organization Assessment Focuses on Customer Satisfaction

Tom Cassidy, Director of Polymer Platforms for the Stepan Company, discusses the company's regular use of balanced scorecard organizational assessments to build high levels of customer satisfaction and drive unmatched competitive advantage:

At multiple times each year, Stepan Company formally assesses the organization's sales performance from the perspective of our customers. The purchase decision makers and influencers at each of our customer organizations are contacted and score Stepan on how well we are meeting their expectations across each facet of our business that comes into contact with customers. This sales organization audit include customers' evaluations of sales representative contacts and helpfulness, ease of doing business, product quality, competitive pricing, order and delivery processes, research and new product development, technical support, and even our billing processes. In addition to rating our performance on each of these business areas, customers also explain their reasoning behind their ratings by discussing what we are doing well and where can improve. As sales managers, we evaluate this information at multiple levels: the corporate sales organization, by country and geographic area, by product line, by salesperson and territory, and even by individual account. This level of detail in the analyses keeps us in close contact with our customers and allows us to better manage and deploy our sales assets across the organization and in the field. Most importantly, the sales audit provides insightful and actionable information enabling Stepan to maintain its leadership position in this highly competitive and worldwide industry.

Regardless of the definition used, the sales organization must be consistent and develop an information system to track sales based on whatever sales definition is used.

Another consideration is whether to focus on *sales dollars* or *sales units*. This can be extremely important during times when prices increase or when salespeople have substantial latitude in negotiating selling prices. The sales information in Exhibit 9.3 illustrates how different conclusions may result from analyses of sales dollars or sales units. If just sales dollars are analyzed, all regions in the exhibit would appear to be generating substantial sales growth. However, when sales units are introduced, the dollar sales growth for all regions in 2013 can be attributed almost entirely to price increases, because units sold increased only minimally during this period. The situation is somewhat different in 2014, because all regions significantly increased the number of units sold. However, sales volume for region 2 is relatively flat, even though units sold increased. This could be caused either by selling more lower-priced products or by using larger price concessions than the other regions. In either case, analysis of sales dollars or sales units provides different evaluative information, so it is often useful to include both dollars and units in a sales analysis.

EXHIBIT 9.3	Sales Dollars versus Sales Units					
	2012		**2013**		**2014**	
	Sales Dollars	**Sales Units**	**Sales Dollars**	**Sales Units**	**Sales Dollars**	**Sales Units**
Region 1	$50,000,000	500,000	$55,000,000	510,000	$62,000,000	575,000
Region 2	$55,000,000	550,000	$60,000,000	560,000	$62,000,000	600,000
Region 3	$45,000,000	450,000	$50,000,000	460,000	$56,000,000	520,000
Region 4	$60,000,000	600,000	$65,000,000	610,000	$73,000,000	720,000

Given a definition of sales and a decision concerning sales dollars versus units, many types of sales evaluations can be performed. Several alternative evaluations are presented in Figure 9.4. The critical decision areas are the organizational level of analysis, the type of sales, and the method of analysis.

Organizational Level of Analysis

Sales analyses should be performed for all levels in the sales organization for two basic reasons. First, sales managers at each level need sales analyses at their level and the next level below for evaluation and control purposes. For example, a regional sales manager should have sales analyses for all regions as well as for all districts within his or her region. This makes it possible to assess the sales effectiveness of the region and to determine the sales contribution of each district.

Second, a useful way to identify problem areas in achieving sales effectiveness is to perform a hierarchical sales analysis, which consists of evaluating sales results

FIGURE 9.4 Sales Analysis Framework

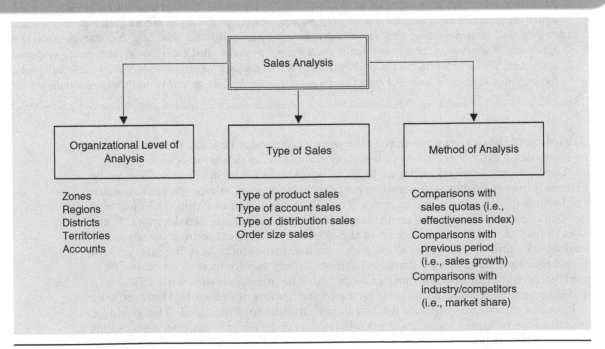

A sales analysis can be performed at a number of organizational levels and for many types of sales, and can use several methods of analysis.

throughout the sales organization from a top-down perspective. Essentially, the analysis begins with total sales for the sales organization and proceeds through each successively lower level in the sales organization. The emphasis is on identifying potential problem areas at each level and then using analyses at lower levels to pinpoint the specific problems. An example of a hierarchical sales analysis is presented in Figure 9.5.

In this example, sales for region 3 appear to be much lower than those for the other regions, so the analysis proceeds to investigate the sales for all the districts in region 3. Low sales are identified for district 4; then district 4 sales are analyzed by territory. The results of this analysis suggest potential sales problems within territory 5. Additional analyses would be performed to determine why sales are so low for territory 5 and to take corrective action to increase sales from this territory. The hierarchical approach to sales analysis provides an efficient way to conduct a sales analysis and to identify major areas of sales problems.

Type of Sales

The analysis in Figure 9.5 addresses only total firm sales at each organizational level. It is usually desirable to evaluate several types of sales, such as by the following categories:

- product type or specific products
- account type or specific accounts
- type of distribution method
- order size

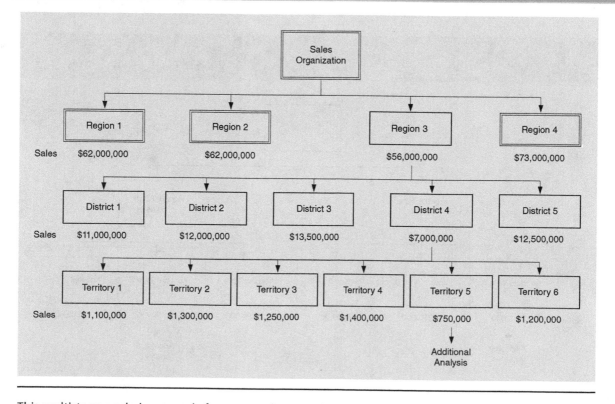

Example of Hierarchical Sales Analysis   **FIGURE 9.5**

This multistage analysis proceeds from one sales organization level to the next by identifying the major deviations and investigating them in more detail at the next lower level. In the present example, region 3 has the lowest sales, so all districts in region 3 are examined. District 4 has poor sales results, so all the territories in district 4 are examined. Additional analysis is indicated for territory 5.

The hierarchical analysis in Figure 9.5 could have included sales by product type, account type, or other type of sales at each level. Or, once the potential sales problem in territory 5 has been isolated, analysis of different types of sales could be performed to define the sales problem more fully. An example analysis is presented in Figure 9.6. This example suggests especially low sales volume for product type A and account type B. Additional analyses within these product and account types would be needed to determine why sales are low in these areas and what needs to be done to improve sales effectiveness.

The analysis of different types of sales at different organizational levels increases management's ability to detect and define problem areas in sales performance. However, incorporating different sales types into the analysis complicates the evaluation process and requires an information system capable of providing sales data concerning the desired breakdowns. "Sales Management in the 21st Century: Diversified Product Types Require Changed Sales Structure at Pfizer" illustrates the growing complexity of sales organizations consisting of diverse product types, multiple types of accounts, and specialized salesforces.

Method of Analysis

The discussion to this point has focused on the actual sales results for different organizational levels and types of sales. However, the use of actual sales results limits the analysis to comparisons across organizational levels or sales types. These within-organization comparisons provide some useful information but are insufficient for a comprehensive evaluation of sales effectiveness. Several additional types of analysis are recommended and presented in Exhibit 9.4.

Comparing actual sales results with sales forecasts and quotas is extremely revealing. A *sales forecast* represents an expected level of firm sales for defined products, markets, and time periods and for a specified strategy. Based on this definition, a sales forecast provides a basis for establishing specific *sales quotas* and reasonable sales objectives for a territory, district, region, or zone (methods for establishing sales quotas are discussed in

FIGURE 9.6   Example of Type-of-Sales Analysis by Product and Account Type

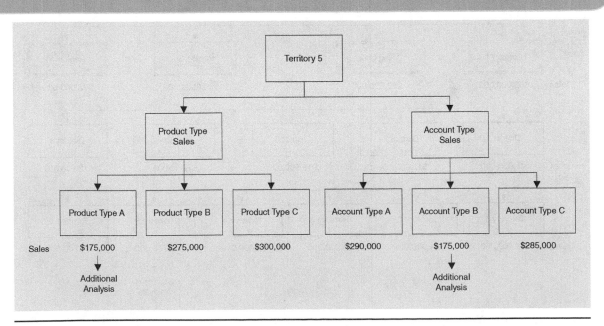

This is a continuation of the hierarchical sales analysis presented in Figure 9.5. Sales in territory 5 are analyzed by product type and account type. The analysis suggests poor sales results for product type A and account type B.

Diversified Product Types Require Changed Sales Structure at Pfizer

Chris Aiken, Certified Medical Representative and Senior Professional Healthcare Representative with Pfizer, Inc. discusses the diversified portfolio of product types and increasingly complex sales organization structure at Pfizer:

Pfizer has moved beyond a reliance on a few blockbuster medicines to a more diversified portfolio. The company has developed clear strategies and established individual business units accountable for each of these product types. This changed sales structure has created a company characterized by accountability, speed, agility and ability to keep commitments to stakeholders by making profitable business decisions that mutually benefit our sales organization and patients. To maximize new opportunities and increase the speed and efficiency for bringing highly innovative medicines to more patients, Pfizer has developed an enhanced commercial operating

structure consisting of nine diverse types of health, care businesses: Primary Care, Specialty Care, Oncology, Emerging Markets, Established Products, Consumer Healthcare, Nutrition, Animal Health, and Capsugel.

The new sales organization incorporates each of these core business types with each business type having a sales executive with clear accountability for results and charged with managing multiple levels of geographic territories and product groups. As a result of this reorganization, each business unit is provided with the resources to pursue attractive growth opportunities and to deliver benefits to all who rely on us around the world. With this sales organization structure, we are able to rapidly capitalize on opportunities to advance our business by increasing support for successful new medicines, forging partnerships with key customers, entering into co-promotion and licensing agreements, investing in new technologies to add value to our core product offerings, and acquiring new products and services from outside the company.

Method of Analysis Examples   **EXHIBIT 9.4**

	District 1	District 2	District 3	District 4	District 5
Sales	$11,000,000	$12,000,000	$13,000,000	$7,000,000	$12,000,000
Sales quota	$11,250,000	$11,500,000	$12,750,000	$10,000,000	$11,000,000
Effectiveness index	98	104	102	70	109
Sales last year	$10,700,000	$11,000,000	$12,250,000	$6,800,000	$10,350,000
Sales growth	3%	9%	6%	3%	16%
Industry sales	$42,000,000	$42,000,000	$45,000,000	$40,000,000	$45,000,000
Market share	26%	29%	29%	18%	27%

Chapter 10). An effectiveness index can be computed by dividing actual sales results by the sales quota and multiplying by 100. As illustrated in Exhibit 9.4, sales results in excess of quota will have index values greater than 100, and results lower than quota will have index values less than 100. The sales effectiveness index makes it easy to compare directly the sales effectiveness of different organizational levels and different types of sales.

Another type of useful analysis is the comparison of actual results to previous periods (i.e., sales growth). As illustrated in Exhibit 9.4, this type of analysis can be used to determine sales growth rates for different organizational levels and for different sales types. Incorporating sales data for many periods makes it possible to assess long-term sales trends.

A final type of analysis to be considered is a comparison of actual sales results to those achieved by competitors (i.e., market share). This type of analysis can again be performed at different organizational levels and for different types of sales. If the comparison is extended to overall industry sales, various types of market share can be calculated. Examples of these comparisons are presented in Exhibit 9.4.

Sales analysis is the approach used most often for evaluating sales organization effectiveness. Sales data are typically more readily available than other data types, and sales results are extremely important to sales organizations. However, developing a sales analysis approach that will produce the desired evaluative information is a complex undertaking. Sales data must be available for different organizational levels and for different types of sales. Valid sales forecasts are needed to establish sales quotas for evaluating sales effectiveness in achieving sales objectives. In addition, industry and competitor sales information is also useful. Regardless of the comprehensiveness of the sales analysis, sales organizations need to perform additional analyses to evaluate sales organization effectiveness adequately.

Cost Analysis

A second major element in the evaluation of sales organization effectiveness is cost analysis. The emphasis here is on assessing the costs incurred by the sales organization to generate the achieved levels of sales. The general approach is to compare the costs incurred with planned costs as defined by selling budgets.

Corporate resources earmarked for personal selling expenses for a designated period represent the total selling budget. The key sales management budgeting task is to determine the best way to allocate these sales resources throughout the sales organization and across the different selling activities. The budgeting process is intended to instill cost consciousness and profit awareness throughout the organization, and it is necessary for establishing benchmarks for evaluating selling costs.

Selling budgets are developed at all levels of the sales organization and for all key expenditure categories. Our discussion focuses on the major selling expense categories and methods for establishing specific expenditure levels within the budget.

Firms differ considerably in how they define their selling expense categories. Nevertheless, all sales organizations should plan expenditures carefully for the major selling and sales management activities and for the different levels in the sales organization structure. The selling budget addresses controllable expenses, not uncontrollable ones. Typical selling budget expense categories are presented in Exhibit 9.5.

Both the total expenditures for each of these categories and sales management budget responsibility must be determined. Sales management budget responsibility depends

EXHIBIT 9.5   Typical Selling Expense Categories in the Budget

Classification	Actual 2014	Original 2015 Budget	2nd Quarter Revision	3rd Quarter Revision	4th Quarter Revision
Compensation expenses					
Salaries					
Commissions					
Bonuses					
Total					
Travel expenses					
Lodging					
Food					
Transportation					
Miscellaneous					
Total					
Administrative expenses					
Recruiting					
Training					
Meetings					
Sales offices					
Total					

on the degree of centralization or decentralization in the sales organization. In general, more centralized sales organizations will place budget responsibility at higher sales management levels. For example, if salesforce recruitment and selection take place at the regional level, then the regional sales managers will have responsibility for this budget category. Typically, the sales management activity occurs at all management levels. For example, training activities might be performed at national, zone, regional, and district levels. In this case, the budgeting process must address how much to spend on overall training and how to allocate training expenditures to the organizational levels.

The basic objective in budgeting for each category is to determine the lowest expenditure level necessary to *achieve the sales quotas*. Notice that we did not say the lowest possible expenditure level. Sales managers might cut costs and improve profitability in the short run, but if expenditures for training, travel, and so forth are too low, long-run sales and profits will be sacrificed. However, if expenses can be reduced by more effective or more efficient spending, these productivity improvements can produce increased profitability in the long run. Achieving productivity improvements has been one of the most demanding tasks facing sales managers in recent years because increases in field selling costs and extremely competitive markets have put tremendous pressure on firm profitability.

Determining expenditure levels for each selling expense category is extremely difficult. Although there is no perfect way to arrive at these expenditure levels, two approaches warrant attention: the percentage of sales method and the objective and task method.

Probably the most often used, the percentage of sales method calculates an expenditure level for each category by multiplying an expenditure percentage times forecasted sales. The effectiveness of the percentage of sales method depends on the accuracy of sales forecasts and the appropriateness of the expenditure percentages. If the sales forecasts are not accurate, the selling budgets will be incorrect, regardless of the expenditure percentages used. If sales forecasts are accurate, the key is determining the expenditure percentages. This percentage may be derived from historical spending patterns or industry averages. Sales management should adjust the percentage up or down to reflect the unique aspects of their sales organization.

The objective and task method takes an entirely different approach. In its most basic form, it is a type of zero-based budgeting. In essence, each sales manager prepares a separate budget request that stipulates the objectives to be achieved, the tasks required to achieve these objectives, and the costs associated with performing the necessary tasks. These requests are reviewed, and, through an iterative process, selling budgets are approved. Many variations of the objective and task method are used by different sales organizations.

In reality, the process of establishing a selling budget is an involved one that typically incorporates various types of analysis, many meetings, and much political maneuvering. However, the process has been streamlined in many firms through the use of computer modeling to rapidly evaluate alternative selling budgets.

After a budget has been determined, cost analysis can be performed. Examples of two types of cost analysis are presented in Exhibit 9.6. The first analysis calculates the variance between actual costs and budgeted costs for the regions in a sales organization. Regions with the largest variation, especially when actual costs far exceed budgeted costs, should be highlighted for further analysis. Large variations are not necessarily bad, but the reasons for the variations should be determined. For example, the ultimate purpose of selling costs is to generate sales. Therefore, the objective is not necessarily to minimize selling costs, but to ensure that a specified relationship between sales and selling costs is maintained. Evaluate a common budgeting challenge that sales managers must deal with in "An Ethical Dilemma."

One way to evaluate this relationship is to calculate the selling costs as a percentage of sales achieved, and then compare this percentage to a budgeted expenditure percentage. Translating actual selling costs into percentages of sales achieved provides a means for assessing whether the cost-sales relationship has been maintained, even though the actual costs may exceed the absolute level in the selling budget. This situation is illustrated by region 4 in Exhibit 9.6, where actual compensation costs exceeded budgeted costs by $300,000, yet actual costs as a percentage of sales achieved (6 percent) were no more than the budgeted expenditure percentage (6 percent).

EXHIBIT 9.6   Cost Analysis Examples

	Compensation Costs			Training Costs		
	Actual Cost	Budgeted Cost	Variance	Actual Cost	Budgeted Cost	Variance
Region 1	$3,660,000	$3,600,000	+$60,000	$985,000	$1,030,000	−$45,000
Region 2	$3,500,000	$3,700,000	−$200,000	$2,110,000	$2,040,000	+$70,000
Region 3	$3,150,000	$3,400,000	−$250,000	$830,000	$1,060,000	−$230,000
Region 4	$4,200,000	$3,900,000	+$300,000	$2,340,000	$2,160,000	+$180,000

	Compensation Costs		Training Costs	
	Actual Cost as % of Sales Achieved	Budgeted Expenditure Percentage	Actual Cost as % of Sales Achieved	Budgeted Expenditure Percentage
Region 1	6.1	6	2.9	3
Region 2	5.8	6	3.1	3
Region 3	5.4	6	2.6	3
Region 4	6.0	6	3.1	3

AN ETHICAL DILEMMA

Diversified Industry Supply recently announced a new performance incentive program for the upcoming year. The program provides significant monetary bonuses to each of the company's 12 regional sales organizations based on the percentage which their individual region's actual sales revenues exceed budgeted revenues for the year. As the sales manager for the Southwest Region, Katy Cook is highly competitive and determined to win the incentive for her region. Although the Southwest Region has potential for exceptional growth in the coming year, Katy and her sales team are considering a plan to better assure the region will win the incentive bonus. This plan would establish a sales budget for the next year which understates forecasted sales in a way that will make the region's year-end sales revenues look significantly better than budgeted and provide her team with a better chance of winning the competition. What do you think Katy should do? Why?

Sales and cost analyses are the two most direct approaches for evaluating sales organization effectiveness. Profitability and productivity analyses extend the evaluation by assessing relationships between sales and costs. These analyses can be quite complex but may provide very useful information.

Profitability Analysis

Sales and cost data can be combined in various ways to produce evaluations of sales organization profitability for different organizational levels of different types of sales. This section covers three types of profitability analysis: income statement analysis, activity-based costing, and return on assets managed analysis.

Income Statement Analysis

The different levels in a sales organization and different types of sales can be considered as separate businesses. Consequently, income statements can be developed for profitability analysis. One of the major difficulties in income statement analysis is that some costs are shared between organizational levels or sales types.

Two approaches for dealing with the shared costs are illustrated in Exhibit 9.7. The full cost approach attempts to allocate the shared costs to individual units based on some type of cost allocation procedure. This results in a net profit figure for each unit. The contribution approach is different in that only direct costs are included in the profitability analysis; the indirect or shared costs are not included. The net contribution calculated from this approach represents the *profit contribution* of the unit being analyzed. This profit contribution must be sufficient to cover indirect costs and other overhead and to provide the net profit for the firm.

An example that incorporates both approaches is presented in Exhibit 9.8. This example uses the full cost approach for assessing sales region profitability and the contribution approach for evaluating the districts within this region. Notice that the profitability calculations for each district include only district sales, cost of goods sold, and district direct selling expenses. A *profit contribution* is generated for each district. The profitability calculations for the region include district selling expenses, region direct

Full Cost versus Contribution Approaches   EXHIBIT 9.7

	Full Cost Approach		**Contribution Approach**
	Sales		Sales
Minus:	Cost of goods sold	Minus:	Cost of goods sold
	Gross margin		Gross margin
Minus:	Direct selling expenses	Minus:	Direct selling expenses
Minus:	Allocated portion of shared expenses		Profit contribution
	Net profit		

Profitability Analysis Example   EXHIBIT 9.8

	Full Cost Approach	Contribution Approach		
	Region	**District 1**	**District 2**	**District 3**
Sales	$300,000,000	$180,000,000	$70,000,000	$50,000,000
Cost of goods sold	$255,000,000	$168,500,000	$58,500,000	$28,000,000
Gross margin	$45,000,000	$11,500,000	$11,500,000	$22,000,000
District selling expenses	$11,000,000	$5,000,000	$3,500,000	$2,500,000
Region direct selling expenses	$10,000,000	—	—	—
Profit contribution	$24,000,000	$6,500,000	$8,000,000	$19,500,000
Allocated portion of shared zone costs	$16,000,000			
Net profit	$8,000,000			

selling expenses that have not been allocated to the districts, and an allocated portion of shared zone costs. This produces a net profit figure for a profitability evaluation of the region.

Although either approach might be used, there seems to be a trend toward the contribution approach, probably because of the difficulty in arriving at a satisfactory procedure for allocating the shared costs. Different cost allocation methods produce different results. Thus, many firms feel more comfortable with the contribution approach because it eliminates the need for cost allocation judgments and is viewed as more objective.

Activity-Based Costing

Perhaps a more accountable method for allocating costs is activity-based costing (ABC). ABC allocates costs to individual units on the basis of how the units actually expend or cause these costs. Costs are accumulated and then allocated to the units by the appropriate drivers, factors that drive costs up or down.

Exhibit 9.9 illustrates how the profitability picture changed for a building supplies company that switched to ABC to assess distribution channel profitability.[7] Notice that with ABC, selling expenses are no longer allocated to each channel based on a percentage of that channel's sales revenues. Instead, costs associated with each activity used to generate sales for a specific channel are allocated to that channel. With ABC, a clearer picture of operating profits per channel emerges. In particular, the original equipment manufacturer channel appears to be much more profitable than the firm's prior accounting system indicates.

ABC places greater emphasis on more accurately defining unit profitability by tracing activities and their associated costs directly to a specific unit. For example, using ABC analysis, the Doig Corporation was able to lower costs by identifying which tasks added value and which ones did not. For instance, it identified which customers could be served just as well by phone, saving both reps and the company time and money.[8] As such, ABC helps foster an understanding of resource expenditures, how customer value is created, and where money is being made or lost.

Return on Assets Managed Analysis

The income statement approach to profitability assessment produces net profit or profit contribution in dollars or expressed as a percentage of sales. Although necessary and valuable, the income statement approach is incomplete because it does not incorporate any evaluation of the investment in assets required to generate the net profit or profit contribution.

The calculation of return on assets managed (ROAM) can extend the income statement analysis to include asset investment considerations. The formula for calculating ROAM is

$$
\begin{aligned}
\text{ROAM} = {} & \text{Profit contribution as percentage of sales} \\
& \times \text{Asset turnover rate} \\
= {} & (\text{Profit contribution/Sales}) \times (\text{Sales/Total assets managed})
\end{aligned}
$$

Profit contribution can be either a net profit figure from a full cost approach or profit contribution from a contribution approach. Assets managed typically include inventory, accounts receivable, or other assets at each sales organizational level.

An example of ROAM calculations is presented in Exhibit 9.10. The example illustrates ROAM calculations for sales districts within a region. Notice that District 1 and District 2 produce the same ROAM but achieve their results in different ways. District 1 generates a relatively high profit contribution percentage, whereas District 2 operates with a relatively high asset turnover. Both District 3 and District 4 are achieving poor levels of ROAM but for different reasons. District 3 has an acceptable profit contribution percentage but very low asset turnover ratio. This low asset turnover ratio is the result of both inventory accumulations or problems in payments from accounts. District 4, however, has an acceptable asset turnover ratio, but low profit contribution percentage. This low profit contribution percentage may be the result of selling low margin products, negotiating low selling prices, or accruing excessive selling expenses.

Activity-Based Costing Example   EXHIBIT 9.9

Profits by Commercial Distribution Channel (Old System)

	Contract	Industrial Suppliers	Government	OEM	Total Commercial
Annual sales (in thousands of dollars)	$79,434	$25,110	$422	$9,200	$114,166
Gross margin	34%	41%	23%	27%	35%
Gross profit	$27,375	$10,284	$136	$2,461	$40,256
SG&A allowance[a] (in thousands of dollars)	$19,746	$6,242	$105	$2,287	$31,814
Operating profit (in thousands of dollars)	$7,629	$4,042	$31	$174	$11,876
Operating margin	10%	16%	7%	2%	10%
Invested capital allowance[b] (in thousands of dollars)	$33,609	$10,624	$179	$3,893	$48,305
Return on investment	23%	38%	17%	4%	25%

Profits by Commercial Distribution Channel (New System: ABC)

	Contract	Industrial Suppliers	Government	OEM	Total Commercial
Gross profit (from previous table)	$27,375	$10,284	$136	$2,461	$40,256
Selling expenses[c] (all in thousands of dollars)					
Commission	$4,682	$1,344	$12	$372	$6,410
Advertising	132	38	0	2	172
Catalog	504	160	0	0	664
Coop advertising	416	120	0	0	536
Sales promotion	394	114	0	2	510
Warranty	64	22	0	4	90
Sales administration	5,696	1,714	20	351	7,781
Cash discount	892	252	12	114	1,270
Total	$12,780	$3,764	$44	$845	$17,433
G&A (in thousands of dollars)	$6,740	$2,131	$36	$781	$9,688
Operating profit (in thousands of dollars)	$7,855	$4,389	$56	$835	$13,135
Operating margin	10%	17%	13%	9%	12%
Invested capital[c]	$33,154	$10,974	$184	$2,748	$47,060
Return on investment	24%	40%	30%	30%	28%

[a]SG&A (selling, general and administrative expenses) allowance for each channel is 25 percent of that channel's revenues.
[b]Invested capital allowance for each channel is 42 percent of that channel's revenues.
[c]Selling expenses and invested capital estimated under an activity-based system.

As illustrated in the preceding example, ROAM calculations provide an assessment of profitability and useful diagnostic information. ROAM is determined by both profit contribution percentage and asset turnover. If ROAM is low in any area, the profit contribution percentage and asset turnover ratio can be examined to determine the reason. Corrective action (e.g., reduced selling expenses, stricter credit guidelines, lower inventory levels) can then be taken to improve future ROAM performance.

EXHIBIT 9.10   Return on Assets Managed (ROAM) Example

	District 1	District 2	District 3	District 4
Sales	$24,000,000	$24,000,000	$24,000,000	$24,000,000
Cost of goods sold	12,000,000	12,000,000	14,000,000	14,000,000
Gross margin	12,000,000	12,000,000	10,000,000	10,000,000
Direct selling expenses	7,200,000	9,600,000	5,200,000	8,800,000
Profit contribution	4,800,000	2,400,000	4,800,000	1,200,000
Accounts receivable	8,000,000	4,000,000	16,000,000	4,000,000
Inventory	8,000,000	4,000,000	16,000,000	4,000,000
Total assets managed	16,000,000	8,000,000	32,000,000	8,000,000
Profit contribution as a percent of sales	20%	10%	20%	5%
Asset turnover	1.5	3.0	.75	3.0
ROAM	30%	30%	15%	15%

Productivity Analysis

Although ROAM incorporates elements of productivity by comparing profits and asset investments, additional productivity analysis is desirable for thorough evaluation of sales organization effectiveness. Productivity is typically measured in terms of ratios between outputs and inputs. For example, as discussed in Chapter 4, one often-used measure of salesforce productivity is sales per salesperson. A major advantage of productivity ratios is that they can be compared directly across the entire sales organization and with other sales organizations. This direct comparison is possible because all the ratios are expressed in terms of the same units.

Because the basic job of sales managers is to manage salespeople, the most useful input unit for productivity analysis is the salesperson. Therefore, various types of productivity ratios are calculated on a per-salesperson basis. The specific ratios depend on the characteristics of a particular selling situation but often include important outputs such as sales, expenses, calls, demonstrations, and proposals. An example of a productivity analysis is presented in Exhibit 9.11.

Exhibit 9.11 illustrates how productivity analysis provides a different and useful perspective for evaluating sales organization effectiveness. As the exhibit reveals, absolute values can be misleading. For example, the highest sales districts are not necessarily the most effective. Although profitability analyses would likely detect this also, productivity analysis presents a vivid and precise evaluation by highlighting specific areas of both high and low productivity. Take the information concerning district 2. Although sales per salesperson is reasonable and expenses per salesperson is relatively low, both calls per salesperson and proposals per salesperson are much lower than those for the other districts. This may explain why selling expenses are low, but it also suggests that the salespeople in this district may not be covering the district adequately. The high sales may be due to a few large sales to large customers.

In any case, the productivity analysis provides useful evaluative and diagnostic information that is not directly available from the other types of analyses discussed in this module. Sales productivity and profitability are highly interrelated. However, profitability analysis has a financial perspective, whereas productivity analysis is more managerially oriented. Improvements in sales productivity should translate into increases in profitability.

	District 1	District 2	District 3	District 4
Sales	$20,000,000	$24,000,000	$20,000,000	$24,000,000
Selling expenses	$2,000,000	$2,400,000	$3,000,000	$3,000,000
Sales calls	9,000	7,500	8,500	10,000
Proposals	220	180	260	270
Number of salespeople	20	30	20	30
Sales/salesperson	$1,000,000	$800,000	$1,000,000	$800,000
Expenses/salesperson	$100,000	$80,000	$150,000	$100,000
Calls/salesperson	450	250	425	333
Proposals/salesperson	11	6	13	9

Productivity Analysis Example   EXHIBIT 9.11

Productivity improvements are obtained in one of two basic ways:

1. increasing output with the same level of input

2. maintaining the same level of output but using less input

Productivity analysis can help determine which of these basic approaches should be pursued.

IMPROVING SALES ORGANIZATION EFFECTIVENESS

Benchmarking

One popular technique for improving sales organization effectiveness is benchmarking. Benchmarking is an ongoing measurement and analysis process that compares an organization's current operating practices with the "best practices" used by world-class organizations. It is a tool for evaluating current business practices and finding a way to do them better, more quickly, and less expensively to better meet customer needs. Using benchmarking, Norwest, the nation's largest mortgage company, was able to consolidate its sales brochures and direct mail campaigns resulting in a savings of more than $1.4 million. It also increased sales by 102 percent using sales road maps. Rank Xerox, the British unit of Xerox, used benchmarking to increase country unit sales from 152 percent to 328 percent and improve new revenue by $200 million.[9] A research study of more than 1,600 U.S. and Canadian organizations found that those companies willing to learn from the best practices of others are more successful at improving customer satisfaction than those that are more reluctant. Perhaps this explains why such firms as IBM, AT&T, DuPont, GM, Intel, Sprint, Motorola, and Xerox use benchmarking.

Figure 9.7 outlines steps in the benchmarking process. A pivotal part of this process is identifying the company or salesforce to benchmark. A literature search and personal contacts are means for identifying companies that perform the process in an exceptional manner. Winning an industry award, being recognized for functional excellence, and receiving a national quality award are three indicators of excellence. Eastman Chemical Company and IBM have used the Malcolm Baldrige National Quality Award criteria as bases on which to evaluate their salesforce, map processes leading to desired results, and focus efforts on continuously improving these processes. Those processes that have the greatest impact on salesforce productivity should be benchmarked. Companies such as Best Practices, LLC (http://www.best-in-class.com), the Benchmarking Network (http://www.benchmarkingnetwork.com), Sales Force Effectiveness Benchmarking Association (http://www.sfeba.com), and American Productivity and Quality Center (http://www.apqc.org) provide useful Web sites for initiating a benchmarking program.

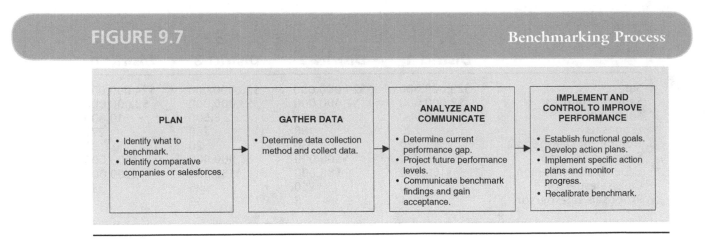

FIGURE 9.7   Benchmarking Process

A benchmarking study should provide several outputs. First, it should provide a measure that compares performance for the benchmarked process relative to the organization studied. Second, it should identify the organization's performance gap relative to benchmarked performance levels. Third, it should identify best practices and facilitators that produced the results observed during the study. Finally, the study should determine performance goals for the process studied and identify areas in which action can be taken to improve performance. Exhibit 9.12 provides some keys to successful benchmarking.

Six Sigma

Six Sigma, a data-driven methodology that attempts to eliminate defects in any process, provides another potentially powerful means for improving salesforce effectiveness. The word *sigma* is a mathematical term for measuring variation, with six sigma indicating a low degree of variability (3.4 mistakes per million opportunities). A form of process improvement, Six Sigma is credited with hundreds of millions of dollars of savings in several large corporations such as Allied Signal, GE, Raytheon and others. This disciplined decision-making approach aims to make processes as perfect as possible by focusing on improving processes and reducing variations through the application of the Six Sigma process as outlined in Exhibit 9.13.[10] Six Sigma can potentially be applied to any process involved in the sales organization (e.g., recruiting, selection, training, etc.) to make it better and improve salesforce effectiveness.

EXHIBIT 9.12   Key to Successful Benchmarking

- Clearly identify critical activities that will improve quality or service or reduce cost.
- Properly prepare and benchmark *only one activity at a time.*
- Make sure that you thoroughly understand your own process first.
- Create a "seek, desire, and listen" environment by choosing curious and knowledgeable people for your benchmark team.
- Verify that your benchmark partner company is the best in its class, and clearly understand your partner's process.
- Provide adequate resources, not only financial, but also knowledgeable personnel.
- Be diligent in selecting the correct partner—do not use a company that may not provide advantages to you.
- Implement the benchmarking action plan.

The Steps of Six Sigma   EXHIBIT 9.13

Michael Webb, author of *Sales and Marketing the Six Sigma Way* (Kaplan, 2006) outlines steps involved in the Six Sigma process:

Define:
Begin at the beginning. What is the defect or problem you are trying to solve? Define the SIPOC (Suppliers, Inputs, Process, Outputs, Customers), and define the process itself as best you can.

Measure:
Collect data (measurements) about the process to gain a better understanding of it.

Analyze:
Try to figure out what the data is telling you. Often, you will go back and forth between the Measure and the Analyze steps to clarify your understanding of how the process really works. This becomes your hypothesis. It is essentially the expression of a theory of cause and effect for your process.

One thing that distinguishes Six Sigma from other approaches is the genius of this insight: cause and effect can be expressed in terms of a mathematical equation:

$$Y = f(x)$$
Y(Output) is the *f*(function) of the x(process)

Improve:
After analyzing the process, you construct an experiment to prove your hypothesis. Your experiment will measurably change one of the independent variables (x)s. If your theory is correct, the result will be a measurable (and positive) change to the dependent variable (Y). If your experiment is on target, you will have reduced the instances of defects.

Control:
It does no good to learn how a process can be improved if the improvement is not institutionalized in some way so the problems do not recur. The control step is doing the things necessary to cause this to happen.

ETHICAL ISSUES

The value of comparing actual expenses with budgeted expenses depends on the accuracy of the expense information provided by salespeople. Although most sales organizations have prepared forms with the expense categories and instructions for salespeople, salespeople often face ethical problems in reporting their expenses. Consider the following situations:

- A salesperson has been on the road for a week and incurs laundry expenses. He knows that if he places the laundry expenses under the miscellaneous expense category in his expense report, he will have to provide receipts. He decides that he can include them under the meals category because receipts are not required for this category as long as he stays under his per-diem allowance.

- A salesperson is trying to get a customer to purchase a new product. He decides to take three individuals from the customer's firm to dinner and a basketball game, even though he knows that he has exceeded his entertainment budget for the month. He thinks about hiding these entertainment expenses in different categories in his expense report.

The decisions that salespeople make in these and similar situations affect the ability of sales managers to evaluate actual and budgeted expenses in an accurate manner. Sales managers themselves, however, may be presented with situations which present them with ethical decisions that they must deal with, as illustrated in "An Ethical Dilemma."

AN ETHICAL DILEMMA

Faith Distributors is a leading wholesaler of religious themed gift items and books. Committed to their faith-based business principles, the company does not allow alcoholic beverages to be used in any of its business activities. This includes marketing conferences and trade shows and even extends to its sales personnel entertaining customers. Royce Richards, sales manager for the Western Region, is discussing the success of saleperson Tim Johnson in gaining a significant opening order from a major buying group along with commitments for the coming year. During their discussion, Tim mentions that, as the result of dinner meetings with the group's regional buyers where they ordered beers and cocktails with their dinner, he is personally out just over $800 because of the company's policy. Tim asks Royce if he could add extra mileage—over and beyond what he actually travels—to his next month's expense report that would add up to what he is out of pocket for the unreimbursed drinks. What do you think Royce should do? Why?

CONCLUDING COMMENTS

As is obvious from the discussion in this chapter, there is no easy way to evaluate the effectiveness of a sales organization. Our recommendation is to perform separate analyses of sales, costs, profitability, and productivity to assess different aspects of sales organization effectiveness. In addition, salesperson performance, which is discussed in the next chapter, must also be evaluated and considered. Each type of analysis offers a piece of the puzzle. Sales managers must put these pieces together for comprehensive evaluations. The objective underlying each of the analyses is to be able to evaluate effectiveness, identify problem areas, and use this information to improve future sales organization effectiveness.

SUMMARY

1. **Differentiate between sales organization effectiveness and salesperson performance.** Sales organization effectiveness is a summary evaluation of the overall success of a sales organization in meeting its goals and objectives in total and at different organizational levels. By contrast, salesperson performance is a function of individual salesperson performance in individual situations.

2. **Define a sales organization audit and discuss how it should be conducted.** The most comprehensive type of evaluation is a sales organization audit, which is a systematic assessment of all aspects of a sales organization. The major areas included in the audit are sales organization environment, sales management evaluation, sales organization planning system, and sales management functions. The audit should be conducted regularly by individuals outside the sales organization. It is intended to identify existing or potential problems early so that corrective action can be taken before the problems become serious.

3. **Describe how to perform different methods of sales analysis for different organizational levels and different types of sales.** Sales analysis is the most common evaluation approach, but it can be extremely complex. Specific definitions of a sale are required, and both sales dollars and units typically should be considered. A hierarchical approach is suggested as a top-down procedure to address sales results at each level of the sales organization with an emphasis on identifying problem areas. Sales analysis is more useful when sales results are compared with forecasts, quotas, previous time periods, and competitor results.

4. **Describe how to perform a cost analysis for a sales organization.** Cost analysis focuses on the costs incurred to generate sales results. Specific costs can be compared with the planned levels in the selling budget. Areas with large variances require specific attention. Costs can also be evaluated as percentages of sales and compared to comparable industry figures.

5. **Describe how to perform an income statement analysis, activity-based costing, and return on assets managed, to assess sales organization profitability.** Profitability analysis combines sales and cost data in various ways. The income statement approach focuses on net profit or profit contributions from the different sales organization levels. Activity-based costing allocates costs to individual units on the basis of how the units actually expend or cause these costs. The return on assets managed approach assesses relationships between profit contributions and the assets used to generate these profit contributions. The different profitability analyses address different aspects of profitability that are of interest to sales managers.

6. **Describe how to perform a productivity analysis for a sales organization.** Productivity analysis focuses on relationships between outputs and inputs. The most useful input is the number of salespeople, whereas relevant outputs might be sales, expenses, proposals, and so on. The productivity ratios calculated in this manner are versatile because they can be used for comparisons within the sales organization and across other sales organizations. Productivity analysis not only provides useful evaluative information but also provides managerially useful diagnostic information that can suggest ways to improve productivity and increase profitability.

7. **Define benchmarking and Six Sigma and discuss how each should be conducted.** Benchmarking is an ongoing measurement and analysis process that compares an organization's current operating practices with the "best practices" used by world-class organizations. It involves identifying the sales organization processes to be benchmarked and whom to benchmark, collecting data on the benchmarked firm, analyzing performance gaps and communicating them to the salesforce, and establishing goals and implementing plans. Six Sigma is a data-driven methodology that attempts to eliminate defects in any process. It involves defining the process problem, collecting data on the process problem, analyzing the data, determining how to improve the process and implementing a process change. Both are conducted to improve processes, thereby enhancing performance.

UNDERSTANDING SALES MANAGEMENT TERMS

sales organization audit
sales analysis
hierarchical sales analysis
effectiveness index
cost analysis
selling budget
percentage of sales method
objective and task method
profitability analysis

income statement analysis
full cost approach
contribution approach
activity-based costing (ABC)
return on assets managed (ROAM)
productivity analysis
benchmarking
Six Sigma

DEVELOPING SALES MANAGEMENT KNOWLEDGE

1. Discuss why it is important to differentiate between sales organization effectiveness and salesperson performance.

2. Discuss what is involved in conducting a sales management audit.

3. Explain how sales managers can utilize benchmarking to improve performance.

4. What is meant by a hierarchical sales analysis? Can a hierarchical approach be used in analyzing costs, profitability, and/or productivity?

5. What is the difference between the full cost and contribution approaches to income statement analysis for a sales organization? Which would you recommend for a sales organization? Why?

6. Explain how a manager evaluating the sales organization's effectiveness might reach different conclusions by analyzing sales dollars or sales units.

7. What are the two basic components of return on assets managed? How is each component calculated, and what does each component tell a sales manager?

8. Identify five different sales organization productivity ratios that you would recommend. Describe how each would be calculated and what information each would provide.

9. What purposes do benchmarking and Six Sigma serve? Discuss what is involved in each process.

10. Discuss how you think new computer and information technologies will affect the evaluations of sales organization effectiveness in the future.

BUILDING SALES MANAGEMENT SKILLS

1. Using the following information provided for the end of the current fiscal year, conduct a sales analysis to evaluate sales organization effectiveness. The company anticipated sales growth of 5 percent. Explain your findings.

	Region 1 ($000)	Region 2 ($000)	Region 3 ($000)	Region 4 ($000)
Sales	$8,100	$9,500	$8,500	$5,000
Sales quota	$8,250	$8,500	$8,150	$7,800
Sales last year	$7,850	$8,750	$8,000	$4,850
Industry sales	$23,000	$25,000	$27,000	$21,000
Previous year market share	36%	35%	30%	25%

2. Sales and cost data can be combined in various ways to produce evaluations of sales organization profitability for different organizational levels or different types of sales. Three types of profitability analysis are useful for evaluating effectiveness: activity-based costing, income statement analysis, and return on assets managed analysis. Examining Exhibit 9.9, point out differences in operating profits by commercial distribution channel between the company's old and new (ABC) system, and explain why they differ. What would the ABC system lead you to believe regarding the effectiveness of each channel? Using the information in Exhibit 9.9 and the following information, conduct an income statement analysis and return on assets managed analysis. Explain the results of your analyses.

	Contract ($000)	Industrial Suppliers ($000)	Government ($000)	OEM ($000)
Accounts receivable	$26,578	$16,840	$72	$1,633
Inventory	$26,578	$16,840	$73	$1,634

3. Several sites are available on the Web that provide benchmarking services. One such site is Best Practices, LLC (http://www.best-in-class.com), a research and consulting firm that provides business insight and analysis of how world-class companies achieve exceptional economic and operational performance. Access this site and review its services.

a. How can a company such as this be useful to a sales manager attempting to improve the sales organization?

b. From the Best Practices, LLC home page, click on the "Products and Services" tab. Next, locate and click on "Best Practices Database" from the list of products and services and then select "Sales Leadership." You do not need to be a subscribing member to look through their database of best practices in sales leadership. Notice the different areas of sales leadership for which they provide best practices. Click on "Sales Force Effectiveness" and examine the diverse reports available. Select one that offers Free Excerpt to Non-members and read through the excerpt. Look through the other areas comprising the Sales Leadership section and some of the other free excerpts available.

 Identify two reports that might be helpful for improving a sales organization's effectiveness and briefly explain how each report's information might be used.

c. Locate another benchmarking service on the Web. Identify its address and briefly describe its services. Compare and contrast its services to those of Best Practices, LLC.

ROLE PLAY

4. **Role Play**

Situation: Read the Ethical Dilemma on p. 266.

Characters: Katy, southwest region manager; Brenda, one of Katy's top salespeople

Scene: *Location*—local restaurant for lunch. *Action*—Katy tells Brenda about her plan to understate the budgeted sales revenue targets for the southwest region in order to win the competition. Brenda is skeptical. The two discuss the pros and cons of taking this action and consider other alternatives Katy might take.

5. Using the following information, conduct a productivity analysis. Based on your analysis, do you have any concerns? Explain.

	District 1	District 2	District 3	District 4
Sales	$15,000,000	$18,000,000	$15,000,000	$18,000,000
Selling expenses	$1,500,000	$1,800,000	$2,250,000	$2,250,000
Sales calls	6,750	5,625	6,375	7,500
Proposals	165	135	195	203
Number of salespeople	15	23	15	23

MAKING SALES MANAGEMENT DECISIONS

CASE 9.1: ALLIED NOVELTY COMPANY

Background

Allied Novelty Company markets a broad mix of toys and games to retailers throughout the United States. The salesforce is organized into five regions, each comprised of five districts. A national sales executive oversees the five regional sales managers. Each regional manager is responsible for the effectiveness of his or her region and is compensated according to the achievements of their region.

Current Situation

Kerri Ross is the northern region sales manager for Allied Novelty. The fiscal year just ended, and Kerri has compiled data to help her analyze her region's effectiveness. Although her region has had what she believes to be a very successful year, she wants to analyze each district closely. She hopes to use her analysis to identify and correct problems. Moreover,

she needs to complete her analysis for her upcoming meeting with her national sales manager, Greg Rich. Market shares for each district were fairly sizable (30 percent, 32 percent, 34 percent, 31 percent, and 28 percent for districts 1 through 5, respectively) at the beginning of the fiscal year. Kerri had expected these to remain relatively stable over the past year. The company had anticipated a sales growth of 2 percent. In addition, selling costs were budgeted at 10 percent of forecasted sales. If Kerri's region did not increase sales by 2 percent and stay within the sales budget, her performance appraisal, and subsequently her compensation, would suffer. Kerri knew her boss would carefully scrutinize her analysis. She hoped to be able to identify any problem areas so that she could develop solutions and implement them in the upcoming year. She was scheduled to meet with Rich in three days. Kerri compiled the following information (shown in the table below).

	District 1 ($000)	District 2 ($000)	District 3 ($000)	District 4 ($000)	District 5 ($000)
Sales	16,400	19,000	20,900	27,500	16,800
Cost of goods sold	9,840	11,020	12,958	16,500	9,240
Compensation	1,230	1,620	1,470	2,280	1,260
Transportation	82	134	84	140	100
Lodging and meals	34	60	32	82	42
Telephone	16	20	24	28	18
Entertainment	20	16	30	24	24
Training	160	190	210	250	220
District accounts receivable	2,340	2,800	2,900	4,840	2,300
District inventory	4,000	7,000	6,400	10,500	5,000
Number of salespeople	16	18	22	24	20
Sales quota	16,200	19,500	20,500	28,250	16,600
Sales last year	15,000	18,500	20,500	27,850	16,400
Industry sales	52,904	59,376	61,472	91,667	60,000

Questions

1. What analyses should Kerri perform with this data? Conduct these suggested analyses being careful to document your work and your answers.

2. What problems can you identify from your analyses?

3. What solutions would you recommend to solve these problems and improve sales effectiveness in

the future? Explain why your recommendations are appropriate.

Role Play

Situation: Read Case 9.1.

Characters: Kerri Ross, northern region sales manager; Greg Rich, national sales manager.

ROLE PLAY

Scene: *Location*—Meeting room at Allied Novelty Company headquarters. *Action*—Kerri presents her findings from analyzing the data about the effectiveness of her salesforce. She makes a number of suggestions for solving the problems that her analysis revealed. Greg Rich offers several responses to her analysis and findings. He then asks Kerri about the performance of her salespeople and whom, if anyone, she thinks the company should let go.

CASE 9.2: TECHNOLOGY SOLUTIONS, INC.

Background

Chicago-based Technology Solutions is a leading provider of business systems and productivity software applications. The company operates throughout the United States and is divided into five regions, each consisting of four districts with a district sales manager in charge of each one. Each sales region is overseen by a regional sales manager and a national sales manager is charged with the ultimate responsibility for the overall sales organization. Technology Solutions' salespeople are well qualified, have college degrees, and experience in the design, sales, and operation of business productivity systems. The average tenure on the salesforce is seven years.

Current Situation

Technology Solutions competes head on with IBM and other major players comprising this industry and has managed to do quite well in terms of sales, profitability, and market share. In fact, Technology Solutions has earned the reputation as a capable, innovative, and aggressive competitor. Nevertheless, Kim Martin, Technology Solutions' president believes that the company can do much better. The following is a conversation she recently had with her national sales manager, Gage Waits.

Kim: I believe that the key to our growth lies in having a successful salesforce.

Gage: Absolutely. We have made great strides over the past three years, consistently increasing our sales volume.

Kim: Sales growth is a must. However, we need to measure up to the performance of our competition in other ways.

Gage: What do you mean?

Kim: If we want to reach the top, we have to have a salesforce that performs like those at the top. How convenient and quick is our service? How long does it take from order to delivery and setup?

Gage: I suppose we could always improve our service. However, our salespeople are well qualified and do a competent job.

Kim: What about our user training program? Can it be made more convenient for customers? Is it possible to accomplish it more quickly and less expensively without sacrificing the quality of the training?

Gage: We seem to be doing OK in this area. There haven't been a lot of complaints that I am aware of, so I assume everything is going well.

Kim: If we are going to be the best, we have to have the best salesforce. Gage, I'm counting on you to lead our salesforce to the top. I can't stress how important it is for us to have a high-performing salesforce. I'd like to meet with you in two weeks to discuss your plan for addressing these issues.

Gage: Perhaps it's time to take a closer look at our sales organization. I'll do my best.

Questions

1. How could Gage use benchmarking to address Kim's concerns?

2. Outline a benchmarking study that could be used to help make Technology Solutions' salesforce more effective.

3. What else can be done to ensure that Technology Solutions' salesforce is performing effectively?

Role Play

ROLE PLAY

Situation: Read Case 9.2.

Characters: Kim Martin, president; Gage Waits, national sales manager.

Scene 1: *Location*—Wait's office. *Action*—Role-play the conversation between Kim and Gage as outlined in the case.

Scene 2: *Location*—Kim's office, two weeks later. *Action*—Gage is meeting with Kim to discuss his plan for improving the sales organization. He outlines his plan and Kim provides her thoughts.

EVALUATING THE PERFORMANCE
OF SALESPEOPLE

OBJECTIVES

After completing this chapter, you should be able to

1. Discuss the different purposes of salesperson performance evaluations.

2. Differentiate between an outcome-based and a behavior-based perspective for evaluating and controlling salesperson performance.

3. Describe the different types of criteria necessary for comprehensive evaluations of salesperson performance.

4. Compare the advantages and disadvantages of different methods of salesperson performance evaluation.

5. Explain how salesperson performance information can be used to identify problems, determine their causes, and suggest sales management actions to solve them.

6. Discuss the measurement and importance of salesperson job satisfaction.

SMALL DATA OUTPERFORMS BIG DATA IN SALES MANAGEMENT

In recent years, Big Data has emerged as a popular concept and tool for developing business insight. Nevertheless, Jason Jordan, partner in Vantage Point Performance, a leading sales management training and development firm, observes that their research indicates that Small Data is most useful for sales management.

In essence, Big Data is a super-sized collection of data aggregated from many unrelated sources of data that is not easily analyzed. The attractiveness of Big Data is its ability to reveal trends and insights that would not be discerned without the variety and mix of data provided by the combination of various data sources. However, Jordan observes that sales managers don't need enormous sets of data and the extensive reports that are generated by today's generation of CRM systems to do their jobs: "What sales managers need is some very basic information about what their sales reps are doing and how they're performing. We'd put this data on the opposite end of the spectrum from Big Data. It's discrete data points on individual salespeople. Just for kicks, let's call it Small Data."

Jordan explains that Small Data doesn't reside in the cloud waiting to be analyzed by supercomputers. Instead, "Small Data may not exist in a database at all. It may only reside in coaching conversations between a manager and salesperson. How is the salesperson performing against quota? Which sales objectives are they pursuing, and how are they doing? Which sales activities will they focus on this week, and how can the sales manager help them execute more effectively?" This is the type of data most useful for sales management, and it does not come in CRM reports.

"In reality, useful data points don't always need to be aggregated with large amounts of other data points to be useful. Did the rep complete the two online training courses that they agreed to take? If so, what did they learn? Did the sales rep go on three sales calls with a peer as you suggested? If so, how did it go? Did the sales rep make the eight prospecting calls last week that they intended to make? If so, how many qualified leads did they uncover?" Rather than focusing on CRM reports and Big Data, sales managers just need to focus on the few things that their salespeople need to do in order to be successful and positively impact their daily sales performance.

Source: Jason Jordan, "With Data, Size Matters, But Not How You Think," *Sales and Marketing Management,* February 24, 2014.

Whereas Chapter 9 focused on evaluating sales organization effectiveness, this chapter examines the task of evaluating salesperson performance and job satisfaction. Evaluations of sales organization effectiveness concentrate on the overall results achieved by the different units within the sales organization, with special attention given to determining the effectiveness of territories, districts, regions, and zones, as well as identifying strategic changes to improve future effectiveness. These effectiveness assessments examine sales organization units and do not directly evaluate individuals. Nevertheless, sales managers are also responsible for the effectiveness of their assigned, individual salespeople.

The Small Data that is specific to an individual salesperson discussed by Jason Jordan in the opening vignette is essential for effective sales management. This specific level of salesperson performance information results from an interactive process designed to determine salesperson's objectives, uncover their problems, develop solutions, improve communication, and provide direction for continued development. To evaluate salesperson performance, sales managers must understand why and how performance evaluations are conducted, as well as how to use the information gained from these evaluations.

The purpose of this chapter is to investigate the key issues involved in evaluating and controlling the performance and job satisfaction of salespeople. The purposes of salesperson performance evaluations are discussed initially. Then, the performance evaluation procedures currently used by sales organizations are examined. This is followed by a comprehensive assessment of salesperson performance evaluation. The assessment addresses the criteria to be used in evaluating salespeople, the methods for evaluating salespeople against these criteria, and the outcomes of salesperson performance evaluations. The chapter concludes by discussing the importance and measurement of salesperson job satisfaction and relationships between salesperson performance and job satisfaction.

PURPOSES OF SALESPERSON PERFORMANCE EVALUATIONS

As the name suggests, the basic objective of salesperson performance evaluations is to determine how well individual salespeople have performed. However, the results of salesperson performance evaluations can be used for many sales management purposes:

1. To ensure that compensation and other reward disbursements are consistent with actual salesperson performance.

2. To identify salespeople who might be promoted.

3. To identify salespeople whose employment should be terminated and to supply evidence to support the need for termination.

4. To determine the specific training and counseling needs of individual salespeople and the overall salesforce.

5. To provide information for effective human resource planning.

6. To identify criteria that can be used to recruit and select salespeople in the future.

7. To advise salespeople of work expectations.

8. To motivate salespeople.

9. To help salespeople set career goals.

10. To relate salesperson performance to sales organization goals.

11. To enhance communications between salesperson and sales manager.

12. To improve salesperson performance.

These diverse purposes affect all aspects of the performance evaluation process. For example, performance evaluations for determining compensation and special rewards should emphasize activities and results related to the salesperson's current job and situation. Performance evaluations for the purpose of identifying salespeople for promotion into sales management positions should focus on criteria related to potential effectiveness as a sales manager and not just current performance as a salesperson. To be effective, sales performance reviews should also be action-oriented and tied to real-time selling activities. "Sales Management in the 21st Century: Oracle Emphasizes Action-Oriented, Continuous Performance Reviews for High-Performance Sales Teams" describes the use of a continuous performance evaluation process that occurs naturally as part of the sales manager's coaching and feedback.

SALESPERSON PERFORMANCE EVALUATION APPROACHES

It would be impossible to describe in detail all the performance evaluation approaches used by sales organizations. However, it is possible to catalog a number of general observations which provide a glimpse into current practices in evaluating salesperson performance.

1. Most sales organizations evaluate salesperson performance annually, although many firms conduct evaluations semiannually or quarterly. Recently, there has been a growing trend toward the use of more frequent performance reviews and even continuous reviews that flow out of the coaching and feedback relationships between sales manager and salesperson.

2. Most sales organizations use combinations of input and output criteria that are evaluated by quantitative and qualitative measures. However, emphasis seems to be placed on outputs, with evaluations of sales volume results the most popular.

3. Sales organizations that set performance standards or quotas tend to enlist the aid of salespeople in establishing these objectives. The degree of salesperson input and involvement does, however, appear to vary across firms.

4. Many sales organizations assign weights to different performance objectives and incorporate territory data when establishing these objectives.

5. Most firms use more than one source of information in evaluating salesperson performance; client and peer feedback are some of the common sources of information.

Oracle Emphasizes Action-Oriented, Continuous Performance Reviews for High-Performance Sales Teams

R&D at Oracle reports that 57 percent of employees-rate their performance reviews as neutral to not useful. Far too may reviews are limited to a backward-looking process documenting what happened over the previous year, but do not provide meaningful and actionable feedback. The challenge is that most performance reviews focus on compliance and timelines rather than enabling quality conversations between sales managers and representatives.

Managers of high-performance sales teams have moved beyond the once a year, backward-looking performance review in favor of a forward-looking and more continuous process that occurs as sales managers and salespeople collaborate on projects and plan future activities. It is a natural outcome of the manager's coaching and feedback. Why not do shorter and more-targeted performance review sessions tied to real-time sales activities that allow capturing the in-the-moment thoughts and enhance the relevance of action oriented feedback?

6. Most salesperson performance evaluations are conducted by the field sales manager who supervises the salesperson. However, some firms involve the manager above the field sales manager in the salesperson performance appraisal.

7. Most sales organizations provide salespeople with a written copy of their performance review and have sales managers discuss the performance evaluation with each salesperson. These discussions typically take place in an office, although sometimes they are conducted in the field.

Although performance appraisal continues to be primarily a top-down process, changes are taking place in some companies leading to the implementation of a broader-based assessment process. An increasingly popular assessment technique, dubbed 360-degree feedback, involves performance assessment from multiple raters, including sales managers, internal and external customers, team members, and even salespeople themselves. As part of its 360-degree review, sales managers at Knowledgepoint, a human resources software provider, solicit feedback from coworkers in areas such as rapport with clients, time management, and presentation skills when evaluating salespeople.

Among its many benefits, 360-degree feedback helps managers better understand customer needs, detect barriers to success, assess developmental needs, create job involvement, reduce assessment bias, and improve performance. Because this evaluation method tends to make employees feel valued, they stay with the organization longer. However, when using the process, keep in mind that bias may still exist. Individuals may be less forthright in giving feedback and less accepting of feedback from others if they believe it will have damaging consequences. Furthermore, top salespeople tend to underestimate their performance, while bottom performers overestimate.[1] Also, other ratings and self-ratings tend to differ significantly most of the time.[2] Thus, it may be best to use feedback in conjunction with other appraisal techniques. Exhibit 10.1 provides keys to implementing an effective 360-degree feedback system.[3] To facilitate this process, some companies use Web sites to distribute and collect multiple evaluations. Companies such as Training Technologies, Inc. (http://www.surveytracker.com), and Cognology (http://www.cognology.com.au) use the Internet to conduct 360-degree feedback surveys for companies.

Another evaluation approach that moves away from the traditional top-down appraisal is referred to as performance management. This approach involves sales managers and

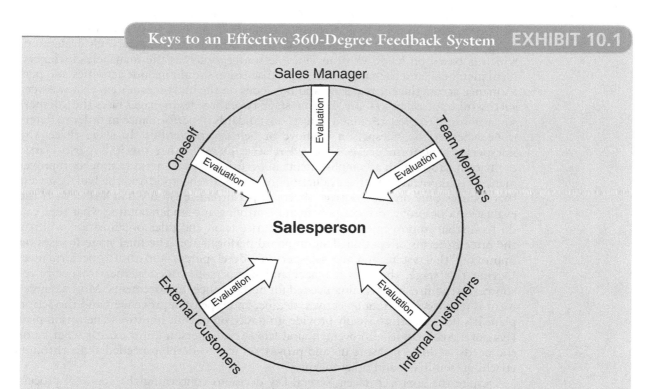

Keys to an Effective 360-Degree Feedback System   EXHIBIT 10.1

1. Ensure that participants willingly provide honest feedback by distributing the feedback instrument confidentially, aggregating responses by rating source, having rating forms sent directly to the person or group organizing the data, and including feedback from at least three respondents in each rater group (e.g., customers, coworkers, team members). Allow participants some input in selecting raters.
2. Explain to all participants how the data will be used.
3. Ensure that the data sources remain confidential, so those being rated do not know specifically who did the rating.
4. Verify that the data are accurate. The assessment tools used to gather the data should be reliable and valid.
5. Ensure that subjects can use the data to improve their performance. Present the feedback from the different groups (perspectives). It should be in a format that is easy to use and interpret. Compare feedback from others with one's own perceptions. Feedback should be linked to development tools and processes.
6. Determine how the system will affect the organization overall and systematically evaluate its effectiveness.
7. Do not rely exclusively on 360-degree feedback. Timely feedback concerning day-to-day performance is important.

salespeople working together on setting goals, giving feedback, reviewing, and rewarding. With this system, salespeople create their own development plans and assume responsibility for their careers. The sales manager acts as a partner in the process, providing feedback that is timely, specific, regular, solicited, and focused on what is within the salesperson's control to change. Salespeople are compensated on the value of their contributions to the organization's success. To facilitate the review process, sales managers may want to use software applications, such as Performance Now Enterprise Edition, which provide a framework for implementing a comprehensive performance management system.

Performance management ultimately focuses on improving salesperson performance by finding new and better ways to satisfy customers. A study of 437 U.S. companies in 58 industries reported that companies following a performance management approach had greater financial and productivity performance relative to other companies in their industry.[4]

The typical approach to performance evaluation incorporates four distinct stages. In stage one, the sales manager and salesperson discuss the salesperson's evaluation, which is based on feedback from multiple sources, such as the manager, customers, team members, and the salesperson. This discussion should include activities and performance across the entire period and not focus on the most recent item that was very successful or possibly a failure. During stage two, the sales manager rates the salesperson according to predetermined criteria or standards of performance in order to determine whether the salesperson is above or below expectations. In stage three, the salesperson's performance is reviewed relative to his or her previous performance evaluation to ascertain accomplishments in performance and areas that need improvement. It is important that the evaluation include both the good and the bad. A review that focuses only on the positive aspects of performance is only half a review. If the evaluation does not assist salespeople in identifying and understanding what they can do to further improve performance, the entire team and sales organization will pay the price in terms of continued substandard performance. The final stage focuses on improving the system and the salesperson's development and future performance. During this stage, the sales manager and salesperson work together to specify resources, structure, and training needed for performance improvements. Mutual agreement is reached regarding objectives, degree, and type of improvement and the action plan. It's not enough to simply provide guidance on how to improve. The action plan lays out a roadmap to improvement and lets the salesperson know exactly what he or she needs to do to measure up and provides a way to develop needed skills through coaching, seminars, and other means.[5]

Despite the approach taken, several key decisions concerning the appraisal process must be made. The remainder of this chapter addresses the key decision areas and alternative methods for developing comprehensive evaluation and control procedures.

KEY ISSUES IN EVALUATING AND CONTROLLING SALESPERSON PERFORMANCE

A useful way to view different perspectives for evaluating and controlling salesperson performance is presented in Exhibit 10.2. An outcome-based perspective focuses on objective measures of results with little monitoring or directing of salesperson behavior by sales managers. By contrast, a behavior-based perspective incorporates complex and often subjective assessments of salesperson characteristics and behaviors with considerable monitoring and directing of salesperson behavior by sales managers.

The outcome-based and behavior-based perspectives illustrated in Exhibit 10.2 represent the extreme positions that a sales organization might take concerning salesperson performance evaluation. Although our earlier review of current practice indicates a tendency toward an outcome-based perspective, most sales organizations operate somewhere between the two extreme positions. However, emphasis on either perspective can have far-reaching impacts on the salesforce and important implications for sales managers. Several of these key implications are presented in Exhibit 10.3. See how placing too much focus on outcomes may lead to undesirable behavior as illustrated in "An Ethical Dilemma."

On balance, these implications provide strong support for at least some behavior-based evaluations in most selling situations, including internationally. Research finds a positive relationship between behavior-based control and salesperson outcome performance, and sales organization effectiveness. In the absence of any behavior-based measures and limited monitoring and direction from sales management, salespeople are likely to focus on the short-term outcomes that are being evaluated. The process of obtaining the desired outcomes may be neglected, causing some activities that produce short-term results (e.g., selling pressure, unethical activities) to be emphasized and activities related to long-term customer relationships (e.g., customer orientation, post-sale service) to be minimized.

Perspectives on Salesperson Performance Evaluation EXHIBIT 10.2

Outcome-Based Perspective	**Behavior-Based Perspective**
• Little monitoring of salespeople • Little managerial direction of salespeople • Straightforward, objective measures of results	• Considerable monitoring of salespeople • High levels of managerial direction of salespeople • Subjective measures of salesperson characteristics, activities, and strategies

The perspectives that a sales organization might take toward salesperson performance evaluation and control lie on a continuum. The two extremes are the outcome-based and behavior-based perspectives.

Outcome-Based versus Behavior-Based Implications EXHIBIT 10.3

The more behavior-based (versus outcome-based) a salesperson performance evaluation is,

- The more professionally competent, team-oriented, risk-averse, planning-oriented, sales-support-oriented, and customer-oriented salespeople will be.
- The more intrinsically and recognition-motivated salespeople will be.
- The more committed to the sales organization salespeople will be.
- The more likely salespeople will be to accept authority, participate in decision making, and welcome management performance reviews.
- The lower the need for using pay as a control mechanism.
- The more innovative and supportive the culture is likely to be.
- The more inclined salespeople are to sell smarter rather than harder.
- The better salespeople will perform on both selling (e.g., using technical knowledge, making sales presentations) and nonselling (e.g., providing information, controlling expenses ethically) behavioral performance dimensions.
- The better salespeople will perform on outcome (e.g., achieving sales objectives) performance dimensions.
- The better the sales organization will perform on sales organization effectiveness dimensions (e.g., sales volume and growth, profitability, and customer satisfaction).
- The greater salespeople's job satisfaction will be.

AN ETHICAL DILEMMA

As sales manager for ACE Chemical, Tim Ryburn is reviewing year-end sales reports for each of his salespeople. ACE offers salespeople a significant annual bonus based on (a) the percentage of sales revenue over budget and (b) the annual gross profit percentage for each salesperson. Tim has noticed an unusually high spike in December gross profit percentages on the report for Kylie Evans. This spike correlates with information Tim has received about several of Kylie's customers calling in about their volume discounts not being reflected on recent invoices resulting in overpriced purchases and bumping up Kylie's gross margin. The accounting department has made the corrections and reinvoiced the customers. However, Tim is curious about the discounts being left off so close to year-end—meaning that any corrections impact next year's revenue and gross profit numbers and not the year under review. Kylie has sold for ACE for five years and does not make this kind of mistake. Tim is concerned that Kylie might have purposefully not entered the sales discounts in order to inflate her gross profit and qualify for a larger bonus. What should Tim do? Why?

A reasonable conclusion from this discussion is that sales organizations should use both outcome-based and behavior-based measures when evaluating salesperson performance. Hybrid approaches incorporating both outcome-based and behavior-based measures place considerable emphasis on the following: supervision; evaluation of attitude, effort, and quantitative results; and complete, accurate paperwork. However, the relative emphasis on outcome-based and behavior-based measures depends on environmental, firm, and salesperson considerations. Limited research finds that behavior-based control is emphasized when the selling environment is uncertain, the salesforce is small, outputs and the cost of measuring them are inadequate, means for measuring behaviors are available, products are less complex, the percentage of routine activities is high, and salespeople are more educated. In addition, when formalization is high, outcome-based control can reduce its negative impact on role ambiguity and organizational commitment. Establishing the desired emphasis should be the initial decision in developing a salesperson performance evaluation and control system. Once this emphasis has been established, the sales organization can then address the specific criteria to be evaluated, the methods of evaluation, and how the performance information will be used. Regardless of the relative emphasis, however, some research suggests that greater control leads to higher levels of salesperson job satisfaction, organizational commitment and job performance, and lower levels of role stress.[6]

Criteria for Performance Evaluation

The typical salesperson job is multidimensional. Salespeople normally sell multiple products to diverse customers and perform a variety of selling and nonselling activities. Therefore, any comprehensive assessment of salesperson performance must include multiple criteria.

Although the specific criteria depend on the characteristics of a given selling situation and the performance evaluation perspective, the four performance dimensions illustrated in Figure 10.1 should be considered: behavioral and professional development (behavior-based perspective) and results and profitability (outcome-based perspective). Regardless of the specific evaluative criteria chosen, it is important that salespeople know and

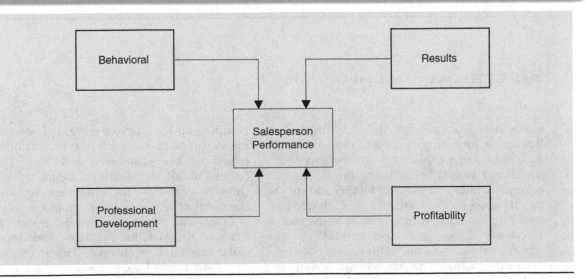

FIGURE 10.1   Dimensions of Salesperson Performance Evaluation

A comprehensive evaluation of salesperson performance should incorporate criteria from these dimensions. Sales organizations using a behavior-based perspective would focus on behavioral and professional development criteria, whereas those using an outcome-based perspective would emphasize results and profitability criteria.

understand the criteria to achieve desired performance. Moreover, sales managers should explain the rationale underlying the use of specific criteria. They may even want to let salespeople help in determining the evaluation criteria. When salespeople believe that the criteria upon which they are being evaluated is appropriate, they are likely to be more satisfied with their job.

Behavior

The behavioral dimension consists of criteria related to activities performed by individual salespeople. The emphasis is on evaluating exactly what each salesperson does. These behavioral criteria should not only address activities related to short-term sales generation but should also include nonselling activities needed to ensure long-term customer satisfaction and to provide necessary information to the sales organization. Examples of typical behavioral criteria are presented in Exhibit 10.4.[7]

As might be expected, most sales organizations focus on the number of sales calls made as the key behavioral criterion. However, other activities are also important to at least some sales organizations. At Motorola, for instance, customer satisfaction is measured to determine goal achievement. Part of salespeople's compensation at IBM is based on customer satisfaction. When salespeople's rewards are based on a customer satisfaction rating, salespeople are likely to demonstrate a higher level of customer service activity. This helps to explain research that finds that when buyers rate salespeople highly, they tend to give the salesperson's organization higher performance ratings.

Salespeople have the most control over what they do, so evaluations of their performance should include some assessment of their behaviors. Interestingly, foreign subsidiaries of U.S.–based multinationals appear to rely more heavily than U.S. firms on behavioral

Behavioral Criteria EXHIBIT 10.4	
Base	**Percentage of Firms Reporting Using**
Calls	
Number of customer calls	48
Number of calls per day (or period)	42
Number of planned calls	24
Number of calls per account	23
Number of calls per number of customers— by product class (call frequency ratio)	18
Average time spent per call	8
Number of unplanned calls	7
Planned to unplanned call ratio	3
Ancillary Activities	
Number of required reports turned in	38
Number of days worked (per period)	33
Selling time versus nonselling time	27
Training meetings conducted	26
Number of customer complaints	25
Number of formal presentations	22
Number of quotes	21
Percentage of goods returned	17
Number of dealer meetings held	17
Number of service calls made	15
Number of formal proposals developed	15
Advertising displays set up	13
Number of demonstrations conducted	12
Dollar amount of overdue accounts collected	10
Number of letters/phone calls to prospects	9

criteria for evaluating salesperson performance. This may be because behavior-based systems have been found to be better than compensation at promoting selling techniques among salespeople in other cultures, particularly Europe.[8] As discussed in Exhibit 10.3, the use of behavior-based criteria will also facilitate the development of a professional, customer-oriented, committed, and motivated salesforce.

Professional Development

Another dimension of considerable importance in evaluating the performance of individual salespeople relates to professional development. Professional development criteria assess improvements in certain characteristics of salespeople that are related to successful performance in the sales job. For example, if product knowledge is critical in a particular selling situation, then evaluations of the product knowledge of individual salespeople over various periods should be conducted. Examples of professional development criteria are presented in Exhibit 10.5.[9]

Many sales organizations incorporate multiple professional development criteria into their salesperson performance evaluations. This is appropriate, because salespeople have control over the development of personal characteristics related to success in their selling situation. The professional development criteria introduce a long-term perspective into the process of salesperson performance evaluation. Salespeople who are developing professionally are increasing their chances of successful performance over the long run. Although the professional development and behavioral criteria might be combined into one category, the preferred practice is to keep them separate to reflect their different perspectives.

EXHIBIT 10.5   Professional Development Criteria

Base	Percentage of Firms Reporting Using
Communication skills	88
Product knowledge	85
Attitude	82
Selling skills	79
Initiative and aggressiveness	76
Appearance and manner	75
Knowledge of competition	71
Team player	67
Enthusiasm	66
Time management	63
Judgment	62
Cooperation	62
Motivation	61
Ethical/moral behavior	59
Planning ability	58
Pricing knowledge	55
Report preparation and submission	54
Creativity	54
Punctuality	49
Resourcefulness	49
Knowledge of company policies	48
Customer goodwill generation	41
Self-improvement efforts	40
Care of company property	39
Degree of respect from trade and competition	38
Use of promotional materials	37
New product ideas	35
Use of marketing/technical backup teams	33
Good citizenship	22

Base	Percentage of Firms Reporting Using
Sales	
Sales volume in dollars	79
Sales volume to previous year's sales	76
Sales volume by (versus) dollar quota	65
Percentage of increase in sales volume	55
Sales volume by product or product line	48
Sales volume by customer	44
Amount of new account sales	42
Sales volume in units	35
Sales volume to (versus) market potential	27
Sales volume by customer type	22
Sales volume to physical unit quota	9
Sales volume per order	7
Sales volume per call	6
Sales volume by outlet type	4
Percentage of sales made by telephone or mail	1
Market Share	
Market share achieved	59
Market share per quota	18
Accounts	
Number of new accounts	69
Number of accounts lost	33
Number of accounts buying the full line	22
Dollar amount of accounts receivable	17
Number of accounts (payment is) overdue	15
Lost account ratio	6

Results Criteria   EXHIBIT 10.6

Results

The results achieved by salespeople are extremely important and should be evaluated. Examples of results criteria used in salesperson performance evaluations are listed in Exhibit 10.6.[10]

A potential problem with the use of results criteria in Exhibit 10.6 is that the overall results measures do not reflect the territory situations faced by individual salespeople. The salesperson with the highest level of sales may have the best territory and may not necessarily be the best performer in generating sales. In fact, some research shows that rewards for achieving results have a negative effect on performance and satisfaction because salespeople may view the rewards as arbitrary if the goals are beyond their control. Aside from the impossible task of developing territories that are exactly equal, the only way to address this potential problem is to compare actual results with standards that reflect the unique territory situation faced by each salesperson. These standards are generally called sales quotas.

A sales quota represents a reasonable sales objective for a territory, district, region, or zone. Because a sales forecast represents an expected level of firm sales for a defined geographic area, time period, and strategy, there should be a close relationship between the sales forecast and the sales quota. Any of the several forecasting approaches discussed in Appendix 4 might be used to develop sales forecasts that are translated into sales quotas.

Accurate sales forecasts are critical for establishing valid sales quotas at all sales organization levels. To increase the accuracy of sales forecasts and subsequently quotas, they should be developed quarterly, particularly in highly dynamic environments.

EXHIBIT 10.7   Elements Important in Assigning Sales Quotas

Statement	Mean[1,2]	Rank
Concentration of businesses within the sales representative's territory is important in determining the amount of quota.	1.82	1
The geographical size of territory is important in determining the amount of quota.	1.95	2
Growth of businesses within the sales representative's territory is important in determining the amount of quota.	2.11	3
Commitment by the sales manager to assisting the sales representative is important in determining the amount of quota.	2.23	4
Complexity of products sold is important in determining the amount of quota.	2.50	5
The sales representative's past sales performance is important in determining the amount of quota.	2.54	6
Extent of product line is important in determining the amount of quota.	2.59	7
The financial support (e.g., compensation) a firm provides sales representatives is important in assigning quota.	2.76	8
The relationship of your product line is important in determining the amount of quota.	2.82	9
The amount of clerical support given to a sales representative is important in determining the amount of quota.	3.13	10

[1]The rating scale and weights used to rate the importance of each statement were as follows: 1 strongly agree; 2 agree; 3 neutral; 4 disagree; and 5 strongly disagree.
[2]The responses numbered 186.

Although forecasts provide the basis for developing quotas, they must be adjusted to determine each individual's quota. Exhibit 10.7 shows results of a survey indicating the relative importance placed on various factors by sales managers when assigning sales quotas.[11] Research suggests that salesperson performance can be enhanced by assigning more challenging quotas to experienced salespeople who have demonstrated exceptional competence or to novices who quickly exhibit high potential. Likewise, performance may be enhanced by setting fair, consistent, and realistic quotas and by explaining to salespeople the rationale behind the quota assignment.[12]

Web-based applications such as Synygy Quotas, by Synygy, Inc. (http://www. synygy .com), facilitate the quota-setting process. This application provides companies a means for setting corporate sales goals, allocating quotas, communicating them, making field adjustments, tracking changes, and tying quotas to incentive compensation programs. Quota allocation methods are derived from over 10 years of industry-leading best practices. Sales managers can use market potential, historical data, revenue, gross margin, profit, or any other measure or combination of measures to set quota.[13]

Although it varies from company to company, some research indicates that a majority of companies require salespeople to achieve 100 percent or more of quota to be considered a strong performer. Over 26 percent of the respondents in this research claimed that achieving 111 percent or more of quota is necessary to be considered a strong performer. However, most companies (72 percent) consider salespeople who make 90 percent or less of quota to be average performers.[14] As seen in Exhibit 10.8, this research also found that sales managers often work closely with salespeople to improve their performance when they fail to achieve quota.[15]

Examples of Managerial Actions Resulting from Failure to Achieve Assigned Quota					EXHIBIT 10.8
	Percentage Agreement				
Action to Salesperson	**Strongly Disagree**	**Disagree**	**Neutral**	**Agree**	**Strongly Agree**
Nothing	12.7	38.2	18.5	25.4	5.2
Informal reprimand to do better	9.2	16.1	19.0	47.1	8.6
A stern verbal warning	10.7	30.5	23.4	29.7	5.7
Sales manager works closely with salesperson to improve	7.6	7.0	17.4	48.8	19.2
Formal probation	12.2	34.9	24.4	22.1	6.4

Profitability

A potential problem with focusing on sales results is that the profitability of sales is not assessed. Salespeople can affect profitability in two basic ways. First, salespeople have an impact on gross profits through the specific products they sell and/or through the prices they negotiate for final sale. Thus, two salespeople could generate the same level of sales dollars and achieve the same sales/sales quota evaluation, but one salesperson could produce more gross profits by selling higher margin products and/or maintaining higher prices in sales negotiations.

Second, salespeople affect net profits by the expenses they incur in generating sales. The selling expenses most under the control of salespeople are travel and entertainment expenses. Therefore, two salespeople could generate the same levels of total sales, the same sales/sales quota performance, and even the same levels of gross profits, but one salesperson could contribute more to net profits through lower travel and entertainment costs. Examples of profitability criteria are listed in Exhibit 10.9.[16]

Sales organizations are increasingly incorporating profitability criteria into their salesperson performance evaluations. The most frequently used profitability criterion is net profit dollars. Selling expenditures relative to budget is also heavily emphasized. The need to address profitability criteria is especially important during a slow-growth, competitive environment in which sales growth is so difficult and productivity and profitability so important.

Comment on Criteria

Conducting a comprehensive evaluation of salesperson performance typically requires consideration of behavioral professional development, results, and profitability criteria. Each set of criteria tells a different story as to how well salespeople have performed and provides different diagnostic information for control purposes. Michael Maretich, Global Sales Manager for the Stepan Company, explains the company's unique and highly effective sales performance evaluation system in "Sales Management in the 21st Century: Stepan Company's Unique Continuous Salesperson Evaluation Process." This ongoing performance evaluation is integrated into sales managers' coaching of individual salespeople and incorporates multiple performance criteria and real-time feedback for performance improvement.

Performance Evaluation Methods

Sales managers can use a number of different methods for measuring the behaviors, professional development, results, and profitability of salespeople. Ideally, the method used should have the following characteristics.

- *Job relatedness:* The performance evaluation method should be designed to meet the needs of each specific sales organization.

EXHIBIT 10.9 Profitability Criteria

Base	Percentage of Firms Reporting Using
Sales	
Net profit dollars	69
Gross margin per sales (a percentage of sales)	34
Return on investment	33
Net profit as a percent(age) of sales	32
Margin by product category	28
Gross margin (in dollars)	25
Margin by customer type	18
Net profit per sale	14
Return on sales cost	14
Net profit contribution	—
Order(s)	
Number of orders secured	47
Average size of order secured	22
Order-per-call ratio (a.k.a. batting average)	14
Number of orders canceled	11
Net orders per repeat order	10
Number of canceled orders per orders booked	4
Selling Expense	
Selling expense versus budget	55
Total expenses	53
Selling expense to sales	49
Average cost per call	12
Selling expense to quota	12
Expenses by product category	7
Expenses by customer type	3

SALES MANAGEMENT IN THE 21ST CENTURY

Stepan Company's Unique Continuous Salesperson Evaluation Process

Michael Maretich, global sales manager for Stepan Company, discusses their unique and action-oriented model of continuous salesperson evaluation that fuels Stepan's position as a worldwide leader in the fast-paced and competitive field of industrial chemical manufacturing and distribution.

Our process of evaluating sales performance begins with each salesperson having a clear understanding of their functional responsibilities, expected results, performance metrics, and the resulting impact on overall corporate business goals. Regional sales managers meet with each of their salespeople to identify current and new sales opportunities that would exceed growth and profit goals if converted. A mutually agreed-upon annual call-plan is created that identifies all accounts, contacts (decision makers and influencers), visit frequency, and time required to maximize each opportunity. This plan is the basis for all sales effort and activity for the year.

Sales managers assist each salesperson using different leadership styles depending on their competence (knowledge and skill) and commitment (motivation and confidence) on each performance objective. Newer salespeople, who are developing, receive needed direction and encouragement to build skill, confidence, and motivation. Salespeople who have demonstrated competence receive more support than direction and collaborate often with leadership on decisions that impact their business. This approach results in a highly motivated sales team. Sales managers are expected to coach each salesperson three to five hours each month (in person, by phone or by email) reviewing call plans, opportunities, and sales performance. Salespeople are continuously measured on other competencies that impact performance, including customer focus, drive for results, ownership, negotiating, business acumen, problem solving and strategic agility. This individualized management approach has resulted in increased sales performance, enhanced salesperson engagement and satisfaction, along with increasing our commitment to customer satisfaction and loyalty.

- *Reliability:* The measures should be stable over time and exhibit internal consistency.
- *Validity:* The measures should provide accurate assessments of the criteria they are intended to measure.
- *Standardization:* The measurement instruments and evaluation process should be similar throughout the sales organization.
- *Practicality:* Sales managers and salespeople should understand the entire performance appraisal process and should be able to implement it in a reasonable amount of time.
- *Comparability:* The results of the performance evaluation process should make it possible to compare the performance of individual salespeople directly.
- *Discriminability:* The evaluative methods must be capable of detecting differences in the performance of individual salespeople.
- *Usefulness:* The information provided by the performance evaluation must be valuable to sales managers in making various decisions.

Designing methods of salesperson performance evaluation that possess all these characteristics is a difficult task. As indicated in Exhibit 10.10, each evaluative method has certain strengths and weaknesses. No single method provides a perfect evaluation. Therefore, it is important to understand the strengths and weaknesses of each method so that several can be combined to produce the best evaluative procedure for a given sales organization.

Graphic Rating/Checklist Methods

Graphic rating/checklist methods consist of approaches in which salespeople are evaluated by using some type of performance evaluation form. The performance evaluation form contains the criteria to be used in the evaluation as well as some means to provide an assessment of how well each salesperson performed on each criterion. An example of part of such a form is presented in Exhibit 10.11.

This method is popular in many sales organizations. It is especially useful in evaluating salesperson behavioral and professional development criteria. As part of its assessment process, Eastman Chemical Company asks its customers to evaluate their satisfaction with the company by using a rating scale. As evident from Exhibit 10.12, Eastman's salespeople are responsible for several behavior-based performance factors.[17] Rating methods

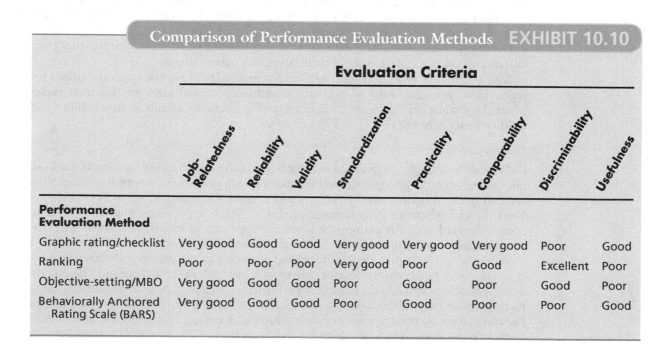

Comparison of Performance Evaluation Methods   EXHIBIT 10.10

Evaluation Criteria

Performance Evaluation Method	Job-Relatedness	Reliability	Validity	Standardization	Practicality	Comparability	Discriminability	Usefulness
Graphic rating/checklist	Very good	Good	Good	Very good	Very good	Very good	Poor	Good
Ranking	Poor	Poor	Poor	Very good	Poor	Good	Excellent	Poor
Objective-setting/MBO	Very good	Good	Good	Poor	Good	Poor	Good	Poor
Behaviorally Anchored Rating Scale (BARS)	Very good	Good	Good	Poor	Good	Poor	Poor	Good

EXHIBIT 10.11   Graphic Rating/Checklist Example

1. Asks customers for their ideas for promoting business
   Almost Never   1   2   3   4   5   Almost Always   N/A

2. Offers customers help in solving their problems
   Almost Never   1   2   3   4   5   Almost Always   N/A

3. Is constantly smiling when interacting with customers
   Almost Never   1   2   3   4   5   Almost Always   N/A

4. Admits when he/she doesn't know the answer,
   but promises to find out
   Almost Never   1   2   3   4   5   Almost Always   N/A

5. Generates new ways of tackling new or ongoing problems
   Almost Never   1   2   3   4   5   Almost Always   N/A

6. Returns customers' calls the same day
   Almost Never   1   2   3   4   5   Almost Always   N/A

7. Retains his or her composure in front of customers
   Almost Never   1   2   3   4   5   Almost Always   N/A

8. Delivers what he or she promises on time
   Almost Never   1   2   3   4   5   Almost Always   N/A

have been developed to evaluate all the important salesperson performance dimensions. There are even employee-appraisal software programs, such as Performance Now!, available to assist in the review process. The program asks users to rate employees by goals, development plans, and competencies.[18]

As evident from Exhibit 10.10, graphic rating/checklist methods possess many desirable characteristics, especially in terms of job-relatedness, standardization, practicality, and comparability. The reliability and validity of these methods, however, must be continually assessed and the specific rating scales improved over time.

The major disadvantage of graphic rating/checklist methods is in providing evaluations that discriminate sufficiently among the performances of individual salespeople or among the performances on different criteria for the same salesperson. For example, some sales managers may be very lenient in their evaluations; they may try to play it safe and give all salespeople ratings around the average. In addition, when evaluating an individual salesperson, some sales managers are subject to a *halo effect,* meaning that their evaluations on one criterion affect their ratings on other criteria.

The advantages of graphic rating/checklist methods clearly outweigh the disadvantages. However, care must be taken to minimize potential sales management biases when the evaluation forms are completed, and continuous attention to reliability and validity issues is necessary.

Ranking Methods

Otherwise similar to graphic rating/checklist methods, ranking methods rank all salespeople according to relative performance on each performance criterion rather than evaluating them against a set of performance criteria. Companies such as Ford, General Electric, and Microsoft use ranking methods. Many approaches might be used to obtain the rankings. An example of a ranking approach in which salespeople are compared in pairs concerning relative communication skills is presented in Exhibit 10.13.

Ranking methods provide a standardized approach to evaluation and thus force discrimination as to the performance of individual salespeople on each criterion. The process of ranking forces this discrimination in performance. Despite these advantages, ranking methods have many shortcomings, as indicated in Exhibit 10.10. Of major concern are the constraints on their practicality and usefulness. Ranking all salespeople against each performance criterion can be a complex and cognitively difficult task. The ranking task

Eastman Chemical Company Customer Satisfaction Survey   EXHIBIT 10.12

Importance: Rate the importance of each statement (your buying criteria) by asking, "Would I place additional business with a supplier who improved performance in this category from 'average' to 'outstanding'?"

Performance: Rate Eastman performance and your best "other supplier" on each criteria.

	Importance 5—Definitely Would 4—Probably Would 3—Uncertain 2—Probably Would Not 1—Definitely Would Not N/A—Not Applicable	Performance 5—Outstanding 4—Good 3—Average 2—Fair 1—Poor N/A—Not Applicable	
		Eastman	Best Other Supplier
Product			
1. Product Performance: Supplier provides a product that consistently meets your requirements and performance expectations.			
2. Product Mix: Supplier offers a range of products that meets your needs.			
3. Packaging: Supplier has the package type, size, and label to meet your needs.			
4. New Products: Supplier meets your needs through timely introduction of new products.			
5. Product Availability: Supplier meets volume commitments and is also fair and consistent during times of restricted supply.			
6. Product Stewardship: Supplier provides information about the transportation, storage, handling, use, recycling, disposal, and regulation of products and product packaging.			
Service			
7. Order Entry: Supplier has a user-friendly system to place orders that is flexible and responsive to routine order changes as well as urgent or special requests.			
8. Delivery: Supplier consistently delivers the right product on time and in satisfactory condition.			
9. Technical Service: Supplier provides timely technical support through training, information, problem solving, and assistance in current and new end-use applications.			
10. Sharing Information: Supplier is a resource for product, market, industry, and company information that helps you better understand business issues.			
11. New Ideas: Supplier offers new ideas that add value to your business.			

(continued)

EXHIBIT 10.12	Eastman Chemical Company Customer Satisfaction Survey (*continued*)

	Importance	Performance	
		Eastman	Best Other Supplier
Pricing/Business Practices			
12. Pricing Practices: Supplier is consistent with the marketplace in establishing pricing practices.			
13. Paperwork: Supplier provides clear and accurate paperwork and business documents that meet your needs.			
14. Commitment to total quality management: Supplier exhibits strong commitment to total quality management in all aspects of their business.			
15. Responsiveness: Supplier listens and responds to your business needs in a timely manner.			
Relationship			
16. Integrity: Supplier is credible, honest, and trustworthy.			
17. Dependability: Supplier follows through on agreements.			
18. Supplier Contact: Supplier is easy to contact and provides the right amount of interface with the appropriate personnel.			
19. Problem Solving: Supplier provides empowered employees to solve your problems.			
Supplier Commitment			
20. Industry Commitment: Supplier exhibits a strong commitment to your industry.			
21. Regional Commitment: Supplier has the appropriate resources in place in your region to provide products and services needed.			
22. Customer Commitment: Supplier is strongly committed to helping your business be successful.			

can be simplified by using paired-comparison approaches like the one presented in Exhibit 10.13. However, the computations required to translate the paired comparisons into overall rankings can be extremely cumbersome.

Even if the evaluative and computative procedures can be simplified, the rankings are of limited usefulness. Rank data reveal only relative ordering and omit any assessment of the differences between ranks. For example, the actual differences in the communication skills of salespeople ranked first, second, and third may be small or large, but there is no way to tell the degree of these differences from the ranked data. In addition, information obtained from graphic rating/checklist methods can always be transformed into

	Ranking Method Example EXHIBIT 10.13					
Performance Criterion: Communication Skills						
	Much Better	**Slightly Better**	**Equal Better**	**Slightly Better**	**Much Better**	
Jane Haynes	X	___	___	___	___	Ron Castaneda
Ron Castaneda	___	X	___	___	___	Bill Haroldson
Bill Haroldson	___	___	X	___	___	Jane Haynes

rankings, but rankings cannot be translated into graphic rating/checklist form. Despite their limitations, many companies find forced rankings to be an effective way to identify and reward core competencies. However, given their limitations, it is suggested that ranking methods for salesperson performance evaluations be used as a supplement to other methods.

Objective-Setting Methods

The most common and comprehensive goal-setting method is management by objectives (MBO). Applied to a salesforce, the typical MBO approach is as follows:

1. mutual setting of well-defined and measurable goals within a specified time period

2. managing activities within the specified time period toward the accomplishment of the stated objectives

3. appraisal of performance against objectives

As with all the performance evaluation methods, MBO and other goal-setting methods have certain strengths and weaknesses (see Exhibit 10.10). Although complete reliance on this or any other goal-setting method is inadvisable, the incorporation of some goal-setting procedures is normally desirable. This is especially true for performance criteria related to quantitative behavioral, professional development, results, and profitability criteria. Absolute measures of these dimensions are often not very meaningful because of extreme differences in the territory situations of individual salespeople. The setting of objectives or quotas provides a means for controlling for territory differences through the establishment of performance benchmarks that incorporate these territory differences.

Quotas can be established for other important results criteria and for specific behavioral, professional development, and profitability criteria. Each type of quota represents a specific objective for a salesperson to achieve during a given period. Actual performance can be compared with the quota objective and a performance index calculated for each criterion being evaluated. The individual performance indices can then be weighted to reflect their relative importance and combined to produce an overall performance index. An example of this procedure is shown in Exhibit 10.14.

This example illustrates an evaluation of Laura, David, and Kendra on sales, gross profit, and demonstration quotas. The unequal weights reflect that the firm is placing the most importance on gross profits, followed by demonstrations and then sales. Laura has performed the best overall, but she did not reach her sales quota for this period. David has performed reasonably well on all criteria. Kendra's situation is interesting in that she performed the best on the sales quota but poorly overall due to low performance indices for gross profits and demonstrations. Perhaps she is concentrating too much on short-term sales generation and not concerning herself with the profitability of sales or the number of product demonstrations. In any case, the use of quotas provides an extremely

EXHIBIT 10.14   Quota Evaluation Example

Salesperson	Actual Quota	Weight	Weighted Performance	Index	Performance
Laura					
Sales	600,000	3	552,000	92	276
Gross profits	150,000	6	180,000	120	720
Demonstrations	200	4	250	125	500
Overall performance					115
David					
Sales	700,000	3	710,000	101	303
Gross profits	170,000	6	174,000	102	612
Demonstrations	200	4	200	100	400
Overall performance					101
Kendra					
Sales	550,000	3	650,000	118	354
Gross profits	140,000	6	100,000	71	426
Demonstrations	180	4	150	82	332
Overall performance					86

useful method for evaluating salesperson performance and highlighting specific areas in which performance is especially good or especially poor.

Behaviorally Anchored Rating Scales

The uniqueness of behaviorally anchored rating scales (BARS) is due to its focus on trying to link salesperson behaviors with specific results. These behavior-results linkages become the basis for salesperson performance evaluation in this method.

The development of a BARS approach is an iterative process that actively incorporates members of the salesforce. Salespeople are used to identify important performance results and the critical behaviors necessary to achieve those results. The critical behaviors are assigned numbers on a rating scale for each performance result. An example of one such BARS rating scale is presented in Figure 10.2.

The performance result in this example is achieving cooperative relations with sales team members. Seven behaviors have been assigned numbers on a 10-point rating scale to reflect the linkages between engaging in the behavior and achieving the result. This scale can then be used to evaluate individual salespeople. For instance, the example rating of 5.0 in the figure suggests that the salesperson occasionally supports the sales team on problems encountered in the field and thus achieves only a moderate amount of cooperation with sales team members.

As indicated in Exhibit 10.10, the BARS approach rates high on job relatedness. This is because of the rigorous process used to determine important performance results and critical salesperson behaviors. The results and behaviors identified in this manner are specific to a given selling situation and directly related to the job of the salespeople being evaluated. Research indicates that positive feedback about sales behaviors has a greater impact on salesperson behavior than positive output feedback, perhaps because it gives salespeople direction for improving selling. The really unique aspect of BARS is the focus on linkages between behaviors and results. No other approach incorporates this perspective.

In sum, the basic methods for evaluating salesperson performance include graphic rating/checklist methods, ranking methods, objective-setting methods, and BARS methods. Each approach has specific strengths and weaknesses that should be considered. Combining different methods into the salesperson performance evaluation process is

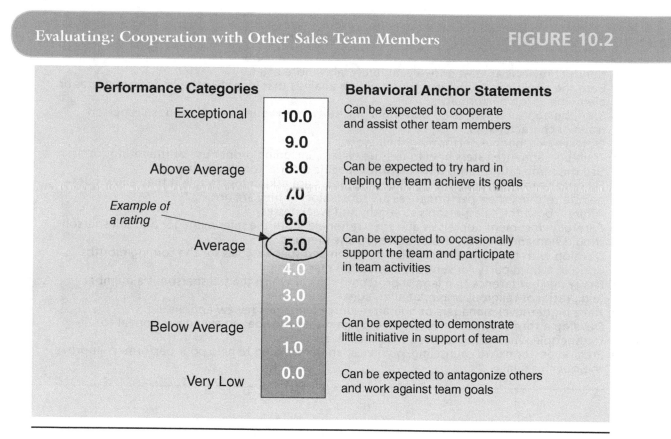

Evaluating: Cooperation with Other Sales Team Members   FIGURE 10.2

This scale evaluates a salesperson's cooperation with other sales team members. The example rating of 5.0 suggests a moderate level of cooperation in which the salesperson gives only occasional support to the sales team.

one way to capitalize on the strengths and minimize the weaknesses inherent in each approach.

Performance Evaluation Bias

Sales managers must be careful to avoid bias when assessing salespeople. For instance, sales managers tend to give more favorable performance ratings to those with whom they have closer personal relationships and less favorable performance ratings to those with whom they maintain formal role-defined relationships. Similarly, sales managers are more likely to discount internal responsibility while bolstering external explanations when appraising salespeople with whom they work well and are socially compatible. In addition, these salespeople are less likely to receive coercive feedback. Sales managers also tend to rate individuals in more difficult territories higher in ability and performance than those in less difficult territories. Furthermore, supervisors are more likely to rate those who are better at impression management (the ability to shape and manage a self-image that positively influences others), which tend to be males, more favorably when using subjective evaluations.

Sales managers must likewise be careful to avoid outcome bias. Outcome bias occurs when the outcome of a decision rather than the appropriateness of the decision influences an evaluator's ratings. When sales managers rate the quality of a salesperson's decision, outcome information (e.g., salesperson did or did not make the sale) often influences their ratings across all criteria when the decision is perceived to have been inappropriate. Using the BARS scale to assess behavioral and professional development criteria helps reduce outcome bias.

EXHIBIT 10.15 Guidelines for Withstanding Discriminatory Appraisal Lawsuits

- Conduct reviews at least once a year, preferably more often.
- Base the appraisal system on a thorough job analysis that identifies the important duties or elements of job performance.
- Base the appraisal system on behaviors or results, not vague or ambiguous salesperson traits or characteristics.
- Observe salespeople performing their work.
- Train performance raters how to use the system, including proper use of the rating forms.
- Use the same rating form, that measures specific criteria, for all salespeople.
- Fill out the rating form *honestly*. Sales managers are asking for trouble if they allow salespeople to think their performances are satisfactory if they are not.
- Address both the salesperson's strengths and weaknesses.
- Carefully document appraisals and their rationale. Both the sales manager and salesperson should sign and date the evaluation after the meeting.
- Develop with the salesperson a plan of action and specific goals for the coming months.
- Bring in a third party for sensitive evaluation meetings.
- Never make reference to a legally protected class of which the salesperson is a member (e.g., racial or religious origin, gender, age).
- Have higher-level managers or human resource managers review appraisals.
- Develop a formal appeal mechanism or system that provides an avenue of appeal to salespeople who are dissatisfied with their evaluations.
- Provide performance counseling, guidance, and/or training to help poor performers improve their performance.

AN ETHICAL DILEMMA

As the Western district manager for Chicago Container Corporation (CCC), you are responsible for evaluating the performance of 11 salespeople. These annual performance appraisals play a large part in your salespeople's bonus and promotion opportunities. Your supervising manager recently came to you and encouraged you to look favorably on one of your salespeople, Kari Shepherd, during her upcoming performance appraisal. It is your understanding that a regional sales management position has opened up in another district and suspect that Kari may be in line for the promotion—particularly if her performance evaluation is good. While Kari is a good salesperson, her performance has not exactly been outstanding. The dilemma is further complicated by your star salesperson actually being a good candidate for the sales manager position—although you would hate to lose him. What would you do? Explain.

Performance evaluation bias not only is harmful to the individual being rated but could result in legal action. Personnel actions that discriminate unfairly are unlawful. A performance appraisal system is more likely to withstand a legal challenge if the guidelines in Exhibit 10.15 are adhered to in developing and implementing the system. "An Ethical Dilemma" illustrates potential difficulties a sales manager may face when evaluating salesperson performance.

Evaluating Team Performance

Sales organizations employing sales teams must also consider how to evaluate them. When designing the appraisal process for teams, sales managers must still consider the

Teamwork Effectiveness and Measurement   EXHIBIT 10.16

ORCA TECHNOLOGIES, INC.
TEAMWORK EFFECTIVENESS EVALUATION

TEAM MEMBER BEING EVALUATED: # Bart Waits

Team Communication	Never				Always
1. Listens effectively	1	2	3	4	(5)
2. Is open-minded and receptive to ideas of others	1	2	(3)	4	5
3. Is organized in written and verbal communication	1	2	3	4	(5)
4. Initiates and participates in discussions	1	2	(3)	4	5
5. Responds promptly to requests	1	2	3	4	(5)
6. Confirms important communication in writing	1	2	3	(4)	5

Major Communication Strength:

Positive Suggestion for Improving Communication Skills:

Team Productivity	Never				Always
1. Is industrious and effectively uses time	1	2	(3)	4	5
2. Meets targets and deadlines	1	(2)	3	4	5
3. Produces accurate and quality work	1	2	3	(4)	5
4. Organizes and plans effectively	1	2	(3)	4	5
5. Focuses on high-priority projects	1	2	(3)	4	5
6. Stays within team budgets	1	(2)	3	4	5

Major Productivity Strength:

Positive Suggestion for Improving Productivity Skills:

Team Relationships	Never				Always
7. Is sensitive to the needs of other team members	1	2	3	4	(5)
8. Is supportive of and concerned for other members	1	2	3	4	(5)
9. Is flexible and cooperates with team members	1	2	3	(4)	5
10. Is dependable and keeps commitments	1	2	3	(4)	5
11. Is pleasant and maintains a positive attitude	1	2	3	4	(5)
12. Is patient and maintains control	1	2	(3)	4	5

Major Relationship Strength:

Positive Suggestion for Improving Relationship Skills:

criteria on which members will be evaluated and the methods used to evaluate performance. In addition, it is important that sales managers establish a link between team performance and positive outcomes to promote individual and team effort. The process is fostered by allowing team members to participate in developing team goals and objectives. Furthermore, members are more willing to participate when individual goals are linked to team goals. Individual and group assignments necessary for reaching goals should be prioritized to help the team better manage its time.

Generally, the team as a whole should be evaluated, in addition to assessing individual member performance. Team performance can be measured by team members as well as by the sales manager. Exhibit 10.16 provides an example of a multidimensional approach team members can use to evaluate teammates' critical skills and behaviors. The measurement allows sales managers to develop a composite performance appraisal, merging each team member's viewpoint. The process helps strengthen teams, enhance morale, and contribute to a healthy working climate. In addition, the team and its members must be

> **EXHIBIT 10.17** **Steps for Measuring Team Performance**
>
> 1. Develop team and individual performance standards and measures that will be used to gauge the level of performance achieved.
> 2. Map the standards and measures to relevant individual and team-level activities that will contribute to the achievement of the team.
> 3. Define the terminology precisely and review the criteria with team members to ensure both awareness and understanding.
> 4. Integrate inputs from management and team members to develop relative importance weights for the performance standards.
> 5. Decide how to collect the data and track performance for each standard and feed this information back to the team.
> 6. Take action based on the evaluations in order to recognize and reward appropriately.

evaluated against predetermined performance criteria. Exhibit 10.17 outlines a process for measuring team performance.

For sales managers, it is important to note that less than effective team performance is often not the fault of individual team members, but of management. The commitment and support of top management has significant weight as a key determinant of a team's achievement. This commitment includes appropriate use of teams, provision of start-up support and training, enabling cross-team communication, and establishing accountability for team performance.

Using Performance Information

Using different methods to evaluate the behavior, professional development, results, and profitability of salespeople provides extremely important performance information. The critical sales management task is to use this information to improve the performance of individual salespeople, sales teams, and the overall operations of the sales organization. Initially, it should be used to determine the absolute and relative performance of each salesperson. These determinations then provide the basis for reward disbursements, special recognition, promotions, and so forth.

The second major use of this performance information is to identify potential problems or areas in which salespeople need to improve for better performance in the future. If salespeople are evaluated against multiple criteria, as suggested in this chapter, useful diagnostic information will be available. The difficulty exists in isolating the specific causes of low performance areas. A framework for performing this analysis is given in Figure 10.3.

The first step in this analysis is to review the performance of each salesperson against each relevant criterion and summarize the results across all salespeople being supervised. The purpose of this step is to determine whether there are common areas of low performance. For example, the situation is different when most salespeople are not meeting their sales quotas than when only one or two salespeople are not meeting their sales quotas.

Once the poor performance areas have been identified, the sales manager must work backward to try to identify the cause of the poor performance. Merely determining that most salespeople did not meet their sales quotas is not sufficient to improve future performance; the sales manager must try to uncover the reason for this poor performance. The basic approach is to try to answer the question, "What factors affect the achievement of this performance dimension?" For instance, in regard to achieving sales quotas, the key question is, "What factors determine whether salespeople achieve their sales quotas?" All the factors identified should be reviewed to isolate the cause of any poor performance. Several factors that might cause poor performance in different areas are presented in Exhibit 10.18.

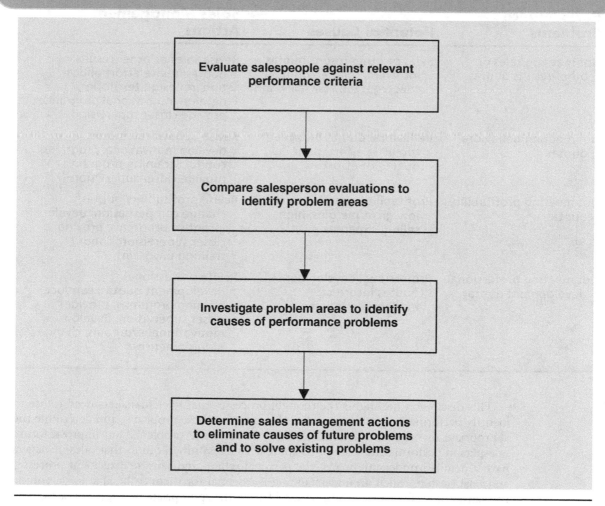

Framework for Using Performance information   FIGURE 10.3

Sales managers need to be able to use the information provided by salesperson performance evaluations in a diagnostic manner. The basic diagnostic approach is to determine problem areas, identify the causes of these problems, and take appropriate action to eliminate the causes and to solve problems that are already present, thus improving future salesperson performance.

After identifying the potential causes of poor performance, the sales manager must determine the appropriate action to reduce or eliminate the cause of the problem so that performance will be improved in the future. Examples of potential management actions for specific problems are also presented in Exhibit 10.18.

Consider again poor performance on sales quota achievement. Assume that intense review of this problem reveals that salespeople not meeting sales quotas also do not make many product demonstrations to prospects. This analysis suggests that if salespeople were to make more product demonstrations, they would be able to generate more sales and thus achieve their sales quotas. The sales management task is to determine what management actions will lead to more product demonstrations by salespeople. Possible actions include more training on product demonstrations, direct communication with individual salespeople about the need for more product demonstrations, or some combination of these or other management actions.

EXHIBIT 10.18   Sample Problems, Causes, and Management Actions

Performance Problems	Potential Causes	Sales Management Actions
Not meeting sales or other results quotas	Sales or other results quotas incorrect; poor account coverage; too few sales calls	Revise sales or other results quotas; revise effort allocation; redesign territories; develop motivational programs; provide closer supervision
Not meeting behavioral quotas	Behavioral quotas incorrect; too little effort; poor quality of effort	Revise behavioral quotas; develop motivational programs; conduct training programs; provide closer supervision
Not meeting profitability quotas	Profitability quotas incorrect; low gross margins; high selling expenses	Revise profitability quotas; change compensation; develop incentive programs; provide closer supervision; conduct training programs
Not meeting professional development quotas	Professional development quotas incorrect; inadequate training	Revise professional development quotas; conduct training programs; provide closer supervision; develop motivational programs; change hiring practices

This discussion highlights the thought processes that sales managers need to use to identify performance problems, isolate the causes of these problems, and determine the appropriate management actions necessary to solve the problems and improve future salesperson performance. Using this approach successfully requires that sales managers have a detailed understanding of the personal selling and sales management processes and relationships. Such an understanding is essential for them to be able to determine the causes of performance problems and identify the appropriate management actions to solve these problems.

Our discussion and examples have emphasized problems affecting many salespeople. The same basic approach can be used for performance problems that are unique to one individual salesperson. In fact, many sales organizations use performance reviews as a means for a sales manager to meet with each salesperson, analyze the salesperson's performance on each criterion, and suggest ways to improve future performance. These performance reviews provide one means for communicating the *performance feedback* that is so important to salespeople. Performance feedback is also an important determinant of salesperson job satisfaction, which is discussed next.

SALESPERSON JOB SATISFACTION

In addition to evaluating salesperson performance, sales managers should be concerned with the job satisfaction of salespeople. Research results have consistently found relationships between salesperson job satisfaction and turnover, absenteeism, motivation, and organizational commitment. Salespeople who are satisfied with their job tend to stay with the firm and work harder than those who are not satisfied.

Other research has investigated relationships between salesperson performance and salesperson satisfaction. This research has produced conflicting findings concerning the direction of the relationship between performance and satisfaction. In other words, it has not been established whether achieving high performance causes salesperson satisfaction or whether salesperson satisfaction determines salesperson performance. However, there is some evidence that salespeople's job satisfaction has a positive effect on customer satisfaction.[19] It is clear, however, that sales managers should be concerned with both the performance and satisfaction of their salespeople. Of importance to sales managers is how salesperson satisfaction might be measured and then how this satisfaction information might be used.

Measuring Salesperson Job Satisfaction

Because job satisfaction is based on individual perceptions, measures of salesperson satisfaction must be based on data provided by individual salespeople. In addition, there are many different aspects of a salesperson's job, and these different areas should be incorporated into the satisfaction evaluation. Fortunately, a scale for evaluating the job satisfaction of salespeople, termed INDSALES, has been developed, validated, and revised. Portions of the revised scale are presented in Exhibit 10.19.[20,21]

On this scale, salespeople indicate their level of agreement with statements concerning their particular sales job. These statements are designed to measure their satisfaction in seven general areas: satisfaction with the job, fellow workers, supervision, company policy and support, pay, promotion and advancement, and customers. Answers to the specific questions for each area are summed to produce a separate satisfaction score for each job dimension. These individual job dimension scores can then be summed to form an overall salesperson satisfaction score. Sales managers can then view the dimensional or overall satisfaction scores for each salesperson or for specified groups of salespeople.

Using Job Satisfaction Information

INDSALES provides extremely useful evaluative and diagnostic information. Because sales managers can evaluate the degree of salesperson satisfaction with specific aspects of the sales job, areas in which satisfaction is low can be investigated further by looking at

Sample Questions from Revised INDSALES Scale **EXHIBIT 10.19**

Component	Total Number of Items	Sample Items
The job	4	My work gives me a sense of accomplishment. My job is exciting.
Fellow workers	4	My fellow workers are selfish. My fellow workers are pleasant.
Supervision	4	My sales manager really tries to get our ideas about things. My sales manager keeps his or her promises.
Company policy and support	4	Top management really knows its job. Management is progressive.
Pay	4	My pay is low in comparison with what others get for similar work in other companies. I'm paid fairly compared with other employees in this company.
Promotion and advancement	4	My opportunities for advancement are limited. I have a good chance for promotion.
Customers	4	My customers are loyal. My customers are trustworthy.

the individual questions for that dimension. For example, if salespeople tended to express dissatisfaction with the supervision they were receiving, management could investigate the answers to the specific questions designed to evaluate the supervision dimension (see Exhibit 10.19). The sales manager in this example might find that most salespeople responded negatively to the statement, "My sales manager really tries to get our ideas about things." The sales manager could then try to increase salesperson satisfaction by using a more participative management style and trying to incorporate salesperson input into the decision-making process.

One useful approach is to perform separate analyses of salesperson satisfaction for high-performing and low-performing salespeople. Research results suggest that there may be important differences in job satisfaction between high performers and low performers. Not incorporating these differences could lead sales managers to make changes that would tend to reduce the turnover of low performers but not of high performers.

Research has also found an important relationship between salesperson satisfaction and performance feedback. Interestingly, negative output feedback does not lower satisfaction with supervisors, whereas negative behavioral feedback appears to improve satisfaction marginally. This suggests salespeople are open to feedback that helps improve their sales performance. Further support for this finding comes from studies showing that sales managers' leadership and role-modeling behaviors positively affect salespeople's job satisfaction. This suggests a sales manager can become an effective leader by doing many of the activities involved in performance appraisal: providing feedback on what salespeople need to improve; offering recognition and rewards in a manner that acknowledges individuals and teams; and helping and supporting salespeople in developing their talents and careers. Carefully evaluating salesperson performance and satisfaction, identifying problem areas, and solving these problems is really what sales management is all about.

SUMMARY

1. **Discuss the different purposes of salesperson performance evaluations.** Performance evaluations can serve many different purposes and should be designed with specific purposes in mind. They may serve to determine appropriate compensation and other reward disbursements, to identify salespeople who should be promoted or fired, to determine training and counseling needs, to provide information for human resource planning to identify criteria for future recruitment and selection of salespeople, to advise salespeople of work expectations, to motivate salespeople, to help salespeople set career goals, to tie individual performance to sales organization goals, to enhance communications, and to ultimately improve salesperson performance.

2. **Differentiate between an outcome-based and a behavior-based perspective for evaluating and controlling salesperson performance.** An outcome-based perspective focuses on objective measures of results, with little monitoring or direction of salesperson efforts by sales managers. By contrast, a behavior-based perspective focuses on close supervision of salesperson efforts and subjective measures of salesperson characteristics, activities, and strategies. The perspective taken by a sales organization will affect salespeople and has important implications for sales management.

3. **Describe the different types of criteria necessary for comprehensive evaluations of salesperson performance.** The multifaceted nature of sales jobs requires that performance evaluations incorporate multiple criteria. Although the specific criteria depend on the characteristics of a particular selling situation, comprehensive evaluations of salesperson performance require that four dimensions be addressed: behavioral, professional development, results, and profitability criteria. Addressing each of these areas is necessary to get a complete picture of salesperson performance and to produce the diagnostic information needed to improve future performance.

4. **Compare the advantages and disadvantages of different methods of salesperson performance evaluation.** Sales managers can use four basic methods to evaluate salesperson behaviors, professional development, results, and profitability: graphic rating/checklist methods, ranking methods, objective-setting methods, and behaviorally anchored rating scales (BARS). Each method has certain strengths and weaknesses that must be understood and can be compensated for by using other methods in combination. Special attention should be directed toward developing performance benchmarks or quotas that reflect the unique characteristics of each territory.

5. **Explain how salesperson performance information can be used to identify problems, determine their causes, and suggest sales management actions to solve them.** The suggested approach is to first identify areas of poor performance, then work backward to try to identify the cause by asking, "What factors affect the achievement of this performance dimension?" Finally, the most effective sales management action to remove the cause of the problem and improve future performance must be determined. Examples of possible actions are given in Exhibit 10.18.

6. **Discuss the measurement and importance of salesperson job satisfaction.** Dissatisfied salespeople tend to be absent more, leave the firm more, and work less hard than satisfied salespeople. The INDSALES scale can be used to measure salesperson satisfaction in total and for specific job dimensions. Analysis of the satisfaction with individual job dimensions can be used to determine appropriate action to increase salesperson job satisfaction.

UNDERSTANDING SALES MANAGEMENT TERMS

360-degree feedback	profitability criteria
performance management	graphic rating/checklist methods
outcome-based perspective	ranking methods
behavior-based perspective	management by objectives (MBO)
behavioral criteria	behaviorally anchored rating scales (BARS)
professional development criteria	outcome bias
results criteria	job satisfaction
sales quota	

DEVELOPING SALES MANAGEMENT KNOWLEDGE

1. Discuss the different purposes of an evaluation of salesperson performance and how each purpose affects the performance evaluation process.

2. Characterize the salesforce of a firm that uses an outcome-based perspective for evaluating salespeople.

3. Why should sales managers pay more attention to behavioral criteria when evaluating salespeople?

4. Compare and contrast the graphic rating/checklist and ranking methods for evaluating salesperson performance.

5. Consider the different types of ethical issues that sales managers might encounter in the process of conducting sales performance evaluations. List three of these ethical issues and explain how sales managers might effectively avoid and/or deal with each one.

6. Discuss the importance of using different types of quotas in evaluating and controlling salesperson performance.

7. What is unique about the BARS method for evaluating salesperson performance?

8. Explain the strengths and weaknesses of using the management by objectives (MBO) approach as a sales performance evaluation method.

9. Why should sales managers be concerned with the job satisfaction of salespeople?

10. How can evaluations of salesperson performance and satisfaction be used by sales managers?

BUILDING SALES MANAGEMENT SKILLS

1. Develop a method that can be used to evaluate salespeople's performance in the following areas: communication skills, attitude, initiative and aggressiveness, appearance and manner, knowledge of competition, enthusiasm, cooperation, and time management. Explain any advantages and/or disadvantages associated with your measurement method.

2. Using the following scale (1 to 5, with 1 being "strongly disagree" and 5 "strongly agree") and the statements in Exhibit 10.19, interview three salespeople and determine the level of job satisfaction of each. Explain areas of dissatisfaction and offer suggestions for improving satisfaction.

3. Following is an evaluation of salesperson Sally from the XYZ Corporation that was filled out by her sales manager. The company requires all its sales managers to use this form when evaluating salespeople.

The following scale was used: Almost Never   1   2   3   4   5   Almost Always

	Sally's Score
Asks customers for their ideas for promoting business	2
Offers customers help in solving their problems	1
Is constantly smiling when interacting with customers	4
Admits when she does not know the answer, but promises to find out	4
Generates new ways of tackling new or ongoing problems	1
Returns customers' calls the same day	2
Retains her composure in front of customers	5
Delivers what she promises on time	1
Remains positive about the company in front of customers	5
Knows the design and specification of company products	4
Knows the applications and functions of company products	2
Submits reports on time	2
Maintains company specified records that are accurate and complete	2
Uses expense accounts with integrity	3
Uses business gift and promotional allowances responsibly	3
Controls costs in other areas of the company (order processing and preparation, delivery, etc.) when taking sales orders	3

Identify any problems that you see with Sally and make suggestions for improving her performance. In your analysis, be sure to consider the reasons why Sally may be doing a poor job in some of these areas. How could information like this be used to improve the performance of the sales organization?

ROLE PLAY

4. **Role Play**

   Situation: Look at the evaluation of Sally from question 3. Identify problems you see with Sally.

   Characters: Brandon, sales manager; Sally, salesperson.

   Scene: *Location*—Brandon's office. *Action*—Brandon is discussing Sally's performance evaluation with her. He makes suggestions for improvements.

Sally does not take the suggestions well. She becomes upset. She believes that Brandon is biased against her because she is a woman and lets him know this in no uncertain terms. In fact, she threatens to bring a lawsuit against him.

ROLE PLAY

5. **Role Play**

   Situation: Read the Ethical Dilemma on p. 302.

   Characters: Ralph, Western district sales manager; Lisa, supervising district sales manager and Ralph's boss.

   Scene: *Location*—Ralph's office. *Action*—Lisa is paying a visit to Ralph to solicit his thoughts about Kari Shepherd. She is very excited about Kari and makes suggestions about how she might be evaluated. Ralph discusses his thoughts about Kari and suggests who he thinks would make a good candidate for the sales management position opening up next month.

6. Use the Internet to search for two performance evaluation software packages. You may want to Google "performance evaluation software" or "performance appraisal software." Provide the name of the software package and the company that provides it. Then, list the pros and cons of using each software package to help sales managers evaluate salespeople. Finally, of the two software packages you evaluated, if you were a sales manager, which would you choose to use and why?

MAKING SALES MANAGEMENT DECISIONS

CASE 10.1: WESTERN STEEL FABRICATORS

Background

Kevin Durant is a district sales manager for Western Steel Fabricators, a manufacturer and marketer of a wide variety of steel components for the construction industry. Prior to joining Western, Kevin was a salesperson for one of Western's major competitors. He was recruited and hired by Western partly because of his philosophy on personal selling. Kevin's philosophy is customer-oriented and based on three premises. First, to succeed in sales requires the proper attitude. That is, a salesperson should have a positive, forward-looking, nondefeatist, cooperative attitude. Second, a salesperson should show initiative. Kevin believes "that things don't happen until you take the right actions to make them happen." Third, salespeople should be aggressive, but never manipulative or unethical. Kevin is convinced that honest and ethical behaviors lead to long-term, trusting relationships.

Current Situation

Kevin is now in the process of a year-end evaluation of his salespeople. When the year began, he met with each salesperson to explain the criteria on which their performance would be judged. Several quotas were determined, including a sales dollar quota, new account quota, and sales call quota. The relative importance of each of these quotas was determined by the following weighting system: a weight factor of 4 for new accounts, 3 for sales dollars generated, and 2 for sales calls. It was also explained to the salespeople that their performance would also be evaluated by the number of customer complaints received and by the extent to which they submitted required reports. Finally, salespeople would be judged on their ability to meet customer needs. This includes salespeople's ability to suggest ideas for promoting business, helping customers solve problems, finding answers to customer questions not readily known, returning customers' calls, and delivering what is promised.

At a recent leadership seminar, Kevin learned about the 360-degree performance appraisal process that involves getting feedback from multiple sources. Kevin thought this would be an ideal way to evaluate his salespeople and decided he would have each salesperson give a questionnaire to a customer, a sales team member, and a member of Western's customer service unit to evaluate that salesperson's performance. Each questionnaire contained the following questions: (1) How often did you have contact with this salesperson over the course of the year? (2) Were you able to work closely with this salesperson to satisfy your needs? (3) Overall, how would you evaluate this salesperson's performance? (4) How satisfied are you with this salesperson? The questionnaire was to be signed by the respondent and returned to the salesperson who would then submit it to Kevin for review. Kevin figured that if he noticed something in the responses he did not like, he would discuss it with the salesperson. Kevin thought that evaluating quota achievement would be a fairly straightforward process and that he could easily determine discrepancies and make salespeople aware of their shortcomings.

Questions

1. Assess Kevin's use of 360-degree feedback for performance appraisal. Can you make any suggestions for improving this process?

2. What do you think about the type of feedback Kevin is willing to provide his salespeople? How do you suggest performance feedback be handled?

3. What can Kevin do to ensure that his salespeople make efforts to improve their performance in the areas he deems important?

ROLE PLAY

Role Play

Situation: Read Case 10.1.

Characters: Kevin Durant, district sales manager; Mike Humphreys, regional sales manager

Scene: *Location*—Mike Humphreys' office. *Action*—Humphreys is meeting with Kevin to review how things have been going for him during his first year at Western. Kevin explains his performance review process to Humphreys. Humphreys makes some suggestions for improving Kevin's appraisal methods and performance feedback.

CASE 10.2: CONTOUR PLASTICS

Background

Contour Plastics produces custom molded plastic parts for use by other manufacturers as components in producing automobiles and trucks, household tools and small appliances, and children's toys. Based in Dallas, Contour has been in business for over 30 years and is recognized as a leader in the industry. The company does business throughout North America and employs 360 salespeople. Its sales organization consists of three regions with four districts in each region. There are three regional sales managers and 12 district sales managers.

Last year, Ralph Smith was promoted to district sales manager at Contour Plastics. He had been a salesperson with a competing firm for five years prior to joining Contour two years ago. Ralph was dissatisfied with the work environment at his previous employer, so when he arrived at Contour, he was eager to take on new challenges with a company he viewed as progressive.

Current Situation

As Ralph reflected on his first year as district sales manager, he was concerned. His district had experienced higher-than-expected turnover among his salespeople during the year, and he was puzzled. In his opinion, Contour offered excellent pay and benefits, a cooperative work environment, a challenging and rewarding job, strong company support, and opportunity for promotion.

Although Ralph was very satisfied at Contour, he began to believe that his salespeople might not be as happy. As a salesperson, he had noticed that dissatisfied colleagues' job performance often suffered. However, his salespeople's performance on the whole was not significantly down. Like many salesforces, his salespeople's performances ranged from less than average to outstanding. Nevertheless, he knew the importance of being satisfied. It was job dissatisfaction that led to his departure from his previous job.

In an attempt to measure the level of job satisfaction among his salespeople, Ralph administered INDSALES to his salesforce. When the results were tabulated, he was surprised to find several areas in which salespeople expressed dissatisfaction. Salespeople seemed to be dissatisfied with their pay, thinking that it was low in comparison with what others were getting for similar work in other companies. Much to his dismay, Ralph's salespeople seemed to be dissatisfied with him. They thought that he did not attempt to solicit their ideas about things and did not live up to his promises. Salespeople also expressed their dissatisfaction with the promotion policy, believing that it was unfair. They did not think that promotion was based on ability. Although Ralph was satisfied with the company's training

program, his salespeople were not. Finally, salespeople did not believe they were receiving adequate support from the home office. Although Ralph was surprised and disappointed at the level of dissatisfaction among his salespeople, he was glad he took steps to analyze their job satisfaction. He was eager to take steps to bring about greater satisfaction. Ralph decided to draw up plans for improving satisfaction and present them to his boss at their meeting scheduled for next week.

Questions

1. What steps can Ralph take to increase the level of satisfaction among his salespeople?

2. Rather than examining overall salesforce job satisfaction, what might be a more useful approach to examining salesforce job satisfaction with INDSALES?

3. What do you perceive the relationship to be between job satisfaction and turnover at Contour?

ROLE PLAY

Role Play

Situation: Read Case 10.2.

Characters: Ralph Smith, district sales manager; Bill Jones, regional sales manager and Ralph's boss; Betty Hudson, member of Ralph's salesforce.

Scene 1:   *Location*—Jones's office. *Action*—Ralph explains to Jones his plans for improving satisfaction amongst his salespeople. Jones provides his reaction, including his assessment of Ralph's method for determining salesforce job satisfaction.

Scene 2:   *Location*—in the car en route to a sales call. *Action*—Ralph is accompanying one of his salespeople, Betty Hudson, on a sales call. He asks Betty why his salespeople think he does a poor job soliciting their ideas and following through on promises and how she thinks he could improve in these areas. Betty provides her thoughts and ideas.

C A S E S

315

SPECTRUM BRANDS, INC.:
THE SALESFORCE DILEMMA

> We are in the business of building our strengths by managing brands . . . as retailers get bigger . . . we get bigger to fight fire with fire. I'm now in the business of managing BRANDS, not simply PRODUCTS!

It was November 2005, and Bob Falconi, vice president of sales and marketing for the Canadian division of Spectrum Brands Inc., was sitting in his New Brantford, Ontario office, pondering his next steps regarding his salesforce. During the course of the last year, the company had gone through a number of changes at the global level. Spectrum Brands (Spectrum), a global consumer products company formerly known as Rayovac Corporation, had made a number of acquisitions to diversify and expand its product and brand portfolio. With these changes, Spectrum had become a leading supplier of consumer batteries, lawn and garden care products, specialty pet supplies, and shaving and grooming products.

Falconi, charged with the task of creating a national salesforce from the teams of the newly merged companies, sat in his office trying to make sense of the new business. He knew that creating an effective sales team—one which would capitalize on the synergies across the various businesses—would be very difficult, since these companies each operated differently with regards to the role of their salesforces, customers targeted, and products sold. Knowing the importance of the sales function to each of these companies, Falconi wanted to ensure, despite the differences amongst the diverse groups, that he still maintained a team that would effectively and efficiently continue to increase the sales of each business unit.

The task ahead of him was big, but Falconi knew that a plan needed to be implemented immediately to avoid disrupting the growth momentum of the company's individual brands, to maintain customer relationships, and to preclude competition from taking advantage of any perceived disruptions during this time of change.

THE CONTEXT

The consumer brands industry had become highly competitive on a global basis. Numerous acquisitions and mergers had taken place over the past decade, resulting in a select group of large companies with extensive brand portfolios. These companies had developed numerous product lines that allowed them to compete in a variety of markets and product categories, and also strengthened their relationships with retailers.

With the growth of large retail chains across North America through retail consolidation, the balance of power had shifted away from manufacturers. Small players could no longer compete effectively, as strong relationships with retailers had become essential in order to compete for limited and valuable shelf space within stores. Manufacturers built alliances with other consumer brand companies in order to gain strength and power in the retail market. As a result, companies such as Procter & Gamble (P&G), Unilever, S.C. Johnson, and others with large portfolios of popular consumer brands, dominated the shelves in traditional retail channels including grocery (e.g. Loblaw, Dominion), drug stores (e.g. Shoppers Drug Mart, Katz Group), hardware retailers (e.g. Home Hardware), home and garden retailers (e.g. RONA, The Home Depot) and mass merchandisers (e.g. Wal-Mart). Internet and direct-to-consumer sales had not proven to be valuable alternate channels for these companies, as retailers would retaliate by de-listing products of those manufacturers who tried to go in this direction.

Companies competing against the brands under the umbrellas of these large companies continued to struggle for position and, ultimately, for market

Richard Ivey School of Business
The University of Western Ontario

Joe Falconi wrote this case under the supervision of Professor Don Barclay solely to provide material for class discussion. The authors do not intend to illustrate either effective or ineffective handling of a managerial situation. The authors may have disguised certain names and other identifying information to protect confidentiality.

share, mainly because of the established relationships that these large firms had with the retailers. The trend was towards companies such as Spectrum Brands who had a presence in batteries, shaving and grooming products, lawn and garden products, and specialty pet supplies.

CONSUMER BRANDS MARKETS

Battery Market

North American consumers of household batteries (AAA, AA, C, D and nine-volt standard batteries) sought convenience and quality when purchasing batteries and tended to gravitate towards the brand names they knew and trusted. Duracell and Energizer continued to dominate the market due to their brand recognition, their relationships with distributors and retailers, and their established presence in the large one-time-use alkaline battery category. These two firms were leaders in this market for decades because of their ability to adapt to consumer needs and to merge with other consumer goods companies to create brand portfolios, thus gaining valuable negotiating power with retailers. For example, the Duracell battery brand was owned by the largest and most recognized consumer products company in the world—Procter & Gamble (P&G)—while the Energizer battery brand was owned by Energizer Holdings Inc., which also owned the Shick Razors brand. Each company held a 40 percent market share within the battery industry.

Household batteries were sold through wholesalers, distributors, professionals and OEMs, but the large majority were sold through traditional retail channels. Of these retailers, mass merchandisers, home and garden centers, and niche electronic stores accounted for more than 60 percent of sales.

As of 2005, the alkaline battery was the predominant type of household battery in North America, and was offered by all major competitors in all sizes. The growth within this segment had become relatively flat, at only 1 to 2 percent annually, yet, due to its size, it was expected to dominate the market for the next five to 10 years. In 2005, the overall battery market in Canada was estimated to be $300[1] million, with the alkaline category representing 70 percent, the rechargeable category making up 10 percent, and other battery chemistries, including zinc, representing 20 percent.

The market for household batteries was highly seasonal. The large majority of sales occurred during the months leading up to and following Christmas sales of electronics and other battery-operated devices. Close to 70 percent of battery sales occurred during this period.

[1] All funds are in Canadian dollars unless otherwise indicated.

Shaving and Grooming Products Market

The shaving and grooming products industry was dominated by a select group of companies selling electric shavers and accessories, electric grooming products and hair care appliances. Electric shavers included both rotary and foil designs for men and women, and accessories included replacement parts, pre-shave products and cleaning agents for shavers. Electric grooming products included beard/moustache trimmers, nose and ear trimmers, haircut kits and related accessories. Hair care appliances included hairdryers, setters, curling irons, crimpers, straighteners and hot air brushes.

The shaving and grooming products market was growing at a rate of 3 to 4 percent annually, and this trend was likely to continue. The market for electronic shaving and grooming products was highly seasonal with peaks during the months leading up to and following the Christmas holiday season and around Father's Day and Mother's Day weekends. The majority of these products were purchased as gifts, and thus the sales cycle followed these gift-giving seasons.

The primary competitors in the shaving market included: Norelco, Braun and Remington. Norelco was a division of Koninklijke Philips Electronics (Philips), which was one of the world's biggest electronics companies and the largest one in Europe. Braun was a member of the Gillette family of products which was now part of P&G, while Remington was part of Spectrum. Norelco only sold rotary shavers, Braun only offered foil shavers, while Remington was the only company competing in both segments. Quality, price, and brand awareness were the main factors influencing sales in this segment.

The major competitors in the hair care market were Remington, Norelco, Conair Corporation and Helen of Troy Limited. Each company offered a complete line of hair care products and accessories and competed on quality and price within this category.

Competitors within both of these segments sold their products largely through traditional retail channels with a heavy emphasis on mass merchandisers and specialty retailers such as salons and hair and body care shops. Like all consumer product companies, those firms able to maintain or increase the amount of retail shelf space allocated to their respective products could gain share of mind and, potentially, a share of the market.

Lawn and Garden Market

The lawn and garden market was a U.S.$4 billion industry in North America, with an additional U.S.$1 billion in sales of household insect control products. Companies manufactured and marketed fertilizers, herbicides, outdoor insect control products, rodenticides, plant foods, potting soil, grass seeds, and other growing media. The lawn and garden industry had been driven largely by affluent baby boomers who enjoyed gardening and also by increasing home ownership levels. Growth in this market had been between 4 and 5 percent annually and was expected to continue at this pace. In North America, more than 80 percent of households were participating in at least one lawn and garden activity in 2004.

The main competitors within the lawn and garden segment included: United Industries (United)/Nu-Gro, Scotts Miracle-Gro Company (Scotts) and Central Garden & Pet Company (CGPC). Scotts marketed products under the Scotts and Miracle-Gro brand names. They led this market with a 30 percent market share. CGPC sat behind United with a 17 percent market share. They sold garden products under the Amdro, Image, and Pennington Seed brand names.

Growth in the insect control market had been generated by population growth in the insect-prone Sunbelt region and the heightened awareness of insect-borne diseases such as West Nile virus. Growth in this market had been slightly higher than historical levels since 2002 with a 7 to 8 percent annual growth rate.

In the insect control market, the major competitors included United, Scotts and S.C. Johnson & Son, Inc. Scotts, once again the market leader, sold products under the Ortho and Roundup brand names, while S.C. Johnson marketed their insecticide and repellent products under the Raid and OFF! brands.

Competitors within both of these markets sold mainly through mass merchandisers, home centers, independent nurseries, and hardware stores. Home centers and mass merchandisers typically carried one or two premium brands and one value brand on their shelves. Obtaining and maintaining share of shelf within these retailers was critical, as 50 to 60 percent of sales passed through these two channels.

The lawn and garden market was also highly seasonal. Products were shipped to distributors and retailers beginning as early as March in preparation for the spring season. Demand for products typically peaked during the first six months of the calendar year. This seasonality created a major risk within this industry, as there was a heavy dependence on weather to drive sales. A poor season greatly hindered the bottom line.

Specialty Pet Supply Market

The specialty pet supply industry had historically been one of the fastest growing consumer product categories with annual growth between 6 and 8 percent. This category consisted of aquatic equipment (i.e., aquariums, filters, pumps), aquatic consumables (i.e., fish food, water treatments, conditioners) and specialty pet products for dogs, cats, birds and other small domestic animals. In North America, this was an U.S.$8 billion market in 2004, and was expected to grow to over U.S.$11 billion by 2007.

Much of this growth could be attributed to the increasing levels of pet ownership. On average, households with children under the age of 18, and adults over 55 (who were typically "empty nesters"), tended to keep pets as companions and had more disposable income and leisure time to spend with them. In North America, both of these categories have expanded rapidly with the aging of the baby boomer population. As of 2004, 62 percent of households in the United States owned a pet, and 46 percent owned two or more pets. In addition to these trends, the growing movement towards pet humanization—the tendency of pet owners to treat pets like cherished members of the family—had also factored greatly into this market expansion.

The specialty pet supply industry was highly fragmented. There were over 500 manufacturers in North America, consisting of both small companies with limited product lines and larger firms. No company held a market share of greater than 10 percent. The largest competitors included: CGPC, United Pet Group/Tetra and the Hartz Mountain Corporation. CGPC led the market with a 9 percent market share.

Products within this segment were sold through specialty pet stores, independent pet retailers, mass merchants, grocery stores and through various professional outlets. Mass merchandisers, supermarkets and discounters increasingly supplied pet products, but they focused mainly on a limited selection of items such as pet food. The majority of sales were made through pet supply stores, of which there were over 15,000 in the United States and more than 5,000 in Canada. There were only two national retailers in this industry: PetsMart and PetCo. PetsMart accounted for 10 percent of North American pet product net sales in fiscal 2004. PetCo reflected similar statistics, but no other retailer accounted for more than 8 percent of industry retail sales.

Sales in this segment remained fairly stable throughout the year, since pets needed to be maintained continuously.

COMPETITIVE CONTEXT

In all of these industries, some competitors had gained significant market share and had explicitly committed significant resources to protecting share and/or stealing share from others. In some product lines, competitors had lower production costs and higher profit margins, enabling them to compete more aggressively through advertising and by offering retail discounts and other promotional incentives to retailers, distributors and wholesalers. This aggressive strategy obviously provided additional strength in attracting retailers and consumers. The ability to retain or increase the amount of retail shelf space allocated to their respective products provided competitive advantages in each of these market spaces.

SPECTRUM BRANDS, INC.

Spectrum brands products were available through the world's top 25 retailers, in over one million stores throughout North America, Europe, Asia Pacific, the Middle East, Africa, Latin America, and Brazil. Overall, the company was generating U.S.$2.8 billion in annualized revenues from its brand portfolio (see Exhibits 1 and 2 for Spectrum pre-merger and consolidated financial information).

Similar to its competitors, Rayovac had acquired other consumer brand companies to enhance its ability to gain retail presence. Beginning in 2003, Rayovac acquired Remington Products Inc., a company specializing in consumer shaving and grooming products. In February 2005, Spectrum Brands was created when the Rayovac Corporation acquired United Industries Corporation (a leading U.S. manufacturer of consumer lawn and garden care, and insect control products), Nu-Gro Corporation (the Canadian subsidiary of United, specializing in lawn and garden care products), and Tetra Holdings Inc. (a leading supplier of fish and aquatics supplies). Continued growth and strategic acquisitions allowed the company to leverage global distribution channels, purchasing power, and operational processes. These mergers provided the company with an extended brand portfolio. This allowed all of the brands to access a number of new retailers where they had not previously been able to gain shelf space. In turn,

---

EXHIBIT 1 (Numbers Based on Fiscal Year Ending September)

Rayovac Corporation Net Sales Breakdown

Consolidated Net Sales by Product line (U.S.$ millions)	2005	2004*
Batteries	$968	$939
Lights	$94	$90
Shaving and Grooming	$271	$272
Personal Care	$143	$116
Lawn and Garden	$447	N/A
Household Insect Control	$150	N/A
Pet Products	$286	N/A
Totals	$2,359	$1,417

*United/Nu-Gro was acquired by Rayovac mid-2005

Rayovac & Remington

(US$ millions)	Rayovac		Remington	
	2004	2003	2004	2003*
Net Sales	$1,029	$922	$388	N/A
Gross Profit	42.8%	38.1%	47.0%	N/A
Operating Income	$109	$60	$47	N/A
Net Income	$39	$15	$17	N/A

*Remington was acquired by Rayovac mid-2003

United Industries and Tetra

North America (U.S.$ millions)	United 2005	Tetra 2005
Net Sales from External customers	$787	$96
Segment Profit	$79	$10
SP as % of Net Sales	10.0%	10.4%

Spectrum Brands, Inc. and Subsidiaries Consolidated Statements of Operations (years ended September 30, 2005, 2004) (U.S.$ 000s)		EXHIBIT 2

	2005	2004
Net Sales	$2,359,447	$1,417,186
Cost of goods sold	$1,465,096	$811,894
Restructuring and related charges	$10,496	$(781)
Gross Profit	$883,855	$606,073
Operating Expenses:		
Selling	$473,834	$293,118
General and Administration	$160,382	$121,319
Research and Development	$29,339	$23,192
Restructuring and related charges	$15,820	$12,224
	$679,375	$449,853
Operating Income	$204,480	$156,220
Interest expense	$134,053	$65,702
Other income, net	$(856)	$(14)
Income from continuing operations before taxes	$71,283	$90,532
Income tax expense	$24,451	$34,372
Income from continuing operations	$46,832	$56,160
Loss from discontinued operations, net of tax benefits	$-	$380
Net Income	$46,832	$55,780

Source: 2005 Spectrum Brands Inc. Annual Report.

(continued)

| EXHIBIT 2 | Spectrum Brands, Inc. and Subsidiaries Consolidated Balance Sheets (years ended September 30, 2005, 2004) (U.S.$ 000s) *(continued)* |

Assets

Current Assets:

Cash and cash equivalents	$29,852	$13,971
Receivables:		
Trade A/R, net of allowances	$362,399	$269,977
Other	$10,996	$19,655
Inventories	$451,553	$264,726
Deferred income taxes	$39,231	$19,233
Assets held for sale	$108,174	$9,870
Prepaid expenses and other	$45,762	$51,262
Total Current Assets	$1,047,967	$648,694
Property, plant and equipment, net	$304,323	$182,396
Deferred charges and other	$47,375	$35,079
Goodwill	$1,429,017	$320,577
Intangible assets, net	$1,154,397	$422,106
Debt issuance costs	$39,012	$25,299
Total Assets	$4,022,091	$1,634,151

Liabilities and Shareholder's Equity

Current Liabilities:

Current maturities of LT debt	$39,308	$23,895
Accounts payable	$281,954	$226,234
Accrued liabilities:		
Wages and benefits	$47,910	$40,138
Income taxes payable	$40,468	$21,672
Restructuring and related charges	$16,978	$8,505
Accrued interest	$31,529	$16,302
Liabilities held for sale	$22,294	$-
Other	$76,935	$60,094
Total Current Liabilities	$557,376	$396,840
Long-term debt, net of current maturities	$2,268,025	$806,002
Employee benefit obligations, net of current portion	$78,510	$69,246
Deferred income taxes	$208,251	$7,272
Other	$67,199	$37,368
Total Liabilities	$3,179,361	$1,316,728
Minority interest in equity of consolidated subsidiary	$-	$1,379
Shareholders' equity:		
Common stock	$666	$642
Additional paid-in capital	$671,378	$224,962
Retained earnings	$267,315	$220,483
Accumulated other comprehensive income (loss)	$10,260	$10,621
Notes receivable from officers/shareholders	$-	$(3,605)
	$949,619	$453,103
Less treasury stock, at cost	$(70,820)	$(130,070)
Less unearned restricted stock compensation	$(36,069)	$(6,989)
Total Shareholders' equity	$842,730	$316,044
Total Liabilities and Shareholders' equity	$4,022,091	$1,634,151

Source: 2005 Spectrum Brands Inc. Annual Report.

this increased the ability for each brand to compete within its given markets. Spectrum became the global leader in aquatic supplies; the number two player in the lawn and garden industry, the household insect control market, and the shaving and grooming supplies industry; and the third largest global company in the battery industry (see Exhibit 3 for a list of brand names under the Spectrum label).

Rayovac

Rayovac was the third largest global consumer battery manufacturer in the world—third largest in North America and second largest in Europe. The company sold batteries and flashlights for various household and industrial uses and was the largest worldwide seller of hearing aid batteries. Their battery product line included one-time-use alkaline and

EXHIBIT 3

Nickel Metal Hydride (NiMH) rechargeable batteries available in all standard sizes (AAA, AA, C, D, nine-volt) to compete in the highly saturated but lucrative household market. Globally, Rayovac held a 14 percent market share, with a 20 percent share of the Canadian market. The division generated U.S.$1.5 billion in annual global revenues in 2004.

The company began operations in 1906, but did not introduce the Rayovac name until the 1930s. Their initial focus was on manufacturing specialty batteries for use in such devices as their patented vacuum tube hearing aids. The company expanded and grew through their continued development of state-of-the-art flashlights and non-traditional batteries, including their successful hearing aid battery line. They eventually entered the competitive household battery market through key acquisitions and by capitalizing on existing distributor and retailer relationships. This was long after the market leaders, Duracell and Energizer, had become well-established within this market. Rayovac made great strides over its last few years in an attempt to gain ground. Acquisitions had been made to gain access to international markets including Europe (Varta Battery Corporation acquired in 2002), China (Ningbo Baowang acquired in 2004), and Brazil (Microlite acquired in 2004).

The leaders in this industry had leading brands and thus greater control over distribution channels, retailers and prices. Rayovac had only been able to secure shelf space in a small number of retailers, including Wal-Mart (making up 40 percent of sales), Canadian Tire (15 percent of sales), Home Hardware (10 percent of sales), and other chains and smaller niche retailers such as Toys R' Us, Radio Shack, and others (35 percent of sales).

Remington Products Company

Remington was a leading designer and distributor of consumer shaving and personal care products in North America and the United Kingdom. They marketed a broad line of electric shaving and grooming products for both men and women, as well as hair care products and other personal care items.

Beginning operations in 1936 as a division of Remington Rand, Remington captured a strong position as a global player in the market by developing new innovative shaving products. Before being bought by Rayovac Corporation in 2003, the Remington Electric Shaver Division had been involved in various mergers: merging with the Sperry Corporation in 1955; being bought by entrepreneur Victor Kiam in 1979; and then acquiring Clairol Inc.'s worldwide personal care appliance business in 1993. Through all of these moves, Remington was able to command a 30 percent market share in North America and a 21 percent share in the United Kingdom, with the number one position in men's foil shavers, women's foil shavers, and men's grooming products, and the number two position in men's rotary shavers globally. Remington had become an established name in the industry, achieving global revenues of U.S.$350 million in 2003.

Remington, like Rayovac, sold its products largely through traditional retail channels. The breakdown of retailers was similar to that of Rayovac, with the niche retailers being salons and specialty hair and body care shops.

United Industries Corporation

United Industries Corporation was a leading manufacturer and marketer of professional and consumer lawn and garden care and insect control products. It produced a wide variety of products, including brand name items and private label products for individual retail chains. United also produced and distributed controlled release nitrogen and other fertilizer technologies to the consumer, professional, and golf industries worldwide under various brand names.

United competed in the United States under the United name. In Canada, the company operated under the Nu-Gro Corporation (Nu-Gro) name. United, which began operations in the early 1950s, acquired Nu-Gro in April 2004 to serve as the Canadian arm of the company. Nu-Gro was established in 1988 as an exclusively Canadian lawn and garden company. Both were leaders within their marketplaces, maintaining a number of top-selling brands including Vigoro, Shultz, and CIL.

Within the lawn and garden industry in North America, United/Nu-Gro was the number two company, holding a 23 percent market share. The company targeted consumers who wanted products comparable to and at lower prices than premium-priced brands, and thus positioned their brands as the value alternatives. In 2004, United/Nu-Gro together generated sales of U.S.$550 million in this market.

In the household insect control industry, United/Nu-Gro generated U.S.$150 million in sales in 2004. With their insect control brands, it was again the number two company, with 24 percent market share in North America.

The consumer division for both of these categories sold its products through various retail outlets, including home and garden centers, large home supply retailers, and general mass merchandisers. The sales breakdown was as follows: Canadian Tire (13 percent), Home Depot (9 percent), Rona (7 percent), Lowe's (6 percent), Home Hardware (5 percent), Wal-Mart (3 percent), independent garden retailers (5 percent), other small retailers and garden stores (12 percent), and their professional division made up 40 percent.

The United/Nu-Gro professional division served two major markets: Professional Turf Care Products for golf courses and lawn care companies, and Professional Pest Control Products and Animal Health Products for pest control operators and farms (making up 25 and 15 percent respectively of the company's overall sales). This division had its own dedicated salesforce and marketing team to manage the diverse needs of the professional customers.

United was also a leading supplier of quality products to the pet supply industry in the United States, under the United Pet Group (UPG) name. UPG operated in the fragmented U.S. pet supply market, manufacturing and marketing premium-branded pet supplies for dogs, cats, fish, birds, and other small animals. Products included: aquarium kits, stand-alone tanks, filters and related items, and other aquarium supplies and accessories, as well as pet treats and supplies. This division was number two in North America, with an 8 percent market share and annual revenues in 2004 totaling U.S.$250 million (figure includes Tetra sales). This division sold its products through large mass merchandisers, while also targeting the larger pet supply chains of PetsMart and PetCo, and the considerable number of independent pet supplies stores.

Tetra Holdings

Tetra Holdings was a global supplier of fish and aquatic supplies, operating in over 90 countries worldwide and holding leading market positions in Germany, Japan, the United States and the United Kingdom. They manufactured, distributed, and marketed a comprehensive premier line of foods, equipment and care products for fish and reptiles, along with accessories for home aquariums and ponds.

Tetra was founded in Germany in the early 1950s, pioneering the development of flake fish foods. The company grew into one of the most recognized global brand names in the pet supplies industry. In addition to the products they offered, they also published hundreds of books on aquarium fish keeping, reptile and amphibian keeping, and water gardening.

Tetra was acquired by United Industries in early 2004, joining the UPG division. Despite the merger, United maintained separate operations for each brand with the exception of combining administrative functions. UPG only operated in the United States, while Tetra operated globally. These groups together held the number two position in the North American pet supply market, with 8 percent market share. Like UPG, Tetra sold its products through large mass merchandisers, while also targeting the larger pet supply chains (PetsMart and PetCo) and smaller pet supplies stores in the countries in which it operated.

BOB FALCONI

Bob Falconi completed his Executive MBA program at the Richard Ivey School of Business in 1990. He had been involved in the battery business for 27 years, working his first 16 with Duracell, where he became vice president of sales. He left Duracell in 1995 for a new start-up battery company, Pure Energy Battery Corporation, which introduced a revolutionary new rechargeable alkaline battery system. He left Pure Energy in 1999 to serve as country manager for Rayovac Canada, and had then taken on the role of vice president of sales and marketing for Spectrum. Throughout his career, he had developed a keen understanding of brand management, and had been given the responsibility within Spectrum to leverage his experiences.

REASONS FOR THE ACQUISITIONS

Through the evolution into Spectrum Brands, Rayovac had become a channel marketer, and purveyor of specialty brands. The Rayovac Corporation had

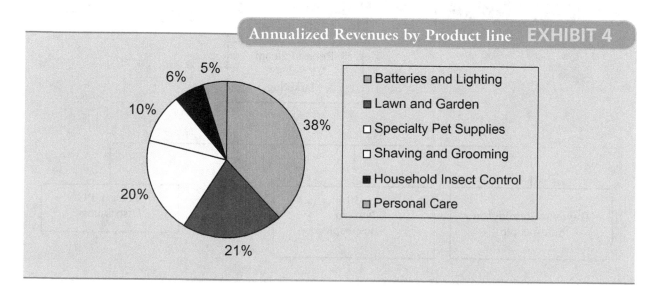

Annualized Revenues by Product line   EXHIBIT 4

- Batteries and Lighting — 38%
- Lawn and Garden — 21%
- Specialty Pet Supplies — 20%
- Shaving and Grooming — 10%
- Household Insect Control — 6%
- Personal Care — 5%

been painted into a corner in the competitive battery market due to its lack of retail strength. In order to compete on a larger scale, greater power within retail channels was required. The company had continually looked for potential acquisitions where it felt that it could add value to the company's operations while at the same time creating a larger and more powerful combined company. Rayovac's goal was to grow through acquisitions that diversified and increased its revenue base while leveraging its strengths and capabilities in global merchandising and distribution.

With the Remington merger, there were many similarities between the two companies in terms of marketing and channel strategies. However, the systems Remington had in place to manage logistic processes were outdated and inefficient. Rayovac saw this as an opportunity to add value to this company through the sharing of best practices. Rayovac acquired Remington and was able to update the company's logistic processes and systems and improve the overall operations of the firm. Through this merger, Rayovac was able to drive U.S.$35million in annual costs out of the combined enterprise while adding the Remington revenues to Rayovac's top line.

With the recent United/Nu-Gro/Tetra acquisitions, Rayovac was looking to continue its growth and expand into new product categories. New products would provide increased negotiating strength with the larger retailers while diversifying the company's revenue base. For example, with this merger, worldwide battery sales represented approximately 40 percent of revenue as compared to the 2004 level of 67 percent. More importantly, the merger served to balance out the sales cycle for the firm given the different seasonalities of the various categories—this meant no down time for the salesforce.

Finally, Spectrum Brands had at least one brand in all of the major retailers in the world, a situation they hoped to leverage into having other brands in many retailers (see Exhibit 4 for annualized revenues by product category).

THE ISSUE

As Falconi looked through his notes on his individual Canadian business units and their competitive markets, he questioned how best to organize the new salesforce in order to capitalize on the strengths of each brand, given the similarities and differences between them. He knew that with the recent acquisitions, the company was looking to leverage any synergies created and reduce costs where possible. However, as overarching objectives, he wanted to make sure that customers would be serviced in the same fashion, if not better, and that sales would not be affected. Falconi decided to take a look at how each business unit currently operated, and how some of their major competitors were organized (see Exhibit 5 for a post-merger organizational chart).

THE CURRENT SALESFORCES

Rayovac and Remington

In Canada, the Rayovac/Remington salesforce was currently organized by distribution channel. The eight sales representatives serving this division were responsible for selling all products under both the Rayovac and Remington brand names to their assigned retailers. This was a small sales team, but it had tremendous support from the U.S. office for large accounts, as well as for marketing and trade promotion campaign design. Sales targeted towards hearing aid professionals and industrial and OEM distributors were handled from the U.S. office.

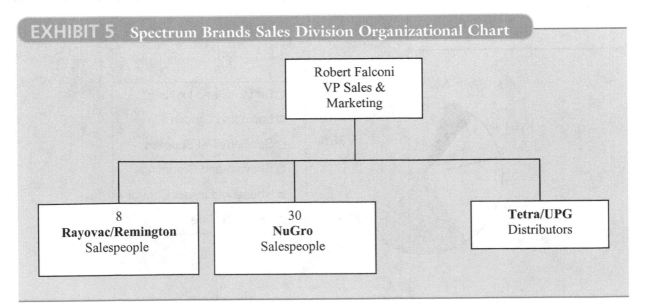

EXHIBIT 5   Spectrum Brands Sales Division Organizational Chart

These sales representatives were organized geographically as well. The allocation was as follows: six in Toronto, and one in each of Vancouver and Montreal. Each representative was responsible for the retailers in their regions. Toronto had a greater number of corporate head offices, thus requiring more representatives to service these accounts.

The average base salary for these sales reps was approximately $70,000, with an overall employee expenditure budget of around $900,000 annually, including bonuses. With these representatives, this division was able to generate a 2004 sales volume of over $50 million in Canada.

Overall, this salesforce had worked well for the company. The division had been able to minimize the size of the salesforce while still achieving their sales goals in an effective and efficient manner.

Nu-Gro

In a similar fashion, Nu-Gro operated customer-focused teams made up of 30 consumer sales reps. Logistics were a very important element within the lawn and garden industry, as shipping costs for these products were significant. For example, a trailer shipment of fertilizer could have a maximum of 1,500 bags valued at $3 a bag, while the same trailer could ship $1 million worth of batteries. As a result, sales reps for Nu-Gro needed to plan carefully with customers in order to minimize costs by ensuring full truck shipments.

As with Rayovac/Remington, sales representative were distributed geographically to service key Canadian locations: seventeen in Ontario, six in Vancouver, three in Montreal, and two in each of Calgary and Winnipeg.

The average base salary for these sales reps was slightly lower than for Rayovac/Remington representatives at $60,000, with an overall employee expenditure budget of approximately $2 million annually, including bonuses. With these sales reps, this division was able to generate a 2004 sales volume of more than $105 million in Canada.

Nu-Gro, however, had been struggling as the company's operations and product offerings were extremely unfocused. Over the past five years, the company had acquired a large number of their smaller competitors and had accumulated their associated brands under the Nu-Gro umbrella. As a result, Nu-Gro experienced a proliferation of products and brands (see Exhibit 6). There were strong arguments to stay in underperforming categories, including contribution toward fixed manufacturing costs, improved transportation economics and account control. On the other hand, the significant working capital required to support these underperforming products could not justify keeping them. Brand and SKU rationalization was needed, and a target of up to a 50 percent reduction over a one-year period was being considered. Ultimately, a more focused product portfolio would facilitate the efforts of the salesforce.

In addition to the large SKU offerings, the sales team was forced to target a wide variety and large number of customers with these brands, including both the large mass retailers and the small "mom and pop" garden stores. These efforts were very time-consuming and uneconomical for the sales team, as the majority of stores were of the smaller garden shop variety that ordered limited quantities.

The professional division that served the two major lawn and garden markets had been fairly successful in the past through its strong established relationships. The salesforce for this division had and would continue to remain independent from Spectrum's consumer (retail) sales division. Nu-Gro

EXHIBIT 6

Major	#SKUs	Revenue By Type/Category		Contribution Margin %	
		$M	% Total	$M	% Sales
Fertilizers	752	29.8	36.40	3.9	13.20
Pesticides	234	21.9	26.80	5.5	25.20
Soils	176	12.3	15.00	0.2	1.30
Seed	143	9	11.00	0.2	1.80
Other	92	8.8	10.80	0.3	10.40
Grand Total	**1,397**	**$82**	**100.00**	**$10**	**12.30**

maintained a separate salesforce beyond the 30 consumer representatives exclusive to this division.

Overall, Nu-Gro's consumer sales operations needed adjustment. A strategy that refocused the sales team's efforts on their large and more important areas, while still finding a way to reach their current customer base, was required to turn this division around.

Tetra/United Pet Group

The salesforce for this division in the United States was regionally based so that each sales rep could ensure an ample supply of product for their distributors and dealers. These sales representatives were responsible for the large accounts such as PetsMart and PetCo, mass merchandisers such as Wal-Mart, and the large number of smaller specialty retailers.

However, in Canada, sales for this division were handled by distributors. These distributors were responsible for the sales to the highly fragmented Canadian specialty pet retailer market. They offered the same services that an internal salesforce could provide, including organizing special promotions and setting up in-store displays. Ultimately, they were able to generate sales from a large number of smaller players more economically than a small internal sales team could. The sales managers for Rayovac/Remington and Nu-Gro were responsible for managing these distributors. The larger retail accounts were managed by the U.S. sales team but serviced by these distributors.

Sales Management

Of the 38 sales reps between the Rayovac/Remington and Nu-Gro divisions, four of them filled the roles of sales manager, two managers for each division. Each rep/manager was responsible for the various representatives in their specific geographic regions. They spent 65 percent of their time selling to their own individual accounts. The remaining 35 percent was spent managing reps, managing distributors, forecasting, strategic planning and analysing their market. For each division, one rep/manager was responsible for the sales reps in the large Ontario market, while the other managed the sales reps in the rest of the country. Regardless of structure of the sales operation going forward, Falconi would likely organize around three regions—the West, Ontario and the East—with one manager responsible for the sales reps within each region. This, of course, raised the issue of the surplus manager and would provide an opportunity to reconsider the incumbents.

COMPETITOR ORGANIZATIONS

Falconi wanted to look at how some of Spectrum's competitors organized their salesforces within Canada. He decided to select a few of the major players from each industry as comparison points. Koninklijke Philips Electronics and P&G operated their sales divisions by product category. Each category had its own dedicated salesforce further divided by specific retail channels and/or customer, depending on the size of the retailer. For example, Norelco's salesforce was responsible exclusively for shaving and grooming products and did not cross-sell other Philips brands such as televisions. Similarly, Braun sales reps would sell both the Braun and Gillette shaving brands, Duracell would have its own sales team, but neither group would cross-sell other P&G brands. In certain circumstances, one purchasing manager for a retailer such as Wal-Mart might deal with a sales rep from each product category but these sales reps would deal exclusively with Wal-Mart as a customer. In other circumstances, the sales reps would interface with different purchasing managers in those retailers where the purchasing function was organized by category.

Both Scotts and CGPC operated their sales divisions in a different manner. Their salesforces were organized by product category, but covered all retail channels. Thus, they had specific sales reps for categories such as fertilizers, soils and seeds, insect control products, and pet supplies (CGPC only), but each sales rep would service clients across multiple channels. Like Philips and P&G, these companies had developed a salesforce with product category expertise, yet they did not concentrate an individual sales rep on a specific retailer.

Due to the size and strength of each of these companies, they had been successful at developing a "pull" strategy with the consumers. Retailers were almost mandated to support and sell these companies' products because of the consumer demand created. In addition, the salesforces had developed strong relationships with retailers, the "push" component.

SALESFORCE OPTIONS

Looking forward, Falconi wanted to evaluate his options regarding how to organize his salesforce to see what alternatives or combinations made sense to Spectrum's operations and the market characteristics.

Separate Salesforces

Maintaining a separate salesforce for each brand line would offer Spectrum the greatest degree of expertise on each brand. These sales reps were already familiar with, and had extensive knowledge about, their brands and would require little, if any, additional training. Sales reps could continue to operate as they already did, and maintain the momentum they had already generated for their product lines. Ultimately, such an organization would allow for a more focused salesforce in that representatives would be in a better position to answer product-related questions and offer product educational services.

On the other hand, maintaining separate salesforces would not take advantage of the synergies that the recent merger had created for the company. There would be little to no expense reduction, as the existing sales rep levels would likely be maintained. In addition, this organization would not offer any efficiency improvements in the use of sales reps during slower seasonal periods. Finally, there would be a significant duplication of efforts as Spectrum would have multiple sales reps calling on the same retailer at any given time.

Merged Salesforce

With a merged salesforce, Spectrum would essentially move to a "one bag" sales rep approach, in that each representative would be responsible for becoming an expert on all product lines and selling every brand to their specified customers. With this option, Falconi would have to define each sales rep's responsibilities relating to whether or not the representative would cover all customers in a geographic area, or be responsible for a specific retail group or nationwide chain.

As with the separate salesforce option, the "one bag" sales rep would offer Spectrum numerous benefits. First, Spectrum would be able to capitalize on the potential synergies of the merger as Rayovac did with the Remington acquisition and integration. With each representative selling the entire Spectrum product line, there would be the opportunity to cross-promote brands, leveraging the strong relationships that certain brands have with particular retailers to sell and promote the other lines. This is especially important, as Spectrum tries to gain presence for all their lines within each major retailer across the country.

Additionally, Falconi would be able to consolidate the existing teams into a smaller unit. Responsibilities for individual retailers could be handled by one or two sales reps selling the entire portfolio of brands, rather than one representative for each individual brand. For example, there are certain customers to whom each business unit has been selling products, including Wal-Mart, the Home Depot, RONA, Canadian Tire, as well as many others across the country. Overall, by merging the salesforce, it is estimated that Spectrum would be able to reduce the salaries and bonus expense to approximately $2 million for the entire Canadian sales division.

Finally, a merged salesforce would create a more efficient team to cope with the seasonality issues inherent in the industries in which Spectrum operates. Sales reps would always have something going on with one of the portfolio brands, allowing them to be in constant contact with retail purchasers.

While there are many benefits to this approach for a diversified company like Spectrum, there could be great difficulty in creating an effective and efficient merged team. First, with the addition of numerous new brands to the company's portfolio, sales reps would need to develop an expertise for a large number of brands and products. In addition, the new products they would be selling are completely different from the current brand category they have experience with (i.e., a battery sales rep selling fertilizer). Additional training would be required for all sales reps to educate them on the unfamiliar brands. This training could ultimately be costly and take a substantial amount of time.

Given the variety of products and brands under the Spectrum name, a merged salesforce may prove to be highly unfocused. A representative may be incapable of attaining a sufficient knowledge base about every product line, or have too much going on to give each brand the necessary focus needed to sustain its current sales levels. This could hinder sales and effectively kill the existing momentum of the brands.

Distributors

Distributors provide sales and logistic services to firms in exchange for commission fees. Such firms are typically hired by smaller companies with limited sales reach, or by companies who are entering new geographic markets but do not yet have a sales team in place. They usually have an advantage over these types of companies as they are well-established, they have existing relationships with retailers, and they operate large sales groups that can service a large number of customers. They typically serve a variety of manufacturers, and thus are able to operate such a sales process in an efficient manner. As a result, distributors are typically given the task of reaching the large number of smaller retailers that prove to be too costly for a small salesforce to target, while the manufacturer's internal sales team targets the smaller number of large customers that contribute greater individual sales.

Though there are many benefits to using professional distributors as the company's salesforce, there are drawbacks as well. The costs associated with these services can be substantial relative to an internal salesforce. The cost of sales through a distributor is approximately 15 percent against revenues, while it is 2 to 3 percent with an internal salesperson. As a result, successful firms that are able to establish large sales teams can ultimately generate sales at a lower cost.

Other Alternatives and Considerations

While each of these alternatives would provide Spectrum with benefits in particular areas, Falconi knew that creating a salesforce based on a combination of one or more of these elements might generate greater returns for the company. For example, one option would be to use a combination of a merged salesforce and distributors in order to reach both large and small retailers more effectively. Another option could be to create "platform teams," where one business manager would be responsible for maintaining the relationships with the retailers, while a group of product experts support the manager during sales pitches. Falconi wanted to further explore these opportunities, and others, to see what benefits might be derived.

Falconi knew that before any changes could be made to the sales strategy, selecting his sales managers would be the first essential step. He would need to ensure that he had the right people in this role, whether they were the current managers or new ones. These individuals would serve as the leaders for the overall salesforce, ensuring continued momentum and performance of the representatives. They would also be the "change agents" responsible for implementing the plans developed by Falconi for any reorganization. If there was a new strategy implemented, Falconi would have to decide how to judge these managers and how best to use them given the chosen system.

Falconi realized he would have to consider the impact that this major change would have on the current employees. The employees recognized that, with such a merger, the company would look for potential synergies to reduce overall company expenses. Other companies in similar situations have typically looked to consolidate employee positions as one option to reduce costs. If there was to be a merger of the sales teams, Falconi would be responsible for selecting the best candidates for the new organization, meaning that nobody's job was safe. As a result, employees from both the Rayovac/Remington and Nu-Gro divisions would be feeling very apprehensive at this point. People are often averse to change and the sales reps would be concerned about their future employment status and the implications of any forthcoming changes to the company.

Falconi knew that dealing with the sensitivities of his employees would be crucial to achieving a successful implementation of a new sales strategy, if, indeed, the company chose to proceed with that option. Changes would need to be made while the company was still in operation; thus, care needed to be given to these issues in order to avoid potential disturbances and to preserve the current momentum of the business. Falconi realized that change management skills would definitely be required to implement a new structure, or to alleviate concerns if no changes were planned, but he wondered how best to deal with these issues moving forward.

Finally, Falconi needed to decide how many sales reps should be kept if a new strategy was to be implemented and by what criteria he should be judging his representatives. He knew that the sufficient number of sales reps would depend on the chosen direction of the salesforce strategy, but he wondered what his team would look like once the dust had settled.

DECISION

Given the nature of the new company, and the industries each business unit competed in, Falconi was unsure what salesforce structure would offer the company the greatest benefits, at the same time allowing it to grow its sales and gain a greater retail presence for the entire Spectrum brand portfolio. How should the new company be structured in terms of reporting, responsibilities and the size of the salesforce? Should Spectrum try to structure itself similarly to its competitors, or did their operation require a different approach?

Additionally, depending on which salesforce structure was selected, Falconi would have to consider how to organize the teams relative to Spectrum's retail customers. He could organize them by geography, by retail channel, by individual retailers, by some combination of these or by another method altogether. Falconi would have to explore the benefits of the options and determine what made the most sense.

The board of directors was meeting next week and Falconi wanted to present them with a full report outlining his proposed strategy regarding the salesforce, and why the other alternatives were dismissed. Overall, Falconi knew that a decision would need to be made quickly in hopes that the new salesforce strategy could be implemented prior to the peak period for the lawn and garden industry. Falconi knew that sufficient time would be needed to implement changes and initiate any training that might be required for the sales team.

BIOMED CO., LTD.: DESIGNING A NEW SALES COMPENSATION PLAN

Ponlerd Chiemchanya had just completed his MBA at the Ivey Business School in May 2006. On the one hand, he was excited about rejoining Biomed Co., Ltd. (Biomed), the family business in Thailand. On the other hand, as the new general manager of Biomed, he had some concerns about the first major decisions he was about to make and implement upon his return. Biomed's parent company, Thai Drugs Co., Ltd. (Thai Drugs), had just revised Biomed's market strategy, a change that created the need to realign the sales compensation system to fit with the new strategy. Chiemchanya was charged with this responsibility. Since Biomed was fundamentally a sales organization working on behalf of Thai Drugs, he knew that getting this right could be the making of Biomed. Of course the opposite also held true. Chiemchanya saw high company risk and high personal risk in this situation.

THE CURRENT SITUATION AT BIOMED

Thai Drugs, a family-owned business, was one of the 170 small-to-medium-sized local Thai pharmaceutical manufacturers. It was overshadowed by the five large firms that accounted for over 50 percent of local manufacturers' sales, and also by foreign manufacturers that accounted for 65 percent of the Thai pharmaceutical market. Thai Drugs' main strength was in the over-the-counter market, selling to drugstores. In 1990, Thai Drugs started to use existing manufacturing capacity to expand into the generic pharmaceutical market. Overall, it provided more than 100 items of prescription and non-prescription drugs to hospitals, drugstores, and clinics.

Biomed was set up as a subsidiary of Thai Drugs and acted as Thai Drugs' sole agent to sell generic pharmaceuticals to the market. Biomed was basically a sales organization, comprising a sales manager, 11 sales representatives, and several sales administration clerks. Despite the total market size of THB14 billion[1] for locally manufactured generics, Biomed sales had been hovering around THB10 million (.07 percent market share). When compared to the over-the-counter arm of Thai Drugs, Biomed sales were minimal. Due to the unsophisticated information systems at Thai Drugs, it was not possible to determine whether these sales were even profitable. This had been of concern to Thai Drugs's management for the past few years.

This concern was exacerbated when changes in GMP (Good Manufacturing Practice)[2] requirements were expected to be effective in 2008, leading to a massive investment to upgrade manufacturing facilities. Most of this investment was to be tied to the manufacturing of Biomed products. Biomed's cost of capital, at 10 percent, had to be considered here. Biomed also knew that it had to cover THB4 million annually in fixed overhead. Given the small market share and small margins in the generics market and the upcoming investment required, management was starting to question the viability of Biomed.

Would it be worth investing in the manufacturing facilities when Biomed may not sell the products? Was Biomed's sales volume actually generating profits? Could Biomed do better, given the market size? Would it be better to close Biomed altogether? These were the questions that management was asking while Chiemchanya was away completing his MBA.

[1] The exchange rate was $1 U.S. = 38.25 Thai Baht (THB) in mid-2006.
[2] GMP is a set of regulations, codes and guidelines for the manufacture of drugs, medical devices, etc.

Richard Ivey School of Business
The University of Western Ontario

Version: (A) 2009-09-14

Management did decide to make an effort to increase Biomed's sales and profitability. To accomplish this, management evaluated the situation and changed Biomed's market strategy. If this was not successful over the next one to two years, Thai Drugs might close down Biomed and abandon the generic pharmaceutical market altogether. Chiemchanya needed to understand what was behind this management decision. He needed to examine the industry, the old market strategy and the existing sales compensation plan, and the new market strategy before he could design an appropriate sales compensation plan.

THE THAI GENERIC PHARMACEUTICAL MARKET

Market Size

With a population of 65 million people in Thailand, the total domestic market for pharmaceuticals (local and foreign companies combined), in 2002 figures, was around U.S.$900 million or THB40 billion at wholesale prices. Foreign companies and their original products accounted for 65 percent of the market. Local Thai companies accounted for the remaining 35 percent of the market. Since all of the Thai manufacturers were formulating drugs but were not involved in the research and development (R&D) of new drugs, 35 percent was a representative figure for the local generic market. This resulted in a THB14 billion market for generics.

Manufacturers

Beyond the top five generics manufacturers, the market was fragmented. There were 175 Thai manufacturers, providing drugs to the THB14 billion market. Five companies accounted for more than 50 percent of the market (see Exhibit 1). The remaining 50 percent of the market was shared among 170 manufacturers, which were small private or family-owned businesses.

Market Segments

Hospitals

According to 2002 figures, hospitals accounted for 70 percent of the market for domestically manufactured pharmaceuticals. In April 2001, the government implemented the "30-baht universal health care" scheme whereby everyone received universal health care at hospitals by paying THB30 per visit. This new scheme put pressure on public hospitals. Under this scheme, hospitals received funding on a per-capita basis, as opposed to having 100 percent funding of a hospital's annual expenditures. Public hospitals were forced to find ways to cut costs in order to manage and service patients within budget. This led to a dramatic increase in generic substitution. Most hospitals automatically substituted all original products with generics whenever there was a generic version available.

There were two major implications for generic manufacturers resulting from the 30-baht scheme. First, the new government scheme favored generic manufacturers due to the substitution of branded products by generics. However, the second implication worked against these manufacturers. Hospitals in the same province and region collectively formed buying groups to bargain for the lowest generic prices. The process started with sellers proposing their price in a bidding process. The provider with the lowest price would win the bid and then became the primary provider of the drug throughout the province or region. The second and third runners-up would be back-up providers. The result was that only those few providers with the lowest costs could sell to public hospitals and make a profit. Manufacturers that did not have low-cost structures, or who were not interested in pursuing low-cost strategies, could sell only those low-volume products that did not end up in a bidding process. They could also decide to simply abandon this market.

EXHIBIT 1 Top Five Thai Drug Manufacturers

Manufacturer	Sales (million THB)	Market Share
Siam Bhaesaj	1,975	14%
GPO	1,702	12%
Biolab	1,468	10%
Berlin Pharm	1,261	9%
Thai Nakorn Patana	963	7%
Total of top five	7,369	53%
Total generics market	14,000	100%

Source: epsicom business intelligence, World pharmaceutical markets: Thailand, March 2004.

Drugstores

From 2002 figures, drugstores accounted for most of the remaining 30 percent of the market for domestically manufactured pharmaceuticals. There were an estimated 11,000 drugstores in Thailand, most of which were privately owned by pharmacists or were "mom and pop"-style pharmacies. Although there were foreign drugstore chains (e.g., Boots, Watson's), these chains were geared more towards selling beauty products and food. When drugs were prescribed in chains, most of the time the original-version drug would be used. Most generics were prescribed through privately owned drugstores.

Patients viewed drugstores as a cheap and convenient alternative compared to a visit to the hospital or a doctor's clinic. Pharmacists in drugstores had the autonomy to prescribe prescription drugs without a prescription from a physician. This latitude made drugstores a good choice for people with lower incomes, since they could receive an immediate diagnosis and prescription while avoiding waiting times and doctors' fees. Generics were widely prescribed in drugstores due to their lower cost. Drugstores purchased generics either through distributors or directly from a manufacturer such as Biomed.

Doctor Clinics

The market for drugs in clinics was relatively small when compared to hospitals and drugstores. Doctor clinics held drug inventory to service their patients. Patients were diagnosed and given medicine at the clinic. Most clinics were privately owned by the attending doctor. Generics were also widely used in clinics due to their lower cost. Generics were purchased through either distributors or directly from the manufacturer.

BIOMED'S MARKET STRATEGY

Management looked at Biomed's existing market strategy and found a disconnect between the strategy and the changing market environment.

Existing Market Strategy for Generics

Biomed's overall value proposition to customers was to provide high-quality drugs backed by excellent service.

Market Focus

Biomed targeted all three markets (hospitals, drugstores, and clinics) throughout Thailand. There was no specific strategy to emphasize one market segment over another.

Products

Biomed offered more than 100 items of generic products covering almost all types of drugs, e.g., analgesics, antibiotics, vitamins, allergy and respiratory drugs, electrolytes and supplements, gastrointestinal drugs, topical agents, and pediatric drugs. Most Biomed products were undifferentiated, commodity-type products. A typical example was Amoxycillin 500 mg × 1,000 capsules packaged in a plain plastic container. However, a small percentage of Biomed's product line was geared more towards drugstores and clinics. These products had some degree of differentiation, mostly in the unique color and shape of tablets or capsules. Due to the low education level of the general population, drugstores and clinics that prescribed drugs with unique appearances could have a competitive advantage in the community, since the patient would come back to the drugstore/clinic asking for "the drug," which he or she could not find anywhere else.

Price

Biomed products were priced in the medium-high to high range of the generics market. Volume discounts were offered on a case-by-case basis. Biomed seldom used aggressive price promotions with its customers. It could not afford price discounts because of its lack of economies of scale in production, which led to a high unit cost, based on full cost accounting.

Distribution

Biomed utilized third-party transportation companies to deliver products directly to customers. Biomed was not in a position to incur additional costs by using distributors.

Communications

The Biomed salesforce was the single contact and means of communication with the customer. No other means of advertising (journal ads, television ads, radio ads) were employed.

Existing Sales Strategy

Sales Role

Given that the sales representative was the only person who touched the customer, the role of the salesperson was complex. The current role and goals could be described as:

- Generate sales according to quota.
- Find new accounts.
- Build and maintain relationships between customers and Biomed.
- Negotiate prices with customers within a given range.
- Decide whether customers should receive 30-day credit or 60-day credit.
- Take orders.
- Listen to customer complaints and provide feedback to management.
- Gain and share market intelligence.

Existing Compensation Plan

The existing compensation plan had three components:

Salary: The current salary was THB5,000 per month (THB60,000 annually).

Commission: Sales reps received 1.5 percent of sales volume with a progressive ramp. Sales above 100 percent of targeted annual sales were compensated at 3 percent. Targeted annual sales per rep were THB2 million, on average.

Quarterly bonus: A bonus was paid at the end of each quarter if the year-to-date sales quota was achieved for the quarter. This bonus was retroactively paid whenever year-to-date sales reached quotas.

Overall, the compensation package was on par with the rest of the industry (see Exhibit 2).

Expenses

Each sales representative received a basic allowance of THB380 per day. This was to cover all costs, e.g., fuel, hotel costs, entertainment expenses, and cell phone. This level of allowance typically covered a basic hotel room and daily meals. No additional expenses were reimbursed. The expense allowance had an incentive portion. Regardless of territory, if year-to-date sales reached a certain level, the daily allowance would increase as follows:

Sales Volume YTD (THB)	Allowance/day
0–500,000	THB380
500,000–1,000,000	THB420
1,000,000–2,000,000	THB460
2,000,000 and above	THB500

Other Benefits

Sales reps were entitled to the same basic benefits as other Thai Drugs employees. This included a medical insurance plan and a company contribution of 7 percent of salary to the provident (retirement) fund.

Strategy Review

In assessing the existing strategy against the current environment, management found two major flaws. The first concerned a lack of direction in terms of product/market focus, and the second concerned price.

There was no discipline in approaching the three different market segments (hospitals, drugstores, doctor clinics). Sales representatives called on any customer where they thought they could generate sales. Management came to believe that Biomed's products were not suitable for hospitals. Since most hospitals used a bidding process to purchase drugs, only the lowest cost providers could win in this segment. Given Thai Drugs' limitation in terms of increasing manufacturing efficiency, and given management's preference not to compete solely on price, it was felt that the hospital segment should not be a target.

Complementing this view was that Biomed actually had strength in the drugstore segment. Since Biomed sales representatives could also sell Thai Drugs' leading over-the-counter products, which were in demand in drugstores, Biomed sales representatives could leverage this to get in the door and start a conversation with the owner. Moreover, some of Biomed's products were already designed for drugstores. Thus, it would be sensible, both from a product standpoint and a sales standpoint, to focus more on drugstores and clinics.

EXHIBIT 2   Existing Compensation Plan

Component	Base Salary with Commission and Bonus		
Base Salary	THB60,000		
Commission on sales volume*	Performance To Goal		Commission rate
	To 100%		1.5%
	Beyond 100%		3%
		Performance	Bonus
Quarterly bonus	Q1	Achieve 100% of Q1 YTD Goal	THB3,000
	Q2	Achieve 100% of Q1-2 YTD Goal	THB4,000
	Q3	Achieve 100% of Q1-3 YTD Goal	THB5,000
	Q4	Achieve 100% of Q1-4 YTD Goal	THB6,000
*Bonus for previous quarters are retro-backed when YTD goal is achieved			

Sales were credited when money was collected.

As to the second observation, Biomed's existing strategy was to price at a medium-high to high price point. This was based on the belief that customers would pay a premium price in exchange for good service and a rewarding relationship with Biomed. Management was becoming concerned that this was no longer a compelling argument. In selling commodity-type products, having a competitive price is the No. 1 key success factor. This did not mean that Biomed would have to have the lowest price, since some customers were willing to pay more as long as the price was not too high, the seller had a good relationship, and good service was provided. However, if the price was out of the acceptable range, no matter how good the relationship or service level were, the value to the customer would not justify the higher price.

New Market Strategy

Although management decided on changes in market focus, products and price, the overall value proposition would remain the same, i.e., high-quality products backed by excellent service. The key changes inherent in the new market strategy were:

Product Market Focus

From the strategy review, management decided that Biomed's products could not compete in the low-price hospital market. The new product market focus was to be on drugstores and doctor clinics.

Product

Instead of selling more than 100 items, the new strategy was to focus on only 10 to 15 items and to reduce the prices on these select items. The rationale was that by focusing on the right items at the right price, it would be possible to gain larger orders with two subsequent benefits. First, Biomed would lose fewer orders because of price. Second, combining large orders of fewer items would make it possible to have longer production runs. This would yield economies of scale and lower the unit cost of these selected products. This would lead to more contribution and provide more room if further price cuts were required.

The items selected would have three main characteristics. From a cost perspective, there must be enough room to be able to lower the price to the same range as competitors. Since Thai Drugs had strength in manufacturing sugar coated tablets and formulating multivitamins, which were skills that not all manufacturers had, these drugs would be preferred over other basic tablets and capsules. Finally, products that had sold well in the past were also good candidates, since it meant that customers valued these products as high-quality products.

Price

Selling prices would be reduced to the low-medium to medium price range. However, not all prices would be reduced. Price reductions would tie into the reduced set of products upon which Biomed decided to focus.

THE NEW MARKET STRATEGY AND BIOMED'S SALES STRATEGY

After digesting the new strategy, Chiemchanya was in a position to think about the implications for Biomed's sales strategy. Before jumping into redesigning the compensation system, he knew that it made sense to review the overall implications for the sales strategy, and then to revisit the role of the sales rep under the new strategy. (See Exhibit 3 for a visualization of the new market strategy.)

Implications for the Sales Strategy

In the new market strategy, the biggest changes included reducing market scope, lowering selected prices, focusing on 10 to 15 items, and the resulting challenge of generating both volume and THB contribution from this sharper product/market focus. Chiemchanya thought that, instead of focusing on sales volume, looking at each sale on a contribution basis might make sense. This would mean that reps would have to consider the cost of the products, transportation costs, and ordering costs before deciding to accept an order. This would require training.

In addition, each sales representative would have to promote the same selected 10 to 15 products so that, collectively, the sales volume for each item from all territories would increase dramatically. This would lead to economies of scale in production and lower unit costs. Sales representatives would have to learn how to convince customers to purchase the items upon which Biomed wanted to focus. This would change the conversation when visiting customers. Sales reps would have to sell versus simply taking orders for any products that the customer wanted.

Finally, hospitals would not be targeted. This change would have minimal impact on sales reps, whose volume came from drugstores. However, there were some sales reps who had a lot of sales activity within the hospital segment. How could Chiemchanya encourage these reps to change their planning and working style to focus away from hospitals?

The New Sales Role and Goals

The salesforce would remain as the single point of contact with the customer. Sales reps would still have a complex set of tasks, and many of the tasks in the old strategy would transfer to the new. As Chiemchanya reflected, he thought the new sales role would have as its overarching purposes: being the single point of contact with the customer, and being the THB contribution generator for the company. He thought the following tasks would make up the sales role.

EXHIBIT 3   New Market Strategy

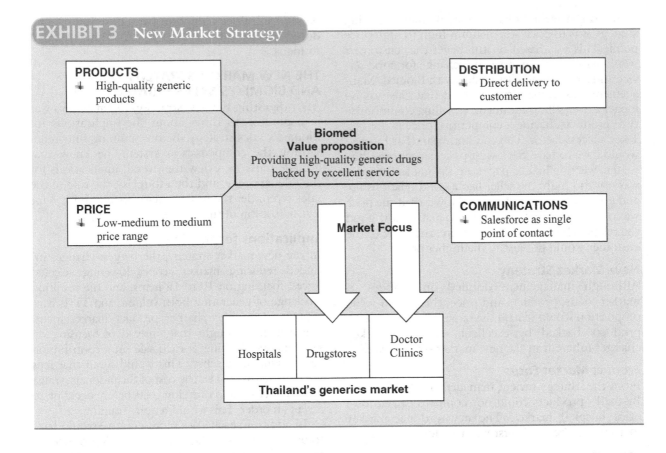

- Generate THB contribution, which included the tasks of:
  - Price negotiation—sales representatives would have autonomy to negotiate prices with customers within a range.
  - Credit evaluation/provision—sales representatives would have autonomy to decide whether a customer should receive a 30-day or 60-day credit.
  - Taking orders.

Focusing on contribution margin would fit perfectly with the new strategy. Biomed's new market strategy had prices going down, so reps need to combine these decreases in unit contribution with increased volumes on an order-by-order basis to ensure company profitability. Reps would be informed of the "loaded" cost of goods, including the variable cost of the product, the transportation cost for each order, and the ordering costs. They would be responsible to negotiate with the customer to reach the price and order quantity that maximized THB contribution.

- Focus selling efforts in drugstores and doctor clinics.

- Find new accounts.
- Build and maintain relationships between the customer and Biomed.
- Focus selling efforts on 10 to 15 items selected by management.
- Listen to customer complaints and provide feedback to management.
- Gain and share market intelligence.

Chiemchanya was still not comfortable jumping to a compensation system that would encourage the accomplishment of the tasks inherent in the new sales role. He thought it was important to set explicit goals against each of these tasks. In the past, only one goal had been set: a sales volume goal. He wanted to be much clearer under the new sales strategy and came up with a specific list of tasks and their associated goals (see Exhibit 4).

DESIGNING THE COMPENSATION SYSTEM AND NEXT STEPS

Chiemchanya believed that he was now set to revamp the sales compensation system at Biomed to reflect the new market strategy. He knew that he was following a logical path since he had translated

Sales Tasks and Goals EXHIBIT 4	
Task	**Goal**
Generate THB contribution	THB contribution against a quota which might vary by territory
Focus selling efforts on drugstores and clinics	At least 60% of contribution derived from drugstores and clinics (with allowances for reps who currently have a large number of hospital accounts)
Find new accounts	Number of new accounts/year, which might vary by territory
Build and maintain relationships between customer and company	Volume of repeat sales
Focus selling efforts on 10 to 15 items selected by management	75% of contribution derived from the focused items (derived from management's estimate of what is required to achieve economies of scale)
Listen to customer complaints and provide feedback to management	Monthly report of customer complaints, feedback
Gain and share market intelligence	Monthly market intelligence report

the market strategy into a new sales strategy with a revised sales role and associated goals. He wondered how he would judge the new system as he designed it. Although Chiemchanya was confident that he had developed a logical approach to redesigning the compensation system, he knew that his task did not end with the compensation system documented on a piece of paper. Two other issues still dogged him.

The first was the implementation of the new plan. Anytime a manager makes decisions that potentially have an impact on someone's wallet, careful thought needs to be given to the communication of the proposed changes. There also has to be consideration of any protection that might be given to reps as they move from one system to the next. In addition, if the new plan required the use of territory-specific targets or quotas, deriving these would have to be done in a manner deemed to be fair and equitable by the sales reps. The first person to get on board would be the sales manager. He could act in concert with Chiemchanya to sell the new approach, although Chiemchanya surmised that the initial reaction of the sales reps would be negative. The new plan required changes in behavior, and the sales reps may feel that their income would be at risk as a result.

The second issue that kept Chiemchanya awake at night was the sense that, although important in supporting the new strategy, there were many other things required from the sales program in order to ensure the success of the new market strategy. Chiemchanya needed to think through any training interventions that would be required. He also had to think through whether or not all the sales reps were suited to the new sales role. It is different selling on volume than selling on contribution to a focused market segment with a focused set of products. What if some reps could not make the switch? He also needed to determine whether or not there was a place for recognition, in addition to rewards, to encourage the desired behaviors under the new strategy.

The fun was about to begin.

CANDYM ENTERPRISES: FALLING SALES IN TERRITORY #61

Brian Matheson, president and founder of Candym Enterprises, a giftware wholesaler, faced a difficult decision. It was November 2003, and he was debating about what to do about the underperformance of Territory #61 in West Toronto. During a recent meeting, it was discovered that this territory's performance was not on par with its East Toronto counterpart, Territory #60. The underperformance in Territory #61 was linked to a decline in sales of one of the product lines. With the January Gift Show, a prime selling event, fast approaching, Matheson needed to make a decision soon.

COMPANY INFORMATION

Background

Candym Enterprises (Candym) was established in 1974, as a Canadian wholesaler specializing in producing, importing and exporting several types of giftware items. Candym's head office, located in Markham, Ontario, consisted of office space, as well as a warehouse and distribution centre. As a large giftware wholesaler, Candym employed 75 staff in-house. A network of 40 independent sales representatives was managed by Sales Manager Bruce Brown, who reported to Matheson (see Exhibit 1).

As Candym grew over the years, management made the decision to cleave the organization into two separate companies: Candym Enterprises and Accent Imports. The companies were managed as one entity but each carried different product lines. The division into two companies allowed for a better organization of the salesforce within a single territory, as one rep represented Candym product lines, and a different rep represented Accent product lines. However, in limited volume territories, reps sometimes carried both Candym and Accent product lines.

Candym Enterprises' product lines were Gund and BabyGUND plush toys, TAG Home Decor & Accessories, Rosemary & Time Garden and Christmas & Home Decor. Accent Imports product lines were Pine Ridge art calendars & stationery products, Nutcracker Designs, Boston Warehouse Home Decor, Kurt Adler Christmas, Greenleaf & Willowbrook fragrances, as well as Riddle & Company tapestries and custom throws.

As holders of exclusive Canadian distribution rights to all of their product lines, Candym was the only company allowed to sell these lines to Canadian retailers. These exclusive rights were a huge benefit since, over the years, Candym had acquired the rights to several popular and in-demand brands, such as TAG Home Décor and GUND Plush. For example, GUND was recognized worldwide as having top-quality plush toys, and any Canadian retailer wishing to carry the GUND plush line had to buy the product from Candym.

Candym had also developed three popular in-house brands: Rosemary & Thyme, Nutcracker Designs, and Pine Ridge Art. These product lines were not only distributed by Candym, but were also developed and owned by the company and exported to different markets.

In addition to the product lines that they offered, each year, Candym performed trend forecasting a service valued by their customers. Because North American trends typically trailed European trends by one year, Candym employees made annual trips abroad to predict which colors, styles and themes would be popular in North America during the following year. Candym had created a strong competitive advantage with this service since many national retailers, such as the Hudson Bay Company, invited Candym to submit their trend forecasts to them. As a result, Candym was in a prime position to then offer these retailers the exact products that would be in demand in the coming year.

Ivey

Richard Ivey School of Business
The University of Western Ontario

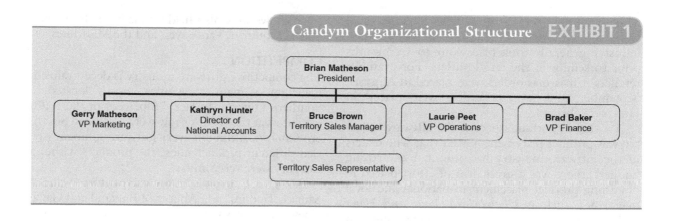

Candym Organizational Structure   EXHIBIT 1

CUSTOMERS
There were two main customer types in the giftware industry: independent retailers and national retail accounts.

Independent Retailers
For the past 30 years, Candym's focus had been on supplying small independent retailers with a wide variety of giftware items. Candym currently serviced approximately 3,500 independent retailers, using a network of 40 independent sales representatives across Canada. These customers ranged from toy stores, to small "ma and pa shop" gift stores, to hospital gift shops. These retailers generally specialized in giftware and home accessories, and typically purchased in small quantities from a variety of suppliers, depending on the nature of their store. For example, a gift shop may offer the entire line of GUND plush toys, yet purchase its home decor items from a competing company.

Two types of sales calls existed for Candym reps. A "cold call" began with the sales rep browsing the store as a shopper to determine fit between the Candym product lines and the store's product mix. Next, the rep would call the store and request an appointment. If successful, the rep then met with the purchaser and made a brief presentation. This informal presentation usually consisted of the rep leafing through the catalogs and pointing out which items and product lines would sell well in the store. Although all items were sold using the catalogs, reps also could take samples to show the customers. In addition, customers were always invited to browse Candym's extensive showroom, which showcased every item they had for sale. Other important aspects of this sales call were answering any questions the customer might have and providing information on how to do business with Candym, such as details on minimum order sizes and delivery information.

A second type of sales call was designed to build relationships in order to maintain active accounts. This call provided the reps with an opportunity to get reacquainted with customers and introduce any new products. Additionally, these visits gave the reps an opportunity to increase the size of their active accounts by promoting more purchases.

In both types of sales calls, if a sale was made, the order was placed via Palm Pilot, and the following day, the rep confirmed the order and the product availability. If products were unavailable or the delivery time needed to be altered, the rep and customer would then adjust the order to suit the customer's needs. The cost of sales for independent retail accounts was approximately 15 percent, which included commissions and other costs to the company. A territory with a sales volume of $300,000 incurred sales costs of $45,000.

National Retail Accounts
National retail accounts were a relatively small part of Candym's strategy until 1999, when a new growth initiative called for a push into the national retail accounts market. At this point, Kathryn Hunter, a product manager, took over the initiative to penetrate this potentially lucrative market. National accounts were large corporations who made the purchasing decisions for their own network of retail stores. For example, the Toys R Us buyer mades the purchasing decisions for stock in all of their Toys R Us stores across Canada. Although there were only approximately 40 national retail accounts, their purchases were typically high volume and high value, with average annual average purchases of $200,000.

CANADIAN GIFTWARE INDUSTRY
The competitive Canadian giftware industry comprised a large number of small- and medium-sized

wholesale/importers and fewer large-sized wholesale/importers. Purchasing in the giftware industry generally took place four to six months prior to selling in the retail outlets. For example, retailers' Christmas orders were placed in August/September, and summer orders were placed in January/February.

Another important aspect of the giftware industry was product placement. Given that wholesalers in the giftware industry had minimal advertising budgets, there was a great deal of effort placed in obtaining product placement in national and local magazines, such as *Chatelaine, House and Home* and the *LCBO magazine*. This placement ensured constant awareness for their product lines among retailers and consumers alike.

Canadian Gift and Tableware Association

The most important trade association for the giftware industry was the CTGA, the Canadian Gift Tableware Association. This association's mission was:

> To improve our members' competitive capability and business effectiveness by enhancing global opportunities for retailer/supplier interaction; offering services that contribute to bottom-line success; and supporting personal and corporate growth through quality educational programs and events.[1]

One of the most important services offered by the CGTA to its retail and wholesale members was the CGTA Gift Show. The association owned and managed a trade fair each January and August. The emphasis of the January show was on spring/summer merchandise, and the emphasis of the August show was on fall/winter merchandise. This show was a forum providing wholesalers with an opportunity to display their products and retailers with the opportunity to browse the distributors' new products and place orders for their stores. In addition, seminars and demonstrations were offered to retail buyers. The CGTA Gift Show was also a prime event for networking between sales representatives, wholesale companies, and retail buyers. The event was held at the Toronto Congress Centre and the International Centre and attracted more than 28,000 retail buyers in the spring and more than 26,000 in the fall. Furthermore, each show offered retail buyers access to more than 1,100 exhibitors in more than one million square feet of display space. Although the CTGA shows were the largest and most important shows for Canadian retailers and wholesalers, other trade shows were also held annually in the United States, Montreal, Vancouver, and the Maritimes.

COMPETITION

The competitive giftware industry is decentralized, made up of many companies, mostly located in Southern Ontario. In fact, 75 percent of the 1,100 exhibitors at the CGTA show were located in Southern Ontario. Although every giftware company carried different product lines, the products within a category were very similar.

Some of Candym's main competitors included Samaco Trading Ltd., Abbott of England and Ganz. These companies were Candym Enterprises' biggest competitors as they were also large-sized wholesalers who carried a wide variety of high-quality and well-known product lines that were similar to Candym's.

Samaco Trading was located in Richmond Hill, Ontario, and competed with Candym on their home accessories, Christmas giftware, and gardening giftware. Abbott of England (www.abbottcollection.com) was located in Toronto, Ontario, and sold a wide variety of giftware items. Finally, Ganz (www.ganz.com) was located in Woodbridge, Ontario, and competed with Candym on plush, as well as candles, fragrances, and home and cottage decor items.

SALESFORCE

Background

Candym believed its independent salesforce was the most important factor in its success. As Bruce Brown, sales manager, states:

> Sales reps are extremely important to a company such as Candym as they are not only the link between the product and the company but "the relationship" of the company to the customer. Good product with a known brand name is a definite advantage, however, people still like to buy from people that they like and that's where the relationship between the rep and customer is of paramount importance.

The salesforce consisted of a network of 40 independent sales representatives throughout Canada. Although not encouraged, it was not uncommon for a Candym sales representative to work as a rep for other companies as well. However, Candym did prohibit their reps from selling competing product lines. If Candym felt that reps were not putting in enough effort with Candym product lines, their contract would be terminated. Despite generally high turnover rates in the industry, Candym enjoyed a below average turnover rate. In fact, many sales reps had represented Candym for more than 15 years.

[1]*CGTA website www.cgta.org.*

Compensation

Candym Enterprises' sales representatives were completely independent and worked on a 100 percent commission basis. These reps were not employees of Candym, and received no benefits, allowances, or expense accounts as would a typical rep. Consequently, they were responsible for all of the expenses incurred to do business. In some cases, customers required special treatment, such as extended payment terms, discounted pricing, or free shipping. The cost of the special treatment was covered by the rep and the company, by means of a discounted commission. For example, a customer who demanded free shipping might receive it, if the rep agreed, but the sales rep would take a reduction in the regular industry standard 10 percent commission rate. Sales representatives with Candym Enterprises earned about the same as other reps in the giftware industry.

The lowest paid Candym rep earned about $20,000 (gross) per year, while the highest paid rep earned about $150,000 (gross) per year. As previously stated, some reps worked for other companies as well, which supplemented their total income. For example, the Candym rep earning $150,000 worked for Candym alone, while the rep earning $20,000 per year with Candym earned $40,000 from another company and $30,000 from yet another company. Overall, a rep's average total income was approximately $90,000 (gross).

In previous years, Candym had used a quota and bonus system for its reps, however, the company found this system had no significant payback since reps were not bringing in more business. In lieu of a bonus, annual targets were set by Candym's sales manager, Bruce Brown, in order to provide the rep with a goal to work towards. A rep who continually achieved sales below target could face termination. These targets were based on many factors, including market conditions, sales history, product line, and territory size and potential. Brown and the reps reviewed these targets every three months. If the rep disagreed with the target, further discussion would ensue in order to come up with an agreed upon target. Brown believed that attainable targets were a key motivating factor for his salesforce. For that reason, he spent most of his time managing his sales team by undertaking performance reviews and reviewing sales orders. Although the reps were independent, he still believed that his job as sales manager was to mentor and motivate his team to increase sales. Performance reviews were used as a formal way to evaluate reps' performances and to suggest how and where they should be focusing their efforts.

Territories

Sales reps were allocated by geographical location, population, and product line (Candym or Accent).

A less populated province, such as Saskatchewan, would have one rep selling both Candym and Accent products because the market potential was rather small. On the other hand, a heavily populated area with thousands of retail outlets, such as the Greater Toronto Area (GTA), had several reps, each selling different product lines in the same territory. For example, the City of Toronto was divided into Territory #61 (West Toronto) and Territory #60 (East Toronto). One rep, Alex Hanson, sold Accent product lines to both territories in Toronto. Another rep sold Candym product lines to East Toronto, while a different rep sold Candym products to West Toronto.

More than half of the company's annual sales were in Ontario. When a territory grew so large that a single rep could not make calls as frequently as the company would like, Brown had to decide whether or not to contract an additional rep. This decision was important since the existing rep should not feel as though sales were being lost. As Brown put it: "more calls equals more business, if there aren't enough calls being made, it's time to add a new rep to maximize the sales potential." These decisions were implemented with great care to ensure that the reps were happy. New hires to an existing territory usually started off with the smaller, newer accounts, while the existing reps remained on the older, often more lucrative, accounts that they had spent time developing.

Training

Training at Candym had been very limited. Regardless of their location, new hires were required to visit the head office in Markham for a two-day training period. During this period, they attended product knowledge meetings with the managers for the lines they would be selling. Also, the new reps were shown around the office and introduced to the administration personnel. This was especially important to the reps who worked in other provinces, as it gave them an opportunity to "put a face to the name." Finally, reps were introduced to the Palm Pilot order-taking system and trained on how to read and interpret Candym sales reports.

In February 2004, Candym introduced a new sales training program called "President's Club." This correspondence-based training program, offered by the Sandler Sales Institute, was recommended to Candym by their U.S. GUND supplier and was mandatory for all new hires as well as selected older ones.

THE PROBLEM

Although Territory #61 had a significant number of retail stores in which Accent product lines could be sold, the potential was not being exploited. Brian Matheson examined past sales reports and noticed a significant decline in Territory #61's active Accent Import accounts. Upon closer examination, Matheson and Brown recognized that Alex Hanson, the sales rep who sold Accent products in Territories #60 and #61, was not focusing enough of his time building and maintaining relationships in West Toronto. In particular, he wasn't spending time on cold calls to new potential customers, which were essential to begin a relationship with a customer and to establish a foothold into an account. Instead, Hanson focused his energy on maintaining the larger, more lucrative accounts in East Toronto (Territory #60). As a result, many of the accounts in #61 who had previously purchased Accent products had decided to take their business elsewhere, and many new potential customers in the area simply had not been visited.

OPTIONS

Replace Alex Hanson

The first alternative that Matheson and Brown considered was to replace Hanson. However, they were hesitant to take such drastic action since they both recognized that Hanson was one of their top-selling reps and that the problem lay more in account management than sales skills. Brown pointed out that their new Sandler Sales Training program might help Hanson build his territory management skills, which might lead him to refocus his attention on Territory #61. They also worried that replacing Hanson would be detrimental to their sales of Accent products, since retailers, especially in East Toronto, had a great relationship with Hanson. Given the importance of relationships to many of these retailers, replacing Hanson might lead some important active accounts to start looking elsewhere.

On the other hand, Brown thought back to a similar situation he had dealt with. A few years ago, Brown had discovered that their accounts in Alberta were concentrated in one small area of Calgary. Brown recognized that Alberta's rep, Suzanne Hanes, was earning a good salary by servicing a small number of large accounts. During a visit to the area, Brown realized that, like Territory #61, the potential was completely unexploited. The decision to replace Suzanne Hanes was a difficult one, since she had built up strong relationships with these large accounts, and the company feared that these customers would remain loyal to Hanes instead of to Candym. Despite this possibility, Brown made the decision to replace her with a different rep that would be more willing to scope out new prospects and extend her reach beyond the city of Calgary. The outcome was a 30 percent increase in sales, and Brown wondered whether or not replacing Hanson in Toronto could yield similar results.

The timing was perfect to hire another rep. Aline Bruneau, a strong candidate with eight years' experience selling giftware, had just stopped by to enquire about a selling position with Candym. She had just moved from Quebec City and had been referred to Candym by one of Quebec reps. She was an independent rep and enjoyed the thrill of working on a 100 percent commission basis. In fact, she had also been hired by a noncompeting company to sell one of their smaller product lines. During discussions, she assured Candym that she could take on another company's products.

Relocate Alex Hanson

Another option was to relocate Hanson to a different territory. This would oblige him to build up relationships in a new area rather than rely on the comfort of the stability in his current accounts. Another benefit to relocating Hanson was that the new rep assigned to his territory would be unfamiliar with the West Toronto customers as well as the East Toronto customers and would likely spend time on building up relationships with all of the accounts.

An opportunity had arisen as Beth Jones, the Accent rep for Oakville/Mississauga/Burlington/Brampton had just resigned her accounts since she was expecting a baby. Jones even offered to show the new rep around her territory and introduce her customers. Matheson and Brown also felt that moving Hanson to this territory was acceptable since this area represented roughly the same number of accounts as his Toronto territories and was close to his Mississauga home. In addition, he was already familiar with the Accent product lines.

Despite Jones's offer to show the new rep around, Matheson recognized that Hanson's complete unfamiliarity with the retail mix in this area might have a negative impact on sales in both Toronto territories as well as the Oakville/Mississauga/Burlington/Brampton one. Matheson also feared that the increased travel time required to service these accounts might lead to less face time with customers, which was what customers loved about Hanson. Matheson had to consider the tradeoff he would be making between building up new relationships and losing out on the relationships that Hanson had already spent much time and energy on in Toronto.

Introduce Salaried Sales Reps

The final alternative was a completely new concept to Candym. Matheson had recently read an article on the concept of business development management and wondered if he could apply this concept to his company. This would involve hiring a second sales rep to take over selling Accent products in Hanson's Territory #61. Hanson would then be free to focus all of his efforts on selling to East Toronto (#60). Matheson also thought that Hanson's sales in this territory alone would increase dramatically if he were no longer burdened with having to service the West Toronto (#61) accounts. Instead of an independent, commission-based rep, West Toronto would now be serviced by a rep on a straight salary. This salaried rep would not be independent, but an employee of Candym Enterprises. Matheson believed that a salary would provide this rep with a stable income and, in return, the rep would be more inclined to spend the time building up the critical relationships in this territory, scoping out new potential accounts and hopefully recapturing the accounts they had previously lost.

Brown pointed out to Matheson that: "developing new accounts takes time and patience . . . issues that a commissioned rep is sometimes not willing to cope with due to the fact that there is not an immediate pay off." The starting salary for the salaried rep was in the $30,000 to $35,000 range per year, plus car allowances and non-travel expenses. Annual car allowances and non-travel expenses were estimated to be between $5,000 and $7,000. Despite these perceived benefits, Matheson recognized that a rep on salary may lack the necessary motivation offered by a commission and that the sales potential would still not be reached. He also worried that the few accounts that Hanson was servicing well in West Toronto might be upset that he had been replaced and might consider buying from new suppliers.

DECISION

It had been a few months since Matheson recognized that he had to make a change in Toronto, and he knew he had to act quickly if he was going to capitalize on the potential in Territory #61. He and Bruce Brown sat down in his office and settled in for what they both knew was to be a long night. What were they going to do?

360-degree feedback An assessment technique that involves performance assessment from multiple raters.

A

absorption training A method of sales training that involves furnishing trainees or salespeople with materials that they peruse without opportunity for immediate feedback and questioning.

account targeting strategy The classification of accounts within a target market into categories for the purpose of developing strategic approaches for selling to each account or account group.

achieving congruence The process of matching the capabilities of a sales recruit with the needs of the organization.

achieving realism The process of giving a sales recruit an accurate portrayal of the sales job.

activity-based costing (ABC) A method that allocates costs to individual units on the basis of how the units actually expend or cause these costs.

ADAPT A questioning methodology that can lead to productive interactions with buyers. ADAPT suggests that questions be used to Assess the buyer's situation, Discover their needs, Activate the buying process, Project the impact of having the buyer solve a problem or realize an opportunity, and make a Transition to the sales presentation or next step in the buying process.

adaptive selling The ability of a salesperson to alter their sales messages and behaviors during a sales presentation or as they encounter different sales situations and different customers.

AIDA An acronym for the various mental states the salesperson must lead their customers through when using mental states selling: attention, interest, desire, and action.

amoral management A form of management in which management is neither moral nor immoral, but decisions lie outside the sphere to which moral judgments apply.

apathetics A salesperson who is low on commitment to the organization and low on involvement in his or her selling job.

assessment center Centers that offer a set of well-defined procedures for using techniques such as group discussions, business game simulations, presentations, and role-playing exercises for the purpose of employee selection or development.

B

background investigation A reference check on the job candidate that can help verify the true identity of the person and possibly confirm his or her employment history.

behavior approach A category of research that tries to uncover what makes an effective leader. It seeks to catalog behaviors associated with effective leadership.

behavior-based perspective A perspective that incorporates complex and often subjective assessments of salesperson characteristics and behaviors with considerable monitoring and directing of salesperson behavior by sales managers.

behavioral criteria Criteria for performance evaluation that emphasize exactly what each salesperson does.

behavioral simulations A method of sales training in which trainees portray specified roles in staged situations.

behaviorally anchored rating scales (BARS) A performance evaluation method that links salesperson behaviors with specific results.

benchmarking An ongoing measurement and analysis process that compares an organization's current operating practices with the "best practices" used by world-class organizations.

bottom-up forecasting approaches A forecasting approach that consists of different methods for developing sales forecasts for individual accounts; these forecasts are then combined by sales managers into territory, district, region, zone, and company forecasts.

breakdown approach An approach used for calculating salesforce size that assumes an accurate sales forecast is available, which is then "broken down" to determine the number of salespeople needed to generate the forecasted level of sales.

business consultant A role the salesperson plays in consultative selling where he or she uses internal and external (outside the sales organization) sources to become an expert on the customer's business. This role also involves educating customers on the sales firm's products and how these products compare with competitive offerings.

business marketing A marketing situation in which business is the target market.

business strategy An organizational strategy level that must be developed for each strategic business unit (SBU) in the corporate family, defining how that SBU plans to compete effectively within its industry.

business unit portfolio A firm's portfolio of their SBUs.

buying center The many individuals from a firm who participate in the purchasing process.

buying needs Buying behavior that can be personal and organizational. The organizational purchasing process is meant to satisfy the needs of the organization; however, the buying center is made up of individuals who want to satisfy individual needs.

Buying Power Index (BPI) A market factor calculated for different areas by the equation $BPI = (5I + 2P + 3R) \div 10$ where I = Percentage of U.S. disposable personal income in the area, P = Percentage of U.S. population in the area, and R = Percentage of U.S. retail sales in the area.

buying process Organizational buyer behavior that consists of several phases: Phase 1 is recognition of problem or need; Phase 2 is determination of the characteristics of the item and the quantity needed; Phase 3 is description of the characteristics of the item and quantity needed; Phase 4 is search for and qualification of potential sources; Phase 5 is acquisition and analysis of proposals; Phase 6 is evaluation of proposals and selection of suppliers; Phase 7 is selection of an order routine; Phase 8 is performance feedback and evaluation.

C

career fair An event in which several employers are brought together in one location (physically or virtually) for recruiting purposes.

candor Salespeople must communicate with candor, or honesty, to build trust-based relationships with customers. Acting otherwise can ruin a business relationship, perhaps forever.

centralization The degree to which important decisions and tasks in an organization are performed at higher levels in the management hierarchy.

change agent A key role played by salespeople as they stimulate sales cycles and help customers reach buying decisions as soon as reasonably possible. By being a catalyst for change, salespeople are involved in diffusion of innovation and can have a positive impact on economic cycles.

channel conflict Occurs when the interests of different channels are not consistent.

classroom/conference training Sales training that features lectures, demonstrations, and group discussion with expert trainers serving as instructors.

coaching A leadership function in which a sales manager concentrates on continuous development of salespeople through supervisory feedback and role modeling.

code of ethics A written code of ethical business behavior that members of an association are urged to adhere to.

coercive power Power in an interpersonal relationship that is based on a belief that one party can remove rewards and provide punishment to affect behavior.

cognitive feedback Information about how and why the desired outcome is achieved.

commission base Commission pay based on sales volume or some measure of profitability.

commission payout event Commission pay that is given when the order is confirmed, shipped, billed, paid for, or some combination of these events.

commission rate Commission pay in which a percentage of the commission earned is paid to the salesperson.

commission splits Commission pay that is divided between two or more salespeople or between salespeople and the employer.

communications agent A key role performed by salespeople who are involved in two-way communications between their customers and their employers. This exchange of information has economic and strategic value for both customers and sales organizations.

compensation rewards Organizational rewards that are given in return for acceptable performance or effort.

competitive knowledge Knowledge of a competitive product's strengths and weaknesses in the market.

conflicts of interest Job conflicts that place the salesperson in a position that could violate customer demands to benefit the company, or that could violate company policy to benefit customer demands.

constant rate A commission rate in which the salesperson is paid a constant percentage of what he or she sells.

consultative selling The process of helping customers reach their strategic goals by using the products, services, and expertise of the sales organization.

contingency approach A category of research that tries to uncover what makes an effective leader and recognizes the importance of the interaction between situational factors and other factors.

continued affirmation An example of stimulus response selling in which a series of questions or statements furnished by the salesperson is designed to condition the prospective buyer to answering "yes" time after time, until, it is hoped, he or she will be inclined to say "yes" to the entire sales proposition.

contribution approach An approach to determining an organization's profitability that only uses direct costs, not indirect or shared costs; net contribution is calculated from this approach.

corporate citizens A salesperson who is highly committed to the organization, but who does not strongly identify with his or her selling role.

corporate mission statement A statement that provides direction for strategy development and execution throughout the organization.

corporate strategy An organizational strategy level that consists of decisions that determine the mission, business portfolio, and future growth directions for the entire corporate entity.

cost analysis The assessment of costs incurred by the sales organization to generate the achieved levels of sales.

current spendable income Money provided in the short term that allows salespeople to pay for desired goods and services.

customer compatibility Refers to the customer's perception that a salesperson is a good person to do business with. Personal characteristics such as a pleasant personality can enhance compatibility, but professionalism and making it easy for the customer to do business with the selling firm also determine compatibility.

customer knowledge Information relating to customers' needs, buying motives, buying procedures, and personalities.

customer orientation A customer orientation can be demonstrated through behaviors such as determining the buyer's unique needs before recommending a purchase, preventing and correcting problems, and sincere listening during sales calls.

customer relationship management (CRM) A business strategy to select and manage the most valuable customer relationships. It requires a customer-centric business philosophy and culture to support effective marketing, sales, and service processes.

customer survey A survey intended to define customer expectations.

customer value The customer's perception of what they receive (e.g., products, services, information) in exchange for what they give up (e.g., time, effort, and money). Customer value is influenced by the buyer's situations, needs, and priorities.

customer value agent A key role of salespeople which includes creating, communicating, delivering, and continually increasing customer value.

D

decision model An analytical approach to the allocation of selling effort in which mathematical formulations are used to achieve the highest level of sales for any given number of sales calls and to continue increasing sales calls until their marginal costs equal their marginal returns.

decomposition method Method for developing company forecasts by breaking down previous company sales data into four major components: trend, cycle, seasonal, and erratic events.

Delphi method A structured type of jury of executive opinion method that involves selection of a panel of managers from within the firm who submit anonymous forecasts for each account.

dependability Salespeople demonstrate dependability by simply doing what they say they will do. Dependability is essential for building customer trust.

detailer A salesperson in the pharmaceutical industry working at the physician level to furnish valuable information regarding the capabilities and limitations of medications in an attempt to get the physician to prescribe their product.

differentiation strategy A type of generic business strategy. It involves the creation of something perceived industrywide as being unique and provides insulation against competitive rivalry because of brand loyalty and resulting lower sensitivity to price.

diffusion of innovation The process whereby new products, services, and ideas are distributed to the members of society.

direction Salespeople choose where their efforts will be spent among various job activities.

distributors channel Middlemen that take title to the goods that they market to end users.

E

economic stimuli Something that stimulates or incites activity in the economy.

effectiveness index A type of sales analysis that can be computed by dividing actual sales results by the sales quota and multiplying by 100.

employee referral programs Interorganizational programs in which existing employees are used as sources for recruiting new salespeople because they have a good understanding of the type of person sought for a sales position.

expense account padding Expense reimbursement in which a salesperson seeks reimbursement for ineligible or fictional expenses.

expert power Power in an interpersonal relationship that is based on the belief that a person has valuable knowledge or skills in a given area.

exponential smoothing A type of moving averages method that weights company sales in the most recent year differently than company sales in the past years.

extensive problem solving The lengthy decision-making process to collect and evaluate purchase information in new task-buying situations.

extrinsically motivated Motivation occurring when salespeople are rewarded by others.

F

farmers Sometimes referred to as order-takers, these salespeople try to increase sales with existing customers.

financial compensation mix The relative amounts to be paid in salary, commission, and bonus.

financial contributor A key role played by salespeople as they produce revenue for their organizations and improve profitability by enhancing sales organization productivity.

forecast A prediction for a future period; forecasts provide the basis for making sales management decisions.

full cost approach An approach that deals with shared costs in an organization by allocating the shared costs to individual units based on some type of cost allocation procedure that results in a net profit figure.

functional specialization Term used to describe a salesforce in which salespeople specialize in a required number of selling activities.

G

generic business strategies The most popular of classification schemes used in developing a business unit strategy. These generic strategies are low cost, differentiation, or niche.

geographic specialization Term used to describe a salesforce whose salespeople are typically assigned a geographic area and are responsible for all selling activities to all accounts within the assigned area.

global account management (GAM) A type of major account organization that serves the needs of major customers with locations around the world.

government organizations Federal, state, and local government agencies.

graphic rating/checklist methods Approaches in which salespeople are evaluated by using some type of performance evaluation form.

H

hierarchical sales analysis A way to identify problem areas in achieving sales effectiveness that consists of evaluating sales results throughout the sales organization from a top-down perspective.

hunters Salespeople who focus on gaining new customers; these salespeople increase market share for their companies by adding new customers. Hunters may also be called order-getters and pioneers.

hybrid sales organization A sales organization structure that incorporates several of the basic structural types; the objective of a hybrid structure is to capitalize on the advantages of each type while minimizing the disadvantages.

I

immoral management A form of management in which management decisions, actions, and behavior imply a positive and active opposition to what is ethical.

income statement analysis A type of profitability analysis that studies the different levels in a sales organization and different types of sales.

incremental approach An approach used for calculating salesforce size that compares the marginal profit contribution with the marginal selling costs for each incremental salesperson.

independent representatives Independent sales organizations that sell complementary, but noncompeting, products from different manufacturers; also called manufacturers' representatives or reps.

industrial distributors Sales channel middlemen who take title to the goods they market to end users.

influence strategies A type of communication strategy sales managers can use on their salesforce that can be based on threats, promises, persuasion, relationships, and manipulation.

initial interviews Brief interviews used to screen job applicants in order to replace a review of resumes or application forms.

initiation to task The degree to which a sales trainee feels competent and accepted as a working partner.

institutional stars A salesperson who is highly committed to the organization and highly involved in his or her selling job.

institutions Public and private organizations.

integrated marketing communication (IMC) The strategic integration of multiple marketing communication tools in the most effective and efficient manner.

integrative meeting A sales meeting in which several sales and sales management functions are achieved.

intensity The amount of mental and physical effort put forth by the salesperson.

intensive interviews Interviews conducted to get an in-depth look at a job candidate.

interviewer bias Something that occurs when an interviewer allows personal opinions, attitudes, and beliefs influence judgments about a job candidate.

intrinsically motivated Motivation occurring when salespeople find their jobs inherently rewarding.

J

job analysis The process of investigating the tasks, duties, and responsibilities of the job.

job application form A form job applicants fill out designed to gather all pertinent information and exclude unnecessary information.

job description A written summary of the job.

job involvement A strong attachment by the salesperson to the job itself.

job preview The process of giving a sales recruit an idea of what the sales job constitutes and how the job is performed.

job qualifications The aptitude, skills, knowledge, personal traits, and willingness to accept occupational conditions necessary to perform the job.

job rotation The exposure of the sales trainee to different jobs.

job satisfaction A salesperson's happiness with his or her job.

job security Job reward in which the salesperson feels comfortable that his or her job will last.

jury of executive opinion method A bottom-up forecasting approach in which the executives of the firm use their expert knowledge to forecast sales to individual accounts.

L

Leader–Member Exchange (LMX) model A sales leadership model that focuses on the salesperson–sales manager dyad as a reciprocal influence process.

leadership The use of influence with other people through communication processes to attain specific goals and objectives.

legitimate power Power in an interpersonal relationship that is associated with the right to be a leader, usually as a result of designated organizational roles.

limited problem solving The decision-making process that occurs in a modified rebuy buying situation that involves collecting additional information and making a change when purchasing a replacement product.

line sales management Sales management position that is part of the direct management hierarchy within the sales organization. Line sales managers have direct responsibility for a certain number of subordinates and report directly to management at the next highest level in the sales organization.

lone wolf A salesperson who is often enthusiastic about his or her selling job (high involvement), but who is not bound to his or her organization (low commitment).

long-term ally A role the salesperson plays in consultative selling where he or she supports the customer, even when an immediate sale is not expected.

low-cost strategy A type of generic business strategy. It involves aggressive construction of efficient-scale facilities, vigorous pursuit of cost reductions from experience, tight cost, and overhead control, usually associated with high relative market share.

M

major account organization A type of market specialization based on account size and complexity; an organization that handles major accounts, or large, important accounts.

major account selling The development of specific programs to serve a firm's largest and most important accounts.

management by objectives (MBO) A performance evaluation method that involves the (1) mutual setting of well-defined and measurable goals within a specified time period, (2) managing activities within the specified time period toward the accomplishment of the stated objectives, and (3) appraisal of performance against objectives.

management levels The number of different hierarchical levels of sales management within the organization.

manipulation An influence strategy that involves sales managers controlling circumstances to influence the target of influence.

market bonus A one-time payment given upon hiring that recognizes an existing imbalance in the supply and demand in a given labor market to entice a sales recruit to join the organization.

market factor method Method for breaking down company forecasts that involves identifying one or more factors that are related to sales at the zone, region, district, territory, or account levels and using these factors to break down the overall company forecast into forecasts at these levels.

market specialization Term used to describe a salesforce that assigns salespeople specific types of customers and are required to satisfy all needs of these customers.

marketing mix A marketing offer designed to appeal to a defined target market.

marketing strategy An organizational strategy level that includes the selection of target market segments and the development of a marketing mix to serve each target market.

mental states selling An approach to personal selling that assumes that the buying process for most buyers is essentially identical and that buyers can be led through certain mental states, or steps, in the buying process; also called the formula approach.

mentor A coach or sales trainer who observes and informs sales trainees on how to improve their sales performances.

merchandiser Sales support personnel who support the retail sales effort by setting up point-of-purchase displays, rotating stock, and keeping store personnel informed about new products and sales promotions.

misrepresentation Something that occurs when incorrect information is given about a job to entice a sales recruit into taking that job.

missionary salespeople Salespeople who usually work for a manufacturer but may also be found working for brokers and manufacturing representatives. Sales missionaries are expected to "spread the word" to convert noncustomers to customers.

modified rebuy buying situation A situation that exists when an account has previously purchased and used the product.

moral management A form of management in which management activity conforms to a standard of ethical, or right, behavior.

motivation A measurement of an individual's intensity, persistence, and direction.

moving averages Method for developing company forecasts by calculating the average company sales for previous years.

multilevel selling A variation of team selling in which the emphasis is to match functional areas between the buying and selling firms.

N

national account management (NAM) A type of major account organization that focuses on meeting the needs of specific accounts with multiple locations throughout a large region or entire country.

need satisfaction selling An approach to selling based on the notion that the customer is buying to satisfy a particular need or set of needs.

needs assessment A process performed to compare the specific performance-related skills, attitudes, perceptions, and behaviors required for salesforce success with the state of readiness of the salesforce.

new task buying situation A situation in which an organization is purchasing a product for the first time.

niche strategy A type of generic business strategy. It involves service of a particular target market, with each functional policy developed with this target market in mind. Although market share in the industry might be low, the firm dominates a segment within the industry.

noncompensation rewards Organizational rewards that include factors related to the work situation and wellbeing of each salesperson.

nonfinancial compensation Job rewards that include career advancement through promotion, sense of accomplishment on the job, opportunities for personal growth, recognition of achievement, and job security.

O

objective and task method A type of zero-based budgeting in which each sales manager prepares a separate budget request that stipulates the objectives achieved, the tasks required to achieve these objectives, and the costs associated with performing the necessary tasks.

observation The process in which sales managers monitor their salespeople during field selling activities.

on-the-job training (OJT) Sales training that puts the trainee into actual work circumstances under the observant eye of a supportive mentor or sales manager.

opportunities for personal growth Job reward such as college tuition reimbursement programs and seminars and workshops on such topics as physical fitness, stress reduction, and personal financial planning.

opportunity for promotion Job reward in which a salesperson obtains a higher job position on the organizational chain.

order-getters Salespeople who actively seek orders, usually in a highly competitive environment.

order-takers Salespeople who specialize in maintaining existing business.

organizational commitment A psychological bond to an

organization or a bond demonstrated through behavior over time.

original equipment manufacturers (OEM) Organizations that purchase products to incorporate into products.

outcome bias The prejudice that occurs when the outcome of a decision rather than the appropriateness of the decision influences an evaluator's ratings.

outcome feedback Information about whether a desired outcome is achieved.

outcome-based perspective A perspective that focuses on objective measures of results with little monitoring or directing of salesperson behavior by sales managers.

P

percentage of sales method A method of cost analysis that calculates an expenditure level for each category by multiplying an expenditure percentage times forecasted sales.

performance bonus A type of current spendable income used to direct effort toward relatively short-term objectives.

performance management An approach that involves sales managers and salespeople working together on setting goals, giving feedback, reviewing, and rewarding.

performance testing A method used to determine sales training needs that specifies the evaluation of particular tasks or skills of the salesforce.

persistence The salesperson's choice to expend effort over time, especially when faced with adverse conditions.

personal selling Personal communication with an audience through paid personnel of an organization or its agents in such a way that the audience perceives the communicator's organization as being the source of the message.

persuasion An influence strategy in which sales managers use expert and referent power to imply that the target of influence must first change his or her attitudes and intentions to produce a subsequent change in behavior.

pioneers Salespeople who are constantly involved with either new products, new customers, or both. Their task requires creative selling and the ability to counter the resistance to change that will likely be present in prospective customers.

planned earnings An advantage of fixed salaries in which management can predict easily what individuals will be paid.

planning activities The first step in the salesperson recruitment and selection process; they include (1) conducting a job analysis, (2) establishing job qualifications, (3) completing a written job description, (4) setting recruitment and selection objectives, and (5) developing a recruitment and selection strategy.

planning and control unit The first step in territory design; an entity that is smaller than a territory.

portfolio models An analytical approach to the allocation of selling effort where each account served by a firm is considered as part of an overall portfolio of accounts; therefore, accounts within the portfolio represent different situations and receive different levels of selling effort attention.

private employment agency An external source for recruiting salespeople in which a fee is charged by the agency that is paid by the employer or the job seeker, as established by contract before the agency begins work for either party.

problem-solving selling An extension of need satisfaction selling that goes beyond identifying needs to developing alternative solutions for satisfying these needs.

product knowledge Knowledge about a product's benefits, applications, competitive strengths, and limitations.

product specialization Term used to describe a salesforce that assigns salespeople selling responsibility for specific products or product lines.

productivity analysis A form of analysis that is measured in terms of ratios between outputs and inputs.

professional development criteria Criteria for performance evaluation that assess improvements in certain characteristics of salespeople that are related to successful performance on the sales job.

professional organizations Professional organizations sales executives join to establish a network of colleagues who have common interests.

profitability analysis An analysis that combines sales and cost data to produce a measure of how profitable an organization is.

profitability criteria Criteria for performance evaluation that assess the profitability of sales.

progressive rate A commission rate in which the percentage a salesperson is paid increases as he or she reaches prespecified selling targets.

promises An influence strategy in which sales managers can use reward power to achieve desired behaviors.

R

ranking methods Approaches in which salespeople are evaluated according to a relative performance on each performance criterion rather than evaluating them against a set of performance criteria.

recognition Job reward that can be informal such as "nice job" accolades, or formal such as group competition or individual accomplishments representing improved performance.

recruitment The second step in the salesperson recruitment and selection process; it is the procedure of locating a sufficient number of prospective job applicants.

recruitment and selection strategy A plan formulated after the recruitment and selection objective have been set that requires the sales manager to consider the scope and timing of recruitment and selection activities.

referent power Power in an interpersonal relationship that is based on the attractiveness of one party to another.

regressive rate A commission rate in which the percentage a salesperson is paid declines at some predetermined point.

relationship strategy A determination of the type of relationship to be developed with different account groups.

relationships An influence strategy containing two types of influence processes: one based on referent power that builds on personal friendships, or feelings of trust, admiration, or respect; the other based on legitimate power over another party by virtue of position in the organizational hierarchy.

resellers Organizations that purchase products to sell.

results criteria Criteria for performance evaluation that assess the results achieved by salespeople.

return on assets managed (ROAM) A calculation that can extend the income statement analysis to include asset investment considerations.

revenue producers Something that brings in revenue or income to a firm or company.

reward power Power in an interpersonal relationship that stems from the ability of one party to reward the other party for a designated action.

reward system management The selection and use of organizational rewards to direct salespeople's behavior toward the attainment of organizational objectives.

role definition A salesperson's understanding of what tasks are to be performed, what the priorities of the tasks are, and how time should be allocated among the tasks.

role playing A method of sales training in which one trainee plays the role of the salesperson and another trainee acts as the buyer; role playing is videotaped or performed live for a group of observers, who then critique the performance.

routinized response behavior The process in which a buyer is merely reordering from the current supplier.

S

salary compression A narrow range of salaries in a salesforce.

salary plus incentive Payment plans for salespeople that feature some combination of salary, commission, and bonus pay.

sales analysis An important element in evaluating sales organization effectiveness in which the organization studies its sales progress.

sales channel strategy The process of ensuring that accounts receive selling effort coverage in an effective and efficient manner.

sales contests Temporary programs that offer financial and/or nonfinancial rewards for accomplishing specified, usually short-term, objectives.

sales dialogue Business conversations which take place over time as salespeople attempt to initiate, develop, and enhance relationships with customers.

sales expenses Expenses incurred while on the job that include travel, lodging, meals, entertainment of customers, telephone, and personal entertainment.

sales leadership Activities that influence others to achieve common goals for the collective good of the sales organization and the company.

sales management Activities related to the planning, implementation, and control of the sales management process.

sales meeting A gathering of salespeople, sales managers, and sometimes other business functions to achieve specific objectives, such as salesperson motivation, recognition, or training.

sales organization audit A comprehensive, systematic, diagnostic, and prescriptive tool used to assess the adequacy of a firm's sales management process and to provide direction for improved performance and prescription for needed changes.

sales process A series of interrelated steps beginning with locating qualified prospective customers. From there, the salesperson plans the sales presentation, makes an appointment to see the customer, completes the sale, and performs post-sale activities.

sales productivity The ratio of sales generated to selling effort used.

sales professionalism Common elements of sales professionalism include the use of customer-oriented, truthful, non-manipulative sales strategies and tactics to satisfy the long-term needs of customers and the selling firm. Sales professionalism also requires that salespeople work from a dynamic, ever-changing knowledge base.

sales quota A reasonable sales objective for a territory, district, region, or zone.

sales supervision Activities related to working with subordinates on a day-to-day basis.

sales support personnel A firm's personnel whose primary responsibility is dissemination of information and performance of other activities designed to stimulate sales.

sales techniques Fundamental procedures salespeople can follow to make sales.

sales trainer A mentor for salespeople in their organization who provides advice and information for improving sales performance.

sales training media Communications and computer technology used in the sales training process.

sales training objectives Objectives sales managers set during sales training that force the manager to define the reasonable expectations of sales training.

salesforce audit A systematic, diagnostic, prescriptive tool, that can be employed on a periodic basis to identify and address sales department problems and to prevent or reduce the impact of future problems.

salesforce composite method A bottom-up forecasting approach that involves various procedures by which salespeople provide forecasts for their assigned accounts, typically on specially designed forms or electronically via computer.

salesforce deployment Important sales management decisions involved in allocating selling effort, determining salesforce size, and designing territories.

salesforce socialization The process by which salespeople acquire the knowledge, skills, and values essential to perform their jobs.

salesforce survey A survey in which sales managers monitor their salesforce in an attempt to isolate sales training needs.

salesperson competence Salesperson competence, or expertise, is an important dimension required to build customer trust. Customers expect salespeople to know what they are doing and to get answers if they don't already know the answer.

selection The third step in the salesperson recruitment and selection process; it is the process of choosing which candidates will be offered the job.

self-management An individual's effort to control certain aspects of his or her decision making and behavior.

selling budget Corporate resources earmarked for personal selling expenses for a designated period.

selling strategy Involves the planning of sales messages and interactions with customers. Selling strategy can be defined at three levels: for a group of customers, i.e., a sales territory; for individual customers; and for specific customer encounters, referred to as sales calls.

sense of accomplishment Job reward that emanates from the salesperson's psyche.

sexual harassment Lewd remarks, physical and visual actions, and sexual innuendos that make individuals feel uncomfortable.

single factor models An analytical approach to the allocation of selling effort in which the typical procedure is to classify all accounts on one factor and then to assign all accounts in the same category the same number of sales calls.

Six Sigma A data-driven methodology that attempts to eliminate defects in any process.

span of control The number of individuals who report to each sales manager.

SPIN selling A problem solving approach to selling that assesses the customer's Situation, determines a customer Problem, analyses the Implications of those problems, and proposes a solution (Need payoff).

specialization A concept in which certain individuals in an organization concentrate on performing some of the required activities to the exclusion of other tasks.

staff sales management Sales management position that does not directly manage people, but is responsible for certain functions (e.g., recruiting and selecting, training) and is not directly involved in sales-generating activities.

stimulus response selling An approach to selling in which the key idea is that various stimuli can elicit predictable responses from customers. Salespeople furnish the stimuli from a repertoire of words and actions designed to produce the desired response.

straight commission A form of payment in which salespeople are paid by commission only.

straight rebuy buying situation A situation wherein an account has considerable experience in using the product and is satisfied with the current purchase arrangements.

straight salary A form of payment in which salespeople are paid one set salary.

strategic account organization Represents a type of market specialization based on account size and complexity.

strategic business unit (SBU) A single product or brand, a line of products, or a mix of related products that meets a common market need or a group of related needs, and the unit's management is responsible for all (or most) of the basic business functions.

strategic orchestrator A role the salesperson plays in consultative selling in which he or she arranges the use of the sales organization's resources in an effort to satisfy the customer.

stress interview An interview designed to put job candidates under extreme, unexpected, psychological duress for the purpose of seeing how they react.

supervision The day-to-day control of the salesforce under routine operating conditions.

survey of buyer intentions method A bottom-up forecasting approach that asks individual accounts about their purchasing plans for a future period and translates these responses into account forecasts.

T

target market A specific market segment to be served.

task-specific self-esteem The feeling salespeople have about themselves relating to performing and accomplishing job-related duties; high levels have been linked to improved performance and job satisfaction.

team selling The use of multiple-person sales teams in dealing with multiple-person buying centers of their accounts.

telemarketing A sales channel that consists of using the telephone as a means for customer contact to perform some of or all the activities required to develop and maintain account relationships; also called telesales.

territory A designated area that consists of whatever specific accounts are assigned to a specific salesperson.

threats An influence strategy in which a manager might specify a desired behavior and the punishment that will follow if the behavior is not achieved.

time and territory management (TTM) Salesperson's training to teach salespeople how to use time and efforts for maximum work efficiency.

top-down forecasting approaches A forecasting approach that consists of different methods for developing company forecasts at the business unit level that are then broken down by sales managers into zone, region, district, territory, and account forecasts.

total quality management (TQM) An approach that incorporates a strong customer orientation, a team-oriented corporate culture, and the use of statistical methods to analyze and improve all business processes, including sales management.

trade shows A typically industry-sponsored event in which companies use a booth to display products and services to potential and existing customers.

trait approach A category of research that attempts to determine the personality traits of an effective leader.

transactional selling Sales approaches that advocate putting pressure on the customer to "say yes" rather than truly satisfy the customer's needs. Transactional selling focuses on maximizing the outcomes of individual transactions rather than on longer-term relationships with customers.

transformational leadership A sales leadership model in which the leaders are charismatic, inspirational, and driven by a sense of mission.

trust-based relationship selling In contrast to transactional selling, trust-based relationship selling seeks to initiate, develop, and enhance long-term customer relationships by earning customer trust, focusing on customer needs, and having the salesperson play a key role in building the value received by the customer.

trust-building To be successful at trust-building with their customers, salespeople should demonstrate five key attributes: customer orientation; competence or expertise; dependability; candor or honesty; and compatibility.

U

users Organizations that purchase products and services to produce other products and services.

W

workload approach An approach used for calculating salesforce size that first determines how much selling effort is needed to cover the firm's market adequately and then calculates the number of salespeople required to provide this amount of selling effort.

Chapter 1

[1]Andris A. Zoltners, Prabhakant Sinha, and Sally E. Lorimar, "Sales Force Effectiveness: A Framework for Researchers and Practitioners," *Journal of Personal Selling and Sales Management* (Spring 2008): 115–131.

[2]"Selling Power 500: The Largest Sales Forces in America," *Selling Power* (July/August/September 2013): 29–32.

[3]Michael Moorman, Torsten Bernewitz, Marshall Solem, and Ty Curry, "Building a Customer-Focused Growth Engine: Establishing Sales Force Effectiveness Priorities," *Selling Power* (Special Edition 2012): 6.

[4]Eli Jones, Steven P. Brown, Andris A. Zoltners, and Barton A. Weitz, "The Changing Environment of Selling and Sales Management," *Journal of Personal Selling & Sales Management* (Spring 2005): 105–112. Nigel Piercy, "Evolution of Strategic Sales Organizations in Business-to-Business Markets," *Journal of Business & Industrial Marketing* (25/5 2010): 349–359.

[5]Thomas W. Leigh and Greg W. Marshall, "Research Priorities in Sales Strategy and Performance," *Journal of Personal Selling & Sales Management* (Spring 2001): 83–94; Thomas N. Ingram, Raymond W. LaForge, and Thomas W. Leigh, "Selling in the New Millennium: A Joint Agenda," *Industrial Marketing Management* 31, no. 6 (October 2002): 559–567; Nigel Piercy, "Evolution of Strategic Sales Organizations in Business-to-Business Markets," *Journal of Business & Industrial Marketing* (25/5 2010): 349–359.

[6]Heather Baldwin, "Deeper Value Delivery," *Selling Power* (September/October 2010): 16–17.

[7]Theodore Kinni, "Cleaning Up," *Selling Power* (July/August 2010): 39–41.

[8]Christine Birkner, "A Plan for Demand," *Marketing News* (April 2013): 8–9.

[9]Heather Baldwin, "Knowledge is (Sales) Power," *Selling Power* (April/May/June 2013): 10–11.

[10]Heather Baldwin, "Cost Consciousness," *Selling Power* (July/August/September 2013): 10–11.

[11]Heather Baldwin, "Rx for Success," *Selling Power* (July/August/September 2012): 10–11.

[12]Heather Baldwin, "Ties That Bind," *Selling Power* (October/November/December 2012): 10–11.

[13]Henry Canaday, "A Truckload of Sales Transformation," *Selling Power* (October/November/December 2012): 35–37.

[14]Henry Canaday, "Students of the Marketplace," *Selling Power* (November/December 2010): 25–27.

[15]Barbara Giamanco and Kent Gregoire, "Tweet Me, Friend Me, Make Me Buy," *Harvard Business Review* (July/August 2012): 88–93.

[16]David W. Cravens, "The Changing Role of the Sales Force," *Marketing Management* (Fall 1995): 54; Thomas N. Ingram, Raymond W. LaForge, and Thomas W. Leigh, "Selling in the New Millennium: A Joint Agenda," *Industrial Marketing Management* 31 (2002): 559–567; Thomas N. Ingram, Raymond W. LaForge, William B. Locander, Scott B. Mackenzie, and Philip M. Podsakoff, "New Directions in Sales Leadership Research," *Journal of Personal Selling & Sales Management* 25 (Spring 2005): 137–154.

[17]Adapted from William Keenan, Jr., "The Man in the Mirror," *Sales & Marketing Management* (May 1995): 95.

[18]*The Chally World Class Sales Excellence Research Report* (2007): 2.

[19]Heather Baldwin, "Direct Effort," *Selling Power* (July/August 2010): 12–13.

[20]The Sales Educators, "The Revolution in Sales Management" (2005): 10–21.

[21]*Selling Power* Editors, "The Top 10 Sales Management Innovations," *Selling Power* (November/December 2010): 68–70.

[22]This section is synthesized from Chally Group, "Building a World-Class Sales Team," *Industrial Supply* (November/December 2010): 20–25, http://www.industrialsupplymagazine.com/pages/Print-edition—NovDec10_BuildingWorldClassSalesTeam.php; "Driving Sales Results in Any Economy: Executive Summary of the 2010 Miller Heiman Sales Best Practices Study," Miller Heiman Executive Summary (2010): 1–5, http://store.millerheiman.com/kc/abstract.aspx?itemid=0000000000000714; Nigel Piercy, "Evolution of Strategic Sales Organizations in Business-to-Business Marketing," *Journal of Business & Industrial Marketing* (25/5 2010): 349–359.

[23]Joseph Kornik, "The Comeback Kids," *Sales & Marketing Management* (April 2007): 18–23.

[24]Dawn R. Deeter-Schmelz, Karen Norman Kennedy, and Daniel J. Goebel, "Understanding Sales Manager Effectiveness: Linking Attributes to Sales Force Values," *Industrial Marketing Management* (2002): 617–626; Dawn R. Deeter-Schmelz, Daniel J. Goebel, and Karen Norman Kennedy, "What Are the Characteristics of an Effective Sales Manager? An Exploratory

Study Comparing Salesperson and Sales Manager Perspectives," *Journal of Personal Selling & Sales Management* (Winter 2008): 7–20.

[25]Maryann Hammers and Gerhard Gschwandtner, "Tap into the 7 Qualities of the Best Sales Managers," *Selling Power* (May 2004): 60–65.

Chapter 2

[1]The definition of marketing according to the American Marketing Association as shown at http://www.marketingpower.com (accessed March 26, 2014).

[2]"The Largest Sales Forces in America," *Selling Power* (July/August 2013): 29–46.

[3]"Tyco National Account Manager Position Description," as it appeared on http://www.firesecurity.taleo.net/careersection (accessed April 16, 2014).

[4]Thomas N. Ingram, Raymond W. LaForge, Charles H. Schwepker, Jr., Ramon A. Avila, and Michael R. Williams, *Sell*, 4th ed. (Stamford, CT: Cengage Learning, 2015).

[5]John E. Swan and Johannah Jones Nolan, "Gaining Customer Trust: A Conceptual Guide for the Salesperson," *Journal of Personal Selling & Sales Management*, 5 (November 1985): 39–48.

[6]Carew International "Do the Right Thing," *Message from the Mentor*, November 1, 2012.

[7]Chally Group Worldwide, "How to Select a Sales Force That Sells," http://chally.com/how-to-select-a-sales-force-that-sells/ (accessed April 10, 2014).

[8]Robert F. Gwinner, "Base Theory in the Formulation of Sales Strategy," *MSU Business Topics* (Autumn 1968): 37; Mack Hanan, *Consultative Selling*, 7th ed. (New York: American Management Association, 2004).

[9]Neil Rackham, *SPIN Selling* (New York: McGraw-Hill Book Company, 1988).

[10]Kevin J. Corcoran, Laura J. Petersen, Daniel B. Baitch, and Mark F. Barrett, *High Performance Sales Organizations* (Chicago: Richard D. Irwin, 1995): 44.

[11]Hanan, p. 5.

[12]Information compiled from www.indeed.com (accessed April 1, 2014).

[13]Geoffrey James, "The Consultative Approach to Selling," *Selling Power* (March/April 2010): 29–32.

[14]Thomas N. Ingram, "Future Themes in Sales and sales Management: Complexity, Collaboration, and Accountability," *Journal of Marketing Theory and Practice* (Fall 2004): 1–11; Thomas N. Ingram, Raymond W. LaForge, William B. Locander, Scott B. MacKenzie, and Philip M. Podsakoff, "New Directions in Sales Leadership Research," *Journal of Personal Selling & Sales Management*, 25 (Spring 2005): 137–154.

[15]"2014 Gold Stevie Award Winner: DHL Freight Forwarding, Bonn, Germany, Cigdem Wondergem,

Global Head of Sales Training," The Stevie Awards for Sales & Customer Service, www.stevieawards.com/pubs/sales/awards/426_2940_24874.cfm (accessed April 18, 2014).

[16]Mathew Sweezey, "5 Keys to Sales and Marketing Alignment," *ClickZ*, January 23, 2014, www.clickz.com/clickz/column/2324296/5-keys-to-sales-and-marketing-alignment (accessed April 13, 2014); Christine Crandell, "Sales and Marketing Alignment Begins with the Customer," *Forbes*, April 5, 2013, www.forbes.com/sites/christinecrandell/2013/04/05/sales-and-marketing-alignment-begins-with-the-customer/.

Chapter 3

[1]Betsy Cummings, "Getting Reps to Live Your Mission," *Sales & Marketing Management* (October 2001): 15.

[2]Matt Murray, "GE Says It Will Combine Appliances, Lighting Units," *Wall Street Journal Online* (August 30, 2002): 1–2.

[3]Robert Schoenberger, "GE Finds Merger Pays Off in Profits," *The Courier-Journal* (September 13, 2003): F1–F2.

[4]Michael E. Porter, *Competitive Strategy* (New York: The Free Press, 1980): 34.

[5]Madhubalan Viswanathan and Eric M. Olson, "The Implementation of Business Strategies: Implications for the Sales Function," *Journal of Personal Selling & Sales Management* (Winter 1992): 45.

[6]Adapted from John F. Tanner, Jr., Michael Ahearne, Thomas W. Leigh, Charlotte H. Mason, and William C. Moncrief, "CRM in Sales-Intensive Organizations: A Review and Future Directions," *Journal of Personal Selling & Sales Management* (Spring 2005): 169–170.

[7]Alex R. Zablah, Danny N. Bellenger, and Wesley J. Johnston, "An Evaluation of Divergent Perspectives on Customer Relationship Management: Towards a Common Understanding of an Emerging Phenomenon," *Industrial Marketing Management* 33 (2004): 475–489.

[8]Lisa Gschwandtner, "It's All About Strategy," *Selling Power* (January/February 2010).

[9]Darrell K. Rigby, Frederick F. Reichheld, and Phil Schefter, "Avoid the Four Perils of CRM," *Harvard Business Review* (February 2002): 101–110.

[10]Julia Chang, "CRM at Any Size," *Sales & Marketing Management* (August 2004): 33–34; "John Deere Would Have Been Proud," *Sales & Marketing Strategies and News* (May 2004): 22–23.

[11]Henry Canaday, "Three Ways Sales and Marketing Can Collaborate to Boost Revenue," *Selling Power* (January/February 2012).

[12]Michael V. Copeland, "Best Buy's Selling Machine," *Business 2.0* (July 2004): 93–102.

[13]Adapted from Dominique Rouzies, Erin Anderson, Ajay K. Kohli, Ronald E. Michaels, Barton A. Weitz, and Andris A. Zoltners, "Sales and Marketing Integration: A Proposed Framework," *Journal of Personal Selling & Sales Management* (Spring 2005): 113–122.

[14]Ernest Waaser, Marshall Dahneke, Michael Pekkarinen, and Michael Weissel, "How You Slice It: Smarter Segmentation for Your Sales Force," *Harvard Business Review* (March 2004): 105–111.

[15]Henry Canaday, "Segmenting Customers for Profit," *Selling Power* (October 2007): 111–112.

[16]Reported in Chad Kaydo, "You've Got Sales," *Sales & Marketing Management* (October 1999): 30.

[17]*Ibid.*, 34.

[18]Mike McCue, "Solutions That Make a Difference," *Sales & Marketing Management* (October 2007): 19–21.

[19]Henry Canaday, "A Cool Duo," *Selling Power* (September 2007): 76–80.

[20]Andy Cohen, "Herman Miller," *Sales & Marketing Management* (July 1999): 60.

[21]Louise Lee, "It's Dell vs. the Dell Way," *Business Week* (March 6, 2002): 61–62; Jack Ewing, "Where Dell Sells with Brick and Mortar," *Business Week* (October 8, 2007): 78.

[22]Henry Canaday, "Independent Rep's Comp," *Selling Power* (January/February 2001): 79.

[23]Adapted from Harold J. Novick, "The Case for Reps vs. Direct Selling: Can Reps Do It Better?" *Industrial Marketing* (March 1982): 90–98; "The Use of Sales Reps," *Small Business Report* (December 1986): 72–78.

[24]Tricia Campbell, "Who Needs a Sales Force Anyway?" *Sales & Marketing Management* (February 1999): 13.

[25]Adapted from Michael D. Hutt, Wesley J. Johnston, and John R. Rouchelto, "Selling Centers and Buying Centers: Formulating Strategic Exchange Patterns," *Journal of Personal Selling & Sales Management* (May 1985): 34. Used with permission.

[26]Adam Bluestein, "In-Your-Face-Selling," *INC. Magazine* (November 2006): 35–36.

[27]Jeffrey L. Josephson, "Is Inbound Marketing Right for B2B?" SalesAndMarketing.com, January 31, 2014, http://salesandmarketing.com/content/inbound-marketing-right-b2b.

[28]Eilene Zimmerman, "Making the Dysfunctional Functional," *Sales & Marketing Management* (September 2004): 30–31.

[29]Henry Canaday and Gerhard Gschwandtner, "The Name's the Game," *Selling Power* (October 2007): 80–82.

[30]Christopher Palmer, "Giving the Booth a Boost," *Business Week* (April 16, 2007): 12.

[31]Megan Sweas, "High-Tech Trade Shows," *Sales & Marketing Management* (February 2004): 12.

[32]Deborah L. Vence, "Trade Show Magic," *Marketing News* (November 11, 2002): 4.

Chapter 4

[1]Dave Kahle, "How Sharp Is Your Sales Structure?" *American Salesman* 58(8) (2013): 8–14.

[2]Reported in "Structuring the Sales Organization," in *Sales Manager's Handbook,* ed. John P. Steinbrink (Chicago: The Dartnell Corporation, 1989): 90.

[3]See Robert W. Ruekert, Orville C. Walker, Jr., and Kenneth J. Roering, "The Organization of Marketing Activities: A Contingency Theory of Structure and Performance," *Journal of Marketing* (Winter 1985): 13, for a more complete presentation of structural characteristics and relationships. The discussion in this section borrows heavily from this article.

[4]Steven W. Martin, "Is Your Sales Organization Good or Great?" *HBR Blog Network*, February 25, 2013, http://blogs.hbr.org/2013/02/is-your-sales-organization-goo/.

[5]*Ibid.*, 20–21.

[6]From David W. Cravens, *Strategic Marketing,* 7th ed. (New York: McGraw-Hill): 541. Reprinted by permission of The McGraw-Hill Companies.

[7]Andris A. Zoltners, Prabhakant Sinha, and Sally E. Lorimer, "Match Your Sales Force Structure to Your Business Life Cycle," *Harvard Business Review* (July/August 2006): 81–89.

[8]Maurie Cushman, "Geographic Sales Territories—Pros and Cons," *Aspen Grove Investments*, August 17, 2013,http://aspengroveinvestments.com/geographic-sales-territories-pros-and-cons/.

[9]Christian Homburg, John P. Workman, Jr., and Ove Jensen, "Fundamental Changes in Marketing Organization: The Movement Toward a Customer-Focused Organizational Structure," *Journal of the Academy of Marketing Science* (Fall 2000): 459–478.

[10]Keith Regan, "Yahoo Reshuffles Ad Sales Unit from Top Down," *E-Commerce Times* (June 25, 2007): 1–3.

[11]George S. Yip and Audrey J.M. Bink, "Managing Global Accounts," *Harvard Business Review* (September 2007): 103–111.

[12]Adapted from Benson P. Shapiro and Rowland T. Moriarity, *Organizing the National Account Force* (Cambridge, MA: Marketing Science Institute, April 1984): 1–37.

[13]John P. Workman, Jr., Christian Homburg, and Ove Jensen, "Intraorganizational Determinants of Key

Account Management Effectiveness," *Journal of the Academy of Marketing Science* (Winter 2003): 3–21.

[14]Marji McClure, 'Major Opportunities," *Selling Power* (July/August 2006): 34–37.

[15]From David W. Cravens and Raymond W. LaForge, "Salesforce Deployment," in *Advances in Business Marketing,* ed. Arch G. Woodside (1990): 76.

[16]Raymond W. LaForge, David W. Cravens, and Clifford E. Young, "Improving Salesforce Productivity," *Business Horizons* (September/October 1985): 54. Copyright © 1985 by the Foundation for the School of Business at Indiana University. Reprinted by permission.

[17]Robert C. Dudley and Das Narayandas, "A Portfolio Approach to Sales," *Harvard Business Review* (July/August 2006): 16–18.

[18]See Raymond W. LaForge, David W. Cravens, and Clifford E. Young, "Using Contingency Analysis to Select Effort Allocation Methods," *Journal of Personal Selling & Sales Management* (August 1986): 23, for a summary of productivity improvements from decision model applications.

[19]Andy Cohen, "Profits Down? Time to Add to Your Headcount," *Sales & Marketing Management* (August 2002): 15.

[20]Scott Hensley, "As Drug-Sales Teams Multiply, Doctors Start to Tune Them Out," *Wall Street Journal Online* (June 12, 2003): 1–4.

[21]Arlene Weintraub, "The Doctor Won't See You Now," *Business Week* (February 5, 2007): 30–32.

[22]Betsy Wiesendanger, "Temp Reps," *Selling Power* (May 2004): 68–71.

[23]LaForge, Cravens, and Young, "Improving Salesforce Productivity," 57.

[24]Ken Grant, David W. Cravens, George S. Low, and William C. Moncrief, "The Role of Satisfaction with Territory Design on the Motivation, Attitudes, and Work Outcomes of Salespeople," *Journal of the Academy of Marketing Science* (Spring 2001): 165–178.

Chapter 4 APPENDIX

[1]Naresh Sadarangani and John A. Gallucci, "Using Demand Drivers for a Collaborative Forecasting Success," *The Journal of Business Forecasting* (Summer 2004): 12–15.

[2]For other classification schemes and more detailed discussion of individual forecasting methods, see John T. Mentzer and Mark A Moon, *Sales Forecasting Management: A Demand Management Approach* (Thousand Oaks, CA: Sage Publications, 2005). For more on the Delphi technique, see Victoria Story, Louise Hurdley, Gareth Smith, and James Saker, "Methodological and Practical Implications of the Delphi Technique in Marketing Decision-Making: A Re-Assessment," *The Marketing Review* (2001): 487–504; Harry R. White,

Sales Forecasting: Timesaving and Profit-Making Strategies That Work (Glenview, IL: Scott, Foresman and Company, 1984): 6; David M. Georgoff and Robert G. Murdick, "Manager's Guide to Forecasting," *Harvard Business Review* (January/February 1986): 113; J. Scott Armstrong, Roderick J. Brodie, and Shelby McIntyre, "Forecasting Methods for Marketing: Review of Empirical Research," *International Journal of Forecasting* 3 (1987): 355.

[3]See John T. Mentzer, "Forecasting with Adaptive Extended Exponential Smoothing," *Journal of the Academy of Marketing Science* (Fall 1988): 62, for discussion and examples of different exponential smoothing methods.

[4]Mark Barash, "Eliciting Accurate Sales Forecasts from Market Experts," *Journal of Business Forecasting* (Fall 1994): 24.

[5]Kenneth B. Kahn and John T. Mentzer, "The Impact of Team-based Forecasting," *Journal of Business Forecasting* (Summer 1994): 18.

[6]Norton Paley, "Welcome to the Fast Lane," *Sales & Marketing Management* (August 1994): 65.

[7]Dianne Ledingham, Mark Kovac, and Heidi Locke Simon, "The New Science of Sales Productivity," *Harvard Business Review* (September 2006): 124–133.

[8]These and other recommendations are available in Robin T. Peterson, "Sales Force Composite Forecasting —An Exploratory Analysis," *Journal of Business Forecasting* (Spring 1989): 23; James E. Cox, Jr., "Approaches for Improving Salespersons' Forecasts," *Industrial Marketing Management* 18 (1989): 307.

[9]For a review and more complete discussion of this approach, see Adrian B. Ryans and Charles B. Weinberg, "Territory Sales Response," *Journal of Marketing Research* (November 1979): 453; Adrian B. Ryans and Charles B. Weinberg, "Territory Sales Response Models: Stability over Time," *Journal of Marketing Research* (May 1987): 229. For specific examples of regression analysis used to establish territory sales quotas, see David W. Cravens, Robert B. Woodruff, and James C. Stamper, "An Analytical Approach for Evaluating Sales Territory Performance," *Journal of Marketing* (January 1972): 31; David W. Cravens and Robert B. Woodruff, "An Approach for Determining Criteria of Sales Performance," *Journal of Applied Psychology* (June 1973): 240.

[10]From "A Market Response Model for Sales Management Decision Making" by Raymond LaForge and David Cravens. Copyright © 1981 by Pi Sigma Epsilon. From *Journal of Personal Selling & Sales Management* (Fall/Winter 1981–1982): 14. Reprinted with permission of M.E. Sharpe, Inc.

[11]Adapted from Adrian B. Ryans and Charles B. Weinberg, "Territory Sales Response Models: Stability over Time," *Journal of Marketing Research* (May 1987): 231, published by the American Marketing Association.

[12]John T. Mentzer and Mark A Moon, *Sales Forecasting Management: A Demand Management Approach* (Thousand Oaks, CA: Sage Publications, 2005).

[13]Zuhaimy Haji Ismail and Maizah Hura Ahamad, "Delphi Improves Sales Forecasts: Malaysia's Electronic Companies' Experience," *Journal of Business Forecasting* (Summer 2003): 22–29.

[14]See Benito E. Flores and Edna M. White, "A Framework for the Combination of Forecasts," *Journal of the Academy of Marketing Science* (Fall 1988): 95, for an examination of different combination approaches.

[15]John T. Mentzer and Mark A Moon, *Sales Forecasting Management: A Demand Management Approach* (Thousand Oaks, CA: Sage Publications, 2005).

Chapter 5

[1]Michael Munson and W. Austin Spivey, "Salesforce Selection That Meets Federal Regulation and Management Needs," *Industrial Marketing Management* 9 (February 1980): 12.

[2]http://www.census.gov. Accessed October 1, 2013.

[3]Rene Darmon, "Where Do the Best Sales Force Profit Producers Come From?" *Journal of Personal Selling & Sales Management* 3 (Summer 1993): 17.

[4]Fred Yager, "Five Tips for Hiring the Right Candidate," *Dice*, http://resources.dice.com/report/the-cost-of-bad-hiring-decisions/ (accessed October 1, 2013).

[5]Presentation by Daniel Mahurin, District Marketing Manager with Federated Mutual Insurance, October 15, 2013.

[6]Herbert Greenberg and Patrick Sweeney, *How to Hire and Develop Your Next Top Performer: The Qualities That Make Salespeople Great* (New York: McGraw-Hill Company, 2013 2nd ed.).

[7]Fred Yager, "Five Tips for Hiring the Right Candidate," *Dice*, http://resources.dice.com/report/the-cost-of-bad-hiring-decisions/ (accessed October 1, 2013).

[8]Georgia Chao, Anne O'Leary-Kelly, Samantha Wolf, Howard Klein, and Philip Gardner, "Organizational Socialization: Its Content and Consequences," *Journal of Applied Psychology* 79 (October 1994): 730.

[9]Christine Galea, "Selective Employment," *Sales & Marketing Management*, 157 (March 2005): 9.

[10]Taken from "New Business Sales Rep" position description at http://jobs.adp.com/kansas/sales/jobid4079993-new-business-sales-rep-jobs (accessed October 2, 2013).

[11]Benson Smith, "Taller Is Better," *Gallup Management Journal* (June 9, 2005). David Mayer and Herbert Greenberg, "What Makes a Good Salesman," *Harvard Business Review*, 84 (July/August 2006): 164–71.

[12]Susan Greco, "When Is It Safe to Hire?" Inc. Magazine 29 (January 2007): 52–53.

[13]Taken from The Sales Educators, *Strategic Sales Leadership: Breakthrough Thinking for Breakthrough Results* (Mason, OH: Thomson, 2006): 200.

[14]John S. Hill and Meg Birdseye, "Salesperson Selection in Multinational Corporations: A Study," *Journal of Personal Selling & Sales Management* 9 (Summer 1989): 39.

[15]Erika Rasmusson, "Can Your Reps Sell Overseas? How to Make Sure They Have What It Takes," *Sales & Marketing Management* 150 (February 1998): 110.

[16]Position description taken from Hewlett Packard, "Jobs at HP" http://h30631.www3.hp.com/conway/sales-operations/jobid4116472-sales-development-representative-jobs (accessed October 2, 2013).

[17]This ad appeared in *Selling Power* (August/September 2013).

[18]Adapted from *Industrial Marketing Management* (March 1995), 24: 135–144, "Guidelines for Managing an International Sales Force" by Earl Honeycutt and John Ford. Copyright © 1995, with permission from Elsevier.

[19]Gina Ruiz, "Recruiters Cite Referrals as Top Hiring Tool," *Workforce Management*, October 23, 2006: 10.

[20]James A. Breaugh, Leslie A. Greising, James W. Taggart, and Helen Chen, "The Relationship of Recruiting Sources and Pre-Hire Outcomes: Examination of Yield Rations and Application Quality," *Journal of Applied Social Psychology* 33 (November 2003): 2267–2287.

[21]Steven G. Rogelberg, *Encyclopedia of Industrial and Organizational Psychology*, 2 (Thousand Oaks, CA: Sage, 2007): 666–670.

[22]Interview with Patrick Cunningham, District Marketing Manager with Federated Mutual Insurance, November 3, 2010.

[23]Andy Bargerstock and Hank Engel, "Six Ways to Boost Employee Referral Programs," *HR Magazine* 39 (December 1994): 72; Kathryn Tyler, "Employees Can Help Recruit New Talent," *HR Magazine* 41 (September 1996): 57.

[24]Fay Hansen, "Recruitment & Staffing," *Workforce Management*, 85 (June 26, 2006): 59–61.

[25]Darmon, "Where Do the Best Sales Force Profit Producers Come From?"

[26]Martha Frase-Blunt, "Make a Good First Impression," *HR Magazine* 49 (April 2004): 80–84.

[27]Drawn from: "Focus on . . . Writing for Online Recruitment," *Personnel Today* (November 1, 2005): 36; Technojobs, "Writing and Online Recruitment Job Advert," http://www.technojobs.co.uk/info/recruiter-guides/writing-an-online-recruitment-job-advert.phtml (accessed September 8, 2010); Tracey Bowyer, "How to Write an Effective Online Employment Advertisement," Host Careers, http://www.hostcareers

.com/index.php?page=en_Effective+Ad (accessed September 15, 2010); Susan Wareham, "How to Write an Effective Recruitment Advertisement," Ezine Articles, (June 25, 2010), http://ezinearticles.com/?How-to-Write-an-Effective-Recruitment-Advertisement&id=4553621 (accessed September 8, 2010).

28Jorgen Sundberg, "The State of Social Recruiting in 2013 [Infographic]," Jobvite Survey, http://theundercoverrecruiter.com/social-recruiting-state/ (accessed October 11, 2013).

29Lain Ehmann, "Too Good to Fail," Selling Power (September/October 2010): 74–75.

30Jobcast, "Features," www.jobcast.net/features/ (accessed October 7, 2013).

31Gillian Flynn, "E-Recruiting Ushers in Legal Dangers," Workforce 81 (April 2002): 70–72; Judith Marshall, "Don't Rely Exclusively on Internet Recruiting," HR Magazine 48 (November 2003): 24. Alex Johnson, "Lack of computer skills foils many job-seekers," MSNBC.com, (July 29, 2010), http://www.msnbc.msn.com/id/33106445/ (accessed September 8, 2010).

32Steven G. Rogelberg, Encyclopedia of Industrial and Organizational Psychology, 2 (Thousand Oaks, CA: Sage, 2007): 666–670.

33Taken from The Sales Educators, Strategic Sales Leadership: Breakthrough Thinking for Breakthrough Results (Mason, OH: Thomson, 2006): 215.

34Michael S. Cole, Hubert S. Field, William F. Giles and Stanley G. Harris, "Recruiters' Inferences of Applicant Personality Base on Resume Screening: Do Paper People Have a Personality?" Journal of Business Psychology, 24 (2009): 5–18.

35Flynn, "E-Recruiting Ushers in Legal Dangers."

36Ibid.

37William Cron, Greg W. Marshall, Jagdip Singh, Rosann L. Spiro, and Harish Sujan, "Salesperson Selection, Training, and Development: Trends, Implications, and Research Opportunities," Journal of Personal Selling & Sales Management, 25 (Spring 2005): 123–136.

38Interview with Patrick Cunningham, District Marketing Manager with Federated Mutual Insurance, November 3, 2010.

39"Interviewing the Candidate," Sales Consultants International, Inc., Cleveland, OH.

40Taken from "How to Find the Right Rep," SellingPower.com Sales Management Newsletter (February 1, 2006), http://www.sellingpower.com/html_newsletter/sales/article.asp?id=2315&nDate=February+ . . . (accessed on February 2, 2006).

41Taken (with permission) from William C. Byham, "Can You Interview for Integrity?" Across the Board Magazine (March/April 2004).

42Wesley J. Johnson and Martha C. Cooper, "Industrial Sales Force Selection: Current Knowledge and Needed Research," Journal of Personal Selling & Sales Management 1 (Spring/Summer 1981): 49.

43Greg W. Marshall, Miriam B. Stamps, and Jesse N. Moore, "Preinterview Biases: The Impact of Race, Physical Attractiveness, and Sales Job Type on Preinterview Impressions of Sales Job Applicants," Journal of Personal Selling & Sales Management 18 (Fall 1998): 21; Thomas E. Ford, Frank Gambino, Hanjoon Lee, Edward Mayo and Mark A. Ferguson, "The Role of Accountability in Suppressing Managers' Preinterview Bias against African-American Sales Job Applicants," Journal of Personal Selling & Sales Management, 24 (Spring 2004): 113–124.

44G. Stoney Alder and Joseph Gilbert, "Achieving Ethics and Fairness in Hiring: Going beyond the Law," Journal of Business Ethics, 68 (Spring 2006): 449–464.

45Henry Canaday, "Begin with the Best," Selling Power (March 2006): 90–93.

46For more on these see Peter Schulman, "Applying Learned Optimism to Increase Sales Productivity," Journal of Personal Selling & Sales Management, 19 (Winter 1999): 31–37; Sarah Maxwell, Gary Reed, Jim Saker and Vicky Story, "The Two Faces of Playfulness: A New Tool to Select Potentially Successful Sales Reps," Journal of Personal Selling & Sales Management, 25 (Summer 2005): 215–229; Seymour Adler, "Personality Tests for Salesforce Selection: Worth a Fresh Look," Review of Business 16 (Summer/Fall 1994): 27.

47Dawn R. Deeter-Schmelz and Jane Z. Sojaka, "Personality Traits and Sales Performance: Exploring Differential Effects of Need for Cognition and Self-Monitoring," Journal of Marketing Theory & Practice, 15 (Spring 2007): 145–157.

48Henry Canaday, "Smart Selection," Selling Power (April/May/June 2013): 42–43.

49William Cron, Greg W. Marshall, Jagdip Singh, Rosann L. Spiro and Harish Sujan, "Salesperson Selection, Training, and Development: Trends, Implications, and Research Opportunities," Journal of Personal Selling & Sales Management 25 (Spring 2005): 123–136.

50Based on Samual J. Maurice, "Stalking the High-Scoring Salesperson," Sales & Marketing Management (October 7, 1985): 63; George B. Salsbury, "Properly Recruit Salespeople to Reduce Training Cost," Industrial Marketing Management 11 (April 1982): 143; Richard Kern, "IQ Tests for Salesmen Make a Comeback," Sales & Marketing Management (April 1988): 42.

51Chally Group, "Chally Case Studies," http://www.chally.com/results/case-studies/cardinal-health/ (accessed October 15, 2013).

52Tara Pepper, Sonia Kolesnikov-Jessop and Matt Hermann, "Inside the Head of an Applicant," Newsweek, http://msnbc.msn.com/id/6934467/site/newsweek/page/2/print/1/displaymode/1098/ (accessed February 27, 2006).

[53]William Cron, Greg W. Marshall, Jagdip Singh, Rosann L. Spiro and Harish Sujan, "Salesperson Selection, Training, and Development: Trends, Implications, and Research Opportunities," *Journal of Personal Selling & Sales Management,* 25 (Spring 2005): 123–136.

[54]E. James Randall, Ernest F. Cooke, and Lois Smith, "A Successful Application of the Assessment Center Concept to the Salesperson Selection Process," *Journal of Personal Selling & Sales Management* 5 (May 1985): 53.

[55]Eleanor Beaton, "Digital Drivers," *Profit,* 27 (May 2008): 32–33.

[56]Presentation by Daniel Mahurin, District Marketing Manager with Federated Mutual Insurance, October 15, 2013.

[57]Marty Nemko, "Earn an MBA in 3 Minutes," *Kiplinger's Personal Finance,* 60 (October 2006): 93.

[58]Henry Canaday, "Two Steps to Better Sales Hiring," *Selling Power* (July/August/September 2013): 70.

[59]"Background/Reference Checks May Provide Defense to Discrimination Suit," *Fair Employment Practices Guidelines* (December 1, 2003): 4–5.

[60]Susan M. Heathfield, "Do You Know Who You're Hiring?" *About.com,* http://humanresources.about.com/od/selectemployees/qt/candidate-background-checking.htm (accessed October 16, 2013).

[61]Larry Besnoff and Arthur Cohen, "Hazardous Hires," *Waste Age,* 38 (April 2007): 106–110; William J. Woska, "Legal Issues for HR Professionals: Reference Checking/Background Investigations," *Public Personnel Management,* 36 (Spring 2007): 79–89.

[62]*How to Select a Sales Force That Sells,* 3d ed. (Dayton, OH: The HR Chally Group, 1998): 14. Reprinted with kind permission from HR Chally Group.

[63]William J. Woska, "Legal Issues for HR Professionals: Reference Checking/Background Investigations," *Public Personnel Management* 36 (Spring 2007): 79–89.

[64]Reuters, "The Facts About Drug Testing During the Hiring Stage," (April 1, 2009), www.reuters.com/assets/print?aid=USTRE5305E120090401 (accessed September 24, 2010).

[65]Gatewood and Feild, *Human Resource Selection.*

[66]Taken from The Sales Educators, *Strategic Sales Leadership: Breakthrough Thinking for Breakthrough Results* (Mason, OH: Thomson, 2006): 218.

[67]W.E. Patton III and Ronald King, "The Use of Human Judgement Models in Sales Force Selection Decisions," *Journal of Personal Selling & Sales Management* 12 (Spring 1992): 1.

[68]G. Stoney Alder and Joseph Gilbert, "Achieving Ethics and Fairness in Hiring: Going Beyond the Law," *Journal of Business Ethics* 68 (Spring 2006): 449–464. *Source*: U.S. Equal Employment Opportunity Commission,

"Laws Enforced by EEOC: The Genetic Information Nondiscrimination Act of 2008," www.eeoc.gov/laws/statutes/index.cfm (accessed October 21, 2015).

[69]C. David Shepherd and James Heartfield, "Discrimination Issues in the Selection of Salespeople: A Review and Managerial Suggestions," *Journal of Personal Selling & Sales Management* 11 (Fall 1991): 67.

[70]G. Stoney Alder and Joseph Gilbert, "Achieving Ethics and Fairness in Hiring: Going Beyond the Law," *Journal of Business Ethics* 68 (Spring 2006): 449–464.

[71]"Interviewing Job Applicants: Watching What You Say," *Fair Employment Practices Guidelines* (July 2005): 1–3.

[72]Munson and Spivey, "Salesforce Selection," 15.

[73]For more discussion of what information should not be sought in a job interview, see John P. Steinbrink, ed., *The Dartnell Sales Manager's Handbook,* 14th ed. (Chicago: The Dartnell Corporation, 1989): 820; Shepherd and Heartfield, "Discrimination Issues."

[74]Jon M. Hawes, "How to Improve Your College Recruiting Program," *Journal of Personal Selling & Sales Management* 9 (Summer 1989): 51.

[75]Adapted from "What Would You Do?" *Sales & Marketing Management* 154 (March 2002): 64.

Chapter 6

[1]Alan J. Dubinsky, Roy D. Howell, Thomas N. Ingram, and Danny N. Bellenger, "Salesforce Socialization," *Journal of Marketing* 50 (October 1986): 195.

[2]Mark W. Johnston, A. Parasuraman, Charles M. Futrell, and William C. Black, "A Longitudinal Assessment of the Impact of Selected Organizational Influences on Salespeople's Organizational Commitment during Early Employment," *Journal of Marketing Research* 27 (August 1990): 341.

[3]Jeffrey K. Sager, "How to Retain Salespeople," *Industrial Marketing Management* 19 (May 1990): 155.

[4]Judy A. Siguaw, Gene Brown, and Robert E. Widing II, "The Influence of the Market Orientation of the Firm on Sales Force Behavior and Attitudes," *Journal of Marketing Research* 31 (February 1994): 106.

[5]Federated Insurance, "Training & Development," www.federatedinsurance.com/wstest/fi/Careers/TrainingDevelopment/index.htm (accessed December 16, 2013).

[6]Gilbert A. Churchill, Jr., Neil M. Ford, Steven W. Hartley, and Orville C. Walker, Jr., "The Determinants of Salesperson Performance: A Meta-Analysis," *Journal of Marketing Research* 22 (May 1985): 117.

[7]ASTD Staff, "Leading Sales Organizations Provide More Training," *T+D* (February 8, 2013): 22.

[8]Henry Canaday, "Begin with the Best," *Selling Power* (March 2006): 90–93. See also Howard Stevens and Theodore Kinni, *Achieve Sales Excellence* (Avon, MA: Platinum Press, 2007).

[9]Maureen Hrehocik, "The Best Sales Force," *Sales & Marketing Management,* 159 (October 2007): 22–27.

[10]"Training scheme cuts staff attrition rate by nearly 90%," *Personnel Today* (June 3, 2008): 4.

[11]Salopek, Jennifer J., "The Power of the Pyramid," *T+D* (May 2009): 70–76.

[12]"Sales Training Investment," *The Controller's Report* (July 2008): 7.

[13]Seonaid Farrell and A. Ralph Hakstain, "Improving Salesforce Performance: A Meta-Analytic Investigation of the Effectiveness and Utility of Personnel Selection Procedures and Training Interventions," *Psychology & Marketing* 18 (March 2001): 281–316.

[14]Jim Dickie and Barry Trailer, *Optimizing the ROI of Sales Training* (Mercer Island, WA: Sales Readiness Group, n.d.), http://pages.csoinsights.com/myleadlife/Repository/CSOInsights/Documents/Sales-Training-ROI.pdf?mkt_tok=3RkMMJWWfF9wsRoku6rJZKXonjHpfsX56OwtUbHr08Yy0EZ5VunJEUWy2oAARNQhcOuuEwcWGog8wx9XE%252B6GdYdI7uY%253D (accessed December 17, 2013).

[15]"Training: S&MM PULSE," *Sales & Marketing Management,* 158 (May 2006): 19.

[16]Brandon Hall, "Should Corporate Shareholders Care about Training," *Training* 41 (May 2004): 16.

[17]"Welcome to the 2006 Training Top 100," *Training* 43 (March 2006): 8.

[18]Ashraf M. Attia, Earl D. Honeycutt, Jr. and Mark P. Leach, "A Three-Stage Model for Assessing and Improving Sales Force Training and Development," *Journal of Personal Selling & Sales Management* 25 (Summer 2005): 253–68.

[19]Darren Short and Danielle Livingston, "Sales Training," *Training* (November/December 2013): 72–73.

[20]See Alan J. Dubinsky and Richard W. Hansen, "The Sales Force Management Audit," *California Management Review* 24 (Winter 1981): 86.

[21]Joseph O. Rentz, C. David Shepherd, Armen Tashchain, Pratibha A. Dabholkar, and Robert T. Ladd, "A Measure of Selling Skill: Scale Development and Validation," *Journal of Personal Selling & Sales Management* 22 (Winter 2002): 13–21.

[22]Betsy Cummings, "Wake Up, Salespeople!" *Sales & Marketing Management* 154 (June 2002): 11.

[23]Lee Perlis, Paul Terry, and Christina Mandzuk, "State of Sales Training, 2012" ASTD Webcast, April 11, 2013, http://webcasts.astd.org/webinar/674 (accessed December 17, 2013).

[24]Lee Perlis, Paul Terry, and Christina Mandzuk, "State of Sales Training, 2012" ASTD Webcast, April 11, 2013, http://webcasts.astd.org/webinar/674 (accessed December 17, 2013).

[25]C. David Shepherd, Stephen B. Castleberry, and Rick E. Ridnour, "Linking Effective Listening with Salesperson Performance: An Exploratory Investigation," *Journal of Business & Industrial Marketing* 12 (Fall 1997): 315.

[26]Sue Melone and Gary Summy, "Sales Training 101: Best Practices for Keeping Pace with Rapid Change in Selling," presentation at the National Conference in Sales Management, April 5, 2002.

[27]William Cron, Greg W. Marshall, Jagdip Singh, Rosann L. Spiro and Harish Sujan, "Salesperson Selection, Training, and Development: Trends, Implications, and Research Opportunities," *Journal of Personal Selling & Sales Management* 25 (Spring 2005): 123–136.

[28]Howard Stevens and Theodore Kinni, *Achieve Sales Excellence* (Avon, MA: Platinum Press, 2007).

[29]Bernard L. Rosenbaum, "Do You Have the Skills for 21st Century Selling? Rate Yourself with This Exercise," *American Salesman* 45 (July 2000): 24–30. Reprinted by kind permission of the author.

[30]"Bluevolt, Blue Hawk Develop Online Training Tools," *Snips* 79 (September 2010): 27.

[31]Marc Hequet, "Product Knowledge: Knowing What They're Selling May Be the Key to How Well They Sell It," *Training* (February 1988): 18.

[32]Alan J. Dubinsky and Thomas N. Ingram, "A Classification of Industrial Buyers: Implications for Sales Training," *Journal of Personal Selling & Sales Management* 2 (Fall/Winter 1981–1982): 49.

[33]Julia Chang, "Multicultural Selling," *Sales & Marketing Management* 155 (October 2003): 26.

[34]Victoria Davies Bush and Thomas N. Ingram, "Adapting to Diverse Customers: A Training Matrix for International Marketers," *Industrial Marketing Management* 25 (September 1996): 373; Strout, Brewer, and Kaydo, "Are Your Salespeople Tech Savvy?"

[35]From "Global Do's and Don'ts," by Andy Cohen, *Sales & Marketing Management* 148 (June 1996): 72. Reprinted by permission of Reprint Management Services. Phillip R. Cateora, Mary Gilly and John Graham, *International Marketing,* 16th ed. (Boston, MA: McGraw Hill-Irwin, 2016): 521.

[36]Taken from James, Geoffrey, "The More You Know," *Selling Power* (January/February 2010): 25–28.

[37]Harish Sujan, Barton A. Weitz, and Mita Sujan, "Increasing Sales Productivity by Getting Salespeople to Work Smarter," *Journal of Personal Selling & Sales Management* 8 (August 1988): 9.

[38]Scott A. Inks and Amy J. Morgan, "Technology and the Sales Force: Increasing Acceptance of Sales Force Automation," *Industrial Marketing Management* 30 (June 2001): 463–472; Robert C. Erffmeyer and Dale

A. Johnson, "An Exploratory Study of Sales Force Automation Practices: Expectations and Realities," *Journal of Personal Selling & Sales Management* 21 (Spring 2001): 167–175.

[39]Mark P. Leach, Annie H. Liu and Wesley J. Johnston, "The Role of Self-Regulation Training in Developing the Motivation Management Capabilities of Salespeople," *Journal of Personal Selling & Sales Management* 25 (Summer 2005): 269–281.

[40]Colette A. Frayne and J. Michael Geringer, "Self-Management Training for Improving Job Performance: A Field Experiment Involving Salespeople," *Journal of Applied Psychology* 85 (June 2000): 361–372.

[41]Jared F. Harrison, ed., *The Sales Manager as a Trainer* (Orlando, FL: National Society of Sales Training Executives, 1983): 7.

[42]Sarah Boehle, "Global Sales Training's Balancing Act," *Training* 47 (January 2010): 29–31.

[43]Adapted from Linda Cecere, "Picking the Perfect Training Program," *Sales & Marketing Management* (July 1994): 38.

[44]Federated Insurance, "Training & Development," www.federatedinsurance.com/wstest/fi/Careers/TrainingDevelopment/index.htm (accessed December 17, 2013).

[45]Julian Birkinshaw and Jordan Cohen, "Make Time for Meaningful Work," *Businessline*, October 15, 2013.

[46]John O'Reilly, *Supply House Times* 53 (March 2010): 50.

[47]Thomas Brashear, Danny Bellenger, James Boles and Hiram Barksdale, Jr., "An Exploratory Study of the Relative Effectiveness of Different Types of Sales Force Mentors," *Journal of Personal Selling & Sales Management* 26 (Winter 2006): 7–18.

[48]Michelle Marchetti, "The Case for Mentors," *Sales & Marketing Management* 156 (June 2004): 16.

[49]ASTD Staff, "Leading Sales Organizations Provide More Training," *T+D* (February 2013): 22.

[50]Celemi, "Celemi Apples & Oranges. Version: Manufacturing—Sales," www.celemi.com/What-we-do/Business-Simulations/Apples-Oranges/Manufacturing-Sales/ (accessed December 19, 2013).

[51]Paradigm Learning, "Zodiak®: Sales Professionals," www.paradigmlearning.com/products-and-services/zodiak-game-of-business-finance-and-strategy/zodiak-sales-professionals.aspx (accessed December 19, 2013).

[52]Kevin Glover and Connie Muray, "Simulations for Selling Success," *T+D* (January 2012): 80.

[53]Margery Weinstein, "Even Better Than the Real Thing?" *Training* 43 (June 2006): 33–39.

[54]For guidelines for enhancing role playing, see "Skills," *Personal Selling Power* (January/February 1995): 54.

Also see Thomas N. Ingram, "Guidelines for Maximizing Role-Play Activities," in *Proceedings,* National Conference in Sales Management, Dallas, TX, 1990.

[55]Federated Insurance, "Training & Development," www.federatedinsurance.com/wstest/fi/Careers/TrainingDevelopment/index.htm (accessed December 17, 2013).

[56]Henry Canaday, "Students of the Marketplace," *Selling Power* (November/December 2010): 25–27.

[57]Marty Rosenheck, "The Modern Medicine Show," *Chief Learning Officer,* 9 (June 2010): 46–48

[58]James, Geoffrey, "A 15-Minute Training Bonanza," *Selling Power* (October 2009): 73.

[59]Henry Canaday, "Students of the Marketplace," *Selling Power* (November/December 2010): 25–27.

[60]Jim Day, Sandy Dick, and Tori Eggleston, "Sales Training at Cisco Systems Goes Digital-and Interactive," *Velocity,* Q1 (2010): 13–16; Kate Day and Lisa Maria Fedele, "Learning at the Speed of Life," *T+D* (June 2012): 60–63.

[61]ASTD Staff, "Leading Sales Organizations Provide More Training," *T+D* (February 8, 2013): 22.

[62]Marty Rosenheck, "The Modern Medicine Show," *Chief Learning Officer* 9 (June 2010): 46–48.

[63]Kathy Chin Leong, "Video E-Mail Goes Corporate," *Computerworld* (March 21, 2005): 23–24.

[64]Heather Baldwin, "The Five-Minute Training Trend," *SellingPower.Com Sales Management Newsletter* (June 14, 2006), www.sellingpower.com/html_newsletter/PrintNewsletter/?NLID=537.

[65]Richard Castle, "Mobile Learning: Is Your Content Fit for Purpose," *Training & Development* (April 2013): 22–23.

[66]Brandon Hall, "Five Approaches to Sales Training," *Chief Learning Officer* (November 2010): 18.

[67]Michele Marchetti, "Tapping Top Talent," *Sales & Marketing Management* 156 (August 2004): 14.

[68]www.remaxshowcase.com/rs.htm (accessed on December 19, 2013).

[69]Taken from Geoffrey James, "Staged Right," *Selling Power* (November/December 2010): 33–36.

[70]Jim Day, Sandy Dick, and Tori Eggleston, "Sales Training at Cisco Systems Goes Digital-and Interactive," *Velocity* Q1 (2010): 13–16.

[71]*Ibid.*

[72]Henry Canaday, "Talent Search," *Selling Power* (July/August 2010): 61.

[73]Sarah Boehle, "Global Sales Training's Balancing Act," *Training* 47 (January 2010): 29–31.

[74]Malcom S. Knowles, *Self-Directed Learning: A Guide for Learners and Teachers* (New York: Association Press, 1975).

[75]Andrew B. Artis and Eric G. Harris, "Self-Directed Learning and Sales Force Performance: An Integrated Framework," *Journal of Personal Selling & Sales Management* (Winter 2007): 9–24.

[76]Mike Schultz, "The Seven Keys for Training for Maximum Impact," *T+D* (March 2013): 52–57.

[77]Jon M. Hawes, Stephen P. Hutchens, and William F. Crittenden, "Evaluating Corporate Sales Training Programs," *Training and Development Journal* 36 (November 1982): 44.

[78]Kate Day and Lisa Maria Fedele, "Learning at the Speed of Life," *T+D* (June 2012): 60–63.

[79]Ashraf M. Attia, Earl D. Honeycutt Jr. and Mark P. Leach, "A Three-Stage Model for Assessing and Improving Sales Force Training and Development," *Journal of Personal Selling & Sales Management* 25 (Summer 2005): 253–68.

[80]Melone and Summy, "Sales Training 101: Best Practices for Keeping Pace with Rapid Change in Selling."

[81]Charles Gottenkieny, "Proper Training Can Result in Positive ROI," *Selling* (August 2003): 9.

[82]Mark P. Leach and Anie H. Liu, "Investigating Interrelationships among Sales Training Evaluation Methods," *Journal of Personal Selling & Sales Management* 23 (Fall 2003): 327–339.

[83]For more on how to assess the return on investment of sales training, see Clive Shepherd, "Assessing the ROI of Training," http://www.fastrak-consulting.co.uk/tactix/features/tngroi/tngroi.thm (accessed January 7, 2014).

[84]David McGeough, "Measuring ROI," *Training* (March/April 2011): 27.

[85]Jason Jordan, "Management Best Practices," *Sales & Marketing Management* 162 (January 2010), 22.

[86]*Ibid.*

[87]The Sales Educators, *Strategic Sales Leadership: Breakthrough Thinking for Breakthrough Results* (Mason, OH: Thomson, 2006): 81.

[88]Gail Johnson, "Forget Me Not," *Training* 41 (March 2004): 12.

[89]"Training: S&MM Pulse," *Sales & Marketing Management* 158 (July/August 2006): 21.

[90]Alan J. Dubinsky, Marvin A. Jolson, Ronald E. Michaels, Masaaki Kotabe, and Chae Un Lim, "Ethical Perceptions of Field Sales Personnel: An Empirical Assessment," *Journal of Personal Selling & Sales Management* 12 (Fall 1992): 9; Karl A. Boedecker, Fred W. Morgan, and Jeffrey J. Stoltman, "Legal Dimensions of Salespersons' Statements: A Review and Managerial Suggestions," *Journal of Marketing* 55 (January 1991): 70.

[91]Scott Inks, Ramon Avila, and Joe Chapman, "A Comparison of Buyers' and Sellers' Perceptions of Ethical Behaviors Within the Buyer-Seller Dyad," *Marketing Management Journal* (Spring 2004): 117–128.

[92]To learn more about a technique for using cases for ethical sales training, see John A. Weber, "Business Ethics Training: Insights from Learning Theory," *Journal of Business Ethics*, 70 (2007): 61–85.

[93]Melone and Summy, "Sales Training 101: Best Practices for Keeping Pace with Rapid Change in Selling."

[94]Boedecker et al., "Legal Dimensions of Salespersons' Statements."

[95]Sean Valentine, "Ethics Training, Ethical Context, and Sales and Marketing Professionals' Satisfaction with Supervisors and Coworkers," *Journal of Personal Selling & Sales Management* 29 (January 2009): 227–42.

Chapter 7

[1]The figure and discussion are adapted from Thomas N. Ingram, Raymond W. LaForge, William B. Locander, Scott B. MacKenzie, and Philip M. Podsakoff, "New Directions for Sales Leadership Research," *Journal of Personal Selling & Sales Management* (Spring 2005).

[2]Karen Flaherty, "Understanding the Relationship Between the Role of the Salesperson and the Role of the Sales Manager," in *The Oxford Handbook of Strategic Sales and Sales Management*, eds. David W. Cravens, Kenneth Le Meunier-Fitzhugh, and Nigel F. Piercy (Oxford, England: Oxford University Press, 2011): 51–76.

[3]Lain Ehmann, "A New Outlook," *Selling Power* (January/February/March 2012): 38–41.

[4]Philip M. Podsakoff, Scott B. MacKenzie, Robert H. Moorman, and Richard Fetter, "Transformational Leader Behaviors and Their Effects on Followers' Trust in Leader, Satisfaction, and Organizational Citizenship Behaviors," *Leadership Quarterly* (1990): 107–142.

[5]Daniel Goleman, "Leadership That Gets Results," *Harvard Business Review* (March–April 2000): 78–90; Daniel Goleman, Richard Boyatzis, and Annie McKee, *Primal Leadership: Realizing the Power of Emotional Intelligence* (Boston: Harvard Business School Press, 2002); Fernando Jaramillo, Douglas B. Grisaffe, Lawrence B. Chonko, and James A. Roberts, "Examining the Impact of Servant Leadership on Sales Force Performance," *Journal of Personal Selling & Sales Management* (Summer 2009): 257–275.

[6]Rosemary R. Lagace, "An Exploratory Study of Trust between Sales Managers and Salespersons," *Journal of Personal Selling & Sales Management* 11 (Spring 1991): 49; David Strutton, Lou E. Pelton, and James R. Lumpkin, "The Relationship between Psychological Climate and Salesperson–Sales Manager Trust in Sales Organizations," *Journal of Personal Selling & Sales Management* 13 (Fall 1993): 1; Karen E. Flaherty and James M. Pappas, "The Role of Trust in Salesperson–Sales Manager Relationships," *Journal of Personal Selling &*

Sales Management 20 (Fall 2000): 271–278; Howard J. Klein and Jay S. Kim, "A Field Study of the Influence of Situational Constraints, Leader–Member Exchange, and Goal Commitment on Performance," *Academy of Management Journal* 41 (February 1998): 88.

[7]Karen Flaherty, "Understanding the Relationship Between the Role of the Salesperson and the Role of the Sales Manager," in *The Oxford Handbook of Strategic Sales and Sales Management*, eds. David W. Cravens, Kenneth Le Meunier-Fitzhugh, and Nigel F. Piercy (Oxford, England: Oxford University Press, 2011): 51–76.

[8]Based on John French, Jr. and Bertram Raven, "The Bases of Social Power," in *Studies in Social Power*, ed. D. Cartwright (Ann Arbor, MI: The University of Michigan Press, 1959).

[9]Interview with Marty Reist, June 15, 2008.

[10]From Gerhard Gschwandtner, "Personal PR Strategies for Creating Power and Influence" in *Personal Selling Power* (October 1990): 20. Reprinted with permission of Personal Selling Power, Inc.

[11]This discussion of influence strategies is largely based on Madeline E. Heilman and Harvey Hornstein, *Managing Human Forces in Organization* (Homewood, IL: Irwin, 1982): 116.

[12]Jerome A. Colletti and Mary S. Fiss, "The Ultimately Accountable Job: Leading Today's Sales Organization," *Harvard Business Review* 84, 7/8 (July–August 2006): 125–131.

[13]Henry Canaday, "Tactical Gains," *Selling Power* (October/November/December 2012): 60–61.

[14]Harry Campbell, "Phone Efficiency," *Sales & Marketing Management* (May 2004): 16.

[15]Henry Canaday, "A Socially Salable World," *Selling Power* (April/May/June 2012): 46–50.

[16]Mark C. Johlke, Dale F. Duhan, Roy D. Howell, and Robert W. Wilkes, "An Integrated Model of Sales Managers' Communication Practices," *Journal of the Academy of Marketing Science* 28 (Spring 2000): 263–277.

[17]Heather Baldwin, "Talk to Me," *Selling Power* (January/February/March 2012): 10–13.

[18]Heather Baldwin, "Coaching Ops," *Selling Power* (July/August/September 2013): 23–25.

[19]Heather Baldwin, "Talk to Me," *Selling Power* (January/February/March 2012): 10–13.

[20]Compiled from Barry J. Farber, "Sales Managers: Do Yourself a Favor," *Personal Selling Power* (April 1990): 33; "First Train Them, Then Coach Them," *Sales & Marketing Management* (August 1987): 64–65; Stuart R. Levine, "Performance Coaching," *Selling Power* (July/August 1996): 46; Bill Cates, "A Coach for All Reasons," *Selling Power* (June 1996): 64–65.

[21]"Basic Principles for Coaching," *Air Conditioning, Heating & Refrigeration News*, 227, 2 (January 9, 2006): 51.

[22]Susan Greco, "Let's Start with an Icebreaker," *Inc. Magazine* (June 2008): 450.

[23]Compiled from Rayna Skolnik, "Salespeople Sound Off on Meetings," *Sales & Marketing Management* (November 1987): 108; Hank Trisler, "Million Dollar Meetings," *Selling Power* (March 1996): 66–67.

[24]Mark McMaster, "Sales Meetings Your Reps Won't Hate," *Sales & Marketing Management* 153 (May 2001): 63–67.

[25]3M Visual Systems Division, "Six Secrets to Holding a Good Meeting," Copyright © Minnesota Mining and Mfg. Co. Reproduced by permission.

[26]Mark Roberti, "Meet Me on the Web," *Fortune* 144 (Winter 2002): 37.

[27]John D. Hansen and Robert J. Riggle, "Ethical Salesperson Behavior in Sales Relationships," *Journal of Personal Selling & Sales Management* (Spring 2009): 151–166.

[28]Archie B. Carroll, "In Search of the Moral Manager," *Business Horizons* 30 (March/April 1987): 12. Copyright © 1987 by the Foundation for the School of Business at Indiana University. Reprinted by permission.

[29]Hansen and Riggle, "Ethical Salesperson Behavior in Sales Relationships."

[30]Excerpted from Sales and Marketing Executives, *International Certified Professional Salesperson Code of Ethics* (Cleveland: Sales and Marketing Executives International, 1994). Reprinted by permission of SME International at 800–999–1414.

[31]O.C. Ferrell, Mark W. Johnston, and Linda Ferrell, "A Framework for Personal Selling and Sales Management Ethical Decision Making," *Journal of Personal Selling & Sales Management* (Fall 2007): 291–299.

[32]Charles H. Schwepker, Jr. and David J. Good, "Transformational Leadership and Its Impact on Sales Force Moral Judgment," *Journal of Personal Selling & Sales Management* (Fall 2010): 299–317; Thomas N. Ingram, Raymond W. LaForge, and Charles H. Schwepker, Jr., "Salesperson Ethical Decision Making: The Impact of Sales Leadership and Sales Management Control Strategy," *Journal of Personal Selling & Sales Management* (Fall 2007): 301–315.

Chapter 8

[1]Data from U.S. Department of Labor, Bureau of Labor Statistics, "May 2013 National Occupational Employment Statistics," http://www.bls.gov/oes/current/oes_nat.htm (accessed May 1, 2014).

[2]Steven P. Brown, Kenneth R. Evans, Murali K. Mantrala, and Goutam Challagalla, "Adapting Motivation, Control, and Compensation Research to a New Environment," *Journal of Personal Selling & Sales Management* 25 (Spring 2005): 155–167.

[3]Ruth Kanfer, "Work Motivation: Theory, Practice, and Future Directions," in *The Oxford Handbook of*

Organizational Psychology, ed. Steve W.J. Kozlowski (Oxford, United Kingdom, 2012): 455–460.

[4]Thomas Steenburgh and Michael Ahearne, "Motivating Salespeople: What Really Works," *Harvard Business Review* 90 (July/August 2012): 71–75.

[5]"Trends in Strategic Market Pricing for Sales Professionals," *Bloomberg BNA* (May 2013): 8.

[6]Jeanne Greenberg and Herbert Greenberg, *What It Takes to Succeed in Sales: Selecting and Retaining Top Producers* (Homewood, IL: Dow-Jones Irwin, 1990): 112.

[7]"Sales Compensation Changes, with Mixed Salary Levels," *Bloomberg BNA* (May 2013): 1–2.

[8]http://www.accountpro.com/mod137.htm (accessed April 28, 2014).

[9]"Seeing the CEO and the Sites: Planners Search for the Right Mix of Team-Building Events and Unstructured Time," *Sales and Marketing Management* (October 4, 2013), www.salesandmarketing.com/content/seing-ceo-and-sites.

[10]"Surya Awards Winners in Sales Force Contest with $100K in Prizes," *Home Textiles Today* (October 22, 2012): 20.

[11]The Sales Educators, *Strategic Sales Leadership: Breakthrough Thinking for Breakthrough Results* (Mason, OH: Thomson, 2006).

[12]Affordable Colleges Online, "Fortune 500 Companies Picking Up the Tuition Tab," www.affordable-collegesonline.org/financial-aid/top-company-college-tuition-reimbursement-programs/ (accessed April 20, 2014).

[13]Paul Shearstone, "Creating Sales Incentive Programs that Work, Part 2," http://sbinfocanada.about .com/cs/marketing/a/incentiveprogps_2.htm (accessed May 2, 2014).

[14]Sample expense report from Expensable.com, http://www.expensable.com/products/expense-report-sample.htm (accessed January 3, 2011).

[15]Concur Technologies, http://www.concur.com/search.html?q=default&p=http://www.concur.com/solutions/exp/default.htm (accessed January 5, 2011).

[16]Automatic Data Processing, "Tricks Employees Use to Pad Their Expenses," www.adp.com/tools-and-resources/newsletters/~/media/CBC4D674B-62F4990A3F67C209C579012.ashx (accessed April 12, 2014).

[17]The Forum for People Performance Management and Measurement, "Match Employee Awards to Specific Organizational Objectives for Optimal Success," Executive White Paper, http://www.performanceforum.org/Match_Employee_Awards_to_Specific_Organizational_Objectives.64.0.html (accessed January 3, 2011).

[18]William H. Murphy, "Sales Contest Research: Business and Individual Difference Factors Affecting Intentions to Pursue Contest Goals," *Industrial Marketing Management* 8 (January 2009): 109–118; Noah Lim, Michael J. Ahearne, and Sung H. Ham, "Designing Sales Contests: Does the Prize Structure Matter?" *Journal of Marketing Research* 46 (June 2009): 356–371; Jason Garrett and Srinath Gopalakrishna, "Customer Value Impact of Sales Contests," *Journal of the Academy of Marketing Science* 38 (December 2010): 775–786; F. Juliet Poujol and John F. Tanner, Jr., "The Impact of Contests on Salespeople's Orientation: An Application of Tournament Theory," *Journal of Personal Selling & Sales Management* 30 (Winter 2010): 33–46; Barbara Scofidio, " This Is Your Motivation Strategy?" *Corporate Incentives and Meetings* (March 2010): 13–16; Scott Ladd, "May the Force Be with You," *HR Magazine* (September 2010): 105–107; The Forum for People Performance Management and Measurement, "Making the Case for Sales Incentives to the Tune of 10 Percent ROI," Executive White Paper, http://www.performanceforum.org/Making_the_Case_for_Sales_Incentives.66.0.html (accessed January 4, 2011).

[19]"Security Dealers Share the Best & the Worst of Sales Contests," *SDM Magazine* (October 14, 2010), http://www.sdmmag.com/articles/security-dealers-share-the-best-the-worst-of-sales-contests.

[20]Rymax Marketing Services, "MaxSite Catalog," http://www.rymaxinc.com/Maxsite/Homepage/Default.aspx (accessed February 15, 2014).

[21]William H. Murphy, Peter A. Dacin, and Neil M. Ford, "Sales Contest Effectiveness: An Examination of Sales Contest Design Preferences of Field Sales Forces," *Journal of the Academy of Marketing Science* 32 (Spring 2004): 127–143.

[22]Maritz, "Maritz Motivation," http://www.maritz .com/About-Maritz/Our-Businesses/Motivation .aspx. (accessed January 15, 2014).

[23]Steven P. Brown, Kenneth R. Evans, Murali K. Mantrala, and Goutam Challagalla, "Adapting Motivation, Control, and Compensation Research to a New Environment," *Journal of Personal Selling & Sales Management,* 25 (Spring 2005): 155–167.

[24]Sarah Sluis, "Sales Management Tools and Trends to Watch: Transform Sales With Technology," *Customer Relationship Management* (February 2014): 29–32.

[25]Brent Adamson, Matthew Dixon, and Nicholas Toman, "Why Individuals No Longer Rule on Sales Teams," *HBR Blog Network*, January 9, 2014, http://blogs.hbr.org/2014/01/why-the-individual-no-longer-rules-in-sales/.

[26]Alex Palmer, "Taking Employee Recognition Mobile," Incentive, April 25, 2014, www.incentivemag.com/News/Industry/Articles/Taking-Employee-Recognition-Mobile/.

[27]John F. Tanner, Jr. and George Dudley, "International Differences—Examining Two Assumptions about Selling," reported in *Baylor Business Review* (Fall 2003): 44–45.

[28]Fay Hansen, "Currents in Compensation and Benefits," *Compensation and Benefits Review*, 40 (May/June 2008): 5–6.

[29]Xavier Baeten, "Global Compensation and Benefits Management: The Need for Communication and Coordination," *Compensation and Benefits Review*, 42 (September/October 2010): 392–402; Thomas Shelton, "Global Compensation Strategies: Managing and Administering Split Pay for an Expatriate Workforce," *Compensation and Benefits Review*, 40 (January/February 2008): 56–60.

[30]From "Global Gamble," by Michele Marchetti, *Sales & Marketing Management* 148 (July 1996): 64–69. Copyright © VNU Business Media Inc. Reprinted by permission.

[31]Sales & Marketing Management's SSM, "Fast-track Motivation: Makana Motivator Case Study," (July 31, 2010), http://www.salesandmarketing.com/article/fast-track-motivation-makana-motivator-case-study.

[32]Betsy Cummings, "Hearing Them Out," *Sales & Marketing Management* 157 (January 2005): 10.

[33]Hinda Incentives, "innergE," http://www.hinda.com/products-innerge.html (accessed January 8, 2014).

Chapter 9

[1]Adapted from David W. Cravens, Thomas N. Ingram, Raymond W. LaForge, and Clifford E. Young, "Behavior-Based and Outcome-Based Salesforce Control Systems," *Journal of Marketing* 57 (October 1993): 47–59. Reprinted by permission of American Marketing Association.

[2]David W. Cravens, Thomas N. Ingram, Raymond W. LaForge, and Clifford E. Young, "Hallmarks of Effective Sales Organizations," *Marketing Management* 1 (March 1992): 56.

[3]From "The Sales Force Management Audit" by Alan J. Dubinsky and Richard W. Hansen. Copyright © 1981, by The Regents of the University of California. Reprinted from the *California Management Review*, 24(2). By permission of The Regents.

[4]Meridian's, http://www.meridianise.com/Testimonials.htm (accessed July 3, 2007).

[5]From Dubinsky and Hansen, "The Sales Force Management Audit."

[6]From "Measuring Sales Effectiveness," by Geoffrey Brewer, *Sales & Marketing Management* 152 (October 2000): 136. Copyright © VNU Business Media Inc. Reprinted by permission.

[7]Reprinted by permission of *Harvard Business Review*. From "Measure Costs Right: Make the Right Decisions," by Robin Cooper and Robert S. Kaplan (September/October 1988): 96–103. Copyright © 1988 by the Harvard Business School Publishing Corporation, all rights reserved.

[8]Bridget McCrea, "A-B-C, Easy as 1-2-3," *Industrial Distribution* 92 (October 2003): H1–H4.

[9]Best Practices LLC Web site, http://www3.best-in-class.com/bestp/domrep.nsf/pages/716AD479AB1F512C85256DFF006BD072!OpenDocument (accessed June 27, 2007).

[10]Michael J. Webb, "Do You Know the Answers to These Questions?" Sales Performance Consultants, question 4. Available at http://www.salesperformance.com/ FAQ.aspx (accessed July 6, 2007). Copyright © 2004 Sales Performance Consultants, Inc. Used by permission.

Chapter 10

[1]Fernando Jaramillo, Francois A. Carrillat, and William B. Locander, "Starting to Solve the Method Puzzle in Salesperson Self-Report Evaluations," *Journal of Personal Selling & Sales Management* 23 (Fall 2003): 369–377.

[2]Fernando Jaramillo, Francois A. Carrillat, and William B. Locander, "A Meta-Analytic Comparison of Managerial Ratings and Self-Evaluations," *Journal of Personal Selling & Sales Management* 25 (Fall 2005): 315–328.

[3]Adapted from Allan Church, "First-Rate Multirater Feedback," *Training & Development* 49 (August 1995): 42–43; and Scott Wimer and Kenneth M. Nowack, "13 Common Mistakes Using 360-Degree Feedback," *Training & Development* 52 (May 1998): 69–78; Bret J. Becton and Mike Schraeder, "Participant Input into Rater Selection: Potential Effects on the Quality and Acceptance of Ratings in the Context of 360-Degree Feedback," *Public Personnel Management* 33 (Spring 2004): 23–32.

[4]Helen Rheem, "Performance Management: A Progress Report," *Harvard Business Review* (March/April 1995): 11.

[5]Adapted from SellingPower Online, "Performance Review Basics," *SellingPower Sales Management Newsletter* (January 5, 2004); SellingPower Online, "Talking About Employee Performance," *SellingPower Sales Management Newsletter* (March 17, 2003).

[6]David W. Cravens, Greg W. Marshall, Felicia G. Lassk, and George S. Low, "The Control Factor," *Marketing Management* 13 (January/February 2004): 39–44.

[7]Donald Jackson, Jr., John Schlacter, and William Wolfe, "Examining the Bases Utilized for Evaluating Salespeople's Performance," *Journal of Personal Selling & Sales Management* 15 (Fall 1995): 57–65.

[8]Dominique Rouzies and Anne Macquin, "An Exploratory Investigation of the Impact of Culture on Sales Force Management Control Systems in Europe," *Journal of Personal Selling & Sales Management* 23 (Winter 2003): 61–72.

[9]Jackson, Schlacter, and Wolfe, "Examining the Bases Utilized for Evaluating Salespeople's Performance."

[10] *Ibid.*

[11] From "Selling and Sales Management in Action," by David J. Good and Robert W. Stone. Copyright © 1991 by Pi Sigma Epsilon. From *Journal of Personal Selling & Sales Management,* 11(3) (Summer 1991): 57–60. Reprinted with permission of M.E. Sharpe, Inc.

[12] Charles H. Schwepker, Jr. and David J. Good, "Understanding Sales Quotas: An Exploratory Investigation of Consequences of Failure," *Journal of Business & Industrial Marketing* 19 (2004): 39–48.

[13] http://www.synygy.com/quotas/problems.html (accessed September 16, 2007).

[14] David J. Good and Charles H. Schwepker, Jr., "Sales Quotas: Critical Interpretations and Implications," *Review of Business* 22 (Spring 2001): 32–36.

[15] *Ibid.*

[16] Jackson, Schlacter, and Wolfe, "Examining the Bases Utilized for Evaluating Salespeople's Performance."

[17] Eastman Chemical Company, "Checking Customer Value through Continual Improvement" survey.

[18] http://hrtools.com/StrategicAlliances/Content/Products/performance_now.asp (accessed September 16, 2007.

[19] Christian Homburg and Ruth M. Stock, "The Link between Salespeople's Job Satisfaction and Customer Satisfaction in a Business-to-Business Context: A Dyadic Analysis," *Journal of the Academy of Marketing Science* 32 (Spring 2004): 144–158.

[20] For a complete discussion of the scale, see Gilbert A. Churchill, Jr., Neil M. Ford, and Orville C. Walker, Jr., "Measuring the Job Satisfaction of Industrial Salesmen," *Journal of Marketing Research* (August 1974): 254. For validation support, see Charles M. Futrell, "Measurement of Salespeople's Job Satisfaction: Convergent and Discriminant Validity of Corresponding INDSALES and Job Descriptive Index Scales," *Journal of Marketing Research* (November 1979): 594; Rosemary Lagace, Jerry Goolsby, and Jule Gassenheimer, "Scaling and Measurement: A Quasi-Replicative Assessment of a Revised Version of INDSALES," *Journal of Personal Selling & Sales Management* 13 (Winter 1993): 65. See also Sarath A. Nonis and S. Altan Erdem, "A Refinement of INDSALES to Measure Job Satisfaction of Sales Personnel in General Marketing Settings," *Journal of Marketing Management* 7 (Spring/Summer 1997): 34.

[21] James M. Comer, Karen A. Machleit, and Rosemary R. Lagace, "Psychometric Assessment of a Reduced Version of INDSALES," *Journal of Business Research* 18 (1989): 295–296. Reprinted by permission of Elsevier Science.

Page numbers in **bold** refer to figures, page numbers in *italic* refer to tables.